The Executor's Manual

Books by Charles K. Plotnick and Stephan R. Leimberg

Die Rich
Get Rich, Stay Rich
So You Want to Be an Executor

Also by Stephan R. Leimberg

The Tools and Techniques of Estate Planning
Computing the Federal Estate Tax
Introduction to Tools and Techniques of Estate Planning
Estate Administration in Pennsylvania
Presenting IRAs and SEPs
The Tax Reform Act of 1984—What It Says—What It Means to You
Federal Income Taxation
Money and Retirement
Section 6166 Installment Payouts—Buy the Numbers (cassette/workbook)
Section 303 Stock Redemptions—Buy the Numbers (cassette/workbook)

The Executor's Manual

Everything You Need to Know to Settle an Estate

Charles K. Plotnick and Stephan R. Leimberg

DOUBLEDAY & COMPANY, INC.
GARDEN CITY, NEW YORK
1986

Library of Congress Cataloging in Publication Data

Plotnick, Charles.
    The executor's manual.

    1. Executors and administrators—United States.
2. Decedents' estates—United States.   3. Probate law
and practice—United States.   I. Leimberg, Stephan R.
II. Title
KF778.Z9P56   1986   346.7305′2   84-25900
ISBN 0-385-23489-9
ISBN 0-385-27948-5(pbk.)   347.30652

Published by Doubleday & Company, Inc.
Copyright © 1986 by Charles K. Plotnick and Stephan R. Leimberg
All Rights Reserved
Printed in the United States of America
First Edition

DEDICATION

To my father, Benjamin Plotnick, who so thoroughly enjoyed being with us all for eighty years.

CHARLES K. PLOTNICK

To my sister, Marcia D. Leimberg, and my brothers, Gary and Eugene Leimberg: It's good to get to know you.

STEPHAN R. LEIMBERG

Contents

Contents

Introduction

The telephone rings. It's your Uncle Stanley's lawyer. He tells you that Uncle Stanley has died and has named you the executor of his estate. He wants to meet with you as soon as possible to probate the estate, as there are certain details that must be taken care of immediately.

At first you feel pleased and flattered by your new appointment. Of course, you are saddened by your uncle's death, but feel an inner sense of pride that Uncle Stanley has appointed you to this important position. After a short while, however, the realization of what has taken place begins to sink in, and you realize that you have absolutely no idea what it is you are supposed to do.

You know generally that an executor is someone who is supposed to handle the affairs of a deceased person, but you have no specific idea how to go about getting the job done. In fact, not only are you unaware of the duties of an executor, but you also do not know what your responsibilities will be to the other members of Uncle Stanley's family, to the creditors and other business associates of Uncle Stanley, and to the state and federal government to which Uncle Stanley's estate may be responsible for death taxes.

Because the gift of immortality has not yet been granted to any of us, the chances of being called upon to act as executor, or personal representative, of the estate of a deceased friend or close relative are quite good. When that time comes, we hope to be blessed with competent advisors to help us settle the estate of the deceased person for whom we will act as executor. Despite the hoped-for presence of wise and friendly advisors, the ultimate decisions and the responsibilities fall on the personal representatives themselves. It would seem to be extremely helpful, therefore, to have an available source of specific information and ideas to guide the personal representative throughout his or her tenure in office.

The purpose of this book is to perform exactly that task. This book is not written specifically for the attorney, trust officer, accountant or other advisor or professional executor (although in many instances it will be of considerable value to them). The purpose of this book is to inform the individual lay executor exactly what he or she is, or will be, required to do in order to properly handle the affairs of a deceased person.

The book discusses those intricate and potentially dangerous areas where the unwarned executor can become mired in a quicksand of personal liability, because of failure to act promptly and in the best interest of the estate and its beneficiaries.

First, read the Table of Contents at the beginning of the book and the Summary at the end of each chapter. Then, read this book once from cover to cover as quickly as you can. Go back and underline those points you need to remember, and put question marks near those you don't understand. Many of your questions will be answered as you read various chapters a second time. Bear in mind that executors can be (and many times have been) held personally liable for their mistakes. In less euphemistic terms, this means that courts have required them at times to reach into their own pockets to pay for their errors, omissions or tardiness.

While the book is extensive in scope, and is intended to cover practically every facet of handling an estate that a personal representative might encounter, it is not meant as a substitute for competent advisors. In fact, the book devotes an entire chapter to the problem of how to select and when to use the other members of the estate settlement team (as well as how to negotiate with them *before* they begin working for the estate). You should familiarize yourself with this chapter as quickly as possible, so that you will know if and when you will require the services of an attorney, accountant, appraiser, real estate agent, stockbroker or any other advisor that may be warranted by the specific facts of the estate that you are handling. Nowhere is the phrase "He who has himself for attorney has a fool for client" more true than in the case of the do-it-yourself executor.

The book also talks about insurance, government benefits and state and federal taxes. While this information was accurate at the time the book was prepared, tax laws and government interpretation of tax laws change rapidly. Therefore, before finalizing any tax returns or making any decisions based on tax information, you should be certain that you are utilizing the very latest tax information available.

We sincerely believe that if you use this book, which is without question the most extensive, up-to-date and easy-to-read treatment of an executor's duties and opportunities, you will be able to greatly expedite the handling of an estate of a decedent. If you read and carry out our suggestions, we are convinced you can perform the work involved more efficiently and with much greater benefit to the family, business associates and other beneficiaries of the decedent. Follow our checklists, and you can minimize or eliminate the risk of becoming personally liable for mistakes in judgment or timely filing of returns, for making improper investment decisions or failing to follow the accepted procedures in handling the specific assets of the estate.

The Executor's Manual

The Personal Representative: A Job Description

The Need for a Personal Representative

In most instances, when a person dies owning property of any real value, it is necessary to have someone appointed to administer the deceased individual's estate. That person (it could be one or several persons, a bank or trust company, or both), who acts for, or "stands in the shoes of," the deceased person, is called the "personal representative."

As we shall see, the duties and responsibilities of the personal representative, and even the title of the personal representative, will change depending on the state laws and circumstances involved.

Before reviewing the details of the appointment, and the duties and responsibilities that go along with the position, let's first determine why there is a need for someone to "stand in the shoes of the deceased person."

Tom and Irene Anderson were a successful married couple in their early forties. They had two children—Ted, age twenty-one, and Sally, nineteen. Tom had a small consulting business. Irene is a high school teacher. On the way back from a consulting job upstate, Tom's car was run off the road by a drunken driver. Tom died within hours of the accident.

As a result of his death, Tom's company will not open for work. But someone must be available to handle or terminate the work in progress, pay the outstanding bills, collect the outstanding obligations, and make the big decision as to what ultimately will happen with the business.

Tom might have had other outstanding obligations apart from his business interests. Someone would have to settle up these accounts, as well as collect any outstanding debts owed to Tom personally.

There might be other issues for the personal representative to handle aside from those involving financial considerations. Tom might have had a child by a previous marriage for whom he was paying support. There could have been an outstanding agreement under which Tom, or Tom and Irene, were to purchase real estate, with the settlement or closing date after the date of Tom's death.

Even if Tom's affairs were precisely in order and there were no outstanding personal or business debts, a personal representative might be necessary to distribute Tom's assets between Irene and the children. If Tom had any property in his name alone, in all likelihood a personal representative would be needed to transfer the property from Tom to his wife and children. A bank account in Tom's name, for example, could not, in most circumstances, be closed out by anyone except the duly appointed personal representative of Tom's estate.

There are, therefore, very few situations in which property of a decedent (deceased individual) could be transferred at death without the appointment of a personal representative.

Of the almost two million Americans who die each year, a significant number will need someone to represent them when they are no longer living. That someone must be able to make the necessary decisions and take the actions that they would otherwise take in regard to their affairs. That person or institution, regardless of the technical name given by the facts of the situation (or the state in which he or she lived), will be the personal representative of the deceased person's estate.

The Executor or Executrix

The title of the personal representative will depend on the method by which he or she (or it, in the case of a bank or trust company) was selected or appointed. If a deceased person specifically names a person or institution to act for him or her in his or her will, and if the will is accepted as valid, the named personal representative is known as the "executor" (male) or "executrix" (female). In those cases where more than one individual or an individual and institution are appointed to act, the joint designation is usually "executors." Corporate executors (banks and trust companies) are also called executors. For the sake of simplicity, in most cases we will use the term "executor," interchangeably with "personal representative," to stand for a person of either sex.

The Administrator or Administratrix

If the deceased person dies without a valid will, and therefore has failed to designate his or her personal representative, a personal representative will be appointed by the Probate Court or the Register of Wills office having jurisdiction over decedent's estate. This will usually take place in the state and county of the decedent's domicile. In most instances, the statutes of the state will determine the person entitled to be the administrator.

Usually, the order of preference will be similar to the order in which the estate would pass to the family of a decedent who died without a will. In other words, the spouse or adult children would usually be next in line to have the right to be named administrator. It is possible, however, that this could extend to distant family members, to brothers, cousins or the like, and possibly to creditors or other strangers to the estate and to the decedent. If the decedent failed to take advantage of his or her right to name a personal representative, and if no persons with close relationships to the decedent were available, the court, in its discretion, might appoint someone completely foreign to the decedent and his or her affairs. This would especially be the case if the court was concerned about possible conflicts of interest, or felt it necessary in order to preserve the rights of creditors or other beneficiaries.

Suppose, for example, there was an obvious objective conflict between two brothers who otherwise would be next in line to be appointed administrators, or co- (equal in right) administrators. Assume this conflict was brought to the attention of the court having jurisdiction over the appointment. The court, in order to avoid the potential conflict and the resultant complex problems, might appoint someone or some institution who would impartially handle the decedent's affairs in a manner that would not show favoritism to either of the conflicting brothers.

As can be readily seen, the results of such action on the part of the court might not coincide with the original wishes of the decedent. This highlights the importance of naming your own personal representative, rather than leaving the decision to the discretion of the court.

Duties and Responsibilities

When a person dies, the law states that his or her property must be collected. After debts, taxes and expenses are paid, the remaining assets are distributed to decedent's beneficiaries. Distribution is determined by the person's will, or the "intestate laws" (laws which govern the distribution of your estate if you die without a valid will) of the state in which the decedent was domiciled at his or her death. It is the executor's or the administrator's responsibility to collect and distribute the assets and to pay the death taxes and expenses of the decedent.

While many executors and administrators perform these designated tasks in an expeditious and prudent manner, unfortunately this is not always the case. Although not necessarily held to the highest degree of care, state law usually holds the personal representative to the standard of care of a "reasonable, prudent individual" under all of the circumstances. To the dismay of the executor, what is reasonable and prudent to the executor when performing his tasks is not always so to the beneficiaries, especially retrospectively.

The various decisions to be made by the personal representative—for example, whether to sell or hold certain securities, the rate of return that investments should be earning for the beneficiaries, and whether to carry on or sell decedent's business—can often result in criticism by the beneficiaries. Sometimes this criticism can escalate into personal lawsuits against the personal representative(s).

If the court feels that the personal representative has not acted reasonably and in the best interest of the estate and beneficiaries, it is possible for the executor or administrator to be "surcharged." A surcharge means that the executor is personally liable for undue mistakes made in the administration of the decedent's estate.

One of the purposes of this book is to set out in detail those areas in which the executor should exercise the utmost care, caution and restraint, so as to minimize or completely eliminate the possibility of lawsuits or attempts by the estate's beneficiaries to place any personal liability on the executor for duties performed in the administration of the decedent's estate.

Fees

A question always arises concerning the fees to which a personal representative is entitled. The first place to check is the statutory law of the state where the estate is probated. Some states have standard fixed fees. There are also local county rules and customs that govern what the personal representative is entitled to charge for services rendered to the estate.

Professional executors such as banking and trust institutions advertise fixed fee schedules. However, in estates in excess of $1 million, it may be possible to negotiate a lower fee. These negotiations will occur between the prospective executor and the person making the initial designation (the individual desiring to name the institution as personal representative in his or her will). An attorney specializing in estate administration may be invaluable in negotiating a lower fee for a large estate.

In all cases, the executor or administrator is entitled to reasonable compensation for services. Fees should not be determined solely on the basis of the monetary amount of the assets of the decedent, but should also take into account the nature of the work involved, the time spent, the complexity of the problems, the professional background and competence of the executor, and the ultimate results and benefits passed on to the decedent's heirs.

For example, two executors might be handling estates for two decedents, with each estate having a value at the decedent's death of $100,000. The first estate might have consisted of five certificates of deposit with a total value of $100,000. The principal duties of the executor might have been to contact the bank, have all the certificates of deposit placed in one estate account, pay the necessary taxes and distribute the balance to the decedent's widow.

The asset in the estate of the second executor was a retail shoe store owned by the decedent and valued at $100,000. It was necessary for the executor to decide whether the business would be terminated immediately, or kept open so that it could be sold as a going concern. The executor had to review the insurance, watch the cash register, be physically present at the store to make sure that decedent's estate received the full value from any sales; locate a purchaser and negotiate the terms of the purchase; then sell the business, allocate the proceeds among the beneficiaries, pay the taxes and file an elaborate accounting with the court in order to be formally discharged from his duties.

In the first instance, the time spent to properly perform the duties of executor was minimal. In the case of the retail shoe store, however, there is no question but that the executor might have easily spent hundreds of hours in the performance of his or her duties. Therefore it can be seen that renumeration for services should bear a reasonable relationship to the time spent by the personal representative, as well as the quality of the work and the results achieved for the benefit of decedent's heirs.

The best advice for the personal representative in regard to charging for his or her time is to keep a detailed record of the time spent, services performed and expenses paid on behalf of the estate. Furthermore, the executor should always make periodic written reports to the beneficiaries in regard to the services being performed, and, if the situation permits, submit periodic bills for services rendered.

In any event, negotiate and settle (in writing) the issue of fees *before* any work is begun. The entire question of fees should be adequately discussed and thoroughly reviewed with all concerned parties at some time near the inception of the personal representative's work. It is much easier to have a frank discussion about fees at a point when the beneficiaries are aware of the complexities of the personal representative's duties and are only too happy to have someone else take on this responsibility. Later, when the beneficiaries are aware of the amount in the pot to be distributed to them, it will be much harder.

Psychologically, many beneficiaries will have their shares "spent" before they receive them. The subsequent announcement that the personal representative expects to receive a significant portion of that amount for services performed will doubtless be met with some serious resistance. This is especially true if the beneficiaries were not periodically apprised of the work being performed and had no prior knowledge of the anticipated amount of the personal representative's fee.

In those instances where the personal representative is an immediate member of the family, no such problems might occur. For example, if the wife is the executrix and sole beneficiary, it might be far more advantageous for her to receive the net proceeds of the estate as an inheritance from her husband rather than to charge an executor's fee that will ultimately come out of her own pocket. The reason for this is that executor's commissions or fees are taxable for income tax purposes, and usually at a far higher rate than would be the case if the sole tax involved were the state inheritance tax, or even, in some instances, the federal estate tax. (Both the inheritance tax and the federal estate tax will be discussed in detail in subsequent chapters.)

Again, if the beneficiaries were other immediate family members, the decision of the personal representative as to whether or not to submit a bill for services, or whether to reduce the fee because of the relationship of the personal representative to the beneficiaries, would certainly be a personal one and beyond the scope of this chapter.

Lastly, there is the question of the division of the fee in the event that two or more individuals are serving as co-executors or coadministrators. When two or more of the personal representatives are individuals, the fee is usually divided equally. But when a corporate executor is serving with an individual coexecutor, courts have often awarded the corporate executor (bank or trust company) a higher percentage. For example, the bank would receive its usual fee and the individual executor might be awarded one half of the bank's fee.

Of course, if the decedent had specifically provided for the payment of fees in his or her will, the courts, in most instances, would be guided by the decedent's wishes in determining the fees to be charged and the allocation between executors.

SUMMARY

1. The personal representative (executor/executrix or administrator/administratrix) is someone who stands in the shoes of a deceased person and acts on behalf of his or her estate.

2. There are many transactions begun by the deceased which the personal representative must finish, as well as tasks directly caused by or related to the death that must be handled by the personal representative.

3. The duties of the personal representative (collection of the decedent's property, payment of debts, expenses and taxes, and distribution of the remaining assets) must be accomplished with care and with the best interests of the beneficiaries placed foremost. The personal representative can be held personally liable and surcharged for his errors.

4. One or more individuals or banks (or a combination) can be personal representatives. Fees are determined under state law and local customs, as well as by prior negotiation and provision in the decedent's will. The size of the fee should be related to the size and complexity of the estate, the nature of the work involved, the time spent, the professional background and competence of the executor, and the ultimate results and benefits to the heirs.

2

The Selection Process

The Attributes of a Good Personal Representative

What does it take to be a good executor? This chapter will attempt to answer that question for you. However, as you read about the many qualities deemed necessary or useful for a competent personal representative, you must be aware that a great many intangible factors go hand in hand with the objective criteria we have listed.

It is always possible for the personal representative, if lacking knowledge in certain areas, to learn more about the subject. But the intangible attribute of "caring" about the performance of one's duties cannot always be measured objectively. That is why, in the final analysis, the human factor plays such an important part in the evaluation of the executor's functions.

For example, if two banks of comparable size were each named executors of estates, and the estates' assets were fairly similar, the reaction of the beneficiaries to the performance of the executor might be based solely on the beneficiaries' personal contacts with the individual or individuals at the bank responsible for administering the estate. The intangible factor of the personal attention received by the beneficiaries, as well as the objective handling of the estates' assets, would certainly play a significant role in the beneficiaries' evaluation of the banks' performance.

No list of standards, therefore, can be complete unless due consideration is given to the personal image of the executor as a "caring" individual in regard to the psychological as well as financial needs and the individual circumstances of the beneficiaries of the decedent's estate.

Competence

Although it would seem too elementary to even include in a book of this nature, the factor of the executor's "competence" must be paramount on any list of qualifications. However, because of the sometimes emotional nature of the appointment, this factor is often overlooked.

Nancy, a dynamic and worldly businessowner, running a virtual empire of interlocking businesses requiring the greatest amount of expertise, named her husband to be her executor. She did this because she did not want to slight him or make him feel that he was not to be included in her estate plan. Unfortunately, because her husband was a college philosophy professor who couldn't even balance the family's checkbook, the results of Nancy's decision (based on emotion rather than logic) were disastrous. The negative impact of her decision fell mainly on the spouse whom she had intended to protect.

Competence in a general sense is not necessarily measured by a complete awareness of all of the decedent's personal affairs or the intricacy of the decedent's business. A competent executor is one who can analyze the decedent's affairs as quickly as possible under the circumstances, determine what facets of the estate can be handled within the bounds of the executor's personal knowledge and capabilities, and then secure professional assistance in those areas in which the executor knows that he or she is lacking. Many individuals are chosen to act as personal representatives by decedents who, while realizing the potential executor's lack of experience in dealing with the decedent's own problems, recognize in the designated personal representative those qualities of organization, understanding, and particularly leadership that will enable the personal representative to overcome his or her lack of familiarity with the subject matter and perform admirably in carrying out the duties and responsibilities of an executor.

The Best Interests of the Beneficiaries

One of the primary reasons for friction between executors and estate beneficiaries is the failure on the part of the executors to appreciate the multifaceted aspects of their appointment and its corresponding obligations.

Executors who perform their duties in an objective vacuum, without giving due consideration to the interests of the beneficiaries, may often find that they have succeeded in putting out the fire only after the building has been destroyed. While it is true that the executor must "stand in the shoes" of the decedent and attempt to perform his or her duties in a fashion similar to the manner in which the decedent would have performed them, the executor's ultimate responsibility is to handle the estate and preserve and transfer its assets in the most efficient manner under all attending circumstances.

To put the matter in its harshest light, very few children would ever think of suing their father because he does not give them the gifts or allowance to which they feel they are entitled. If the children are adults, however, and a stranger is handling their father's money, the aura of parenthood is no longer present. The sooner the executor realizes that he or she is dealing with individuals with their own opinions, concerns and feelings, the sooner the executor will be in a position to discharge the duties of the office with minimal likelihood of interference or hostility on the part of the estate's beneficiaries.

This is not to say that the best interests of the beneficiaries can be objectively characterized, because this can sometimes be far from the truth.

For example, a nineteen-year-old son of the decedent who insists that the executor immediately release sufficient funds to enable him to buy a Corvette because he must have transportation to college does not necessarily have to have his own way. If the executor determines that transportation is in fact essential, and that the respective share to which the son is entitled can afford adequate but not luxurious transportation, the recommendation of a good, used automobile at one quarter the price might be the preferred solution. It would be clearly in the best interest of the beneficiary, and one which would receive the court's support should the issue be legally contested.

Many important decisions that an executor might be called upon to make can have lasting effects on the beneficiaries. The decision whether or not to sell a business can be greatly affected by the interest and active participation of the beneficiaries in the business. Whether to place investment securities in investments with guaranteed returns, or with long-term growth potential, also has to be weighed. The personal representative must understand that, although he was in essence hired by the decedent, he is in fact performing his work on behalf of the decedent's heirs, the estate's beneficiaries. Only the personal representative who appreciates this fact will accurately perceive the true nature of his position.

Knowledge of Beneficiaries' Needs and Subject Matter of Estate

In many instances, a decedent with foresight will have selected an executor who has personal knowledge of the subject matter of the decedent's estate and of the specific needs of the beneficiaries. Familiarity with the specific assets would, of course, be a tremendous help to the executor, with resultant benefits to the estate and the beneficiaries. For example, if one of the principal assets of the estate was a business owned by the decedent, and if the executor was also active in the business, the advantage to the estate of continuity and experience could be quickly translated into dollars and cents.

Again, a prior familiarity would be of considerable benefit if decedent's assets were varied and located in different areas. By reviewing the nature of the assets and giving the proposed executor the benefit of consultation during his or her lifetime, the decedent could greatly simplify the eventual tasks of the executor and at the same time enable the executor to realize a great deal more from these assets, to the eventual benefit of the decedent's heirs.

Prior knowledge of the specific needs of the beneficiaries would also be extremely helpful. Because beneficiaries are people, and people's needs are, of course, varied, it is impossible to lump them all together. They may be something as specific as the necessity to have money always available for the purchase of insulin for a diabetic child, or to provide an elderly mother with cash to pay for the daily necessities of life —expenses which may have been previously paid by the decedent.

Experience

You can read twenty books on how to ski, but until you actually experience what it's like to try to put all your weight on your downhill ski while coming down the side of a mountain, you will never really be a good skier.

Experience is of similar value to the personal representative. The brightest twenty-one-year-old son or daughter, or the most intelligent spouse, may lack experience in handling a decedent's affairs. Until they have to make decisions of major significance and have acquired the necessary experience, they lack a vital characteristic of a good executor. Therefore, the decedent who has chosen an experienced executor will have given his heirs a distinct edge.

Professional executors, banks and trust companies are in the business of knowing how to collect the decedent's assets. They have separate departments to handle businesses and evaluate them, supervise and sell real estate, and analyze the relative merits and demerits of the securities that are in the decedent's portfolio.

Likewise, if the decedent has nominated as executor an accountant or stockbroker with expertise in all or some of these areas, quite often a similar advantage can be passed on to the estate.

But while there is no substitute for experience, intelligent individuals who have the ability to obtain the necessary information and experience, as well as the time required to administer the estate, can still do a credible and often outstanding job if they are willing to put time and effort into the performance of their duties.

We do not pretend that this book can be a substitute for experience. However, it can and should be a blueprint for the inexperienced as well as for the experienced personal representative (the wise man—and woman—learns from the mistakes of others). By adhering to the procedures outlined in this book, both the experienced and the inexperienced executor can be certain that he or she has not overlooked any of the crucial elements necessary to the fulfillment of his or her fiduciary obligations. At the same time, by familiarizing themselves with the various components that go into administering an estate and by dealing with each of the components on an individual basis, executors will receive much of the "field experience" that will enable them to successfully perform their duties.

Familiarity with the Decedent's Business

There is no more difficult an asset for an executor to administer than the business interests of a decedent. When the decedent has made plans prior to his or her death for the disposition of the business, the executor's task is greatly simplified. For example, assume decedent had been in a two-person partnership and had signed a business "buy/sell agreement." Suppose the agreement provided that upon the death of either the decedent or the decedent's partner, the surviving partner would be obligated to buy—and the decedent's executor would be obligated to sell—the decedent's interest to the survivor for a preascertained price. That would mean the executor's job would be predetermined. All that the executor would have to do would be to transfer the decedent's business interest to the survivor. In return, the executor would receive the agreed-upon payment. If the surviving partner owned insurance on the life of the decedent, then the surviving partner could pay the proceeds of the policy to the executor in return for decedent's business interest. The executor would then have cash, which could easily be handled as part of the estate.

On the other hand, if no such arrangements were made, it would be necessary for the executor to assume whatever role the decedent had in the business. Depending on the circumstances of the appointment and nature of the business, the business could be either continued or terminated by the executor. If decedent had a will specifically providing for the continuation of the business, the executor could perform his or her duties without the undue pressure of finding an immediate buyer. If, on the other hand, the personal representative is acting without a will, in most cases it would be advisable to secure the approval of the court before continuing to run the business.

Without knowledge of the details of the business, or without any expertise in the specific area involved, the executor or administrator would obviously be working under a considerable handicap. Even a professional executor, such as a bank or trust company, might not have the particular expertise if decedent's business was in a specialized or personalized area in which particular or unique knowledge was necessary in order to survive in the marketplace.

Clearly, the executor who has an understanding of the inner workings of decedent's business has a tremendous edge over the neophyte executor. (Precisely what must be done, and how it must be done, are covered in detail in Chapter 16.)

Management Experience

When a decedent has chosen a bank or trust company to handle his or her affairs, one of the reasons for the choice is the management experience of these large fiduciary institutions. They have the background and the personnel, and have managed many estates that will have much in common with the estate of the individual in question.

In the same vein, the decedent who has selected as executor a member of his family who operates a large business, is trying to obtain for his beneficiaries the management experience of this particular individual.

The President of the United States often selects, as members of his Cabinet, individuals who have obtained their management experience as chief executives of large corporations. Governors and senators running for office often stress their prior management experience. The same necessarily holds true for the position of personal representative. It stands to reason that someone with past management experience would be in a better position to step in and take control of decedent's affairs, using prior expertise as a guide in the handling of decedent's estate.

The personal representative without prior management experience must look on his or her appointment as one in which managerial talents, if not experience, are essential. In most instances, the executor will be controlling the assets of the estate and dealing with the beneficiaries and with various supporting personnel, such as lawyers, insurance agents, stockbrokers and accountants. Therefore, the personal representative must be able to function as kingpin of the administrative management team of the decedent's estate.

Investment Knowledge

If an individual's estate is comprised largely of investment-type securities, he or she would be well advised to select a personal representative with investment knowledge. Again, bank and trust companies figure prominently in this category, since they have entire departments geared specifically to following market conditions and advising their clients, both estates and others, as to current market trends and investment possibilities.

Individuals who have had long and profitable relationships with persons in the investment field, stockbrokers and the like, might want to include these advisors in their estate plan, either as sole executors or as advisors to their designated executor.

Without extensive investment knowledge, an executor should secure the services of skilled advisors and investment personnel. Often, when the estate consists of constantly fluctuating securities, lack of action can be just as serious as improper investment decisions. The executor who retains a security in the estate for many years and watches its value decrease rapidly, or else ignores it completely, can be subject to personal liability despite the fact that he or she took no action whatsoever in regard to that security. It therefore makes sense for the individual nonprofessional executor to secure competent advice when dealing with the securities that comprise the estate of the decedent.

Ability to Serve

Quite often, in deciding whom to appoint as executor, the decedent will have failed to take into consideration the ability of the chosen person or persons to serve. Make no mistake about it, the duties and responsibilities of a personal representative can often require considerable time and effort. (Most moderate or large estates take at least six to nine months to settle, and many take three or more years.) If the designated executor does not have the time available, then the heirs of the decedent might suffer the consequences. It is therefore incumbent on anyone choosing an executor to select a party who will have the necessary time and ability to serve. If not, then at the very least the individual should serve together with a professional executor such as a bank or trust company.

Lack of Conflicts

One area that decedents have often failed to take into consideration is that of potential conflicts caused by their choice of a certain individual, or group of individuals, to act as their personal representative. For example, the decedent might have felt that an older child would be well qualified to manage his or her affairs. While this might very well be true, a conflict could arise between the personal interest of the older child and his or her younger siblings or their mother.

An estate owner sometimes chooses a business associate to act as a personal representative, without considering the effect that the associate's handling of the business might have on the apportionment of profits or proceeds between the associate and the family of the estate owner. For these reasons, it is often advisable to take the necessary steps in advance to prevent potential conflicts. If children are chosen as co-executors, it might be advantageous to have a bank as the third executor, so that any tie-vote decisions could be broken by an independent third party. In the same vein, it might be more advantageous to have the third independent party act as sole executor, thus reducing the possibility of conflict.

Proximity to Estate and Beneficiaries

Another major consideration is the proximity of the proposed executor to the estate and to the beneficiaries. A close relative, such as a brother, living three thousand miles away is sometimes appointed by the decedent in order to ensure that the executor will act in the best interests of the beneficiaries. Unfortunately, in spite of its merits, such an appointment fails to consider that the executor will be far removed physically from the beneficiaries and the assets of the estate. In these instances it would be better if the decedent had appointed a local executor—perhaps a bank or trust company or a nearby relative—with the distant relative keeping close touch with the estate and perhaps serving unofficially as the estate's "advisor." If smaller children were involved, and it was decedent's intention to have them live with the distant relative, then the distant relative could be appointed the guardian of the person of the minor children and would therefore have the right to keep close watch over the interests of his or her wards.

Added Insurance—Your Lawyer

While the proposed executor may not have all of the attributes described in this chapter, there is a method by which the potential of the executor to properly perform his or her duties can be greatly enhanced. Whenever an individual has a good working relationship and rapport with his or her attorney, and when the attorney is experienced in estate matters and knowledgeable about the client's family and business and the client's plans for his or her beneficiaries, the testator or testatrix (the person making a will) could recommend that his or her executor retain the services of the decedent's attorney as attorney for the estate. This gives the decedent added insurance that the provisions of his or her will will be carried out in a manner that is most beneficial for the beneficiaries of the estate.

A skilled and knowledgeable attorney, familiar with decedent's affairs and decedent's wishes, can be a tremendous asset to the executor and can more than make up for the executor's lack of knowledge and experience. While in many states the executor makes the final decision in appointing an attorney for the estate (and, if he is uncomfortable with the attorney who drew the will, should exercise his right to select counsel on his own), in most cases the executor should retain the attorney recommended by the decedent in decedent's will. (The executor should still negotiate the attorney's legal fee and request a satisfactory written explanation of how the fee will be determined *before* the attorney begins the work.)

SUMMARY

1. The attributes of a good executor are (a) caring, (b) competence, (c) an understanding of the needs and circumstances of the beneficiaries, (d) an appreciation of the values and nature of the decedent's assets, (e) experience, (f) familiarity with the decedent's business, (g) management experience, (h) investment expertise, (i) ability to serve, (j) lack of conflicts of interest, and (k) proximity to the estate's assets and its beneficiaries.

2. The employment of a skilled and knowledgeable attorney—one familiar with the decedent's family, business and plans—can often make up for the attributes the executor is missing. The executor usually has the right to select the attorney for the estate. If the testator recommended the use of a particular attorney in the will, the executor should be guided by the testator's wishes—unless there is a valid reason (e.g., greater expertise) to choose another attorney.

3

What an Executor Must Know About the Psychological Aspects of Death and Dying

Facing Faces

As executor, your most difficult task may be that of dealing with the decedent's survivors; you may even be one yourself. Therefore, as executor, you must learn not only to face facts and figures; you must learn to face faces. A good executor should have the skill and sensitivity to work with people who are in shock, disorganized and experiencing extremely volatile emotions. These emotions include feelings of guilt, loss, loneliness and depression.

The Dying Person—A Guide to Understanding the Grief of Survivors

If you understand how grief is experienced by a dying person, you will have a much better grasp of the way in which survivors will handle that awesome experience.

Basically, a dying person experiences five stages of grief (which can occur in any order and at any time): (1) denial, (2) anger, (3) bargaining, (4) depression, and (5) acceptance.

Denial. This is a temporary defense. At almost any age, there is the "it can't happen to me" reaction to thoughts of death. Denial is the healthy way we use to deny our mortality. It is the means by which a dying person deals with the painful and uncomfortable fact of impending death.

Bargaining. This is the "let me live one more year and I'll be good to my wife/husband/children" or "I'll donate money to my church/synagogue" plea. Bargaining is an attempt on an emotional level to postpone what is inevitable on the intellectual and physical levels.

Depression. This reaction is a common response to the actual loss of health or use of part of the body. It is a preparatory measure to the impending loss of life.

Acceptance. Acceptance is often the final stage. The dying person is void of feelings and usually expresses an increased desire and need for sleep. The dying may also experience panic (terror that they have lost control of their fate and that decisions are made without their knowledge or consent), anger (often the dying resent being made to feel like dehumanized objects instead of persons), and depression (sometimes triggered by feelings of loss of importance or control or by feelings of guilt and inadequacy as husbands/fathers, wives/mothers, sons/daughters and brothers/sisters).

It is important to understand that survivors will often experience these same symptoms of grief while the dying person is dying and, almost always, directly afterward.

How Will a Given Person React to Death?

It is impossible, of course, to predict exactly how any given person will react to the death of someone close. The determining factors include (1) how close the bereaved were to the deceased and how they saw him or her ("good," "bad," or a little of both); (2) how emotionally or financially dependent on the deceased they were (if they looked to the deceased for guidance and support, the bereaved may feel helpless and frightened); (3) how much energy and time the bereaved spent helping the deceased (if a father spends his entire life helping his son, the son's death may make the father feel purposeless); and (4) how many other important relationships the bereaved have (they will feel more empty, helpless and depressed if there is little likelihood of replacing the deceased in their lives).

Normal Reactions to Death

Intense discomfort, coupled with mixed responses, can be expected as normal reactions to death. These feelings are typically expressed in the form of palpitations, rapid breathing, sweating, sleeplessness, loss of appetite and constipation.

It has been said that the bereaved are "restless." This is because the comforting routine of normal activity is broken; the housewife no longer has a husband to cook for, and the widower no longer has a wife to whom he can "bring home the bacon." The activities that formed an essential part of these relationships seem to have no purpose once the relationship has ended.

There is often a wish for things to be as they were. This "I can't believe she is gone" thought is expressed by a denial of the person's death or, in more extreme cases, by the lack of any outward display of emotion.

It is common for the bereaved to withdraw from people: much as you pull back when you burn your hand in a fire, a person who has lost a loved one tends to avoid that which led to his or her suffering—a close human relationship. Such a person will keep others at arm's length, may reject old friends and often shun expressions of condolence.

Effect of Death on the Survivors

A breadwinner's death results in drastic changes in the life of the family. These include loss of security and an end to the survivors' dependence on the decedent. Survivors will be required to take over many of decedent's roles and tasks, accept a strange new schedule, and shoulder what are sometimes actually (and are almost always perceived as) harsh and awesome new responsibilities. Especially for widows, this often means a sudden involvement in business and financial affairs.

In every substantial estate, the widow (if there is one) has major roles to perform. Yet in most situations she lacks even a modicum of previous exposure or training to function efficiently in handling legal, business, probate or taxation problems. Quite often she's never balanced a checkbook, let alone handled an $800,000 estate. She has not been shown how to do things which will be her certain responsibility. Nor has she been taught to avoid acts which she should not even attempt.

Ironically, at the very time the widow is first involved in these matters, she is in the worst possible frame of mind. She is depressed, unhappy and insecure, and her entire social life has changed. After the few days when her friends, relatives and close family are there to comfort her, they will return to their normal lives. The widow is left— alone and lonely. Confronting her with strange and complex legal duties is like throwing her into a pitch-black room. She loses all sense of direction, doesn't know where the light switch is and is afraid to move because all sorts of risks and impediments are there in the darkness.

How does the widow feel? One widow said, "I feel like one of those spiraled shells washed up on the beach. Poke a straw through the twisting tunnels inside and nothing is there—no flesh, no life. Whatever lived there has dried up and gone!"

And, although the male pronoun is commonly used to designate the breadwinner/ decedent, it is quite often the *man* who survives. Studies show that a widower faces even more serious emotional problems than many widows do. Men seldom have a support system to hold them up—and *keep* them up.

The word "widow" is appropriate—it comes from Sanskrit and it means "empty."

The shock of that emptiness is not always immediately felt. Another widow said, "It took me some time to grasp the meaning of what happened. The word 'death' didn't mean anything to me. All I thought of was that it would be impossible for Marty to be here one day and gone the next. It was as if the earth had just opened up and swallowed him. My shock turned to panic; I felt lost. I didn't want to see or talk to anyone. The thought of going to bed frightened me because I would always wake up in the middle of the night trying to stifle a scream. I couldn't believe Marty was dead."

Years ago, we had the benefit of a socially accepted collection of rites and ceremonies to help survivors make the transition. In some societies, these rites were performed for weeks or even months after an individual's death. But today, we don't often have elaborate wakes, mourning clothes or annual remembrances. Many of society's rules, rites and ceremonies of the past are gone. And so survivors are not really sure how to cope with death—they have to make their own decisions as to what to do and how to react. This uncertainty produces anxiety.

Survivors experience guilt for what they did or did not do in life to or for the deceased, or simply embarrassment for having lived while the deceased died. Survivors may feel guilty because the death of the deceased has relieved them from heavy, emotionally and financially draining burdens ("If he'd die already, the financial nightmare would end").

At the same time, the bereaved may feel anger at being deserted and left to face life's problems. A young daughter, speaking of her father who had just died, told us, "I felt as though he didn't have the right to die. I wasn't ready for him to die."

Perhaps the most difficult of all emotions that survivors must overcome is a deep sense of loneliness and resentment at being left alone. There are ten million widows in our country—one out of every six women over age twenty-one. A study of over seventeen hundred widows showed that loneliness is the single most serious problem of widowhood. One of those widows said, "It's funny, but it's love and companionship that you miss. You don't get someone out of your system so easily after twenty-six years . . . Being lonesome is a big void that can't be filled."

The second most serious problem of widowhood is the financial pressure of raising children without a father.

So beside their emotional problems, families are likely to have financial problems, or at least concern as to how they will pay current bills and continue to get along after the breadwinner's death. One widow said, "After my husband died, there was the emotional shock. The pain was so deep—so consuming—it seemed unendurable. But I learned to live with it. The economic shock was something else. It didn't strike as fast or hit as furious. It's the sort of thing you don't even notice at first. But after a while, the shock of your economic plight begins to creep into your consciousness like some black, oozing reality that you can't believe or escape. It's true . . . money can't compensate two children for the loss of their father; money can't reach out in the night and caress you; money can't come home at night with a briefcase, a twinkle and a hug; but money can give you some peace of mind." And so survivors must be concerned, among other things, with the need for money—because, to the extent the decedent didn't provide it, his or her survivors have the problem of raising it—or doing without it. This in turn creates incredible psychological pressures.

Bereavement is not a commonplace occurrence in our lifetimes. The whirlwind shock of sudden change is a crisis with which many family members feel particularly unable to cope. Quite often a real, and almost always a perceived, imbalance exists between the difficulty and importance of the problems and the resources available to deal with them. Obviously, professional psychiatric and psychological help may be required.

Survivors must release their ties with the deceased. They must adjust to their new environment and form new relationships. The family must allow mourning to occur, relinquish the memory of the deceased as a force in family affairs and activities, and realign themselves in terms of readjusting responsibilities and needs.

It is particularly important that all (both children and adults) who are touched by the death of the decedent be given an opportunity to adequately work out their feelings about the event. You can expect problems to occur when a person of any age is unable to express grief or tries to hold back natural responses. Symptoms of the morbid and abnormal reactions which tend to occur when there is an unnatural delay include:

1. Exhausting overactivity.
2. Symptoms similar to those manifested in the last illness of the deceased, or the outbreak of other psychosomatic illnesses such as asthma or colitis. (This is a combination of normal mourning and the "It should have been me" feeling.)
3. Furious (and usually unreasonable) hostility against specific persons (often including the estate's executor).
4. Agitated and acute depression (sometimes leading to suicidal thoughts).
5. Extreme and prolonged difficulty in sleeping.

6. Preoccupation with the image of the deceased (you may find dozens of pictures of the deceased suddenly appear throughout the house).

7. Difficulty in continuing normal social interaction and a withdrawal of interest in the outside world.

About the Will and Probate—What They Mean to the Survivors

The will and the probate process itself fulfill important functions in the process of emotional repair known as "mourning." The will is the last communication of the deceased. It has unique emotional meanings because in it the decedent states many of his feelings about the bereaved. Of course, his thoughts are usually not implicit in the words used. But in terms of *who* receives property, *how* that property is to be received, and *when* it will be received, the testator has expressed approval (or disapproval), gratitude (or revenge), and confidence (or a lack of confidence). Likewise, the terms of a will may emphasize that the testator recognized one child's need or another child's deservingness. Or the testator may have favored a blood relative over someone who is loved but is not related (or vice versa).

It is important to recognize that what the testator meant to say when he wrote his will may not be how it is taken by the beneficiaries. A devoted but less needy son who gets less than a proportionate part of his father's estate may resent the injustice of being left less than his less worthy brother.

Choice of Executor—What It Means

You probably have been selected as an executor because the testator trusted and had confidence in you. You may have had a close or very deep emotional relationship.

A bereaved executor, in performing his duties, facilitates the process of coming to terms with the testator's death. By carrying out the wishes of the deceased the executor is retaining and strengthening his relationship with the deceased, but at the same time, as he goes through the stages of the probate process, he is gradually "letting go."

Of course, the opposite is true in some situations. For instance, assume a widow had always been dependent on her husband for every decision. If the couple's son or a bank is named as executor, the sense of helplessness precipitated by the loss of her husband is increased by the lack of control she continues to experience. Her helplessness may generate fear and distrust. The result may be that every move the executor makes may be questioned or viewed with suspicion.

What Can—and Should—the Executor Do?

One of the positive results of the estate planning process is to give survivors a feeling of control, a sense of usefulness and the satisfaction of completing the decedent's (and their own) unfinished business. As executor, you should increase the family members' dignity by empowering them with as much control as possible. Keep in mind that it is not enough to give survivors a voice; you must also give them a listener. Only then can they be active participants in the decision-making process. Hopelessness and depression are precipitated and are exacerbated when individuals can't (or perceive they can't) act on their environment.

Any steps you take as executor to bring all family members into the decision-making process will relieve their feelings of helplessness. The death of a loved one will be experienced as less absurd, and may become more tolerable, if the family knows that the life of the deceased had meaning. So, as executor, you must do what you can to give the family a sense of pride in what the deceased had accomplished.

Accumulating an estate, buying life insurance, preparing the will and trust are all like buying a car, filling it with gas, and expecting that a wife or child who has never been in a car can get in and drive that vehicle in heavy traffic. We can't, of course, make survivors into mechanics, but we can help them learn where the steering wheel is, how to make the car go, how to put on the brakes and how to read road signs. The more you can do to explain "what comes next" and how the family can take the wheel, the better off they will be.

SUMMARY

As executor, then, you must be extremely conscious of the trauma of the bereaved. Understanding the five stages of grief experienced by a dying person (denial, anger, bargaining, depression and acceptance) will help you understand what survivors experience. Every person will react to death differently than others. How the bereaved react is largely dependent on their relationship with the deceased, their emotional and financial dependence, the energy and time they have devoted to the deceased, and how many other important relationships they may have.

Death often results in drastic life-style changes. These are coupled with various physical symptoms of grief that can be normally anticipated, as well as abnormal reactions that occur when the mourning process is delayed or repressed.

Probate is an important part of the "letting go" process; it is also a means of completing the unfinished business of the deceased and at the same time a beginning of the family's taking control.

As executor, any steps you take to bring the survivors into the probate process and give them control will help relieve their feelings of helplessness and help them readjust.

4

How and When to Use the Other Members of the Estate Team

DECEDENT'S APPOINTMENTS

Co-executor

In many instances, people select more than one individual to serve as personal representative under their wills. A husband can name his wife and his bank as co-executors. A widow might appoint her two surviving children as co-executors. If all the executors named in the will choose to serve, there is an obvious need for cooperation.

We should point out that an executor named under the will of a decedent is not required to accept the appointment. It is not unusual for one or more of several named executors (if there is more than one, each is a "co-executor") to decide for some reason that they wish to "renounce" their right to serve as such. This is usually done by filing a "renunciation." The renunciation—a form setting forth their wish not to serve—is filed with the local probate office. This might be done, for example, when a brother and sister are named co-executors and the brother lives thousands of miles from the state of decedent's domicile. In cases where there are close family ties and no possibility of conflicts, this could greatly expedite the handling of the estate and also reduce unnecessary expenses. Some states, for example, require the out-of-state executor to post bond even if the will states otherwise. Distance and travel always cause problems and delays in decision making that could be avoided with a local executor. Sometimes decedents name multiple executors so as not to exclude a member of a class, such as a child, and if this is the only purpose, then renunciation might very well be in order.

In other cases, co-executors are chosen because each has something specific to offer. If, for example, a decedent appointed his bank to serve as co-executor with his wife, two functions are fulfilled. The expertise of the bank is coupled with the widow's personal knowledge of the family's situation, and, in this instance, there is no need for a renunciation. Usually the bank or other selected professional will assist with most of the detail work, and the family member will be advised and consulted at all times with regard to any important decisions. The family member is thereby relieved of the day-to-day tasks that are a necessary and often unwelcome part of being a personal representative.

Major decisions involving the estate should always be made jointly by all the executors serving as such, because errors in judgment or other problems involving the estate will be the responsibility of all the executors. As we stress in Chapter 5, you can become personally liable for the acts of another co-executor. So it is apparent that there must be the utmost cooperation between you. A major problem in this area is that beneficiaries, or other persons or institutions affected by the acts of the executor, can bring suit against the executors personally for their actions. This often results in costly delays and obvious inconvenience, regardless of the ultimate outcome of the suit.

It is therefore absolutely essential for the executors to be in complete agreement on all major issues. Individuals who anticipate possible conflicts among their executors might make provision for this in the will. Decedents have named individuals and banks as executors, and given one or the other precedence in case of disagreement. For the same reason, decedents have appointed either one or three persons to serve as executors, so that there can be a unanimous decision or, at the very least, a majority decision in every instance.

We strongly recommend that you consult with your co-executor on any major decision, and make certain that each co-executor is continually advised of the day-to-day handling of decedent's estate. When one executor has an obvious field of expertise —for example, if an individual appoints his son and his own accountant to serve as co-executors—then the expertise should obviously be utilized to its fullest advantage. In this case, be sure that the nonexpert is fully aware of what is going on. If you are the nonexpert, you should remember that ignorance of the law is no excuse. If you accept the appointment, the obligation goes along with it. Having a co-executor can relieve the burden of handling all of the estate's affairs yourself—but the responsibility always remains on your shoulders.

Trustee

A testator might have selected a trustee to manage the property of one or more beneficiaries of his estate. Trustees are often appointed to handle funds for minor children or incompetent persons. Trustees are also appointed in order to take advantage of tax-saving devices such as the setting up of a marital deduction trust or a qualified terminable interest trust. The exact reason for establishing these trusts is beyond the scope of this work, but an excellent explanation is contained in our book *Get Rich, Stay Rich* (Stein & Day, 1984).

Trustees are often chosen because they are equipped to handle the property in question for the beneficiaries. This is true in situations where the decedent has named a bank, a trust company, or a competent family member or other professional to act as trustee. In most situations, the decedent will have advised the trustee in advance of the appointment. Trusts that are contained in decedent's will are called "testamentary trusts" and do not take effect until the death of the decedent. However, the decedent might have set up a trust during his lifetime, in which case it would be called a "living trust" or *"inter vivos* trust." If decedent had a living trust, some of the assets from the estate often will "pour over" from the will into the trust that is already established. For example, a testator might leave all his personal property (furniture, jewelry, automobiles, etc.) at his death to his wife. He might then provide in his will that the residue of his estate (the rest of his property) is payable to the trust that he had established with the XYZ Bank during his lifetime. So property passing under his will is poured over into the living trust.

In cases where estate moneys are to be paid to trustees for beneficiaries, the money or property must first be administered by the executor. It is your duty and responsibility to administer the estate, and only after the administration has been completed to turn the assets of the estate over to the trustee. Therefore, in most instances, trustees will require a formal accounting from the executor so that they will know exactly what property they are receiving. The trustees will also know the exact amount of the administrative costs taken out of the share to which the beneficiary of the trust would otherwise have been entitled. Since this is the case, you should be especially careful to keep accurate records in order to prepare a proper accounting for the trustee, and to keep in constant touch with the trustee in regard to the progress of the estate. While calling on the trustee's services is not usually required during the administration of the estate, there are often situations where we would recommend that this be considered.

An individual might have selected his or her spouse to act as executor, but chosen a corporate trustee (a bank or trust company) to handle the property in the residue of the estate for his or her spouse and children. In these cases, especially when important business or investment decisions are to be made, it could be beneficial to all concerned if the executor consulted with the trustee and utilized the trustee's services for investment advice, evaluation of decedent's business, or other matters that are beyond the personal knowledge of the individual executor.

Guardian

There are two types of guardians that might be appointed under the decedent's last will. The "guardian of the person" is an individual (or individuals) chosen to take personal care of the decedent's children. Since a surviving parent would, in most instances, be the natural guardian of decedent's children, the right to appoint a guardian of the person usually belongs solely to the surviving parent. In the typical situation, decedent's children would live with the guardian of the person, either in decedent's home or in the guardian's home. In these cases the executor would have to be someone other than the surviving spouse of the decedent, and unless the same person were chosen as both guardian of the person of decedent's children and executor of decedent's estate, it would be necessary for the executor to keep in constant touch with the individual or individuals caring for decedent's children.

An executor should make certain that the needs of the minor beneficiaries are being met, to the greatest extent possible, from the assets of the estate that the executor is administering. This means that benefits to which the children are entitled, such as social security and veteran's or civil service or work-related benefits (discussed in detail in Chapter 11) must be applied for on behalf of the children, and that the estate funds in your hands are invested in such a way that the children are being "properly provided for." What "properly provided for" means, will of course depend on the individual circumstances of the estate. Factors to be considered are the standard of living of the children during decedent's lifetime and the availability of funds in the estate as measured against the future needs of the children. For example, $100,000 might seem sufficient to care for a five-year-old child. But when prorated over the life of the child, and with education costs included in the equation, $100,000 may not go far. So, as executor, you must be aware of the needs of the beneficiaries and at the same time administer the estate as economically as possible. The guardian of the person usually serves until the minor attains majority. The age of majority usually varies from eighteen years to twenty-one years, depending on the laws of the state where the minor resides.

Guardian of the Property

A guardian of the property of the beneficiary may have been selected by the decedent to handle funds or other property of the beneficiary when the latter is unable to handle his or her own funds because of age or for some other reason, such as incompetence, and when the decedent has not chosen to have a trustee appointed to manage the beneficiary's funds. In other words, where there is a need for a person or an institution to manage property for someone else, the testator has the choice of setting up a trust which will be managed by a trustee, or having the property managed for the beneficiary by the guardian of the property. Again, the reasons for selecting either a trustee or a guardian are beyond the scope of this book, but are discussed in detail in the book *Get Rich, Stay Rich*. A guardian of the property, however, has much less flexibility in handling the funds for the minor or incompetent.

If a guardianship is established because of the minority of a child, the guardianship will terminate when the minor attains his or her majority, regardless of the minor's ability to handle money at that time and regardless of the size of the estate to which the minor will then be entitled. Your relationship with the guardian will not differ greatly from the relationship you might have with a trustee. It will be your responsibility to deliver to the guardian of the property the assets to which the beneficiary is entitled under decedent's will or under the intestate laws.

In either event, you should advise the guardian of the property as to the assets available to the beneficiary. You should keep in periodic touch with the guardian. You must in all instances be able to account in detail to the guardian for all the funds you administered for the child or other beneficiary, and present a complete accounting when you close the estate and deliver the property of the minor or incompetent to the guardian.

Attorney

If the decedent died intestate (without a will), the estate's administrator has absolute freedom to select an attorney to help administer decedent's estate. Where the decedent died testate (with a valid will), the executor will typically have the same flexibility, even if the testator specifically mentioned in the will that he wanted his executor to employ the services of a particular attorney: this, under the law of most states, is usually considered merely a suggestion on the part of the decedent and is not binding on you as executor. You have, in most instances, the right to employ an attorney of your choice to help administer a decedent's estate. Since the attorney is an essential part of the estate administration team, many executors prefer to have an individual with whom they can work effectively in the administration of the estate. Whether the attorney is the one originally selected by the decedent or a different one selected by you as personal representative, the services of the attorney are vital to the successful handling of many estates.

Regardless of the asset structure of the estate, in practically every case there are legal as well as tax matters that must be handled properly. The Executor's Checklist (see Appendix) spells out in detail many of the "deadlines" that must be met. Most attorneys familiar with estate work have appropriate procedures for ensuring the timely preparation and filing of the tax forms and other information as needed.

One of the major causes of lawsuits against executors is their improper handling of decedent's business. Does the executor in fact have the right to manage and continue operating the business? How far can the executor go in making changes in the business? These are questions that require the attention of a skilled attorney. The question of "who gets what" is another major problem area. If decedent left his stock in the Mighty Oak Tree Company to his daughter, and the executor wants to sell the stock or take advantage of an option available to that company's stockholders, what should the executor do? If decedent owned a farm, should the executor value the farm on the basis of its present use as a farm or base valuation on the amount that the building developer just offered decedent for the property?

The services of the attorney to the estate are therefore not only important but in many, many instances essential. The attorney should be the executor's sounding board for all but routine decisions. If, for any reason, you feel that you are not getting proper advice, you should seek other counsel. There are cases in which executors who relied on their lawyer's advice were still held responsible by the court for improperly administering decedent's estate. Therefore, choose your lawyer carefully. When you know you have the right lawyer (after reading this book you'll be better able to tell), consult with him or her as frequently as you feel necessary.

Insurance Representative

Often, one of the real heroes on the estate administration team is decedent's insurance representative. Many insurance agents have had a great deal of experience with the financial problems associated with death and can be extremely helpful. A call to the insurance agent who sold the policies should bring fast, *no cost* help. You give the insurance agent (1) a death certificate, (2) a "short certificate" (explained in Chapter 12), (3) the policy itself (be *sure* to photostat the entire policy before letting it out of your hands), and (4) a claim form for the proceeds (the agent will provide you with this form). Alternatively, you can present these documents at the office of the local agency for the insurance company or mail them (return receipt requested, registered mail) to the company's claims department (the home office address is usually on the first page of the policy). You should utilize the services of the insurance agent and the agent's company to assist you in such matters as selection of the appropriate settlement option, proper investment of the proceeds, how best to utilize the vast resources of the insurance company for the benefit of the estate, and a review of the present casualty and property insurance covering the assets of the estate. The insurance representative can also make suggestions to the executor and members of the decedent's family in regard to their new insurance needs.

If you can't locate or don't want to use the decedent's insurance agent, try to find an agent who is a CLU (chartered life underwriter). This designation connotes that its bearer has completed a series of examinations in financial security areas and should be much more helpful than the typical agent. (A good alternative is a ChFC—a chartered financial consultant.)

How can insurance proceeds be used to pay estate expenses and debts? As executor, you may be able to borrow cash from the parties who received the insurance or sell estate assets to that party in exchange for the cash. But be sure to discuss such transactions with the estate's attorney before you execute them.

Cash proceeds (especially since they are usually income tax free) are always a welcome addition to any estate. In most instances, insurance that has been set up properly will not be paid directly to the estate, and therefore technically it will not become your responsibility to administer. (The executor is legally responsible for obtaining the proceeds if the estate has been named beneficiary, or if the executor has been named beneficiary, or if the beneficiary named in the policy predeceased the decedent and no contingent beneficiary was named.) So, although you may help the beneficiaries obtain the proceeds, legally that money isn't payable to you as executor, and you are not responsible for its disposition. That's advantageous. Why? Because proceeds that don't officially come into the estate are treated more favorably in many states' inheritance tax laws. Furthermore, insurance proceeds payable to beneficiaries other than the estate will not become subject to creditors or other claims against the estate.

Stockbroker

Another individual with whom decedent might have had a close relationship, and who can provide you with a wealth of knowledge in regard to the decedent, the decedent's investments and the decedent's investment goals, is his stockbroker. If you are impressed with the stockbroker and with the stockbroker's performance on behalf of the decedent, you can continue with the services of the stockbroker in regard to handling and investing decedent's assets.

There is no liability on the part of the stockbroker to reinvest or change the structure of decedent's investments. That responsibility belongs to you. If, for example, a corporation in which the decedent invested makes a limited offering available to its stockholders, and you, through neglect, fail to take advantage of this opportunity to the detriment of the beneficiaries, you can be held personally liable for your failure to take action. You should therefore obtain all the information possible from decedent's stockbroker concerning decedent's investments and decedent's investment goals, obtain the stockbroker's advice on the proper present approach to decedent's investments, and make certain that the stockbroker was, and is now, acting in the best interests of decedent and decedent's estate. Brokerage firms today have the latest computerized equipment, and make it a point to permit customers to take full advantage of their multifaceted investment services. There is no reason why you should not utilize these services to the fullest advantage of the estate.

PERSONAL REPRESENTATIVE'S APPOINTMENTS

A Little More About the Attorney

As mentioned in the preceding section, the attorney is probably the keystone of the estate administration team. If the personal representative is not satisfied with decedent's attorney, or if the decedent gave no indication of his or her choice of attorney for the estate, the personal representative should, in practically every instance, obtain the services of an attorney qualified in the area of administering decedents' estates. In the case of a very simple estate situation—such as a single jointly owned bank account, the proceeds of one life insurance policy, or jointly owned family home—the functions of the attorney (and *especially the attorney's fee)* should be greatly reduced. In most instances, however, where the estate does consist of property of any real value, we absolutely recommend that the personal representative employ the services of an attorney. As indicated earlier in this chapter, the attorney should be consulted in regard to day-to-day decisions, the legality of investments, the proper procedure for handling decedent's business and, most important, the executor's duties and obligations to the estate and the beneficiaries as set forth under the laws of decedent's domicile. It is impossible in today's society for a nonprofessional executor to be aware of the many intricacies and pitfalls involved in the administration of a decedent's estate, and anyone entering into this jungle without a well-informed guide can expect to become prey to the legal lions and tigers that roam the probate forests.

One word of caution: this applies particularly to the estate's attorney, but also to each and every party you hire to assist you in probating the estate. Be sure—*before they begin to work*—that an hourly or other reasonable fee is agreed upon. *Demand that the fee structure be in writing and signed by the professional* (reasonable fees vary from city to city and according to the expertise of the professional). We recommend that—before you sign *anything*—you talk to at least two or three attorneys. (Keep in mind, however, that they sell time and knowledge, and deserve to be compensated for the time you take to "shop around.") Read the fee structure carefully *before* you sign it. Do *not* be embarrassed to ask "what if" questions. Remember, *when retaining an attorney for the estate, you are in charge, and it is a "buyer's market!"*

Accountant

Although the services of an accountant may not be required in rather uncomplicated estates, the accountant in many instances is an extremely valuable member of the estate team. Where decedent had an ownership interest in a business, and where valuating and business decisions have to be made, the services of an accountant are a must. In placing a value on decedent's business, a review of tax returns, comparisons with other businesses and a review of present business operations are essential. You should first consult with decedent's accountant and, if satisfied, continue those services. If there was no regular accountant, or if you feel that another accountant would best serve the interests of the estate at this point, then obtain such services. Not only are you responsible for death tax returns, state and, in many instances, federal estate tax returns, but there is also the area of gift tax returns to be reviewed, and always income taxes. As will be discussed in detail in Chapter 20, there are many options in regard to taxes, and these apply both to decedent's income taxes and the income taxes of the estate, as well as estate, inheritance and possibly gift taxes. In many instances the attorney is qualified to discuss many of the above, but quite often the services of a CPA will be invaluable in making the necessary tax decisions, in preparing the myriad tax forms that are required, and in doing the valuations discussed in depth in Chapter 26.

Professional Appraisers

When a decedent's assets consist of real estate or business interests or collectible items, the services of professional appraisers may be needed. Most taxing authorities of the states and federal government require real estate appraisals for real estate included on tax returns.

Since the value of the property involved can vary considerably, the executor would be well advised to obtain a competent professional appraiser, and not just another real estate agent. As with all good tax returns, the more qualified information you furnish to the taxing authorities, the more favorably they will look upon your conclusion. A competent appraisal by a respected appraiser can often be well worth the cost.

The need for an appraisal in real estate is obvious. Appraisals for business interests are also a must. While the value of the stock of a company listed on the New York Stock Exchange can be found in a few minutes, the value of a family-owned corporation is far from certain, and requires painstaking evaluation to be given proper credence. A careful and accurate appraisal of the business interest is important not only for tax reasons, but also for setting the value of the business as a going concern in the event of a possible sale and to fix the value at which the beneficiaries receive their interest.

Another area in which appraisals are necessary is that of collectibles. If the decedent had a stamp collection, coin collection, antiques, art, old guns or any other type of valuables, these should also be appraised by someone with expertise in that particular area. While you certainly cannot be expected to assign a value to these assets, it is your responsibility to find someone qualified to appraise property whose value must be professionally determined.

Real Estate Agents

If the estate contains real estate that must be sold, the executor should obtain the services of a qualified real estate agent. The real estate office should be one that serves the area in which the property is located; it should specialize in the particular type of property (residential, commercial or industrial) and should charge a commission that is fair and reasonable in the circumstances and commensurate with commissions being charged by similar offices in the area. In practically every instance, we would recommend that you informally discuss the real estate involved with at least three different real estate offices, utilizing the above criteria before agreeing to sign an exclusive listing for the property in question.

Bank or Trust Company

Although decedent might not have named a bank or trust company as executor or trustee, bank services that are designed to assist in the handling of decedents' estates are also available to individual executors. These services may be obtained on a "fee for service" basis—in other words, you can hire a trust company or bank to assist you. You can also take advantage of the expertise of trust companies by permitting them to handle and invest the estate's assets in a "custodial" account, in which the bank is only acting as custodian of the estate's funds. This relieves you of the responsibility of handling and investing the funds and gives you freedom to deal with the other aspects of the estate. If you don't want to undertake the investment responsibility of the estate, this is an alternative to be considered. (Warning! The track records of banks will vary considerably. Demand evidence of investment performance by at least two or three companies before deciding which one to use. Local newspapers often do these comparisons in an annual review of trust company performance. Banks also will provide, upon your request, the overall portfolio rate earned on common trust funds.)

COURT APPOINTMENTS

Guardian of the Estate

In some cases, it will be necessary for the court to appoint persons or institutions to supervise the handling of funds for particular estate beneficiaries.

In cases where decedent died intestate and property is to pass to minor beneficiaries, the court must appoint a guardian of the property of the minor. This is also true when the beneficiary of decedent's estate is incompetent.

You should never deliver property to a minor or incompetent. Where decedent appointed a guardian or trustee, this problem does not arise. But if the decedent's will did not make provisions for minors or incompetents, or if decedent died intestate, then someone, possibly a parent or close relative of the minor or incompetent, must petition the court having jurisdiction over the minor or incompetent to appoint a guardian. If there is no such person to petition the court, you must take that action as executor.

If the property in question is small, the court, in some instances, may appoint a parent or close relative as guardian with the limitation that the funds be placed in an insured bank account and not be removed until the minor attains majority. In those cases where considerable funds are involved, the courts often prefer the services of a corporate guardian (bank or trust company) to handle the funds of the minor or incompetent's estate.

Guardians and Trustees "Ad Litem"

It may happen in the administration of the estate that someone has to be appointed to look after the interests of an individual or class of individuals. For example, the provisions of a will might be interpreted in more than one way. Assume that, under one interpretation, a nephew of the decedent would receive a share of the estate while under another interpretation the nephew would receive nothing. If the nephew is a minor, someone should be appointed to represent the nephew in presenting his position to the court. In such cases the court, upon the petition of the executor or the administrator, or of another interested party, or by the court's own volition, will appoint counsel to look after the interests of the minors or other class of beneficiaries. These court-appointed persons are often called "guardians *ad litem*" or "trustees *ad litem.*" They are appointed solely for the purpose of representing the interests of the beneficiaries in a particular situation, and serve as such until a determination has been made by the court.

Although the nature of their appointment and the services rendered to the beneficiaries and the estate as a whole are of a technical nature, you should be aware of the circumstances under which guardians and trustees *ad litem* might be called upon to serve during the administration of an estate. A typical example is that of a minor who is a civil lawsuit defendant.

SUMMARY

It is important to remember that you do not have to serve as executor and that you have a right to "renounce." Renunciation is appropriate if you don't wish to serve or there is a good reason why you can't.

If you do decide to serve as executor, and co-executors have been named, you must share information and make all major decisions jointly with them. You can be held personally liable for each other's errors in judgment or breaches in fiduciary duty.

When a trust has been named a beneficiary under the will, it is your duty to prepare an accounting to enable the trustee to know what property will be received and when it will be transferred.

You must contact the "guardian of the person" of any minor beneficiaries and make certain they are "properly provided for." Take appropriate action to apply for benefits such as social security on their behalf. If a "guardian of the property" of a minor has been appointed, you must advise the guardian of the assets available, deliver to that person at the proper time any assets to which the beneficiary is entitled, and present a complete accounting when you close the estate.

As executor you have the right to select any attorney you wish as the attorney for the estate, whether or not that individual drew the will. This is true even if the will suggests that you should employ the drafting attorney. You have the right (if not the duty) to negotiate with the attorney you select with regard to fees. Be satisfied with the fee arrangement before you allow work on the estate to begin. Demand that the estimate and hourly fee be in writing. Use the attorney as frequently as you feel necessary. If the attorney is not responsive to your calls or inquiries or you feel you are not receiving sound advice, seek other counsel.

Life insurance agents are an excellent source of fast, no-cost assistance. A knowledgeable agent (try to find one with a CLU designation) can assist you in selecting settlement options, investing policy, proceeds, and reviewing the life and disability insurance needs of the survivors.

Contact the decedent's stockbroker for information on investments, but keep in mind it is your responsibility to keep estate assets both protected and productive.

Accountants are an invaluable aid in many phases of the administration process. Utilize an accountant not only to prepare the income tax returns of the estate, but also to assist you and the estate's attorney in the valuation of assets and in decisions concerning the operation of any business the decedent owned. Post-death tax decisions should not be made until you have consulted a CPA.

If an estate comprises real estate or business interests or collectible items, professional appraisers are essential both for tax purposes and to fix the value at which beneficiaries will receive their interests. If the decedent had a coin, stamp, gun, art or antique collection, this should be appraised by an independent expert.

Real estate agents are often needed to assist you in the sale of property. Select a local agent who specializes in the type of property in question and who charges a fair and reasonable commission.

Banks and trust companies can be hired on a "fee for service" basis to relieve you of certain responsibilities such as the handling and investment of funds. Demand evidence of investment performance and compare at least three institutions before making your selection.

If the decedent died intestate or the will did not provide for minors or incompetents, the court should be petitioned to appoint a guardian. If there is no parent or close relative of the minor or incompetent, it is your duty to petition the court. You should not (without court permission) deliver property to a minor or incompetent.

Guardians *"ad litem"* should be requested by you in cases where the interests of a particular minor or other beneficiary are in question.

5

Avoiding Fiduciary Liability

Financial Quicksand

It's been said that fiduciary liability is like quicksand. The problem is not always readily apparent and, unfortunately, a liability can entrap you before you realize it. The oversight, all too often, will be quite costly.

Beneficiaries are not content to sit back and let things happen, as they once did. If you leave questions unanswered, or beneficiaries neglected, you may find that attorneys have been retained and litigation is ensuing. "Surcharge" will become an all too meaningful word to you. Even the problems which do not end up in court and are resolved through settlement may adversely affect your relationship with the beneficiaries.

You can minimize the risks of conflict and deter liability. Here are the guidelines:

Duties of the Fiduciary

The most fundamental duty you owe, as an estate's executor, is loyalty. The relationship between you and the estate's beneficiaries arises out of the very nature of the duties of an executor.

Every action you take must be for the benefit of those individuals. Confidentiality is inherent in the duty of loyalty. You should never disclose information about the estate or its affairs to unauthorized persons.

Another extremely important duty related to the duty of loyalty is that of avoiding conflicts of interest. This means that, as an executor, you must never put yourself in a position that might favor your interest over the interests of the beneficiaries you are representing. Furthermore, aside from a fee for the services you are rendering (assuming the will does not prohibit such a fee, and assuming you have not agreed to serve without a fee), you must not derive any personal advantage from, or realize a profit in, dealing with the estate.

As a fiduciary, you have a duty to exercise care, diligence and prudence in dealing with the estate's property. But what is meant by exercising "care, diligence and prudence?" The answer is that your conduct will be considered reasonable if you act as a "prudent man." This "prudent man" theory means that you must act with the care and skill that a prudent man would exercise in his own affairs. (Corporate and other professional fiduciaries are deemed to have special skills or expertise superior to those of a prudent man, and are typically held by courts to a higher standard.)

As a fiduciary, you are under a duty to preserve and protect the assets in your custody. This is particularly important in the case of assets such as real estate, household furniture, furnishings and coin, stamp, art and other collections. Obviously, you'll have to provide adequate security and protection for such items. One of your first roles as executor is to have an insurance agent review all of the estate's assets and immediately obtain sufficient insurance coverage. You may be held personally accountable for any loss which occurs to uninsured or underinsured assets.

With respect to investing, your first duty is to protect capital. But you're also under a duty to use reasonable care and skill to make property productive, within the guidelines of the will and the provisions in it (as well as state law restrictions). With regard to your powers, you must consider both inflation and the cost of undue risk. Obviously, if you invest estate money in speculative ventures you are risking personal liability in the event a loss is sustained (unless that investment is specifically authorized by the terms of the will). The bottom line is that you must exercise prudence, discretion and intelligence to safeguard the estate's principal, but at the same time generate as much income as possible.

Fortunately it is your conduct, rather than the investment performance, which is judged by the courts. You will be personally liable only when losses result from your imprudent conduct, rather than because investment performance has not been as good as possible. You may retain non-income-producing assets, but only if the will specifically authorizes you to hold those assets, or if there is some other good reason for keeping them.

Maintaining accurate records is another important duty. You must account periodically to the beneficiaries (letting them know what is going on is an extremely good way to avoid litigation), and maintaining accurate records greatly reduces the possibility of your violating the duty of loyalty. Conversely, if you do not maintain good records you will be held liable if there is a loss or expense that can be traced to your failure to do so.

As executor, you cannot delegate your fiduciary responsibility. This duty "not to delegate" is derived from the very nature of your position as executor. Obviously, you are entitled to employ legal counsel, accountants and others to help in your tasks. But you have a personal duty to perform the responsibilities of an estate's executor; and, even though you may delegate certain administrative or "ministerial" tasks, you have a duty to the beneficiaries of the estate to supervise the conduct of the people you hire. As stated in various cases, it is the executor who is responsible for the filing of an estate tax return even though an attorney was employed to do so. These cases have held the executor personally liable for the interest and penalty charges the estate had to pay, even though it was the attorney who was late in filing the return.

If you are one of several co-executors, each of you is under a duty to the beneficiaries to participate in the administration of the estate and to use reasonable care to prevent other co-executors from breaching fiduciary responsibilities.

What Happens If?

What happens if you do breach one of the duties discussed above? If you violate (or don't perform) any duty which you owe to the beneficiaries of the estate, and if that breach of duty is intentional or negligent and you are personally at fault, you will be held liable for damages resulting from that breach. In other words, a beneficiary can recover those values that he would have enjoyed had there been no breach.

Here are some examples:

1. If you sell an asset without authority to do so and the beneficiaries who are entitled to that asset lose their interest in that asset because of your action, you are liable for the full present value of the asset. In fact, if a beneficiary can show willful misconduct on your part, a court may grant punitive damages as well. Of course, if the loss would have occurred even in the absence of your breach of fiduciary duties, you may not be chargeable with the loss.

2. If you unnecessarily spend estate money, courts may consider your actions negligent. Likewise, any action (or omission) that results in a loss can be considered "waste," and you can be held liable. Obviously, you must avoid speculation since your primary duty is to preserve and protect the estate's assets. In this regard, undue delay in accomplishing your duties may be considered negligent. For instance, you should ascertain as quickly as possible the amount of cash required to administer the estate. Make an estimate of how much money you'll need and which assets have to be sold to pay taxes and for other estate administration expenses. If estate assets depreciate in value while you have unduly delayed selling them, you may be held liable. In one estate, the beneficiary sought to surcharge the executor for negligence because too much time was allowed to elapse and the value of the corporate stock held by the estate had fallen precipitously. The executor had only sold a few shares of stock to cover cash needs. Fortunately, the executor in that case was given absolute discretion by the will to hold property and refrain from immediately diversifying a large block of stock received at the decedent's death. But a lack of attention in administering the estate and failure to notice a drop in stock values could cause you to be surcharged.

A way to safeguard against such problems is to continually inform—and consult with—the beneficiaries concerning investment decisions, and to keep such communications in writing. Litigation can often be avoided by combining prompt action with constant information and consulting with the beneficiaries. You must make a reasonable, conscious effort to exercise judgment in arriving at investment decisions. If you do—and can prove it—the courts will look beyond the performance of any stocks, bonds or other investments.

3. Where there is a conflict of interest or self-dealing, you will clearly be held liable. For example, in one famous case, three art dealers, executors of the estate of a famous artist, were engaged in self-dealing. They sold his art work substantially below the fair market value of the paintings. The court not only awarded the beneficiaries the actual value of the paintings, but also added an award for "appreciation" damages. The executors' liability exceeded $9 million dollars. In that particular case, two of the executors were considered not to have exercised good judgment and to have violated their duty of undivided loyalty. The third executor was deemed only to have lacked good judgment; but, because he was aware of the conflict of interest of the other two executors and did nothing about it, his liability exceeded $6 million.

How should these individuals have proceeded? Where there is any question at all of a conflict of interest, it is important to instruct your attorney to seek court approval ahead of time before you sell any estate assets.

4. As we mentioned above, at times you will have to hire experts to advise or assist you. Keep in mind that you may only delegate so-called ministerial acts—acts which are administrative and do not involve major decisions requiring judgment and discretion. Certain decisions, such as whether or not to make certain tax elections, may only be made by you as executor. Here, again, the advice of counsel is essential.

5. As executor, you are liable not only for your own acts, but for the acts of your co-executors as well. You have a duty to carry out your own responsibilities in a prudent manner, as well as to be certain that your co-executors also act prudently. If you approve a breach of fiduciary duty on the part of another co-executor, you are as responsible as if you had committed the breach yourself. The $6 million surcharge against the third executor in the case described above illustrates this point quite clearly. It is also extremely important, if you are taking over the duties of a prior executor, that before you accept the appointment you have counsel thoroughly review all the acts of any previous executor. Why? Because if your predecessor committed a breach of duty, and if you do not take appropriate action on behalf of the beneficiaries, you are guilty of your "own malfeasance." In other words, if you don't force a previous executor to make the beneficiaries "whole," you are permitting a known breach to continue and you can be held guilty of a breach of duty yourself.

About Investing Estate Assets

In many cases, beneficiaries have surcharged executors because estate assets have been depleted. The rules discussed above indicate how important it is to invest trust property prudently. Your most important job is to meticulously document what investment decisions you are making and why you are making them. If you can show the courts (and beneficiaries) why you made these particular decisions, and also that you periodically reviewed your investment decisions, you significantly reduce the potential for a successful lawsuit against you.

You must be more concerned with safety of principal than in "making a fortune." Obviously, this means that all your client's assets should not be in one investment (remember Penn Central stock?). Diversification is the key to safety in this area. Is there a provision in the will relieving you from the obligation of diversifying assets? Even with this special language, you must maintain records to show why you did not diversify. Many states impose a duty to diversify, and if you ignore that rule you may be held liable for any loss that occurs.

If you are going to make any investment changes, timeliness is the key. This means that you must implement your plans as quickly as possible after prudent decisions have been made.

Filing Tax Returns

An astonishing number of cases involve an executor's failure to file tax returns in a timely manner. Many of these cases involve individuals who have relied upon the advice of an attorney or accountant as to when the return should be filed. It is your duty to know the appropriate filing dates and to be sure a return has been filed. Unless you have reasonable cause for not complying with the time requirement, you will be held personally liable if the tax is late or not paid.

You must also show that you have given consideration to tax planning. As shown in Chapter 21, you as executor can make a number of elections. You should use that chapter as a checklist to document (in the form of a written memo) that you have considered each one of those elections and your reasons for accepting or rejecting them.

Communicating with Beneficiaries

Perhaps the key reason executors are sued is that they have failed to give personal attention to the beneficiaries. Regardless of whether you are a corporate or individual executor, a strong relationship with the beneficiary, fostered by constant, thorough and humanistic communication, will serve as a natural deterrent to conflict and minimize the possibility of liability. By taking the time to discuss estate transactions, you invite discussion and settlement rather than litigation.

It is suggested that you keep beneficiaries informed by telephone (but keep written memos of your conversations in writing) and, whenever possible, in person.

Before you take action, contact and consult with the estate's attorney, accountant and other professionals.

Taking the Time and Being Timely

Every beneficiary wants his or her share of an estate—yesterday! Certainly, the one thing you will learn from this book is that you cannot make immediate distributions of all estate assets without incurring great personal risk in the form of liability to creditors and taxing authorities. (You may be able to make partial distributions, but you should not do so without consulting the estate's attorney.)

You are, however, responsible for acting in a decisive, organized and timely manner. This means that you should promptly return the phone calls of beneficiaries and professionals retained to work with you. It also means that "tough" decisions should be made without undue delay.

Unfortunately, the very nature of probate and administration is time consuming. The Federal Estate Tax Return, for example, is normally not filed until at least nine months (often with extensions) have passed. But beneficiaries should be informed when certain things can be expected to occur, and it is your job to ensure that the process is not extended beyond its built-in time delays.

Protecting Yourself by Agreements

There is no such thing as a "model" estate. Every estate has its unique problems, and difficult decisions are often associated with those problems. There are several ways you can protect yourself legitimately for the actions you must take.

It is extremely important that you obtain a receipt for any assets you distribute to a beneficiary. That receipt should describe the assets in detail so that you can prove what has been distributed, to whom and when. It also shows that the beneficiary has accepted the asset from the estate; if he has signed a "receipt in full" for his share, the burden is shifted to him to prove that he has not received everything to which he is entitled.

If you are in the process of changing investments, as mentioned earlier, you should obtain the written consent of all beneficiaries who are of legal age. The written consent given by individuals who have full knowledge of all relevant facts, and of their legal rights, protects you from the consequences of the act. In other words, if a competent adult beneficiary consents in writing to a new investment, assuming he or she was under no inducement to act, that beneficiary cannot later hold you liable for losses arising out of the change in investment. Of course, if that consent is withdrawn before you purchase the new asset, you are not protected by the original written consent. Although you do not have to obtain consent to make investments allowed by the terms of the will, a written consent from a competent adult beneficiary will protect you from a charge that you are acting outside the scope of your authority.

If there are several beneficiaries, they must all consent to an act you are about to take. A beneficiary who does not consent has the right to question your action and is not bound by consents given by other beneficiaries. For instance, a consent you obtain from an income beneficiary (one entitled to income, rents or dividends produced by the property) does not protect you from remaindermen (beneficiaries entitled to principal at a later date) who question your actions.

One of the most important techniques that protect you, as executor, from liability is the "release." A release is a document which discharges you from liability for actions (or omissions) of the past. A consent is a written document exonerating you for what you are about to do. A release is what you obtain if you have not gotten a consent. But a release is not effective unless the beneficiary had knowledge of all relevant facts and you have not used any improper conduct to influence the beneficiary to consent to a transaction that has already taken place.

Another extremely important method to prevent a beneficiary from holding you liable for breach of your duties as executor is to obtain a court order. A court order authorizing a particular action will protect you from future liability. For instance, in most states an "accounting" (discussed in detail in Chapter 28) is required before you can be released from your duties. You must account for what came in, what went out and to whom it went. You must show that you have properly carried out the terms of the will under which you are acting. If the court accepts that accounting (after the beneficiaries have been given proper notice and opportunity to be heard), you will be protected from future liability for the acts you have disclosed in the accounting. In many cases, the will may not be clear. It is extremely important for you to petition the court for direction so as to avoid (or settle) disagreement among the beneficiaries (or among your co-executors). If you do not seek court approval and petition the court before taking action, you in essence expose yourself to unnecessary liability.

The most expeditious way to limit your liability is to enter into a settlement agreement with all the beneficiaries. If there is conflict between you and the beneficiaries, a private out-of-court settlement may be the most appropriate way to minimize conflict and deter liability.

SUMMARY

Throughout this book you will find that, as executor, you have accepted a multiplicity of duties and responsibilities. These are both time-consuming and often extremely significant in terms of the decisions you must make. Compounding these problems are the duties of the fiduciary: confidentiality; avoiding conflicts of interest; duty to exercise care, diligence and prudence; duty to preserve and protect estate assets; duty to maintain accurate records and account periodically to beneficiaries; duty not to delegate responsibilities involving major judgments and discretion; and duty to act in a timely manner.

6

Pre-death Planning Techniques

You may be facing the uncomfortable task of dealing with a dying friend or relative. It is extremely important that you consider and implement the appropriate devices and techniques to (1) ease administration, (2) increase the size of the estate going to beneficiaries, (3) reduce transfer taxes, (4) decrease income taxes, (5) provide cash to pay taxes and other expenses, and (6) defer the payment of transfer taxes. The right steps taken in the weeks, days, or even hours before death can simplify the job of the executor and increase the financial security of the beneficiaries by thousands of dollars.

Easing Administration

The first step to ease administration is to have the friend or relative sign a "durable power of attorney." This is a legal document giving you or some other specified person the right to act on behalf of the dying person. The power can be drawn broadly so that the "attorney in fact" (you don't have to be a licensed lawyer) can sign tax returns, make gifts or take other tax-saving actions on behalf of the person who executed the power. The power should be "durable." This means it should specifically state that it is to continue in the event of disability or incompetence of its maker.

POWER OF ATTORNEY

KNOW ALL MEN BY THESE PRESENTS, that I, Brett A. Rosenbloom, of Delaware County, Pennsylvania, hereby revoke any general power of attorney that I have heretofore given to any person, and by these Presents do constitute, make and appoint my brother, Eric J. Rosenbloom, of Delaware County, Pennsylvania, my true and lawful attorney.

1. To ask, demand, sue for, recover and receive all sums of money, debts, goods, merchandise, chattels, effects and things of whatsoever nature or description which are now or hereafter shall be or become owing, due, payable, or

belonging to me in or by any right whatsoever, and upon receipt thereof, to make, sign, execute and deliver such receipts, releases or other discharges for the same, respectively, as he shall think fit.

2. To deposit any moneys which may come into his hands as such attorney with any bank or bankers, either in my or his own name, and any of such money or any other money to which I am entitled which now is or shall be so deposited to withdraw as he shall think fit; to sign mutual savings bank and federal savings and loan association withdrawal orders; to sign and endorse checks payable to my order and to draw, accept, make, endorse, discount, or otherwise deal with any bills of exchange, checks, promissory notes or other commercial or mercantile instruments; to borrow any sum or sums of money on such terms and with such security as he may think fit and for that purpose to execute all notes or other instruments which may be necessary or proper; and to have access to any and all safe deposit boxes registered in my name.

3. To sell, assign, transfer, and dispose of any and all stocks, bonds (including U. S. Savings Bonds), loans, mortgages or other securities registered in my name; and to collect and receipt for all interest and dividends due and payable to me.

4. To invest in my name in any stock, shares, bonds (including U. S. Treasury Bonds referred to as "flower bonds"), securities or other property, real or personal, as to vary such investments as he, in his sole discretion, may deem best; and to vote at meetings of shareholders or other meetings of any corporation or company and to execute any proxies or other instruments in connection therewith.

5. To enter into and upon my real estate, and to let, manage, and improve the same or any part thereof, and to repair or otherwise improve or alter, and to insure any buildings thereon; to sell, either at public or private sale or exchange any part or parts of my real estate or personal property for such consideration and upon such terms as he shall think fit, and to execute and deliver good and sufficient deeds or other instruments of warranty or otherwise as he shall see fit, and to give good and effectual receipts for all or any part of the purchase price or other consideration; and to mortgage my real estate and in connection therewith to execute bonds and warrants and all other necessary instruments and documents.

6. To contract with any person for leasing for such periods, at such rents and subject to such conditions as he shall see fit, all or any of my said real estate; to give notice to quit to any tenant or occupier thereof; and to receive and recover from all tenants and occupiers thereof or of any part thereof all rents, arrears of rents, and sums of money which now are or shall hereafter become due and payable in respect thereof; and also on non-payment thereof or of any part thereof to take all necessary or proper means and proceedings for determining the tenancy or occupation of such tenants or occupiers, and for ejecting the tenants or occupiers and recovering the possession thereof.

7. To commence, prosecute, discontinue or defend all actions or other legal proceedings pertaining to me or my estate or any part thereof; to settle, compromise, or submit to arbitration any debt, demand or other right or matter due me or concerning my estate as he, in his sole discretion, shall deem best and for such purpose to execute and deliver such releases, discharges or other instruments as

he may deem necessary and advisable; and to satisfy mortgages, including the execution of a good and sufficient release, or other discharge of such mortgage.

8. To execute, acknowledge and file all Federal, State and Local tax returns of every kind and nature, including without limitation, income, gift and property tax returns.

9. To engage, employ and dismiss any agents, clerks, servants or other persons as he, in his sole discretion, shall deem necessary and advisable.

10. To convey and transfer any of my property to trustees who shall hold the same for my benefit and/or the benefit of my children and other members of my immediate family upon such trust terms and conditions as to my attorney shall deem desirable.

11. To make gifts to my wife and/or issue upon such terms and conditions as he in his discretion shall determine.

12. In general, to do all other acts, deeds and matters whatsoever in or about my estate, property and affairs as fully and effectually to all intents and purposes as I could do in my own proper person if personally present, giving to my said attorney power to make and substitute under him an attorney or attorneys for all the purposes herein described, hereby ratifying and confirming all that the said attorney or substitute or substitutes shall do therein by virtue of these Presents.

13. In addition to the powers and discretion herein specifically given and conferred upon my attorney, and notwithstanding any usage or custom to the contrary, to have the full power, right and authority to do, perform and to cause to be done and performed all such acts, deeds and matters in connection with my property and estate as he, in his sole discretion, shall deem reasonable, necessary and proper, as fully, effectually and absolutely as if he were the absolute owner and possessor thereof.

14. In the event of my disability or incompetency, from whatever cause, this power of attorney shall not thereby be revoked.

15. The following is an example of the signature of the person I am appointing my true and lawful attorney:

_____
ERIC J. ROSENBLOOM

IN WITNESS WHEREOF, I have hereunto set my hand and seal this   day of   , 19   .

_____ (SEAL)
BRETT A. ROSENBLOOM

STATE OF PENNSYLVANIA:

            SS.

COUNTY OF DELAWARE

Before me, the undersigned, a Notary Public within and for the County of Delaware, Commonwealth of Pennsylvania, personally appeared Brett A. Rosenbloom, known to me to be the person whose name is subscribed to the within instrument, and acknowledged that he executed the same for the purposes therein contained.

IN WITNESS WHEREOF, I have hereunto set my hand and official seal
this _____ day of _____ , 19 ____ .

_____

NOTARY PUBLIC

SOURCE: *Get Rich, Stay Rich* by Plotnick and Leimberg, Stein & Day Publishers, Briarcliff Manor, N.Y.

Locating and listing all important documents should be second on the list of priorities of the executor-to-be. These documents (including bank accounts; life, health, fire, liability, and other insurance policies; real estate deeds; wills and trusts; stocks, bonds, and other securities; birth certificates, marriage licenses and marital agreements; military service records; social security information, etc.) should be placed in a safe-deposit box with an inventory of its contents. The names, addresses and phone numbers of bankers, insurance agents, brokers, accountants, attorneys and other advisors should also be placed in the safe-deposit box. Other persons' property should be removed from the box.

All wills, life insurance policies and employee benefit beneficiary designations should be reviewed and changed if appropriate and necessary.

A revocable trust should be considered to ease estate administration. Placing property into a revocable trust can provide for property management both during and after the lifetime of the dying individual. A revocable trust allows a smooth transition and may also eliminate some of the cost, delay and uncertainty encompassed in the probate process. The estate owner may be both the primary trustee and the primary beneficiary, and can also designate another person to take over at the estate owner's death or incapacity as a secondary or "step up" trustee.

A "living will" should be considered. If an individual desires that extraordinary means of life support not be used to prolong life, that desire should be formally expressed. Several states (including Arkansas, California, Idaho, New Mexico, North Carolina, Oregon and Texas) have already enacted laws making it easier for doctors or family members to honor such wishes. In other states a living will has no legal effect.

Proposed Living Will

DECLARATION MADE THIS _____ DAY OF _____

I, _____ being of sound mind, willfully and voluntarily make known my desire that my dying shall not be artificially prolonged under the circumstances set forth below, do hereby declare:

If at any time I should have an incurable injury, disease or illness certified to be a terminal condition by two physicians who have personally examined me, one of whom shall be my attending physician, and the physicians have determined that my death will occur whether or not life-sustaining procedures are utilized and where application of life-sustaining procedures would serve only to artificially prolong the dying process, I direct that such procedures be withheld or withdrawn and that I be permitted to die naturally with only the administration of medication or the performance of any medical procedures deemed necessary to provide me with comfort care.

In the absence of my ability to give directions regarding the use of such life-sustaining procedures, it is my intention that this declaration shall be honored by my family and physicians as the final expression of my legal right to refuse medical or surgical treatment and accept the consequences from such refusal.

I understand the full import of this declaration and I am emotionally and mentally competent to make this decision.

Signed _____

City, County, State of Residence _____

_____

The declarant has been personally known to me and I believe him or her to be of sound mind.

Witness _____

Witness _____

SOURCE: *Get Rich, Stay Rich* by Plotnick and Leimberg, Stein & Day Publishers, Briarcliff Manor, N.Y.

Forms for anatomical gifts, if desired, should be signed and the appropriate hospitals or other donees should be notified of the impending gift. Individuals who feel strongly that no gift should be made of any part of their body should so state clearly in the will as well as in a "letter of instructions."

A letter of instructions is a private, informal, nonlegal document, usually left with immediate relatives, explaining one's wishes with respect to highly personal matters that shouldn't be stated publicly in the will. This letter should contain a list of financial advisors, such as CLUs (chartered life underwriters), ChFCs (chartered financial consultants), CFPs (certified financial planners), attorneys, accountants, or others who can be relied upon for advice and assistance.

If a business is involved, arrange for successor management while the business owner is still alive. You can often do these things more easily and profitably while the estate owner is alive than at a time when you are more likely to be emotionally distraught.

Establish domicile to avoid state death taxation by more than one state. If decedent lived in two or more houses in the course of one year, more than one state may attempt to tax his or her property unless it is clear that decedent's home was in one state. To establish domicile, the individual should (1) register to vote in the desired state; (2) apply for a certificate of domicile if the state (such as Florida) issues one; (3) transfer all bank accounts to the desired state; (4) purchase all securities in that state and have them located in the broker's local office or in a safe-deposit box; (5) address credit card correspondence to the appropriate office in the desired state; (6) apply for a driver's license in the desired state; (7) affiliate with a religious organization in the desired state; (8) have Social Security checks and other correspondence mailed to the house in the desired state; (9) file all tax returns from the desired state; and (10) live in the house in the desired state for more than six months.

Increasing the Size of the Estate

Following are several ways to increase the amounts that will go to the estate owner's heirs.

All life insurance policies should be checked for a "waiver of premium" clause. This clause requires the insurer (assuming the requirements specified in the insurance contract are met) to continue the policy in full force. The policy owner is relieved of the burden of paying premiums. In fact, the insurer must also repay every dollar of premium paid after the insured became totally disabled. (Money that otherwise would have been used to pay premiums can be used for living expenses or given away.) The policy cash values and dividends build up while premiums are waived, just as if the policy owner had continued to pay the full premium.

If the policy does not contain a waiver of premium provision or for some reason it doesn't apply, check with the insurer about "extended term" insurance. The insurance company takes the whole life policy and converts it to a term policy (at no charge). This relieves the policy owner of the burden of making premium payments and continues the full amount of coverage for a limited period of time.

Flower bonds are U.S. government issues that can be purchased at banks or from a stockbroker. The Treasury Department of the federal government will buy these bonds back from a decedent's estate at 100 cents on the dollar even though they may have been purchased a few days before for an amount significantly below face value. In other words, flower bonds (they have an engraving of a flower on their reverse side) can be bought at a discount (mainly because they pay a very low rate of interest) even on one's deathbed and are redeemable at face value in payment of the federal (but not state) estate tax. It is important to note that these bonds must be purchased (either by the estate owner or by someone acting on his or her behalf under a power of attorney) while the estate owner is alive and must be owned by the estate owner at death; they cannot be purchased after death by the estate's executor and then used to pay federal estate taxes.

Some individuals continue to work until shortly before their deaths. Increasing the salary of such individuals may enlarge death benefits under certain fringe benefit plans. If the estate owner controls the business and if pension, group life insurance, or other employee benefits are based on a multiple of salary, an increase in salary may significantly increase the amount payable at death. For instance, if group insurance payments are twice the salary for all covered employees, a five-thousand-dollar increase in salary results in a ten-thousand-dollar increase in life insurance coverage.

Reducing Transfer Costs

The cost of transferring property from one individual to another can be greatly reduced by a few simple steps:

Check every married estate owner's will. Has it been updated since September 13, 1981? An important change of law on that date makes it possible to save an incredible proportion of estate taxes. But if the will has not been changed since that date, it may not qualify for the unlimited federal estate tax marital deduction. Roughly half of the estate may be needlessly subjected to federal estate taxes. Be sure to check with legal counsel and see that all wills and trusts signed before that date are reviewed.

Repay life insurance policy loans. Most states treat life insurance more favorably than any other property for death tax purposes. For example, in Pennsylvania, if an individual left $100,000 in cash to a brother, the state death tax would amount to $15,000. If the same person left the same brother $100,000 in the form of life insurance, there would be no tax at all. The $15,000 difference is only part of the savings. None of the life insurance is subject to probate costs, legal fees or other transfer expenses.

If decedent has named his estate as beneficiary of life insurance (or if the beneficiary named has predeceased the insured), suggest he or she change the beneficiary designations—*immediately!* Otherwise, the insurance proceeds may needlessly be subjected to both state inheritance taxes and the claims of creditors.

Use the $10,000 per donee annual federal gift tax exclusion. Each person may give up to $10,000 in cash or in the form of any other type of property—entirely gift tax free—to anyone (whether or not related) year after year. Once the gift is made, it is removed from the estate even if the donor (the person making the gift) dies within a day of the time the gift is made. All income and appreciation earned by the gifted property from the day of the gift is removed from the estate and escapes taxation and legal fees. So a dying individual with three married children and six grandchildren could give twelve gifts (one to each child, one to each child's spouse, and one to each grandchild) of $10,000 and remove the whole $120,000 from his or her estate. These gifts also avoid probate and are typically not subject to a will contest. A broadly drawn durable power of attorney will enable the "attorney in fact" to make these gifts on behalf of the estate owner.

Decreasing Income Taxes

A reduction in income taxes translates into an increase in the amount a person's heirs will receive. Here is one way to reduce income taxes:

Estate owners who plan to make gifts to charity in their will should consider making those gifts before death. Often the income tax savings on the immediate gift outweigh the estate tax deduction available at death. This is especially true for most married couples and individuals with modest estates. A lifetime charitable contribution is almost always preferable to one made after death. Furthermore, lifetime gifts remove the property from the possibility of an attack on the will and may save probate and legal costs as well.

Providing Cash and Deferring the Time to Pay the Tax

Individuals who own closely held businesses have two unique opportunities: (1) they can arrange for their businesses to pay their estate taxes through what is known as a "Section 303 stock redemption"; and (2) they can also delay the payment of federal estate taxes and spread payments out over fourteen years from the date of death under what is called a "Section 6166 installment payout."

As in the case of all tax-planning devices, you should consult the estate owner's attorney and accountant to ensure qualification for a Section 303 stock redemption. In a nutshell, if the value of the closely held business exceeds a specified proportion of the estate (it must exceed 35 percent of the gross estate after certain adjustments), the corporation can pay cash or other property to the estate in return for stock. Arranged properly, the transaction will permit a tax-free bailout of otherwise taxable cash from the corporation and provide cash to pay (1) federal estate taxes, (2) state death taxes, and (3) funeral and administrative expenses. Lifetime planning can help ensure that an individual's estate will qualify for this extremely favorable means of obtaining cash for estate liquidity needs. The form on p. 46 can be used to test qualification.

Deferring the payment of federal estate taxes is possible with approval of the IRS. It is also allowed under Section 6166 of the Internal Revenue Code as a matter of right to an estate if certain tests are met. One test is basically identical to the Section 303 "more than 35 percent" test. In both cases, planning while the estate owner is alive can make it more likely that the estate will qualify. In some cases, gifts or sales of assets will enable an otherwise nonqualifying estate to utilize these two important provisions.

SUMMARY

There are many steps you should take to ease administration, increase the financial security of beneficiaries, lower the costs of transferring estate assets, provide cash to pay taxes, and delay the time those taxes must be paid if a friend or relative is dying. Although you have no duty or right to act before you are officially appointed executor (and of course this cannot occur until the estate owner's death), actions taken even immediately prior to death can make a meaningful difference.

Premortem planning tools and techniques include the durable power of attorney (authority to act on the estate owner's behalf); location and listing of all documents and the names of key advisors; the review and updating of wills, life insurance policies, and employee benefit plans; and the creation of a revocable trust. A living will (stating the desire that extraordinary means of life support not be used) should be considered. Likewise, an individual's desires concerning anatomical gifts and other highly personal matters should be stated in a letter of instructions. Domicile should be clearly established to avoid death taxation in two or more states.

The size of the estate should be increased through waiver of premium, extended term life insurance, and the use of flower bonds to pay the federal estate tax at a discount. In some cases increasing salary may have the effect of increasing benefits.

Transfer costs can be reduced by revising certain wills and trusts drawn before September 13, 1981. You should repay policy loans and make sure the estate is not

Determination of Whether Estate Qualifies for Sec. 303 Stock Redemption

(1) FEDERAL ESTATE TAX VALUE OF CORPORATE
STOCK INCLUDED IN GROSS ESTATE . . . . $ _____
(The value of stock of two or more corporations
can be aggregated if 20% or more of the value
of the outstanding stock of **each** such corporation
is included in the decedent's gross estate.)

(2) 35% of ADJUSTED GROSS ESTATE
(Form 102, line 5) . . . . $ _____

_____ Does qualify   _____ Does **not** qualify

If line 1 **exceeds** line 2, a redemption under Section 303 is
considered a sale or exchange rather than a dividend **to the
extent** the selling stockholder's interest is reduced
directly or the stockholder is bound to contribute to the
payment of

    (a) deductible funeral and administration
        expenses . . . . $ _____

    (b) federal estate taxes . . . . $ _____

    (c) state death taxes . . . . $ _____

    (d) interest collected as part of above
        taxes . . . . $ _____

Maximum allowable Section 303 redemption . . . . $ _____

SOURCE: *Get Rich, Stay Rich* by Plotnick and Leimberg, Stein & Day Publishers, Briarcliff Manor, N.Y.

named as beneficiary of life insurance or pension proceeds. Use the $10,000 annual gift tax exclusion to remove assets from the estate.

Income taxes can be reduced by making lifetime as opposed to death-time charitable gifts.

Cash can be provided for the estate of a business owner through a tax-free bailout of cash via a Section 303 stock redemption in which the corporation buys (and pays for with cash or other property) and the estate sells stock in the business. Federal estate tax payments can be deferred for four years and then paid in equal annual increments over the next ten years, a fourteen-year payout. Both of these provisions are available only if the value of the business comprises a significant portion (more than 35 percent) of the estate (after certain adjustments). Pre-death planning may help the estate meet the requisite tests.

7

Getting Organized

Search for Will and Related Documents

Whenever a property owner dies, someone somewhere must determine what will happen to the deceased individual's property. The first inquiry must be: "Did the decedent leave his own instructions as to disposition of his property at death?" In other words, did the decedent make a valid, enforceable will during his lifetime?

This is the exact point at which plans to handle the decedent's affairs commence. Anyone familiar with the reams of material written about the search for the authentic last will and testament of the late Howard Hughes, will know that this is not always a routine matter. In the case of the death of a husband or wife, if both had their will prepared by the same attorney there should be no problem. At the other extreme, however, where you may have a recluse living alone, with no professional contacts, the search can be a long, costly and involved procedure.

Without examining in detail the laws of each particular state, logic tells us that the law will not treat kindly anyone who chooses to conceal or attempts to destroy the will of a deceased person. The law requires the possessor of the will of a deceased person to present it to the personal representative chosen in the document, so that it can be duly admitted to probate. (In most states, a person known to have possession of the decedent's will can be compelled to produce it. Any party at interest can direct the Register of Wills to issue a citation directed to the person alleged to have the will to show cause why it should not be deposited with the Register of Wills.) If a deceased person had made a will and the will has not been discovered, the estate will be probated as an intestacy.

The persons who are the statutory recipients of a decedent's property under state intestacy laws are often not the same persons who would have been recipients under the decedent's will.

Survivors (including family, friends or professional advisors) must therefore make a thorough search of the decedent's residence and business, coupled with extensive inquiries, to ascertain specifically whether or not the deceased person had made a will. Inquiries can be directed to attorneys and accountants with whom the decedent had contact during lifetime, banks and safe-deposit companies with whom the decedent did business, and, of course, relatives and close friends of the decedent.

Many states have no specific time period following the decedent's death in which a valid will may be produced, and therefore if the estate is handled as intestate (i.e., the deceased person is assumed to have died without a valid will) and a valid will is later discovered, the confusion and the necessary readjustments can easily result in a legal nightmare for everyone involved.

What is or is not a "valid will" is beyond the subject matter of this chapter (see Chapter 8 on will contests). Formal requirements vary from state to state. Any written documents that indicate in any way that they are disposing of the decedent's property at death should be brought to the attention of an attorney. There are myriads of cases involving what is or is not a valid will, and many seemingly innocuous pieces of paper have been held by the courts to pass title to millions of dollars. Never ever assume that what you have found is not a valid will, even if it fails to comply with the formalities that you think necessary. Handwritten notes signed at the end by the decedent can in many instances pass title to the decedent's property, and all of these should be carefully examined by experts before they are disregarded. Copies of wills can, in many states, be probated if it can be shown that the original was lost or destroyed without the testator's consent.

Anatomical Gifts

During his or her lifetime, the decedent may have made provisions for a particular part, or all, of his or her body to be given to individuals needing transplants or to hospitals, medical schools or other specified donees. If this is the case, chances are that such provisions were made known to one or more close family members or are contained in a separate document, so that they could be acted on immediately after death. Because many vital organs must be transplanted within hours of death, the appropriate steps should obviously be taken by the family without delay. In the event that decedent made no provision for anatomical gifts, many state statutes provide that members of decedent's family may donate part or all of decedent's body to transplants or research.

If the anatomical gift was made in decedent's will, it should be acted upon immediately. In most cases, the anatomical gift—if it was made in good faith—will not be affected even if the will is later contested, because obviously it will be too late to do anything about it. This is an area in which time is quite often of the essence, and the immediate family will usually be in a better position than a nonrelated executor or attorney to take whatever action is necessary immediately following the decedent's death.

Funeral and Burial

In most cases, the funeral and burial will take place before the formal appointment of an executor or administrator. If decedent's will contains specific directions about the funeral or burial, these directions should be complied with wherever possible and practical. In any event, according to the dictates of our society, typically the funeral and burial must take place within days of the decedent's death.

The necessary arrangements for the funeral and burial are usually the responsibility of the immediate family, although the executor will, in the end, be furnished with the bill and asked to pay the costs from the assets of decedent's estate. The choice of the type of funeral and burial arrangements will again depend on the particular thoughts and desires of decedent's family, with the religious practices of the decedent's faith obviously requiring close adherence by the survivors.

If the surviving family members or friends are to make the funeral arrangements, the only practical guideline is to select a funeral director with a good general reputation. Detailed arrangements should be made by the bereaved next of kin. We strongly recommend that an unemotionally involved person accompany the family members to the funeral director's office. When the decedent's surviving spouse or children make funeral arrangements, because of their emotional involvement they often tend to pay more than they reasonably should. (This problem should be alleviated somewhat by disclosure regulations of the Federal Trade Commission requiring funeral directors to provide certain cost information.)

If the decedent and his or her family had previously arranged for a family cemetery plot, then the cemetery deed should be immediately located. Many individuals are now making their own funeral arrangements. This, of course, can relieve family members of having to make difficult decisions under the pressure of time and can result in lower expenditures. Sam Brodsky, Vice-President of Joseph Levine & Son, funeral directors in Philadelphia, in referring to the proper costs that a family should pay for funeral arrangements, sums it up concisely: "Don't spend more emotionally than you can afford financially."

Analyzing the Will

Following the death, after immediate matters such as funeral, burial and anatomical gifts, if any, have been taken care of, the formal probate process described in Chapter 8 takes place. If the decedent had a valid will in force at death, then "letters testamentary" are obtained (see Chapter 8). If decedent left no will, then the administrator has no guidelines to use in administering the estate and must rely on his own knowledge of the situation, coupled with the advice of the other members of the estate administration team (specifically discussed in Chapter 4).

If the decedent did have a will, the personal representatives should first review the will in order to "capture the decedent's thinking" in regard to the handling of the estate. For example, suppose the decedent wanted to make certain that a daughter would be financially secure throughout her life. Let's assume the decedent had established a trust to make periodic payments of income and had named a corporate trustee in order to protect and invest the daughter's principal. These facts should put the personal representative on notice that the decedent was concerned that the daughter might not be fully capable or desirous of managing and investing the property that had been left for her. Another example might be that of a decedent who was a partner in a business and whose will specifically stated that the personal representative should comply with the terms of the buy/sell agreement in effect at decedent's death. In this case, the executor is put on notice that his handling of decedent's business is limited to compliance with the lifetime agreement between the decedent and his or her partner.

Specific references as to investment limitations must also be reviewed by the executor. For example, the testator may have been strongly opposed to investments in arms manufacturers.

In many cases the testator will want his business sold as quickly as possible after his death, while others want the business continued no matter what. Obviously, the executor must be guided by the dispositive provisions in the will. This means you must make certain that the property of the decedent goes to the persons specifically indicated in the will. Where specific assets are bequeathed, they must not be otherwise disposed of. In general, the personal representative should have a thorough understanding of where the decedent wished assets to go and the manner in which they were to be given to the respective beneficiaries of the estate. If the will is unclear, or if the property specified cannot be found, or if the intended beneficiary has died before the testator, you should consult an attorney before proceeding.

SUMMARY

Survivors must make a thorough search for a will when a property owner dies. If the will is in the possession of an individual who refuses to present it to the estate's executor, that person can be compelled by law to produce it.

Anatomical gifts of all or a specific part of a decedent's body must be acted upon immediately. In many states, if no provision for anatomical gifts was made, members of the decedent's family may make donations of part or all of the body (in the absence of directions to the contrary).

An emotionally uninvolved person should accompany the family members to the funeral home.

Analysis of the decedent's will should be given high priority. The personal representative should use the will to ascertain who is to receive the decedent's probate assets, as well as when and in what manner this is to be accomplished.

8

The Formal Appointment: Probating the Estate

What Is Probate?

Probate, in the formal and most narrow sense, is the legal process of proving the validity of the will and the competence of the testator to make that will. It is also the procedure by which a personal representative is appointed to handle the affairs of a deceased person. Most of the formalities involved in appointing the personal representative are in many respects similar throughout the country. But keep in mind that there are fifty separate states, each with different laws governing probate, and, in many states, individual counties have their own regulations that must be followed. Regardless of the technical formalities, however, this chapter will give the prospective personal representative a clear understanding of the appointment process.

Is Probate Always Necessary?

The answer is no. Some estates do not have to be probated. What determines whether or not you must probate an estate? Here are some guidelines:

First, probate is not necessary if all a person's assets will pass automatically under the terms of joint ownership. One of the most important functions of the executor or administrator is to pass title from the decedent to the beneficiary. If title to property is transferred immediately at death (as is the case with jointly held property), there is no need for probate. For example, if the decedent was married, and the only assets of value he owned when he died were owned jointly with his wife, there might be no necessity for probate. This is a common situation. Say the decedent and his spouse owned a home and a bank account at the time of death. If both the home and the bank account were titled in joint names with the "right of survivorship," in most states at his death title would pass immediately and automatically to the spouse without probate. There will be no "probate assets," since all of the decedent's property was owned jointly by the decedent and his spouse at death and passed automatically to the survivor. In such cases there is no need to appoint a personal representative to pass title.

Second, probate may not be necessary if the only asset of value is life insurance payable to a beneficiary (other than the insured person's estate). Title to the insurance proceeds passes automatically to the party named as beneficiary in the policy.

Third, the same principle applies to employee benefits such as pension or profit-sharing proceeds payable to a named beneficiary (other than the estate). If there are no other assets of significance, probate may not be necessary since the retirement plan money will go automatically to the beneficiary. There is no need to have a person appointed merely to pass title.

Fourth, many states have "small estate" exemptions from probate that apply to estates consisting solely of particular classes of assets. An example of an asset that might not require probate, if it were the only asset in decedent's name, would be unpaid salary or a work-related fringe benefit such as vacation pay and sick leave. In estates of very modest size, you should talk to the decedent's employer and then call the Register of Wills in the county in which the decedent lived to see if probate can be avoided.

Fifth, assets placed in trust during the decedent's lifetime typically do not have to be probated. The reason is that "beneficial title" or interest in the property in that trust will pass automatically at decedent's death according to the terms of the trust. While this procedure may save certain probate costs, transfer costs may still be imposed by the state or federal government. This depends on the form of the trust and the size of the assets involved. Therefore, if you find yourself administering a rather large estate in which it appears that no probate will be necessary because all the assets will be held in trust, we would strongly suggest that you consult a knowledgeable estate attorney before deciding to bypass the probate procedure completely. The amount of the assets involved certainly warrants the additional expenditure of at least a consultation.

Checking with an attorney can save you, the personal representative, as well as the beneficiaries, considerable future grief and give you some assurance that the decedent's affairs are handled in a proper, legal manner. Federal and state taxing authorities carefully scrutinize devices that are specifically designed to avoid or greatly reduce taxes of any type, and, in particular, death taxes. This is not to say that legitimate tax savings plans such as living trusts should not be considered—far from it. However, you should realize that where the assets are considerable, so will be the interest of the taxing authorities to make certain that all the *t*'s have been crossed and the *i*'s dotted.

Never assume that any technical plans made by the decedent will automatically absolve you, the personal representative, of any liability for their enforcement. Rather, you should be acutely aware of the fact that when the chips are down the buck will stop with you, and therefore an ounce of prevention and a dollar spent for advice can well be worth the effort and the slight loss in funds to the beneficiaries. It also will go a long way toward relieving you of personal responsibility should you later discover that probate was necessary or that taxes will be due and owing by virtue of the decedent's death. It is especially important to remember that interest and penalties on unpaid taxes usually begin to accrue as early as nine months, and in some cases even sooner, following decedent's death.

As you've probably realized by now, it is not the size of an estate that determines whether or not you must probate the estate; a $9 million estate consisting of $3 million worth of joint property, $3 million worth of life insurance and $3 million in pension benefits may not (theoretically at least) have to be probated.

You do not have to probate an estate just because there are taxes to be paid. There is no direct correlation between the necessity of paying state death taxes and the need to probate an estate. So, although your state may impose a death tax, a surviving spouse or other beneficiary may be able to pay that tax without going to the expense and trouble of probate. A good rule for determining whether to probate an estate is to first decide whether decedent will have, at the time of death, property in his or her name that will require the appointment of a personal representative to pass title to the surviving beneficiaries.

Should You Have a Lawyer?

Retaining the services of a lawyer may not be necessary if, after reading the pertinent sections of this book and reviewing the assets of the estate, you can determine either that no probate is necessary or that the executor's duties and responsibilities will be of such a routine and minor nature that you can handle them without any complications. If, however, you have any question concerning the administration of the estate—although you feel that you are competent to handle most of the important duties yourself—we strongly recommend that you consult an attorney knowledgeable in estate matters at an early point in your handling of the decedent's estate. Hiring an attorney helps to avoid costly mistakes.

Why else might you decide to hire an attorney? One good reason is that an attorney who works in this field will see things or know things that you wouldn't. (Keep reading and you'll learn many of them.) Let's use insurance as an example. In one case, a man was hospitalized several months before his death. His widow was advised by her attorney that the husband's insurance at work and his Blue Cross and Blue Shield insurance provided duplicate coverage. That meant the widow was entitled to an additional $25,000 in cash from one of the carriers, since the other carrier had paid the hospital bill directly. The widow was pleasantly surprised, since all of the family's income had been used up because of the prolonged last illness of the decedent. Here the $25,000 uncovered by the attorney was well worth the modest fee he charged for his services to the estate.

A probate attorney may point out certain options which you might have overlooked: these might be opportunities which, while not directly affecting the death taxes or related benefits, might later prove advantageous to the decedent's beneficiaries.

Bear in mind that the purpose of this book is to give the personal representative as much detailed information as possible, since the executor's duties cannot be properly performed without an awareness of their exact nature. Nevertheless, when the personal representative becomes aware of specific problem areas, he or she would be well advised to secure the services of a skilled attorney. Even though the executor is now in a position to diagnose the estate's condition, we do not recommend attempting the equivalant of an appendectomy without qualified assistance.

How to Find the Right Attorney

For those of us who are old enough, it's nice to think back to the days of the corner grocery store, when the typical doctor was a general practitioner and the lawyer down the block could solve all your problems. If we are completely honest with ourselves, however, we can remember that the corner grocery store often did not have what we wanted, that our general practitioner missed a *few* diagnoses, and that we might have done much better in a particular case if our lawyer had been a specialist.

Make no mistake about it, estate work, commonly known as estate administration, is a specialty in the law. It is definitely an area in which all lawyers are *not* created equal. This is not to say that the average lawyer is not qualified to make an average will for an average person or to handle an uncomplicated estate. But as the very size of this book attests, the complexities of handling a decedent's estate are such that it is physically impossible for every lawyer to have in-depth knowledge of this particular specialty. We therefore recommend the selection of an attorney skilled in the areas of estate planning and administration to assist the executor with his or her duties.

The personal representative of the decedent's estate assumes the difficult decisions and burdensome responsibilities of that office and therefore has the right to select an attorney of his or her choice. In most cases, as executor, you are not bound by law to use the decedent's attorney, or even the attorney who prepared the will. Of course, a given situation might very well warrant selecting decedent's attorney, and/or the attorney who prepared the will, to act as attorney for the estate; but the final decision should be made by the personal representative.

If decedent's business was rather complicated and the entire family agrees that the decedent's attorney was an extremely helpful and competent advisor, then by all means consider retaining that attorney for guidance with decedent's business. Keep in mind, however, that you are still free to retain an estate attorney to help you administer the estate and fulfill the duties and responsibilities set forth herein.

Good attorneys, like qualified individuals in every profession and business, have good reputations. Various organizations, such as the National Association of Estate Planning Councils, deal specifically with estate planning situations. Ask if the attorney in question is a member. Through continuing legal education, attorneys can obtain specific knowledge of the different areas of the law, including estate administration.

There are many, many qualified attorneys who can help you—and, whether you read this book next month or next year, take our word for it that it is still a buyer's market. If you have a good working relationship with an attorney who does not specialize in this area, that attorney should be more than pleased to recommend an expert to you. Also, the estate planning or trust officer of your bank or trust company can refer you to qualified attorneys who specialize in this area. Ask the trust officer for a list of four or five names and qualify them yourself. Your accountant or your insurance advisor may be able to recommend an estate planning specialist with whom he or she has worked in the past. At the first meeting with the attorney, don't be afraid to ask questions. Get an idea of the attorney's background, have the attorney give you an idea of the work that he or she will perform for you, make sure that this is an individual you would feel comfortable working with in a long-term relationship, and, lastly, don't be afraid to talk fees.

How to Keep the Fees as Low as Possible

The subject of fees can sometimes create a barrier between the attorney and client that can severely hamper the relationship and have a negative effect on the results that the executor hopes to attain. There are two obvious extremes, neither one of which is likely to produce the desired results. If you shop for a lawyer on a price basis only, you might indeed end up with the cheapest lawyer, but also perhaps with one of the least knowledgeable in the field. Conversely, the lawyer who charges the highest fee is not necessarily the most qualified. How then do you solve the problem?

You attack the fee problem from the standpoint of one professional fiduciary engaging the services of another. Never forget that your duty to the estate and its beneficiaries is to provide them with the highest degree of service, and to do this you must, in most instances, retain the services of a qualified attorney. The work of the attorney necessarily reflects on your performance. But, as a fiduciary of the estate, you also have an obligation not to unduly burden the estate with excessive costs and fees. As we have warned before, beware of the attorney who quotes the fee before discussing the services to be performed. The attorney should be fairly and adequately compensated according to the time involved, the nature of the work, the attorney's background, experience and professional qualifications, and, where indicated, the beneficial results achieved for the estate and the heirs.

If you already know an attorney who can satisfy the above criteria, by all means hire that individual right away. If you are not sure, then contact the indicated sources, get the names of several qualified attorneys, meet with at least two personally, and make your decision on the basis of your discussions of the work to be performed and the fees to be charged. Consider, too, your gut reaction as to whether a given person is someone you wish to be associated with. If you have absorbed the underlying reasoning in this section, you will indeed have obtained the services of the most qualified attorney at a fair and reasonable cost to the decedent's estate. Before the attorney begins to work, ask for a written statement of the hourly fee and a rough estimate of how many hours it will take to do the job.

Where to Probate (The Question of Domicile)

Domicile has been defined as an individual's permanent home. Your domicile is the place to which, regardless of where you are currently living, you intend to return to live permanently.

It is absolutely necessary to correctly determine the domicile of the decedent. Why? Because the state of domicile will impose inheritance or estate taxes on decedent's property. Domicile is also important because that state will determine (and interpret) the rules and regulations governing the distribution of the assets of the estate.

In most cases, where there is no question as to the decedent's permanent residence, domicile will not be a significant issue. However, because of Americans' increased mobility and because many of them today own homes in more than one state, the question of decedent's domicile can present serious problems.

Jerry Smith owns a home in suburban Philadelphia and has a condominium in Florida. Jerry has just retired; he plans to spend May through October in Philadelphia, and November through April in Florida. If Jerry were to die while in Philadelphia, should his estate be probated in Pennsylvania or Florida?

Since Florida has more liberal tax laws, if Jerry had been aware of this potential problem he might have taken steps to avoid it. For example, he might have redrafted his will indicating that he was a resident of the State of Florida and have it signed and notarized in Florida. He could have used his Florida address for voting purposes and as his main address on income tax returns; he could have registered his automobile in Florida and used the Florida address on his driver's license. All of these would constitute evidence of Jerry's intent to make Florida his permanent home.

Regardless of how well the decedent documented his or her domicile, it is the duty of the executor or administrator to thoroughly analyze the relevant criteria for a determination of decedent's domicile, hoping then to be in a position to support that decision in the event of an attack by the other state.

In addition to the question of the state of domicile, in most instances the will will be probated, or the administrator will apply for letters of administration, in the county in which decedent resided in the state of domicile.

Ancillary Probate

As we have previously noted (and will review in depth in the chapters on jointly held property and life insurance), not every asset owned at the time of death is probate property. This means probate may not be needed to pass title to the survivor at decedent's death. The probate office in which decedent's estate is probated will typically not have any jurisdiction or any say in the disposition of nonprobate property. It will pass by survivorship if a joint tenancy, or by contract if the person receiving the property was named as beneficiary of a life insurance policy. (Both of these subjects will be discussed in great detail, in Chapter 12 and Chapter 17.)

There is one other type of property over which the local probate office or court will not have jurisdiction—namely, real estate owned by decedent in another state or owned property that cannot be collected or managed and against which no state death taxes could be charged in the state of domicile. In such cases a second personal representative must be appointed in the state in which that property is located. This procedure is called "ancillary probate," and an ancillary administration is necessary for such property.

In the above example, even if Jerry was domiciled in Florida, an ancillary administration in Pennsylvania would still be necessary because of the real estate Jerry owned in Pennsylvania. Letters of administration would have to be taken out in Pennsylvania (probably by a second attorney, located in that state), and inheritance taxes paid on the Pennsylvania real estate.

Procedure Varying with Locality

Although most of the procedures discussed in this book are relevant to the probate process regardless of the locality in which the probate takes place, the personal representative must be familiar with the laws of the state in which the will or the estate is probated and the particular rules and regulations of the county probate office.

In the Appendix, you will find the most recent state tax laws and procedures in effect when this book was written. These, however, are given to you for illustrative purposes only, and it is absolutely essential that you verify the information in this book against the latest death tax laws and procedural requirements of your state, as well as the regulations of the local probate office, which should be readily obtainable at the office itself.

Probate with a Will

If the decedent had a valid will, and if the will named you as the executor, then the probate procedure is relatively simple. As the named executor you go to the probate office, together with witnesses to the will if they are available, and you sit down with a representative from the probate office who will prepare the necessary petition. In most cases, you must also bring a copy of the death certificate. Together with a clerk, you prepare a "petition." This petition merely recites the fact that decedent has died, states the place, time and cause of death, and supplies basic information concerning the will, including the fact that you are the executor appointed under the will. If you have hired an attorney, he or she can quite often simplify the probate procedure by having all necessary documents prepared beforehand. The witnesses attest to the fact that the signature is that of the decedent, and, in some states, must declare that they were present when the will was signed.

What do you do if you cannot find the witnesses? Where witnesses are required by state law and are not available, the law may require other witnesses to attest to the authenticity of the signature at the end of the will or conform to other formalities prescribed by the state or the county office in particular.

Many states today have accepted "self-proving wills." At the end of these wills, the testator and the witnesses state that the will was signed in the presence of all of them and that the testator realized that he or she was preparing a will. Typically, the signing is done in the presence of a notary public who places a seal on the last page of the will. When this "self-proving" will is presented at the probate office it will be accepted without the necessity of bringing witnesses.

Your state's laws should be consulted in regard to the requirements of witnesses, signatures and other formalities.

As indicated in the following section, you have the right to refuse to act as executor. This can be especially important if more than one executor is named in the will.

If the named executor dies before the decedent and no successor is named in the will, then an administrator will have to be chosen who will act under the terms of the will. In effect, the administrator will be acting as an executor would have and is said to be an administrator "CTA," which stands for a Latin phrase meaning "with the will attached." In other words, there is a valid will, but you are performing the duties of the executor named in the will, acting in his place.

If an executor dies or becomes incompetent after commencing his or her duties but before the estate is formally closed, a successor executor is chosen in accordance with the local requirements. Usually the procedure is the same as or similar to the one followed in the selection of an administrator.

In any event, the actual probate of the will can usually be accomplished quickly and with minimal fuss if you understand the procedure, and thus avoid any undue concern.

Executor's Right to Renounce

A person who makes a will, appoints an executor in the will and fails to notify the executor of this fact may be committing a great disservice, not only to the executor but also to the beneficiaries of his or her estate. The size of this book alone indicates the vast scope of the potential duties and responsibilities of an executor. Thrusting this responsibility on an unwilling recipient can precipitate disaster.

If, for whatever reason, you do not wish to act as executor, in most cases you have the right to "renounce" and be released from your responsibilities. This can be usually accomplished by filing a renunciation form in the probate office that has jurisdiction over the estate. You should file this form before you perform any duties or take any actions on behalf of the estate.

Renunciation makes sense if the estate could be handled much more efficiently by a lesser number of executors. For example, if a brother and sister were named co-executors and there was no possibility of any conflict between them, and if the sister lived two thousand miles away from the locality in which the estate was being probated, it might be easier for all concerned if the brother acted as the sole executor.

Renunciation should also be considered in another instance—namely, where the situations of the parties have changed considerably since the will was prepared and the designation of executor was not changed. In such cases, logic would suggest (but not demand) that the named executor no longer act as such. For example, the named executor might be a former spouse, a former business associate, or a former close friend who has since moved to a different country.

Probate Where There Is No Valid Will—Intestacy

It has been said that no one dies without a will. Either you prepare a will for yourself or the state in which you are domiciled at your death will "make a will" for you. This so-called will that the state makes for you is referred to as the "intestacy law" of the state. The intestacy laws govern the distribution of decedent's assets. Provision is first made for decedent's spouse. Children, grandchildren, parents, brothers and sisters and their children follow next (depending on the particular state intestacy law).

Where either a husband or a wife dies, survived by one or more children, state law might provide for a larger share to be paid to the spouse, with the children's share to be divided equally among them. The percentage to be allocated to the spouse and children is often determined by the number of children surviving the decedent. For example, if decedent were to die survived by a spouse and one child, state law might provide for the estate to be divided equally between the spouse and the surviving child; if the decedent had two or more children, the spouse might be limited to one third, with the children equally sharing two thirds.

Some states provide for the spouse to receive a specific amount plus a percentage of the excess, with the remainder for the children. For example, the surviving spouse might be entitled to the first $20,000, with a given percentage of the balance divided between the spouse and the children. While a summary of the intestacy laws of each state is included in the Appendix, be sure to check with your attorney before making any decision based on this information, since state laws change frequently.

In relatively uncomplicated situations where decedent failed to make a will (or the will he made is for some reason held to be invalid) and was survived by a spouse and children, letters of administration could be granted to the spouse. The only formal requirements are that the spouse obtain a death certificate and provide the probate official with other relevant data, as is the case in the probate of a will.

Intestacy is an unfortunate occurrence in most cases because the decedent has forfeited the right to say (1) *who* gets his property (state law decides this), (2) *how much* each beneficiary receives (regardless of how much each person needs or how much the decedent would have wanted each person to get), (3) *when* they get the property (the money or other property must be distributed to them when they reach majority), and (4) *how* each person receives the property (it passes outright upon the beneficiary's majority regardless of how well that person can manage or invest the property).

Who Is Entitled to Act as Personal Representative or Administrator

If there is no valid will, most states establish a priority list of potential administrators starting with the decedent's spouse. If, for example, there is no widow or if for some reason she does not serve as administratrix, decedent's children, parents, brothers or sisters or other close relatives would then have the right to serve. Individuals who have priority but do not desire to serve could renounce their right in favor of others further down on the list. In the event that no relatives were available or willing to serve and decedent had a creditor anxious to have claims paid from the assets of the estate, the creditor could petition the court to be appointed as administrator. Legal proceedings would then take place. Relatives of the decedent would be given notice of the creditor's action. Unless a relative were willing to act as administrator or had a sufficient legal basis to dispute the creditor's right to act as such, the court could appoint the creditor as administrator.

How to Qualify as Executor or Administrator

Almost anyone over the legal age in the state where the decedent was domiciled at death can qualify to act as a personal representative. In order to formally qualify if you have been named as executor in the decedent's will (or as the administrator of the estate of someone who has died without a will), you must go to the local probate office, file the necessary petition and have "letters testamentary" or "letters of administration" issued. These letters, or documents, are legal proof that you are qualified to act as the decedent's personal representative. Here are the details:

The Mechanics of Probate—Petition—Letters Testamentary—Letters of Administration—Bond

The mechanics of probating the estate of a deceased individual are, in the vast majority of cases, quite simple. Contrary to public misconception, probate itself is relatively inexpensive.

First, you must go to the local county office responsible for the probate of wills. The precise name of the office varies with the state and sometimes with the county of domicile. It may be called the Register of Wills, Probate Office, Probate Court, Orphans' Court, or Surrogate Court.

Second, you must present evidence of death. This requirement is usually satisfied by giving the clerk a duly issued and sealed death certificate.

Third, a petition is either prepared at the probate office or prepared beforehand by the personal representative and attorney and presented at the probate office for review, approval and signatures.

Fourth, if the decedent had a will, then the *original* of the will must also be presented (copies are not accepted by most state laws except under very limited circumstances), and the witnesses to the will, if available, should be present.

What happens next? The appropriate official reviews the death certificate, verifies the information on the petition, questions the witnesses as to the validity of decedent's signature, and determines whether the personal representative must post bond before taking charge of the estate.

A bond (insurance to protect the heirs in case the personal representative steals or misappropriates estate assets) is often required by the appropriate probate authorities to protect the estate's beneficiaries and creditors. Most lawyers include a provision in the will which exempts the executor from this requirement. In some instances, courts may direct that bond be posted even where the will states that no bond is necessary, but this would occur only if the court felt security was needed (for example, if the personal representative were not a resident of the state where the probate takes place).

A bond can usually be obtained without much difficulty through a bonding company representative. You can get the names, addresses and phone numbers of several by asking the clerks at your local probate office. (Be sure to "shop around," as you would with any other insurance.) If you have hired counsel, that attorney can usually obtain the bond, and you need not appear in person at the bonding office.

As soon as the probate official has been satisfied that your petition to be named the personal representative is in order, and when the bond, if required, has been posted, the probate office issues "letters testamentary" to you as the executor. As mentioned, these letters (or, in the case of intestacy, letters of administration) are official evidence that you have been appointed executor (or administrator) of decedent's estate.

Since you will need to furnish proof of your appointment in order to perform many of the required duties, the probate officials will issue shortened versions—in effect, summaries—of the letters testamentary or letters of administration. These shortened versions (often called "short certificates") indicate the formal appointment, the date of death of the decedent, and the date of the appointment by the court of the personal representative.

Settling Small Estates

Many states have laws to enable a decedent's family to entirely bypass the probate process. These laws apply to estates which lack valuable assets or whose assets are limited to certain classifications, such as unpaid wages, salaries, employee benefits, motor vehicles, or even bank accounts with balances of, for example, less than a thousand dollars.

In some states, title to real estate passes automatically and immediately on the death of the decedent to the decedent's heirs or beneficiaries, so there is no need for a personal representative to be appointed in order to pass title. Not all states have these laws, however, and there is a wide discrepancy in the provisions of the laws of the various states. You should therefore check the applicable provisions of the law of the state in which decedent was domiciled at death before deciding whether the normal probate process can be bypassed. We strongly advise that you confer with an attorney who practices in the county of decedent's domicile and who can help you make that decision.

Will Contests—Why Courts Invalidate Wills

Regardless of the intentions of the deceased individual when he prepared his will, and regardless of the skill and draftsmanship of the lawyer who prepared it, there is always the possibility that someone will "contest" the will.

As a practical matter, in most instances the reason for a will contest is that the contesting person(s) did not receive the property they had expected to get from the decedent. Will contests, therefore, generally are brought by disinherited children, by close friends of either sex who were misled into believing that they would be "remembered" in decedent's will, or by someone who was more closely related to the decedent than the beneficiaries actually named in the will.

Fortunately, a will cannot be set aside merely because someone isn't happy with what it says. There must be "grounds" for contesting the will. The law of each state specifies certain formal requirements which must be met for a will to be "valid." If one or more of these key tests are not met, the will can be disregarded by the court, and an intestacy will result. Check with an attorney for the requirements in your state.

Reasons frequently given by potential heirs who seek to have a will invalidated are that (1) the decedent lacked "testamentary capacity" (legal ability to make a valid will) because of weakened intellect; (2) the decedent was the victim of "fraud" (the decedent signed what he thought was a document other than a will or was deceived into thinking a beneficiary was dead who really wasn't); (3) "undue influence" (persuasion strong enough to overcome decedent's freedom of choice); (4) the signature or the will itself was a forgery; and (5) the will did not comply with the statutory formalities required of a valid will in the state of decedent's domicile (for instance, it was not signed by the decedent at the appropriate place or was not properly witnessed).

In most states, the contestants of the will bear a heavy burden in attempting to prove to the court that the will should be set aside. Obviously, the courts want to encourage people to prepare wills. Therefore, as a general rule, wills will not be invalidated unless the court has been convinced by strong evidence that the will does not represent the wishes of the decedent.

If the will is held to be invalid by the court, then a question will arise as to who then would be entitled to the proceeds of decedent's estate. The law of the probating state will again govern the court's decision. Typically, the court has two alternatives: (1) the estate could be distributed in accordance with the intestacy laws if the court finds that no valid will was in effect at decedent's death; and (2) if decedent had a prior will which was revoked by the will found by the court to be invalid, the court could hold that the prior will now becomes the valid last will of the decedent and is entitled to be probated. (This is a good example of why a will should not be destroyed even if a new will has since been executed.)

Executor's Role in Will Contests

If you have been formally appointed as executor, and the will under which your appointment was made is being contested, you should immediately determine the extent of your duties and obligations for the duration of the will contest. In most cases, you as executor will be expected to continue to perform your regular functions, with the expectation of being duly compensated for the time you spend on behalf of the estate (unless the will provides that you are to serve without fee or unless you elect to forego that fee). To neglect to perform these duties because of the will contest might result in financial losses to the estate. Therefore, if there is any question at all as to what services you are to perform during the hiatus caused by the will contest, you should obtain written directions either from counsel or from the court to make sure that you will be protected regardless of the outcome of the will contest.

SUMMARY

1. Probate is not necessary if all a person's stocks, real estate or other assets pass automatically under the terms of a joint title, by life insurance, or through a pension, profit-sharing or IRA plan, or if the value or type of assets involved qualify under the "small estate" exemptions of your state.

2. An attorney specializing in probate and estate administration may help you avoid needless and costly mistakes and point out valuable tax-saving opportunities.

3. Attorneys who are members of an Estate Planning Council and who are recommended by your local bank or trust company will probably be less costly and more effective than those who don't specialize in estate administration areas.

4. Discuss fees, demand a written hourly fee statement, and understand and be satisfied with the terms of your arrangement before you allow an attorney to proceed.

5. A will must be probated in the county of the decedent's domicile.

6. If the decedent owned assets in a state other than that of his domicile, you may have to hire an attorney in that state to file state death tax returns and administer those assets (this is called "ancillary administration").

7. To actually probate the will, you (and the witnesses) will go to the appropriate county office, with the will and with a copy of the death certificate, and petition to be appointed as executor (or administrator if there is no valid will).

8. If for any reason you do not wish to serve, renounce the position of executor before you begin to perform any duties or accept any responsibilities.

9

After Probate

Bank Accounts—Checking, Savings or Combination

In the administration of an estate, setting up the proper checking and savings accounts holds a high priority. This is an area of estate administration in which banks are especially helpful.

One of your most important duties is record keeping. As personal representative of an estate, you are required to account to three separate and distinct entities or groups of people. First, to the beneficiaries of the estate; second, to the respective taxing authorities—local, state and federal; and third, to the courts if and when you must give a formal accounting of what money and other property came in and what went out to various creditors, taxing authorities, and agents and representatives and employees of the estates.

The initial record-keeping tool of the estate administrator should be the estate checking account. All moneys, regardless of the source, should be funneled through one central account—the checking account of the estate—so as to establish a permanent record which can be verified by the records of the banking institution. As indicated later in the book when we talk about investing the estate's assets, we strongly recommend that you do not tie up a considerable amount of the decedent's property in a non-interest-bearing checking account. Keep just enough in the account to meet bills as they fall due. The checking account should be a funnel through which all of the liquid assets pass, so that it will always show exactly how much cash you have received, when you disbursed it and to whom.

Most banks will establish a special account for an estate. A bank officer will provide you with a separate checkbook that clearly identifies you as the personal representative. That will make it easier for you to administer the cash that flows through the account and put the payee of any check on notice as to the origin of the payment. With the advent of interest-paying checking accounts, the availability of insured money market funds, and the entry into the market of savings institutions with checking accounts, you have a wide diversity of options available. While we cannot recommend one type of banking institution over another, we would strongly urge you, before you set up an account, to "shop around" and talk to at least three different bankers to determine the type and the cost of accounts and services available to the estate. Savings accounts should be insured. Other factors to be considered include the advisability, in some circumstances, of using the same banking institution in which decedent had the bulk of his accounts, the advisability of using a banking institution with which you have previously done business, and the suggestions of the estate's attorney. Obviously, an attorney who specializes in estate administration and who has considerable practical experience with local banks can be invaluable in helping you select the right bank and the proper type of account.

Regardless of the type of account or accounts, the personal representative should be certain that every cent that comes into the estate is funneled through one central account upon which checks can be drawn. Sufficient moneys should be kept on hand for everyday expenses, but the bulk of the money should be earning the "highest possible fully insured interest rate reasonably available to the estate."

Safe-Deposit Boxes

A valuable source of information about the decedent's assets, as well as a potential depository of some of these particular assets, will be the decedent's safe-deposit box. Quite often, personal papers of value, placed by a decedent in a safe-deposit box, will be essential in handling affairs after his death. They could include deeds, mortgages, insurance policies, stock certificates, business agreements and other valuable documents. Cash and jewelry are sometimes kept in safe-deposit boxes, together with other valuables of limited size, such as coin collections or stamp collections.

If the family has no personal knowledge of the safe-deposit box, and if circumstances suggest that the effort is warranted, you as personal representative should ascertain whether the decedent did in fact own a safe-deposit box. At the very least, you should inquire at the banking institutions with which the decedent did business, and, where appropriate, address written inquiries to other banking institutions in the area in which the decedent lived or conducted business.

State laws vary widely in regard to accessibility to safe-deposit boxes. Some states permit the surviving spouse access to the contents of a box in joint names at any time, with no qualifications, following the death of the other spouse. If the decedent was an officer in a corporation, other corporate officers with access to the box could gain access to it following decedent's death without undue formality. In many states, however, the state or local taxing authorities will require that the box be sealed by the bank at the date of decedent's death and only entered in the presence of a representative of the state or local government. The purpose of the limitation on entry is to prevent possible tax evasion, i.e., the accumulation of unreported cash or other valuables by the decedent. Most states and the banking institutions will permit access to an otherwise locked safe-deposit box in order to see if it contains decedent's will or to withdraw from it a burial lot deed or insurance policies. On such occasions a representative of the bank would most probably be present so that nothing could be removed from the box without a record of it being made.

When entry is limited, the personal representative must usually schedule an appointment with the bank and with the appropriate governmental official in order to gain entrance to the box. In addition, if you are not in possession of a key to the box, the bank must also obtain the services of someone to "drill" the box open. This will require coordinating the schedules of everyone involved.

If there is any question as to your right of entry following decedent's death, you should consult an attorney before attempting to gain access to the box. For example, if a box were in the joint names of a mother and her daughter, and if the mother died and state law prohibited the daughter from entering the box following death, the daughter would be in violation of state law if she gained access to the box after her mother's death. If she entered the box within hours or even days following her mother's death, the bank might very well not have notice and would not bar her entrance. The daughter's action, however, might have violated state law, in which case she would be subject to civil or even criminal prosecution and of course would become a prime suspect in the event that any articles of the decedent which might be expected to be in the box could not be located. With this in mind, we strongly urge that survivors familiarize themselves with the laws of their particular state before attempting to enter a safe-deposit box following the death of a co-owner of the box. Of course, if the personal representative's name was not on the signature form for the box, he or she could not gain access to the box without the banking institution being fully aware of decedent's death.

Notice and Advertising

One of the first duties of the personal representative is to ascertain that everyone who had contact with the decedent during decedent's lifetime is notified of his or her death. You must also be certain that you are kept fully apprised of all matters relevant to the decedent and therefore important to you as the decedent's personal representative.

In order to put the world on notice of the decedent's death, and to inform the public that you have been appointed personal representative and now act for the decedent, you should make certain that you receive all mail directed to the decedent. You should notify the post office to direct the decedent's mail to you. As executor, you should also be in contact with any individuals with whom the decedent had business interests, and naturally all creditors, as well as debtors, of the decedent.

Most states have laws governing the procedures you should follow as personal representative to advertise that you have been granted letters testamentary or (where there is no will) letters of administration to act for the decedent. The laws provide when and where the advertisements should be placed. Many states will not permit you to be formally discharged from your duties unless these advertisements have been properly made.

One purpose of the advertisements is to give formal notice of decedent's death to any possible creditors and to anyone with whom the decedent had a business relationship. The court, therefore, will not authorize payment to the decedent's beneficiaries without first ascertaining that all of decedent's creditors have been notified of the death and without giving them the opportunity to present any outstanding claims. The sooner you meet these statutory requirements the better, since the statute of limitations for creditors does not begin to run until you have duly advertised your appointment. After a specified period of time, if the creditors have not notified you of the decedent's debt to them and received payment, they lose the right to make claims against the estate. The statute of limitations typically runs from six months to a year. (Be sure to check with the Register of Wills office about this law.)

Notice is also important to make certain that there are no "long-lost" potential beneficiaries of the estate (such as children of a deceased relative).

Determining What Claims the Estate Has

Before the executor can prepare an inventory of decedent's assets, he or she must determine whether decedent had any outstanding claims at death and whether these claims can be reduced to cash for the estate and the beneficiaries. Legally, these claims can be classified under the general heading of "causes of action." A cause of action is a legal, enforceable claim of the decedent at death. For example, suppose the decedent owned a retail store and sold a pair of shoes on credit prior to his or her death. The outstanding bill for the shoes would be an asset of the estate, under the general heading of "accounts payable" to the business. Personal loans or other fixed obligations owed to the decedent at death would come under this category. It should not be difficult for you to determine what accounts are outstanding and owed to the estate at decedent's death. Be sure to check through all of decedent's records to make certain that no such claim is overlooked.

More difficult are the claims that are not so easily ascertainable or easily translated into dollars and cents. The decedent might have had an automobile accident several months before death. He or she might have intended to file a formal lawsuit because of injuries or other losses sustained in the accident, but formal procedures might not have been set in motion at the time of decedent's death. A tenant in a building owned by the decedent might have moved out several months before the latter's death, leaving unpaid rent due on the lease.

Before preparing a formal inventory, you must know the precise extent of your duty in making a formal claim on behalf of the estate for all potential assets.

We suggest the following procedure:

1. Conduct as extensive a review of the decedent's books and records as possible under the circumstances.

2. Make a list of all potential claims of the estate.

3. Determine whether these claims can be reduced to cash. Don't assume the responsibility of deciding the value of a claim or the practicality of collecting it. If it involves a potential lawsuit, secure the opinion of a competent attorney (and, if you decide not to follow through with the case, be sure you can prove that you discussed the merits of the case with the attorney and can document good reasons for not going to court). If the claim involves a debt that you feel is not worth the time and expense to the estate to try to collect, have supporting documentation in your file so that you can justify your position.

4. Be sure to document your awareness of the potential asset and the steps taken to effect collection. Should one of the beneficiaries later raise a question about the asset, you will certainly be in a far stronger position if your records indicate your awareness of the problem, the actions taken by you on behalf of the estate, and the supporting documentation of the professional whose advice you obtained before deciding not to follow through with collection.

Inventorying the Assets

At this point the personal representative should have a fairly clear picture of the assets that comprise the estate of the decedent. Since the executor must practically always prepare an inventory, even though it may not have to be formally filed and approved in every case, a first draft should now be prepared. The personal representative will then be aware of the size and extent of the estate, can determine how to go about collecting and securing all property listed in the inventory, and—more important at this point—can decide which matters should be given top priority.

It is essential, at the same time, that the personal representative understand what legally does or does not constitute an asset of the estate. We discuss in depth in Chapter 17 the legal effects of jointly owned property. If title to property was in decedent's name alone, undoubtedly that property constitutes an asset of the estate, and one which must be administered by the executor. In many cases, property in joint names, such as property owned by husband and wife, will pass to the wife at the husband's death by survivorship, and this property will be the wife's asset, controlled by her, and not an asset of the estate to be administered by you as the estate's personal representative. Obviously, therefore, ownership must be determined in order to establish who has the right to the property and to its administration.

The following sample inventory indicates the type of property to be included and the format to be used.

Will No. 481, 1985

REGISTER OF WILLS

INVENTORY

COMMONWEALTH OF PENNSYLVANIA   )
) SS:
COUNTY OF MONTGOMERY   )

JAMES JOHNSON, Executor

of the Estate of WALTER HARRIS, Deceased, being duly sworn according to law, deposes and says that the items appearing in the following inventory include all of the personal assets wherever situate and all of the real estate in the Commonwealth of Pennsylvania of said decedent, that the valuation placed opposite each item of said inventory represents its fair value as of the date of the decedent's death, and that decedent owned no real estate outside of the Commonwealth of Pennsylvania except that which appears in a memorandum at the end of this inventory.

Sworn to and subscribed before me
this 20th day of January, 1985.

_____
JAMES JOHNSON, EXECUTOR

ATTORNEY   Name   Samuel Smith, Esquire
             Address   7885 Main Street, Norristown, PA 19401

Date of Death	Last Residence	Decedent's Social Security No.
10/28/84	8800 DeKalb Pike Norristown, PA 19401	168-05-4190

1	Real Estate: Premises known as 8800 DeKalb Pike, Norristown, PA 19401. Acquired 6/28/71, Sylvia Lewis to Walter Harris, widower, by deed in Volume 496, Page 267, Recorder of Deeds of Montgomery County, Pennsylvania	$ 58,000.00
2	Household furnishings and personal effects at 8800 DeKalb Street, Norristown, Pennsylvania	3,525.00
3	1983 Plymouth Coupe	4,000.00
4	Coins—5 U.S. Proof Sets—1972 at $6.50	32.50
5	The Long Life Assurance Society of the U.S., dividend	28.40
6	JFK Industries, Inc., Hourly Pension Trust, period ending 7/31/83	50.12
7	Continental Casualty Co., refund insurance premium on homeowner's policy	40.85
8	Insurance Company of North America, refund of partial premium and cancellation of homeowner's policy	161.22
9	The Norristown Saving Fund Society, Norristown, PA, Savings Acct. No. 648,281 balance 10/28/84	10,024.88

10	Fourth Pennsylvania Bank
	    Savings Account No. 85-684-3
	        balance 10/28/84
		1,240.12

	Checking Account No. 0841-6214 balance 10/28/84	425.02
11	Monumental Bank & Trust Co. 340 shares capital stock at 13¾	4,675.00
	10/1/84 dividends	77.50
	10/1/84 proceeds from fractional share of stock	12.87
12	Morris-Lynch Ready Assets Trust, No. 487-631-8, balance	22,781.64
	TOTAL . . .	$105,075.12

Determining Priorities

While every estate is different, and matters that have priority in one might not in another, we can set general guidelines as to what should be given priority in a given situation.

The executor should first attend to those matters in which time is a factor in preserving or creating property for the estate. These priority matters can vary considerably. Some situations obviously require prompt attention: if, for example, decedent owned a business dealing in perishable items, such as fruit, it is essential to dispose of the property before it becomes worthless. Then there is the not-so-obvious situation in which the executor must renew the fire insurance on decedent's home or risk being held personally accountable should a fire occur and the insurance not be in force. Another matter that requires prompt attention is the investment decision in which a time factor is involved. A six-month certificate of deposit might be maturing, and absent timely reinvestment the estate could lose considerable interest. Stock options might have to be exercised by a given date. There could be outstanding contractual relationships in which the decedent was involved at the time of death and which must be fulfilled, or changed by reason of decedent's death, within a prescribed time. Obviously these decisions cannot be made without a knowledge of all the matters in which the decedent was involved at the time of death, and failure to act responsibly in these matters can often lead to serious problems for the personal representative.

Preparing Executor's Checklist

Although estate priorities and timetables may vary in part, certain specific duties must be performed within stated time periods.

The list of the executor's primary duties on p. 71 will give the personal representative an excellent outline to follow.

Executor's Primary Duties

1. Probate of will.
2. Advertise Grant of Letters.
3. Inventory of safe deposit box.
4. Claim for life insurance benefits—obtain Form 712 from insurance company.
   a. Consider mode of payment.
5. Claim for pension and profit-sharing benefits.
   a. Consider mode of payment.
   b. Obtain copies of plan, IRS approval and beneficiary designation.
6. Apply for lump sum Social Security benefits and V.A. benefits.
7. File Form 56—Notice of Fiduciary Relationship.
8. Open estate checking and savings accounts.
9. Write to banks for date of death value.
10. Value securities.
11. Appraisal of real property and personal property.
12. Obtain 3 years of U.S. individual income tax returns and 3 years of cancelled checks.
13. Obtain 5 years financials on business interest plus all relevant agreements.
14. Obtain copies of all U.S. gift tax returns filed by decedent.
15. Obtain evidence of all debts of decedent and costs of administering estate.
16. Were any of decedent's medical expenses unpaid at death?
17. Has the estate received after death income taxable under Section 691 of the IRC?
18. Prepayment of state inheritance tax—check state law to determine if permissible and advantages and if so, the applicable deadlines.
19. Consider requesting prompt assessment of decedent's U.S. income taxes.
20. File personal property tax returns—due February 15 of each year estate in administration.
21. File final U.S. and state individual tax return (IRS Form 1040)—due April 15 of the year after the year in which death occurs and gift tax returns—due by time estate tax return due.
22. Is the estate subject to ancillary administration?
23. Are administration expenses and losses to be claimed as an income or estate tax deduction?
24. Obtain alternate valuation date values for federal estate tax return.
25. Payment of U.S. estate tax with flower bonds—must be tendered to Federal Reserve with Form within 9 months of death.
26. Consider election of extension of time to pay U.S. estate tax (Sections 6161 or 6166)—must be filed on or before due date of U.S. estate tax returns including extensions.
27. Consider election to defer payment of inheritance tax on remainder interests —where permitted, determine deadline for election.
28. Consider election for special valuation of farm or business real estate under IRC Section 2032A—must be made with timely filed U.S. estate tax return.

29. File form notice to IRS required by Section 6039A of IRC—due with final U.S. individual income tax return or U.S. estate tax return.
30. Elect (or do not elect) to qualify certain terminable interest property for marital deduction.
31. Ascertain if credit for tax on prior transfers is allowable.
32. File inheritance and federal estate tax return—federal due within 9 months of death—extensions may be requested—check local state law for due date and possible extensions.
33. File inventory—check local state law for requirements and due date.
34. Consider requesting prompt assessment of U.S. estate tax return.
35. Apply for U.S. I.D. number if estate will file U.S. income tax returns.
36. File U.S. Fiduciary Income Tax Return (Form 1041)—choice of fiscal year.
37. Consider redemption under IRC Section 303.
38. Apply for tax waivers.
39. File account or prepare informal family agreement.
40. Prepare audit notices and statement of proposed distribution.
41. File schedule of distribution if applicable.

Source: *Tools and Techniques of Estate Planning,* 4th ed., The National Underwriter Co., Cincinnati, Ohio.

Meeting with and Assisting the Beneficiaries

If you are a close friend or relative of the decedent, you will most likely be familiar with the needs of the beneficiaries of the estate. If not, then as soon as conveniently possible you should meet with the primary beneficiaries of the estate. It is of the utmost importance that the beneficiaries be provided for during the administration of the estate. Make certain that the surviving spouse and children, for example, have sufficient income to carry them over the period of adjustment, which may be as long as one year. Determine whether there are sufficient funds on hand to meet the immediate expenses of the beneficiaries, and, if necessary, arrange for the sale of assets in order to provide these funds. Next, obtain as much information as possible from the beneficiaries to facilitate the handling of the estate. The decedent's family may be able to tell you of any open business transactions of the decedent, the name of the decedent's broker and insurance agent, and the whereabouts of assets which have not come to your attention.

As personal representative you should advise the beneficiaries of the various steps in the administration process. The beneficiaries' awareness of your timetable will prevent frequent and unnecessary contacts on their part to find out when they will finally receive their share of the estate. A logical and informative discussion of the administrative process will not only provide the beneficiaries with information to which they are entitled but will also give them confidence in, and respect for, your work and responsibilities as the estate's personal representative.

The Family's Rights

The surviving members of decedent's family have certain specific rights at decedent's death. Which of them has such rights and exactly what any survivor is entitled to are determined by the law of the state in which decedent was domiciled at death.

Most states specify that a certain minimum amount of property which goes to the spouse alone, or to the spouse and children, is exempt from both taxation and the claims of creditors. This family exemption may apply to a specific amount of money or to a particular property, such as the family home.

State laws often give the surviving spouse a "nonforfeitable" interest in the deceased spouse's estate. This can take the form of election by the surviving spouse to take his or her statutory share of the decedent's estate, or, under some state laws, the right of the surviving spouse to interests in the decedent's property that are comparable to or in lieu of dower or curtesy. The term "dower" refers to the centuries-old English law providing for a widow's support and the support of her children out of the lands or property of her husband. "Curtesy" refers to the assets to which a man would be entitled on the death of his wife under English common law. Some states still use these technical terms, while others define the rights of surviving spouses as their "right of election," their right to "take against" the will of their deceased spouse (to take a share specified by state statutes *regardless* of what the will provides).

In some states, for example, a surviving spouse could have a right of election equivalent to one third of the estate of the decedent. If, say, a deceased husband had a net estate of $100,000 and left it all to his girlfriend, his wife would have a right to elect to receive a minimum of one third, or $33,333. To qualify for this election, the wife might have to exercise her right thereto within a certain period of time—six months, for example—and also be willing to relinquish any other property she might have received from her husband (her half of the family house, for example). The summary of state laws in the Appendix shows what rights a deceased spouse has in your state. In some states, certain rights are also given to children who have not otherwise been provided for in decedent's will.

If there is any indication that the decedent's will did not provide for a spouse or child, you should be extremely careful in regard to the practical, ethical and perhaps legal question involved—namely, the question of your duty to advise the spouse or child—who has been "cut off" from decedent's assets—of his or her rights. If the spouse is relying on you for guidance and you are not aware of the six-month grace period from the date of death during which the right of election may be exercised, the spouse might hold you personally responsible for failure to so advise her. On the other hand, if you do advise her, have you acted equitably toward the other beneficiaries of the estate, toward whom you also have a fiduciary duty?

If, therefore, you have any indication whatsoever of a potential problem such as the one described above, we strongly recommend that you obtain competent legal counsel to advise you how best to handle the problem. Remember also that there may be qualifications to the rights given by state law to the surviving spouse or children. A wife, for example, might lose her right of election if she deserted her husband and was absent from the family home for more than one year before his death.

The summary of state laws that we have provided should be used only as an initial guideline. Once you are involved in a family situation that calls for further expertise, you must obtain the services of a qualified lawyer. Failure to do so might result in your personal liability to the spouse or children or to the remaining beneficiaries of the estate.

SUMMARY

An estate checking account to control and record cash flow in and out of the estate is essential. Investment of amounts in excess of current needs is another top priority.

Safe-deposit boxes owned by the decedent should be found, opened and inventoried.

Notice of the decedent's death must be given to creditors and debtors, as well as potential beneficiaries, by advertising the executor's appointment. Mail should be directed to the executor.

The executor must ascertain if there are causes of action on behalf of or against the decedent and take appropriate measures.

All assets owned by the decedent must be inventoried. An Executor's Checklist should be prepared (see Appendix) to help establish priorities and to pinpoint the individual responsible for each task.

As executor, you must meet with the beneficiaries and explain their rights under law (obviously, with competent legal counsel participating).

10

Tangible Personal Property

Keep It Safe

Quite often, one of the most time-consuming and least productive of the executor's tasks is that of handling the "tangible" personal property of the decedent. By tangible personal property we mean specific items that we can touch and see, such as automobiles, jewelry and furniture (as opposed to "intangibles," a category in which the only assets in our possession represent the value of an article but are not the asset itself: for example, certificates of stock, savings certificates and insurance policies—which, of course, do not have value in themselves but represent the monetary interest that stands behind them).

In situations involving close family members, the executor's duties can be limited to inventorying and appraising the property in question. If the executor represents the estate of a husband who died leaving all his personal property to his wife, it will be the duty of the executor to appraise the property, determine whether it was owned individually by the decedent or jointly with decedent's wife, and have appraisals made where indicated. However, if the decedent lived alone, and especially if valuable personal property is involved, it is the executor's duty to secure (and in some cases seal) the premises and take every precaution to make certain that the tangible personal property will remain intact. For example, if decedent was a single woman living alone and her closest beneficiaries were relatives who resided several thousand miles away, and if decedent kept valuable works of art in her apartment, her executor should take immediate precautions, in some instances even before being formally appointed, to ensure the safety of the articles in decedent's apartment. In all events, a prompt inventory should be taken, locks changed where circumstances warrant it, and insurance policies checked to make certain that valuables are properly and adequately covered.

Jewelry and Collectibles

Where decedent left valuable jewelry or other valuable collectible items such as coins or stamps, we recommend that these be placed in an estate safe-deposit box as quickly as possible. Once the executor becomes aware of the existence of these valuables, it becomes his or her responsibility to see that they are preserved in their entirety for the estate's beneficiaries.

Appraisals

In almost every instance, the executor will need to obtain an appraisal of the tangible property involved prior to distributing it according to the terms of the will or selling it. The appraisal can, according to the circumstances, be relatively brief, as in the case of household articles or furnishings that have no particular value. For example, a list of household articles indicating their approximate value will in most cases be sufficient. On the other hand, if decedent owned a valuable collection of old pipes or antique crystal, its value should be determined by a competent appraiser.

Automobiles

In the case of automobiles titled in joint names with right of survivorship, the surviving joint owner can usually obtain title from an appropriate agency, such as an automobile club, or a notary public that specializes in this area. If the automobile was titled in decedent's name alone, then the executor will have to personally transfer the title. In some states it is possible to avoid probating an estate if the only asset that would require probate is decedent's automobile, and therefore the rules and regulations of the State Department of Motor Vehicles in each state should be reviewed. State laws vary, and the executor should contact the Department of Motor Vehicles located in the capital of his state if it appears that time and expense could be saved through an expeditious transfer of the automobile to a proposed buyer or beneficiary. In all other instances, possession and disposition of the automobile should be treated in the same way as other tangible assets of the estate.

Selling Tangible Property

When the decedent specifically leaves an article of tangible personal property to a beneficiary (e.g., "my diamond bracelet to my daughter, Mary"), then the executor should make certain that the article in question is distributed to the named beneficiary after being inventoried and appraised. If tangible property has not been specifically bequeathed or if the estate is in need of funds to pay taxes and other expenses and the items of personal property must be sold to produce these needed funds, the executor should then proceed to have the property sold.

If a sale of tangible property seems to be in order, we recommend that an executor set the wheels in motion for the sale as quickly as possible. This will prevent possible loss of the property itself or depreciation in the value of the property. Written notice (preferably by certified mail) should be given to the beneficiaries of the sale, so that the executor cannot later be accused of permitting articles of sentimental value to leave the estate without giving family members the opportunity to purchase them at their fair value. Unfortunately, there is usually no ready market for used and outdated furniture, clothing and the like, so the executor must decide whether to dispose of it by public auction or private sale. An alternative is to donate such articles to charity, which should result in a valuable income tax deduction for the estate.

If any conflict with the beneficiaries over the manner of disposal of the tangible personal property seems likely, we strongly recommend that, at the very least, you review your plans with the beneficiaries. Obtain their written consent where possible, so that no questions will be raised later as to whether you chose the most profitable means of disposing of the tangible property. In all events, a careful inventory should be made of all the property before the sale takes place.

One other word of caution: where there is any possibility of a conflict of interest on the part of the executor, he or she should refrain from purchasing or otherwise retaining any tangible asset of the estate. Self-dealing on the part of the executor is one area of the law treated harshly by courts. Anyone whose actions indicate that his or her primary motive was self-gain, and not the best interest of the estate, is subject to strong and unpleasant court action.

SUMMARY

The executor should promptly take steps to safeguard decedent's tangible property, and have the property properly inventoried and appraised. Where property is specifically bequeathed, it should be distributed after it is inventoried and appraised. The executor should make certain that valuable property, where necessary, is placed in the estate's safe-deposit box, and that all tangible property is adequately insured. If any tangible property must be sold, the executor should take whatever reasonable action is necessary to obtain the highest possible price for the property in question. Where possible, the executor should consult the beneficiaries before disposing of the tangible personal property: this gives them the opportunity to purchase the property from the estate, and also permits the executor to obtain their agreement as to the type of sale or other disposition of the property in question.

11

How to Collect Government and Fringe Benefits

Social Security, Railroad Retirement and Civil Service Benefits

Governmental and work-related fringe benefits are not always treated as assets of decedent's estate, so that technically the collection of these benefits may not be the legal responsibility of the executor. In many instances, however, the amounts payable to beneficiaries from these sources can be greater than those passing through probate, and it is the executor's responsibility to make the beneficiaries aware of the potential benefits to which they are entitled. If the benefits are paid to the decedent's estate, then their collection will be the executor's responsibility. If paid directly to named beneficiaries, the latter must still be fully informed by the executor of the nature and size of the benefits and the name of each recipient.

Social Security benefits, benefits payable under the Railroad Retirement Act, and benefits payable to the spouse and dependent children of government employees covered by Civil Service are paid directly to named beneficiaries, and not to decedent's estate.

Veterans' Benefits

If the decedent was a veteran, the estate may be entitled to a burial allowance and the beneficiaries to a pension, depending on the service or disability status of the deceased veteran and the income of the beneficiaries. Since families of deceased veterans may be entitled to both service- and nonservice-connected benefits, as well as to other death-related benefits and benefits often provided by local governmental agencies, these should be pursued in the case of any decedent who served in the armed forces, regardless of whether or not the individual was in the military service at the time of death. You should contact the Veterans Administration or a veterans' service organization to make sure that all benefits to which the survivors are entitled have been applied for, and should also ascertain whether the Veterans Administration Life Insurance was in force at decedent's death.

Making Direct Contact

Experience has shown that in dealing with the family of a deceased, personal contact produces the most efficient results. Since every working American is usually covered under one or more of the above programs, the personal representative should at the very least make certain that the beneficiaries apply to the respective governmental agency for death benefits or for continuing pension benefits. Whenever you as the personal representative have assumed full responsibility for all of decedent's affairs, you should make direct contact with the agency in question, submit the necessary documentation, fill out the required forms, and follow through until payments are in fact received.

Work-related Benefits

In addition to Social Security and other governmental related benefits, work-related fringe benefits might be available to named beneficiaries or to decedent's estate if the decedent was ever employed. Since there are often time limitations and possibly loss of interest if these benefits are not timely applied for, the executor should advise and, where applicable, assist the beneficiaries in obtaining decedent's work-related benefits.

In most cases, these benefits will be payable to named beneficiaries and are not the responsibility of the executor. If, however, the named beneficiaries are deceased, or if decedent failed to name a beneficiary, the proceeds will often be payable to the estate and will be the direct responsibility of the executor. The executor should then make sure that all available benefits are collected.

Group Life Insurance

Heading the list of these work-related fringe benefits is group life insurance. Since many companies insure employees for a multiple of earnings, group life insurance benefits are often quite high, and constitute one of the largest assets the beneficiaries will receive. When the proceeds are paid to adult beneficiaries, the executor's duties may be limited to advising or assisting the beneficiaries in making their claims. However, when the assets of the estate exceed the minimum requirements for filing a federal estate tax return, the executor will have to obtain a Form 712 from the insurance company. This form, which states the amount and exact disposition of the proceeds, is required when filing Form 706, as indicated in Chapter 21, and it is therefore the executor's responsibility to make certain that there is a Form 712 for every policy in which the decedent owned any interest at death. If no beneficiary is named, or the named beneficiary has died and no contingent beneficiary was listed, the proceeds will be paid to the estate to be administered by the personal representative. There are options available to the beneficiaries as to how the proceeds should be paid, and the personal representative can assist in selecting the proper settlement option.

Pension and Profit-sharing Plans

Pension and profit-sharing plans can be significant. Here, again, the personal representative should be aware of the amount and nature of the benefits and, in particular, whether a beneficiary has been selected by the decedent. The exact amount and nature of the benefits should be listed—and benefits taxed, where applicable—on the appropriate state inheritance tax return and on federal Form 706. Qualified pension and profit-sharing plans usually contain settlement options available to the beneficiary, with varying income tax consequences; therefore, care must be taken that the beneficiaries are informed of these tax consequences before selecting the appropriate option. The executor who is not knowledgeable in this area should advise the beneficiaries to consult tax counsel, or their accountant, before reaching a decision on how to receive benefits from these plans.

Besides pension or profit-sharing plans, other plans in which tax considerations are essential—and to which named beneficiaries or decedent's estate might be entitled—include savings plans, employee stock option plans and other employee benefit plans.

Be Certain You Have It All

How can you be certain that all of the above benefits have been applied for and collected? Take the following two steps: (1) Conduct an extensive search of decedent's personal papers and belongings. Most large companies issue periodic statements identifying the benefits to which an employee is entitled upon disability, death, or other termination of employment. Group insurance certificates should be available, and payroll slips will often indicate deductions for various company plans. (2) As executor, you should write to the last employer of the decedent, and all prior employers, to be informed about every work-related benefit to which the decedent's beneficiaries or estate are entitled. You should also request information on any accumulated vacation or sick pay benefits to which decedent was entitled. (Be sure to keep copies of all correspondence.)

Medical Insurance

If the decedent had a prolonged illness before death, there could be large outstanding medical and doctor bills, and the personal representative should make certain that all available medical coverage is utilized. In some cases, decedent's estate might be entitled to double coverage—for example, if decedent was covered at work as well as by private medical insurance. Decedent's death may also have been caused by circumstances that would bring into play other types of payments. For example, if decedent's death was caused by an automobile accident in a state where no-fault insurance was in effect, the estate might be entitled to payment of decedent's medical bills by his or her own hospitalization carrier and by the insurance company that insured decedent's car (through no-fault personal injury protection payments). The estate or beneficiaries might also be entitled to damages from the party responsible for the accident which caused decedent's death.

If decedent's death was work-related, the estate or beneficiaries may be entitled to benefits under the state Workmen's Compensation law. Therefore, where there is any question as to the cause of death, you should investigate the possibility of third-party payments to the estate and to other beneficiaries. Failure to do so could be considered negligence on your part.

If there is any doubt at all as to potential recovery of medical bills and costs, or damages under Workmen's Compensation, or a negligence or tort claim—where another party could be held responsible for injuries or death to the decedent—you should consult with an attorney knowledgeable in these matters and should document the advice given you. Many death-related claims must be brought within a limited time following decedent's death, and if that time lapses without appropriate action being taken you may be held responsible for failing to act in a timely manner.

SUMMARY

While the personal representative is not primarily responsible for collecting government and work-related benefits payable to named beneficiaries, he or she should make certain that the beneficiaries in question are aware of the potential benefits to which they are entitled and should verify that benefits have been applied for and are paid. The personal representative who fails to do so will not know whether insurance or other group benefits are being paid to beneficiaries or to the estate. Also, certain forms must be obtained (such as Form 712) in order to file state and federal death tax returns.

In those instances where other benefits might be available, or where a third party can be held responsible in whole or in part for decedent's death, the personal representative must be careful to take appropriate legal action to protect the estate's interest in these potential benefits within the prescribed time.

12

Life Insurance

When a person dies, life insurance is often one of the most valuable assets left to the survivors. Life insurance can provide the cash to pay debts and expenses of the estate as well as income for the survivors. Despite its considerable value, it is usually not difficult for the beneficiary or the executor to collect the proceeds.

Executor's Responsibility

While the collection of life insurance proceeds payable to a named beneficiary is not technically your responsibility (since the moneys paid will not constitute an asset of the estate), you must be aware, for both tax and cash flow and control reasons, of all insurance policies on the life of the decedent at his or her death. If the beneficiaries are relying on you as the executor to handle all of decedent's affairs, including the collection of nonprobate assets, you should take an active role in helping them collect the proceeds.

Life Insurance Payable to the Estate

If insurance on the life of the decedent is payable to his or her estate, or if the proceeds are payable to a named beneficiary who predeceased the decedent and no contingent or substitute beneficiary was named, then the proceeds will be paid to decedent's estate. It is the responsibility of the executor to collect the proceeds of insurance on the life of the decedent, payable to his or her estate. In cases where proceeds were payable to a named beneficiary who predeceased the insured, the proceeds will also be payable to the estate of the insured.

In addition to handling insurance proceeds payable to the estate, the executor must have insurance information available for preparation of the federal estate tax return (and state inheritance tax returns where applicable). Insurance companies furnish Form 712 (at no cost) to the beneficiaries, as well as directly to the executor, but only when requested in writing to do so. Form 712 contains all the relevant data concerning the amount of the proceeds payable, the amount of any outstanding loan, dividends, and specific information as to the ownership of the policy.

Collecting the Proceeds

The actual collection of the life insurance proceeds is usually not an involved or time-consuming process. To facilitate collection, you as the executor should contact the agent or local office of the life insurance company which issued the policy, find out exactly what documentation will be required, and ask the company to send you a claim form. The insurance company immediately establishes a file. It also requests a duly certified death certificate and the policy itself (if it has been lost, the insurer will still pay the claim as long as the policy was in force at the time of death of the insured) or other relevant information. Life insurance policies are written with contestable periods, usually of one to two years. This means, with very rare exceptions (e.g., in case of obvious fraud), that most companies will not delay payment of the proceeds once the contestable period has elapsed. Insurance contracts also contain a limited period following purchase during which payment will not be made if the insured commits suicide. Aside from these two considerations, proceeds typically are payable within a few weeks of decedent's death.

Be sure to photostat the entire policy—especially the application—before releasing it to the insurance agent or mailing it to the insurance company. The information may be vital evidence in the event of a dispute with the insurer or in certain tax matters. Use registered mail and request a receipt.

Accidental Death

Many life insurance policies contain added benefits, such as double indemnity (i.e., double the face amount of the policy), payable in cases of death from other than natural causes. You must therefore check to see if this type of coverage was in force. Other policy features may provide additional benefits. The policy should therefore be thoroughly reviewed, if necessary by an expert such as an attorney or a CLU (chartered life underwriter), before it is surrendered to the insurer. In any event, as mentioned above, we recommend that you make copies of all insurance policies for your records in case of future questions concerning the type and amount of coverage or the statements in the original application.

Review of Prior Records

Most life insurance policies contain provisions known as "nonforfeiture" provisions. These indicate the value of the policy in the event that the policy owner decides to discontinue payment or otherwise change the present status of the insurance. Nonforfeiture provisions in policies with cash value usually include the right to cash in the policy for a stated amount and the right to purchase a reduced paid-up policy commensurate with the premiums paid to date.

A third option, and quite often the option that the insurance company will select if payment is stopped and no other option is selected, is known as the "extended term" option. Under this extended term option, the company will continue the policy in force, in effect utilizing its cash value to purchase a term policy that will expire in a given amount of years and months. All of these nonforfeiture guarantees are clearly indicated in a chart within the policy. Therefore it is entirely possible that death benefits are due to beneficiaries, or to the estate of the decedent, from a policy for which no premiums have been paid for months or even for years prior to decedent's death. Never throw out a policy without writing to the insurance company for confirmation as to its status.

While you can certainly not be held responsible for specific knowledge of everything the decedent did at any time, we suggest that you review decedent's checkbooks and other records to see if there are any payments to or receipts from insurance companies for policies. If you are not able to determine whether the decedent did own a policy of insurance in a particular company, or whether a policy once owned but discontinued still has any value, then in every instance you should request specific information on any particular policy from the insurance company involved, and keep a documented record of its response for your permanent file.

Settlement Options

Most insurance policies give the beneficiaries the option of selecting the manner in which the proceeds are to be paid. While the growing tendency has been for beneficiaries to take the proceeds in a lump sum and invest the proceeds themselves, any decision on part of the executor and the beneficiaries should be based on a thorough knowledge of all the available options.

These options include leaving the money to earn interest with the insurance company. Interest will usually begin to accrue either from the date of death or from the date the claim is received by the company. (Be sure to check immediately, since interest may not begin to accrue until you submit a death claim.) There is also an installment option under which the beneficiary can receive a certain monthly amount for as long as the proceeds (together with interest) last. Alternatively, the beneficiary can select a term of years (e.g., five, ten, fifteen or twenty years) and have the proceeds paid monthly, together with interest, during that period. If installment payments are elected, and if the beneficiary is the spouse of the decedent, the spouse is entitled to a spouse's special, $1,000 income tax exemption. This can offset up to $1,000 of the interest payable under the installment option. Proceeds of insurance are not otherwise subject to income taxes, but when the proceeds are invested the interest on the proceeds is taxable. Therefore the spouse's special, $1,000 annual income tax exemption should be considered before electing to take the total proceeds in a lump sum settlement.

Other Insurance

As indicated in Chapter 11, the executor should be aware of all death-related benefits to which decedent would be entitled. In addition to the standard life insurance contract discussed above, or other insurance and fringe benefits discussed in Chapter 11, decedent might also have had more limited insurance contracts in force that would provide a recovery depending on the cause of the death. For example, a decedent might have purchased travel accident insurance before being killed in an airplane accident. A decedent who travels regularly or who is particularly concerned about accidental death may own "accident only" coverage, which means that payment may be limited to cases of accidental death or, more limited still, to accidental death while traveling by public conveyances or other modes of travel. In the event of death by accidental cause, every effort should be made to ascertain if decedent had insurance that would specifically cover the circumstances of decedent's death. Check particularly with credit card companies such as American Express, Diner's Club and Carte Blanche, which may offer group term coverages on an automatic basis, and travel clubs such as the Automobile Association of America.

SUMMARY

Collecting life insurance proceeds is usually not a complicated matter, and is the primary responsibility of the named beneficiaries of the policy. The executor, however, must be aware of all coverage on decedent's life and have documentation of the coverage for the estate. It's good practice to obtain a Form 712 from the insurance company for each policy, regardless of whether the insurance was paid to a named beneficiary or to decedent's estate. The executor should also make certain that there is no insurance in force for which claims have not been made, and should carefully review decedent's records for any evidence of old policies on which no payments have been recently made but which may be still in force. If decedent died by other than natural causes, a search should be made to determine whether there was insurance in force specifically covering the circumstances of decedent's death.

13

Cash, Bank Accounts and Listed Securities

Cash

If the decedent had cash on his or her person or at home or in a safe-deposit box at the time of death, an accurate record of the surrounding circumstances should be made. For example, the executor should note that "$400 was found in decedent's top dresser drawer" or that "$150 was in an envelope in decedent's safe-deposit box with decedent's son's name on the envelope." This will help establish the source or ownership of the funds, if relevant, and is especially important where there might be a question whether the cash represents decedent's income or the property of others. Once discovered, the cash should be deposited in the estate's checking account for a permanent record, and any cash not destined to be used in the immediate future should be invested in an insured account at interest.

Handling Checking Accounts, Savings Accounts and Certificates of Deposit

After a thorough search of decedent's documents and papers, and after preparing an inventory as discussed in Chapter 9, the executor should be aware of decedent's bank accounts. In those situations where the money is unproductive (for example, if decedent had $10,000 in a non-interest-bearing checking account at time of death), the executor should immediately transfer these funds to the estate checking account and then write a check payable to an interest-bearing account, unless the estate checking account itself pays a reasonable amount of interest.

It is extremely important that the executor have proper documentation of all bank account moneys for the inventory, the final accounting, and the state and federal tax returns. You, or the attorney for the estate, should promptly write to each bank, giving the account number and title and requesting an up-to-date statement of the moneys in each account, and in particular the date-of-death value. While most banking institutions post interest at stated intervals, it will be necessary to have the interest stated to the date of decedent's death. You should also request the date on which the account was first established, and ask whether the decedent had any other accounts or safe-deposit boxes in that bank. A sample executor's letter follows.

1924 Old Sage Road
Philadelphia, PA 19100
December 20, 1985

The Philadelphia Bank & Trust Company
1400 Market Street
Philadelphia, PA 19100

Re: Estate of Edward Anderson
   Account No.'s 47651 and 525-314

Gentlemen:

I am the executor of the estate of the late Edward Anderson who died on December 10, 1985, and I am enclosing a short certificate issued by the Register of Wills of Philadelphia evidencing my appointment as executor.

The estate's records indicate that the late Mr. Anderson had the above accounts with your bank. Would you please send me written confirmation of the above, and the following information for these accounts, and for any other accounts that Mr. Anderson had with your bank, regardless of whether these accounts were in his name alone, or in joint names with other persons:

1. The date-of-death balance in each account, including interest stated to the date of death.

2. The date on which the account was first opened at the bank.

3. The exact name or names in which the account is titled on your records. If a change has been made since the account was first established, please include the date that the title of the account was changed.

Would you also advise if Mr. Anderson had, at the date of his death, or ever had, a safe-deposit box at The Philadelphia Bank.

Your cooperation in this matter is sincerely appreciated.

Very truly yours,

James Jefferson
Executor of the Estate
of Edward Anderson

If there is any indication of the potential existence of other bank accounts, then the form of letter described above should be sent to all banks in which decedent had any prior accounts, as well as to other banking institutions in the area in which decedent worked or resided. (Be sure to write to banks in cities where the decedent had a vacation home, as well as where the decedent did business.)

Certificates of Deposit

It is especially important when dealing with certificates of deposit in decedent's name that the executor be aware of the maturity date and the terms of the certificate. Quite often when a certificate matures you will need to take steps to change the investment, or it will be automatically rolled over into a new certificate or placed in a low-interest savings account. The ultimate beneficiary of the certificate might be upset if the certificate were reinvested for a period of years at a much lower return than could otherwise be earned. On the other hand, there is no necessity for the executor to immediately cash in certificates in the decedent's name that are paying an attractive rate of interest. Unless the cash is otherwise needed by the estate, the executor may permit the money to remain at the current interest rate until the certificate matures.

Banking regulations usually permit the death of the insured to accelerate the maturity date of a certificate of deposit. For example, suppose a decedent who died in March 1985 had a certificate that matured in January 1986. You will probably be able to cash it in and receive full interest to the date the certificate is terminated, without the usual penalty imposed for cashing it in before the maturity date.

Jointly Owned Bank Accounts

If the decedent had a checking account, savings account or certificate of deposit in joint names with another person at the time of his or her death, it is particularly important to ascertain the precise interest of the estate in the account. The executor must determine who has the legal right to possession and ownership, who is responsible for paying taxes on that particular property, and who has the right to spend the money in the account following decedent's death. If, for example, decedent had a $10,000 certificate of deposit in his name and his wife's name, as joint tenants with the right of survivorship, then, as indicated in Chapter 17, in most states the money would automatically belong to the surviving spouse. However, decedent's executor would have to include that property in the federal estate tax return, and in the state death tax return if required. If, in fact, the account were taxable, the executor might want some guarantee that funds would be available to pay the proportional share of the tax attributable to that jointly held property.

If decedent had a bank account in his or her name in trust for another person, then, in most states, the account would be taxable to the decedent, but the property would pass to the beneficiary. This is called a "totten trust" (named after the individual involved in the first case that dealt with this technique), sometimes known as the "poor man's will." By this device, the decedent can pass property to another without having to prepare a will. This, however, leaves the executor in a precarious position because of the tax, and it might be in order for the executor to request that the bank arrange to have the state death tax paid, or money withheld, at the time of distribution of the proceeds to the beneficiary. Chapter 17 discusses the handling of jointly owned property, but whenever any question arises regarding the respective rights of the estate and the surviving co-owner, the executor should act only after obtaining proper legal counsel as to the respective ownership rights of the parties.

Handling Decedent's Securities

While decedent's personal records may indicate what—if any—securities were owned at the time of death, the executor should take care to ascertain the full extent of decedent's investment portfolio. We suggest that the executor obtain this information by contacting all known brokerage houses with which the decedent conducted business during the three to five years preceding his or her death. This is especially important if any securities that were purchased were not personally received by the decedent but were held by the brokerage house in its own account. (Look through canceled checks and tax returns of the past five years for records of such transactions.)

In some cases, decedent's broker might have had outstanding orders or authority to purchase and sell securities on decedent's behalf. Therefore prompt notice of decedent's death should be given. Stock purchases made after decedent's death might be interpreted as actions taken on behalf of yourself as the executor (and for which the beneficiaries may try to hold you personally liable in the event that the investment in question is a poor one).

You should immediately take possession of all of decedent's securities, write to the brokerage houses in question for a complete record of decedent's transactions, request that all stock certificates and other evidences of investment be immediately turned over to you, and request that all outstanding orders be immediately canceled. It will be extremely helpful to obtain copies of all transactions of the decedent for the past few years. If these records are not available from decedent, they should be requested from the broker.

In addition to writing to the brokerage house for an accounting of all securities owned by decedent at the date of death, the executor will need other information concerning the securities in question. You must know the purchase date and purchase price of the securities and their value as of the date of death. In Chapter 21 we discuss the method of valuing listed securities, and you can obtain this information from the brokerage house in question, from the stock pages of *The Wall Street Journal,* the New York *Times* or your local newspaper, or from your bank or trust company. (You should save the copy of *The Wall Street Journal* published on or following the date of death.)

Usually, as executor, you have the right to sell securities unless decedent's will states otherwise. If you are not certain about the advisability of selling securities, you should obtain the written consent of the beneficiaries before converting the stock into cash. This would be particularly desirable in cases where the beneficiaries might have preferred receiving the securities themselves as part of the distribution, and assuming that other sources could readily be drawn on to cover the various expenses of decedent's estate.

How to Transfer Securities

While brokers' procedures as well as state regulations with respect to the sale of securities may differ somewhat, some general guidelines should be applicable in most cases. If the stock is registered solely in decedent's name and the executor sells the stock, considerable delays can result, with consequent loss in value, dividends or the availability of funds to the estate. Some brokerage firms will put through a sale order immediately when the executor sells decedent's stock, but will delay making payment of the funds until the time-consuming process of changing title from the decedent to the executor has been completed. This process can last from three to five weeks, and can create hardship if the funds are needed immediately. Therefore, whenever selling the stock or converting it into cash within a reasonably short time appears to be necessary, the executor should have the stock transferred from decedent's name to the executor's name (in his or her capacity as executor of decedent's estate).

The stock certificate should be registered in the name of "Mary Roe, Executrix of the Will of Richard Roe, Deceased" (or whatever wording is used in your locality). Once the stock has been transferred to the executor, it can be sold and payment made within the customary five-day period. Stock transfers can be made through the broker with whom the decedent or the executor has regularly conducted business, or the executor can write directly to the transfer agent indicated on the security itself (usually a bank or trust company). The documents usually required by transfer agents are a "short certificate" (often the requirement is that the short certificate be updated to within sixty days of the date of transfer) and the stock certificate signed by the personal representative. (If there are many certificates, or for other convenience reasons, the executor can execute a "stock power," evidencing a transfer of ownership of stock but kept physically separate from the stock for security purposes.) Stock power forms can be obtained from legal stationery stores. The transfer agent often requests that signatures be guaranteed at a commercial bank familiar with the executor's signature. In addition to the above, transfer agents can require an affidavit of domicile attesting that decedent was domiciled in the state where the will was probated. Depending on the circumstances or on the particular regulations of the transfer agent, other documents may be requested.

Obtaining the necessary information and having securities processed through brokerage houses and transfer agents can often be time-consuming. We therefore recommend that the process be started as quickly as possible once the decision to sell the securities has been made. If the securities are in the joint names of the decedent and a survivor, usually the identical information must be furnished to the transfer agent in order to have the securities placed in the name of the survivor.

Securities which are in bearer forms, such as municipal bonds and similar instruments, should immediately be placed in a secured area, preferably a safe-deposit box titled in the name of the executor, so that there can be no doubt that the property in question is an asset of decedent's estate.

Investment Responsibilities

What is the obligation of the executor who is charged with handling various security investments of a decedent? (For a detailed discussion, see Chapter 15.) If you are acting under a will which gives you broad investment powers, then your authority to handle decedent's securities and other investments is broader (and safer) than would be the case if you had to rely solely on state investment law. Therefore, in order to answer this question we must first look at the source of the executor's rights—the decedent's will.

If decedent specifically limited the executor's duties, or if the decedent gave instructions that all securities were to be sold immediately following his death, then you should comply with this request as expeditiously as is reasonably possible under the circumstances. In the absence of specific authority, the executor is governed by the "reasonable and prudent man" rule. Some states have held that, where the executor has particular expertise, he or she (or "it" where a corporate executor is involved) can be held to a higher standard of care than a nonprofessional executor. What steps can protect the executor in these circumstances and what constitutes reasonable action on the part of the executor in regard to decedent's investments? While no specific answer would fit every case, the following guidelines are applicable:

1. As soon as possible after decedent's death, review decedent's investment portfolio with acknowledged professionals. These would include the trust or investment departments of local banking institutions and experienced securities brokers.

2. Consider the needs of the estate and the beneficiaries. If cash is needed for taxes or other liquidity problems or to meet beneficiaries' immediate needs, then the estate and the executor may not be able to afford the luxury of gambling on a possible future increase in the value of the securities. Under these circumstances, it might very well be necessary to immediately sell the investments and not risk a loss in value which could result in tax deficiencies, lack of needed capital, or personal hardship to the beneficiaries (as well as personal liability on your part).

3. When the size of the estate warrants it, discussions should take place with tax counsel and/or certified public accountants. If decedent had employed the services of an accountant or tax attorney who would be familiar with decedent's personal affairs and overall tax picture, then it would be wise for the executor to obtain from one or both of these professionals their evaluation of decedent's financial status. However, since the ultimate decision will be yours, we recommend a second or third opinion if you feel you are not getting proper advice. A well-intentioned executor who receives poor advice from the wrong source can still be held personally liable for unsatisfactory results. In any event, the beneficiaries can take legal action against the executor, which will be expensive and time-consuming (regardless of whether or not the executor is ultimately held to be personally at fault). Obviously, a lawsuit is to be avoided wherever possible.

4. Keep on top of all investments. The easiest way to get in trouble in administering decedent's investments is to ignore them. Market conditions change, and decisions that make sense at any given time might be absolutely wrong only a short time later. Then, too, investments are not always passive, and many involve timely decisions. For example, stock options might become available which must be exercised in a timely manner by the executor.

5. Make certain that you have taken every reasonable step to locate all of decedent's assets. If, for example, the decedent had regularly purchased securities from different brokerage houses, a check of decedent's withdrawals and checkbook stubs through the preceding five years might indicate the purchase of a security or an investment not otherwise evidenced. Keep a close watch on incoming mail, especially for dividends and other information that can help you to effectively obtain and verify all of the investment information possible in regard to decedent's securities. There are

also many situations in which decedent owned securities jointly with other persons. In most instances, the discussion of jointly owned bank accounts in this chapter and the information contained in Chapter 17 should prove extremely helpful to the executor.

Mutual Funds and Tax-free Securities

The obligations of the executor in regard to mutual funds, tax-free bonds and other investments are similar to those discussed above for securities in general. It should be pointed out that while many municipal-type bonds or bond funds are exempt from federal income tax (and in some cases from state income tax), they are in most cases subject to death taxes and are still, of course, assets of the estate to be administered by the executor. While listed securities might fall in value more precipitously than municipal bonds, the executor still has to decide whether to sell or to retain more conservative types of investments, such as corporate bonds and Series E bonds. In these cases, however, since almost complete safety is assured and the downside risk, if any, is greatly minimized, the executor's potential liability in retaining such assets is proportionately diminished.

SUMMARY

It is the duty of the executor to collect all cash and bank accounts, to properly inventory them and to transfer them into the estate's bank accounts as expeditiously as possible. Care should be taken to ensure that the estate is receiving the highest reasonable and safe interest possible at any given time. The executor must also be aware of the estate's interest in all jointly owned accounts.

The executor is responsible for collecting all securities and other investments belonging to the decedent. Because of the volatile nature of many securities, the executor must act as a reasonable, prudent individual in protecting the estate's interest in this property.

The executor should promptly review decedent's investment portfolio with a knowledgeable professional, give careful consideration to the needs of the estate and the beneficiaries, if necessary review the situation with an accountant or tax counsel, keep on top of all investments, and make every possible effort to locate all of decedent's securities.

14

Real Estate

The Big Difference

Most states treat real estate differently from other property of the decedent, and you should be aware of this difference, and of your duties and responsibilities in handling real estate. Unlike title to other property of the decedent, title to real estate usually passes automatically at death. Title can pass to a surviving joint owner, to the beneficiaries of the real estate under decedent's will or, in cases of intestacy (i.e., if decedent died without a valid will), to decedent's heirs. With this difference in mind, let's look at the duties of an executor in regard to decedent's real estate.

Rented Property

If decedent did not own real estate but was renting at the time of death, decedent's lease should be reviewed to determine the contractual obligations of the estate. Many landlords are sympathetic in these instances, and many are quite indifferent. The executor must find out how long the estate will be obligated to continue the rental payments and should make whatever arrangements are legally and practically possible to reduce the estate's liability. If there is any question as to the legal liability of the estate, legal counsel should be consulted, since the executor can be held personally accountable for making rental payments in excess of what would otherwise be legally required. For example, the lease may contain an option—exercisable shortly after decedent's death—under which decedent might have given notice to the landlord and therefore terminated liability under the lease. If this option period expires without any action on the part of the executor, the estate may continue to be held responsible under the lease.

Determining Decedent's Interest

If decedent owned real estate at the time of death, the first question is to determine decedent's interest in the real estate. If the property in question is titled solely in decedent's name, the executor need look no further. In many instances, however, real estate is titled in the names of two or more persons. It then becomes essential to determine the interest of decedent's estate or heirs or named beneficiaries of the real estate following decedent's death. The information contained in Chapter 17 may help determine the effects of death on property in the names of two or more persons. In many instances, the family home will be titled in the name of decedent and his or her spouse. At the death of one spouse, the property in most cases will be owned solely by the survivor, and for all practical purposes the executor will have very few responsibilities in regard to the home. However, care must be taken to ascertain the state's legal requirements before the executor can be extricated from responsibility for the home.

If the decedent was one of several owners of commercial real estate, a question of major consequence is whether decedent's interest passed to the surviving joint owners or to decedent's heirs. If decedent's property passed by survivorship, as in cases where the property was owned jointly with right of survivorship, then the survivor will not only take over ownership of the property, but in most cases the responsibility for care and management of the property. If, however, the property was owned by the decedent and others as tenants in common and not as joint tenants with the right of survivorship, then decedent's interest in the property passes to his or her devisees (the person or persons to whom decedent gave the property under his or her will) or, in the absence of a will, to decedent's heirs at law. In these cases, while title will usually vest immediately in the beneficiaries or heirs, the executor may, depending on local laws, have the responsibility for the property until the estate's administration has been completed. How do you, as an executor, make a determination as to the ownership interest in real estate of a decedent?

Secure the originals, or obtain copies, of all deeds and other evidences of title. If the deed indicates that the property was owned solely by the decedent, there should be no problem in regard to title. If the property was in the names of decedent and his or her spouse, then you must ascertain the legal consequences—the result being, in most instances, that the surviving spouse becomes the sole owner of the entire property. If property was owned jointly by two or more persons and the other joint owner or owners are not the spouse of the decedent, then a legal interpretation of the documents in question should be obtained as soon as possible after your appointment has been formalized.

Appraisals

While the actual right to administer the property as between the executor and the title owner on record can vary depending on the state and jurisdiction involved, it is usually always the executor's responsibility to file the necessary death tax returns for the estate. In order to determine the value of the real estate in question at decedent's death, as well as for other tax purposes (such as computing the date-of-death value of real estate which is to be sold), accurate appraisals are necessary.

The kind of appraisal required depends on the relative value of the property as well as the value of the entire estate. In the case of a decedent and surviving spouse with a relatively small estate, if their jointly owned home is valued at $75,000, for example, and the remainder of their probate estate at $20,000, an appraisal by a qualified real estate appraiser familiar with the area in which decedent resided should suffice. If, on the other hand, the property in question is a valuable commercial property, then, in order to substantiate the valuation for tax purposes or for other purposes involving the sale or distribution of the property, the executor should obtain an in-depth appraisal. The appraiser should take into consideration other relevant factors, such as rental income, or particular features that might affect valuation. (See Chapter 26 for a detailed discussion on valuation.) Care should be taken to check the requirements of local taxing authorities. For sale purposes or for filing death tax returns, local law or practice might require, for example, two separate appraisals from appraisers who are qualified to act before the respective taxing authorities.

Administering and Maintaining the Real Estate

Since title to the property in practically every instance passes at decedent's death to the beneficiaries or heirs of the decedent, the executor should ascertain exactly what his or her duties are in regard to administering and supervising the property. These duties will depend on two factors—first, the nature of the property itself, and second, the applicable state law. If, for example, the executor is a third party and the property in question is a home owned jointly by the decedent and decedent's wife, and if decedent's wife continues to reside in the home, there will be little, if anything, for the executor to do to maintain and administer the property. Once it is ascertained that the appropriate insurance coverage is in effect and provisions are made for payment of any outstanding mortgage, the decedent's spouse should be able to assume responsibility for the normal day-to-day maintenance of the home. Serious problems can arise, however, in cases where the real estate interest of the decedent is other than the above.

Among the responsibilities of anyone charged with administering real estate are the following:

1. Maintaining the premises in general. If the property is rented, not only must the rent be collected, but the administrator must check the premises to make sure they are being kept up properly. Serious problems can arise in the case of vacant property. Simple day-to-day activities like cutting the grass must be provided for if the property is not to appear vacant and so constitute an open invitation to vandalism and theft.

2. Checking insurance policies to make certain that coverage is adequate and that premiums have been timely paid. If there is any question whatsoever on whom the ultimate responsibility for caring for the real estate in question falls, then the executor and beneficiaries should make a joint determination as to who will be responsible for maintaining the real estate in question.

3. Monthly or other periodic payments for expenses such as utilities (water, gas, sewer, etc.) and taxes on the property.

Mortgages, Liens, Leases and Contracts

The real estate to be administered by the personal representative at decedent's death must be limited to the amount of decedent's interest in the property at the time of death. Therefore, outstanding obligations or liens against the real estate must be taken into consideration by the personal representative in valuing and describing the decedent's real property. If decedent had previously made an agreement to sell or lease the property, then, as the personal representative, you are responsible for carrying out the terms of the particular contract. In all cases, you should make a diligent search to ascertain the exact status of the real estate, because, in many jurisdictions, liens can be placed against the real estate for failure to comply with mortgage provisions and payments. In case of an outstanding mortgage, mortgage payments should be kept current until a final determination is made as to the property—whether to sell it or pay off the mortgage, or whether it is in the best interest of the estate and the beneficiaries to continue the mortgage, as would be the case if the outstanding mortgage had a much lower interest rate than the currently prevailing market rate.

Sale of Real Estate

State laws vary as to the executor's right to sell real estate, and therefore these laws must be consulted before the executor unilaterally decides to sell. Some states give the executor the right to sell real estate in every instance, while others give the executor the right to sell real estate in order to raise necessary cash to pay taxes and other expenses. Many states require the executor to obtain permission from the court before selling real estate and distributing the proceeds of the sale. The right to sell real estate can be specifically given under the terms of decedent's will or can be agreed to by the executor and the beneficiaries.

How can the executor be sure that he or she is acting properly in selling decedent's real estate?

1. Have the property accurately and adequately appraised to determine its fair market value; and

2. obtain written permission from the estate's beneficiaries to sell the property at the indicated price; or

3. obtain court approval for the sale at the specified price, with the indicated distribution (in certain jurisdictions, courts may require the executor to post bond or additional bond to cover the proceeds from the sale of the real estate until the proceeds are distributed to the beneficiaries); and

4. make certain that the entire procedure surrounding the sale has been reviewed by competent legal counsel.

Real Estate Located in Another State

Most states maintain the right to tax real estate located within their borders at the death of the owner of the property. Therefore a personal representative must usually be appointed to administer the property and see that taxes are paid. This chapter indicates what rights you as the executor have to deal with real estate located in the state of decedent's domicile, which is the state in which you have been appointed. You do not, however, have authority to handle decedent's real estate in another state: your responsibility in this regard should, in most instances, be limited to making certain that another executor or administrator (usually called an "ancillary" administrator or representative) is appointed in that state. You are also responsible for including reference to that out-of-state property in preparing federal estate tax returns and state tax returns (even though the property will be taxed in the state where it is located and not in the state of decedent's domicile).

SUMMARY

The executor must be aware of the fact that, in most instances, title to real estate passes automatically at death either to the beneficiaries under decedent's will or to decedent's heirs at law. Title to real estate is often placed in more than one name, and a determination must be made as to the interest of decedent's estate in the real estate in question.

It is the responsibility of the executor to obtain appraisals of the real estate in order to ascertain its value at decedent's death, so that this value can be used for the necessary death tax returns, as well as in the event of a future sale of the property. Although title to the property may be in the beneficiaries, in many states the executor still has the responsibility of administering and maintaining the property.

Care should be taken to maintain adequate insurance, to collect rents, to make certain that the property is adequately cared for, and that all expenses and taxes are timely paid. Proper authority to sell the property should be obtained from the heirs or beneficiaries or from the court which has jurisdiction over decedent's estate. In the case of out-of-state property, make certain that an ancillary representative is appointed.

15

Investing Estate Assets

Among the many duties of an executor, one of the most important is to preserve and protect the assets of the estate until they are distributed. We have discussed investment responsibilities as we reviewed each type of asset. However, because of the overall importance of the executor's investment decisions in the estate's administration, we feel the subject deserves its own separate chapter.

Investing Estate Funds

Generally speaking, you are under no specific obligation to invest funds belonging to the estate. This does not mean, however, that you cannot be held accountable by the beneficiaries if you leave estate assets idle. Your obligation to "protect" estate assets implies that you have a duty to invest funds and earn interest. Furthermore, your obligations may be specified in the decedent's will or in your state laws. In addition, if there is an unusual delay in settling the estate and making the final distribution, you will be expected to keep estate assets productive during the intervening period.

What investments can you make? Your best and safest route is to start with the provisions of the will and stay within those guidelines. If the will does not expressly authorize you to invest estate assets, have your attorney apply to the Probate Court for permission.

Another course of action open to you is to make investments that conform to state law. Many states provide a list of investments (or types of investments) which are deemed "reasonable." These are fairly conservative investments. Your duty, as one Pennsylvania court has stated, is to invest in such assets "as an ordinary prudent man of intelligence and integrity, who as a trustee of the moneys of others, would purchase in the exercise of the reasonable care, judgment, and diligence, under the circumstances existing at the time of purchase, having due regard for the management, reputation, and suitability of the issuer and the character of the particular securities . . ."

Most importantly, before you invest you must be certain that after you make the investment the estate will be liquid enough to quickly pay debts, taxes and administration expenses, and that the appropriate distribution can then be made to the estate's beneficiaries.

Reread Chapter 1 on the executor's duties. Note that one of the primary obligations is that of using care, diligence and prudence. You are legally responsible to beneficiaries of the estate, and your breach of fiduciary duty could result in being surcharged by them. The ultimate test is whether your conduct was "reasonable under the circumstances." Perhaps the test used to determine an executor's liability to beneficiaries is also the test you should use in making investments. That test is: "How much interest would have been earned on estate funds in your hands if you had exercised reasonable care and diligence and invested in income-producing securities or deposits?"

So you're caught between the proverbial rock and a hard place. You've got to keep estate assets reasonably invested, yet at the same time keep investments liquid enough to pay the estate's debts, taxes and expenses, and enable you to distribute each beneficiary's share when you complete probate.

Where to Start

The best place to start is—as always—at the beginning. Since you can't invest assets you don't have, you must locate assets or secure pertinent information so you can identify and inventory each asset. Your duty to identify and collect all of the decedent's assets extends not only to those assets you can quickly locate, but to all assets that you can identify through "reasonable investigation."

We suggest you have a meeting with the decedent's family and ask questions about savings and checking accounts the decedent might have had, not only in the decedent's last domicile but also in cities where the decedent lived in the recent past. Next, contact the post office and have it forward all mail to you as executor.

As indicated in Chapter 13, contact all the banks in the immediate area to ascertain if the decedent had any account relationships. You should also examine two other things: first, look over the tax returns (both business and personal) filed by the decedent during the last five years; second, check casualty insurance policies the decedent paid (search through the last five years' checking accounts for canceled checks to insurance companies) for assets covered by the policies but not found in the decedent's home or office.

If you want to be extra safe, contact Commerce Clearing House, Inc. (4025 West Peterson Avenue, Chicago, Ill. 60646) and purchase its reprint of "Examination Technique Handbook for Estate Tax Examiners." The handbook is used as a guideline by the IRS in auditing federal estate tax returns. You will certainly find this handbook a good source of information for locating, inventorying and properly valuing estate assets.

Need for Liquidity

Once you know how large the estate is and what types of assets the estate encompasses, you should begin to estimate what debts the estate must pay and what specific cash bequests you'll have to make. You also have to "guesstimate" how much money you'll need to pay taxes and administration expenses. Why must you do all these things? Because you have an obligation to determine if the estate has sufficient liquidity to meet financial demands. If the estate does not, your duty is to formulate an orderly investment plan to increase estate liquidity.

If there isn't enough cash to pay these expenses when the time comes (but there was enough value when you took over as executor), you could be surcharged for "speculating on the continued maintenance of estate values."

Here's what we suggest you do:

1. Value assets as quickly as possible. You can use the worksheet form titled "Property in Gross Estate" (see Appendix, p. 393).

2. Draw up a list of estimated debts, taxes, expenses and other cash needs. Use the worksheet entitled "Determination of Cash Requirements" (see Appendix, p. 394).

3. Compute the difference between liquidity and cash needs.

4. See how much of the estate consists of cash or "near cash" (bonds or savings instruments with a maturity date prior to the date you'll need cash).

5. If your analysis shows you don't have enough cash, decide which permanent asset(s) should be sold to meet the estate's needs.

6. See if any assets should be disposed of immediately to avoid destruction or loss (such assets including stocks or bonds which may fall in value or vacant non-income-producing real estate).

7. Consider selling small or odd-lot holdings as well as underproductive assets.

Be sure, before you make any sales, that you confer with the beneficiaries. Obtain written approval from them or see if they would like you to hold certain assets (also obtain written consent for "holding" assets you otherwise feel you should sell).

8. You are allowed to surrender certificates of deposit to the issuer before maturity without penalty (if the bank gives you any trouble, mention Federal Reserve Regulation Q).

Flower Bonds

"Flower bonds" are bonds which have been purchased below par value. The federal government will redeem them in payment of the federal estate tax at par value (see Chapter 21). You should make an estimate of the federal estate tax burden to see if the estate has excess bonds. Many estates will have more flower bonds than necessary, since quite a few people bought bonds to pay death taxes before the unlimited marital deduction and increased unified credit became law. If more bonds were purchased than were needed, it would not be prudent to hold the excess. Why? Because flower bonds generally yield less than 5 percent.

Be sure to obtain the advice of counsel before you sell flower bonds. The reason is that these bonds are includable in the decedent's gross estate at par, rather than at their much lower market value, if they can be used to pay federal estate taxes. The problem is that the IRS may make adjustments in the estate's federal estate tax liability, and what you thought was "excess" may not be. Then you're faced with the problem of paying federal estate taxes on bonds which the estate no longer owns and can use. Again, seeking—and obtaining—the written advice of counsel on this specific problem can protect you from surcharge.

How to Invest Money

By now, you should realize that estate beneficiaries could sue you if you leave a sizable amount of cash uninvested for a significant amount of time.

What can you invest in that will be safe? Practically all commercial banks and savings and loan institutions offer money market accounts that are federally insured. Obviously, daily money market accounts offer the most flexibility and liquidity; in the event that money is needed quickly, they should be given the first consideration. It is our feeling that the prudent executor should not invest the estate's funds in an account that is not fully covered by some recognized federal insurance agency. If a large sum of money will not be needed for longer periods of time, then six-month Treasury bills, for example, can be considered by the executor, since they are backed by the full faith and credit of the federal government.

Certain situations might arise in which it would be more beneficial to have tax-exempt investments in order to reduce the income tax consequences. In that event, a qualified stockbroker or banker should be contacted to make certain that any tax-exempt investments provide the greatest degree of safety.

Whenever it seems inadvisable to invest all of the funds in an insured money market account or in United States government securities, the executor should obtain competent investment advice from a stockbroker, banker, or insurance agent.

Where Do We Go from Here?

So far you've collected and preserved estate assets, you've raised estate liquidity to meet cash requirements and disposed of questionable or risky assets in the estate. Now what do you do with the remaining assets in the estate?

What about long-term or permanent investments? We do not recommend that you become involved in long-term investment decisions, which should be left to the judgment of the beneficiaries or to the trustee of the trust to which you'll turn over estate assets.

SUMMARY

To summarize, your obligations as executor include collecting and preserving estate assets and taking whatever steps are necessary to protect estate property against undue depreciation, damage or loss. These duties encompass the need to immediately identify and collect estate assets and determine any potential liquidity shortfall. Once you have decided how much the estate needs in cash to pay its various obligations, you must sell estate assets to raise that cash. Once the cash is raised, it should be invested until it is paid out. Suitable investments include insured savings accounts, U.S. government securities, negotiable certificates of deposit, commercial paper or money market funds. Generally speaking, you should not make any long-term investments such as stock, bonds or real estate.

16

Handling a Family Business

The Problems

Without question, the most difficult asset to administer in any estate is a family business. There are at least four major problems whenever a family business is concerned: (1) lack of liquidity—not enough cash to pay administration expenses, death taxes and specific bequests; (2) lack of investment diversification—quite often, all or most of a decedent's wealth is in one (often shaky) business; (3) nonmarketability—it's hard, and sometimes impossible, to sell a minority interest in a family-owned business (since ownership of less than 51% of the voting shares can't control the actions of the board of directors, force the payment of dividends, or assure the hiring or firing of corporate employees or the payment of dividends); and (4) the family's emotional involvement and company-employee relationships—difficulties are often encountered because decisions are not always rationally made.

Before You Accept

Before you accept the formidable responsibility of being the executor of an estate consisting mainly of a business interest, you should be able to give positive answers to the following questions:

1. Does the company have (or can it get) experienced and qualified management?

2. Is there enough business-generated income, after paying reasonable salaries and bonuses, to pay appropriate dividends to the beneficiaries?

3. Can the business survive in the hands of others? (It's unlikely that a personal-service business, such as a professional practice, will survive the death of its owner.)

4. Is retention of the business primarily to create employment opportunities for family members who are qualified or willing to run it?

5. Are you as executor capable (either personally or through agents) of managing the business? (Geographically, how far away is it?)

6. Is there adequate liquidity—outside the business (through life insurance proceeds or other cash equivalent investments)—to cover death taxes and administration expenses and to provide for the surviving spouse and children not actively engaged in the business?

7. Can you effectively control the direction of the business? (Or do you have to share control with co-fiduciaries who may have conflicts of interest or may not have good business judgment?)

The General Rule

As a general rule, as executor you do not have the legal right to continue the decedent's business. Your job is to conserve estate assets and liquidate them as soon as reasonably possible. This means that you continue the business at your own risk. Any income and gains go to the beneficiaries, while you are responsible for any losses. Don't let the nature of the business mislead you into thinking that you can handle the business without proper authority. A situation as uncomplicated as that of a single practitioner's medical practice recently resulted in a lawsuit when the doctor's widow sold the practice without court approval.

Exceptions to the General Rule

You can safely continue a business under certain conditions. First, the will may specifically allow you to do so without personal risk. Second, state law (check with your attorney and obtain written confirmation) may allow business continuation. Third, you may have your attorney petition the Probate Court for permission to continue the business. Fourth, you could safely continue the business with the written consent of all interested parties as long as they are fully informed of the facts and as long as they are all competent adults. If you are going to run the business using provisions in a will as your authority, note that those provisions must be both definite and explicit. It must be quite clear that the decedent gave you such permission.

If you are going to continue the business under the authority of state statutes, you should know that most state laws permit you to continue only long enough to "wind up" the business. This does not mean you have to close the doors the day after a person dies, but you cannot continue running the business indefinitely. Here again, written advice from an attorney is recommended.

The safest authority to continue a business can be found in written court orders. Your attorney can obtain a court order allowing you to continue the business for several months or up to a year or longer, depending on the particular circumstances involved.

What's the Problem?

As an executor managing a business of a deceased person, you can be sued by any number of people for any number of reasons. You could be sued by a recently divorced spouse, a beneficiary, a stockholder of the deceased, a creditor or anyone else interested in the estate. For example, if the family unit consisted of parents, a son and a daughter, and if the son worked for his father in the family business, the son might automatically conclude that he had the right to take over the business and operate it for the benefit of his mother and sister following his father's death. In this situation, if the son were to make an improper business decision resulting in a financial loss to the business, he could be liable to his mother and sister for the loss, because he had no proper authority to manage the business and make the decision that resulted in the loss.

You could be sued for mismanaging any phase of the business or for the improper use, operation or distribution of the enterprise. In managing a business, you are held to the standard of care that an ordinary, prudent business person should exercise. If loss or injury occurs, therefore, you must either be adequately insured or pay the expenses personally. Of course, if your actions were prudent you will not be surcharged. (But you may still incur significant court costs and legal expenses in the process of defending yourself.)

Who decides whether or not the executor's acts are those of an ordinary, prudent business person? The answer is that if the parties cannot agree between themselves that the actions of the executor were proper and consistent with normal business customs and usages, and that the executor acted as an ordinary, prudent business person would act under the circumstances, then the courts will have to decide. Unfortunately, this can often result in long delays and a great deal of inconvenience and expense to the estate and to the executor.

Where Does the Money Come From?

Before you accept the position of executor of an estate with a family business, you should determine the amount of the operating funds of the business. Why is this important? Because you have no right to use money from the decedent's general estate. The only funds you can use to carry on the business are those invested in the business at the time the decedent dies.

Even obtaining loans to run the business may be difficult under state law. To mortgage estate property as security for any loan, you must have express or implied authority from the will or from state laws. If you continue a nonincorporated business, you subject each and every asset in the estate (in addition to assets invested in the business) to the liability of any new business creditors.

Who Does the Work?

If you are thinking that you can hire somebody to run the business and then forget about it, you may want to think again. As executor, you are obligated to personally perform all acts and duties requiring the "exercise of discretion." This means that you can hire others to do only "ministerial" duties. Major business decisions cannot be made by others. In fact, you must act as a prudent person in both what you do and whom you hire. You can be held accountable for hiring somebody who is not suited for the job.

How Much Authority Do You Have?

If you decide to operate an unincorporated sole proprietorship, you have complete authority to make business decisions (and complete responsibility for decisions you make). Your exposure to surcharge by beneficiaries and others is quite broad.

If the decedent owned stock in a corporation, you have a much narrower scope of rights and responsibilities. The property you are responsible for is the corporate stock, and through the exercise of that right you must protect the estate's interest. The more stock the decedent owned, the more power you will have, as executor, in the management of the business. You are obligated to act as a "reasonably prudent stockholder" would under the circumstances.

If the decedent was a partner, you cannot become a partner unless the other partners consent. Your rights are (1) to receive income earned by the partnership (to the extent of the decedent's partnership interest) and (2) to obtain reasonable information about what is going on within the business. Unless there is consent by the other partners, neither you nor the estate can become a partner or continue the business. In most circumstances a partnership, unless otherwise provided for, terminates upon the death of one of the partners.

Keeping It Up

Can you make repairs to business property? The answer is that you cannot unless the will expressly or implicitly authorizes you to do so. The question is, what is a repair as opposed to an improvement? In today's economy, business equipment becomes old and ineffective quickly. Should you buy new machinery or office technology? First, check for specific authority in the will. Then try to obtain court permission. If the will does not give you clear and unequivocable guidance, and if you cannot obtain court permission and the business cannot be run effectively with its present equipment, you should sell or liquidate the business.

Can I Make It Grow?

It should be obvious from the paragraphs above that you need specific direction just to continue a decedent's business. You must have even greater authority if you want to expand the business or its products or services. Your job is to conserve estate assets rather than to continue or expand the enterprise. Therefore, be extremely conservative about expanding an existing business without proper authority. It's a one-way street. The beneficiaries have everything to gain, while you, the executor, will lose if you act without proper authority and your actions result in losses to the business.

Where Do I Go from Here?

Let's take first things first. Have an attorney examine the will and give you a written interpretation of it. Be sure that the advice you receive is clear—have your attorney state that he or she has studied the will and state law and that either you can (or cannot) safely continue the business. If the will is silent or ambiguous and state law provides no help, the next step should be to either petition the court for permission to continue the business or obtain the written consent of all beneficiaries.

In any event, you must adequately insure and protect the business and keep it running until it can be decided whether to sell it or continue it.

Here's What to Check Before Deciding

Before you determine whether the business should be sold or continued, you ought to document—in writing—answers to the following questions:

1. What type of business is it, and are there people capable of running it?

2. What is the condition of the physical assets involved?

3. Who is presently running and operating the business, and are they capable of continuing it over an extended period?

4. What are the net worth and overall financial condition of the business?

5. Is the business expected to become more—or less—profitable in the future?

6. What is the morale of the employees after the owner's death?

7. Is there reliable second-line management who can step in and take the place of senior management, or can other outside people be brought in at a reasonable expense?

8. Is there a buy/sell agreement? If so, what are its terms? (The existence of a buy/sell agreement might eliminate all other problems. If the agreement is effective and adequately funded, you as executor will receive cash and will no longer be tied to the financial fortunes of the business.)

9. What are the current, long-term or potential liabilities of the business?

10. How quickly do beneficiaries need cash, and do they have other large capital needs?

11. Can the business be sold and, if so, to whom and at what price?

12. Can money be borrowed to maintain, improve or expand the business?

13. If the business is unincorporated, should it be incorporated? (If so, consider what assets should be retained by the estate and its heirs, and which should be contributed to the corporation.)

14. Can the business provide cash to pay the estate's other expenses?

SUMMARY

The continuance of a business for any time beyond that necessary to obtain an adequate price involves high risk to you as executor. Absent specific and unambiguous authorization in the decedent's will, state law, court approval or consent of all interested parties, you have no power to continue a decedent's business. Your duty is to conserve the business and liquidate it as soon as reasonably possible. If you do continue the business without specific authority, you do so at your own risk. You must pay over any income and gains to the beneficiaries, and you are *personally* liable for any losses incurred in operating the business. If you decide to run the business, you are held to the standard of care of the ordinary, prudent business person. To operate the business, you must use only funds in the business at the time the estate comes into existence, and may not use funds from the general estate of the decedent. You may delegate only those tasks which are ministerial. Absent specific instructions to the contrary, your job is to sustain the business and usually not to expand it. Before you decide whether to carry on the decedent's business, you must review the entire situation and obtain answers to a series of relevant business questions.

Even more than most other decisions you'll have to make as executor, the decision to continue a business should be made only after consulting both the estate's attorney and accountant. We also suggest that, after you have carefully listed the pros and cons of whatever course of action you have chosen, you obtain written consent from the beneficiaries before executing your plan.

17

Jointly Owned Property

The executor is charged with the responsibility of administering all of decedent's probate property. This consists of property in decedent's name alone, and also property that was jointly owned by the decedent and other persons at the time of decedent's death and in which decedent's interest passed to decedent's estate at his or her death, and not to the other surviving joint owners of the property. Since it is the executor's duty to administer all of decedent's probate property, regardless of its source, the executor must have a working knowledge of the laws of jointly owned property in order to determine decedent's interest in any property owned jointly by the decedent and others at the time of death.

Tenancy in Common

Two or more people (such as a mother and daughter or uncle and nephew) will often purchase property and hold title to it as tenants in common. This means each person owns a proportionate share (e.g., four tenants in common each own one fourth) and can sell it, give it away or leave it to whomever he or she wishes. Each party has an "individual interest." This means that, if one party dies, decedent's interest passes under decedent's will and therefore becomes subject to probate. It will not pass to the surviving joint tenant in common (unless it does so under the decedent-tenant's will or by the laws of intestacy). If an asset was held by someone as a tenant in common, you must treat it as an asset of the estate and dispose of it as dictated under the terms of the will (or intestacy law, if appropriate).

Tenancy by Entireties

A tenancy by the entirety is a form of property ownership that is available only to husband and wife. Neither party during lifetime (except with the consent of the other) can dispose of his or her interest. At the death of either tenant, the property is owned solely and completely by the survivor—regardless of what the will or intestacy law may provide. Technically, such property is not a probate asset and so, as personal representative, you have no legal obligation to assist the family with this type of property. In practice, however, you will be called upon to advise the surviving spouse and assist in collecting and distributing such assets.

Joint Tenancy with the Right of Survivorship

A certain type of property ownership is referred to as "joint tenancy" or "joint property." It exists when two or more persons (who need not be husband and wife or even related in any way) hold property in such a way that, upon the death of either, the property passes automatically to the survivor.

Assisting the Family

You can transfer the title to stocks, bonds or other securities held by the decedent as a tenant by the entirety or as a joint tenant with right of survivorship through the transfer agent designated on the stock certificate or through a stockbroker. Typically, you will need

1. the original stock certificate;

2. an "assignment of title" signed by the surviving joint tenant(s) and guaranteed by a commercial bank or stockbroker;

3. a death certificate; and

4. an affidavit of domicile.

Your stockbroker can assist you with the transfer of title and tell you what specific steps you must take.

Title to bank accounts held jointly (either as tenants by entireties or held jointly with right of survivorship) is transferred by submitting a death certificate to the bank.

Be sure to examine all jointly owned assets carefully to ascertain whether they are subject to probate. Remember, also, that even nonprobate assets are often subject to federal and/or state death taxes. Furthermore, the valuation you place on those assets will have an impact on the potential gain to be realized on a future sale, since death tax valuation generally establishes an asset's income tax basis. (See Chapter 26.)

SUMMARY

A decedent's interest in tenancy in common property is the direct responsibility of the estate's personal representative and passes under the terms of the decedent's will or the state intestacy laws.

Although the handling of property under tenancy by the entirety and under joint tenancy with right of survivorship is not among your legal duties, as a practical matter it is incumbent upon you to perform this task. The valuation of all such assets is your responsibility and has significant implications for federal and state death and income taxes.

18

Trusts and Guardianships

The executor will often have to deal with a variety of trusts or guardianships that have been established either by the decedent during his lifetime or under the provisions of decedent's will, to take effect after decedent's death. Therefore, it is necessary that the executor understand the purpose and function of trusts and guardianships and be aware of the duties and responsibilities in regard to property that is now, or will become, trust property.

In Chapter 4 we discussed the duties of trustees and guardians. In this chapter we will discuss the different classifications of trusts and guardianships and how the executor should react in each situation.

GUARDIANSHIPS

The Need for a Guardian

In just about every state and jurisdiction, the law will not permit an executor to distribute property of considerable value to a minor or to an incompetent unless an individual or an institution has been appointed to administer the property during the period of minority or incompetency. The executor therefore should be aware of the age of majority in the state of decedent's domicile and not pay any legacy to anyone not legally competent to receive it.

Some cases are easy to classify. A gift of $25,000 to a three-year-old child obviously requires that someone handle the money until the child becomes of age. But how about a bequest of an automobile to a seventeen-year-old son? Or what if the executor transfers a large sum of money to an elderly person whose overt manifestations of senility might have been apparent had some investigation been made? Suppose the son has a car accident or the recipient loses or squanders the money within a short time after the executor makes payment. Is there any liability on the part of the executor?

If you as the executor have any question at all about making payment to a beneficiary or heir of an estate for any of the above reasons, you should

1. ascertain the age of majority in your state;

2. be aware of the local rules for making payment of limited amounts or distributing specific articles without the necessity of formalized appointments.

3. be hypersensitive to any indication of a possible problem, such as a large bequest to a mentally slow, retarded or elderly person, or gifts to minor children, or the fact that a beneficiary has been recently institutionalized; and

4. take the following steps: (a) secure legal counsel, (b) have the court appoint guardians if necessary, and/or (c) obtain the court's approval for the distribution in question.

Guardian of the Person

In most jurisdictions, only the surviving parent can appoint a testamentary guardian of the person of his or her minor children in his or her will. If no testamentary guardian is appointed and a minor beneficiary is involved, it will probably be necessary for the court to appoint a guardian. The guardian stands "in loco parentis," or in the place of a parent, to the minor child. In most cases this means that the child will live with the guardian and the guardian will supervise the child's day-to-day care, sign his or her report card, purchase clothing and perform the usual routine tasks of a parent. These do not include investing the child's money, but the funds needed for the child's routine care and maintenance are funneled through the guardian of the person.

If there are minor children and if the children's mother (or father) is still living, then money for the care of the children that belongs to the children and not to the mother (or father) can be paid to the mother (or father) for their daily care and maintenance. If, however, you are the executor of an estate where there are no surviving parents and funds are needed for the care of children prior to the final distribution of the estate, then you can and should make payments to the testamentary guardian if one has been named in decedent's will. As in practically every instance of payments from the estate's assets, careful records should be kept and receipts obtained for all payments. When money must be paid for the care of minor children and no parent or guardian is available, the executor should take whatever steps are necessary to have a guardian appointed for the children.

Guardian of Property

Where property is left directly to minor children and no testamentary guardian or trustee has been named in decedent's will, it will be necessary, with few exceptions, to have a guardian appointed to administer the property for the minors until they attain their majority. If the proceeds of an insurance policy are payable to a minor child, the life insurance company will usually require the appointment of a guardian. For example, if a bequest in a will leaves $15,000 to a twelve-year-old minor son, then at the time of making distribution from the estate the executor should be certain that a guardian has been appointed to receive these proceeds. Usually, this is a fairly routine procedure. A relative, a friend or a bank or trust company is selected to handle the money and make any necessary payments during minority. A petition to that effect is filed with the local court having jurisdiction over minors and estates, and the court will usually approve the appointment expeditiously after ascertaining that the guardian will, in fact, handle the funds for the benefit of the minor involved. The guardian is usually required to file an account with the court at the time that final distribution is made to the minor at majority.

Guardian Ad Litem

A guardian "ad litem" is usually a lawyer or other qualified individual appointed by the court to represent the interests of minors or incompetents in a specific matter before the court. If, for example, a question arises over the interpretation of a clause in a will that might in effect reduce the share to be received by a particular class of minors (such as the grandchildren of the deceased individual), then the court might have a guardian ad litem appointed, either on its own initiative or at someone's request on behalf of the minors. The guardian ad litem will conduct an investigation, make a report to the court, or represent the minors in any legal proceedings to make certain that their interests are fully protected.

TRUSTS

Inter Vivos or Living Trust of the Decedent

In the case of a trust set up by decedent during his or her lifetime and providing for disposition of the trust assets following decedent's death, these assets will continue to be handled by the trustee of the trust and will not constitute part of the estate's probate assets to be administered by the executor (but may be part of the gross estate for computation of the federal or state death tax). In such cases the executor's only responsibility in regard to the assets of the trust will be to determine the legality and validity of the trust, by making certain that the property is not, in fact, part of decedent's estate. If, on the other hand, the decedent had set up a trust during lifetime with the proceeds payable to his or her estate or payable under his or her will at death, then these proceeds would be part of the probate estate, to be handled and administered by the executor or administrator.

Living or Inter Vivos "Pourover" Trust

One of the most popular estate planning tools is the "pourover" or "insurance" trust. Under this type of plan, assets are poured over from the probate estate into a preexisting trust. An individual will set up a trust during lifetime which may or may not be funded with income-producing assets prior to death. In some cases, assets can be placed in the trust during lifetime, and the trustee can invest these assets and pay out the income, with additional assets being paid into the trust at decedent's death. Quite often, one of the principal sources of post-death funding for these trusts will be life insurance on the life of the decedent. When the individual dies, the life insurance proceeds are paid directly to the trust and completely bypass decedent's estate.

Another, often used feature of this type of plan is that it allows decedent's will to leave property to the trust. For example, decedent's will might first dispose of his personal property (leaving that to his wife and children), with the residue of his estate (all other property in his name alone) to be paid to the trustee of the living trust. (The trust must be in effect before the will is, so that the will may leave property to the trust

—but usually both are prepared at the same time, the trust being executed prior to the will.)

If you are the executor of an estate in which a trust is a beneficiary, then you should pay particular attention to your accounting procedures. Usually, the only difference in making payments to a named beneficiary or to a trust is that in some cases a more detailed accounting may be required for payments made to a trust. You should maintain a clear distinction between what is principal and what is income, so that a final accounting and distribution to the trustee can be made without any questions arising.

You should be aware that your duties and responsibilities as executor are considerably different than those of the trustee. The executor's duties are to collect the assets of the estate, satisfy the outstanding obligations and make payment to the beneficiaries. Once you have made payment, you will be discharged as executor.

The trustee, on the other hand, is in fact one of the beneficiaries of the estate. The trustee's duties do not begin until the executor has transferred the assets or trust property to the trustee. From that point on, the trustee's duties and responsibilities are governed by the trust instrument itself. For example, the trust might say that the trustee is responsible for paying certain income to decedent's wife for her lifetime, or holding the property in trust until the children reach certain ages and then making distribution to them.

In spite of the differences, a common thread ties together the executor's and the trustee's duties and responsibilities: they are both, in fact, handling the same property. Since the executor handles the property until it is turned over to the trustee, the trustee has a considerable and vital interest in what the executor does with the potential trust property. We therefore recommend that the executor consult with the trustee, where feasible, over important matters such as death and income taxes on the property in question or the sale or exchange of potential trust property during the administration of the estate.

Testamentary Trust

If a trust is established under the provisions of decedent's will, it is called a "testamentary trust." Testamentary trusts become operative only through decedent's will, and therefore do not take effect until decedent's death. Where the will establishes a trust, the executor's duties are similar to those described for cases in which the property in the will is poured over into an inter vivos (living) trust. The executor is responsible for administering the property in question, collecting all the assets, paying all debts, and then making distribution to the trustee rather than to an individually named beneficiary. The trustee is therefore another named beneficiary under decedent's will, and, upon ultimately receiving the property from the executor, will then hold and administer the property pursuant to the trust provisions set out in the will.

The executor should keep a careful accounting of the trust property, and, in those jurisdictions that require it, make a clear distinction between principal and income. The executor should also consult with the trustee for major decisions about taxes or about the sale or distribution of, or change in, the trust property. In most cases, especially when banks or other corporate trustees are involved, a formal accounting and approval by the court is usually required before the trustee accepts the trust property from the executor.

Trustee Ad Litem

Although it will not frequently do so, the court might appoint a trustee ad litem, usually an attorney, to represent the interest of unascertained persons in a particular matter before the court. In most situations which involve distribution of the estate to close family members, no problems of this nature will arise. Sometimes, however, a question may arise as to the rights of unascertained beneficiaries (for example, an unborn grandchild). To protect yourself and ensure fair and conclusive administration and accounting of the estate, you can request the court to appoint a trustee ad litem (if the court on its own volition does not appoint one) to represent the interest, if any, of these unascertained persons or beneficiaries.

SUMMARY

In the administration of the estate, the executor will be dealing with other fiduciaries, including guardians and trustees, and should be aware of the different functions of each and the interrelatedness of their duties. The executor should guard against making any distributions to minors or to otherwise incompetent persons. You should make certain, in every case where a question could arise, that payment is only made to a duly appointed guardian, with the explicit approval of the court where warranted.

As executor, you should be aware of the contrast between your duties and those of a trustee. If the trust was set up during decedent's lifetime, then the trust property will not, in most cases, be part of decedent's estate or subject to administration by the executor. However, if the trust is set up under decedent's will or if decedent's will pours over property into a trust set up by decedent during his or her lifetime, then the executor is responsible for handling that property during the administration of the estate. In these cases, the executor has sole responsibility for handling the property during administration, but should consult with the trustee when making major decisions in regard to taxes or in regard to a sale or change in the asset structure of the property to be transferred to the trust.

19

Paying Debts and Expenses

The executor's duties can be divided into three distinct categories: (1) collecting and administering the assets; (2) paying the outstanding obligations of the estate, including its debts, expenses and taxes; and (3) making distribution to the beneficiaries.

Up to this point, we have discussed the executor's duty to assemble the assets and make certain that they are properly administered so as to conserve them for the use of the ultimate beneficiaries. Now we will discuss the executor's second major function—paying the debts and taxes of the estate.

Before going into the details of death taxes, let's first look at the general debts and expenses of the estate. These can be divided into three general categories: funeral and related expenses, administrative expenses, and debts and claims of the estate.

Funeral and Last Expenses

One of the first bills, and frequently one of the largest you must pay, is the funeral bill. Funeral expenses, cemetery expenses and related costs—e.g., the cost of religious services, cremation or grave markers—are normal estate expenses and should be paid out of the estate's assets, unless the executor feels that the charges are unreasonably high or are not the same as previously agreed upon.

If the decedent was ill for some time prior to death, then in addition to the funeral expenses there may be unpaid bills for doctors or hospitalization. Care should be taken to ascertain all of decedent's medical insurance coverage. In today's world of escalating medical bills, hospital bills amounting to tens of thousands of dollars are not infrequent. We strongly suggest, therefore, that you conduct a careful search of decedent's documents to make sure that all private insurance, work-related coverage and governmental benefits have been exhausted before utilizing the estate's assets to cover these costs. You should promptly notify creditors of receipt of a bill to avoid any legal action on their part. Note, however, that it is much easier to pay a bill a little later than to obtain return of estate's funds from a medical provider when the provider has already received renumeration from an insurance carrier or governmental agency.

Administrative Expenses

In the first two chapters of the book, we talked specifically about the question of fees and the competence of the executor and the attorney for the estate. Executor's fees and attorney's fees are quite frequently the largest element of the administrative expenses, and, as such, are always subject to court approval. Any contractual agreement between the executor and the attorney with regard to fees can still be questioned by the beneficiaries of the estate when the estate is called for audit. This also applies to any fees charged by the executor. Of course, it is reasonable to pay for services on a periodic basis; but remember that if you, as executor, pay an attorney a fee that the court later holds to be excessive, you could be surcharged by the court for the amount of the overpayment.

What should you do, as executor, in regard to payment for your services and for the estate's attorney's services? The surest and safest thing to do is to allocate and set aside the appropriate amount, but to withhold any payment until the court has approved your final accounting, which indicates the fees to be paid to the executor and counsel. However, if it seems that the administration of the estate will be protracted, perhaps over a period of years, this obviously is not a completely fair procedure. In this case, periodic payments in an amount that would be unquestionably reasonable can be made, with the understanding that, regardless of any other agreements made, the court will have the final say on the reasonableness of the amount of the fee.

Aside from the executor's and attorney's fees, other reasonable costs can be paid when incurred (for example, travel expenses, postage and shipping costs, storage and insurance expenses, and the normal and reasonable costs of administering the estate).

Other Debts and Obligations of the Estate

A date-of-death balance sheet listing (in addition to assets) all of decedent's obligations is the best way for you to ascertain the total amount of outstanding bills owed at the date of death. These obligations, plus other continuing obligations of the decedent (and now of his estate), are the responsibility of the executor. Usually, a will contains a clause directing the payment of all unpaid debts. Even in the absence of such direction, most obligations have to be satisfied before any moneys are paid to beneficiaries. Problems can arise when assets are insufficient to pay all of decedent's debts and satisfy any bequests in the will, and also where any property is mortgaged or encumbered.

For example, if decedent left real estate with an outstanding mortgage and the real estate in question was given to decedent's son, who is responsible for paying the mortgage—the son or decedent's general estate? Suppose that, at decedent's death, decedent had left debts in the amount of $10,000, a bank account to his daughter with a balance of $8,000 and, to his son, an automobile worth $15,000. From which of these assets must the executor obtain the money to pay the creditors?

Although it seems that these questions might arise frequently and should have readily available answers, this, unfortunately, is not the case. The executor must obtain the answers by first thoroughly examining decedent's will to see if it contains helpful directions (e.g., "I give and bequeath my real estate located at 651 Shore Drive

to my son, DAVID DOE, *free and clear of all encumbrances")* and, second, consulting ^A^
the law of the state of domicile to determine how that state treats this particular
problem in legal terms. Obviously, seeking legal assistance is imperative in these and
similar situations.

Before satisfying any creditor's claim, the executor must be certain that the claim is
genuine. If there is any question as to the authenticity of the claim, no payment should
be made. By advertising the existence of the estate as discussed in Chapter 9, you have
given notice to all creditors of decedent's death and have indicated where claims
against the estate should be presented. Any unsubmitted claims will be discharged at
the same time that the court discharges you of your responsibility. If you have a
question as to the amount or nature of the claim, you should so inform the court. The
court will then rule on the validity and amount of the claim prior to the "final
adjudication of the estate's account" (this is the accounting the executor must submit
and have approved before being released from his or her obligations). State laws and
local court regulations vary as to the exact procedure required when submitting a
formal claim to an estate; therefore, in any case involving a disputed claim, you should
obtain legal advice before making or permanently withholding payment.

SUMMARY

The executor has the duty and responsibility of satisfying all the legitimate outstanding claims of the estate. The executor should promptly pay all reasonable funeral
and related expenses, and should make certain that all insurance or governmental
benefits are utilized to the fullest degree for unpaid medical bills before using the cash
or other assets of decedent's estate.

Since administrative fees and expenses are always subject to court approval, care
should be taken to avoid payment of excessive fees to the executor or to the attorney
for the estate before court approval is obtained. Other debts and obligations of the
estate can be satisfied from the general assets of the estate if there appears to be no
problem of insolvency. Whenever questions arise as to the sufficiency of the estate
assets to satisfy both the estate's creditors and the bequests in decedent's will, or as to
who is responsible for liquidating an encumbrance against a particular asset, then the
executor should obtain legal advice and, in some instances, specific court approval
before paying the claims in question.

20

State Death Taxes

We have included in the Appendix a summary of each state's death tax laws. These summaries are for your general reference only, and you must ascertain what tax schedules in your state were actually in effect when your decedent died. It is important to check with your local attorney to see (1) if these laws apply and (2) if they have been modified in any way since this book was printed. The purpose of this chapter is to give you a basic outline of how state death tax laws operate.

Almost every estate will incur some state death tax. In many cases the state death tax will equal or exceed the federal death tax. The amount of these taxes will be quickly "guesstimated" by the estate's attorney or accountant so that you can begin to assemble enough cash to meet the demands.

Types of Property Subject to Tax

There are three types of property—real property, tangible personal property and intangible personal property.

Real property (such as land, buildings and houses) can be taxed only by the state where the property is located (the so-called situs of the property), regardless of where decedent was domiciled at the time of his or her death. In other words, no state can tax real property outside its borders.

Tangible personal property (furniture, cars, art, jewelry, etc.) can be taxed only by the state where the property is located. This rule is identical to the rule governing real property, so that a state cannot tax tangible personal property which is in another state.

Intangible personal property (such as stocks, bonds and bank accounts) is taxed by the state in which the decedent was domiciled at the time of his or her death. This rule is applied regardless of where the securities or other evidences of ownership were located when the decedent died. But intangible personal property may also be taxed (with the possibility of double or even multiple taxation of intangible personal property) by any other state which "afforded some direct protection to the decedent's rights in such property."

The Concept of Domicile

You may remember that we discussed the question of domicile in Chapter 8. While every person has one and only one domicile for death tax purposes, unfortunately states often disagree on which state that is. The problem is that each state claiming domicile can tax all the intangible personal property of the decedent regardless of where the property is located. In one case, an estate composed largely of intangible personal property was almost completely consumed by the death taxes imposed by as many as four states. Fortunately, many states have enacted legislation that minimizes or eliminates unfair double or multiple taxation. Many states expressly exempt the intangibles of nonresidents or provide for reciprocal exemption. In other words, one state won't tax the intangible personal property of a nonresident if the state of residence will provide the same protection for the other state's domiciliaries.

Inheritance Tax Defined

Almost every state imposes an inheritance tax. An inheritance tax is a tax imposed on the right to inherit property. This should be compared with an estate tax, which is a tax imposed on the right to transfer property. Why is the distinction important? Because an inheritance tax is levied on the share of each beneficiary individually and not on the estate as a whole. The importance of this distinction is that the closer the relationship to the decedent, the greater the exemption (if there is one) and the lower the rate of tax. For instance, some states don't tax transfers to surviving spouses, while others provide a lower rate of tax for transfers to children, parents or surviving spouses.

The Estate Tax

Some states impose a tax known as an estate tax in addition to or in place of the inheritance tax. Typically, the estate tax is levied in addition to the inheritance tax, and is designed to absorb the credit allowed against the federal estate tax. What does this mean? In simple terms, federal estate tax law allows credit (a dollar-for-dollar reduction of the tax) to be applied against the federal estate tax payable. This federal credit is for state death taxes actually paid. In the instructions to the federal estate tax return (Form 706) you will find tables that show the maximum limits on this federal estate tax credit. The additional estate tax is designed to guarantee that—to the extent there is a credit and that credit has not already been "used up" by the inheritance tax —it will be used up by an additional state estate tax. In essence, the state is saying, a given amount of tax is going to be collected, either by the federal government or by our state; so it might as well be—up to those limits—our state.

The form and amount of such "additional estate taxes" vary considerably among the various states. It is important to examine the summaries in the Appendix as well as to check with a local attorney. In many cases where the decedent was survived by a spouse, the federal law will not allow a credit for state death taxes, and therefore no additional state estate tax should be imposed.

What Transfers Are Taxable?

All states tax property transferred by will or by intestacy laws, so the property actually owned by the decedent at the time of his death will be subject to state death taxes. There are exceptions: for instance, if an individual renounces his or her legacy (that is, disclaims all rights to that transferred property) no tax will be imposed on that individual. What if there is a valid will and the heirs argue over the interpretation of various provisions? In a will dispute, most states will tax the original beneficiaries regardless of the way that property is actually distributed. Some states, however, will impose their inheritance taxes in accordance with the actual distribution of property after a compromise, rather than by the terms of the will.

What if a decedent has forgiven a debt someone owed him? The forgiveness of a debt in a will results in the debt being treated as a taxable transfer, on the assumption that the debtor is solvent and the debt is still legally binding. Are bequests to executors —in place of regular commissions—taxable? The answer is yes. The state has the right to tax a bequest to an executor just as though it were a normal bequest. Likewise, if an individual signs an antenuptial agreement which requires that property be transferred at his or her death, when property is transferred pursuant to that agreement by will it is taxable under state death tax laws.

Gifts in Contemplation of Death

Most states tax transfers made within prescribed periods before death. Typically, if an individual makes a transfer within one, two or three years before death, the state law may treat that transfer as if it were still in the decedent's estate at the time of death.

Many states use what is known as a "contemplation of death" statute. This means that nothing is taxable unless the state can prove the decedent gave the gift with the intention of avoiding the state death tax. If the survivors can prove that the decedent had a "living" motive (such as the desire to minimize income taxes), this would mean that the gift was not made in contemplation of death and therefore would not be subject to a state death tax.

The trend is for state death tax laws to follow the federal law. Under the new federal statute, but with notable exceptions, gifts made within three years of death are not—generally—brought back into the taxable estate.

Transfers "Taking Effect at Death"

Most states tax transfers "taking effect at death." These include transfers under which the decedent retained a life income ("You can have the stock now, but I'm keeping the dividends as long as I live") or life estate ("The house in Wildwood is yours, but I'm going to live in it until I die") or the right to designate who will receive either the property or the income or both. Transfers taking effect at death also include property placed in revocable trusts. Since these trusts can always be changed, a transfer does not take place for tax purposes until the death of the person who established the trust. A third type of transfer taking effect at death is the one in which the rights of the donee (the recipient of the gift) are not certain (or, as lawyers would say, "vested") until and unless he or she survives the person who made the gift. A fourth type of transfer taking effect at death is one under which the decedent had retained power (either in himself or in conjunction with someone else) to alter, amend or terminate the donee's enjoyment of the gift. For instance, if an individual establishes a trust but reserves the right to alter, amend, revoke or terminate the trust, state death taxes will be imposed when that individual dies as if the trust had never been established.

Powers of Appointment

Powers of appointment sometimes attract state death taxation. A power of appointment is a right given by one person to designate who will receive property. Under a "general power" of appointment, individuals who are given the right to designate the recipients of the property can take the property themselves or name their estate, their creditors or the creditors of their estate as recipients of the property. A "special power" is one in which individuals with the right to appoint a property can only appoint it to a specified or limited group of people (which does not include those individuals themselves, their estate, their creditors or the creditors of their estate).

Some states tax the property subject to a power of appointment in the estate of the donee (the person with the power to appoint the property) only if the power is general. Other states impose a tax only if the general power is exercised. In most states, transfers under limited or special powers are not taxed. In at least one state (Pennsylvania), if an individual dies while possessing a general power of appointment, none of the assets will be taxable.

Jointly Owned Property

Jointly owned property (property which the decedent owned jointly with right of survivorship) becomes the property of the survivor immediately upon the death of the other owner. Some states tax such jointly held property under the "percentage of contribution" rule. This means the entire value of the property will be subject to state death taxes except to the extent that any survivors can prove their contribution. If survivors can prove that they contributed 90 percent and the decedent contributed only 10 percent of the purchase price, then only 10 percent of the date-of-death value of the property will be subject to tax. Other states use the "fractional" method, where the date-of-death value of the property is divided by the number of owners. For example, if there are four owners, only one fourth of the value of the property will be includable in the decedent's estate. Some states do not tax property owned jointly with the right of survivorship if that property is owned jointly by husband and wife.

Community Property

Community property states typically impose an inheritance tax on one half of the community property at the death of either spouse. There are eight community property states—Arizona, California, Idaho, Louisiana, Nevada, New Mexico, Texas and Washington.

Life Insurance

How is life insurance taxed? Most states treat life insurance—if it is payable to the estate of the insured (or the executor or administrator of the insured)—like any other property. Life insurance will also be taxable if it is paid directly to a creditor of the insured. Some states (for example, Pennsylvania) exempt life insurance proceeds—regardless of amount—no matter who the recipient of the proceeds is.

Most states exempt fully or partially the proceeds of life insurance payable to a named beneficiary or to a trustee for the benefit of specified beneficiaries.

Qualified Retirement Plans

Payments under qualified pension and profit-sharing plans—IRAs, HR-10 plans (Self-Employed Individuals Retirement—often called Keogh—plans) and other retirement plans or systems—are sometimes exempted fully or partially from state death taxes. Many states follow federal law, which no longer allows an exemption. If the proceeds are payable to the plan participant's estate, any exemption is usually lost.

Preparing and Filing Tax Returns

Each state usually has its own forms for inheritance tax or other death tax returns. We recommend that executors obtain these forms at the earliest possible date, so that they will be familiar with the nature of the tax, the property to be included, and other information required by the state. As executor you will then be aware in advance of your responsibilities and can accumulate the necessary information during the administration of the estate.

You must, as soon as reasonably possible, become familiar with the time requirements for filing the state death tax returns. Some states give a discount for early payment, and this early payment can be due several months after decedent's death. The tax return is often due in less than a year, with penalties for late payment. The executor who does not take advantage of discounts where they make good financial sense, and who does not pay the tax on time, with no justification for failure to pay, can be personally liable for penalties and interest.

In some cases it is impossible to pay the tax on time—as in the case of undiscovered assets or assets whose values cannot be determined within the prescribed period. It may also be impossible if, for example, the only asset is real estate of considerable value which must be sold in order to produce the funds to pay the taxes. Most states have requirements for requesting extensions within which to pay the tax, and these requirements must be complied with in all cases. Quite often, it might be wise for the executor to make a payment on account, so that interest (or penalties) will not accrue on the full amount of the unpaid tax. If requests for extensions are timely filed, the estate will be relieved of penalties for failure to pay the tax, although in most cases interest will still accrue.

Most states allow certain deductions, credits and exemptions that differ from those indicated in Chapter 21 for the federal estate tax. For example, some states have a "family exemption," which is available if the beneficiaries were members of decedent's household at decedent's death. Some states have a "homestead" allowance for the family home. Other states have credits and exemptions for close family members. Some relieve married persons from any tax on jointly held property at the death of the first one to die, while in other states the amount of the exemptions and credits might relieve the entire estate from all tax obligations.

Allocation of the Tax Among the Beneficiaries

In most states the executor is responsible for paying state death taxes, but this responsibility only applies to the property passing through the probate estate. In many cases, nonprobate property will also be subject to inheritance tax. Property held in the names of two brothers, for example, might pass to the surviving brother when one of them dies. The surviving brother, and not the executor, will have the responsibility of paying the state inheritance tax on the share of the property owned by the deceased brother. In spite of this, however, the executor may still be responsible for advising the state of the fact that decedent died owning property jointly with his brother. Therefore the executor must be careful to include all required information concerning decedent's assets on the state death tax return.

If decedent left a will, then the provisions of the will must be examined to determine upon whom the tax burden will lie. For example, if decedent bequeathed certain gifts to his children and left the residue of his estate to his wife, and if the will indicates that all taxes shall be paid from the residue of the estate, the children will receive their gifts free of any tax obligations.

State death tax laws must be examined to determine whether a particular tax should be apportioned pro rata among the estate's beneficiaries or charged to certain named beneficiaries. In the case of property left to a particular individual under a decedent's will, that individual will often be responsible for the inheritance tax on that property. Unfortunately, every case will not be that clear, and the executor therefore has two distinct responsibilities:

1. to be certain of the amount of the tax and make payment; and
2. to allocate the tax burden to the proper beneficiary.

SUMMARY

Most states impose inheritance or estate taxes on the property of the decedent. The executor must check the state of domicile and the tax information in the Appendix to ascertain the nature of the tax imposed on decedent's property and the rate of tax to be paid.

If decedent owned property in two or more states, the nature of the property will determine which state has the right to tax it. Real estate is taxed in the state where it is located, while intangible and other property is usually taxed in the state of domicile. The executor must be familiar with the time requirements for filing the returns and the proper method of allocating the tax among the beneficiaries.

21

Filing the Federal
Estate Tax Return

Introduction

An executor must complete and file Form 706, the U.S. Estate Tax Return, if the size of the estate exceeds certain thresholds (described below). Although a great deal of the mathematics involved is simple and the compilation and gathering of data seem to be merely legwork, this task should not be attempted without the assistance of competent tax counsel. The tax payable, the options forfeitable, and the penalties that may be imposed are too high for the layperson to attempt to dispense with counsel.

Nevertheless, as a nonprofessional executor you can be of great assistance and can save a great deal of time and money if you are aware of what must be done and how that task (and it can be a very difficult one) is to be done.

Many of the words and phrases in the text that follows are used in a special way by tax attorneys and accountants: almost all of these are in quotation marks, to alert you to their special usage. In most cases, a definition will follow the words or phrases, and you can find a more technically complete definition in the Glossary at the conclusion of this book.

You will find a sample filled-out Form 706 in the Appendix. If you refer to this as you are reading, you will find the text much more useful.

When to File the 706

The 706, or federal estate tax return form, must be filed within nine months after a person's death. (It is possible to receive an extension of time for both filing and paying the tax. These extensions will be discussed below.)

Who Must File the 706

The 706 must be filed by the executor. To guarantee that someone will be responsible, the tax law defines the term "executor" as the court-appointed person or persons named in the decedent's will, or—if there is no valid will—the person named by the court to act as the decedent's administrator. What if no executor or administrator has been appointed by the court? In that case, anyone (and everyone) who has actual or "constructive" possession of any of the decedent's property is considered an executor and is therefore legally responsible for filing a federal estate tax return.

Form 706 must be filed by the estate's executor for the estate of any person who was a U.S. citizen or resident if that person's (1) "gross estate" (defined below) *plus* (2) his or her "adjusted taxable gifts" (the taxable portion of gifts made after 1976) exceed the following:

Year of Death	Threshold Amount
1983	$ 275,000
1984	$ 325,000
1985	$ 400,000
1986	$ 500,000
1987	$ 600,000

A person's "gross estate" means all property in which the decedent had an interest. This definition is very broad and includes real and personal property titled in a person's name as well as

1. certain transfers made during the decedent's life (not counting those made for adequate and full consideration);

2. certain annuities;

3. joint tenancies in property with survivorship interests;

4. life insurance proceeds;

5. property over which the decedent possessed a "general power of appointment" (defined below); and

6. "community property" interests of the decedent.

These are all explained in more detail below.

Where Must the 706 Be Filed?

You can hand-carry an estate tax return to the office of your local IRS district director. Most executors mail the form (we suggest you use certified mail with return receipt requested) to the appropriate IRS Service Center (i.e., serving the area in which the decedent was domiciled at time of death). The service centers' addresses are listed below.

State	*Mailing Address of IRS Service Center*
New Jersey, New York City, and Nassau, Rockland, Suffolk and Westchester counties	HOLTSVILLE, NY 00501
New York (all other counties), Connecticut, Maine, Massachusetts, New Hampshire, Rhode Island and Vermont	ANDOVER, MA 05501
Alabama, Florida, Georgia, Mississippi and South Carolina	ATLANTA, GA 31101
Michigan and Ohio	CINCINNATI, OH 45999

State	Mailing Address of IRS Service Center
Arkansas, Kansas, Louisiana, New Mexico, Oklahoma and Texas	AUSTIN, TX 73301
Alaska, Arizona, Colorado, Idaho, Minnesota, Montana, Nebraska, Nevada, North Dakota, Oregon, South Dakota, Utah, Washington and Wyoming	OGDEN, UT 84201
Illinois, Iowa, Missouri and Wisconsin	KANSAS CITY, MO 64999
California and Hawaii	FRESNO, CA 93888
Indiana, Kentucky, North Carolina, Tennessee, Virginia and West Virginia	MEMPHIS, TN 37501
Delaware, District of Columbia, Maryland and Pennyslvania	PHILADELPHIA, PA 19255

Who Must Sign the 706?

The executor or administrator (if more than one, then all) must sign the 706. Your signature verifies the statements on the return, and, in every case, you sign under penalty of perjury. So if you ask yourself, How will they know if I don't list an item on the return? the answer is another question: Are you willing to risk criminal prosecution and perhaps jail—not to mention stiff cash penalties and fines? The Criminal Investigations Division of the IRS has means of uncovering assets left unlisted (such as crosschecks with past years' income tax returns, insurance policies and cancelled checks).

In many cases, an attorney or accountant will be preparing the return. If it is prepared by someone other than the person who is filing it, the return must also be signed at the bottom of the first page by the preparer. Each individual executor must list his or her Social Security number on the form or on a separate, attached sheet.

Does the Will Have to Be Filed with the 706?

A certified copy of the will must be filed with the federal estate tax return if the decedent was a citizen or resident and died "testate" (with a valid will). Certain other documents must also be filed, including a certified copy of the death certificate. (In most estates, you will need at least ten copies of this. The cost should be paid by the estate and is deductible as part of administration expenses.) You must also file copies of any trust instruments in which the decedent held a "power of appointment" (the right to say who receives the property in the trust) and, if the state death tax has been paid, a copy of the state certification of payment of death taxes.

What Else Should Be Filed with the 706?

Other documents that may have to be attached to the 706 are the following:

1. Copy of decedent's will.
2. Copy of the order admitting the will to probate.
3. Copies of any relevant trust documents.
4. Real estate appraisals.
5. Supporting documents to indicate how the value of a business interest was determined, including copies of any buy/sell agreements, copies of balance sheets and earnings and profits statements for five years preceding death.
6. Letters from stockbrokers confirming the absence of value of worthless securities.
7. Verification letters from banks indicating date-of-death balances for all accounts and certificates of deposit.
8. Statement verifying reason for taking discount on notes payable.
9. Form 712 for every insurance policy on the life of the decedent and for every policy that decedent owned on the life of some other person.
10. Proof of the survivor's contribution to jointly owned property such as deeds, bills of sale or copies of gift tax returns.
11. Appraisals for valuable items or collections.
12. Statement discussing valuation problem involving pending litigation.
13. Copies of trust instruments containing powers of appointment.
14. Affidavits of attorney and executor in regard to fees.
15. Information to verify special use valuation (affidavits as to the use of the property).
16. Evidence of payment of state death taxes.

Simplified Procedure for Small Estates

If the total gross estate (line 1 under "Tax Computation" on the 706) is $500,000 or less in 1986 or $600,000 or less in 1987, you complete and file the first three pages of the 706, but you don't have to fill out or file schedules A through M, O or P.

Procedure for Large Estates

If the total gross estate is more than the amounts mentioned directly above, you must file the first three pages of the 706 as well as all required schedules.

COMPLETING THE FORM

Form 706 has sixteen consecutively numbered pages. In the Appendix, these are perforated so that you can remove them for copying and filing. Staple all the required pages together when you send in the form.

On each schedule, you will list the items that belong in that category. Land owned by the decedent in his or her own name, for example, will be listed on Schedule A, "Real Estate." Number the items you list on each schedule. Then, total all listed amounts at the bottom of each schedule. When you have completed all the schedules, enter the totals on page 3, under "Recapitulation."

The value of the items you list on the return should be rounded: Any amount smaller than 50 cents is dropped, while amounts that show 50 to 99 cents are raised to the next highest dollar.

Let's go through the form page by page, starting at the top of the first page. (As the IRS changes the form from time to time, it is important to request the form appropriate for the year of the decedent's death and follow the instructions to that year's form.)

Page 1

Page 1 requires you to state the name and "domicile" of the decedent, as well as the year that domicile was established. (The concept of domicile is important for both federal estate tax and state tax and state property law interpretation purposes.) You must also state the decedent's date of death and social security number and the name, address and social security number of the estate's executor(s). Similar information must be given for the estate's attorney.

The second half of the page is devoted to the federal estate tax computation, which cannot be completed until all the schedules have been filled out and the "Recapitulation" on page 3 is completed. We'll come back to the tax computation after discussing these tasks.

Page 2

Page 2 requests further general information such as the decedent's business or occupation and marital status. It requires a breakdown of the estate to show how much of it was (or is to be) received by the decedent's spouse and other heirs. This is to ascertain the estate tax marital deduction discussed below.

An extremely important decision must be made on this page. Line 8 requests the executor to state whether or not the "alternate valuation date" is to be used. The alternate valuation date is the earlier of two dates—either the date six months after the date of death or the date on which an asset is sold, exchanged, distributed or otherwise disposed of. This makes it imperative to wait until six months have elapsed in order to determine what the alternate values are. The decision has both estate and income tax implications. Keep in mind that the right to elect alternate valuation is forfeited unless the 706 is filed on time. As is the case with most of the tax decisions in the administration of an estate, this one should not be made without the advice of both your attorney and your accountant. The alternate valuation date is discussed in more detail below.

If the decedent owned a farm or other closely held (not a publicly owned) business real estate, you may want to elect "special use" valuation. Special use valuation (line 9) allows you to value certain farm and closely held business real estate at its farm or business use value rather than at the highest price it might bring on the general market. Whether or not you think you can meet the tests for this favorable provision, you should file what is called a "protective election." Basically, this means that you are retaining the right to use special use valuation even if it appears that you don't qualify when you initially file the return.

A very important decision is the "Q.T.I.P." election. Certain interests in property may not have passed outright, or in a manner tantamount to outright, to the decedent's surviving spouse. For example, a decedent may have left property to his wife for life (she gets the income), but at her death the property goes to his children. The wife's interest terminates at her death. Absent this Q.T.I.P. (*q*ualified *t*erminable *i*nterest *p*roperty) election, such "terminable interest property" would not qualify for the federal estate tax marital deduction. But if certain requirements are met, the entire value of such property can be deductible in the present decedent's estate. The cost of the Q.T.I.P. election, however, is that when the second (surviving) spouse dies, that spouse's estate will include (for estate tax purposes) the value of the Q.T.I.P. property.

Page 3

Page 3 continues the compilation of general information. This is followed by a schedule entitled "Recapitulation," which is used to total the values in the schedules of assets and deductions that follow.

Page 4: Schedule A—Real Estate

You must complete Schedule A if the total gross estate is more than $600,000 and contains any real estate owned by the decedent in his own name. Real estate owned in "joint tenancy" or "tenancy by the entirety" or as part of an unincorporated business is reported on another schedule—either on Schedule E as jointly owned property or on Schedule F as part of the valuation of a business interest.

Each parcel of real estate owned solely by the decedent (or that the decedent had contracted to purchase in his own name) must be listed and numbered. It must be described in enough detail so that the IRS can inspect and value it if necessary.

When property is subject to a mortgage, the full value of the property must be recorded if (1) the creditor can proceed against assets of the decedent other than the property subject to the mortgage or if (2) the decedent was personally liable for the debt. For instance, in the typical home mortgage, the documents the borrower signs entitle the lender to proceed not only against the house itself, but also against the personal assets of the borrower who fails to make payments. So if you buy a $100,000 house in your own name, borrow $60,000 and die, the full, fair market value of the home, $100,000, is listed on Schedule A. Of course, in this example, the unpaid amount of the debt, $60,000, may be taken as a deduction of the estate on Schedule K.

If the decedent's estate is not liable for the mortgage and the property itself is the only security for the loan, report only the net value of the property—the value of the property less the indebtedness. For example, say you bought a $1 million office building and borrowed $900,000 to help finance it. If the bank could only proceed against the building and had no right to attach your personal assets for nonpayment of the mortgage, you would enter only the net value, $100,000, on Schedule A. In this case, there would be no Schedule K deduction.

As in the case of other property listed on Form 706, real estate must be listed at its "fair market value," the highest price at which property would change hands between a hypothetical willing buyer and willing seller who both have knowledge of the relevant facts (an exception is made for "special use" valuation property).

As the estate's executor, you must hire a qualified appraiser who should consider the following factors in valuing the real estate:

1. The prices obtained on the prior sales of the property in question or for similar properties located nearby.

2. The size, age, condition, use and income-generating capacity of the property in question or of similar properties; and

3. The value of the property according to a capitalization of the net annual income it produces. In other words, what would an investor pay for the property if a given rate of return was assumed appropriate for the type and condition of the property, and the net income was known? For example, if a given building produced a net annual income of $50,000 a year and an interest rate of 15 percent was appropriate, the property should be worth about $333,333. This is found by dividing the net income by the rate of return an investor would demand on his capital in the situation.

Before you do your best to lower the value you enter on the return, here's something you should consider. As in the case of the estate tax valuation of stocks, bonds and other assets likely to be sold before the death of the beneficiary of the estate, the lowest valuation is not always the most advantageous. This is because the fair market value that is settled upon for estate tax purposes becomes the recipient's income tax basis for determining gain or loss when the property is later sold. Likewise, it is the recipient's income tax basis for determining the limit on cost recovery (depreciation) deductions. High valuation (which may or may not mean a higher estate tax), will result in a higher cost basis, which means less gain and therefore less tax upon a subsequent sale of the property or higher depreciation deductions if the property is depreciable.

For example, if you buy real estate (or any other asset) for $1,000 and sell it for $5,000, your gain is the difference between the amount you realize on the sale, here $5,000, and your cost (tax professionals call this your "basis"). At a person's death, the basis of most assets changes. The basis of assets is "stepped up" (or down) to its federal estate tax value; so, in the example we've been using, if death occurred when the property was worth $8,000, its new basis is "stepped up" to $8,000. If you, as executor, sell the property for $8,000, there is no gain. Why not? Because the amount you realize on the sale, $8,000, does not exceed your $8,000 basis. The bottom line is, Be sure to consider the income as well as the estate tax implications of your valuations. We'll have more to say on this planning technique—and others—in our chapter on the tax elections available to an executor.

Any property listed on Schedule A should be described according to the examples given in the instructions for the 706. It is also important to attach to the 706 all supporting documents and appraisals. Absent such documentation and description, the estate tax examiner is much more likely to audit the return.

Page 5: Schedule B—Stocks and Bonds

All stocks and bonds that were titled by the decedent in his own name must be entered on this schedule. You must indicate the following:

For stocks—

1. number of shares;
2. whether common or preferred;

3. exact name of corporation;
4. price per share; and
5. stock exchange where sold.
   For bonds—
1. quantity and denomination;
2. name of obligor;
3. date of maturity;
4. interest rate;
5. interest due date; and
6. stock exchange where sold.

WHERE TO OBTAIN STOCK PRICES

Prices of stocks can be obtained from *The Wall Street Journal* for the appropriate date. Many stockbrokers subscribe to computerized services which can list this information quickly. The printout will probably be acceptable as an attachment to this schedule. Alternatively, you can obtain the information you need in most libraries.

VALUING STOCKS IN GENERAL

How is the fair market value of a stock determined? The fair market value is the mean between the highest and the lowest quoted selling price on the valuation date.

VALUING BONDS IN GENERAL

Corporate bonds are valued similarly to stocks. The mean of the highest and lowest selling prices on or near the applicable valuation date is used.

If there were no sales on or reasonably close to the valuation date, the value of the bonds would be determined by (1) ascertaining the soundness of the security, (2) comparing the interest yield on the bond in question to yields of similar bonds, (3) examining the maturity date, (4) comparing prices for listed bonds of corporations engaged in similar types of business, (5) checking the extent to which the bond is secured, and (6) weighing all other relevant factors such as the opinions of experts, the business's position in the industry and the economy in general.

VALUING CLOSELY HELD STOCK

How do you value stock in a closely held corporation? If the estate holds stock that is not traded on an exchange or over the counter, eight factors should be considered (and here an accountant working with an attorney can be invaluable). The eight factors are: (1) the nature and economic history of the business; (2) the economic outlook in general and for the specific industry; (3) the book value of the corporation and financial condition of the business; (4) the company's earning capacity; (5) the corporation's dividend-paying capacity; (6) the existence or nonexistence of goodwill; (7) stock sales and size of the block of stock to be valued; and (8) the fair market value of stock of comparable corporations engaged in the same or a similar line of business.

No single fixed formula of valuation has yet been devised that is applicable to closely held corporations. All the factors that would add to or subtract from value must be considered.

A reduction in value may be allowed because the shares being valued represent a minority interest. Executors typically take from 10 to 30 percent off the value because the stock isn't a controlling interest. Certainly, stock has less value if its holder is unable to force the payment of dividends, compel the liquidation of the corporation or control corporate policy.

EFFECT OF BUY/SELL AGREEMENT ON VALUE

Stock has less value if it cannot be freely traded or if there is no active market for it. Most closely held stock is subject to some type of restriction on its marketability. A buy/sell agreement, for example, may set a ceiling on the price that will be paid for stock. The IRS will typically go along with the price that was set in the buy/sell agreement if the following conditions are present:

1. The agreement was made between the parties as the result of arm's-length bargaining, and

2. The price set in the agreement was fair and adequate at the time the agreement was signed, and

3. The decedent was bound to offer the stock back to the corporation or its shareholders during his lifetime before he could offer it to anyone else, and

4. The decedent could not sell the stock for a higher price during his lifetime than his estate was entitled to at his death (this being required to prevent an artificially low death-time price designed to result in a lower estate tax), and

5. The executor is bound to sell the stock at the decedent's death at the price fixed in the agreement, and

6. The price per share payable for the stock either is specifically fixed by the agreement or is determinable according to a formula in the agreement.

Buy/sell agreements between family members are closely scrutinized by the IRS to determine whether the agreement is a bona fide business agreement or is merely a device to pass the decedent's shares to the objects of his bounty for a price that does not reflect the stock's fair market value.

Whenever a decedent's estate includes closely held stock, you must submit copies of the corporation's balance sheet (particularly the one nearest to the valuation date). The IRS also requires copies of the corporation's last five years' earnings and profits statements.

VALUING BONDS

There are four types of bonds:

The first category—state, local, private and foreign bonds—must be shown at the mean of the bid and asked market quotations on the applicable valuation date. Interest on such bonds that has accrued from the last payment date to the date of death must be shown as a separate item.

Series E U.S. savings bonds make up the second category. These bonds must be shown at the total of their cost plus the increase in value due to any semiannual accruals up to the date of the decedent's death.

The third category also consists of U.S. bonds—Series H, J and K. These must be listed at par value.

Flower bonds comprise the fourth category. These are bonds which are redeemable by the federal government at their par value to the extent of the federal estate tax. Therefore, to the extent of the estate's federal estate tax liability, flower bonds must be shown at par value, and, to the extent of any excess, listed at the mean of the bid and asked market values (which should be considerably below par).

VALUING WORTHLESS SECURITIES

How are worthless securities handled? Even though a security may have no value, it must be shown on the Form 706. You should attach letters from stockbrokers, from the companies or from your state's Department of Corporations that confirm the absence of value. Such documentation may prevent an audit.

HOW TO HANDLE DIVIDENDS

Dividends on stock owned by the decedent at death constitute part of the estate and must therefore be entered on the 706 if the dividend was payable but not received until after death. What do you do if the decedent died after a dividend was declared but between the ex-dividend date and the stockholder-of-record date? (Your stockholder can explain these terms and help you obtain the appropriate price.) In such a case, the market price of the stock will have fallen by the amount of the dividend. But since the dividend was payable to the estate, the amount you must list is the sum of the depressed market price and the dividend received by the estate.

Page 6: Schedule C—Mortgages, Notes, and Cash

If any mortgages or notes were payable to the decedent at time of death, list them here. Group the items in the following categories and list the categories in the following order:

1. Mortgages. State (a) face value and unpaid balance, (b) date of mortgage, (c) date of maturity, (d) name of maker, (e) property mortgaged, and (f) interest dates and rate of interest.

2. Promissory notes. Same information as for mortgages.

3. Contract by decedent to sell land. State (a) name of purchaser, (b) date of contract, (c) description of property, (d) sale price, (e) initial payment, (f) amounts of installment payments, (g) unpaid balance of principal, and (h) interest rate.

4. Cash and certificates of deposit in the decedent's possession (list separately from bank deposits).

5. Cash in banks, savings and loan associations and other types of financial organizations. State (a) name and address of each such organization, (b) amount in each account, (c) serial number, and (d) nature of account (savings, checking, etc.).

Keep statements from various financial institutions for inspection. (As executor, you should write to all the local banks requesting that an officer of the bank provide you with a letter verifying the following information.) The date-of-death balance should be shown for bank accounts. Savings accounts should reflect interest if that interest was both accrued and payable at the decedent's death. Commercial accounts with checks outstanding should be reduced accordingly (unless the checks are shown as debts on Schedule K, in which case the balance should be shown on this schedule).

You should list the balance of any note due to the decedent at death, plus any interest which has accrued, unless (1) there is substantial doubt that the note will be collected and that the security is sufficient, or (2) the rate of interest payable is well below the prevailing prime rate (for example, where the rate is less than two points above prime). In the latter case, a discount should be taken (substantiated by a statement filed with the return which explains why the discount should be allowed and why the amount taken is reasonable).

Page 7: Schedule D—Insurance on the Decedent's Life

This schedule requires information concerning every life insurance policy (including group insurance and insurance obtained through fraternal or religious organizations) on the decedent's life. You must list every policy on the decedent's life, even if you feel it should not be included in the gross estate of the decedent.

REASONS LIFE INSURANCE MUST BE INCLUDED

Life insurance is includable in a decedent's gross estate if (1) it is payable to or for the benefit of his estate, or (2) it is payable to a named beneficiary other than the estate but the decedent held an "incident of ownership" in the policy (see below) at time of death.

Insurance is considered payable to the estate if it is payable to the estate's executor (as executor); or it may be payable to a beneficiary who is obligated by contract or otherwise to use the proceeds to pay the estate tax or any other taxes, debts or charges which are enforceable against the estate.

A decedent is considered to have an incident of ownership in a policy of insurance on his own life if he had any of the following rights:

1. the right to change or name the policy beneficiary;

2. the power to surrender the policy or cancel it;

3. the right to assign the policy or revoke an assignment;

4. the power to pledge the policy for a loan;

5. the right to obtain a loan from the insurer; and

6. a "reversionary interest" (which occurs if the proceeds are payable to the estate of or according to the directions of the insured) with an actuarial value in excess of 5 percent of the policy's value (as of the instant before the insured died).

You should request from each insurance company a statement on Form 712 (the insurance company will have this form) showing how much was paid and the form of payment. If the policy proceeds are paid in a lump sum, go to line 24 on Form 712 and enter that amount on your Form 706. If the proceeds are not paid in a lump sum, go to line 25 on Form 712 and enter that figure.

REASONS NOT TO INCLUDE SOME POLICIES

If for any reason you are not going to include the proceeds of a policy on the decedent's life, you should explain the reason for the noninclusion. In certain instances, a policy on the life of a person should not be included in decedent's estate. For example, if a son takes out a policy on his father's life and pays all the premiums from his own money, nothing should be included in the father's estate (unless the proceeds were payable to the estate or unless the son was under an obligation to use the proceeds to pay taxes or expenses of the estate). If the decedent owned a policy on his own life but made an irrevocable transfer of the policy more than three years before death, the proceeds are not includable in his estate.

Be sure to photostat each policy and any other papers before you send them to the insurance company to obtain the death proceeds. These photostats may be useful if litigation with the IRS over a policy detail becomes necessary (or if litigation with the insurer occurs).

Page 8: Schedule E—Jointly Owned Property

You must enter on Schedule E all property, whether "real" or "personal" (any property or property rights other than real estate), in which the decedent held an interest as a "joint tenant with a right of survivorship" or as a "tenant by the entirety." Property held as a "tenant in common" should be listed on Schedule A rather than on this schedule.

Jointly held property is divided into two categories: (1) "qualified joint interests" and (2) other joint interests.

QUALIFIED JOINT INTERESTS—THE FIFTY/FIFTY RULE

Qualified joint interests are interests whereby the decedent held title to the property as tenant by the entirety or as a joint tenant with right of survivorship if the only joint tenants were the decedent and his or her spouse. Qualified joint interests are listed in Part I of Schedule E. They are so called because only one half of the estate tax value of such interests is includable in the decedent's gross estate, regardless of which spouse dies first or when the property was purchased or how much each spouse contributed to the purchase price. So if a married couple purchased a home for $80,000 and the wife dies at a time when the home is worth $200,000, then 50 percent, or $100,000, of the value of the home, is included in her estate. But this fifty/fifty rule applies only if the property is held solely between husband and wife.

OTHER JOINT TENANTS—THE "PERCENTAGE OF CONTRIBUTION" RULE

All joint interests other than qualified joint interests must be entered in Part II of Schedule E. A different inclusion rule applies to such interests. You must include the entire value of the property except to the extent that the surviving tenant can prove that he or she contributed to the purchase of the property or that a part of the property originally belonged to the surviving co-tenant. The consideration paid by the co-tenant will only be counted to the extent that it was not a gift from the decedent.

If the survivor(s) can prove contribution, then only a percentage of the estate tax value will be includable in the decedent's estate. You may exclude from the full value of the property an amount proportionate to the consideration furnished by the survivor. Let's assume a father paid $20,000 and his adult son paid $80,000 (money he saved from salary) for a parcel of land. Let's further assume that the land was worth $500,000 at the father's death. How much would be included in the father's estate? Only 2/10 (20,000/100,000) of the $500,000 value would be includable in the father's estate, since the son could prove he contributed $80,000 of the original purchase price and could also prove none of the money was a gift from his father.

The rule discussed directly above is called the "percentage of contribution" rule (some attorneys call this the "consideration furnished" rule). In order to use the rule to exclude part or all of the property from the decedent's estate, you must be able to prove the extent, origin and nature of both the decedent's and the survivor's interests.

What kind of evidence is acceptable? The IRS will typically go along with records of the original purchase (such as deeds or bills of sale) or copies of gift tax returns filed by donees other than the decedent (remember that property received gratuitously from the decedent and contributed by the donee toward the purchase of the joint tenancy doesn't count). Although in some instances the IRS will accept oral and circumstantial evidence of the survivor's contribution, it is often necessary to litigate a case in order to receive credit for such testimony.

Page 9: Schedule F—Miscellaneous Property

Schedule F is the place to enter all the items includable in the gross estate that are not includable in any other schedule. You would enter on Schedule F such items as debts owed to the decedent (other than notes and mortgages), interests in a sole proprietorship, royalties, shares in trusts established by others (be sure to attach a copy of the trust document), livestock, farm equipment and automobiles.

SOLE PROPRIETORSHIPS AND PARTNERSHIPS

Where the decedent had owned an interest in a sole proprietorship or partnership, you must attach a balance sheet for the valuation date as well as for the five years preceding that date. Earnings and profit statements for the same five years must also be filed with the return. The business must be valued essentially as you would value a closely held corporation. This means that any goodwill ("going concern") value attached to the business must be considered in your valuation process.

JEWELRY, ART, FURS, ETC.

Articles of intrinsic or artistic value such as jewelry, furs, silverware, books, statuary, rugs, art and coin and stamp collections must be noted and fully described. If any one such article or collection is valued at more than $3,000, an appraisal must be attached. (Lest larceny conquer duty, the IRS does have ways to uncover assets which "disappear." Typically, the IRS examiner will request canceled checks and insurance policies covering valuable collections or objects of art. Since you, the executor, sign all tax returns under penalty of perjury, and since perjury is a crime, it pays for you to be honest.) The appraisal must be made by an expert, who signs the appraisal of value under oath, and it must be accompanied by a statement of his qualifications. Your phone book's yellow pages will probably list the names of several such appraisers (your attorney or trust officer probably can suggest an expert in this area). Be sure to discuss the appraiser's fee before you authorize him or her to proceed.

INSURANCE ON THE LIFE OF ANOTHER

One asset that must be listed on Schedule F but is often overlooked or misplaced is insurance on the lives of others. If the decedent owned a policy on the life of some other person, the value of that policy must be included in the decedent's gross estate. This value will be figured at no cost to you by the insurer and provided to you on Form 712 (don't forget to request it from the insurer). You can write directly to the home office of the company or have your agent contact the company. Form 712 should be attached to Schedule F.

One very important note of warning: if, as executor, you are holding a policy on the life of a person who dies after you have begun your probate, do not select the alternate valuation date (without consulting counsel). Why not? Because if you elect the alternate valuation date (six months after decedent's death), his estate will include the proceeds on the life of the other insured. For instance, say Don and Gene are co-shareholders and each purchases a $500,000 policy on the life of the other to fund a business buy/sell agreement. Don dies and you are named his executor. If Gene dies within the next six months and you select the alternate valuation date, the entire $500,000 of proceeds will be considered an asset of Don's estate. (This problem is discussed in more detail in Chapter 25.)

CLAIMS IN LITIGATION

A decedent may have been litigating claims against others at the time of his death. If there is pending litigation that could result in an estate asset, the estimated value of such a claim should be entered on Schedule F. But what if the value of the claim is impossible to ascertain? Usually it is best to file the 706 and show no value but attach a statement explaining the valuation problem. Obviously, this will trigger an IRS audit.

AMOUNTS FROM THE ESTATES OF OTHERS

In some instances, a decedent will have been entitled to the proceeds of someone else's estate at the time of his death. You should use actual amounts received if the distributions have been made to you as executor by the time the 706 must be filed. But if any distributions are yet to be made, you should use an estimated amount. Then you'll have to file an amended return when the actual amount is known.

Page 10: Schedule G—Transfers During Decedent's Life

There are five types of lifetime transfers that must be reported on this schedule. They are (1) certain gift taxes, (2) certain transfers within three years of death, (3) transfers in which the decedent retained a "life estate," (4) transfers which take effect at death, and (5) revocable transfers.

INCLUSION OF GIFT TAXES ON GIFTS WITHIN THREE YEARS OF DEATH

Schedule G requires you to enter the amount of any gift tax paid by the decedent (or his estate) on gifts the decedent made within three years before his death. Tax practitioners call this a "gross up" of the estate by the amount of the gift tax. This "gross up" rule requires you to review all gift tax returns (IRS Form 709) filed within three years prior to decedent's death. You must determine what part of the total gift taxes reported on these returns is attributable to gifts made within three years of death. You must also attach copies of those returns to Form 706.

LIFE INSURANCE TRANSFERRED WITHIN THREE YEARS OF DEATH

Certain other gratuitous transfers made within three years of death must also be included. If a life insurance policy on the life of the decedent was transferred by him within three years of death, the policy proceeds must be included in his gross estate.

Lifetime Gifts Where a Power Is Retained

Likewise, if the decedent made lifetime gifts but retained certain powers over the property given away, and if those powers were given up within three years before his death, the property subject to the powers would be includable. For example, if a mother gave her son $300,000 worth of stock but retained the right to the income from the stock, the value of the stock on the date of her death would be includable in her estate. Under the "gifts within three years of death" rule, the property would still be includable—even if she gave up the right to the income—if she released the right to the stock's dividends within three years of death.

Transfers in which the decedent had retained for life the right to the income or enjoyment of the property or the right to designate the person or persons who would possess or enjoy the transferred property must be entered on Schedule G.

For instance, if the decedent put $160,000 of stock in trust for his daughter but retained the right to the dividends from the stock, the stock would be in his estate at its federal estate tax value. Likewise, if the decedent had given a summer home in Wildwood to his son, the house would be in the decedent's estate if he had retained the right to live in it (or to say who could).

The tax law also requires you to list on this schedule any lifetime gratuitous transfers of stock if the decedent had retained or acquired voting rights in a "controlled corporation." A controlled corporation is one in which the decedent owned—actually or constructively—(or had the right to vote—alone or with any other person) at least 20 percent of the total combined voting power of all classes of stock.

Transfers which take effect at death comprise another type of gratuitous lifetime transfer that must be shown on Schedule G. In essence, these are transfers in which the beneficiary cannot take possession of or enjoy the property unless he or she survives the decedent and the property will return to the decedent's estate if the beneficiary does not survive. This is called a "but if . . . back to" type of transfer because the decedent, when he gave away the property, provided: "But if you don't survive me, the property is to come back to me or to my estate." (The rules here are highly technical and before you list such property be sure—as you should throughout the process of filing a 706—to work with a tax attorney.)

A further type of gratuitous lifetime transfer which must be included on Schedule G is a revocable transfer. If the decedent had given property away but had reserved the right to alter, amend, revoke or terminate the gift in any significant manner, its value will be includable. Here are three common examples: (1) The decedent set up a trust and put property into the trust, but provided in the trust that he could change its terms or decide who would receive the property in the trust or choose when trust beneficiaries would receive the property. (2) The decedent established a "revocable" trust, which he could terminate or whose terms he could alter at any time during his lifetime. (3) A woman put $8,000 into a Uniform Gifts to Minors Account (UGMA) for her twelve-year-old daughter. If the mother is custodian for the minor child at the time of the mother's death, the value of the money in the account must be included in her estate because of her right as custodian to determine the time of payouts.

Schedule G requires you to list the name of the transferee, state the date of the transfer and give a complete description of the property. Where the transfer was by trust, you should attach a copy of the trust document to the 706.

Page 10: Schedule H—Powers of Appointment

A "power of appointment" is a right to designate who will receive someone else's property. For example, a grandfather may set up a trust. The terms of that trust provide "income to my wife for her life," and further state: "then at her death, any capital in the trust is to be distributed in equal shares to my grandchildren." The grandfather could give his wife or his son (or both) a "power of appointment," a right to change the distributive pattern.

If the power is "limited," (some attorneys call this a "special power of appointment"), the holder of the power would only have the right to divide trust assets among the class of people or organizations designated by the person who set up the trust. For instance, the grandfather may have given his son a power to give income or capital to one or more of the son's children. The son could only exercise the power in favor of one or more of his children, but could not use the property in the trust for his own benefit.

The power could also be "general." This means that the power is very broad and the son could exercise the power for his own benefit. He could take the money or other property and use it as he pleased, and his right over trust property would be nearly the same as outright ownership.

GENERAL POWER IS INCLUDABLE

Where a decedent had, at the time of his death, a "general power"—an unlimited right to funds in a trust established by someone else, exercisable in favor of himself, his estate, his creditors or the creditors of his estate—the property subject to that power must be included in his estate and listed on Schedule H. In essence, a general power gives a person the right to take the property in someone else's trust whenever he wants or use it for his benefit or to satisfy his debts. Therefore, under the estate tax law, that right over property is taxed accordingly (even if the holder of the power, the son in the example above, never actually owned the property or took it out of the other person's trust or exercised his power in any other way).

No federal estate tax inclusion is required where the decedent merely held a limited power of appointment over the assets in someone else's trust. So you don't have to list the property on Schedule H if, according to a trust provision, the son can direct only that the trust assets be paid to or among a designated class of individuals or organizations—no matter how broad that class is—as long as it does not include the holder of the power (the son) or his estate or creditors.

You must attach to the 706 a certified or verified copy of the trust instrument giving the decedent the general power of appointment. In fact, the instructions to the 706 require you to file the copy even if you feel that the power was limited and no property should be included under this schedule.

Page 11: Schedule I—Annuities

Includable on this schedule are certain arrangements that fall into two general categories: (1) "joint and survivor annuities" purchased from insurance companies and (2) nonqualified deferred compensation plan payments and payments under qualified retirement plans.

Joint and survivor annuities provide that payments will be made during the joint lifetimes of two people and, upon the death of one annuitant, continued for the life of the other person. The contract provides that the same or a reduced payment will be made to the survivor after the first annuitant's death. If all payments are to cease at the death of an individual, the annuity is not "joint and survivor" and is not includable, since no property will be transferred at death.

In your description of the annuity, you should include the name and address of the party paying the annuity. If the annuity is payable for a term of years, rather than over the survivor's lifetime, the length of the term and the date on which the annuity began should be specified. The survivor's birthdate and sex should be stated.

VALUATION OF THE SURVIVOR'S RIGHTS

Typically, joint and survivor annuities are purchased from an insurance company. The value of a commercial joint and survivor annuity in the estate is the amount it would cost to buy an annuity contract for the survivor which would pay the same amount under the same conditions as the contract purchased by the decedent.

Private individuals can promise to pay others an annuity. These "private annuities" are valued by using actuarial tables which can be found in government regulations.

It is only the portion of the purchase price of the annuity which the decedent pays that is includable. So if the decedent contributed only 60 percent of the purchase price, only 60 percent of the value of the annuity is includable in his estate. If the decedent had contributed the entire purchase price, the entire value of the cost of a comparable contract (to provide income to the survivor) would be in the decedent's estate.

VALUING NONQUALIFIED DEFERRED COMPENSATION (SALARY CONTINUATION) PLANS

A "nonqualified deferred compensation plan" (often called a "salary continuation plan") is an employer-sponsored plan which provides income after retirement to an employee and payments after the employee's death to his or her designated beneficiary. Such arrangements are a form of joint and survivor annuity since they provide that, upon the death of one annuitant, payments will be continued for the life of another. The present value of the survivor's right to receive payments must be included in the decedent's estate. The value is ascertained through government actuarial tables, which are reprinted in the Regulations to the Internal Revenue Code. But the IRS has an actuarial department which will assist you or your counsel in making the computations.

Page 12: Schedule J—Funeral Expenses and Expenses for Property Subject to Claims

Schedule J is the proper place to list deductible expenses incurred in connection with the decedent's funeral and the probate of the estate.

Funeral expenses include the cost of the burial plot, the cost of monuments or gravestones and markers, the cost of perpetual care for the lot in which the decedent is buried and the expenses of religious observances.

Among the other expenses you can claim on this schedule are court costs, filing fees, transfer fees, accountant's fees and other expenses incurred in safeguarding and distributing the estate.

It is important to keep receipts of all expenditures no matter how small or seemingly trivial. The deductible expenses listed above will be deductible on both federal and state death tax returns.

DEDUCTION REQUIREMENTS

To be deductible, death-related expenses must be necessary, reasonable, allowable under state law, and must have been paid (or be payable) by the estate. The term "necessary" implies that the IRS will attempt to disallow deductions for expenses which are not necessary to pay the debts or taxes of the estate or to preserve the estate or distribute it. For example, if property is sold that is not needed to raise funds for the estate, the cost of the sale will not be deductible since the expense benefits the heirs personally rather than the estate.

The "reasonableness" requirement precludes the deduction of funeral expenses significantly above the decedent's station of life. (Don't panic with respect to this rule—the IRS and the courts are fairly liberal with respect to funerals.)

The third requirement, that the expense must be allowable under local law, is to ensure that the outlay is within the local probate law's scope of legitimate expenses incurred in the estate's best interest.

The fourth requirement is designed to prohibit a deduction for an expense that will not be paid or one that will be reduced by Social Security or a veteran's burial allowance.

DEDUCTION FOR EXECUTOR'S COMMISSIONS AND ATTORNEY'S FEES

A deduction for executor's commissions and attorney's fees is allowable to the extent permitted under local law (a local Probate Court serves as a watchdog in this respect). If these fees have not been paid by the time the 706 is due, the deduction should still be taken. An affidavit should be signed by both the executor and the attorney stating the amount which must be paid. This statement should be attached to the 706.

Choosing the Tax Return on Which to Take a Deduction

It is extremely important to consult tax counsel before claiming certain deductions. The reason is that it may pay for the executor to waive the executor's commission, since this will be taxable as ordinary income.

If the executor's income tax bracket is higher than the estate tax rates and the executor is also the sole beneficiary under the will, the additional estate tax incurred by foregoing the deduction for the executor's commission on the estate tax return is outweighed by the tax savings realized if the heir does not have to report the income.

Another reason to consult tax counsel is that an estate has the option to claim administration expenses either on the estate's income tax return (while the estate is open, it is a tax-paying entity separate and apart from its beneficiaries) or on the estate tax return. The deduction may be more valuable if taken on the fiduciary income tax return, since the tax bracket may be higher.

The IRS will accept a reasonable estimate of expenses if you cannot determine the exact amount at the date you file the return.

Page 13: Schedule K—Debts of the Decedent and Mortgages and Liens

Among the items which fall into this schedule are medical expenses not reimbursed by insurance, unsecured notes, miscellaneous bills, any unpaid income taxes due when you computed the decedent's final income tax return, and any real estate taxes which were a lien at death.

REQUIREMENTS FOR DEDUCTIBILITY

A debt is deductible only if (1) the decedent owed the money personally at the time of his death and (2) the claim was legally enforceable at the date of death. If the debt is disputed or is the subject of litigation, you should take a deduction only for the amount (if any) you concede to be a valid claim. If you are going to contest a claim, state that fact on Schedule K.

Another requirement that must be met for a claim to be deductible is that there must be adequate and full consideration for the debt. This prevents a dying parent from giving children an IOU for, say, $300,000 and then allowing the estate's executor to claim that amount as a deductible debt.

An exception to this rule applies to certain pledges to charity. An enforceable claim based on a decedent's promise or agreement to make a contribution or gift to (or for the use of) a charitable, public, religious or other similar organization will be deductible to the extent that state law would allow the deduction.

In listing unsecured debts, you should give (1) the name of the payee, (2) the face amount, (3) the unpaid balance, (4) date and term, (5) interest rate and (6) date to which interest was paid before death. You should also include the exact nature of the claim and name of the creditor.

MEDICAL EXPENSES—CHOOSING THE TAX RETURN
ON WHICH TO TAKE THE DEDUCTION

A decedent's medical expenses and expenses of his last illness can be claimed on Schedule K for estate tax purposes or on the decedent's final income tax return (or partially but not fully on both returns). Here again, an executor should consult tax counsel as to possible tax savings. Typically, it will be advantageous to take the deduction on the return in the highest bracket, but the effect on various beneficiaries should also be considered.

DEDUCTING PROPERTY TAXES

When deducting property taxes, you are limited to the taxes accrued before the decedent's death. Likewise, you can deduct any taxes owed on income received while the decedent was alive. Taxes owed on income received after the decedent's death are not deductible.

INCLUSION RULE WHERE PROPERTY IS SUBJECT TO A MORTGAGE

If the decedent was personally liable for a debt in connection with the purchase of property (i.e., if the creditor can go beyond any particular property and claim any of the decedent's assets), you must include the full value of the property on the appropriate schedule. Then you may deduct the mortgage or the lien here. But if the property itself was the sole collateral for the loan and the decedent's estate is not liable, only the net value of the property (value of the property less the amount of the debt) should be listed in the gross estate.

For example, if a woman purchased a home for $90,000 subject to a $40,000 mortgage and (as is almost always the case) the bank could go beyond the house itself and reach her personal assets if she defaulted on the debt, you would enter the $90,000 amount on Schedule A, "Real Estate," and then take a deduction here on Schedule K for the outstanding balance on the date of her death. But if a $1 million building was mortgaged for, say, $700,000 and the bank lending the money had agreed to accept the building as the sole collateral for the loan, you would enter the building on Schedule A at its net value of $300,000 (assuming death occurred while the outstanding balance was still $300,000). No further reduction would be allowed.

Page 13: Schedule L—Net Losses During Administration and Expenses for Property Not Subject to Claims

LOSSES INCURRED DURING ADMINISTRATION

If a fire, storm, shipwreck or other sudden or unexpected casualty occurs during the settlement of the estate, you may take a deduction to the extent the loss is not offset by insurance.

You must describe the loss and its cause, and, if you did receive any insurance, state the amount you collected.

If you elected the "alternate valuation date," you have probably already reduced the value of any damaged or lost item when you listed that item in the gross estate. You cannot take a deduction on this schedule for the amount by which you have already reduced the value of the item.

CHOOSING THE TAX RETURN ON WHICH TO TAKE THE DEDUCTION

A casualty loss deduction can be taken either on this estate tax return or on the estate's income tax return, but not on both. You should consult tax counsel as to which return is in the highest bracket.

EXPENSES INCURRED IN ADMINISTERING NONPROBATE PROPERTY

Schedule L has two parts. The first part, described above, pertains to losses incurred during administration. The second part of the schedule deals with expenses incurred in administering "nonprobate property." These expenses (deductible only if paid within three years and nine months from the decedent's death) include costs incurred in the administration of a trust established by the decedent before death.

To be deductible, these expenses must have been incurred as a result of settling the decedent's interest in the property or vesting good title to the property in the beneficiaries.

List the names and addresses of persons to whom each expense was payable and the nature of each expense. Identify the property for which the expense was incurred. You can estimate an expense if you don't know its exact amount. Be sure to keep all vouchers and receipts.

Page 14: Schedule M—Bequests, etc., to Surviving Spouse

Schedule M is the appropriate place to list the items that will pass or have passed to the decedent's surviving spouse in a manner that will qualify them for the federal estate tax marital deduction.

RULES GOVERNING MARITAL DEDUCTION

The tax law governing the marital deduction is highly complex and is strictly construed by both the IRS and the courts. In essence, the deduction is allowed for property passing outright or in a manner tantamount to outright where the surviving spouse receives property or an interest in property

1. as the heir under the decedent's will, or

2. as the surviving joint tenant, or

3. as the beneficiary of a life insurance policy, or

4. as a surviving spouse taking the share of a decedent's estate allowed under state law in the event of intestacy, or

5. as the recipient of any transfer made by the decedent at any time if the property was includable in the decedent's gross estate.

MARITAL DEDUCTION FOR TRANSFERS IN TRUST

Can you take a marital deduction if the property passes in trust to the surviving spouse? The answer is "Yes, if . . . ." If a number of conditions are met, a transfer in trust will qualify for the marital deduction. Because of the complexity of the tax law in this area, the advice of competent counsel is essential.

Q.T.I.P. RULES

"Q.T.I.P." (qualified terminable interest property) is a term which every executor should know. It means that certain property which otherwise would not qualify for the marital deduction can qualify if certain conditions are met.

This very important election must be made by the decedent's executor; once made, it is irrevocable. The election can only be made if the surviving spouse is entitled to all the income from the property and if that income is payable annually or more frequently. For example, an individual may have left property income "to [his] wife for her life," and "then, upon her death, the property is to go to [his] children." Such a bequest would ordinarily not qualify for the marital deduction, but it will if a Q.T.I.P. election is made. There is just one catch: if you make the election on the deceased spouse's estate tax return, when the surviving widow dies the value of any Q.T.I.P. property remaining at her death will be included in her estate (even though she doesn't have the right to dispose of it at her death).

Complete Schedule M by listing each property interest for which you are claiming a marital deduction. Number each item in sequence and describe each item in detail. Describe the instrument (will or trust) or provision of law under which each item passed to the surviving spouse. You should also attach to the 706 a certified copy of the order admitting the will to probate.

Page 15: Schedule N—Section 2032A Valuation

"HIGHEST AND BEST USE" RULE

As a general rule, you must value property at its "highest and best use" value. This means it must be entered at the highest price at which a willing buyer and a willing seller would come to terms. But if certain conditions are met, you can value the estate's real property devoted to farming or closely held business use on the basis of the property's value according to its current use. (See the form on pp. 146–147.)

SPECIAL (CURRENT) USE VALUATION

Farmland is a good example of the type of property for which the special or current use election would be advantageous. Farmland is often valued at the price it might bring if it were to be used for residential or industrial development rather than the price it is worth as farmland. If certain conditions are met, you are entitled to value the farm on the basis of a formula which more realistically represents its value as farmland. One such formula works like this:

Farmer Dick Barrone owns four hundred acres of farmland in Wildwood. About the same acreage of nearby land generates an average of $20,000 in annual gross cash rentals. Average annual state and local real estate taxes are $3,000. Assume the average annual effective interest rate for loans from the Federal Land Bank is 10 percent. Under the general valuation formula, farmer Barrone's land is worth $170,000, or $17,000 ($20,000 less $3,000) divided by 10 percent.

You would not use this general valuation formula if there were no comparable land from which average annual rentals could be determined. You might then decide to value the farmland by another method.

To take advantage of this special valuation, you must list each "qualified heir" (essentially the decedent's immediate family plus his ancestors and certain other relatives) who will receive an interest in the property to be specially valued. Various other documents must also be filed with this schedule, including:

1. a statement signed by every person who has an interest in the property with information about the adjusted value and how it was ascertained;

2. copies of written appraisals of the fair market value of the real property;

3. a legal description of the specially valued property; and

4. a consent statement by all the parties with an interest in the property that if the property is sold or no longer used as farmland (or has no other special use) they agree to a "recapture" (payback) of all or some of the taxes that would have been paid if this advantageous election had not been allowed.

IMPORTANCE OF A PROTECTIVE ELECTION

Whether or not you think the estate meets the requirements for "special use" (some authorities call this "current use") valuation, you should file what is called a "protective election." You protect the right to value property according to its current use by writing "Protective election" across Schedule N and stating on a separate attachment (1) the decedent's name and taxpayer identification number, (2) the relevant qualified

Determination of Whether Estate Qualifies for Current Use
Valuation of Farm Real Estate or Business Real Estate

(1) Gross estate . . . . $ _____

Less

(2) Unpaid mortgages or indebtedness
on property included in estate at
gross value . . . . $ _____

Equals

(3) Adjusted value of gross estate . . . . $ _____

(4) 50% of adjusted value of gross
estate . . . . $ _____

(5) 25% of adjusted value of gross
estate . . . . $ _____

(6) Value of real and personal property
of farm or closely held business
. . . . $ _____

Less

(7) Unpaid mortgages or indebtedness
on farm or closely held business real
or personal property included in
estate at gross value . . . . $ _____

Equals

(8) Adjusted value of real and personal
property of farm or closely held
business . . . . $ _____

(9) Qualified real property . . . . $ _____

Less

        (10) Unpaid mortgages or indebtedness
            on qualified real property included in
            estate at gross value . . . . $ _____

Equals

        (11) Adjusted value of qualified real property
        . . . . $ _____

REAL PROPERTY OF FARM OR CLOSELY HELD BUSINESS QUALIFIES FOR CURRENT-USE VALUATION IF LINE 8 EQUALS OR EXCEEDS LINE 4 **AND** LINE 11 EQUALS OR EXCEEDS LINE 5.

This also assumes that (a) the decedent was a U.S. citizen or resident, (b) the real property passes to a qualified heir, and (c) for 5 out of the last 8 years before the decedent's death, the real property was used in the farm or closely held business, and the decedent or a family member materially participated in the farm or business operation.

* The full highest and best-use value and not the current-use value is used in determining the value of the gross estate for the 50% and 25% tests.

© 1985 by The American College as part of **Advanced Estate Planning I and II courses** use (such as farming) and (3) the location of the real property which you are claiming is used for farming or business.

Page 15: Schedule O—Charitable, Public, and Similar Gifts and Bequests

Schedule O should be used if the decedent left property to a charitable, religious, educational or scientific organization. The deduction is unlimited (there is no percentage limitation) and applies to gifts made in a person's will as well as transfers to charity through life insurance policies, certain transfers in trust, and even lifetime transfers that for some reason were included in the decedent's estate.

You must attach to this schedule a copy of the instrument under which the charitable transfer was made. If the transfer was by will, you should attach a certified copy of the order admitting the will to probate in addition to the will.

Page 16: Schedule P—Credit for Foreign Death Taxes

A "credit" (dollar for dollar reduction of the tax) may be taken for death taxes paid to one or more foreign countries. This credit is allowed if the gross estate of the decedent includes property which was taxed in a foreign country.

If the credit is applicable, you should prepare IRS form 706CE in triplicate. Be sure to retain one copy and send two copies to the appropriate tax official in the foreign country. That person should be requested to certify one copy and forward it to the IRS office where you file the 706.

Page 16: Schedule Q—Credit for Tax on Prior Transfers

If two people die within a short time of one another and the first to die had left property to the survivor (who later died), a credit may be available to alleviate the harshness of two taxes on the same property. This "credit for tax on prior transfers" is available if the later to die decedent had received property from someone else's estate within ten years of his death and an estate tax was paid at the prior death.

AMOUNT OF THE CREDIT

The credit is a percentage of the lower of two amounts: (1) the tax generated by the inclusion of the property in the estate of the present decedent or (2) the tax generated by the inclusion of the property in the estate of the prior decedent.

The percentage is 100 percent if the two individuals die within two years of each other. Then it drops 20 percent every two years. So in the third and fourth year after the first individual's death the credit has dropped to 80 percent of the credit that would have been allowed if death had occurred in the first two years. In the fifth and sixth years the credit drops to 60 percent. By the seventh and eighth years the credit is down to 40 percent. In the ninth and tenth years the credit is only 20 percent of the lower of the two taxes. If the second individual should die after the tenth year, no credit is allowed.

Calculating the Tax

At this point you have completed Schedules A to I, which include all the property that must be entered in the decedent's gross estate. You have also completed Schedules J to Q, the allowable deductions and credits.

Now you will enter the values of both assets and deductions in the "Recapitulation" on page 3 of the 706 and total both gross estate and allowable deductions.

Notice the column entitled "Alternate Value." In each of the gross estate schedules, to the left of the "Value at date of death" column, there are two columns entitled "Alternate valuation date" and "Alternate value." As executor, you have the right to decide whether you will value assets as of the decedent's date of death or as of an alternate valuation date. This alternate valuation date is six months after the decedent's death. Its purpose is to alleviate the hardship that this situation might impose. Assume that an estate values assets at date of death and pays taxes based on these values. Assume also that the assets plunge in value in a rapidly declining market (remember the great Depression?) so that by the time the return is filed the tax is larger than the estate.

If you elect the alternate valuation date, all assets must be valued as of that date. The term "alternate valuation date" typically means six months after death, but it may be a different date if assets were sold, distributed, exchanged or otherwise disposed of before that date—in which case the value as of the date of sale, distribution, exchange or other disposal is used.

Another exception may be made to the general rule for alternate valuation dates if an asset is of the type affected by the mere lapse of time—such as a patent which loses value as each day's monopoly is lost. If the asset's value diminishes merely because of the passage of time, the alternate valuation date is defined as the date of death. But adjustments are allowed for any reduction in value which is not due strictly to the lapse of time—such as an improved competing product on the market or a drastic change in technology which reduces the importance of the asset in question. For example, the value of a corporation which makes a first-generation computer drops drastically when the second- and third-generation products of its competitors are announced.

Importance of the Alternate Valuation Date Decision

Why is the right to select an alternate valuation date so important? The answer is, as was mentioned above, that the finally agreed upon value of an asset has implications beyond the federal estate tax consequences. The value used on the 706 also determines the income tax basis of the property in the hands of its beneficiary. In other words, the basis of an asset is changed ("stepped up" or "stepped down") when a person dies. The new basis (the starting point for determining the gain or loss from a sale or the limit on cost recovery through depreciation) is the asset's federal estate tax value. A higher value may mean higher estate taxes, but it may also mean a lower gain to report if it is sold by the beneficiary, or it may mean larger write-offs.

Alternate valuation may only be elected if the total value of all property in the estate is reduced *and* if the federal estate tax liability is reduced.

Once the decision is made, you can proceed to the actual computation on the first page. (Be sure to read—and reread—the chapter on the tax elections available to the executor.)

The Computation

Page 1 of the 706 is the place for the actual computation of the tax. The "gross estate" (line 1 of the "Tax Computation") is the sum of all amounts subject to tax and is taken from line 10 of page 3. Total allowable deductions (from line 20 of page 3) are then subtracted from the gross estate. This results in the "Taxable Estate," upon which you will compute the "state death tax credit" (line 13). The taxable estate is not —as its name seems to imply—the amount to which the estate tax rates are applied.

APPLYING THE RATES

It is to the amount of the "tentative tax base" (line 5 of page 1) that the rates are applied. The tentative tax base is found by adding to the taxable estate (line 3) any "adjusted taxable gifts" (line 4). These are the taxable portions of any lifetime gifts that are not already reflected in the gross estate: what you add is the taxable portion of any taxable gifts made after 1976 to the taxable estate.

Now go to Table A, reproduced below from the Instructions to IRS Form 706 (page 7 of the Instructions).

Table A

Column A	Column B	Column C	Column D
Taxable amount over	Taxable amount not over	Tax on amount in column A	Rate of tax on excess over amount in column A
			(Percent)
0	$10,000	0	18
$10,000	20,000	$1,800	20
20,000	40,000	3,800	22
40,000	60,000	8,200	24
60,000	80,000	13,000	26
80,000	100,000	18,200	28
100,000	150,000	23,800	30
150,000	250,000	38,800	32
250,000	500,000	70,800	34
500,000	750,000	155,800	37

Unified Rate Schedule

Column A	Column B	Column C	Column D
			Rate of tax on excess over amount in column A
Taxable amount over	Taxable amount not over	Tax on amount in column A	
			(Percent)
750,000	1,000,000	248,300	39
1,000,000	1,250,000	345,800	41
1,250,000	1,500,000	448,300	43
1,500,000	2,000,000	555,800	45
2,000,000	2,500,000	780,800	49
2,500,000	See Table A(1) for year of decedent's death.		

If the amount on line 5 of page 1 is $2,500,000 or less, the tax is shown in Column C of the table (for example, if the line 5 tentative tax base is $1 million, the tax is $345,800). If the amount on line 5 exceeds the Column A amount, then you must multiply the excess by the rate in Column D (for example, if the line 5 tentative tax base were $1,100,000, you would multiply the $100,000 excess by 41 percent. The tax would therefore be $386,800 (345,800 plus $41,000). Enter this tentative tax on line 6 of page 1.

At this point you may subtract the total of any post-1976 gift taxes actually paid (line 7). The result (on line 8) is the gross estate tax.

Note that the maximum federal estate tax rate is 55 percent for estates of individuals dying in 1984, 1985, 1986 and 1987. In 1988 and later years the top rate will be 50 percent on estates in excess of $2,500,000.

REDUCING THE TAX BY THE UNIFIED CREDIT

Fortunately, you are now allowed to reduce this tax by one or more of various credits. The first of these is the "unified credit," allowed to every person during lifetime or at death (this is why it is called "unified"). It offsets the tax on a dollar-for-dollar basis. For decedents dying in 1982, the credit was $62,800. It increased to $79,300 in 1983, and to $96,300 in 1984 (barring any tampering with the credit by Congress). It will continue to rise until 1987, when it will level off at $192,800. This $192,800 credit is roughly equivalent to the allowance of a $600,000 deduction. In other words, if the property actually subject to tax were $600,000 or less, there would be no federal estate tax (assuming the decedent hadn't used up any of the credit during his lifetime).

REDUCING THE TAX BY THE CREDIT FOR STATE DEATH TAXES

After subtracting the unified credit from the gross estate tax, you may also be entitled to a credit for state death taxes (line 13). Go back to the taxable estate amount (line 3). Subtract $60,000. (This is a statutory amount that must be subtracted at this point.) Use the net result to compute your credit according to the applicable rates in Table C (reproduced below).

Table C

Computation of Maximum Credit for State Death Taxes (Based on Federal adjusted taxable estate which is the Federal taxable estate reduced by $60,000)			
Adjusted taxable estate equal to or more than—	Adjusted taxable estate less than—	Credit on amount in column (1)	Rate of credit on excess over amount in column (1)
(1)	(2)	(3)	(4)
			(Percent)
0	$40,000	0	None
$40,000	90,000	0	0.8
90,000	140,000	$400	1.6
140,000	240,000	1,200	2.4
240,000	440,000	3,600	3.2
440,000	640,000	10,000	4.0
640,000	840,000	18,000	4.8
840,000	1,040,000	27,600	5.6
1,040,000	1,540,000	38,800	6.4
1,540,000	2,040,000	70,800	7.2
2,040,000	2,540,000	106,800	8.0
2,540,000	3,040,000	146,800	8.8
3,040,000	3,540,000	190,800	9.6
3,540,000	4,040,000	238,800	10.4
4,040,000	5,040,000	290,800	11.2
5,040,000	6,040,000	402,800	12.0
6,040,000	7,040,000	522,800	12.8
7,040,000	8,040,000	650,800	13.6
8,040,000	9,040,000	786,800	14.4
9,040,000	10,040,000	930,800	15.2
10,040,000	_____	1,082,800	16.0

For example, if the decedent's taxable estate were $900,000, by subtracting $60,000 you would obtain a balance of $840,000, and the tax would be $27,600. If the taxable estate were $1 million, after subtracting $60,000 the balance would be $940,000. The tax would be $27,600 plus 5.6 percent of the $100,000 excess over the $840,000 in Column 1—a total of $33,200.

The amount you have just computed is your maximum allowed credit for state death taxes. Actually, the credit allowed is the lower of two amounts: (1) the amount you have just computed or (2) the amount actually paid. (You may claim the credit you anticipate and figure the federal estate tax on the return before the state death taxes are actually paid.) The credit is allowed for state estate, inheritance, legacy or succession taxes.

You should file the following documents with your federal estate tax return:

1. A certificate from the state showing the tax paid, the amount of any interest and penalties, the total amount paid in cash, and the date of payment (this is important because the federal credit will not be allowed unless the state tax is paid within four years after the return is—or should be—filed).

2. Any additional proof of payment.

REDUCING THE TAX BY OTHER TYPES OF CREDITS

You may be entitled to a credit for federal gift taxes (line 15) if the decedent made certain transfers before January 1, 1977, and those transfers were included in his estate.

Credits are also allowed for foreign death taxes (line 16) and for the taxes paid on transfers from prior decedents. These credits were discussed on page 148.

SUMMARY

1. You must complete a federal estate tax return, Form 706, if the size of the estate exceeds certain thresholds.

2. The return generally must be filed within nine months of the decedent's death.

3. The return should be filed with the IRS office serving the area where the decedent was domiciled when he died.

4. The estate tax return is signed by the executor and preparer and filed together with certain other documents.

5. Form 706 contains a number of "schedules" on which you should list the values of property or property interests owned by the decedent at death. (See Chapter 26 for a detailed discussion of asset valuation.)

6. Certain deductions can be taken before computing the tax. These expenses or other items such as debts and charitable pledges must be shown in separate schedules.

7. You must decide whether or not to value the estate's assets as of the alternate valuation date, which is usually six months after the decedent's death.

8. You must also decide whether to value certain property according to the current special use in which it is placed.

9. Certain allowable credits reduce the payable tax on a dollar-for-dollar basis.

10. The tax is computed on the sum of the taxable portion of certain lifetime taxable gifts and property interests transferred at death.

22

Executor's Duty to File Gift Tax Returns

If the decedent made a taxable gift during his or her lifetime but did not file the required gift tax return, it is your duty to file the return and, if appropriate, to pay the gift tax. The gift tax is a tax levied on the right of one individual to transfer money or other property to another. It is based on the value of the property transferred.

The gift tax is computed on a progressive schedule (i.e., the rates get higher as the amount of total gifts increases) based on cumulative lifetime gifts. In other words, the tax rates are applied to the total of "taxable gifts" (all gifts less exclusions and deductions) made over decedent's lifetime rather than *only* to the taxable gifts he made in the calendar year of his death.

Computing the Tax on Gifts

Gift tax rates are applied to a net figure (the taxable gifts). Before you compute the tax on a gift, you are allowed to make certain deductions: (1) "gift splitting," (2) an annual exclusion, (3) a marital deduction, and (4) a charitable deduction.

Gift Splitting

The tax law permits a married donor—with the consent of the nondonor spouse— to treat a gift to a third party (a child or some other person) as though each spouse had given one half. You may elect such gift splitting on the gift tax return of the donor spouse.

Gift splitting is an artificial mechanism. For computational purposes, even if one spouse makes the entire gift, you will treat that single transfer on the gift tax return as though each spouse had only made one half of the gift. The advantage of gift splitting is that the tax rate for each spouse is separately calculated on the basis of prior gifts made by each one individually. This lowers the rate considerably.

The second advantage of gift splitting is that it "creates" another "annual exclusion" (discussed below).

The privilege of gift splitting is available only with regard to gifts made while the couple was married, so that gifts made before the marriage may not be split, even if the couple was married later in the same calendar year. Likewise, gifts made after the spouses were legally divorced or gifts made by a survivor after one spouse dies may not be split. But gifts made before one spouse dies may be split even if that spouse dies before signing the appropriate consent or election. As executor, you can (and, in most cases, should) elect to split the gift.

Annual Exclusion

Each person is allowed to make up to $10,000 worth of tax-free gifts to each of any number of persons or parties each year. The total maximum excludable amount, therefore, is determined by multiplying $10,000 by the number of persons to whom gifts were made in any one year. For example, if the decedent was unmarried and in the course of one year made outright gifts of $2,000, $8,000 and $16,000 respectively to his brother, father and son, the $2,000 gift and the $8,000 gift would be fully excludable, and the first $10,000 of the $16,000 gift to his son would also be excludable. If the same individual were married and his spouse consented to splitting the gift, each spouse would be deemed to have made one half the gift. As a result, both spouses would receive annual exclusions and none of the $26,000 worth of gifts would be subject to tax. The executor should take advantage of this "extra" annual exclusion through gift splitting. As the executor of an individual who was married at the time a gift was made, you may sign the gift tax return with the surviving spouse regardless of who made the gift. (In fact, the Internal Revenue Service has said that, if no administrator or executor has been appointed, the surviving spouse may consent to the gift split even if he or she has not been legally appointed.)

Gift Tax Marital Deduction

An individual who transfers property to a spouse during his or her lifetime is allowed an unlimited deduction (subject to certain conditions) known as the gift tax marital deduction. The purpose of this marital deduction is to enable spouses to be treated as an economic unit. The deduction eliminates any tax on interspousal transfers made during lifetime. (A similar deduction, allowed at death, was explained in Chapter 20.)

Gift Tax Charitable Deduction

A donor making a transfer of property to a qualified charity is allowed a charitable deduction equal to the value of the gift (to the extent not already covered by the annual exclusion). The net effect of the charitable deduction—together with the annual exclusion—is to eliminate any gift tax liability for gifts to qualified charities.

There is no limit on the amount, gift tax free, that an individual is allowed to give to a "qualified" charity. (Qualified charities include the federal government, state or political subdivisions, certain religious, scientific or charitable organizations, some fraternal societies and some veterans' associations.)

Calculating the Gift Tax Payable

The actual gift tax payable should be calculated by the estate's attorney or accountant. However, as in the case of every major decision, you should know "what's happening." The process begins with a determination of the amount of taxable gifts made in the year of the decedent's death. To compute taxable gifts, you first value all gifts made. Then, if appropriate, you split the amount and consider the decedent as having made one half of the gift. Then you apply any annual exclusion and marital or charitable deduction to the extent appropriate.

The following examples in computational format illustrate this process. These, in turn, are followed by two forms that can be used as guidelines (and may be helpful to your attorney and/or accountant).

Assume a single donor in the last month of 1986 made certain outright gifts: $160,000 to his son, $125,000 to his daughter, $8,000 to his grandson, and $25,000 to The American College (a total of $318,000).

Computing Taxable Gifts

Step 1	*List* total gifts for year		$318,000
Step 2	*Subtract* one-half of gift deemed to be made by donor's spouse (split gifts)	$ 0	
	Gifts deemed to be made by donor		$318,000
Step 3	*Subtract* annual exclusion(s)	$38,000	
	Gifts after subtracting exclusion(s)		$280,000
Step 4	*Subtract* marital deduction	$ 0	
Step 5	*Subtract* charitable deduction	$15,000	
	Taxable gifts		$265,000

Note that, although there were four donees, the annual exclusion was $38,000 and did not total four times $10,000, or $40,000. This is because the annual exclusion is the lower of (a) $10,000 or (b) the actual net value of the property transferred. In this example the gift to the grandson was only $8,000, which limits the annual exclusion to that amount.

A slight change in the fact pattern above will illustrate the computation where the donor is married and his spouse consented to split their gifts to third parties. In this case, only half the gifts made by the donor would be taxable to the donor (half the gifts made by the donor's spouse to third parties would also be included in computing the donor's total gifts). A separate (and essentially identical) computation is made for the donor's spouse.

That computation would show (a) the other half of the husband's gifts to third parties plus (b) half of the wife's actual gifts to third parties (since all gifts must be split if any gifts are split).

Computing Taxable Gifts

Step 1	*List* total gifts for year		$318,000
Step 2	*Subtract* one-half of gift deemed to be made by donor's spouse (split gifts)	$159,000	
	Gifts deemed to be made by donor		$159,000
Step 3	*Subtract* annual exclusion(s)	$ 34,000	
	Gifts after subtracting exclusion(s)		$125,000
Step 4	*Subtract* marital deduction	$ 0	
Step 5	*Subtract* charitable deduction	$ 2,500	
	Taxable gifts		$122,500

(The calculation on the wife's return would parallel this return.)

Note that in this example the annual exclusions were computed *after* the split and each donor's exclusions would be:

(a)	Gift to son	$10,000
(b)	Gift to daughter	10,000
(c)	Gift to grandson	4,000
(d)	Gift to The American College	10,000
		$34,000

If the married donor in the fact pattern directly above had also made an outright gift of $200,000 to his wife, the computation would be as follows:

Computing Taxable Gifts

Step 1	*List* total gifts for year	$518,000
Step 2	*Subtract* one-half of gift deemed to be made by donor's spouse (split gifts)	$159,000
	Gifts deemed to be made by donor	$359,000
Step 3	*Subtract* annual exclusion(s)	$ 44,000
	Gifts after subtracting exclusion(s)	$315,000
Step 4	*Subtract* marital deduction	$190,000
Step 5	*Subtract* charitable deduction	$ 2,500
	Taxable gifts	$122,500

When the total value of taxable gifts for the reporting period is found, the actual tax payable is computed using the following method:

Computing Gift Tax Payable

Step 1	Compute gift tax on all *taxable* gifts regardless of when made (use unified rate schedule)	$ _____
Step 2	Compute gift tax on all *taxable* gifts made prior to the present year's gift(s) (use unified rate schedule)	$ _____
Step 3	Subtract Step 2 result from Step 1 result	$ _____
Step 4	Enter gift tax credit remaining	$ _____
Step 5	Subtract Step 4 result from Step 3 result to obtain *gift tax payable*	$ _____

For instance, a widow gives $1,400,000 to her daughter and $100,000 to The American College in 1987. Both transfers are present-interest gifts. If she had made no previous taxable gifts in the current or prior years or quarters, the computation would be as follows:

Computing Taxable Gifts

Step 1	*List* total gifts for year	$1,500,000
Step 2	*Subtract* one-half of gift deemed to be made by donor's spouse (split gifts)	$ 0
	Gifts deemed to be made by donor	$1,500,000
Step 3	*Subtract* annual exclusion(s)	$20,000

	Gifts after subtracting exclusion(s)	$1,480,000
Step 4	*Subtract* marital deduction	$ 0
Step 5	*Subtract* charitable deduction	$90,000
	Taxable gifts	$1,380,000

To find the gift tax payable on this amount, the procedure would be as follows:

Computing Gift Tax Payable

Step 1	Compute gift tax on all *taxable* gifts regardless of when made ($1,380,000)	$504,200
Step 2	Compute gift tax on all *taxable* gifts made prior to the present gift(s)	$ 0
Step 3	Subtract Step 2 results from Step 1 result	$504,200
Step 4	Enter gift tax (unified) credit remaining (1987)	$192,800
Step 5	Subtract Step 4 result from Step 3 result to obtain *gift tax payable*	$311,400

The Step 1 entry, $504,200, is found by using the unified rate schedule for estate and gift taxes. Note that the unified rate table is used regardless of when the gifts were made.

If the donor in the example above had made $100,000 of additional taxable gifts in 1984 (a total of $1,480,000 of taxable gifts), the computation would be as follows:

Computing Gift Tax Payable

Step 1	Compute gift tax on all *taxable* gifts regardless of when made ($1,480,000)	$547,200
Step 2	Compute gift tax on all *taxable* gifts made prior to the present gift(s)	$ 23,800
Step 3	Subtract Step 2 result from Step 1 result	$523,400
Step 4	Enter gift tax credit remaining (1987)	$169,000
Step 5	Subtract Step 4 result from Step 3 result to obtain *gift tax payable*	$354,400

This illustrates the cumulative nature of the gift tax (the $100,000 prior taxable gifts pushed the present $1,380,000 of taxable gifts into a higher bracket).

What if $200,000 of taxable gifts were made in 1984? The tax computation would be as follows:

Computing Gift Tax Payable

Step 1	Compute gift tax on all *taxable* gifts regardless of when made ($1,580,000)	$591,800

Step 2 Compute gift tax on all *taxable* gifts made prior to the present gift(s) $ 54,800

Step 3 Subtract Step 2 result from Step 1 result $537,000

Step 4 Enter unused gift tax credit $ 54,800

Step 5 Subtract Step 4 result from Step 3 result to obtain *gift tax payable* $399,000

This assumes that the $200,000 taxable gift made in 1984 used up a credit equal to the $54,800 tax it generated.

Credits

A unified credit can be applied against the tax on gifts made either during lifetime or at death or part can be applied against each. The gift tax credit, which provides a dollar-for-dollar reduction of the tax otherwise payable, is as follows:

Donors Making Gifts in	Receive a Credit of
1982	$62,800
1983	79,300
1984	96,300
1985	121,800
1986	155,800
1987 and later years	192,800

In the example directly above since the taxable gifts in prior years used up part of the available credit, to that extent they are not available to reduce the tax liability for the present gifts.

Computing Taxable Gifts   Case # _____

Step 1. **Enter** total gifts for year. $ _____

Step 2. **Subtract** one half of gift deemed to be
made by donor's spouse (split gifts). $ _____

       Gifts deemed to be made by donor $ _____

Step 3. **Subtract** annual exclusions $ _____

       Gifts after subtracting exclusion(s) $ _____

Step 4. **Subtract** marital deduction. $ _____

Step 5. **Subtract** charitable deduction. $ _____

       TAXABLE GIFTS $ _____

Calculating Gift Tax Payable   Case # _____

Step 1. Compute gift tax on all **taxable**
gifts regardless of when made
(use unified rate schedule). Tax on $ _____ is $ _____

Step 2. Compute gift tax on all **taxable**
gifts made prior to the present
gift(s) (use unified rate schedule). Tax on $ _____ is $ _____

Step 3. Subtract Step 2 result from Step 1
result. $ _____

Step 4. Enter gift tax credit **remaining.** $ _____

Step 5. Subtract Step 4 result from Step 3
result to obtain **gift tax payable.** $ _____

Reporting of Gifts and Payment of Tax

Typically, no gift tax return must be filed until a gift made to one individual exceeds $10,000. You must file a return on a calender year basis when a gift to one person in one year exceeds $10,000, even if no gift tax is due. For example, if a married woman had given $15,000 to her son, the transfer would be gift tax free (because each spouse had a $10,000 annual exclusion). However, you would have to file a gift tax return because the gift exceeded the annual exclusion amount (and also because the gift was "split" [that is, treated as if each spouse gave one half], and filing a return is a prerequisite for "splitting" a gift).

The gift tax return must be filed and the gift tax, if any, due on reported gifts must be paid no later than the date on which the donor's federal estate tax return is due (despite any time extensions for filing the donor's income tax return and the fact that the gift tax return is normally due on April 15 of the year following the calendar year of the gift). That date is nine months after the decedent's death.

SUMMARY

You must file a gift tax return and pay the tax on taxable gifts made by the decedent in excess of any allowable credit. You compute the taxable gift by reducing the gross gift by any allowable gift splitting, annual exclusion, marital deduction or charitable deduction. Once taxable gifts are computed, you compute the gift tax (if any) payable. You must usually file the return within nine months of the donor's death.

23

Estate's Income Tax Return

The Estate as a Separate Entity

An estate is a taxable entity just like a person. In other words, during the period of administration, if the gross income of the estate exceeds $600 you must file Form 1041, the Income Tax Return for an Estate. The estate, as a taxpayer, continues to exist until you have distributed all the assets of the estate to its beneficiaries.

The estate's income tax return (IRS Form 1041) is due on the fifteenth day of the fourth month after the estate's tax year closes (assuming you select a fiscal year).

Extensions of Time to File

The IRS will typically allow you an extension of time to file the estate's income tax return. The Application for Extension of Time to File U.S. Partnership, Fiduciary and Certain Exempt Organizations Return (IRS Form 2758) is the appropriate form.

Requesting Prompt Assessment of Tax

To obtain relief from the personal liability you have assumed for payment of the estate's income taxes, you can request the IRS to make a prompt assessment of the tax due. This course of action reduces the IRS's time for assessing any additional tax (normally three years) to a much shorter time—from the date the return was filed until eighteen months from the date you request prompt assessment of any additional income tax.

Paying the Estate's Income Tax

As executor, you are obliged to file an income tax return for the estate and to pay any tax on income received by the estate up until the date you are formally discharged. You must either pay the full tax liability at the time you file the return or (better yet) pay four equal installments over a thirteen-month period (see Chapter 25).

Electing the Estate's Taxable Year

You have the right to choose a calendar or a fiscal year as the reporting period for the estate's income and deductions. Your objective is to minimize the overall impact of taxes on all the parties concerned, the estate and its beneficiaries.

You should work with the estate's accountant and attorney and estimate what future income will be received and what expenses will be incurred by the estate. If the estate has a great deal of income in its early stages and few offsetting deductions, you may want to elect a short fiscal year.

Here is one useful planning technique for selecting a taxable year: if you pay administration expenses just before the estate ends, and if those deductions exceed the income of the estate, the excess deductions may be carried over to the individual income tax returns of the respective beneficiaries. In other words, your payment of administration expenses can be utilized to offset the personal income of the beneficiaries.

Another technique used by professional estate planners involves timing. If an estate distributes all of its income, that income must be reported by each beneficiary. It has the same character (ordinary, capital gain or tax-free income) in the hands of the beneficiaries that it had in the hands of the estate. The beneficiary will be taxed on the distributions, but not until his or her taxable year in which the estate's taxable year ends. For instance, assume the estate's taxable year ends on January 31, 1986. The beneficiary who must report any income from the estate doesn't have to report it until his or her tax return for 1986 is due. That means no tax is payable until April of 1987. Therefore, if you carefully select the estate's taxable year you can defer the beneficiaries' payment of the tax for a considerable period (and earn money on the amount you would otherwise have paid in tax).

Another timing technique involves your ability as executor to accumulate income received by the estate. To the extent you hold income within the estate, it will be taxable to the estate. Once you distribute that income, it is taxable to the beneficiary. Because you can choose how much to pay out and how much to accumulate, you have the flexibility to allocate tax liability between the estate and its beneficiaries. What you must do is consult with the estate's attorney and accountant and decide which taxpayer is in the highest tax bracket. You then try to equalize the incomes of the respective taxpayers so that all income is in the lowest possible overall tax brackets.

When the time comes to distribute the estate, any loss carryovers (losses that are tax-deductible) not fully used by the estate can be used by the beneficiaries.

SUMMARY

An estate is a separate entity for income tax purposes; it must report income and may take deductions and credits. As executor, you must file an income tax return and pay the appropriate tax. Several planning techniques may be used to significantly reduce the estate's income tax liability. One is the proper selection of a taxable year to generate excess deductions, which are then carried over to the tax returns of the beneficiaries. Another, also involving the estate's tax year, pertains to the time when income is reported and can postpone considerably the beneficiary's payment of tax. A third device is to utilize your ability as executor to accumulate or pay out estate income so that it will be reported by the party in the lowest tax bracket.

24

Decedent's Final Income Tax Return

Executor's Duty to File

If you are the executor, it is your duty to prepare a final federal (and state) income tax return for the decedent. That tax return will cover the part of the taxable year of the decedent during which he was alive. If he were required to file a return had he lived, you must file one on his behalf.

The return is due at the same time it would have been due had death not occurred. This means a final return for a "calendar year basis" taxpayer (one who reports income starting January 1 and ending December 31) is due on or before April 15 of the year following the year of death. Regardless of when death occurred, the federal income tax return is due on that date. (Check with the decedent's accountant to find out when the state income tax return is due.)

You may have a duty to file even if it appears that the decedent's income was insufficient to require the filing of a return. This is because of the possible refund of tax withheld or estimated tax paid.

Where do you obtain the necessary information to file someone else's return? We suggest that you examine prior tax returns, deposit slips and canceled checks. The easiest course is to contact the accountant who prepared the decedent's income tax return in the past and hire that individual to prepare the decedent's final income tax returns. Incidentally, the fees you pay the accountant on behalf of the estate are deductible for federal estate tax purposes as an administration cost (or can be deducted on the income tax return if this deduction results in a greater benefit).

Extension of Time to File

The IRS will grant you an automatic two-month extension to file the decedent's last federal income tax return after you complete Form 4868 (Application for Automatic Extension of Time to File U.S. Individual Income Tax Return). However, even though you can extend the time to file, you *cannot* extend the time to pay. You must send payment for any tax due together with your completed Form 4868. (Obviously, you will not know the exact amount and should make the best estimate possible at the time).

If you are delayed by circumstances beyond your control, you may be able to obtain an additional extension of time to pay the tax due. File Form 2688 (Application for Extension to File U.S. Individual Income Tax Return) and state why timely filing and payment are beyond your control.

Requesting Prompt Assessment of Tax

As executor, you will become personally liable for payment of all the decedent's taxes if you make distributions to beneficiaries and have not fully satisfied your tax obligations before you do. You may therefore want to request that the IRS assess the tax due more promptly than it usually does and settle the issue. We suggest that you contact an accountant and/or tax attorney before making such a request (which is likely to trigger an audit). The request must be sent separately from the tax return itself and must be made within three years after the date the return is filed.

How can you be discharged from your personal liability for payment of decedent's income taxes? You write for a release. The IRS will notify you of the amount of the tax within nine months from the date it receives your application, and once you pay that amount you will be discharged from personal liability even if a deficiency is later found.

Obtaining a Refund

In many cases, a refund will be due to the estate. You should complete IRS Form 1310 (Statement of Claim Due Deceased Taxpayer) and attach it to the income tax return. You should also enclose a "short certificate," or shortened version of your authorization to act on behalf of the estate, as granted you by the Register of Wills.

Right to File Joint Returns

As executor, you have the right to file a joint return with the decedent's surviving spouse (even if you *are* the decedent's surviving spouse) or you can elect to file a separate return for the decedent. You probably will file a joint return if the overall tax rates are more favorable in this case than if you were filing for the decedent as a single individual. You may also want to file jointly if the decedent had significant tax losses or deductions that might otherwise be wasted. (Note that you will lose the right to file a joint return if the surviving spouse of the decedent remarries before the end of the taxable year within which the decedent died.)

Election for Certain Government Bonds

Chapter 25 discusses the various options open to you, and possibly quite beneficial, in regard to the decedent's final income tax return. One of these involves estates holding Series E or EE bonds. You have the right to report the increase in the bonds' value year by year or you can defer reporting the income until you redeem the bonds.

If you choose to report the interest currently (which makes sense if the decedent had little or no income), the accrued interest must also be reported in the current year.

Medical Expense Deductions

You have the right to deduct the decedent's final medical expenses either on the decedent's final income tax return or on the federal estate tax return (or take some of the expenses as deductions on each of the two returns). It makes sense to have the decedent's accountant make a comparison of the relative tax advantages. Medical expenses you pay during the year following the decedent's death are deductible on his last income tax return (subject, of course, to the percentage limitation). If you decide to take the deduction there, you must file a form stating that you have not already claimed (or will not claim) the same expenses as a deduction on the federal estate tax return.

Personal Exemption and Dependency Exemptions Allowed

When you file the decedent's last income tax return you must report all income the decedent earned, but you are entitled to deduct the decedent's personal exemption and dependency exemptions in the same manner as if the decedent had lived.

SUMMARY

As executor, you will probably have to prepare a final federal (and state) income tax return for the decedent. The return is due at the same time it would have been due had death not occurred (although extensions are possible). You have the right to file a joint return with the decedent's surviving spouse—even if you are the surviving spouse. You may elect to report or defer reporting the income on Series E or EE bonds. Certain deductions (such as the medical expense deduction) may be taken on the final income tax return or on the decedent's estate tax return—or split between the two. A personal exemption and dependency exemption may be taken just as if the decedent had lived.

25

Tax Elections Available to an Executor

An executor can choose to use—or not to use—a multiplicity of income and estate tax deductions. These options can greatly diminish the overall tax burden facing the estate and its beneficiaries and can result in a dispositive arrangement that meets the needs of the beneficiaries more effectively.

None of the elections discussed below should be made—or allowed to lapse—unless they are carefully considered by competent counsel. An executor can be "surcharged" (held financially accountable) for losses incurred in an estate where less than adequate consideration is given to these highly valuable elections.

An executor must examine each of the following elections and determine:

1. Does this estate qualify for this election?

2. Should the election be taken in light of all the surrounding circumstances? (What are the *non*tax effects?)

3. How much time do we have to make the election?

An executor should create a checklist and keep a written record indicating that each of these issues has been addressed.

Joint Return with Surviving Spouse

The decedent's accountant and attorney should decide whether or not the decedent's income, earned and reportable up to the date of his death, should be shown on a return that also includes the surviving spouse's income. The executor is entitled to file a joint income tax return with the surviving spouse that would include both the decedent's income until the date of death and the surviving spouse's income for the entire year.

To be eligible for this election, the surviving spouse must not remarry until after the regular tax year ends. The surviving spouse must join the estate's executor in signing IRS Form 1040 and thereby consent to the election. (You sign as the surviving spouse *and* in your capacity as executor if you are both.)

The advantage of filing a joint return is that the rates are lower than in the separate return schedules (see the tables beginning on page 412). The overall income tax would therefore be lower. A secondary advantage is that the surviving spouse might have incurred losses that could offset the income of the deceased spouse, or the deceased spouse may have had tax losses or other deductible items that could offset the income earned by the surviving spouse.

This election must be made by the due date of the decedent's final income tax return. The return is due, in the case of calendar year taxpayers, on or before April 15 of the year following the year of the decedent's death.

Series E Bond Accrued Interest

Interest accrued on Series E government bonds (as well as H and HH exchange bonds) can be reported in one of four ways. As the estate's executor, you can choose to report accrued interest on the final income tax return of the decedent. Alternatively, you could report the income on the estate's income tax return. A third possibility is to report the accrued bond income on a later return. Finally, you could decide to cash in the bonds.

There are no special requirements for any of these options. As long as the bonds pass to the executor at the owner's death, any one of the choices above can be made. However, if the bonds pass to someone other than the executor (for example, if the bonds were held jointly with rights of survivorship), the executor could not choose to report the accrued interest on the estate's income tax returns.

The major advantage of the flexibility above is timing; as executor, you can choose to report the accrued income on the return which contains the least amount of income. Rather than piling this additional income on top of substantial amounts of other income, you can place it on the income tax return where it will be subject to the lowest possible rates.

If you choose to report this accrued interest on the decedent's final income tax return rather than on the estate's income tax return, a deduction that might otherwise have been available to the recipient of the income—the deduction for "income in respect of a decedent"—will be lost. (Income that was earned but not received by a calendar-basis taxpayer before death is subject to both federal estate taxes and federal income taxes. The recipient of such income is entitled to an income tax deduction based on the federal and state death taxes generated by the inclusion of this income. The greater the death taxes generated, the larger the income tax deduction.)

One advantage, therefore, of electing to report accrued bond income on the final return of the decedent is that it creates an income tax liability which in turn may be taken as a federal estate tax deduction. There is a second advantage, too. Suppose the decedent died early in the tax year before he had realized much income. If you report all the "built-in" gain from the Series E bond in that tax year, you obtain the low marginal tax rate applicable to that very short tax year. Keep in mind, however, that once you elect to report the income from the bond, you have to continue to report it annually. If the tax you'll have to pay is large, you have a high-cost-of-money factor to consider (you have to pay the tax now, but you have no cash until you cash in the bond).

Accrued bond interest should be reported on the appropriate tax return by the applicable due date.

Unpaid Medical Expenses

An executor can deduct unpaid medical expenses either on the federal estate tax return or on the decedent's income tax return for the year in which the expense was incurred. Note that the income tax deduction will be disallowed unless the medical expense has actually been paid within one year of the decedent's death.

You should choose to take the deduction on the return which produces the greatest tax benefit, typically the return in the highest tax bracket. In most cases, this will be the income tax return since estate tax rates will usually be lower than the income tax rates imposed. Furthermore, if the decedent has left his property to a surviving spouse in a manner that qualifies for the federal estate tax marital deduction, there may be no estate tax. Obviously, the deduction would be wasted if it were not taken on the decedent's final income tax return.

If medical expense amounts are very large, you should consider dividing the deduction. In other words, you can deduct some of the expenses on the decedent's last income tax return, and the balance on the estate tax return. The medical expense deduction must be taken on the appropriate return by the due date of that return.

Whenever possible, the family should pay medical bills prior to death. This has the twofold effect of generating an income tax deduction and reducing the gross estate by the amount of the payment.

Administration Expenses

You can decide to deduct administration expenses either on the estate's income tax return or on the estate tax return.

Deductible administration expenses include executor's commissions—if you paid them to yourself—attorney's fees, court costs, accountant's costs, appraiser's fees and other death-related expenses.

You may split the administration deduction between the two returns.

Be careful. When you choose to take a deduction on the estate's income tax return, you may be increasing the estate tax. This means the estate's "remaindermen" (those who receive property after the income beneficiary's death) receive less. The income tax deduction benefits the income beneficiaries. So be sure to check the will for authorization to take the deduction on either return—or discuss the issue with an attorney.

Quarterly Payment of Estate's Income Tax Liability

The tax law allows the estate's income tax to be paid in installments. One fourth of the tax payable must accompany the income tax return. The balance of the income tax due may be paid in equal installments spread over each of the next three calendar quarters. No interest is payable on the unpaid balance of these installments.

Any estate may elect to make quarterly installment payments of income tax. There are no special requirements.

One of the primary principles of estate planning is, whenever possible, to defer the payment of taxes for as long as possible. Money can be earned by the estate on the unpaid income tax. Certainly, the right to defer payment on the income tax buys time for the estate to liquidate assets and diminishes the need for a forced sale of valuable assets to pay the tax.

You can take advantage of this privilege merely by filing a timely estate income tax return (Form 1041) and paying one quarter of the tax due. If you are electing to pay the income tax in quarterly installments, you should so state on Form 1041.

Distributions from the Estate

Taxation of the income produced by property generally follows the property itself. When the estate makes a distribution of property to an heir, the heir rather than the estate is taxable on the income produced by the property. By either keeping the income or passing it out of the estate, you can shift taxation to the party in the lower bracket.

To accomplish this income shift, it is necessary to actually distribute the property during the estate's fiscal year (the income tax consequences will also be shifted to a beneficiary if the will requires the income to be distributed even if in fact it is not).

The major advantage of shifting income tax consequences by distributing property is that the tax burden can be shifted to a number of taxpayers (thereby lowering the effective rate of tax) and can be shifted to family members who are in the lowest brackets. This illustrates the estate planning technique of dividing income among as many taxpayers as possible in order to use the progressive nature of the tax law against itself. You can apply the same tax-saving principle by making an early distribution to a trust (which is also a separate taxpayer and in a separate tax bracket).

You can make distributions from the estate until the end of the estate's fiscal year. If the decedent's assets produce a great deal of income, significant income tax savings can be realized by keeping the estate open. In other words, by continuing the estate as a separate taxpayer you can divide income by holding some and paying the rest out. The estate will be taxed on what it receives and does not pay out. The estate's beneficiaries will be taxed on what they receive.

How long can you keep the estate open? The estate is permitted to remain in existence for "a reasonable period of administration"—this being defined as the period actually required for you to collect the estate's assets, pay its debts and distribute any legacies and bequests. The longer you can extend the administration, the more income tax savings are possible.

Waiver of Fees by Personal Representative

You are entitled (unless the will specifically prohibits it) to a fee for the services you render on behalf of the estate. But you may "waive" (formally give up) your right to the fee or to a portion thereof.

There are no special requirements under federal law to waive your executor's fees. As in the case of other decisions discussed in this chapter, you should check with counsel about state law requirements.

If you take an executor's fee, to the extent that the amount is reasonable it will be deductible by the estate on the federal estate tax return. This, of course, will result in a lower estate tax, assuming there would be a tax payable (if the unlimited marital deduction is available, any additional deduction may be wasted). On the other hand, the fees you take are taxable to you personally as ordinary income, which will increase your income tax liability.

So the question you must ask is whether the reduction in estate tax is greater than the additional income tax you must pay. If so, take the executor's fee. If your answer is no, waive the fee. But before you decide, consider the non-tax cash flow implications and how the other beneficiaries will react if you do take a fee: Will the potential family friction outweigh the tax advantage?

If you decide to waive your fee, you should so inform the principal beneficiaries in writing. Notice should be given very quickly—if possible, within six months of your appointment as executor. Of course, if you are the principal or only beneficiary of the estate it is highly doubtful that your taking a fee and paying income tax on it would ever pay. Why? Because if you don't take the executor's fee it will pass to you as beneficiary, income tax free. On the other hand, suppose you are one of several beneficiaries. By waiving your fee, you can shift the amount you could have taken to a younger generation of relatives. Best of all, there will be no gift tax payable.

Election Against the Will

In almost every state, a surviving spouse has the right under state law to elect to take a share of a decedent's estate regardless of what the will says. This "right of election" is specified under state statute. The "statutory share" is typically one third of the probate estate of the decedent. (The amount varies from state to state.)

This right to "elect or take against the will" is generally easy to exercise. There is no need to contest the will or to show any fraud, duress, undue influence or improper execution. You should check with counsel about your own state's provisions. (See the summary of state laws beginning on page 325.)

One reason to consider an election against the will is that it may give the surviving spouse a larger portion of the estate than he or she would receive under the will. A larger portion of the estate translates into a larger marital deduction, which means lower federal estate taxes.

If the surviving spouse desires to take his or her elective share, it is necessary to file a written election with the local Probate (Orphans') Court. The election must be made within the time specified under local law, typically within six months after the announcement to the public of the appointment of the estate's executor or within one year of the decedent's death. Failure to file the election within the prescribed period results in permanent loss of the surviving spouse's right to "take against the will" of the deceased spouse.

In some states, children have a similar right, determined by statute, to a share of decedent's estate regardless of what the will provides.

Alternate Valuation

An executor can pick one of two dates for valuation of assets on the federal estate tax return. The first is the date that will be used if no election is made—the date of death. The second date is six months after the date of death, and called the "alternate valuation date." If property is sold, exchanged, distributed or otherwise disposed of between the date of death and six months after death, the latter becomes the alternate valuation date.

If you are required to file a federal estate tax return (Form 706), you are eligible to elect the alternate valuation date.

An obvious advantage of the alternate valuation date is that if the value of estate assets has dropped between the date of death and the alternate valuation date, this election may save federal estate taxes. (To the extent property qualifies for the marital deduction this would not be true, since no federal estate tax would be payable regardless of the value of the property.) For example, suppose a widow died owning assets worth $800,000 at her death. Assume these assets had dropped in value to only $730,000 by the alternate valuation date—six months after her death. By electing to value assets six months after death rather than on the date of death, you would save the amount of the estate tax on $70,000 ($800,000 less $730,000).

In some cases, you should choose the date on which overall estate values were highest. Why? This technique is especially useful in an estate with a great deal of highly appreciated assets that are likely to be sold by the heirs. A higher value is also important where the estate contains highly depreciated assets such as buildings. The reason you may want to pick the date on which assets have a higher value is that the federal estate tax value of an asset also becomes its "basis"—that is, the starting point for determining gain or loss in the event of a sale, or the limit for cost recovery through depreciation deductions. The higher the seller's basis, the lower the gain on a later sale. Likewise, the higher the basis, the greater the income tax deductions that can be enjoyed by the recipients of depreciable property.

For these reasons, you may choose to use the alternate valuation date to obtain a higher rather than a lower value. This would be especially indicated if the income tax brackets of the estate and/or its beneficiaries were higher than the estate tax bracket of the estate. Obviously, if all or a large portion of the estate were to qualify for the estate tax marital deduction, there would be lower or no rates applied against estate assets, regardless of their value. So it would seem to be excellent planning to select the date that would result in the highest estate tax valuation. Unfortunately, this technique is not available. An estate may use alternate valuation only if the election has the effect of reducing (1) the total value of the gross estate and (2) the amount of the estate tax liability.

It is important to remember that you must make the alternate valuation election on page 2 of IRS Form 706 by the date the form itself is due to be filed. (An exception to this rule allows the election to be made on a return filed late, but only if that return is the first filed for the estate, is otherwise properly made, and is filed within one year of its due date.)

Special Use Valuation for Farm or Closely Held Business Real Estate

Real estate used in a farm or closely held business can be valued according to its actual use (for example, as pasture land) rather than its "highest and best use" (for example, at the price it would bring if offered to a real estate developer), but only if certain tests are met.

The amount of the decrease between the property's highest and best use value (the valuation required for most assets) and that special use value is limited to $750,000.

This means that you must have an appraiser figure both the normal fair market value and, in many cases, the special value (although there are formulas that you can use, such as the one on page 146, Chapter 21).

Not all estates are eligible for the special use method of real estate valuation. The form on page 175 outlines the requirements which an estate must meet to qualify for current use valuation.

The major benefit of special, or current, use valuation is the consequent reduction in the federal estate tax. But note that this advantage is coupled with the property's lower tax basis, with the result that, if it is sold, the reportable gain will be greater.

Various disadvantages can be found in the special use valuation. For example, personal liability is required of all heirs to the property; and, if the property is disposed of within ten years of the decedent's death, all or a portion of the estate tax savings will be "recaptured"—that is, the money the estate "saved" in taxes must be paid back to the IRS.

Another disadvantage is that there may be administrative problems (as will inevitably be the case where minors are involved) and intra-family conflicts of interest. The IRS will probably want a special lien placed on the property until the statutory period for recapture of the tax break has expired.

The current use valuation election must be made on a federal estate tax return timely filed (including extensions).

Qualified Terminable Interest Property

Generally, property qualifies for the estate tax marital deduction only if it is left to the decedent's surviving spouse either outright or in a manner tantamount to outright. Therefore, the spouse must be given such control over property that she can leave it or give it to anyone (including a second husband or his children). In fact, even if the surviving spouse left all the property to decedent's children, a second husband could elect against her will and obtain a portion of the property.

On the other hand, if a decedent's will provided "to my husband for life and then to my children," she could be sure her children would (eventually) receive the property, but the bequest would not qualify for the federal estate tax marital deduction.

Congress, in an attempt to eliminate this Hobson's choice, provided that an individual could obtain a marital deduction for property interests which previously did not qualify. These "terminable interests" (in the example above, the husband's interest terminates at his death and he has no right to transfer the property to anyone) can qualify for the marital deduction if you, as the executor, make a Q.T.I.P. election.

Not all property will meet Q.T.I.P. requirements. To satisfy the rules, the surviving spouse must be given the right to all the income from the property. That income must be payable at least annually. None of the capital in the trust (usually this type of property will be in trust, although life insurance proceeds and other forms of transferral vehicles can also qualify) can be paid to anyone but the spouse for as long as he or she lives.

Although the Q.T.I.P. election makes it more likely that no one other than the individual(s) selected by the decedent will obtain the property when the surviving spouse dies, it does not fully ensure that result. For example, in some states a surviving spouse still has a right to elect against the will and take the same share of the estate

Determination of Whether Estate Qualifies for Current Use
Valuation of Farm Real Estate or Business Real Estate

(1) Gross estate (Form 102, line 1)* . . . . . . $ _____

Less

(2) Unpaid mortgages or indebtedness
on property included in estate
at gross value
(Fact Finder, pp. 4, 5, 6, 20) . . . . $ _____

Equals

(3) Adjusted value of gross estate . . . . $ _____

(4) 50% of adjusted value of
gross estate . . . . $ _____

(5) 25 % of adjusted value of
gross estate . . . . $ _____

(6) Value of real and personal property
of farm or closely held business
(Fact Finder, pp. 4 & 5) . . . . $ _____

Less

(7) Unpaid mortgages or indebtedness
on farm or closely held business real
or personal property included in
estate at gross value
(Fact Finder, pp. 4, 5, 6, 20) . . . . $ _____

Equals

(8) Adjusted value of real and personal
property of farm or closely
held business . . . . $ _____

(9) Qualified real property (Form 101) . . . . . $ _____

Less

    (10) Unpaid mortgages or indebtedness
         on qualified real property included
         in estate at gross value
         (Fact Finder, pp. 4, 5, 20) . . . . $ _____

Equals

    (11) Adjusted value of qualified
         real property . . . . $ _____

REAL PROPERTY OF FARM OR CLOSELY HELD BUSINESS QUALIFIES FOR CURRENT-USE VALUATION IF LINE 8 EQUALS OR EXCEEDS LINE 4 **AND** LINE 11 EQUALS OR EXCEEDS LINE 5.

This also assumes that (a) the decedent was a U.S. citizen or resident, (b) the real property passes to a qualified heir, and (c) for 5 out of the last 8 years before the decedent's death, the real property was used in the farm or closely held business, and the decedent or a family member materially participated in the farm or business operation.

* The full highest and best-use value and not the current-use value is used in determining the value of the gross estate for the 50% and 25% tests.

This form is reproduced through the courtesy of The American College and is used as part of its **Advanced Estate Planning I and II courses.**

that would have been available had the decedent died intestate. Still, the odds are higher that the decedent's objectives will be accomplished. The cost of the Q.T.I.P. election—which provides greater assurance of meeting personal objectives—is that, when the surviving spouse dies, any capital remaining will be taxed in his or her estate. In other words, you as executor are agreeing that the property in question be includable in the surviving spouse's estate in return for the allowance of a marital deduction in the present decedent's estate.

You must make the election on the federal estate tax return, and the return should be filed by the appropriate due date.

Installment Payment of Estate Tax

As executor, you can elect to pay the federal estate tax generated by the inclusion of a closely held business in installments. During the first four years, only interest on the unpaid tax is due. Over the next ten years, the estate must pay principal and interest (equal annual principal payments with interest on the declining balance).

The form on page 178 illustrates the mathematical tests to be met for this election. In addition, the enterprise in question must in fact be an active trade or business, and not a mere investment, in order to qualify.

It is quite appealing to be able to stall off principal payments on the federal estate tax for four years and pay a very modest rate of interest during that time. Small estates (where the business generates $345,800 or less in federal estate tax) will pay only 4 percent interest. Actually, this special 4 percent interest rate applies only to the following amounts of tax:

1984	1985	1986	1987
249,500	244,000	190,000	153,000

If the tax generated by a business exceeds these amounts, the interest will be the rate which is charged generally by the IRS on unpaid taxes. This rate (much higher than the 4 percent amount) is changed twice a year and is compounded daily.

You should keep in mind that this election does not provide funds to pay the tax; it merely delays the day of reckoning. Furthermore, consider that you, as executor, are personally liable for the tax, and if there are insufficient funds in the estate you must pay the tax as due from your own personal funds.

Determination of Whether Estate Qualifies for Installment Payout of Tax

Section 6166 (up to 14 years) Installment Payout

(1) Estate tax value of farm or other closely held business
included in gross estate .... $ _____

(2) Adjusted gross estate .... $ _____

(3) 35% of adjusted gross estate .... $ _____

If line 1 **exceeds** line 3, estate can elect to pay that portion of estate taxes attributable to the inclusion of the farm or other closely held business in installments for up to 14 years (first 4 years—no tax due, only interest; up to 10 years—annual installments of tax and interest).

Two or more businesses may be aggregated if the decedent held a 20% or more interest in each such business. (Attribution rules may also make it possible to meet the 20% or more test.)

_____ Does qualify   _____ Does **not** qualify

Computing 6166 Deferral Limitation

Net F.E.T. payable $\times$ $\dfrac{\text{Value of includible closely held business interest}}{\text{Adjusted gross estate}}$

You will be discharged from personal liability only if you furnish a bond (you can charge the cost of the bond to the estate) or have all the parties who have an interest in the property consent to a lien and to the imposition of additional liens if the value of the original property is—or falls—below the total of the unpaid taxes and the aggregate interest owed.

This fourteen-year installment election (tax practitioners call this a "6166" election because Code Section 6166 spells out the eligibility requirements) only defers the federal estate tax attributable to the closely held business. It does not defer administration expenses or the need for cash to pay state death taxes, debts, the remaining portion of the federal estate tax, income taxes, etc.

It would be extremely dangerous to make final distributions to estate beneficiaries before the entire fourteen-year period has expired since, as was mentioned above, you remain personally liable for the unpaid tax.

To take advantage of this election, you must submit notice to the IRS when you file the federal estate tax Form 706. This notice must be filed on a timely return.

Deferral of Estate Tax on Remainder Or Reversionary Interest

A "remainder interest" is a future interest in property that comes into existence after a prior interest terminates. For example, a decedent may have set up a trust under his will and provided in the trust that his wife is to receive the income from the property in the trust for her lifetime, and that the principal at her death is to go to their children. The children receive what is left (the remainder) when the wife's interest terminates. For this reason, the children are called "remaindermen." A "reversionary interest" is a right to recover property at some time in the future. For instance, a person may set up a trust while he or she is alive under which a parent will enjoy the income as long as the parent lives. When the parent dies, the principal of this trust will revert to the person who set up the trust (the "grantor").

The federal tax law recognizes the imposition that would be placed on estates which contained remainders or reversions of great value; there would be tax imposed on the interest, but the estate would not have the interest to sell, pledge or otherwise pay the tax. For this reason, the law provides that the estate tax attributable to the value of either a remainder or a reversionary interest can be deferred for up to six months beyond the date on which the preceding legal interest ends. In the examples above, the executor would have six months from the date the wife (the income beneficiary) died in the case of the remainder interest (example above) and the same length of time from the date the parent died in the case of the reversion example.

The election to defer payment of the federal estate tax is available to any estate in which a remainder or reversionary interest is includable in the gross estate.

It makes sense to make the election if the estate needs cash or the value of the interest is large relative to the values of other estate assets. This election is particularly useful where the decedent had established a "Clifford" (short-term) trust.

You make the election by filing a notice to the IRS on or before the due date for filing the federal estate tax return. The notice should be accompanied by a copy of the document that created the remainder or reversionary interest.

You must also furnish a bond to the IRS for twice the amount of the tax and estimated interest.

Reasonable-Cause Extension to Pay Federal Estate Tax

The IRS may (entirely at its own discretion) allow an estate to extend the due date for payment of the federal estate tax, one year at a time, for up to ten years.

To obtain the extensions, you must prove to the IRS

1. that you are unable to marshal assets to pay the estate tax at the time it is due; or

2. that a substantial part of the estate consists of rights to receive payments in the future; or

3. that the estate has insufficient cash to pay the tax and is not able to borrow the money except on unreasonable terms; or

4. that the estate's assets cannot be collected without litigation; or

5. that sufficient funds are not available, after the exercise of due diligence, to pay the tax in a timely manner; or

6. that there is some other "reasonable cause" for the extensions to be granted.

All of the problems discussed in connection with the fourteen-year installment payout apply to this election. The big advantage is that it does relieve the immediate need for liquidity, but eventually you must raise the cash to pay the tax or be liable personally. To apply for this deferral, you must file IRS Form 4768 with the federal estate tax return by the due date of the return.

Section 303 Stock Redemption

The tax law recognizes the hardships caused by a forced sale of a closely held business, and provides a way for a corporation to make a distribution in redemption of its stock that will not be taxed as a dividend. Specifically, Section 303 allows a corporation to provide cash and/or other property in return for its stock without its being treated as a dividend, and to provide cash for the estate to pay death taxes and other expenses.

The protection afforded under Section 303 is limited; a distribution is afforded "sale or exchange" treatment. (Only the difference between the estate's basis and the amount it receives for the stock will be taxable at all, and that gain, if any, will usually receive long-term capital gains treatment.) Typically there will be no reportable gain, since the estate's basis for the stock is stepped up to the stock's fair market value as of the decedent's death. The new basis therefore is equal to the price the estate receives for the stock, and there is no reportable gain (or only to the extent of the estate's federal and state death taxes and funeral and administration expenses).

The worksheet on page 181 shows the protective limit of Section 303 as well as the mathematical tests the estate must meet to qualify for such stock redemption. Even if these numerical tests are met, the distribution is protected from dividend treatment only to the extent the seller of stock must pay or is liable for the decedent's death taxes or other expenses.

The major advantage of Section 303 is that it affords protection to family-owned corporations from "attribution" (constructive ownership) problems, whereby redemptions of only a part of a family member's stock are almost always taxable as dividends. (If a distribution is classified as a dividend, the entire amount received is taxable at

Determination of Whether Estate Qualifies for Sec. 303 Stock Redemption

(1) FEDERAL ESTATE TAX VALUE OF CORPORATE
STOCK INCLUDED IN GROSS ESTATE . . . . $ _____
(The value of stock of two or more corporations
can be aggregated if 20% or more of the value
of the outstanding stock of **each** such corporation
is included in the decedent's gross estate.)

(2) 35% of ADJUSTED GROSS ESTATE . . . . $ _____

_____ Does qualify   _____ Does **not** qualify

If line 1 **exceeds** line 2, a redemption under Section 303 is
considered a sale or exchange rather than a dividend **to the
extent** the selling stockholder's interest is reduced
directly or the stockholder is bound to contribute to the
payment of

   (a) deductible funeral and administration
       expenses . . . . $ _____

   (b) federal estate taxes . . . . $ _____

   (c) state death taxes . . . . $ _____

   (d) interest collected as part of above
       taxes . . . . $ _____

Maximum allowable Section 303 redemption . . . . $ ===========

ordinary income rates as high as 50 percent, compared to a maximum effective rate of 20 percent on long-term capital gains.)

Section 303 is affected by an agreement between the corporation and the selling shareholder followed by the exchange; the corporation pays cash and/or property, and in return receives stock of equal value.

The redemption must be accomplished within three years and ninety days from the due date of the federal estate tax return; or, if there is a contest regarding the estate's tax liability, within sixty days of the time a tax court decision on the subject is final. A longer time is allowed if the estate is also utilizing a Section 6166 installment payout of estate taxes.

Flower Bonds

Certain U.S. Treasury obligations (which are currently traded at a discount), if owned by a decedent at death, can be redeemed at par value (plus accrued interest) in payment of federal estate taxes. These debt instruments are called flower bonds for two reasons. The first is that flower bonds "blossom." They may be purchased by an individual (or by an individual's agent) at a substantial discount from par because of the very low interest rates they pay. Yet the difference between the purchase price and their value provides a way to pay the federal estate tax at a "discount." The second reason they are called flower bonds is that on their back they have an engraving of a flower.

The major advantages of these bonds are that they can provide some measure of additional liquidity and can be obtained even on one's deathbed.

Flower bonds are subject to probate costs and state inheritance taxes (at market rather than par) and can be used at par only to pay the federal estate tax. Flower bonds are includable in the gross estate at their par value to the extent they can be used to pay the federal estate tax. To the extent of any difference between the par value of the bonds that could be used to pay the estate tax and any excess of bonds, they are includable at market value.

Flower bonds are not accepted directly by the IRS in payment of the estate tax. You must send the bonds, together with a certified copy of the decedent's death certificate, to any Federal Reserve Bank or branch thereof or to the Bureau of the Public Debt, Division of Securities Operations, Washington, D.C. 20226. They should be submitted well in advance of (at least one month before) the date specified for the redemption. The form that should be used is PD 1782, Application for Redemption at Par of United States Treasury Bonds Eligible for Payment of Federal Estate Tax. These forms can be obtained from any Federal Reserve Bank or any of its branches. The entire transaction should be completed well before the time for filing the federal estate tax return.

Disclaimers

A disclaimer (some practitioners call it a renunciation) is an unqualified refusal to accept benefits. For federal estate tax purposes, the person disclaiming is regarded as never having received the property disclaimed. It is as if the disclaimant had predeceased the person leaving the property. As a result of this treatment, no transfer is considered to have been made by the disclaimant for estate tax purposes.

The ability to shift an interest in property without gift tax cost can lead to exciting planning possibilities. For example, if an individual with children and a large estate receives a bequest that would only serve to compound his or her estate tax problems, disclaiming causes the bequest to pass to the next in line. So if the decedent left a million dollars to his multimillionaire nephew if he was living, and otherwise to the nephew's children, the nephew, by disclaiming, in essence makes a tax-free gift of a million dollars to his children.

The disclaimer can be used to shift not only capital but also income. For instance, assume an individual in a high income tax bracket is left a bequest that provides "to my son if he survives me; otherwise to his children." If the children are in a lower income bracket than the son, a disclaimer by him will shift both the property and the income from the property (and therefore the income taxation) to them.

If property is left to a child if living, and otherwise to the decedent's surviving spouse, a disclaimer by that child means that the property will be considered as having passed directly from the decedent to his surviving spouse and may therefore qualify for the estate tax marital deduction. Likewise, if property is left to a child if living, and otherwise to a qualified charity, a disclaimer by the child will result in a charitable deduction in the decedent's estate.

A disclaimer will have the desired tax effects only if it is qualified. A "qualified disclaimer" is an unqualified refusal to accept an interest in property. It must be in writing and must be received by the legal representative of the decedent within nine months of the decedent's death (or the day the transfer became complete, if earlier) or within nine months of the date on which the beneficiary reached age twenty-one. Note that the disclaimer must be made before the property or any of its benefits have been accepted. The interest must pass (or have passed) to the recipient without any direction on the part of the disclaimant.

Although the disclaimer may be effective in spite of local law, it is best to check and meet all local law requirements for disclaimers as well as those outlined above.

There is no specific federal form to be used for a disclaimer. It is best to check with local counsel for state procedural rules. Typically, as noted above, the disclaimer must be made within nine months of the decedent's death.

Fiscal Year of the Estate

The estate is a tax entity separate from its beneficiaries, which results in a great many planning opportunities. As executor, you can select an initial fiscal year for the estate that will end on the last day of any month (within the twelve months immediately following death).

There are no requirements that must be met; you are automatically entitled to choose the first taxable period of the estate.

One advantage of the right to select the length of the first fiscal year is that, by selecting a short year, you may be able to obtain one additional $600 exemption. A second (and perhaps more important) benefit is that you can time income and deductions: that is, you can more evenly offset income with deductions, so as to avoid a lot of income in one tax year and a lot of (wasted) deductions in a different year. This flexibility is particularly important if you are administering the estate of a professional with a great deal of earned but not yet received income at the time of his or her death.

To obtain the benefit of a short fiscal year, you must file the estate's income tax form, Form 1041, by the fifteenth day of the fourth month after the end of the fiscal year.

Estate Administration Expenses

The expenses of administering an estate include attorney's fees, probate costs, accounting fees and many other expenses. You may deduct these costs on either the estate's income tax return (Form 1041) or the federal estate tax return (Form 706). You may also apportion the deductions to both returns, i.e., partly as income tax deductions and partly as estate tax deductions.

The advantage of being able to choose the return is obvious: you can take the deduction where it will do the most good. If little or no federal estate tax is payable, you would take the deduction on the income tax return. For example, little or no tax would be payable if the estate just barely exceeded the "unified credit equivalent"— the amount of estate that anyone can pass, federal estate tax free, to anyone else. There will typically be no estate tax on the federal level if the entire estate qualifies for the estate tax marital deduction because it goes to the surviving spouse. One potential problem, if several different beneficiaries are involved, is that an income tax deduction may favor one group at the expense of another. State law or the will itself may require the income beneficiaries to reimburse the remaindermen for the forfeited estate tax savings.

You make the election by claiming the appropriate amount of deductions on the return you have selected. If you claim a deduction on the income tax return, you must file a waiver stating that you agree not to take the deduction on a later filed estate tax return.

Estate Selling Expenses

There is great flexibility with respect to the expenses the estate incurs when you must sell estate assets to pay taxes or expenses or to meet any other obligations or responsibilities of the estate. You can deduct estate sale expenses—such as brokerage fees, seller's commissions or other transfer costs—on the federal estate tax return as part of the cost of administering the estate. Alternatively, when you report a gain on the sale of an item, you can reduce the sale price in computing the gain. Here again you are comparing the rates on the two returns and will typically take the deduction (or reduction) on the return with the highest rate.

The only requirement for this deduction is that the amount of the expense be reasonable and allowable under state law and necessary to the administration of the estate. If the expense is not deemed necessary and benefits the beneficiaries more than the estate itself (for example, if the expense is incurred to settle a dispute between the heirs), then it cannot be taken as a deduction on the estate tax return. It may, however, be used to reduce the amount reportable if there is a gain on the sale of an item.

You must claim the deduction on the appropriate return before the expiration of the limitations period.

SUMMARY

The many elections available to you as executor can significantly affect how much tax the estate and its beneficiaries will pay. They include: (1) filing a joint return as executor for the estate with the surviving spouse (even if you *are* the surviving spouse) to take advantage of lower joint rates on the decedent's tax losses; (2) reporting Series E bond interest at the time and on the tax return with the least amount of taxable income; (3) taking unpaid medical expenses on the federal estate tax return or on the decedent's income tax return, whichever will produce a bigger deduction; (4) filing the estate's income tax returns quarterly to defer payments and earn money on the unpaid tax; (5) deducting administrative expenses on the tax return (income or estate) which will yield the highest deduction; (6) keeping taxable income of the estate in the estate —or passing it out (depending on which party is in the lower bracket); (7) waiving fees as personal representative to avoid the tax on ordinary income and receive your inheritance income tax free (at the possible cost of higher estate taxes); (8) electing against the will to receive a larger share of the estate than provided under the will; (9) selecting the alternate valuation date other than the date of death to either lower estate taxes or increase the basis of assets for income tax purposes; (10) electing special use (rather than normal) valuation for real estate used in a farm or other closely held business; (11) paying federal estate taxes in installments of up to fourteen years through a Section 6166 election; (12) paying estate taxes with corporate dollars through a Section 303 stock redemption; and (13) electing Q.T.I.P. treatment for assets that otherwise would not be eligible for the marital deduction.

26

Valuation of Assets

One of the most complex and uncertain processes required of an executor is the valuation of property for both federal and state death tax purposes.

Value is a variable. Reasonable minds can and often will differ as to the proper value of any item of property. But value is not determined by a mere flip of the coin. The executor must use appraisals by qualified experts, obtain documentation of recent sales of similar property and submit photostats of any buy/sell agreements to the IRS.

General Rules of Estate Tax Valuation

As executor, you must value every asset at its "fair market value." Fair market value is the price at which the property in question would be acquired by a hypothetical willing buyer from a willing seller, assuming that neither of them is under any compulsion to buy or to sell. A further assumption is that both parties have reasonable knowledge of any and all relevant facts. Remember, too, that the value you may place on property may vary greatly from what the government thinks that property is worth. You should take a reasonable but aggressive position. If your purpose is to reduce federal and state death taxes to a minimum, you should place the lowest possible reasonable value on the property. On the other hand, if you are more interested in obtaining a high cost basis for the beneficiaries in order to lower potential gain if the property is later sold, or to increase cost recovery (depreciation) deductions, you should place a high but reasonable value on the asset.

You should direct appraisers to document those factors which support your position and which, if litigated, would be sustained by the courts.

Date Assets Are Valued

Generally, federal estate taxes are based either on the fair market value of property as of the date the decedent died or on the value of property six months after the date of the decedent's death (the "alternate valuation date"). Once selected for valuation purposes—date of death or alternate valuation date—that date applies to all assets in the estate.

If you select the alternate valuation date and you distribute, sell, exchange or otherwise dispose of property within six months of the decedent's death, you must value it as of *that* date—not the "six months after death" date.

Certain types of property diminish in value over time. For example, the value of a patent diminishes each year, as does the value of an annuity. You must value a property interest whose value is affected by the mere passing of time as of the date the decedent died. Of course, if some external factor has affected valuation (as a new invention might reduce the value of an existing patent), that factor can be used in the valuation process.

Valuation of Real Property

Land is unique. The value of any real property as of a given date is subject to widely differing opinions. If there is no market for the property, it should be valued at (a) the highest price available, or (b) the amount it will bring as salvage, whichever is greater.

If there is a market for real property held by the estate, the factors that you (and/or a qualified professional appraiser) should consider are:

1. The nature and condition of the property, its physical qualities and defects, and the adequacy or inadequacy of its improvements.

2. The size, shape and location of the property.

3. The actual and potential use of the property and how it is affected by development trends and economic conditions. (Is the neighborhood getting better or worse?)

4. How suitable the property is for its actual or intended use.

5. Changes in zoning restrictions.

6. The size, age and condition of the buildings (degree of deterioration or obsolescence).

7. The market value of other properties in the same area.

8. The value of the net income realized from the property. Rentals are often "capitalized." This means the value of the rent is projected to derive a value for the asset. For example, a building which yields $10,000 a year in net rentals is probably worth some multiple of (such as five times) $10,000. Once rental has been capitalized, it must be adjusted for depreciation.

9. Prices at which comparable property in the same area was sold at a time near the applicable valuation date (providing it was an arm's-length transaction for the best price obtainable).

10. How much would it cost to duplicate the property after taking depreciation into account? The appraiser you hire must separate the cost or value of land from the total value. The cost of reproducing the building, using present cost figures, would have to be estimated, and then the loss in value due to depreciation would have to be subtracted from the total of the other two figures.

11. Unusual facts.

If property in the estate is sold within a reasonable time after the decedent's death, the IRS will usually accept the amount received as its value. This assumes, however, that it was sold in an arm's-length transaction to a purchaser who is unrelated to the estate or its beneficiaries. If property is sold at auction, the price will generally be accepted if it appears that no other method would have resulted in a higher price.

Keep in mind that land may have substantial value for federal and state death tax purposes even though it doesn't produce income and even though there is no active market. If land is in or adjacent to a settled community (as at the edge of an expanding shopping center), it might be worth far more to the shopping center developer than it would to a potential buyer in the residential market. Real estate, just like all other assets, must be valued at its "highest and best use" price rather than at the lowest figure the property might bring.

Special Valuation of Certain Farm and Certain Business Real Property

Let's assume the decedent was a farmer. Let's also assume that the farmland is surrounded by new housing developments. The estate tax value of the land as farmland might be considerably lower than the value of the same land if it was subdivided and used for single-family dwellings. The tax law allows you to value farmland (and certain business real property) at its "special use" value. For example, a farmer's executor could choose to value farmland as such rather than as land subdivided and developed.

Essentially, the requirements for "special use" valuation are: (1) At the date the decedent died, the property must be in use as a farm for farming purposes or in a trade or business other than farming. (2) The property in question must comprise a significant portion of the decedent's gross estate. (3) The property must pass to a "qualified heir"—a member of the decedent's family, an ancestor, a lineal descendant, the decedent's spouse, the spouse of a descendant or a lineal descendant of a grandparent. (4) The property in question must have been owned by the decedent or a member of his family and been used as a farm or closely held business for at least five of the eight years prior to his death; during that time, the decedent or a member of his family must have been materially involved in the operation of the farm or other business.

If these requirements (described in simplified form above) are met, the property qualifies for "special" or "current" use valuation. (See the worksheet in the Appendix entitled "Determination of Whether Estate Qualifies for Current Use.")

You can choose one of various formulas to reduce the value of the farmland from its "highest and best use" value (such as the price a developer might pay) to its value as farm (or business) real property.

The most commonly used formula is to (1) compute the average annual gross cash rental from comparable land, (2) subtract the taxes (state and local real estate taxes) that would be paid on comparable land, and (3) divide the result by the average annual effective interest rate for all new Federal Land Bank loans. For instance, assume land comparable to the land you are valuing yields $14,000 a year in gross cash rental. Assume also that real estate taxes on that land are $2,000. You would divide $12,000 by the average annual effective interest rate for all new Federal Land Bank loans (say, 10 percent). The special use value of the land would therefore be $120,000.

If there is no comparable land, or if you choose to value the farm in the same way you might value qualifying closely held business real estate, then you would do one or more of the following: (1) capitalize the income that the property can be expected to yield for farming purposes over a reasonable period of time under prudent management using traditional cropping patterns for the area (taking into account soil capacity, terrain configuration and other relevant factors); (2) compare sale prices of other farms or closely held business land in the same geographical area but far enough removed from metropolitan resort areas to eliminate nonagricultural use as a significant factor in the sale price; and (3) consider any other factor which fairly values the farm (or closely held business) property.

Watch out for "recapture": if, within ten years after the decedent's death and before the death of the "qualified heir," the qualified heir who receives the property disposes of it (by giving it to someone outside the family) or no longer uses it as a farm or for business purposes, the estate tax benefit you are receiving by virtue of the lower valuation is "recaptured." This means that all the tax you would have paid by choosing the "highest and best use" valuation must be repaid (see Chapter 25).

Valuation of Life Insurance

Life insurance on the life of a decedent that is received by or for the benefit of his estate will be taxed in his estate. The proceeds will be includable for federal estate tax purposes in his estate (note that many *state* death taxes do not require inclusion, or provide special partial exclusions for life insurance proceeds). The amount you must include is the amount received by the beneficiary. This includes any dividends and premium refunds paid to the beneficiary.

If the beneficiary selects a "settlement option" (i.e., takes the money in a form other than a lump sum), the amount that would have been payable as a lump sum is the amount you must include in the decedent's gross estate. If the policy never allowed a lump sum payment in the first place, the amount you must include is the "commuted amount" used by the insurance company to compute the settlement option payments. In other words, it's the lump sum the insurance company would apply to make the promised monthly or annual payments to the beneficiary.

Fortunately, all you have to do with regard to life insurance policies is to request the company or agent to provide you with IRS Form 712 for each policy. The insurance company will do all the computations.

What if the decedent owned insurance on the life of someone else? Is anything includable? If so, how much? The answer is that the value of a policy which has not yet matured and which is owned by a decedent on the life of someone else is included in the policy owner's gross estate when he predeceases the insured. The amount includable depends on whether the policy is "new," "paid up," "active" (still in the premium-paying stage but beyond its first year) or "term insurance."

If a new policy (a policy in its first year) is involved, you must list the gross premium paid as the policy's value.

If the policy is "paid up" (i.e., no more premiums were payable when the decedent died), or if it was a single-premium policy, the value is the policy's "replacement cost." This is the single premium which that company would have charged for a comparable contract with the same death benefit on the life of a person who was the same age as the insured at the date of the decedent/policy owner's death.

If the policy is a whole-life policy on which premiums were still being paid, the value is (in slightly oversimplified form) the policy cash value plus the portion of the premium paid beyond the date of death of the policy owner.

If the policy is a term insurance policy, the value is the premium paid beyond the date of death of the policy owner.

Again, as executor, you don't have to compute these amounts. Merely request in writing that the insurance company supply the appropriate figures, which it will do at no charge.

Look out for this tax trap: if the insured dies within six months of the policy owner and you elect the alternate valuation date, you must include the full amount of the proceeds rather than the "living" value of the policy. In other words, if a policy pays off during the six-month period following the policy owner's death and you have selected the alternate valuation date, the entire proceeds are includable in your decedent's estate.

Valuation of U.S. Government Bonds

Series E bonds are valued at the redemption (market) price as of the date of death.

Flower bonds—certain U.S. Treasury bonds redeemable by the Treasury at par value if used to pay federal estate taxes—are valued for federal estate tax purposes (but not for state death tax purposes) at their market price or at their par value, whichever is higher.

Even if such bonds are not used to pay federal estate taxes, courts have consistently held that, to the extent they *could* have been so used, they should be valued at the higher of the two—market value or par value. But to the extent the bonds could not have been applied to pay the federal estate tax, their value is the market value—the mean quoted selling price as of the date of the decedent's death. Your stockbroker can obtain U.S. government bond valuations for you.

Valuation of Household and Personal Effects

In valuing household and personal effects, it is best to itemize each asset, room by room. Generally, when valuing household property and personal effects (watches, rings, clothing, etc.), you use the "willing buyer/willing seller" rule. If household goods include articles of artistic or intrinsic value such as jewelry, furs, silverware, paintings, engravings, antiques, books, statuary, oriental rugs and coin, stamp, gun or other valuable collections, you should hire an independent appraiser. Call your local bank's trust department and ask them to recommend one or more.

Valuation of Listed Stocks

For federal and state death tax purposes, the fair market value per share of a stock traded on an established exchange governs. The fair market value is based on selling prices when there is a market for the stock. This is the mean between the highest and lowest quoted selling price on the valuation date.

What if no sales were made on the valuation date? If there were sales within a reasonable period before and after the valuation date, the fair market value is determined by taking a weighted average of the means between the highest and lowest sales on the nearest date before and the nearest date after the valuation. The average is then "weighted inversely" by the respective number of trading days between the selling date and the valuation date. For example, suppose there were no sales on the date of death because that date was on a weekend or holiday. If the stock was selling at $10 a share two days before death and $12 a share three days after death, you would (a) multiply $10 times three ($30) and (b) multiply two times $12 ($24), then add the two together ($54) and divide by the number of days (five); so the value of the stock would be $10.80 per share.

The prices can be obtained by checking *The Wall Street Journal* or by calling your stockbroker for prices on the date of death.

Valuation of Corporate Bonds

You value bonds similarly to the way you value listed common stock. If there were no sales on the valuation date, you take the weighted mean of the selling prices on or near the applicable valuation date.

If there were no sales and no bid or asked prices within a reasonable number of days before and after the valuation date, you must consider the following factors to determine the value of the bonds: (1) How sound was the security? (2) How does the interest yield on the bond in question compare to yields on similar bonds? (3) What is the date of the bond's maturity? (4) How do prices for listed bonds of corporations engaged in similar business compare? (5) Is the bond secured? If so, by what? (6) Does the business have goodwill? What is the industry's outlook? What is the company's position in the industry? How sound is the company's management?

The Wall Street Journal can be used to find a bond price. Again, your stockbroker and accountant may be helpful in documenting a value.

Valuation of Stocks of Closely Held Corporations

If you are the executor of an estate which holds closely held stock, you have a difficult, time-consuming and potentially costly problem if there is no buy/sell agreement.

Closely held stock is defined as stock with a limited number of shareholders, with restrictions imposed on the shareholders' ability to transfer the stock, with no sales regularly made in national, regional or over-the-counter exchanges, and with an irregular and limited history of sales or exchanges. Because, by definition, closely held stock is seldom traded, it is difficult to value.

How does the IRS approach the valuation problem? In valuing closely held stock, the IRS studies (1) the nature of the business and the entire history of the enterprise; (2) the economic outlook in general and the conditions and outlook for the specific industry in particular; (3) the book value of the stock and the financial condition of the business; (4) the earning capacity of the company; (5) the company's dividend-paying capacity; (6) the existence (or nonexistence) of goodwill; (7) the sales of stock and the size of the block of stock to be valued; (8) the fair market value of stocks of comparable corporations engaged in the same or a similar line of business with stock actively traded in the established market.

Unfortunately, no fixed formula can be used to value closely held corporations. All the facts must be considered in any one case. (Two worksheets, "Valuation of Business Interest" and "Estimated Going-Concern Value," may be helpful and can be found on pages 400 and 402 of the Appendix.)

As executor, you should work closely with the estate's attorney, and particularly with the business's accountant (or an accountant of your own selection). The estate administration team may also want to hire a person or company that specializes in the valuation of closely held stocks if the stakes are high enough.

You should be extremely aggressive in valuing closely held stocks. Definitely, you should take a reduction in value if the shares being valued represent a "minority" (i.e., a less than controlling) interest in the business. A minority interest discount (10 to 30 percent) is often allowed because such shares have no power to force the corporation to pay dividends, liquidate the corporation or control corporate policy. This weakness limits the potential market for closely held stock. It is only the controlling shareholders, probably, who would be interested. Therefore the price at which such shares might be purchased (if at all) would be much lower than other factors would tend to indicate. (Conversely, if the shares in question represent a controlling interest, the IRS may attempt to increase the value of the stock because control does justify a higher value for a specific block of stock.) Remember this, particularly if you are taking a charitable deduction for stock left to a charity.

Many closely held corporations are subject to buy/sell agreements. These are legal agreements which limit the parties to whom the stock can be sold and set certain conditions upon sales or other transfers. If the terms of the buy/sell agreement definitely fix the values of the shares in question, you don't have to examine either book value or earnings. Usually the IRS will go along with the price fixed in the agreement (although it is not bound by it).

For a buy/sell agreement to be persuasive to the IRS,

1. The agreement as to the value per share must have been made at arm's length and must have been fair and adequate at the time the agreement was signed.

2. The agreement must have been binding during the shareholders' lifetimes. This means the shareholders must have been obligated to offer the stock first to the corporation or other shareholders (this is called a first-offer commitment) at the specified offer price before offering it to an outsider.

3. The agreement must have been binding at death: that is, you as executor must have been legally obligated to sell the shares to the corporation (or other shareholders) at the price fixed by the agreement.

4. The price as stated in the agreement must be either fixed (e.g., a fixed dollar price or book value on the purchase date) or determinable according to the formula in the agreement.

Obviously, the IRS will closely scrutinize a buy/sell agreement between family members to determine whether it is a bona fide arm's-length business agreement (in which case the price in the agreement will usually be accepted) or a device to pass the decedent's shares to the natural objects of his bounty for less than adequate consideration (in which case the IRS will probably disregard the price specified in the agreement).

Lowest Value Not Always Best

While the federal estate tax is based on the value of the property interest in the decedent's estate, as executor you should remember that the lowest possible valuation of an asset is not always a proper objective. One example is the estimation of the value of a business interest. A buy/sell agreement which provides a higher price per share will result in more cash for the estate than a formula resulting in a lower price.

Secondly, the additional tax payable due to the increased valuation of closely held stock may be more than offset by the advantages of qualifying for a Section 303 stock redemption or a Section 6166 election to pay federal estate taxes attributable to the business interest in up to ten installments (see Chapter 25). To qualify for either of these favorable elections, the value of the business interest must *exceed* 35 percent of the value of the gross estate after certain adjustments.

Third, and most important, you must be aware not only of the estate tax implications of your actions but also of the income tax results. If the asset in question is likely to be sold shortly after the decedent's death, a higher estate tax valuation can lead to a lower income tax gain in the future. This is due to the "step-up-in-basis" rules, whereby most property included in a decedent's estate acquires a new basis (cost) for income tax purposes. This new basis is the fair market value of the property at the date of the decedent's death (or the applicable alternate valuation date). The higher the estate tax value, the higher the income tax basis. Then, because the beneficiary's basis (cost) is high, there will be a lower income tax liability when the property is later sold by the beneficiary. For example, assume a decedent owned stock traded on a national exchange. If that stock was worth $100 a share when purchased and $1,000 a share on the date of his death, its new basis would be $1,000 in the hands of the estate or its beneficiaries. If the stock were later sold for $1,001, there would be a $1 long-term capital gain, and the tax payable would be negligible. The point is you should be aggressive—but only after you have decided what your objective is. A higher value (especially if there will be an unlimited estate tax marital deduction) may be better than a lower value.

SUMMARY

Valuation is a complex and often uncertain process. But there are ground rules. The general rule governing all estate tax valuation is that property is valued at its fair market value, the price at which the property would change hands between a hypothetical willing buyer and a willing seller, neither being under any compulsion to buy or to sell and both having reasonable knowledge of the relevant facts. Assets are valued as of the date of death or the applicable alternate valuation date. Real property, because of its uniqueness, is valued according to the various factors that would be considered by a hypothetical buyer and seller. Certain farm and certain business real property can be valued at less than their "highest and best" use. They can be valued according to their "special" use, which can be significantly below their normal value. Life insurance is includable in the estate of the insured for federal estate tax purposes if it is payable to or for the benefit of the estate of the insured or if the decedent/

insured held incidents of ownership (e.g., the right to change the beneficiary, receive dividends, or cash in the policy) in the policy at the time of his death.

The amount includable is the amount receivable by the beneficiary. If the decedent owned a policy on the life of someone else, different rules apply. U.S. government bonds are typically valued at their redemption price. Flower bonds (Treasury bonds redeemable by the government in payment of federal estate taxes) are valued at their market price or par value, whichever is higher. Household goods are valued according to the willing buyer/willing seller rule; a room-by-room itemization (with a qualified independent appraiser) is recommended. Listed stocks are typically valued on the mean between the highest and lowest quoted selling price on the valuation date. Corporate bonds are similarly valued. Stocks of closely held corporations are valued according to a multiplicity of factors, and there is no one overriding test or formula.

27

How to Handle
Charitable Bequests

Bequests to charities can sometimes create problems for executors. This chapter will point out the potential problem areas and give you a working knowledge of some of the most common forms of charitable bequests.

Identifying the Charity

Quite often, the decedent's will fails to accurately pinpoint the specific charity that he intended to benefit. General terms, such as "Boy Scouts" or "Methodist Church" or "Temple University's Graduate School," clearly indicate the general intention of the maker of the will to benefit a particular class or group, but still leave much room for interpretation. In the case of a will in which the general intention of the decedent is evident, the courts can apply the doctrine of *cy pres*—namely, they can construe the bequest in accordance with what they consider the general intent of the decedent. So if decedent's will contained a bequest to "our local Boy Scout Chapter to place an additional wing on its lodge in Briar Park," and if Briar Park has since been sold to a real estate developer, the courts can construe the bequest to be a general one to the Boy Scouts of America or to the local Boy Scout chapter.

In any event, whenever a will contains a bequest to a charity, the executor must be certain that the charity can be identified precisely. Payment to the wrong beneficiary, or even the wrong organizational chapter, scout troop, church or synagogue, can lead to legal action against the executor. Therefore, if there is any doubt whatsoever, a formal statement of the executor's interpretation of the identity of the charity should be filed, so that court approval can be given before any money is paid to the charity in question.

Notice Requirements for Charitable Bequests

Because charitable bequests are in the public interest, most states require that the attorney general of the state in which the will is probated be notified that decedent's will contains a gift to charity. This ensures that the charity will have representation in the event the bequest is not paid in full. You should consult local and state laws to make certain that these notice requirements are complied with at every step prescribed by local law in the probate or distribution process.

You should also send written notice to each charitable beneficiary stating the date of the decedent's death and the county where the will has been probated, and stating that it has been named as a beneficiary.

Exemption Certificate

Almost all states provide an exemption from the state inheritance tax for transfers of property to or for the use of religious, charitable, scientific, literary or educational organizations. Some states require you to apply for a certificate of exemption from the state inheritance tax for charitable bequests. Check with counsel before making any charitable distributions.

Gifts for Religious or Charitable Purposes Made Shortly Before Death

A potential problem area is that of the "last-minute charitable gift." A few jurisdictions have laws (called "mortmain" statutes) that invalidate last-minute charitable gifts. The theory behind these laws is that the decedent, being near death, was not acting rationally in leaving his money to charity, or might have been unduly influenced to leave his money to a particular religious charity. The state law attempts to protect the decedent's prior beneficiaries by voiding last-minute charitable gifts. The time involved is often about thirty days; therefore, if decedent's will was executed shortly before his death, gifts to charity should be thoroughly reviewed.

FORM OF THE CHARITABLE BEQUEST

There are different methods by which the decedent can give money to charity under the terms of his will, with varying tax consequences, depending on the form the bequest takes.

Outright Bequests

In the case of an outright gift to charity, such as "I give the sum of $10,000 to Temple University, Philadelphia, Pennsylvania, to be used for the general purposes of the University," then there is no question as to the validity of the bequest, the identity of the recipient, or the fact that this is an outright bequest to charity. Under state and federal death tax laws, the bequest to charity will be tax-exempt (as discussed more fully in Chapter 20), and as long as the executor complies with the notice requirements and the other procedural requirements discussed in this book, payment can be made with no further problems.

Qualified Charities

Contributions to charities—either by will or by some other means of conveyance, such as life insurance—are generally deductible for both federal and state death tax purposes, but only if the charity is "qualified." Qualified charities include:

1. A state, a U.S. possession or political subdivision, or the U.S. government itself.

2. A community chest, corporation, trust, fund or foundation organized or created in the United States, if it is operated exclusively for charitable, religious, educational, scientific or literary purposes, or for the prevention of cruelty to children or animals, or to foster national or international sports competitions. This category includes most schools, colleges, churches and synagogues and many hospitals and medical research organizations.

3. Certain war veterans' organizations.

4. A nonprofit volunteer fire company.

5. Certain other charitable organizations.

Charitable Remainder Interests

The decedent may have kept, for the lifetime of some other individual such as a spouse, the right to use, possess or enjoy property and/or its income. At the same time, the decedent may have given a specified charity the right to the property at the end of that given time. There are four forms such a charitable remainder interest may take. The charity may have been given a remainder interest in

1. a personal residence or farm;

2. the assets of an "annuity" trust;

3. a unitrust; or

4. a pooled income fund.

Each of these forms of charitable gifts is explained below. Note that such gifts often pose questions as to both federal and state death tax valuation, so that the assistance of competent counsel is essential. An immediate deduction is allowed for the present (actuarial) value of the charity's right to (someday) receive the property.

1. Remainder Interest in a Personal Residence or Farm. A typical example of such a bequest is the case of a decedent who has signed a deed transferring a home or farm to a charity subject to the right of the decedent and his spouse to live in the house for the rest of his life. The home need not be the decedent's principal residence, so a vacation home or co-op home can qualify.

2. Charitable Remainder Annuity Trust. This is, for example, an arrangement in which a sum of money, stocks, bonds or other income-producing property has been transferred in trust to the charity, but a specific amount in dollars had to be paid from the trust to the decedent and his spouse each year. At the end of a specified period—or at the death of the donor and his spouse—the property or money in the trust is transferred to the charity. For example, $500,000 may be placed into a trust with $50,000 a year payable to the donor for life and then to the donor's spouse for as long as she lives; then at her death the assets in the trust will pass to a qualified charity.

3. Charitable Remainder Unitrust. Essentially, the unitrust is similar in concept to the annuity trust; income has been retained by the donor and spouse (or other designated beneficiary), but at the end of a given period (or at the death of the income beneficiaries) the principal goes to a designated qualified charity. The difference is that in a unitrust the donor does not receive a guaranteed specific amount of cash each year from the trust. Instead, the income recipients are paid a fixed percentage of the fair market value of the trust's assets—as valued each year. So if assets in the trust grow in value, more income will be paid. The converse is also true. If unitrust assets shrink, annual payments to the income beneficiaries will be lower.

4. Pooled Income Fund. Instead of establishing a personal trust, the decedent may have joined many others in transferring cash or property to an organization which pools their contributions. Each donor would be paid a proportionate share of the income of the fund. The income payment is not fixed in amount and varies with the growth of the pooled funds.

A multiplicity of problems can arise if the estate you are administering includes any of the four charitable gifts described above, and tax counsel is highly recommended.

SUMMARY

The executor's first task with respect to charitable bequests is to identify the appropriate charity. Then you must give proper notice to both the state (usually through the state's attorney general) and the charity itself.

In some cases you must also obtain a certificate exempting the property from state death taxes. Be sure to check state law, if the will was made or revised shortly before the decedent's death, to see if the charity's gift will be voided or reduced.

Outright gifts usually pose no problem. But if the decedent made a remainder interest gift and retained a lifetime right to income for a noncharitable beneficiary, complex problems often arise, and tax counsel should be consulted before any distributions are made or deductions taken.

28

Distribution

Who Is Entitled to Decedent's Property?

After all the assets of the estate have been assembled and made secure and the debts and taxes have been paid, the executor is then in a position to distribute the assets to the beneficiaries. Who gets the property will depend on the terms of decedent's will. If decedent had no will, then distribution will be governed by the intestacy laws of the state of domicile. The Appendix contains a summary of the intestacy statutes of every state. Please note this is for your reference only, and you should ascertain with legal counsel that these laws are in effect and have not been changed at the time you are prepared to make distribution.

If decedent's estate consisted solely of cash and the will left everything to decedent's spouse, who in fact was living at the time of decedent's death, then there is no problem with distribution. Unfortunately, this is not always the case. Beneficiaries can die before receiving their share of the distribution. Property left to a particular individual may have been sold or given away or lost prior to the testator's death. As executor, you must be aware of what problems can arise in making distribution and know how to deal with them before final disposition of the estate's assets.

Property No Longer Owned by Decedent at Death

If the decedent left specific property to a particular beneficiary in his will but sold it or otherwise disposed of it before his death, then that gift to the beneficiary (a gift under a will is called a "legacy" or "devise") is said to have been "adeemed." Ademption, then, means that the property is not available for distribution to the beneficiary named in the will. Assume, for example, decedent had said in his will, "I give and bequeath my 1956 antique Thunderbird automobile to my nephew, JACK." But several years before his death, after making his will, the decedent had sold the Thunderbird. The gift to Jack would be adeemed. That means Jack is not entitled to any other property from the estate in place of the car or its value.

Exceptions to the above rule are possible. If the will specified a gift of "my automobile to my daughter, JANE," the courts could decide—or interpret prior cases to hold —that the decedent did not make a gift of a specific automobile, but of the automobile he owned at his death. Therefore, even though decedent had sold the automobile he owned at the time he made the will, Jane would still be entitled to the one he owned at death. How can the executor determine whether the gift is specific ("my 1956 Thunderbird") or general ("my automobile")? In all cases where doubts arise as to the treatment of a particular bequest, state law must be referred to, and distribution should only be made with the court's approval, or the approval of all interested parties in the estate, so that the executor can be fully protected.

Suppose decedent's will specified a gift of "$5,000 to my son, STEVEN," but six months before decedent died he gave Steven $5,000. In that case, the law in many states would say that the gift to the son under the will was "satisfied" by the gift during decedent's lifetime. The courts could hold that this lifetime gift was an "advance" (the purpose of the law being to secure equality among the children). In this situation, the controlling factor would be decedent's intent when he made the lifetime gift. The executor should therefore have a formal, legal interpretation as to whether in fact the lifetime gift satisfied the bequest in the will. This could be obtained by having the schedule of proposed distribution approved by the court (after you, as executor, have given all beneficiaries written notice and ample opportunity to testify or object), so that any objections can be raised prior to payment of the legacy to the son.

Assets Insufficient to Satisfy a Bequest

Suppose decedent's will left "$5,000 to my daughter, AMY." What happens if assets, after paying administration costs and debts, are insufficient to pay Amy $5,000 and for other gifts and bequests? How can the executor properly apportion decedent's assets if there is not enough to satisfy all of the estate's obligations as well as to distribute all of the bequests in the will?

If there are no assets to satisfy the bequests, or if the assets available are insufficient to satisfy all of the gifts in full, then the gifts or bequests are said to "abate," either entirely or proportionately, according to state law. The executor, therefore, must look to the law of his or her state to determine the order of abatement. This applies when assets are insufficient to pay all claims against the estate as well as to make distribution of the property to the beneficiaries. Each state has its own schedule of priorities. Property bequeathed specifically to decedent's spouse and children usually has top priority. Again, as executor, you must be familiar with the laws of your state and obtain court approval (or at least the approval of *all* interested parties) before making distribution in the above circumstances.

Beneficiary's Death Before Decedent's Death

What happens if a decedent's will includes a bequest of "$5,000 to my daughter, MARY," and Mary dies before her father? In many cases, Mary's estate would not be entitled to the $5,000 she would have received if she had survived her father, unless the will made it clear that Mary did not have to survive in order to receive the money. Mary's bequest would therefore "lapse." However, if the will left "$5,000 to my daughter, MARY, if she survives me, otherwise to her children," then clearly Mary's children would be entitled to the $5,000. Unfortunately, the wording in many wills may not be as clear as in this example, and state law must be consulted and court approval obtained in case of any question about the possible lapsing of a particular bequest.

If the beneficiary cannot be located, and if the executor is not certain whether the beneficiary is alive or dead, then, after a reasonable attempt to locate the beneficiary, court direction should be obtained to properly handle the bequest to that particular individual.

Common Disasters

If a question arises over the order of death of the decedent and of a beneficiary under the will, distribution of the estate can be seriously affected. Many wills contain "common disaster" clauses which are designed to direct the executor, when the order of death is not certain, as to whether the beneficiary or the decedent is presumed to have survived. In other wills, certain "marital deduction" tax clauses might indicate that the spouse of the testator is deemed to survive if the order of death is not clear. Most states have specific statutes dealing with common disasters, and wherever this problem arises the executor must consult the state law, know how to deal with the particular clauses in the will and, whenever in doubt, obtain court approval before making distribution.

Distribution Affecting the Marital Deduction

In Chapter 21 we discussed at length the marital deduction provision of the federal estate tax. When the estate is large enough to be affected by the federal estate tax, the executor should make certain that any distribution of marital property includes only property that would qualify for the marital deduction. Reference should be made to Chapter 21, and, whenever in doubt, the executor should consult with counsel to make sure that the spouse receives only property that can qualify for this particular tax shelter.

Minors or Incompetents

Distribution should never be made directly to a minor or to anyone who the executor feels is suffering from a mental disability. As set forth in detail in Chapter 16, if no guardian or trustee has been appointed to receive the property of an individual suffering a disability because of age or impaired mental health, it is the executor's responsibility to see that someone is appointed to handle the funds of the minor or incompetent before any distribution of the estate's assets is made to that person.

Other Legal Impediments to Distribution

In some cases, bequests to beneficiaries that are otherwise in order can be held by the state of domicile to be improper because they violate state law. For example, in some states beneficiaries to a will can forefeit the right to receive property under it if they have also signed as witnesses. (As a general rule, three persons unrelated to the testator and who are not beneficiaries under the will should sign as witnesses in each other's presence.) Many state laws will not permit anyone causing a person's death to receive property under the decedent's will. Also, in some states, a highly technical "rule against perpetuities" prohibits long-term gifts that will not take effect within twenty-one years of the death of someone who is alive on the date of the gift. For instance, if a will provided that a home in Wildwood was to go to a friend, Marie Chester, but could not be sold by her until fifty years after the death of a certain individual, the gift to Marie may not be valid. In such cases, therefore, the executor must determine how state law will affect the particular situation before making any distribution.

Informal Distribution

Let's assume you are satisfied that none of the problems discussed above exist, that you have handled the administration of the estate in a satisfactory manner, that all outstanding debts and taxes have been paid, and that the beneficiaries are satisfied with your handling of the estate. In that case, a formal accounting and discharge by the court may not be necessary (or may not even be advisable). A great deal of time and effort goes into preparing and filing a formal account and giving the required notice. Filing fees, advertising expenses and legal fees will also raise the cost to the estate. Therefore, in close family situations where everyone is satisfied with the administration of the estate, a "family settlement agreement" can be entered into by all the parties involved. The beneficiaries enter into a written agreement with the executor stating that they have received an account of the income, expenses and property available for distribution in the estate, that a copy of the accounting is attached to the agreement, and that all the beneficiaries agree to the proposed distribution.

Even when questions do arise as to the respective rights of the beneficiaries or the handling of the estate, if all the interested parties (including all the beneficiaries) sign an agreement as to the handling of the estate and the proposed distribution, that agreement will usually be enforced by the courts and can be relied on by the executor.

These family settlement agreements are usually an excellent way to resolve any outstanding questions—the reason being that in most instances such agreements save time, court costs and legal expenses. In most states the executor will file the family settlement agreement, with or without the court's approval of the agreement (depending on the law of the jurisdiction), and the agreement will therefore be on record as a final settlement of the estate.

When all the parties agree to waive a formal accounting in simplified estates or in estates involving close family members, the estate can be settled without ever using the family settlement agreement. The executor supplies the beneficiaries with an informal accounting and obtains their approval of the accounting and their share of the distribution. This is usually accomplished by the executor obtaining a "receipt" from each beneficiary for his or her distributive share of the estate as well as a "release" of the executor from any further liability or obligation to that beneficiary. This simplified "receipt and release" procedure can be used by the executor if no formal accounting is required and if, after a thorough review of this book, the executor is satisfied that there are no outstanding questions to be resolved.

Small Estates

Most jurisdictions provide for the settling of small estates without a formal accounting. For example, a state statute might provide that if the estate of the decedent does not exceed $10,000, exclusive of real estate, wages and salaries, a petition may be filed with the court, with an accounting attached, asking the court to approve the petition, order distribution in accordance with its terms, and discharge the personal representative of further responsibility. The court will usually require that notice be given to all parties in interest, including beneficiaries and creditors, of the filing of the petition and its contents. Because of the savings in time, court costs and expenses, the executor should take advantage of the provisions of his or her state law, and use this procedure if the estate qualifies as a "small estate."

Accounting

Perhaps the executor's single most important duty is the filing of a formal accounting with the court. This means preparing financial statements that will give the court, the beneficiaries and everyone in the estate a clear picture of the property in the estate available for distribution, as well as presenting a history of all the transactions involving the estate's assets and dating back to the time the personal representative first took control of the property. The accounting is, at the same time, a balance sheet, a record of income and expenses, and a vehicle for tracing the history of the original assets left by the decedent and any changes in their form or value during the period of the estate's administration.

The accounting is prepared and filed at the conclusion of the administration of the estate. It forms the basis for the court's order to approve the accounting, direct distribution of the assets, and discharge the executor from his duties and liabilities, and it relieves the requirement of any bond, if one has been filed. If for any reason the executor chooses not to file a formal accounting, then a beneficiary or other interested party in the estate may ask the court having jurisdiction over the estate to require the executor to file the account.

Time, Place and Notice Requirements

The account is usually filed at the end of administration of the estate, unless required earlier by the court upon request by an interested party. For example, if a beneficiary feels that the executor is unduly delaying the administration of the estate or has improperly handled the estate's funds, that beneficiary may request the court to demand that the executor file an account at that time, so that any improprieties can be immediately brought to the court's attention.

State and local laws must be reviewed thoroughly before the preparation of the accounting to determine the form, notice and advertising requirements. State laws usually require that creditors, beneficiaries and other interested parties be given sufficient notice (each state or county has rules that provide how much notice must be given) of the time and filing of the account and the court in which the account will be filed. This is to give the parties an opportunity to present any objections they might have to the accounting at the time it is handed up for audit (i.e., review and approval by the court). At the time of the audit the executor must usually furnish proof to the court that notice to all interested parties was in fact given. Absent such notice, it is always possible that an interested party will later challenge the executor's handling of the estate. Local courts often require that the filing be advertised in local newspapers, so that anyone interested in the estate who is not given specific notice by the executor can appear at the time and place of audit and present any objections that he or she might have.

FORM OF THE ACCOUNTING

The form of account to be used will depend on the form of account prescribed by the local rules of court in the jurisdiction in which your estate is probated. The Appendix includes the model form approved by the Pennsylvania Supreme Court. This form is acceptable in all counties throughout Pennsylvania, but local modifications may also be used. It is presented solely as a guide. You must use the form prescribed by your state's local rules of court. Sample forms are usually available at the courthouse in the county where the decedent lived, or are included in the local rules of the court having jurisdiction over these matters. In most cases, because of the complexity of the account, its contents should be reviewed (and preferably prepared) by counsel and/or by an accountant.

AUDIT

Audit procedures vary considerably with local court custom and state law and must be consulted by the executor or counsel. In general, the purpose of the audit is to have the formal accounting approved by the court, and to prove to the court that anyone with an objection to the account will have the opportunity to be heard. Notice requirements and advertising procedures therefore must be strictly complied with. In many jurisdictions, the court itself will publish the legal advertisement of the audit. Anyone who has objections to the accounting can present them in person at the audit, by notice to the court before the audit or within a prescribed period after the audit date, or else in compliance with any other pertinent rule by the appropriate court. The court might choose to hear the objections at the audit date, or schedule a subsequent hearing date at which all interested parties can present their respective positions to the court for its final adjudication.

Depending on local custom, the executor might prepare a proposed schedule of distribution to be presented on the audit date, or prepare one by direction of the court after the accounting has been approved. In any event, and regardless of the particular format employed by the court, approval of the audit will be accompanied or followed by an approved schedule of distribution.

Receipt and Satisfaction of Awards

Following the court's approval of the accounting and distribution, you should wait until the time has elapsed for appealing the "adjudication" (the court's formalized approval of the accounting and distribution). The time will vary from state to state but typically will not exceed three months. Thereafter you are in a position to deliver the property in question to the beneficiaries in accordance with the court's adjudication, obtain a receipt from each beneficiary for the property transferred and take the necessary steps to have any bond terminated. Then—*and not until then*—you will be relieved of all liability and responsibility for your administration of the decedent's estate.

SUMMARY

After the estate's assets have been assembled and debts and taxes paid, the executor can distribute the estate to the beneficiaries. Problems arise when property bequeathed to an individual is no longer in existence, and when assets are insufficient to pay all creditors and satisfy all legacies. Beneficiaries can predecease the decedent, or the decedent and beneficiary can die at the same time. Special care should be taken when minors or incompetents are involved, and the executor should be familiar with legal impediments to distribution.

The executor can utilize several forms of distribution without having to file a formal account. If all interested parties agree, a family settlement agreement can be entered into. In simplified cases, the executor can make distribution by "receipt and release." Most jurisdictions allow the settling of small estates without a formal accounting, and if few assets are involved the executor should take advantage of these simplified and less costly procedures.

When a formal accounting is indicated, state and local laws must be complied with. Creditors, beneficiaries and other interested parties must be given advance notice of the filing of the account and the time and place of the audit. The audit permits any beneficiaries and creditors with objections to the account to be heard by the court before the account is approved. After formal approval a schedule of distribution is prepared, and the executor is then in a position to deliver the property to any beneficiary in exchange for a receipt, to have any bond terminated, and to be formally relieved of responsibility for the administration of the estate.

29

Anatomical Gifts:
Uncomfortable Conversations

Why Talk About It?

If death and dying are uncomfortable topics, body gifts are even more threatening and less easily discussed.

One way or another, the issue must be faced. If a person wants to make an anatomical gift, he or she should know how to do it. Conversely, anyone who is strongly against a gift of one or more organs after death should be protected from violation of his or her desires by others.

What Is It?

The *Uniform Anatomical Gifts Act* has been enacted in whole or in part in every state and in the District of Columbia. Its purpose is to encourage various types of organ donations and to avoid inconsistency among the various jurisdictions.

The UAGA provides that any person over eighteen may donate his or her entire body or any one or more of its parts. The donation can be made to any hospital, surgeon, physician, medical or dental school, or various organ banks or storage facilities. Organ gifts can be made for education, research, therapy or transplants. These gifts become effective at death and can be made by will. The act also provides that no body or organ gift may be made if there is an express objection to such a gift either by will or in some other document.

How Does It Work?

There are two ways a gift can be made under the UAGA. One is for the donor to designate a specific individual to receive the gift. For instance, a person might specify that one eye be given to a blind sister. A hierarchy of donees can be established, and various body parts can be specified to go to certain donees.

A second way is by granting persons other than the decedent the power to make the gift. In other words, a family member can donate a person's body or organs.

Absent any evidence that the decedent did not want to make an anatomical gift, his or her (1) spouse, (2) adult children, (3) parents, or (4) siblings can make a donation. The UAGA uses this priority system for relatives of the deceased, starting with the spouse and moving down from closest to most distant relatives, who can make—or refuse to allow—anatomical gifts.

The gifts can be made by these third parties unless (1) there is actual knowledge that the decedent would not want to make an anatomical gift, or (2) someone in the same or higher "class" opposes the gift. Donations can be authorized by third parties either before or after an individual's death. Obviously, because of the possibility that an ill-intentioned relative would use anatomical gifts to obtain postmortem revenge, a person's intention regarding such gifts should be clearly specified one way or the other.

What Are the Requirements?

The UAGA requires that gifts be made in writing by the donor and attested by at least two witnesses. The donor must be of sound mind at the time of the writing (although there is no procedure for proving legal capacity in a manner similar to that used in probate). There is no requirement that the will or other documents be delivered by the donor to make the gift valid. When gifts are made by family members, a written document is not a legal requirement, and a telegram, tape recording or taped telephone conversation may satisfy statutory formalities.

Many states provide for the making of anatomical gifts through a notice on a driver's license. But many authorities feel that, because of the wide variety of forms the gift may take and the potential for problems with regard to revoking gifts made in such a way, it is better to either make or object to an anatomical gift through a document other than a driver's license.

When Is the Donor Dead?

The Uniform Anatomical Gifts Act gives no specific definition of death. Most states define death as a "total and irreversible loss of brain function" and require the opinion of at least two physicians to that effect. The UAGA forbids the physicians who certify death (and all members of the medical team involved) to participate in any organ removal or transplant procedure.

If only a part of the body is donated, after that part is removed the surviving spouse or next of kin or other person responsible for the burial must make final disposition of the body.

How to Meet a Decedent's Wishes

A person's wishes should be honored. A traditional funeral service is possible in most cases (check with local clergy) even if an entire body is left for medical research. This will alleviate much of the anxiety regarding anatomical gifts. You might also point out that the anatomical gift is a "post-self" device, a way to continue to have meaning beyond the event of one's physical death.

Documents meeting the requirements of the Uniform Anatomical Gifts Act should be prepared separately and apart from the will. A codicil to the decedent's will can state his intentions regarding anatomical gifts in a way that does not disclose the other provisions of the will. If at all possible, a person should designate a specific donee, such as a family member or medical institution (and there should be "backup" donees in case the primary one can't or won't accept the gift).

Objections to an Anatomical Donation

If a client does not want a gift of body parts to be made, such desires should be clearly and strongly expressed. A "non-consent" document should have been prepared, and as executor you should check the will. Some wills provide that any bequests made to an individual who consents to an anatomical gift will be void.

The discussion of anatomical gifts is one more facet of the uncomfortable—but highly important—non-tax aspects of estate planning. It's part of the process by which the executor must learn not only to face facts but also to face a face.

The Mechanics of Making an Anatomical Gift

A potential donor or donor's representative should contact the prospective donee with respect to specific requirements for the gift. The form that follows has been prepared by the Real Property, Probate and Trust Law Section of the ABA.

STATEMENT REGARDING ANATOMICAL GIFTS

I, _____ of _____, _____ make the following statement regarding anatomical gifts which I have checked and initialed:

SPECIFIC GIFTS

ENTIRE BODY

☐ I give my entire body, for purposes of anatomical study, to _____.
If, for any reason, _____ does not accept this gift, I give my body to _____, for purposes of anatomical study.

GIFTS TO INDIVIDUALS

☐ I give my _____ to _____, if needed by him or her for
        (part or parts)
purposes of transplantation or therapy.

☐ I give my _____ to _____, if needed by him or her for
        (part or parts)
purposes of transplantation or therapy.

GIFTS TO INSTITUTIONS AND PHYSICIANS

☐ I give my _____ to _____,
        (part or parts)   (name of hospital, bank, storage facility, or physician)
for purposes of research, advancement of science, therapy, or transplantation.

☐ I give my _____ to _____,
        (part or parts)   (name of hospital, bank, storage facility, or physician)
for purposes of research, advancement of science, therapy, or transplantation.

PROSTHETIC DEVICES

☐ I give my _____ to _____ for critical
          (type of prosthetic device)   (name of hospital)

evaluation, study, and research.

INTENTION

☐ If any anatomical gift cannot be effectuated because of the donee's non-existence, inability, or unwillingness to accept it, I request that one of the authorized persons make anatomical donations in a manner consistent with my desires expressed in this statement.

☐ I express my desire not to make anatomical gifts under any circumstances. It is my wish that no part be used for transplantation, therapy, study, or research. I request that my personal representative and next of kin respect my wishes.

THIS STATEMENT INCORPORATES ALL OF THE PROVISIONS ON THE REVERSE OF IT.

Signed this ____ day of _____, 19___, at _____.

_____

_____   _____
             Witness   Witness

PRIORITY OF DONATION

A gift of any part to an individual recipient for therapy or transplantation shall take precedence over a gift of that part to any other donee.

INSTRUCTIONS

If I have made any written instructions regarding the burial, cremation or other disposition of my body, I direct that any donee take possession of my body subject to those instructions, if that donee has actual knowledge of those instructions. If there is any conflict between the statements made in this document and any of those instructions, my wishes regarding anatomical gifts shall be given preference over my instructions regarding the disposition of my body.

COUNTERPARTS

I may be signing more that one statement regarding anatomical gifts. I intend that only signed documents be effective and that no person shall give any effect to any photocopy or other reproduction of a signed document.

DEFINITIONS

The terms "bank or storage facility," "hospital," "part," and "physician" have the same meaning which the Uniform Anatomical Gifts Act accords to them. The term "authorized persons" means the persons authorized to make donations under the Uniform Anatomical Gifts Act in the order or priority provided in that Act.

WARNING

This form is designed to be used with the advice of an attorney. It has been drafted in accordance with the provisions of the Uniform Anatomical Gifts Act. Because the law regarding anatomical gifts may vary in each state, attorneys advising on use of this form should be familiar with the law of the relevant jurisdiction.

[This form has been adapted from that of the Real Property, Probate and Trust Law Section of the American Bar Association.]

Glossary

Accidental Death Benefits. The accidental death, or "double indemnity," feature of a life insurance policy will provide a larger additional benefit, often twice the face amount of the policy, if death occurs by accidental means. Insurance policies should be reviewed for this feature when death occurs from other than natural causes.

Accounting. The preparation of financial statements that will give the court, the beneficiaries and everyone involved in the estate a clear picture of the property in the estate available for distribution, and a history of the transactions dating back to the time the personal representative first took control of the property.

Ademption. The extinction or withdrawal of a legacy by disposing of or otherwise preventing a beneficiary from receiving a bequest under a will.

Adjudication. The court's formal approval of the accounting and distribution.

Administration. The management of the estate of a deceased person. It includes collecting the assets, paying the debts and taxes and making distribution to the persons entitled to the decedent's property.

Administrator *(m)*, **Administratrix** *(f)*. The person appointed to manage the estate of a deceased person if the decedent had no valid will or if the will did not provide for an executor or executrix to settle the decedent's estate.

Advancement. Money or property given by a parent to a child or other heir (depending on the state law), or expended by the former for the latter's benefit, by way of anticipation of the share which the child will inherit in the parent's estate and intended to be deducted therefrom.

After-born Child. A child born after the execution of a parent's will.

Alternate Value Date. For federal estate tax purposes, the value of the gross estate six months after the date of death, unless property is distributed, sold, exchanged or otherwise disposed of within six months. In that case, the value of such property is determined as of the date of disposition.

Annual Exclusion. For federal gift tax purposes, an exclusion of $10,000 is allowed the donor each year, provided the gift is a present interest in property (the donee must be given the unfettered, ascertainable and immediate right to use, possession or enjoyment of the property interest).

Attestation Clause. The paragraph at the end of a will indicating by certain persons' signatures that they have heard the testator (testatrix) declare the instrument to be his (her) will and have witnessed the signing of the will.

Audit. The proceeding at which the court approves the executor's account and gives anyone with objections to the account the opportunity to be heard.

Beneficiary. The person who inherits a share or part of the decedent's estate. One who receives a beneficial interest under a trust or insurance policy is also called a beneficiary.

Bequest. A gift of property by will. A specific bequest is a gift of specified property ("my watch" or "automobile"). A general bequest is one that may be satisfied from the general assets of the estate ("I give $100 to my brother, Sam"). If the specific bequest (the watch) was sold before the decedent died, the gift will fail.

Buy/Sell Agreement. A buy/sell agreement, or business agreement, is an arrangement for the disposition of a business interest in the event of the owner's death, disability or retirement or upon the owner's withdrawal from the business at some earlier time. Business purchase agreements take various forms: (1) an agreement between the business itself and the individual owners (a stock redemption agreement); (2) an agreement between the individual owners (cross-purchase agreement); and (3) an agreement between the individual owners and a key person, family member or outside individual (a third-party business buy/out agreement).

Charitable Remainder Annuity Trust. A trust that permits payment of a fixed amount annually to a noncharitable beneficiary, with the remainder going to charity.

Charitable Remainder Unitrust. A trust designed to permit payment of a periodic sum to a noncharitable beneficiary, with the remainder going to charity.

Codicil. A supplement to an existing will to effect some revision, change or modification of that will. A codicil must meet the same requirements regarding execution and validity as a will.

Collateral Relations. A phrase used primarily in the law of intestacy to designate uncles and aunts, cousins, etc.—relatives not in a direct ascending or descending line, like grandparents or grandchildren, who are designated as lineal relatives.

Common Disaster. An accident that results in the death of both the decedent and the intended beneficiary.

Community Property. Property acquired during marriage in which both husband and wife have an undivided one-half interest. Not more than half can be disposed of by the will. In some community property states the husband can control and dispose of community property during marriage. There are currently eight community property states: Arizona, California, Idaho, Louisiana, Nevada, New Mexico, Texas and Washington.

Contingent Interest. A future interest in real or personal property that depends on the fulfillment of a stated condition that may never come into existence.

Contingent Remainder. A future interest in property dependent on the fulfillment of a stated condition before the termination of a prior estate. For example, a husband leaves property to a bank in trust to pay the income to his wife during her lifetime. After her death, the trustee is to transfer the property to decedent's son if the son is then living; otherwise, to his daughter. The son has a contingent remainder interest—contingent upon his outliving his mother. The daughter has a contingent remainder interest which she will only receive if the son does not outlive the mother.

Corpus. A term used to describe the principal or trust estate as distinguished from the income. When we speak of the corpus of a trust, we are talking about the assets in the trust.

Credit Estate Tax. A tax imposed by a state to take full advantage of the amount allowed as a credit against the federal estate tax.

Curtesy. At common law, the estate by which a man was entitled to a life estate in all lands owned by his wife during marriage, provided lawful issue was born of the union. As with dower, modern-day statutes have in many cases repealed or modified common law curtesy.

Decedent. The person who died (whether man or woman).

Descent. The passing of real estate to the heirs of one who dies without a will.

Devise. A gift of real estate under a will, as distinguished from a gift of personal property.

Devisee. The person to whom lands or other real property are devised or given by will.

Disclaimer. The refusal to accept property that has been devised or bequeathed—a renunciation by the beneficiary of his or her right to receive the property in question.

Distribution. The passing of personal property to the heirs of one who dies without a will. Also, the formal act of the personal representative disposing of the estate's assets to the designated beneficiaries.

Domicile. An individual's permanent home. The place to which, regardless of where he or she is living, an individual intends to return.

Donee. The person who receives a gift. Also one who is the recipient of the power of appointment from another person.

Donor. One who makes a gift. Also, a person who gives a power of appointment to another person.

Dower. The right which the law gives a woman in her deceased husband's real estate.

Escheat. In the absence of lawful heirs, and subject to the claims of creditors, the property of a person dying intestate is said to escheat, that is, to "return" to the state.

Estate Tax. A tax imposed on the right of a person to transfer property at death. The tax is imposed not only by the federal government but also by various states.

Executor *(m)*, **Executrix** *(f)*. The person named by the deceased in his or her will to manage the decedent's affairs; the personal representative of the decedent who stands in the shoes of the decedent, collects the assets of the estate, pays the debts and taxes, and makes distribution of the remaining property to the beneficiaries or heirs.

Fair Market Value. The value at which estate property is included in the gross estate for federal estate tax purposes; the price at which property would change hands between a willing buyer and a willing seller, neither being under compulsion to buy or sell and both having knowledge of the relevant facts.

Family Exemption Laws. Laws giving surviving family members of decedent's household specific exemptions from state death taxes.

Federal Estate Tax. An excise tax levied on the right to transfer property at death, imposed on and measured by the value of the estate left by the deceased.

Fiduciary. One occupying a position of trust. Executors, administrators, trustees and guardians all stand in a fiduciary relationship to persons whose affairs they are handling.

Flower Bonds. Certain U.S. Treasury obligations (traditionally traded at a discount) that are owned by a decedent at death and can be redeemed at par value (plus accrued interest) in payment of federal estate taxes. They are called flower bonds because they "blossom" at death and, while purchased at a discount, can be redeemed at their full par value in payment of federal estate taxes.

Gift Tax. A tax imposed on the lifetime gratuitous transfer of property. In addition to the federal gift tax, some states also impose a tax on transfers during lifetime.

Gift Tax Exclusion (for federal gift tax purposes). Anyone, married or single, can give up to $10,000 in cash or other property each year to any number of persons (whether or not they are related to the donor) with no gift tax liability. The exclusion is doubled to $20,000 in the case of a married donor whose spouse consents to "splitting" the gift.

Grace Period. A provision in life insurance policies which gives the insured additional time (usually thirty days) in which to pay the premium without losing the benefits of the policy.

Grantor. A person who creates a trust; also called a settlor, creator, donor or trustor.

Gross Estate. An amount determined by totaling the value of all property in which the decedent had an interest, the inclusion of which in the estate is required by the Internal Revenue Code for federal estate tax purposes.

Guardian. There are two classes of guardians: (1) A guardian of the person is appointed by the surviving spouse in his or her will to take care of the personal affairs of the couple's minor children. Since each parent is the natural guardian of the minor children, only the surviving parent can name the guardian of the person. (2) A guardian of the property of a minor or incompetent is a person or institution appointed or named to represent the interests of a minor child or incompetent adult. A guardian of property can be named in a will or is appointed by a court.

Guardian Ad Litem. A lawyer or other qualified individual appointed by the court to represent the interests of minors or incompetents in a particular matter before the court.

Heir. A person designated by law to succeed to the estate of a person who dies intestate (without a will).

Holographic Will. A will entirely in the handwriting of the testator. In many states, such a will is not recognized unless it is published, declared and witnessed as required by statute for other written wills.

Homestead Exemption Laws. Laws passed in many states allowing the head of a family to designate a house and land as his or her homestead to exempt it from debts and taxes.

Incompetent. An individual who has been legally found incapable of managing his or her own affairs.

Incontestable Clause. A provision in life insurance policies which prevents the insurance company from denying a claim because of any error, concealment or misstatement after the contestable period has expired (usually two years).

Inheritance Tax. A tax levied on the rights of the heirs to receive property from a deceased person, measured by the share passing to each beneficiary (sometimes called a succession tax). The federal death tax is an estate (as opposed to an inheritance) tax. Some states have estate taxes but most have inheritance taxes.

Installment Payments of Estate Tax Under Section 6166. Section 6166 of the Internal Revenue Code provides for the payment of federal estate tax in installments in certain cases in which the deceased had an interest in a closely held business that represented a considerable part of his estate. Under present law, to receive special tax treatment under 6166, the value of the business interest must comprise more than 35% of the adjusted gross estate.

Insurance Trust. A trust composed partly or wholly of life insurance policy contracts.

Intangible Property. Property that does not have physical substance. The item itself is only the evidence of value (for example, a certificate of stock or bond, an insurance policy).

Inter Vivos Trust. A trust created during the grantor's lifetime and operative during lifetime, as opposed to a trust under a will, called a testamentary trust, which does not go into effect until after the grantor dies.

Intestacy Laws. Individual state laws that provide for distribution of property of a person who has died without leaving a valid will.

Intestate. Without a will. A person who dies without a valid will dies intestate.

Inventory. A schedule of all the assets of an estate, to be prepared by the personal representative.

Irrevocable Trust. A trust that cannot be revoked or terminated by the grantor. To qualify the trust as irrevocable for tax purposes, the grantor cannot retain any right to alter, amend, revoke or terminate. The trust can be revoked or terminated by the grantor only with the consent of someone who has an adverse interest in the trust.

Issue. All persons descending from a common ancestor.

Joint Tenancy. The holding of property by two persons in such a way that, on the death of either, the property goes to the survivor. If the persons are husband and wife, then the property is said to be held "by the entireties." This is contrasted to tenancy in common, in which each of the owners has an undivided interest which upon the death of one is passed by probate.

Joint Will. A single instrument that is made the will of two or more persons and is jointly signed by them.

Lapse. The failure of a testamentary gift due to the death of the recipient during the life of the testator (the person who made the will).

Legacy. Technically a gift of personal property by will, but in practice including any disposition by will.

Legatee. A person to whom a legacy is given.

Letters of Administration. A written document issued to the administrator or administratrix (if no will) or to the executor named in a will authorizing him to act as such. After the will is probated or is taken to the appropriate office for formal approval (Register of Wills, Probate, Orphans' or Surrogate Court) the letters of administration (no will) or letters testamentary (will) are granted. They serve as official recognition that the administrator or administratrix or the executor or executrix has the right to take any action that the deceased would have taken in regard to handling and disposing of the decedent's property.

Life Estate. The title of the interest owned by a life tenant; a person whose interest in property terminates at his or her death.

Life Tenant. The person who receives the income from a legal life estate or from a trust fund during his or her own life. This right terminates at death.

Liquid Assets. Cash, or assets which can be readily converted into cash without any serious loss (bank accounts, life insurance proceeds, government bonds).

Literary Executor. A term sometimes used in the will of an author to designate a person authorized by the will to assemble unpublished works of the deceased, and to try to have those works published which the literary executor thinks appropriate, discarding the remainder. Technically, a person designated as literary executor is probably more like the possessor or donee of a power of appointment, and, as such, should be subordinate to the executor of the estate in any matters not dealing directly with the literary material.

Living Will. A living will is a written expression of an individual's desire that no extraordinary means be employed to prolong his or her life. Living wills are legal in some states. In other states, where the living will itself has no legal effect, it can be of help to physicians by enabling them to know of a patient's wishes.

Marital Deduction. For federal estate tax purposes, the portion of a decedent spouse's estate that may be passed to the surviving spouse without its becoming subject to the federal estate tax levied against the decedent spouse's estate. Under present federal estate tax law, the marital deduction is unlimited, provided that the property passes to the surviving spouse in a qualified manner.

Marital Trust. A trust set up to take advantage of the marital deduction provisions of the federal estate tax. It can take the form of a Q.T.I.P. trust or a general power of appointment trust (defined elsewhere in this glossary). The trust property that will pass outside the marital trust will be in a "nonmarital" or residual trust. Typically, the beneficiaries of the nonmarital trust will be the children of the spouse setting up the trust. Assets in the marital trust are taxed when the surviving spouse dies, while assets in the nonmarital trust are not in the surviving spouse's estate and therefore are not taxed when the spouse dies.

"Ministerial" Acts. Acts of an executor or administrator which do not involve major decisions requiring judgment and discretion and whose performance may be delegated to others.

Minor. A person who is under the legal age of majority, which can vary from age eighteen to twenty-one depending on the state law.

Mutual Wills. The separate wills of two or more persons, with reciprocal provisions in each will in favor of the other person(s).

Nonliquid Assets. Assets that are not readily convertible into cash for at least nine months without a serious loss (such as real estate and business interests).

Nonprobate Property. Property that passes outside the administration of the estate, other than by will or intestacy laws (for example, jointly held property, pension proceeds and life insurance proceeds paid to a named beneficiary, or property in an inter vivos trust).

Nuncupative Will. An oral will, declared by the testator in his last sickness before a sufficient number of witnesses, and afterward reduced to writing.

Per Capita. Equally to each individual. In distribution per capita, the takers share equally without a right of representation. For example, each of five sons would take one fifth of the estate. In most states, if descendants are related in equal degree to the decedent, they take per capita; if descendants are of unequal degree (such as four sons and a child of a deceased son), a per stirpes distribution is made (see Per Stirpes below).

Per Stirpes. "By stock." A distribution per stirpes occurs when issue succeed to the shares of their lineal ascendants by representation. For example, if a person dies survived by three children and by two children of a deceased child (the decedent's grandchildren), distribution would be per stirpes. The two grandchildren would succeed to their deceased parent's share, so that one quarter of the estate would go to each of the surviving children, and one eighth to each of the two grandchildren.

Posthumous Child. A child born after the death of his or her father.

Pourover. The transfer of property from an estate or trust to another estate or trust upon the occurrence of an event specified in the instrument. For example, a will can provide that certain property be paid (poured over) to an existing trust. This is called a pourover will.

Power of Appointment. A right given to a person to dispose of property that he or she does not fully own. There are two types of powers of appointment. A general power of appointment is a power over the distribution of property exercisable in favor of any person the donee of the power may select, including himself, his estate, his creditors or the creditors of his estate. A limited power of appointment is the power granted to a donee that is limited in scope. This is sometimes called a special power. An example of a limited power would be giving the donee of the power the right to distribute the property at his death to any of his sister's children that he designates.

Power of Attorney. A written document which enables an individual, or "principal," to designate another person or persons as his or her "attorney in fact," that is, to act on the principal's behalf. The scope of the power can be severely limited or quite broad.

Present Interest. A present right to use or enjoy property.

Pretermitted Heir. A child or other descendant omitted from testator's will. When a testator fails to make provisions for a child, either living at execution of the will or born thereafter, statutes often provide that such child, or the issue of a deceased child, take an intestate share of testator's estate.

Principal. The property comprising the estate or fund that has been set aside in trust, or from which income has been expected to accrue. The trust principal is also known as the trust corpus or res.

Probate. The process of proving the validity of the will and executing its provisions under the guidance of the appropriate public official. The title of the official varies from state to state. Wills are probated in the Register of Wills office and in the Probate or Surrogate Court. When a person dies the will must be filed before the proper officer, and this is called filing the will for probate. When it has been filed and accepted, it is said to be "admitted to probate." The process of probating the will involves recognition by the court of the executor named in the will (or appointment of an administrator if none has been named).

Probate Property. Property that can be passed under the terms of the will or (if no will) under the intestacy laws of the state. Also, property held in the individual name of the decedent or in which the decedent had a divisible interest.

Prudent Man Theory. The theory according to which the duty of an executor is to invest in such assets as an ordinary, prudent man of intelligence and integrity would purchase in the exercise of reasonable care, judgment and diligence under the circumstances existing at the time of purchase.

Publication. A declaration by the testator to the witnesses that the instrument is his will.

Q.T.I.P. Trust (qualified terminable interest property trust). A trust that can qualify for the marital deduction under current tax laws, even though under the trust a spouse is given the income of the trust for life. Assets at death pass to the beneficiaries named by the spouse who set up the trust. Under prior law, only a trust in which the spouse had a general power of appointment over the trust property would have qualified for the marital deduction. This type of trust is called a general power of appointment trust.

Receipt and Release. Informal method of settling estates. The executor gives the beneficiaries an informal accounting and obtains a "receipt" from the beneficiaries for their share of the estate and a "release" discharging the executor from any further liability to the beneficiaries.

Reinstatement. A privilege contained in life insurance policies which enables the insured to reinstate the policy when it has lapsed for nonpayment.

Residuary Estate. The remaining part of the decedent's estate after payment of debts and bequests. Wills usually contain a clause disposing of the residue of the estate that the decedent has not otherwise bequeathed or devised.

Reversionary Interest. A right to future enjoyment by the transferor of property that is now in the possession or enjoyment of another party. For example, a son creates a trust under which his father is going to enjoy the income for life, with the principal of the trust to be paid over to the son at his father's death. The son's interest is the reversionary interest.

Revocable Trust. A trust that can be changed or terminated during the grantor's lifetime and under which the property in the trust can be recovered by him.

Rule Against Perpetuities. A rule of law invalidating interests in property which will vest in the recipient too far in the future, or by which the devisee is restricted in disposing of the property for an inordinate length of time. The common-law rule, which has been changed in many states, holds that "no interest in property is valid unless it must vest, if at all, within a life or lives in being plus twenty-one years."

Rule Against Unreasonable Accumulation of Income. A state law which imposes restrictions upon trusts or other devices to prevent the withholding of the present enjoyment of income from the life tenant to the enhancement of the trust estate.

Section 303 Redemption. Section 303 of the Internal Revenue Code establishes a way for a corporation to make a distribution in redemption of a portion of the stock of a decedent that will not be taxed as a dividend. A Section 303 partial redemption can provide cash and/or other property from the corporation without resulting in dividend treatment and provides cash for the decedent, shareholders or executor to use to pay death taxes and other expenses.

Short-Term Trust (also known as a Clifford trust). An irrevocable trust running for a period of at least ten years and one day or the life of the beneficiary, whichever is shorter, in which the income is payable to a person other than the grantor and established under the provisions of the Internal Revenue Code. The income is taxable to the trust or to the income beneficiary and not to the grantor. The agreement may provide that on the date fixed for termination of the trust, or on the prior death of the beneficiary, the assets of the trust shall be returned to the grantor.

Shrinkage. The reduction in the amount of property that passes at death caused by loss of capital and income resulting from the sale of assets to pay death costs.

Sole Ownership. The holding of a property by one person in such a manner that upon death it passes either by the terms of the will or (if no will) according to the intestacy law.

Sprinkling or **Spray Trust.** A trust under which the trustee is given discretionary power to distribute any part or all of the income among beneficiaries in equal or unequal shares, and authority to accumulate any income not distributed.

Tangible Property. Property that has physical substance—may be touched, seen or felt—and itself has value (such as a house, a car or furniture).

Taxable Estate. An amount determined by subtracting the allowable deductions from the gross estate.

Tenancy by the Entireties. The holding of property by husband and wife in such a manner that, except with the consent of the other, neither husband nor wife has a disposable interest in the property during the lifetime of the other. Upon the death of either, the property goes to the survivor.

Tenancy in Common. The holding of property by two or more persons in such a manner that each has an undivided interest which, upon the death of one, is passed by probate. It does not pass to the surviving tenant in common.

Testamentary. By will. A testamentary document is an instrument disposing of property at death, being either a will in fact or in the nature of a will.

Testamentary Trust. A trust of certain property passing under a will and created by the terms of the will.

Testate. Having left a will or disposed of by will.

Testator. A person who leaves a will in force at death.

Trust. A fiduciary arrangement whereby the legal title of the property is held, and the property managed, by a person or institution for the benefit of another.

Trustee. The holder of legal title to property for the use or benefit of another.

Trustee Ad Litem. Usually an attorney appointed to represent the interest of unascertained persons in a particular matter before the court.

Unfunded Insurance Trust. An insurance trust that is not provided with cash or securities to pay the life insurance premiums. Such premiums are paid by someone other than the trustee.

Unified Credit (for federal gift and estate tax purposes). The unified credit is a dollar-for-dollar reduction against the federal estate and gift tax. For 1983, the credit is $79,300 and protects an estate of $275,000. For 1984, the credit is $96,300 and protects an estate of $325,000. For 1985, the credit is $121,800 and protects an estate of $400,000. For 1986, the credit is $155,000 and protects an estate of $500,000. For 1987, and thereafter, the unified credit is $192,800 and protects an estate of $600,000.

Usufruct. The right to the enjoyment of property owned by another, provided the substance of the property is not changed.

Vested Interest. An immediate fixed interest in real or personal property, although the right to possession and enjoyment may be postponed until some future date or until the happening of some event. For example, if a husband leaves real property and securities to a trustee in trust to pay the income to his wife during her lifetime and at her death to transfer the property to his son and his heirs, the wife has a present vested life interest in the right to the income, and the son has a future vested interest in the right to property. If contributions are made to a pension or profit-sharing plan, and the property regardless of any event is going to the employee, then the employee has a vested interest in that property.

Will. Technically, in law, the expression of what you want to happen to your property when you die. Formal requirements vary by states, but usually, at a minimum, a will must be in writing and signed at the end. Requirements for witnesses vary according to states.

APPENDIX

Executor's Checklist

Stage 1—Preprobate Tasks	Person responsible	Date accomplished
1. Provide physician with accurate information for death certificate—request at least 6 copies from funeral director or state bureau of vital statistics.	_____	_____
2. Arrange for security at homes of decedent and close relatives.	_____	_____
3. Meet with decedent's family/heirs; offer assistance, information; obtain psychotherapeutic aid if needed.	_____	_____
4. Discuss and make decisions on donation of body organs with close family members.	_____	_____
5. Ascertain who has right to make funeral arrangements; render assistance (notify clergy if not already informed).	_____	_____
6. Obtain deed to cemetery plot.	_____	_____
7. Help family prepare obituary.	_____	_____

Stage 1—Preprobate Tasks	*Person responsible*	*Date accomplished*
8. Provide care for minors/family members unable to care for themselves.	_____	_____
9. Provide immediate care/security for plants/pets/business and personal assets (especially perishables) and documents.	_____	_____
10. Determine cash needs of immediate survivors and adequacy and sources of cash to meet demands.	_____	_____
11. Tell all friends and family members to give you receipts for funeral-related expenditures.	_____	_____
12. Arrange for decedent's mail to be held at post office until your formal appointment; then arrange for forwarding. Stop newspapers and other deliveries if appropriate.	_____	_____
13. Notify bank—if named as executor or trustee—of death and request immediate appointment of administration officer.	_____	_____

Stage 2—Obtaining "Letters"	*Person responsible*	*Date accomplished*
1. Locate and examine will.* Advise spouse of right to obtain own attorney and elect against will.	_____	_____
2. Select and meet with attorney to represent estate.	_____	_____
3. Estimate decedent's assets/ liabilities.	_____	_____
4. Prepare petition for "letters" (out-of-state property may require ancillary administration as well).	_____	_____

	Person responsible	Date accomplished
Stage 2—Obtaining "Letters"		

5. Probate will at Register of Wills office and order "short certificates."

6. If necessary, arrange for bond with surety. Ascertain if special procedure for small estates is available and/or if estate can be settled by family agreements.

* If no will can be found after a diligent search, prepare a petition for letters of administration. Then proceed with checklist.

	Person responsible	Date accomplished
Stage 3—Assembling and Converting Assets		

1. Call property casualty insurance agent(s) and have all coverage checked for adequacy. Obtain confirmation in writing.

2. Call life insurance agent:

   (a) Have health and life insurance on survivors reviewed;

   (b) Request claim forms for proceeds on decedent's life (request IRS Form 712) and health/accident claims.

3. Contact bank for opening of safe-deposit box. Open new box for estate.

4. Redraft wills of survivors.

5. List all assets/liabilities. Examine checks, tax returns, insurance policies.

6. Locate and take control of all decedent's property.

7. Arrange for appraisal of personal property.

Stage 3—Assembling and Converting Assets	Person responsible	Date accomplished
8. Arrange for appraisal of real estate.	_____	_____
9. Sell or dispose of all perishables.	_____	_____
10. Analyze and review securities. Put idle funds into money markets or CDs.	_____	_____
11. Notify Social Security/V.A. and county and begin to process forms for obtaining benefits.	_____	_____
12. Contact employer and request unpaid salary/bonus/vacation pay/ pensions/other death-related benefits.	_____	_____
13. Advertise grant of letters.	_____	_____
14. Notify local banks of decedent's death. Request information on accounts/safe-deposit box.	_____	_____
15. Transfer all cash to new checking account in estate's name. Set up accounting and control system and apply for employer identification number from IRS.	_____	_____
16. Obtain all stocks/bonds. Close brokerage accounts. Collect any interest/dividends. Sell securities to extent necessary/appropriate. Place balance in name of executor.	_____	_____
17. Inspect all real estate. Arrange for security, management/payment of taxes, collection of rents.	_____	_____
18. Put all jewelry/furs/art/other valuable personal effects into safe-deposit box or similar protected storage.	_____	_____

Stage 3—Assembling and Converting Assets	*Person responsible*	*Date accomplished*
19. Proceed with, adjust and settle claims/lawsuits.	_____	_____
20. Check will/letter of instructions and consult decedent's heirs and attorney with respect to business continuation. Arrange for immediate supervision and management. Decide on sale/liquidation/continuance.	_____	_____

Stage 4—Filing and Payments of Taxes,** Debts and Expenses	*Person responsible*	*Date accomplished*
1. Request family exemption from state death tax if appropriate. Obtain exemption certificates for charitable gifts.	_____	_____
2. File state and federal income tax returns for (a) period before death and (b) period after death.	_____	_____
3. File federal estate tax return if necessary and pay tax due.	_____	_____
4. File state death tax return(s) (including other states) and pay tax due.	_____	_____
5. Pay personal or real property taxes due.	_____	_____
6. Pay bills, loans, etc.	_____	_____
7. Pay appraiser's/accountant's/ lawyer's/personal representative's fees and court costs.	_____	_____

** Consider state/federal extension of time to pay taxes.

Stage 5—Distribution	*Person responsible*	*Date accomplished*
1. Prepare and file accounting of receipts/disbursements/schedule of distribution.	_____	_____

	Person responsible	*Date accomplished*
Stage 5—Distribution		
2. Notify unpaid creditors and beneficiaries of filing of account and time and date of audit.	_____	_____
3. Notify attorney general of state if charitable gifts are involved.	_____	_____
4. Establish testamentary trusts.	_____	_____
5. Transfer securities and other assets in accordance with court-approved distribution schedule (obtain receipt and release).	_____	_____
6. Petition for surety's discharge.	_____	_____

Sample Forms for Applying for Social Security Benefits

DEPARTMENT OF HEALTH AND HUMAN SERVICES
Social Security Administration

TOE 120/145/155

Form Approved
OMB No 0960-0004

APPLICATION FOR WIDOW'S OR WIDOWER'S INSURANCE BENEFITS*

I apply for all insurance benefits for which I am eligible under Title II (Federal Old-Age, Survivors, and Disability Insurance) and Title XVIII (Health Insurance for the Aged and Disabled) of the Social Security Act, as presently amended. The information you furnish on this application will ordinarily be sufficient for a determination on the lump-sum death payment.

*This may also be considered an application for survivors benefits under the Railroad Retirement Act and for Veterans Administration payments under title 38 U.S.C., Veterans Benefits, Chapter 13 (which is, as such, an application for other types of death benefits under title 38).

If you were receiving benefits as a wife/husband at the time of your spouse's death, you need complete only the circled items. All other claimants must complete the entire form.

(Do not write in this space)

1. (a) PRINT name of deceased wage earner or self-employed person *(herein referred to as the "deceased")* → | FIRST NAME, MIDDLE INITIAL, LAST NAME

(b) Check (√) one for the deceased → ☐ Male ☐ Female

(c) Enter deceased's Social Security Number → __ __ __ / __ __ / __ __ __ __

2. (a) PRINT your name → | FIRST NAME, MIDDLE INITIAL, LAST NAME

(b) Enter your Social Security Number → __ __ __ / __ __ / __ __ __ __

(c) Enter your name at birth if different from item 2(a) → | FIRST NAME, MIDDLE INITIAL, LAST NAME

PART I — INFORMATION ABOUT THE DECEASED

3. Enter date of birth of deceased _____ | MONTH, DAY, YEAR

4. (a) Enter date of death _____ | MONTH, DAY, YEAR

(b) Enter place of death _____ | CITY AND STATE

5. Enter name of the State or foreign country where the deceased had a fixed, permanent home at the time of death. →

6. (a) Did the deceased ever file an application for Social Security benefits. a period of disability under Social Security, supplemental security income, or hospital or medical insurance under Medicare? *(If unknown, so indicate)* → | ☐ Yes *(If "Yes," answer (b) and (c).)* ☐ No *(If "No," go on to item 7.)*

(b) Enter name(s) of person(s) on whose Social Security record(s) other application was filed. → | FIRST NAME, MIDDLE INITIAL, LAST NAME

(c) Enter Social Security Number(s) of person(s) named in (b). *(If unknown, so indicate)* → __ __ __ / __ __ / __ __ __ __

ANSWER ITEM 7 ONLY IF THE DECEASED DIED PRIOR TO AGE 66 AND WITHIN THE PAST 4 MONTHS.

7. (a) Was the deceased unable to work because of a disabling condition at the time of death? → | ☐ Yes ☐ No *(If "Yes," answer (b).) (If "No," go on to item 8.)*

(b) Enter date disability began → | MONTH, DAY, YEAR

8. (a) Was the deceased in the active military or naval service (including Reserve or National Guard *active* duty or active duty for training) after September 7, 1939? → | ☐ Yes *(If "Yes," answer (b) and (c).)* ☐ No *(If "No," go on to item 9.)*

(b) Enter dates of service → | *(Month, year)* FROM: | *(Month, year)* TO:

(c) Has anyone (including the deceased) received, or does anyone expect to receive a benefit from any other Federal agency? → | ☐ Yes ☐ No

Form **SSA-10-BK** (8-84) Destroy prior editions.   Page 1   *(Over)*

ANSWER ITEM 9 ONLY IF DEATH OCCURRED WITHIN THE LAST 2 YEARS.

| 9. | (a) | About how much did the deceased earn from employment and self-employment during the year of death? ⟶ | Amount $ |
| | (b) | About how much did the deceased earn the year before death? ⟶ | Amount $ |

10. Enter below the information requested about each marriage of the deceased, including the marriage to you.

To whom married		When *(Month, Day, and Year)*	Where *(Enter name of City and State)*
Last marriage of the deceased	How marriage ended	When *(Month, Day, and Year)*	Where *(Enter name of City and State)*
	Marriage performed by: ☐ Clergyman or public official ☐ Other *(Explain in Remarks)*	Spouse's date of birth	If spouse deceased, give date of death
	Spouse's Social Security Number *(If none or unknown, so indicate)*		⎯ ⎯ ⎯ / ⎯ ⎯ / ⎯ ⎯ ⎯ ⎯
To whom married		When *(Month, Day, and Year)*	Where *(Enter name of City and State)*
Previous marriage of the deceased **(IF NONE, WRITE "NONE.")**	How marriage ended	When *(Month, Day, and Year)*	Where *(Enter name of City and State)*
	Marriage performed by: ☐ Clergyman or public official ☐ Other *(Explain in Remarks)*	Spouse's date of birth (or, age)	If spouse deceased, give date of death
	Spouse's Social Security Number *(If none or unknown, so indicate)*		⎯ ⎯ ⎯ / ⎯ ⎯ / ⎯ ⎯ ⎯ ⎯

(Use "Remarks" space on back page for information about any other previous marriage)

(11)	Is there a surviving parent (or parents) who was receiving support from the deceased at the time of death or at the time the deceased became disabled under Social Security law? ⟶	☐ Yes ☐ No *(If "Yes," enter the name and address in "Remarks.")*

PART II — INFORMATION ABOUT YOURSELF

12.	(a)	Enter name of State or foreign country where you were born. ⟶	

If you have already presented, or if you are now presenting, a public or religious record of your birth established before you were age 5, go on to item 13.

| | (b) | Was a public record of your birth made before age 5? ⟶ | ☐ Yes ☐ No ☐ Unknown |
| | (c) | Was a religious record of your birth made before age 5? ⟶ | ☐ Yes ☐ No ☐ Unknown |

13. Enter below information about each of your marriages. Indicate your marriage to the deceased by entering deceased's name (if you are applying for widower's benefits, enter the maiden name of the deceased); it is not necessary to repeat other information about this marriage you have already given in item 10. Enter complete information on all other marriages, whether before or after you married the deceased.

To whom married		When *(Month, Day, and Year)*	Where *(Enter name of City and State)*
Your current or last marriage	How marriage ended	When *(Month, Day, and Year)*	Where *(Enter name of City and State)*
	Marriage performed by: ☐ Clergyman or public official ☐ Other *(Explain in Remarks)*	Spouse's date of birth (or age)	If spouse deceased, give date of death
	Spouse's Social Security Number *(If none or unknown, so indicate)*		⎯ ⎯ ⎯ / ⎯ ⎯ / ⎯ ⎯ ⎯ ⎯

13. ontinued	To whom married		When *(Month, Day, and Year)*	Where *(Enter name of City and State)*
Your previous marriage **(IF NONE, WRITE "NONE.")**	How marriage ended		When *(Month, Day, and Year)*	Where *(Enter name of City and State)*
	Marriage performed by: ☐ Clergyman or public official ☐ Other *(Explain in Remarks)*		Spouse's date of birth (or age)	If spouse deceased, give date of death
	Spouse's Social Security Number *(If none or unknown, so indicate)*			___ / __ / ____

(Use "Remarks" space for information about any other marriage)

IF YOU ARE APPLYING FOR SURVIVING DIVORCED SPOUSE'S BENEFITS. OMIT 14 AND GO ON TO ITEM 15.

(14) (a) Were you and the deceased living together at the same address when the deceased died? ⟶
☐ Yes *(If "Yes," go on to item 15.)* ☐ No *(If "No," answer (b).)*

(b) If either you or the deceased were away from home (whether or not temporarily) when the deceased died, give the following:

Who was away? ⟶ ☐ Deceased ☐ Surviving spouse

Date last at home:	Reason absence began:	Reason you were apart at time of death:

If separated because of illness, enter nature of illness or disabling condition.

15. (a) Have you (or has someone on your behalf) ever filed an application for Social Security benefits, a period of disability under Social Security, supplemental security income, or hospital or medical insurance under Medicare? ⟶
☐ Yes *(If "Yes," answer (b) and (c).)* ☐ No *(If "No," go on to item 16.)*

(b) Enter name of person on whose Social Security record you filed other application ⟶

(c) Enter Social Security Number of person named in (b). *(If unknown, so indicate)* ⟶
___ / __ / ____

16. (a) Are you so disabled that you cannot work or was there some period during the last 14 months when you were so disabled that you could not work? ⟶
☐ Yes *(If "Yes," answer (b).)* ☐ No *(If "No," go on to item 17.)*

(b) If "Yes," enter the date you became disabled. ⟶
(Month, day, year)

17. Were you in the active military or naval service (including Reserve or National Guard *active* duty or active duty for training) after September 7, 1939? ⟶
☐ Yes ☐ No

18. Did you or the deceased work in the railroad industry on or at any time after January 1, 1937? ⟶
☐ Yes ☐ No

19. (a) Did you or the deceased ever engage in work that was covered under the social security system of a country other than the United States? ⟶
☐ Yes *(If "Yes," answer (b).)* ☐ No *(If "No," go on to item 20.)*

(b) If "Yes," list the country(ies). ⟶

20. (a) Have you qualified for, or do you expect to qualify for, a pension or annuity (or a lump sum in place of a pension or annuity) based on your own employment and earnings for the Federal Government of the United States, or one of its States or local subdivisions? ⟶

☐ Yes   ☐ No

(If "Yes," check which of the items in item (b) applies to you.)

(If "No," go on to item 21.)

(b) ☐ I receive a government pension or annuity.

☐ I received a lump sum in place of a government pension or annuity.

☐ I applied for and am awaiting a decision on my pension or lump sum.

☐ I have not applied for but I expect to begin receiving my pension or annuity

_____
(Month, year)

(If the date is not known, enter "Unknown")

I AGREE TO PROMPTLY NOTIFY the Social Security Administration if I begin to receive a government pension or annuity, based on my own earnings, from the Federal government or any State (or any political subdivision thereof), or if my present government pension or annuity amount changes.

MEDICARE INFORMATION

If this claim is approved and you are still entitled to benefits at age 65, you will automatically have hospital insurance protection under Medicare at age 65. If you are not also eligible for automatic enrollment in the Supplementary Medical Insurance Plan, this application may be used for voluntary enrollment.

COMPLETE THIS ITEM ONLY IF YOU ARE WITHIN 6 MONTHS OF AGE 65 OR OLDER

Medical insurance under Medicare helps pay your doctor bills. It also helps pay for a number of other medical items and services not covered under the hospital insurance part of Medicare.

If you sign up for medical insurance, you must pay a premium for each month you have this protection. If you get monthly Social Security, railroad retirement, or civil service benefits, your premium will be deducted from your benefit check. If you get none of these benefits, you will be notified how to pay your premium.

The Federal Government contributes to the cost of your insurance. The amount of your premium and the Government's payment are based on the cost of services covered by medical insurance. The Government also makes additional payments when necessary to meet the full cost of the program. (Currently the Government pays about two-thirds of the cost of this program.) You will get advance notice if there is any change in your premium amount.

If you are entitled to hospital insurance as a result of this application, you will be enrolled for medical insurance automatically unless you indicate below that you do not want this protection. If you decline to enroll now, you can get medical insurance protection later only if you sign up for it during specified enrollment periods. Your protection may then be delayed and you may have to pay a higher premium when you decide to sign up.

The date your medical insurance begins and the amount of the premium you must pay depend on the month you file this application with the Social Security Administration. Any Social Security office will be glad to explain the rules regarding enrollment to you.

21. DO YOU WISH TO ENROLL IN THE MEDICARE SUPPLEMENTARY MEDICAL INSURANCE PLAN? ⟶   ☐ Yes   ☐ No

Answer item 22 ONLY if the deceased died before this year.

(22.) **(a)** How much were your total earnings in 1983? ⟶ $ _____

(b) Did you earn more than $410 (if under age 65) or $550 (if age 65 or over) in wages or perform substantial services in self-employment in each month of 1983? ⟶

☐ Yes
(If "Yes," go on to item 23.)

☐ No
(If "No," answer (c).)

(c) Circle each month of 1983 in which you did not earn more than $410 (if under age 65) or $550 (if age 65 or over) in wages and did not perform substantial services in self-employment.

Jan.	Feb.	Mar.	Apr.
May	Jun.	Jul.	Aug.
Sept.	Oct.	Nov.	Dec.

(23.) **(a)** How much do you expect your total earnings to be in 1984? ⟶ $ _____

(b) Did you or will you earn more than $430 (if under age 65) or $580 (if age 65 or over) in wages or perform substantial services in self-employment in all months of this year? ⟶

☐ Yes
(If "Yes," go on to item 24.)

☐ No
(If "No," answer (c).)

(c) Circle each month of 1984 in which you did not or will not earn more than $430 (if under age 65) or $580 (if age 65 or over) in wages and did not or will not perform substantial services in self-employment. ⟶

Jan.	Feb.	Mar.	Apr.
May	Jun.	Jul.	Aug.
Sept.	Oct.	Nov.	Dec.

(24.) Answer this item ONLY if you are now in the last 4 months of your taxable year (Sept., Oct., Nov., and Dec., if your taxable year is a calendar year).

(a) How much do you expect to earn in 1985? ⟶ $ _____

(b) Circle each month of 1985 in which you do not expect to earn more than $ _____ in wages and do not expect to perform substantial services in self-employment. ⟶

Jan.	Feb.	Mar.	Apr.
May	Jun.	Jul.	Aug.
Sept.	Oct.	Nov.	Dec.

(25.) If you use a fiscal year, that is, a taxable year that does not end December 31 (with income tax return due April 15), enter here the month your fiscal year ends. ⟶

Month

IF YOU ARE AGE 65 AND 6 MONTHS OR OLDER, GO ON TO PAGE 6. OTHERWISE, PLEASE READ CAREFULLY THE INFORMATION ON PAGE 7 AND ANSWER ONE OF THE FOLLOWING ITEMS.

(26.) **(a)** I want benefits beginning with the earliest possible month that will be most advantageous. ⟶ ☐

(b) I am age 65 (or will be age 65 within 4 months) and I want benefits beginning with the earliest possible month providing there is no permanent reduction in my ongoing monthly benefit. ⟶ ☐

(c) I want benefits beginning with _____ ⟶ ☐

Explain _____

27. ANSWER THIS QUESTION ONLY IF YOU ARE NOW BETWEEN AGE 61 YEARS, 8 MONTHS, AND AGE 65 AND 6 MONTHS. Do you wish this application to be considered an application for reduced benefits on your own earnings record? ⟶   ☐ Yes   ☐ No

Form **SSA-10-BK** (8-84) Page 5   *(Over)*

(28) It is possible for your Social Security monthly payments to be forwarded directly to your bank, savings and loan, credit union or other financial organization for deposit. If you wish direct deposit you will have to contact your financial organization to complete the necessary form. We will advise you when your direct deposit request is processed. If you do not wish direct deposit, your benefits will be paid by check to your mailing address.

Do you wish to be paid by direct deposit? ⟶ ☐ Yes ☐ No

It is possible that your claim will be ready to be paid before the direct deposit form is returned by your financial organization. Your claim can be processed and any payments due will be sent to you until your direct deposit request is received.

An ANNUAL REPORT of earnings must be filed with the Social Security Administration within 3 months and 15 days after the end of any taxable year in which you earn more than the exempt amount (e.g., $5,160 for 1984 if you were under age 65, or $6,960 for 1984 if you were age 65 or over), if you are under age 70 for at least 1 full month of that year and receive some benefits during the taxable year. I AGREE TO FILE AN ANNUAL REPORT OF EARNINGS. THE ANNUAL REPORT IS REQUIRED BY LAW AND FAILURE TO REPORT MAY RESULT IN A MONETARY PENALTY.

Remarriage prior to age 60 may terminate your benefits. There are certain exceptions which are explained in the informational booklet which you will receive. You must report if you remarry even if you believe an exception applies. We will advise you whether additional evidence is needed and how your benefits may be affected.

I AGREE TO PROMPTLY NOTIFY the Social Security Administration if I REMARRY and to PROMPTLY RETURN ANY BENEFIT CHECK I receive for the month I marry, and for any later month.

REMARKS *(You may use this space for any explanations. If you need more space, attach a separate sheet.)*

_____

_____

_____

_____

_____

_____

_____

I know that anyone who makes or causes to be made a false statement or representation of material fact in an application or for use in determining a right to payment under the Social Security Act commits a crime punishable under Federal law by fine, imprisonment or both. I affirm that all information I have given in this document is true.

SIGNATURE OF APPLICANT	Date *(Month, day, year)*
Signature *(First name, middle initial, last name) (Write in ink)*	
SIGN HERE ▶	Telephone Number(s) at which you may be contacted during the day
	AREA CODE

Mailing Address *(Number and street, Apt. No., P.O. Box, or Rural Route) (Enter resident address in "Remarks" if different)*

City and State	ZIP Code	County (if any) in which you now live

Witnesses are required ONLY if this application has been signed by mark (X) above. If signed by mark (X), two witnesses to the signing who know the applicant must sign below, giving their full addresses.

1. Signature of Witness	2. Signature of Witness
Address *(Number and street, City, State and ZIP Code)*	Address *(Number and street, City, State and ZIP Code)*

PLEASE READ THE FOLLOWING INFORMATION CAREFULLY

HOW YOUR EARNINGS IN 1984 AFFECT YOUR BENEFITS

(a) If You Are Under Age 65 In 1984

You may earn up to $5,160 a year and still receive all your Social Security benefits. *If you earn OVER $5,160, $1 in benefits may be withheld for each $2 of earnings you have over $5,160. For one year only, under a "Monthly Earnings Test" you are entitled to a benefit for any month you do not earn wages of over $430 and do not perform substantial services in self-employment **

(b) If You Are Or Will Be Age 65 Or Older Before 1/2/85

You may earn up to $6,960 a year and still receive all your Social Security benefits. *If you earn OVER $6,960, $1 in benefits may be withheld for each $2 of earnings you have over $6,960. For one year only, under a "Monthly Earnings Test" you are entitled to a benefit for any month you do not earn wages of over $580 and do not perform substantial services in self-employment **

HOW YOUR EARNINGS IN 1983 AFFECT YOUR BENEFITS

(a) If You Were Under Age 65 In 1983

You could earn up to $4,920 a year and still receive all your Social Security benefits. *If you earned OVER $4,920, $1 in benefits may be withheld for each $2 of earnings you had over $4,920. For one year only, under a "Monthly Earnings Test" you are entitled to a benefit for any month you did not earn wages of over $410 and did not perform substantial services in self-employment. **

(b) If You Were Age 65 Or Older Before 1/2/84

You could earn up to $6,600 a year and still receive all your Social Security benefits. *If you earned OVER $6,600, $1 in benefits may be withheld for each $2 of earnings you had over $6,600. For one year only, under a "Monthly Earnings Test" you are entitled to a benefit for any month you did not earn wages of over $550 and did not perform substantial services in self-employment. **

*This yearly period referred to in this and following items is the same 12-month period you use in figuring your income tax.

**THE MONTHLY EARNINGS TEST APPLIES FOR ONE YEAR ONLY — THE FIRST YEAR IN WHICH YOU HAVE A MONTH IN WHICH YOU DO NOT EARN OVER THE MONTHLY EXEMPT AMOUNT AND DO NOT PERFORM SUBSTANTIAL SERVICES IN SELF-EMPLOYMENT. IN ALL OTHER YEARS, THE TOTAL AMOUNT OF BENEFITS PAYABLE WILL BE BASED SOLELY ON YOUR TOTAL YEARLY EARNINGS WITHOUT REGARD TO MONTHLY EARNINGS OR SERVICES RENDERED IN SELF-EMPLOYMENT.

FIGURING YOUR ANNUAL EARNINGS

To figure your total yearly earnings, count all gross wages (before deductions) and net earnings from self-employment which you earn during the entire year. This includes earnings both before and after retirement and applies to all earned income whether or not covered by Social Security.

In figuring your total yearly earnings, however, DO NOT COUNT ANY AMOUNTS EARNED BEGINNING WITH THE MONTH YOU BECOME AGE 70. Count only amounts earned before the month you become AGE 70.

PLEASE READ THE FOLLOWING INFORMATION CAREFULLY BEFORE ANSWERING QUESTION 26.

Benefits may be payable for some months prior to the month in which you file this claim (but not for any month before you reach age 60 (unless you are disabled)) if:

1) you will earn over $5,160 this year AND you are under age 65 for this ENTIRE year;

— OR —

2) you will earn over $6,960 this year AND you have already attained age 65 or will attain age 65 this year

If your first month of entitlement is prior to age 65, your benefit rate will be reduced. However, if you do not actually receive your full benefit amount for one or more months before age 65 because benefits are withheld due to your earnings, your benefit will be increased at age 65 to give credit for this withholding. Thus, your benefit amount at age 65 will be reduced only if you receive one or more full benefit payments prior to the month you are age 65.

RECEIPT FOR YOUR CLAIM FOR SOCIAL SECURITY WIDOW'S OR WIDOWER'S INSURANCE BENEFITS

NAME OF PERSON TO CONTACT ABOUT YOUR CLAIM	SSA OFFICE	DATE CLAIM RECEIVED
TELEPHONE NUMBER(S) TO CALL IF YOU HAVE A QUESTION OR SOMETHING TO REPORT	**BEFORE** YOU RECEIVE A NOTICE OF AWARD	
	AFTER YOU RECEIVE A NOTICE OF AWARD	

Your application for Social Security benefits has been received and will be processed as quickly as possible.

You should hear from us within _____ days after you have given us all the information we requested. Some claims may take longer if additional information is needed.

In the meantime, if you change your address, or if there is some other change that may affect your claim, you—or someone for you — should report the change. The changes to be reported are listed below.

Always give us your claim number when writing or telephoning about your claim.

If you have any questions about your claim, we will be glad to help you.

CLAIMANT	DECEASED S SURNAME IF DIFFERENT FROM CLAIMANTS	SOCIAL SECURITY CLAIM NUMBER

CHANGES TO BE REPORTED AND HOW TO REPORT

Failure to report may result in overpayments that must be repaid, and in possible monetary penalties

▶ You change your mailing address for checks or residence. *To avoid delay in receipt of checks you should ALSO file a regular change of address notice with your post office.*

▶ You go outside the U.S.A.

▶ Any beneficiary dies or becomes unable to handle benefits.

▶ Work Changes—On your application you told us you expect total earnings for 19____ to be $ _____ .

You (are) (are not) earning wages of more than $ _____ a month.

You (are) (are not) self-employed rendering substantial services in your trade or business.

(Report AT ONCE if this work pattern changes.)

▶ Custody Change—Report if a person for whom you are filing or who is in your care dies, leaves your care or custody, or changes address.

▶ Change of Marital Status—Marriage, divorce, annulment of marriage.

▶ You begin to receive a government pension or annuity (from the Federal government or any State or any political subdivision thereof) or present payment changes.

▶ You are confined to jail, prison, penal institution, or correctional facility for conviction of a felony.

▶ **Disability Applicants**

1. You return to work (as an employee or self-employed) regardless of amount of earnings.

2. Your condition improves.

HOW TO REPORT

You can make your reports by telephone, mail, or in person, whichever you prefer.

WHEN A CHANGE OCCURS AFTER YOU RECEIVE A NOTICE OF AWARD, YOU SHOULD REPORT BY CALLING THE APPROPRIATE TELEPHONE NUMBER SHOWN NEAR THE TOP OF THIS PAGE.

In addition, an annual report of earnings must be filed with the Social Security Administration within 3 months and 15 days after the end of any taxable year in which you earn more than the exempt amount. (See explanation on the reverse.)

THE ANNUAL REPORT OF EARNINGS IS REQUIRED BY LAW AND FAILURE TO REPORT MAY RESULT IN A MONETARY PENALTY

Collection and Use of Information From Your Application — Privacy Act/Paperwork Act Notice

The Social Security Administration is authorized to collect the information on this form under sections 202(e), 205(a), and 1872 of the Social Security Act, as amended (42 U.S.C. 402(e), 405(a), and 1395ii). While it is voluntary, except in the circumstances explained below, for you to furnish the information on this form to Social Security, no benefits may be paid unless an application has been received by a Social Security office. Your response is mandatory where the refusal to disclose certain information affecting your right to payment would reflect a fraudulent intent to secure benefits not authorized by the Social Security Act.

The information on this form is needed to enable Social Security to determine if you and your dependents are entitled to insurance coverage and/or monthly benefits. Failure to provide all or part of this information could prevent an accurate and timely decision on your claim or your dependent's claim, and could result in the loss of some benefits or insurance coverage. Although the information you furnish on this form is almost never used for any other purpose than stated in the foregoing, there is a possibility that for the administration of the Social Security programs or for the administration of programs requiring coordination with the Social Security Administration, information may be disclosed to another person or to another governmental agency as follows: 1. to enable a third party or an agency to assist Social Security in establishing rights to Social Security benefits and/or coverage; 2. to comply with Federal laws requiring the release of information from Social Security records (e.g., to the General Accounting Office and the Veterans Administration); and 3. to facilitate statistical research and audit activities necessary to assure the integrity and improvement of the Social Security programs (e.g., to the Bureau of the Census and private concerns under contract to Social Security).

✿ U.S. GOVERNMENT PRINTING OFFICE: 1984-421-185:2302

TOE 120/145/155

DEPARTMENT OF HEALTH AND HUMAN SERVICES
Social Security Administration

Form Approved
OMB No. 0960-0013

APPLICATION FOR LUMP-SUM DEATH PAYMENT*

I apply for all insurance benefits for which I am eligible under Title II (Federal Old-Age, Survivors, and Disability Insurance) of the Social Security Act, as presently amended, on the named deceased's Social Security record.
(This application must be filed within 2 years after the date of death of the wage earner or self-employed person.)

*This may also be considered an application for insurance benefits payable under the Railroad Retirement Act.

1.	(a) PRINT name of Deceased Wage Earner or Self-Employed Person (herein referred to as the "deceased")	*(First name, middle initial, last name)*
	(b) Check (✓) one for the deceased ➔	☐ Male ☐ Female
	(c) Enter deceased's Social Security Number ➔	__ __ __ / __ __ / __ __ __ __
2.	PRINT your name ➔	*(First name, middle initial, last name)*
3.	Enter date of birth of deceased *(Month, day, year)* ➔	
4.	(a) Enter date of death *(Month, day, year)* ➔	
	(b) Enter place of death *(City and State)*	
5.	(a) Did the deceased ever file an application for Social Security benefits, a period of disability under Social Security, supplemental security income, or hospital or medical insurance under Medicare? ➔	☐ Yes *(If "Yes," answer (b) and (c).)* ☐ No ☐ Unknown *(If "No" or "Unknown," go on to item 6.)*
	(b) Enter name(s) of person(s) on whose Social Security record(s) other application was filed. ➔	
	(c) Enter Social Security Number(s) of person(s) named in (b). (If unknown, so indicate) ➔	__ __ __ / __ __ / __ __ __ __
6.	ANSWER ITEM 6 **ONLY** IF THE DECEASED WORKED WITHIN THE PAST 2 YEARS.	
	(a) About how much did the deceased earn from employment and self-employment during the year of death? ➔	Amount $
	(b) About how much did the deceased earn the year before death? ➔	Amount $
7.	ANSWER ITEM 7 **ONLY** IF THE DECEASED DIED PRIOR TO AGE 66 AND WITHIN THE PAST 4 MONTHS.	
	(a) Was the deceased unable to work because of a disabling condition at the time of death? ➔	☐ Yes *(If "Yes," answer (b).)* ☐ No *(If "No," go on to item 8.)*
	(b) Enter date disability began *(Month, day, year)* ➔	
8.	(a) Was the deceased in the active military or naval service (including Reserve or National Guard *active* duty or active duty for training) after September 7, 1939? ➔	☐ Yes *(If "Yes," answer (b) and (c).)* ☐ No *(If "No," go on to item 9.)*
	(b) Enter dates of service. ➔	From: *(Month, Year)* To: *(Month, Year)*
	(c) Has anyone (including the deceased) received, or does anyone expect to receive, a benefit from any other Federal agency?	☐ Yes ☐ No
9.	Did the deceased work in the railroad industry at any time on or after January 1, 1937? ➔	☐ Yes ☐ No

Form **SSA-8-F5** (1-83) Page 1
DESTROY PRIOR EDITIONS

10.	(a) Did the deceased ever engage in work that was covered under the social security system of a country other than the United States? ———————————————————▶	☐ Yes ☐ No *(If "Yes", answer (b).) (If "No" go on to item 11.)*
	(b) If "Yes," list the country(ies). ———▶	

11.	Is the deceased survived by a spouse or ex-spouse? (If "No," go on to item 12. If "Yes," give the following information about all marriages of the deceased including marriage in effect at time of death.) (If you need more space, use "Remarks" section on back page or attach a separate sheet.)	☐ Yes ☐ No

To whom married *(Name at Birth)*		When *(Month, day, year)*	Where *(Enter name of City and State)*
Last marriage of the deceased	How marriage ended	When *(Month, day, year)*	Where *(Enter name of City and State)*
	Marriage performed by: ☐ Clergyman or public official ☐ Other *(Explain in Remarks)*	Spouse's date of birth (or age)	
	Spouse's Social Security Number *(If none or unknown, so indicate)* _ _ _/_ _/_ _ _ _		

To whom married		When *(Month, day, year)*	Where *(Enter name of City and State)*
Previous marriage of the deceased If none, write "None."	How marriage ended	When *(Month, day, year)*	Where *(Enter name of City and State)*
	Marriage performed by: ☐ Clergyman or public official ☐ Other *(Explain in Remarks)*	Spouse's date of birth (or age)	If spouse deceased, give date of death
	Spouse's Social Security Number *(If none or unknown, so indicate)* _ _ _/_ _/_ _ _ _		

12.	The deceased's surviving children (including natural children, adopted children, and stepchildren) or dependent grandchildren (including stepgrandchildren) may be eligible for benefits based on the earnings record of the deceased.

List below ALL such children who are now or were in the past 12 months UNMARRIED and:
- UNDER AGE 18   • AGE 18 TO 19 AND ATTENDING SECONDARY SCHOOL
- DISABLED OR HANDICAPPED (age 18 or over and disability began before age 22)

(If none, write "None".)

Full Name of Child	Full Name of Child

13.	Is there a surviving parent (or parents) of the deceased who was receiving support from the deceased either at the time the deceased became disabled under the Social Security law or at the time of death? ———————————————————▶	☐ Yes ☐ No *(If "Yes," enter the name and address of the parent(s) in "Remarks".)*
14.	Have you filed for any Social Security benefits on the deceased's earnings record before? ———————————————————▶	☐ Yes ☐ No

NOTE: If there is a surviving spouse, continue with item 15. If not, go on to item 19.

15.	If you are not the surviving spouse, enter the surviving spouse's name and address here

16.	(a) Were the deceased and the surviving spouse living together at the same address when the deceased died?	☐ Yes ☐ No
	(b) If either the deceased or surviving spouse was away from home (whether or not temporarily) when the deceased died, give the following:	

Who was away? ———————————————————▶	☐ Deceased ☐ Surviving spouse

Date last home	Reason absence began	Reason they were apart at time of death

If separated because of illness, enter nature of illness or disabling condition.

If you are the surviving spouse, answer Items 17 and 18.

| 17. | (a) Are you so disabled that you cannot work or was there some period during the last 14 months when you were so disabled that you could not work? ⟶ | ☐ Yes ☐ No |
| | (b) If "Yes," enter the date you became disabled. ⟶ | *(Month, day, year)* |

| 18. | Were you married before your marriage to the deceased? *(If "Yes," give the following about each of your previous marriages. If you need more space, use "Remarks" section on back page or attach a separate sheet.)* ⟶ | ☐ Yes ☐ No |

To whom married		When *(Month, day, year)*	Where *(Enter name of City and State)*
Your previous marriage	How marriage ended	When *(Month, day, year)*	Where *(Enter name of City and State)*
	Marriage performed by: ☐ Clergyman or public official ☐ Other *(Explain in Remarks)*	Spouse's date of birth (or age)	If spouse deceased, give date of death
	Spouse's Social Security Number *(If none or unknown, so indicate)* __ __ __ / __ __ / __ __ __ __		

DO NOT ANSWER ITEMS 19 THROUGH 26 IF:
- DEATH OCCURRED AFTER 8-31-81
    OR
- YOU ARE THE SURVIVING SPOUSE WHO WAS LIVING IN THE SAME HOUSEHOLD AS THE DECEASED AT THE TIME OF DEATH.

Instead, turn to page 4 and complete the signature and address portion of the form.

19.	(a) What was the total amount of the burial expenses charged by the funeral home(s) *(hereafter referred to as "burial expenses")*? ⟶	$
	(b) Did you assume responsibility for payment of any part of the burial expenses? ⟶	☐ Yes *(If "Yes," answer (c).)* ☐ No *(If "No," go on to item 21.)*
	(c) Show whether you assumed responsibility for burial expenses: ⟶	☐ Personally ☐ As legal representative of the deceased's estate

| 20. | What amount of burial expenses shown in 19 (a) above did you pay? *(If none, write "None.")* ⟶ | $ |

| 21. | Has an application for the burial allowance been filed (or will it be filed) with the Veterans Administration, other Federal agency of the U.S., or (if death occurred outside the U.S.) any foreign governmental agency? ⟶ *(If "Yes," give the following information.)* *(If "No," go on to item 22.)* | ☐ Yes ☐ No |

Name of Agency	Amount Claimed
☐ Veterans Administration	$
☐ Other *(Give name)*	$
Name of person filing with other agency	

| 22. | What is your relationship to the deceased? ⟶ | |

DO NOT answer Item 23 if you are related to the deceased or if you are the estate's legal representative.

| 23. | Why did you assume responsibility for or pay the burial expenses? |

DO NOT complete items 24 and 25 If there are unpaid burial expenses of at least $255.

24. If you have paid part or all of the burial expenses, have you received or will you receive any cash or property toward the expenses? (Do not include proceeds from an insurance policy or death benefits from a fraternal association, union, or employer.) *(If "Yes," give the following information.) (If "No," go on to item 25).* ⟶ ☐ Yes ☐ No

Source of payment	Date received or expected	Amount
		$
		$

25. Did anyone else assume responsibility for payment of or pay any part of the burial expenses in 19 (a)? *(If "Yes," give the following information.)* ⟶ ☐ Yes ☐ No

Name and address of other person who assumed responsibility or paid	Other person's relationship to deceased	Amount paid by such other person, if any
		$
		$

26. If any of the burial expenses shown in 19 (a) are unpaid, the lump-sum payment (or that part of it equal to the unpaid expenses) can be made ONLY to the funeral home(s). To request such payment, the following must be completed.

I hereby request the Social Security Administration to make payment or give notice of nonpayment of the lump-sum to the:

(Name(s) and address(es) of funeral home(s))

Payment, if made, is to be applied toward the unpaid expenses of ⟶ Amount $

Remarks: *(You may use this space for any explanation. If you need more space, attach a separate sheet.)*

I know that anyone who makes or causes to be made a false statement or representation of material fact in an application or for use in determining a right to payment under the Social Security Act commits a crime punishable under Federal law by fine, imprisonment or both. I affirm that all information I have given in this document is true.

SIGNATURE OF APPLICANT	Date *(Month, day, year)*
Signature *(First name, middle initial, last name) (Write in ink)* ▶	Telephone Number(s) at which you may be contacted during the day Area Code

Mailing Address *(Number and street, Apt. No., P.O. Box, or Rural Route)*

City and State	ZIP Code	Enter Name of County (if any) in which you now live

Witnesses are required ONLY if this application has been signed by mark (X) above. If signed by mark (X), two witnesses to the signing who know the applicant must sign below, giving their full addresses.

1. Signature of Witness	2. Signature of Witness
Address *(Number and street, City, State, and ZIP Code)*	Address *(Number and street, City, State, and ZIP Code)*

RECEIPT FOR YOUR CLAIM FOR THE SOCIAL SECURITY LUMP-SUM DEATH PAYMENT

NAME OF PERSON TO CONTACT ABOUT YOUR CLAIM	SSA OFFICE	DATE CLAIM RECEIVED
TELEPHONE NUMBER		

RECEIPT FOR YOUR CLAIM

Your application for the lump-sum death payment has been received and will be processed as quickly as possible.

You should hear from us within_____days after you have given us all the information we requested. Some claims may take longer if additional information is needed.

In the meantime, if you change your mailing address, you should report the change.

Always give us your claim number when writing or telephoning about your claim.

If you have any questions about your claim, we will be glad to help you.

CLAIMANT	SOCIAL SECURITY CLAIM NUMBER

DECEASED'S NAME (If surname differs from claimant's name)

COLLECTION AND USE OF INFORMATION FROM YOUR APPLICATION - PRIVACY ACT/PAPERWORK ACT NOTICE

I. The Social Security Administration is authorized to collect the information on this form under sections 202(i) and 205(a) of the Social Security Act, as amended (42 U.S.C. 402(i) and 405(a)).

II. While it is voluntary, except in the circumstances explained below, for you to furnish the information on this form to Social Security, no lump-sum death payment may be paid unless an application has been received by a Social Security office. Your response is mandatory where the refusal to disclose certain information affecting your right to payment would reflect a fraudulent intent to secure payment not authorized by the Social Security Act.

III The information on this form is needed to enable Social Security to determine if you are entitled to the lump-sum death payment. It will also enable us to determine if there are any survivors of the deceased who may qualify for monthly Social Security benefits as dependents of the deceased.

IV. Failure to provide all or part of this information could prevent an accurate and timely decision on your claim, and could result in the loss of some benefits for eligible dependents of the deceased.

V. Although the information you furnish on this form is almost never used for any other purpose than stated in Part III, above, there is a possibility that in the administration of the Social Security programs or for the administration of programs requiring coordination with the Social Security Administration, information may be disclosed to another person or to another government agency as follows:

1. To enable a third party or an agency to assist Social Security in establishing rights to Social Security benefits and/or coverage.

2. To comply with Federal laws requiring the release of information from Social Security records (e.g., to the General Accounting Office and the Veterans Administration).

3. To facilitate statistical research and audit activities necessary to assure the integrity and improvement of the Social Security programs (e.g., to the Bureau of the Census and private concerns under contract to Social Security).

DEPARTMENT OF HEALTH AND HUMAN SERVICES   TOE 120/145/155

Social Security Administration

Form Approved
OMB No. 0960-0010

APPLICATION FOR CHILD'S INSURANCE BENEFITS

(Do not write in this space)

I apply on behalf of the child or children listed in item 3 below for all insurance benefits for which they may be eligible under title II (Federal Old-Age, Survivors and Disability Insurance) of the Social Security Act, as presently amended. (If you are applying on your own behalf, answer the questions on this form with respect to yourself.)

If you are applying for benefits based on the earnings record of a Deceased Worker, this may also be considered an application for survivors benefits under the Railroad Retirement Act and for Veterans Administration payments under Title 38 U.S.C., Veterans Benefits, Chapter 13 (which is, as such, an application for other types of death benefits under Title 38).

LIFE CLAIM ☐   DEATH CLAIM ☐

1. (a) PRINT name of Wage Earner or Self-Employed person (herein referred to as the "Worker") ➤

FIRST NAME, MIDDLE INITIAL, LAST NAME

(b) PRINT Worker's Social Security Number ➤

_ _ _ / _ _ / _ _ _ _

2. PRINT your name (unless you are the Worker) ➤

FIRST NAME, MIDDLE INITIAL, LAST NAME

PART I — INFORMATION ABOUT THE WORKER'S CHILDREN

3. The Worker's children (including natural children, adopted children, and stepchildren) or dependent grandchildren (including stepgrandchildren) may be eligible for benefits based on the earnings record of the Worker. For a living Worker, the information below applies to this month or to any of the past 12 months. For a deceased Worker, the information below applies to the date of death or for any period since the Worker's death. Also list any student who is between the ages of 18 and 23 if the student was both: 1. previously entitled to Social Security benefits on any Social Security record for August 1981, and 2. was also in full-time attendance at a post-secondary school for May 1982.

LIST BELOW ALL SUCH CHILDREN (IN ORDER OF BIRTH BEGINNING WITH THE OLDEST) who are now, or who were at the appropriate time (above), UNMARRIED and: • UNDER AGE 18 • AGE 18 TO 19 (OR TO AGE 23 FOR MONTHS PRIOR TO AUGUST 1982) AND ATTENDING SECONDARY SCHOOL • DISABLED OR HANDICAPPED (age 18 or over and disability began before age 22)	Check (✓) Sex of Child		Date of Birth (Mo., day, yr.)	Check (✓) if Child 17 or Older is:		Check (✓) the Column That Shows Child's Relationship to Worker						CHILD'S SOCIAL SECURITY NUMBER
	M	F		Student	Disabled	Legitimate	Adopted	Stepchild	Dependent Grandchild	Other		
FULL NAME OF CHILD												

If you do not wish to be payee for any child or dependent grandchild named above, list the child's name and address in "Remarks" on page 5. You may apply for a child even though you do not wish to be payee for the child's benefits.

4. If any children in item 3 are stepchildren of the Worker, enter the date the Worker married the natural parent. ➤

MONTH, DAY, YEAR

5. Is there a legal representative (guardian, conservator, curator, etc.) for any of the children in item 3? ➤

☐ Yes   ☐ No

Form **SSA-4-BK** (1-84) Destroy prior editions   Page 1   (over)

6.	Have any children in item 3 ever been adopted by someone other than _____ the Worker? (If "Yes," enter the following information):	➤ ☐ Yes ☐ No

Name of Child	Date of Adoption	Name of Person Adopting

7.	Are all the children in item 3 now living in the same household with you? ➤ (If "No," enter the following information about each child not living with you. If uncertain as to the whereabouts of any of these children, explain in "Remarks".)	☐ Yes ☐ No

Name of Child Not Living With You	Person With Whom Child Now Lives	
	Name and Address	Relationship to Child

8.	Has any child in item 3 ever been married? ➤	☐ Yes ☐ No
		(If "Yes," enter the information requested below.)

Name of Child	Date of Marriage (Month, day, year)
How Marriage Ended (If still married, write "not ended")	Date Marriage Ended (Month, day, year)

9.		☐ Yes ☐ No
	Has anyone ever before filed an application with the Social Security Administration for monthly benefits on behalf of any child in item 3?	(If "Yes," enter below the name(s) of the child(ren) and the name(s) and Social Security number(s) of the person(s) on whose earnings record any other claim was based.)

Name of Child	Name of Worker	Social Security Number of Worker
		_ _ _/_ _/_ _ _ _
		_ _ _/_ _/_ _ _ _

If you are applying **ONLY** for a child age 18 or over who is disabled, omit items 10 through 13. In all other cases, answer items 10 through 13.

1983 EARNINGS INFORMATION: Do not complete this item if the Worker died in 1984.

10.	(a) Did any child in item 3 earn more than $4,920 in 1983? ➤	☐ Yes ☐ No
		(If "Yes," answer (b). If "No," go on to item 11.)

(b) Name of Child Who Earned Over $4,920 in 1983	Total Earnings of Child	List Each Month That Child Did Not Earn More Than $410 in Wages and Did Not Perform Substantial Services in Self-Employment
	$	
	$	

1984 EARNINGS INFORMATION:

11.	(a) Do you expect the total earnings of any child in item 3 to be more than $5,160 this year? (Count all earnings beginning with the first of this year and all anticipated earnings through the end of this year.)	☐ Yes ☐ No
		(If "Yes," answer (b). If "No," go on to item 12.)

(b) Name of Child Who Expects to Earn Over $5,160 This Year	Expected Earnings of Child	List Each Month (including the present month) That Child Did Not or Will Not Earn More Than $430 in Wages and Did Not or Will Not Perform Substantial Services in Self-Employment
	$	
	$	
	$	

Form **SSA-4-BK** (1-84) Page 2

Complete item 12 ONLY if any child is now in the last 4 months of the child's taxable year (Sept., Oct., Nov., and Dec., if the taxable year is a calendar year).

1985 EARNINGS INFORMATION:

12.	**(a)** Do you expect the total earnings of any child in item 3 to be more than $_____ in 1985? ➤ ☐ Yes ☐ No (If "Yes," answer (b). If "No," go on to item 13.)

(b)

Name of Child Who Expects to Earn Over $ _____ in 1985	Expected Earnings of Child	List Each Month That Child Will Not Earn More Than $_____ in Wages and Will Not Perform Substantial Services in Self-Employment
	$	
	$	

13.	If any of the children for whom you are filing uses a fiscal year (one that does not end on December 31), print here the name of the child and the month the fiscal year ends. ➤	Name of Child and Month Fiscal Year Ends

14. It is possible for the Social Security monthly payments of the child(ren) to be forwarded directly to your bank, savings and loan, credit union, or other financial organization for deposit to your account. This method of payment is known as direct deposit. If you wish direct deposit you will have to contact your financial organization to complete the necessary form. We will advise you when your direct deposit request is processed. If you do not wish direct deposit the child(ren's) benefits will be paid by check to your mailing address.

Do you wish to be paid by direct deposit? ➤ ☐ Yes   ☐ No

It is possible that your claim on behalf of the child(ren) will be ready to be paid before the direct deposit form is returned by your financial organization. Your claim can be processed and any payments due will be sent to you until your direct deposit request is received.

Complete items 15 and 16 ONLY if the Worker is living. Otherwise, go on to item 17.

15. If any children in item 3 are children adopted by the Worker, print below the name of each such child and the date of adoption by the Worker.

Name of Adopted Child	Date of Adoption

16. Have all of the children in item 3 lived with the Worker during each of the last 13 months (counting the present month)? ➤ ☐ Yes   ☐ No

(If "No," enter the information requested below.)

Name of Child Who Did Not Live With the Worker in Each of the Last 13 Months	List Each Month in Which This Child Did Not Live With the Worker	Person With Whom Child Lived	
		Name and Address	Relationship to Child

PART II — INFORMATION ABOUT THE DECEASED. Complete items 17 through 26 ONLY if the Worker is deceased. Otherwise, go on to the Signature block.

17.	(a) Print date of birth of Worker ➤	MONTH, DAY, YEAR
	(b) Print Worker's name at birth if different from item 1(a) ➤	
	(c) Check (✓) one for the Worker ➤	☐ Male ☐ Female
18.	(a) Print date of death ➤	MONTH, DAY, YEAR
	(b) Print place of death ➤	CITY AND STATE
19.	Print the name of the State or foreign country where the Worker had a fixed, permanent home at the time of death. ➤	
20.	Did the Worker work in the railroad industry at any time on or after January 1, 1937? ➤	☐ Yes ☐ No

Form **SSA-4-BK** (1-84) Page 3

(Turn to page 4)

21.	(a) Was the Worker in the active military or naval service (including Reserve or National Guard active duty or active duty for training) after September 7, 1939?	☐ Yes (If "Yes," answer (b) and (c).)	☐ No (If "No," go on to item 22.)
	(b) Enter dates of service	From: (Month, year)	To: (Month, year)
	(c) Has anyone (including the Worker) received, or does anyone expect to receive, a benefit from any other Federal agency?	☐ Yes	☐ No

22.	Were all the children in item 3 living with the Worker at the time of death?	☐ Yes	☐ No
		(If "No," enter the following information.)	

Name of Child Not Living With the Worker	Person With Whom Child Was Living Name and Address	Relationship to Child

ANSWER ITEM 23 ONLY IF DEATH OCCURRED WITHIN THE LAST 2 YEARS.

23.	(a) About how much did the Worker earn from employment and self-employment during the year of death?	AMOUNT $
	(b) About how much did the Worker earn the year before death?	AMOUNT $

24.	(a) Did the Worker ever engage in work that was covered under the social security system of a country other than the United States?	☐ Yes (If "Yes," answer (b).)	☐ No (If "No," go on to item 25.)
	(b) List the country(ies).		

25.	(a) Did the Worker ever file an application for Social Security benefits, a period of disability under Social Security, supplemental security income, or hospital or medical insurance under Medicare?	☐ Yes ☐ No ☐ Unknown (If "Yes," answer (b) and (c).) (If "No" or "Unknown", go on to item 26.)
	(b) Enter name of person(s) on whose Social Security record other application was filed.	
	(c) Enter Social Security Number of person named in (b). (If unknown, so indicate)	_ _ _ / _ _ / _ _ _ _

ANSWER ITEM 26 ONLY IF THE WORKER DIED PRIOR TO AGE 66 AND WITHIN THE PAST 4 MONTHS.

26.	(a) Was the Worker unable to work because of a disabling condition at the time of death?	☐ Yes ☐ No (If "Yes," answer (b).)
	(b) Enter date disability began	MONTH, DAY, YEAR

An ANNUAL REPORT of earnings must be filed with the Social Security Administration within 3 months and 15 days after the end of any taxable year in which any child earns more than the exempt amount (e.g., $5,160 for 1984) and receives some benefits in that year.
I AGREE TO FILE AN ANNUAL REPORT OF EARNINGS. THE ANNUAL REPORT IS REQUIRED BY LAW AND FAILURE TO REPORT MAY RESULT IN A MONETARY PENALTY.

BENEFITS MAY END if any of the following events occur. However, there are certain exceptions which are explained in the informational booklet which you will receive. You must report each of these events even if you believe an exception applies. We will advise you whether additional evidence is needed and how the benefits may be affected.
I AGREE TO PROMPTLY NOTIFY the Social Security Administration if any of the following events occur and to PROMPTLY RETURN ANY BENEFIT CHECK I receive to which a child is not entitled if:

- Any child MARRIES, is DIVORCED, or has a marriage ANNULMENT.
- A student, age 18 or over, STOPS ATTENDING SCHOOL, REDUCES SCHOOL ATTENDANCE BELOW FULL-TIME, CHANGES SCHOOLS, IS PAID BY AN EMPLOYER TO ATTEND SCHOOL, OR IS INCARCERATED FOR CONVICTION OF A FELONY.
- A disabled child, age 18 or over, GOES TO WORK, IS INCARCERATED FOR CONVICTION OF A FELONY, or the child's DISABLING CONDITION IMPROVES.
- I no longer have responsibility for the care and welfare of any child for whom I am filing.
- Any child for whom I am filing or who is in my care dies, leaves my care or custody, or changes address.

I UNDERSTAND that all payments made to me on behalf of a child must be spent for the child's present needs or (if not presently needed) saved for the child's future needs, and I AGREE to use the benefits that way. I will be held personally liable for repayment of benefits I receive if they are not spent for the child or if I am found at fault with respect to an overpayment of such benefits.

Remarks: (You may use this space for any explanations. If you need more space, attach a separate sheet.)

_____

_____

_____

_____

_____

_____

_____

_____

_____

_____

_____

_____

_____

_____

_____

_____

_____

_____

_____

I know that anyone who makes or causes to be made a false statement or representation of material fact in an application or for use in determining a right to payment under the Social Security Act commits a crime punishable under Federal law by fine, imprisonment or both. I affirm that all information I have given in this document is true.

SIGNATURE OF APPLICANT	Date (Month, day, year)
Signature (First name, middle initial, last name) (Write in ink) **SIGN HERE** ►	Telephone Number(s) at which you may be contacted during the day ___ ___ ___ Area Code

Mailing Address (Number and Street, Apt. No., P.O. Box, or Rural Route) (Enter residence address in "Remarks", if different.)

City and State	ZIP Code	Enter Name of County (if any) in wich you now live.

Witnesses are required ONLY if this application has been signed by mark (X) above. If signed by mark (X), two witnesses to the signing who know the applicant must sign below, giving their full addresses.

1. Signature of Witness	2. Signature of Witness
Address (Number and Street, City, State, and ZIP Code)	Address (Number and Street, City, State, and ZIP Code).

Form **SSA-4-BK** (1-84) Page 5

AN ANNUAL REPORT OF EARNINGS must be filed with the Social Security Administration within 3 months and 15 days after the end of any taxable year in which any child earns more than the exempt amount (e.g., $5,160 for 1984) and receives some benefit payment in that year.
THE ANNUAL REPORT IS REQUIRED BY LAW AND FAILURE TO REPORT MAY RESULT IN A MONETARY PENALTY.

BENEFITS MAY END if any of the following events occur. However, there are certain exceptions which are explained in the informational booklet which you will receive. You must report each of these events even if you believe an exception applies. We will advise you whether additional evidence is needed and how the benefits may be affected.
I AGREE TO PROMPTLY NOTIFY the Social Security Administration if any of the following events occur and to PROMPTLY RETURN ANY BENEFIT CHECK I receive to which a child is not entitled if:
- Any child MARRIES, is DIVORCED, or has a marriage ANNULMENT.
- A student, age 18 or over, STOPS ATTENDING SCHOOL, REDUCES SCHOOL ATTENDANCE BELOW FULL-TIME, CHANGES SCHOOLS, IS PAID BY AN EMPLOYER TO ATTEND SCHOOL, OR IS INCARCERATED FOR CONVICTION OF A FELONY.
- A disabled child, age 18 or over, GOES TO WORK, IS INCARCERATED FOR CONVICTION OF A FELONY, or the child's DISABLING CONDITION IMPROVES.
- I no longer have responsibility for the care and welfare of any child for whom I am filing.
- Any child for whom I am filing or who is in my care dies, leaves my care or custody, or changes address.

I UNDERSTAND that all payments made to me on behalf of a child must be spent for the child's present needs or (if not presently needed) saved for the child's future needs, and I AGREE to use the benefits that way. I will be held personally liable for repayment of benefits I receive if they are not spent for the child or if I am found at fault with respect to an overpayment of such benefits.

Collection and Use of Information from Your Application — Privacy Act/Paperwork Act Notice

I. The Social Security Administration is authorized to collect the information on this form under sections 202(d) and 205(a) of the Social Security Act, as amended (42 U.S.C. 402(d) and 405(a)).

II. While it is not mandatory, except in the circumstances explained below, for you to furnish the information on this form to Social Security, no benefits may be paid unless an application has been received by a Social Security office. Your response is mandatory where the refusal to disclose certain information affecting your right to payment would reflect a fraudulent intent to secure benefits not authorized by the Social Security Act.

III. The information on this form is needed to enable Social Security to determine if you and your dependents are entitled to insurance coverage and/or monthly benefits.

IV. Failure to provide all or part of this information could prevent an accurate and timely decision on your claim or your dependent's claim, and could result in the loss of some benefits or insurance coverage.

V. Although the information you furnish on this form is almost never used for any other purpose than stated in Part III, above, there is a possibility that in the administration of the Social Security programs or for the administration of programs requiring coordination with the Social Security Administration, information may be disclosed to another person or to another government agency as follows:
1. To enable a third party or an agency to assist Social Security in establishing rights to Social Security benefits.
2. To comply with Federal laws requiring the release of information from Social Security records (e.g., to the General Accounting Office and the Veterans Administration).
3. To facilitate statistical research and audit activities necessary to assure the integrity and improvement of the Social Security programs (e.g., to the Bureau of the Census and private concerns under contract to Social Security).

PLEASE READ THE FOLLOWING INFORMATION CAREFULLY

HOW EARNINGS IN 1984 AFFECT BENEFITS

A child may earn up to $5,160 a year* and still receive all the child's Social Security benefits. If a child earns OVER $5,160, $1 in benefits may be withheld for each $2 of earnings over $5,160. Under a "Monthly Earnings Test" the child is entitled to a benefit for any month the child does not earn wages of over $430 and does not perform substantial services in self-employment.**

HOW EARNINGS IN 1983 AFFECT BENEFITS

A child could earn up to $4,920 a year* and still receive all the child's Social Security benefits. If a child earned OVER $4,920, $1 in benefits may be withheld for each $2 of earnings over $4,920. Under a "Monthly Earnings Test" the child is entitled to a benefit for any month the child did not earn wages of over $410 and did not perform substantial services in self-employment.**

* This yearly period referred to in this and following items is the same 12-month period used in figuring income tax.
** Under the "Monthly Earnings Test," a child can get a full benefit for any month in which the child does not earn wages over the monthly exempt amount and does not perform substantial services in self-employment regardless of how much the child earns in the year. For children (including students), the Monthly Earnings Test can be used for two taxable years. The first taxable year in which the monthly earnings test can be used is usually the first year the child is entitled to benefits. The second taxable year in which the Monthly Earnings Test can be used is _always_ the year in which the child's entitlement to benefits stops. In all other years, the total amount of benefits payable will be based solely on a child's total yearly earnings without regard to monthly earnings or services rendered in self-employment.

RECEIPT FOR YOUR CLAIM FOR SOCIAL SECURITY CHILD'S INSURANCE BENEFITS

NAME OF PERSON TO CONTACT ABOUT YOUR CLAIM	SSA OFFICE	DATE CLAIM RECEIVED

TELEPHONE NUMBER(S) TO CALL IF YOU HAVE A QUESTION OR SOMETHING TO REPORT	**BEFORE** YOU RECEIVE A NOTICE OF AWARD
	AFTER YOU RECEIVE A NOTICE OF AWARD

Your application for Social Security benefits on behalf of the child(ren) named below has been received. You will be notified by mail as soon as a decision is made on your claim.

You should hear from us within _____ days after you have given us all the information we requested. Some claims may take longer if additional information is needed.

In the meantime, if you or any child(ren) changes address, or if there is some other change that may affect your claim, you or someone for you should report the change. The changes to be reported are listed below.

Always give us your claim number when writing or telephoning about your claim.

If you have any questions about your claim, we will be glad to help you.

CLAIMANT	SOCIAL SECURITY CLAIM NUMBER

WORKER'S NAME *(If surname differs from name of claimant(s).)*

CHANGES TO BE REPORTED AND HOW TO REPORT

FAILURE TO REPORT MAY RESULT IN OVERPAYMENTS THAT MUST BE REPAID, AND IN POSSIBLE MONETARY PENALTIES.

▶ You or any child changes mailing address for checks or residence. *To avoid delay in receipt of checks you should ALSO file a regular change of address notice with your post office.*

▶ Any beneficiary goes outside the U.S.A.

▶ Any beneficiary dies or becomes unable to handle benefits.

▶ Work Changes—On your application you told us

_____ expected total earnings for 19 ____
(name of child)

to be $ _____ .

_____ (is) (is not) earning wages of
(name of child)

more than $ _____ a month.

_____ (is) (is not) self-employed
(name of child)

rendering substantial services in a trade or business.

(Report AT ONCE if this work pattern changes.)

▶ Custody Change — Report if a child for whom you are filing or who is in your care dies, leaves your care or custody, or changes address.

▶ Change of Marital Status — Marriage, divorce, annulment of marriage of any child.

▶ Change in school attendance.

▶ Any child is confined to jail, prison, penal institution, or correctional facility for conviction of a felony.

▶ Disability Applicants
1. The disabled adult child returns to work (as an employee or self-employed) regardless of amount of earnings.
2. The disabled adult child's condition improves.
3. The disabled adult child is incarcerated for conviction of a felony.

An agency in your State that works with us in administering the Social Security disability program is responsible for making the disability decision on the child's claim. In some cases, it is necessary for them to get additional information about the child's condition or to arrange for the child to have a medical examination at Government expense.

HOW TO REPORT
You can make your reports by telephone, by mail, or in person, whichever you prefer.

WHEN A CHANGE OCCURS AFTER YOU RECEIVE A NOTICE OF AWARD, YOU SHOULD REPORT BY CALLING THE APPROPRIATE TELEPHONE NUMBER SHOWN NEAR THE TOP OF THIS PAGE.

DEPARTMENT OF HEALTH AND HUMAN SERVICES
Social Security Administration

TOE 120/145/155

Form Approved.
OMB No. 0960-0003

(Do not write in this space)

APPLICATION FOR MOTHER'S OR FATHER'S INSURANCE BENEFITS*

The information you furnish on this application will ordinarily be sufficient for a determination on the lump-sum death payment without the filing of a separate application.

*This may also be considered an application for survivors benefits under the Railroad Retirement Act and for Veterans Administration payments under title 38 U.S.C., Veterans Benefits, Chapter 13 (which is, as such, an application for other types of death benefits under title 38).

I apply for all insurance benefits for which I am eligible under Title II (Federal Old-Age, Survivors, and Disability Insurance) and Title XVIII (Health Insurance for the Aged and Disabled) of the Social Security Act, as presently amended.

1.	(a)	PRINT name of deceased wage earner or self-employed person *(herein referred to as the "deceased")* →	FIRST NAME, MIDDLE INITIAL, LAST NAME	
	(b)	Check (✓) one for the deceased →	☐ Male	☐ Female
	(c)	Enter deceased's Social Security Number →	— — — / — — / — — — —	

| 2. | (a) | PRINT your name → | FIRST NAME, MIDDLE INITIAL, LAST NAME |
| | (b) | Enter your Social Security Number → | — — — / — — / — — — — |

| 3. | Enter your name at birth if different from item 2. → | |

| 4. | (a) | Enter your date of birth → | MONTH, DAY, YEAR |
| | (b) | Enter name of State or foreign country where you were born → | |

Please read carefully before answering item 5

You may receive a mother's or a father's benefit for any month in which you have in your care the deceased's child or dependent grandchild who is entitled to a child's benefit if the child is:

- under age 16, or
- disabled or handicapped (age 16 or over and disability began before age 22)

If you are filing as a surviving divorced mother or father, such child must be your son, daughter, or legally adopted child who is entitled to child's benefits on the deceased's earnings record.

Mother's or father's benefits are not payable if the only child in your care is a child age 16 or over who is not disabled.

5.	Has an unmarried child or dependent grandchild of the deceased, who is under age 16 or disabled, lived with you any time from the month of death through the present month? (Include natural child, adopted child, stepchild, and stepgrandchild.) *(If "Yes," enter the information requested below)* →	☐ Yes	☐ No

Name of child	Months child lived with you *(If all, write "All")*

6.	(a)	Have you (or has someone on your behalf) ever filed an application for Social Security benefits, a period of disability under Social Security, supplemental security income, or hospital or medical insurance under Medicare? →	☐ Yes *(If "Yes," answer (b) and (c).)*	☐ No *(If "No," go on to item 7.)*
	(b)	Enter name of person on whose Social Security record you filed other application. →		
	(c)	Enter Social Security Number of person named in (b). *(If unknown, so indicate)* →	— — — / — — / — — — —	

Form **SSA-5-F6** (1-84) Destroy prior editions.   Page 1

| 7. | (a) | Are you so disabled that you can't work or was there some period during the last 14 months when you were so disabled that you could not work? ⟶ | ☐ Yes　　☐ No
(If "Yes," answer (b).) (If "No," go on to item 8.) |
| | (b) | Enter the date you became disabled. | Month, Day, Year |

| 8. | Did you work in the railroad industry on or at any time after January 1, 1937? ⟶ | ☐ Yes　　☐ No |

| 9. | (a) | Have you ever engaged in work that was covered under the social security system of a country other than the United States? ⟶ | ☐ Yes　　☐ No
(If "Yes," answer (b).)(If "No," go on to item 10.) |
| | (b) | If "Yes," list the country(ies). ⟶ | |

| 10. | Is there a surviving parent (or parents) of the deceased who was receiving support from the deceased at the time of death or at the time the deceased became disabled? ⟶ | ☐ Yes　　☐ No
(If "Yes," enter the name and address of the parent(s) in "Remarks".) |

11. Enter below information about each of your marriages. Include information on your marriage to the deceased and any other marriages, whether before or after you married the deceased. If you are applying for father's benefits, enter the maiden name of the deceased.

	To whom married	When *(Month, day, year)*	Where *(Name of City and State)*
Your last marriage	How marriage ended	When *(Month, day, year)*	Where *(Name of City and State)*
	Marriage performed by: ☐ Clergyman or public official ☐ Other *(Explain in Remarks)*	Spouse's date of birth (or age)	If spouse deceased, give date of death
	Spouse's Social Security Number *(If none or unknown, so indicate)*		___ ___ ___ / ___ ___ / ___ ___ ___ ___

	To whom married	When *(Month, day, year)*	Where *(Name of City and State)*
Your previous marriage **(IF NONE, WRITE "NONE.")**	How marriage ended	When *(Month, day, year)*	Where *(Name of City and State)*
	Marriage performed by: ☐ Clergyman or public official ☐ Other *(Explain in Remarks)*	Spouse's date of birth (or age)	If spouse deceased, give date of death
	Spouse's Social Security Number *(If none or unknown, so indicate)*		___ ___ ___ / ___ ___ / ___ ___ ___ ___

(Use "Remarks" space on back page for information about any other previous marriage)

12. Enter below the information requested about each marriage of the deceased, including the marriage to you. (Indicate your marriage to the deceased by entering your name; it is not necessary to repeat other information about this marriage you have already given in item 11.) Enter complete information on all other marriages.

	To whom married	When *(Month, day, year)*	Where *(Name of City and State)*
Last Marriage of Deceased	How marriage ended	When *(Month, day, year)*	Where *(Name of City and State)*
	Marriage performed by: ☐ Clergyman or public official ☐ Other *(Explain in Remarks)*	Spouse's date of birth (or age)	If spouse deceased, give date of death
	Spouse's Social Security Number *(If none or unknown, so indicate)*		___ ___ ___ / ___ ___ / ___ ___ ___ ___

	To whom married	When *(Month, day, year)*	Where *(Name of City and State)*
Previous marriage of the deceased **(IF NONE, WRITE "NONE.")**	How marriage ended	When *(Month, day, year)*	Where *(Name of City and State)*
	Marriage performed by: ☐ Clergyman or public official ☐ Other *(Explain in Remarks)*	Spouse's date of birth (or age)	If spouse deceased, give date of death
	Spouse's Social Security Number *(If none or unknown, so indicate)*		___ ___ ___ / ___ ___ / ___ ___ ___ ___

(Use "Remarks" space on back page for information about any other previous marriage)

13. **(a)** Were you and the deceased living together at the same address when the deceased died? ➤

☐ Yes
(If "Yes," go on to item 14.)

☐ No
(If "No," answer (b).)

(b) If either you or the deceased were away from home (whether or not temporarily) when the deceased died, give the following:

Who was away? ➤	☐ You ☐ Deceased
Reason absence began ➤	
Date last at home ➤	
Reason you were apart at time of death ➤	
If separated because of illness, enter nature of illness or disabling condition ➤	

PLEASE READ CAREFULLY THE INFORMATION ON THE OPPOSITE PAGE

Answer item 14 **ONLY** if the deceased died before this year.

14. **(a)** How much were your total earnings in 1983? ➤ $

(b) Did you earn more than $410 in wages or perform substantial services in self-employment in each month of 1983?

☐ Yes *(If "Yes," go on to item 15).*

☐ No *(If "No," answer (c))*

(c) Circle each month of 1983 in which you did not earn more than $410 in wages and did not perform substantial services in self-employment.

Jan.	Feb.	Mar.	Apr.
May	Jun.	Jul.	Aug.
Sept.	Oct.	Nov.	Dec.

15. **(a)** How much do you expect your total earnings to be in 1984? ➤ $

(b) Did you or will you earn more than $430 a month in wages or perform substantial services in self-employment in all months of 1984?

☐ Yes *(If "Yes," go on to item 16).*

☐ No *(If "No," answer (c))*

(c) Circle each month of 1984 in which you did not or will not earn more than $430 in wages and did not or will not perform substantial services in self-employment.

Jan.	Feb.	Mar.	Apr.
May	Jun.	Jul.	Aug.
Sept.	Oct.	Nov.	Dec.

Answer this item ONLY if you are now in the last 4 months of your taxable year (Sept., Oct., Nov., and Dec., if your taxable year is a calendar year).

16. **(a)** How much do you expect to earn in 1985? ➤ $

(b) Circle each month of 1985 in which you do not expect to earn more than $_____ in wages and do not expect to perform substantial services in self-employment.

Jan.	Feb.	Mar.	Apr.
May	Jun.	Jul.	Aug.
Sept.	Oct.	Nov.	Dec.

If you use a fiscal year, that is, a taxable year that does not end December 31 (with income tax return due April 15), enter here the month your fiscal year ends. ➤

MONTH

17. (a) Have you qualified for, or do you expect to qualify for, a pension or annuity (or a lump sum in place of a pension or annuity) based on your own employment and earnings for the Federal Government of the United States, or one of its States or local subdivisions? ➤

☐ Yes   ☐ No

(If "Yes," check the box in item (b) that applies.
(If "No," go on to item 18.)

(b) ☐ I receive a government pension or annuity.

☐ I received a lump sum in place of a government pension or annuity.

☐ I applied for and am awaiting a decision on my pension or lump sum.

☐ I have not applied for but I expect to begin receiving my pension or annuity

_____
(Month, year)

(If the date is not known, enter "Unknown")

18. It is possible for your Social Security monthly payments to be forwarded directly to your bank, savings and loan, credit union, or other financial organization for deposit to your account. This method of payment is known as direct deposit. If you wish direct deposit you will have to contact your financial organization to complete the necessary form. We will advise you when your direct deposit request is processed. If you do not wish direct deposit your benefits will be paid by check to your mailing address.

Do you wish to be paid by direct deposit? ➤   ☐ Yes   ☐ No

It is possible that your claim will be ready to be paid before the direct deposit form is returned by your financial organization. Your claim can be processed and any payments due will be sent to you until your direct deposit request is received.

An ANNUAL REPORT of earnings must be filed with the Social Security Administration within 3 months and 15 days after the end of any taxable year in which you earn more than the exempt amount (e.g., $5,160 for 1984) and receive some benefits during the taxable year. I AGREE TO FILE AN ANNUAL REPORT OF EARNINGS. THE ANNUAL REPORT IS REQUIRED BY LAW AND FAILURE TO REPORT MAY RESULT IN A MONETARY PENALTY.

BENEFITS MAY END if either of the following events occur. However, there are certain exceptions which are explained in the informational booklet which you will receive. You must report each of these events even if you believe an exception applies. We will advise you whether additional evidence is needed and how your benefits may be affected.

I AGREE TO PROMPTLY NOTIFY the Social Security Administration and to PROMPTLY RETURN ANY BENEFIT CHECK I receive if the check is for a month in or after the month in which:
- I MARRY.
- I NO LONGER HAVE IN MY CARE the deceased's child or dependent grandchild under age 16 or disabled who is entitled to benefits.

REMARKS *(You may use this space for any explanations. If you need more space, attach a separate sheet.)*

_____

_____

I know that anyone who makes or causes to be made a false statement or representation of material fact in an application or for use in determining a right to payment under the Social Security Act commits a crime punishable under Federal law by fine, imprisonment or both. I affirm that all information I have given in this document is true.

SIGNATURE OF APPLICANT	Date *(Month, day, year)*
Signature *(First name, middle initial, last name) (Write in ink)*	Telephone Number(s) at which you may be contacted during the day
SIGN HERE ▶	_____ AREA CODE

Mailing Address *(Number and street, Apt No., P.O. Box, or Rural Route) (Enter resident address in "Remarks" if different)*

City and State	ZIP Code	Enter Name of County (if any) in which you now live

Witnesses are required ONLY if this application has been signed by mark (X) above. If signed by mark (X), two witnesses to the signing who know the applicant must sign below, giving their full addresses.

1. Signature of Witness	2. Signature of Witness
Address *(Number and street, City, State and ZIP Code)*	Address *(Number and street, City, State and ZIP Code)*

Form **SSA-5-F6** (1-84) Page 4

PLEASE READ THE FOLLOWING INFORMATION CAREFULLY

HOW YOUR EARNINGS IN 1984 AFFECT YOUR BENEFITS
You may earn up to $5,160 a year and still receive all your Social Security benefits. *If you earn OVER $5,160, $1 in benefits may be withheld for each $2 of earnings you have over $5,160. Under a "Monthly Earnings Test" you are entitled to a benefit for any month you do not earn wages of over $430 and do not perform substantial services in self-employment.**

HOW YOUR EARNINGS IN 1983 AFFECT YOUR BENEFITS
You could earn up to $4,920 a year and still receive all your Social Security benefits. *If you earned OVER $4,920, $1 in benefits may be withheld for each $2 of earnings you had over $4,920. Under a "Monthly Earnings Test" you are entitled to a benefit for any month you did not earn wages of over $410 and did not perform substantial services in self-employment.**

*This yearly period referred to in this and following items is the same 12-month period you use in figuring your income tax.

**Under the Monthly Earnings Test, you can get a full benefit for any month in which you do not earn wages over the monthly exempt amount and do not perform substantial services in self-employment, regardless of how much you earn in the year. For younger beneficiaries such as mothers and fathers entitled only by reason of child-in-care, the Monthly Earnings Test can be used for two taxable years. The first taxable year in which the Monthly Earnings Test may be used is usually the first year you are entitled to benefits. The second taxable year in which the Monthly Earnings Test may be used is *always* the year in which your entitlement to benefits stops. In all other years, the total amounts of benefits payable will be based solely on your total yearly earnings without regard to monthly earnings or services rendered in self-employment.

FIGURING YOUR ANNUAL EARNINGS
To figure your total yearly earnings, count all gross wages (before deductions) and net earnings from self-employment which you earn during the entire year. This includes all earned income whether or not covered by Social Security.

Collection and Use of Information from Your Application—Privacy Act/Paperwork Act Notice

The Social Security Administration is authorized to collect the information on this form under sections 202(g) and 205(a) of the Social Security Act, as amended (42 U.S.C. 402(g) and 405(a)).

II. While it is voluntary, except in the circumstances explained below, for you to furnish the information on this form to Social Security, no benefits may be paid unless an application has been received by a Social Security Office. Your response is mandatory where the refusal to disclose certain information affecting your right to payment would reflect a fraudulent intent to secure benefits not authorized by the Social Security Act.

III. The information on this form is needed to enable Social Security to determine if you and your family are entitled to monthly benefits.

IV. Failure to provide all or part of this information could prevent an accurate and timely decision on your claim or your family's claim, and could result in the loss of some benefits.

V. Although the information you furnish on this form is almost never used for any other purpose than stated in Part III, above, there is a possibility that in the administration of the Social Security programs or for the administration of programs requiring coordination with the Social Security Administration, information may be disclosed to another person or to another government agency as follows:

1. To enable a third party or an agency to assist Social Security in establishing rights to Social Security benefits.

2. To comply with Federal laws requiring the release of information from Social Security records (e.g., to the General Accounting Office and the Veterans Administration).

3. To facilitate statistical research and audit activities necessary to assure the integrity and improvement of the Social Security programs (e.g., to the Bureau of the Census and private concerns under contract to Social Security).

RECEIPT FOR YOUR CLAIM FOR SOCIAL SECURITY MOTHER'S OR FATHER'S INSURANCE BENEFITS

NAME OF PERSON TO CONTACT ABOUT YOUR CLAIM		SSA OFFICE	DATE CLAIM RECEIVED
TELEPHONE NUMBER(S) TO CALL IF YOU HAVE A QUESTION OR SOMETHING TO REPORT	**BEFORE** YOU RECEIVE A NOTICE OF AWARD		
	AFTER YOU RECEIVE A NOTICE OF AWARD		

Your application for Social Security benefits has been received and will be processed as quickly as possible.

You should hear from us within _____ days after you have given us all the information we requested. Some claims may take longer if additional information is needed.

In the meantime, if you change your address, or if there is some other change that may affect your claim, you — or someone for you — should report the change. The changes to be reported are listed below.

Always give us your claim number when writing or telephoning about your claim.

If you have any questions about your claim, we will be glad to help you.

CLAIMANT	DECEASED'S SURNAME IF DIFFERENT FROM CLAIMANT'S	SOCIAL SECURITY CLAIM NUMBER

CHANGES TO BE REPORTED AND HOW TO REPORT

Failure to report may result in overpayments that must be repaid, and in possible monetary penalties.

▶ You change your mailing address for checks or residence. *To avoid delay in receipt of checks you should ALSO file a regular change of address notice with your post office.*

▶ You go outside the U.S.A.

▶ Any beneficiary dies or becomes unable to handle benefits.

▶ Work Changes—On your application you told us you expect total earnings for 19_____ to be $ _____ .

You (are) (are not) earning wages of more than $ _____ a month.

You (are) (are not) self-employed rendering substantial services in your trade or business.

(Report AT ONCE if this work pattern changes.)

▶ You are confined to jail, prison, penal institution, or correctional facility for conviction of a felony.

▶ Custody Change or Disability Improves — Report if a person for whom you are filing or who is in your care dies, leaves your care or custody, changes address or, if disabled, the condition improves.

▶ Change of Marital Status — Marriage, divorce, annulment of marriage.

▶ You begin to receive a government pension or annuity (from the Federal government or any State or any political subdivision thereof) or present payment changes.

HOW TO REPORT
You can make your reports by telephone, mail, or in person, whichever you prefer.

WHEN A CHANGE OCCURS AFTER YOU RECEIVE A NOTICE OF AWARD, YOU SHOULD REPORT BY CALLING THE APPROPRIATE TELEPHONE NUMBER SHOWN NEAR THE TOP OF THIS PAGE.

Also, an ANNUAL REPORT OF EARNINGS must be filed with the Social Security Administration within 3 months and 15 days after the end of any taxable year in which you earn more than the exempt amount and receive some benefits during the taxable year. THE ANNUAL REPORT IS REQUIRED BY LAW AND FAILURE TO REPORT MAY RESULT IN A MONETARY PENALTY.

Sample Forms for Applying for Veterans Administration Benefits

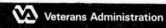 **Veterans Administration**

Form Approved
OMB No. 76-RO668

DETACH AND RETAIN THIS GENERAL INFORMATION SHEET

APPLICATION FOR STANDARD GOVERNMENT HEADSTONE OR MARKER

FOR

INSTALLATION IN A PRIVATE OR LOCAL CEMETERY

BENEFIT PROVIDED

    a. Headstone or Marker - Furnished upon application for the *unmarked grave* of a deceased veteran. Applicant must be sure the grave is *UNMARKED* and a Government headstone or marker is preferred to a privately purchased monument. Applicant may be anyone having knowledge of the deceased.

    b. Memorial Headstone or Marker - Furnished upon application by a relative recognized as the next of kin for installation in a private or local cemetery *or in a national cemetery* to commemorate any veteran whose remains have not been recovered or identified or were buried at sea through no choice of the next of kin. Check box in item 1.

    c. Crypt Marker - If entombment is in a columbarium or mausoleum, complete the application (except item 10) and check the box in item 24. You will be advised of special procedures in such cases.

WHO IS ELIGIBLE - Any deceased veteran of wartime or peacetime service who was discharged under conditions other than dishonorable. To expedite processing, attach a copy of the deceased veteran's discharge certificate or other official document(s) pertaining to military service, if available. Do not send the original.

HOW TO APPLY - Mail both copies of the completed application (VA FORM 40-1330) to: Monument Service (42), Veterans Administration, 810 Vermont Avenue, N.W., Washington, D.C. 20420. No Government headstone or marker may be furnished unless a completed application form has been received (38 U.S.C. 906).

SIGNATURES REQUIRED - The applicant signs in item 15 and then obtains signature of consignee in item 19 and signature of cemetery official in item 22. If there is no official in charge of the cemetery write "NONE" in item 22.

ASSISTANCE NEEDED - If assistance is needed to complete this application, contact the nearest VA Regional Office, National Cemetery, or a local veterans organization. No fee should be paid in connection with the preparation of this application.

INSTALLATION - All costs to install the headstone or marker must be paid from private funds.

TRANSPORTATION - The headstone or marker is shipped without charge to the person or firm designated in item 17 of the application. An address showing Rural Delivery or Post Office Box must show a telephone number in item 18 to expedite delivery.

DUPLICATION OF BENEFITS PROHIBITED - Applicant has the option of requesting a monetary allowance instead of a Government headstone or marker. Application for the monetary allowance must be submitted on VA Form 21-8834, Application for Reimbursement of Headstone or Marker Expenses, available at any VA Regional Office. Application may be filed for *one benefit only.*

CAUTION - After completing the application, please check carefully to be sure you have furnished all required information and that it is accurate. Mistakes cannot be corrected at Government expense after headstone or marker has been ordered from the contractor. A headstone or marker furnished on this application remains the property of the United States Government and cannot be used for any purpose other than to memorialize the deceased veteran.

VA FORM
JUL 1980 **40-1330**

EXISTING STOCK OF VA FORM 40-1330, AUG 1977,
WILL BE USED.

ILLUSTRATIONS OF STANDARD GOVERNMENT HEADSTONE AND MARKERS

NOTE: In addition to the headstone and markers pictured, two special styles of upright marble headstone are available upon request - one for eligible deceased who served with the Union Forces, Civil War, or during the Spanish-American War; and the other for eligible deceased who served with the Confederate Forces, Civil War. Request should be made in item 24 of the application.

UPRIGHT HEADSTONE OF
AMERICAN WHITE MARBLE

This headstone is 42 inches long, 13 inches wide, and 4 inches thick. Weight is approximately 230 pounds.

FLAT MARKERS
AMERICAN WHITE MARBLE OR LIGHT GRAY GRANITE

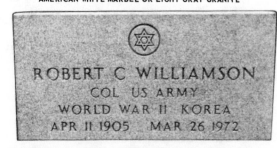

This marker is 24 inches long, 12 inches wide, and 4 inches thick. Weight is approximately 130 pounds.

BRONZE

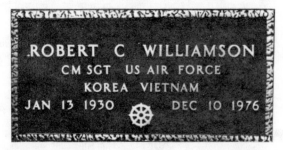

This marker is 24 inches long and 12 inches wide, with 3/4-inch rise above the foundation. Weight is approximately 18 pounds. Anchor bolts for fastening the marker to the foundation are furnished with the marker.

SLATE

This marker is 24 inches long, 12 inches wide, and 3/4-inch thick. Weight is approximately 20 pounds. Color will vary with the contractor's source of supply. ▶

INSCRIPTION INFORMATION

<u>Mandatory items</u> of inscription at Government expense are: Name; Branch of Service; and Year of Birth - Year of Death. Branches of Service are: U.S. Army, U.S. Navy, U.S. Air Force, U.S. Marine Corps and U.S. Coast Guard. Only one may be shown. NOTE: Army Air Corps and Army Air Forces were a part of the U.S. Army and, therefore, are not authorized for inscription at Government expense as Branch of Service.

<u>Optional items</u> which may be inscribed at Government expense are: Grade, Rate or Rank; War Service; Month and Day in the dates of birth and death; and an emblem reflective of a religious or non-religious belief. If any of these items are desired, the information must be clearly shown in the appropriate shaded boxes on the application.

<u>Memorial headstones and markers</u>: The words "In Memory Of" are mandatory and will precede the authorized inscription data.

<u>Additional inscription items</u> may be inscribed at private expense subject to VA approval. Such items may be terms of endearment, emblems and other representations of military and civilian participation or accomplishments. Request should be made in item 24 of the application. Financial and other arrangements are the responsibility of the applicant and contractor. Detailed instructions will be furnished by the VA Monument Service in each case.

IMPORTANT: *Read the General Information sheet before completing this form. Type or print in caps (except signatures).*

Form Approved
OMB No. 76-RO668

1. NAME OF DECEASED TO BE INSCRIBED ON HEADSTONE OR MARKER (NICKNAME NOT AUTHORIZED)	☐ CHECK IF REMAINS NONRECOVERABLE

FIRST (Or initial)	MIDDLE (Or initial)	LAST

NOTE—Shaded blocks are optional inscription items. See Inscription Information.

2. HIGHEST RANK ATTAINED	3. BRANCH OF SERVICE	4. WAS DECEASED AWARDED MEDAL OF HONOR? ☐ YES ☐ NO

5. WAR SERVICE
☐ WWI ☐ WWII ☐ KOREA ☐ VIETNAM ☐ OTHER (Specify in Item 24) ☐ NONE

6. YEAR OF BIRTH *	7. YEAR OF DEATH *

*Give complete dates (month, day, year) if desired on inscription.

8. SERVICE NO., SOCIAL SECURITY NO., OR VA CLAIM NO. OF DECEASED

9. SERVICE INFORMATION (Last period of active duty)

A. DATE ENTERED (Month, day, year)	B. DATE RELEASED (Month, day, year)

10. TYPE OF HEADSTONE OR MARKER REQUESTED (Check one)
☐ UPRIGHT MARBLE ☐ FLAT MARBLE ☐ FLAT GRANITE ☐ FLAT SLATE ☐ FLAT BRONZE

11. DESIRED EMBLEM OF RELIGIOUS OR NON-RELIGIOUS BELIEF (Check one)
☐ CROSS (Christian) ☐ STAR OF DAVID (Jewish) ☐ WHEEL OF RIGHTEOUSNESS (Buddhist) ☐ OTHER (Specify in Item 24) ☐ NONE

FOR USE OF VETERANS ADMINISTRATION

INSCRIPTION DATA

ORDER NO.	DATE ORDERED	CONTRACTOR

12. APPLICANT'S NAME AND ADDRESS (No. and street, city, State and ZIP CODE)

13. AREA CODE AND PHONE NO.	14. RELATIONSHIP TO DECEASED

I accept responsibility for installing the headstone or marker at no expense to the Government. I certify that all statements made are true and correct to the best of my knowledge.

15. SIGNATURE OF APPLICANT	16. DATE

17. NAME AND ADDRESS OF PERSON, CEMETERY, OR FIRM OFFICIAL WHO WILL ACCEPT PREPAID DELIVERY (No. and street, city, State and ZIP CODE)	18. AREA CODE AND PHONE NO.

I agree to accept headstone or marker on behalf of applicant.

19. SIGNATURE OF PERSON TO ACCEPT DELIVERY	20. DATE

21. NAME AND LOCATION OF CEMETERY (City and State)

The headstone or marker of the type checked in item 10 will be permitted on the unmarked plot or grave of the named deceased.

22. SIGNATURE OF CEMETERY OFFICIAL	23. DATE

VA FORM JUL 1980 **40-1330**   (SUBMIT IN DUPLICATE)   **APPLICATION FOR STANDARD GOVERNMENT HEADSTONE OR MARKER**

NOTE—Before making any entries on this side of the form, reverse the carbon paper.

24. USE THIS SPACE, IF NECESSARY, TO CONTINUE YOUR ENTRIES FOR OTHER ITEMS, FOR REMARKS, OR FOR ADDITIONAL INSCRIPTION ITEMS AT PRIVATE EXPENSE.

☐ ENTOMBMENT IS IN A COLUMBARIUM OR MAUSOLEUM

FOR USE OF VETERANS ADMINISTRATION

TO INSCRIPTION	TO ORDER	TO TRANSPORTATION
TO RESOLUTION	SUSPENDED	REACTIVATED
CANCELED	RENEWAL	REPLACEMENT

Form Approved
OMB No. 2900-0013

VETERANS ADMINISTRATION
APPLICATION FOR UNITED STATES FLAG FOR BURIAL PURPOSES

Postmaster or other issuing official: Submit this form to the nearest VA Regional Office. Be sure to complete the stub at the bottom.

LAST NAME - FIRST NAME - MIDDLE NAME OF DECEASED *(Print or type)*

BRANCH OF SERVICE *(Check)*

☐ ARMY ☐ NAVY ☐ AIR FORCE ☐ MARINE CORPS ☐ COAST GUARD
☐ OTHER *(Specify)*

VETERAN'S SERVICE *(Check)*

☐ SPANISH AMERICAN ☐ WW I ☐ WW II ☐ KOREAN CONFLICT ☐ AFTER 1-31-55
☐ OTHER *(Specify)*

CONDITION UNDER WHICH VETERAN WAS RELEASED FROM SERVICE *(Check)*

☐ 1. VETERAN OF A WAR, MEXICAN BORDER SERVICE, OR OF SERVICE AFTER 1-31-55, DISCHARGED OR RELEASED FROM ACTIVE DUTY UNDER CONDITIONS OTHER THAN DISHONORABLE.

☐ 3. BY DEATH IN ACTIVE SERVICE AFTER MAY 27, 1941, AND FLAG NOT FURNISHED BY THE SERVICE DEPARTMENT.

☐ 2. DISCHARGED FROM, OR RELEASED FROM ACTIVE DUTY IN U.S. ARMED FORCES UNDER CONDITIONS OTHER THAN DISHONORABLE, AFTER SERVING AT LEAST ONE ENLISTMENT, OR DISCHARGED FOR DISABILITY INCURRED IN LINE OF DUTY.

☐ 4. SEPARATED FROM PHILIPPINE MILITARY FORCES, UNDER CONDITIONS OTHER THAN DISHONORABLE, AFTER SERVING UNITED STATES IN SUCH FORCES UNDER PRESIDENT'S ORDER OF JULY 26, 1941, AND DIED ON OR AFTER APRIL 25, 1951.

NAME OF PERSON ENTITLED TO RECEIVE FLAG

ADDRESS OF PERSON ENTITLED TO RECEIVE FLAG

RELATIONSHIP TO DECEASED

PERSONAL DATA OF DECEASED *(To be filled in if possible)*

VA FILE NUMBER	SOCIAL SECURITY NUMBER	SERVICE SERIAL NUMBER

DATE OF ENLISTMENT	DATE OF DISCHARGE	DATE OF BIRTH	DATE OF DEATH

DATE OF BURIAL	PLACE OF BURIAL *(Name of cemetery, city, and State)*

REMARKS

I CERTIFY that, to the best of my knowledge and belief, the statements made above are correct and true, the deceased is eligible, in accordance with attached Instructions, for issue of a United States flag for burial purposes, and such flag has not previously been applied for or furnished.

SIGNATURE OF APPLICANT *(Sign in INK)*	ADDRESS	RELATIONSHIP TO DECEASED	DATE

PENALTY--The law provides that whoever makes any statement of a material fact knowing it to be false shall be punished by a fine or by imprisonment of both.

ACKNOWLEDGMENT OF RECEIPT OF FLAG

I CERTIFY that the flag requested by the applicant will be used to drape the casket of the deceased in whose honor it is issued by the Veterans Administration; and that paragraph 7 of the attached Instructions will be complied with.

SIGNATURE OF PERSON RECEIVING FLAG *(Sign in INK)*

DATE FLAG RECEIVED

NAME AND ADDRESS OF POST OFFICE OR OTHER FLAG ISSUE POINT

FOR VA USE

DATE NOTIFICATION FORWARDED TO SUPPLY	INITIALS OF RESPONSIBLE VA EMPLOYEE

VA FORM
FEB 1979 **90-2008**

This stub is to be completed by the POSTMASTER or other issuing official. Upon receipt the VA Regional Office will detach and forward it to the appropriate Supply Officer.

NOTIFICATION OF ISSUANCE OF FLAG

DATE FLAG ISSUED	SIGNATURE OF POSTMASTER OR OTHER ISSUING OFFICIAL *(Sign in INK)*	ADDRESS

FOR VA USE ▶	DATE OF REPLACEMENT

VA FORM
FEB 1979 **90-2008**

EXISTING STOCKS OF VA FORM 60-2008 AND 00-2008, FEB 1979, WILL BE USED.

USE OF THE FLAG

1. This flag is issued on behalf of the Veterans Administration to honor the memory of one who has served our country.

2. When used to drape the casket, the flag should be placed as follows:

(a) Closed Casket.—When the flag is used to drape a closed casket, it should be so placed that the union (blue field) is at the head and over the left shoulder of the deceased.

(b) Half Couch (Open).—When the flag is used to drape a half-couch casket, it should be placed in three layers to cover the closed half of the casket in such a manner that the blue field will be the top fold, next to the open portion of the casket on the deceased's left.

(c) Full Couch (Open).—When the flag is used to drape a full-couch casket, it should be folded in a triangular shape and placed in the center part of the head panel of the casket cap, just above the left shoulder of the deceased.

3. During a military commitment ceremony, the flag which was used to drape the casket is held waist high over the grave by the pallbearers and, immediately after the sounding of "Taps," is folded in accordance with the paragraph below.

4. Folding the flag (see illustration):

CORRECT METHOD OF FOLDING THE UNITED STATES FLAG

(a) Fold the lower striped section of the flag over the blue field.

(b) Folded edge is then folded over to meet the open edge.

(c) A triangular fold is then started by bringing the striped corner of the folded edge to the open edge.

(d) Outer point is then turned inward parallel with the open edge to form a second triangle.

(e) Triangular folding is continued until the entire length of the flag is folded in the triangular shape of a cocked hat with only the blue field visible.

5. The flag should not be lowered into the grave or allowed to touch the ground. When taken from the casket, it should be folded as above.

6. The flag should form a distinctive feature of the ceremony of unveiling a statue or monument, but it should never be used as a covering for the statue or monument.

7. The flag should never be fastened, displayed, used, or stowed in such a manner as will permit it to be easily torn, soiled, or damaged in any way.

8. The flag should never have placed upon it, nor any part of it, nor attached to it, any mark, insignia, letter, word, figure, design, picture, or drawing of any nature.

9. The flag should never be used as a receptacle for receiving, holding, carrying, or delivering anything.

10. The flag, when badly worn, torn, or soiled should no longer be publicly displayed, but privately destroyed by burning in such a manner as to convey no suggestion of disrespect or irreverence.

INSTRUCTIONS

1. No flag may be issued unless a completed application form has been received (38 U.S.C. 901). The person filling out the application must state (under "relationship to deceased") whether he/she is: *(a)* A relative, and degree of relationship (e.g., "Brother"); *(b)* the funeral director; *(c)* a representative of veterans' or other organization having charge of the burial (e.g., "The American Legion"); *(d)* other person having a knowledge of the facts, and acting in the interest of the deceased or his/her family (e.g., "Friend"; "Det. Clerk").

2. One of the numbered conditions listed "under which deceased was separated from service" must be evidenced, normally by a document such as a discharge paper, before a flag may be issued.

(a) The phrase "veteran of a war" (No. 1) requires a showing that the deceased was in service in the United States armed forces during a war period. The phrase "Mexican border service" means active service during the period beginning on January 1, 1911, and ending on April 5, 1917, in Mexico, on the borders thereof, or in the waters adjacent thereto. The phrase "service after January 31, 1955" relates to veterans with active military, naval, or air service after that date.

(b) The phrase "under conditions other than dishonorable" requires a showing of discharge or release from active duty under honorable conditions ("Honorable" or "General") from the indicated period of service in the United States armed forces, or, in absence of such discharge or release from active duty, a determination by Veterans Administration that discharge or release from active duty, was under conditions other than dishonorable.

(c) The phrase "at least one enlistment" (No. 2) is construed to include service of a commissioned officer whose service, computed from date of entrance into commissioned status to date of separation from service, terminated under honorable conditions, and in all cases, relates to peacetime service before June 27, 1950.

(d) When the deceased was honorably discharged for disability, it may be assumed that the disability was "incurred in line of duty."

(e) Issue of flag in in-service cases (No. 3) is required only when deceased was interred outside the United States, or remains not recovered, or where service department cannot supply flag in time for burial. Explanation should be included under "Remarks."

3. When the applicant is unable to furnish documentary proof, such as a discharge under honorable conditions ("Honorable" or "General"), an application may be accepted and a flag issued when statement is made by a person of established character and reputation that he/she personally knows the deceased to have been a veteran of a war, the Mexican border service, or of service after January 31, 1955, discharged or released from active duty, under honorable conditions, or to have been a person discharged from, or released from active duty in the United States Army, Navy, Air Force, Marine Corps, or Coast Guard under honorable conditions after serving at least one complete peacetime enlistment, before June 27, 1950, or for disability incurred in line of duty; or that the deceased was in active service at the time of death and a flag was not obtainable from a military or naval establishment in time for burial.

4. The following classes of persons are ineligible for issue of a burial flag:

(a) A discharged or rejected draftee, or a member of the National Guard, who reported to camp in answer to the President's call for World War I service but who, when medically examined, was not finally accepted for military service.

(b) A person who was discharged from World War I service prior to November 12, 1918, on his/her own application or solicitation, by reason of being an alien, or any person discharged for alienage during a period of hostilities.

(c) A person who served with any of the forces allied with the United States in any war, even though a United States citizen, if he/she did not serve with the United States armed forces.

(d) A person inducted for training and service who, before entering upon such training and service, was transferred to the Enlisted Reserve Corps and given a furlough.

(e) A former temporary member of the United States Coast Guard Reserve.

(f) A reservist who served only on active duty for training unless he/she was disabled or died from a disease or injury incurred or aggravated in line of duty.

5. Flags will not be issued subsequent to burial, except where circumstances render it impossible to obtain a flag in time to drape the casket of a deceased veteran prior to final interment. The applicant must personally sign the application and include (under "Remarks") a statement explaining the circumstances preventing the requesting of a burial flag prior to final interment.

6. In no instance will flags be issued to funeral directors, organizations, or individuals to replace flags loaned or donated by them. Reimbursement may not be allowed for flags privately purchased by relatives, friends, or other parties, nor will any financial settlement be made in lieu of the issue of a flag.

7. *(a)* The flag will be disposed of as follows: When actually used to drape the casket of the deceased, it must be delivered to the next of kin (or to a close friend or associate when no claim is made by next of kin) following interment or inurnment. If there is no living relative, or one cannot be located, and no friend or associate requests the flag, it must be returned to the nearest Veterans Administration office.

(b) The phrase "next of kin," for the purpose of disposing of the flag, is defined as follows with preference to entitlement in the order listed below:

(1) Widow or widower.

(2) Children, according to age (minor child may be issued a flag on application signed by guardian).

(3) Parents, including adoptive, stepparents, and foster parents.

(4) Brothers or sisters, including brothers or sisters of the halfblood.

(5) Uncles or aunts.

(6) Nephews or nieces.

(7) Others—cousins, grandparents, etc.

(c) The phrase "close friend or associate" means any person who establishes by evidence that he/she was a close friend or an associate of the deceased.

Form Approved
OMB No. 2900-0003

Veterans Administration

(DO NOT WRITE
IN THIS SPACE)
VA DATE STAMP

APPLICATION FOR BURIAL BENEFITS

(Under 38 U.S.C., Chapter 23)

IMPORTANT - Read instructions carefully before completing form. YOUR COMPLETE COMPLIANCE WITH ALL INSTRUCTIONS WILL AVOID DELAY.

1. FIRST NAME - MIDDLE NAME - LAST NAME OF DECEASED VETERAN (Type or print)

2A. SOCIAL SECURITY NO. OF VETERAN	2B. VA FILE NO. C-

3A. FIRST NAME - MIDDLE NAME - LAST NAME OF CLAIMANT (Type or print)

3B. MAILING ADDRESS OF CLAIMANT (Number and street or rural route, city or P.O., State and ZIP Code)	4. RELATIONSHIP TO VETERAN

PART I - INFORMATION REGARDING VETERAN

5. DATE OF BIRTH	6. PLACE OF BIRTH	7. DATE OF DEATH	8A. PLACE OF DEATH	8B. DATE OF BURIAL

9. MARITAL STATUS
☐ NEVER MARRIED ☐ MARRIED ☐ WIDOWED ☐ DIVORCED

10. SURVIVING CHILD(REN)?
☐ YES ☐ NO

11. FIRST NAME, MIDDLE NAME, LAST NAME OF SPOUSE (Complete address, if living)	12. FIRST NAME, MIDDLE NAME, LAST NAME OF FATHER (Complete address, if living)	13. FIRST NAME, MIDDLE NAME, LAST NAME OF MOTHER (Complete address, if living)

SERVICE INFORMATION (The following information should be furnished for the periods of the VETERAN'S ACTIVE SERVICE)

14A. ENTERED SERVICE		14B. SERVICE NO.	14C. SEPARATED FROM SERVICE		14D. GRADE, RANK OR RATING ORGANIZATION AND BRANCH OF SERVICE
DATE	PLACE		DATE	PLACE	

15. IF VETERAN SERVED UNDER A NAME OTHER THAN THAT SHOWN IN ITEM 1, GIVE FULL NAME AND SERVICE RENDERED UNDER THAT NAME

PART II - CLAIM FOR BURIAL BENEFITS AND/OR INTERMENT ALLOWANCE IF PAID BY CLAIMANT

NOTE - If claiming Plot Allowance Only, do not complete Part II, but complete Parts III and IV on reverse.

16. PLACE OF BURIAL

17. WAS BURIAL (WITHOUT CHARGE FOR PLOT OR INTERMENT) IN A STATE OWNED CEMETERY, OR SECTION THEREOF, USED SOLELY FOR PERSONS ELIGIBLE FOR BURIAL IN A NATIONAL CEMETERY?
☐ YES ☐ NO (If "No," complete Items 19 and 20)

18. WAS BURIAL IN A NATIONAL CEMETERY OR CEMETERY OWNED BY THE FEDERAL GOVERNMENT?
☐ YES ☐ NO (If "No," complete Items 19 and 20)

19. BURIAL PLOT, MAUSOLEUM, ETC. COST IS: (Check one)
☐ PAID BY ANOTHER PERSON(S) ☐ PAID BY CLAIMANT FOR BURIAL
☐ DUE FUNERAL DIRECTOR ☐ NONE
☐ DUE CEMETERY OWNER

20. IF PLOT/INTERMENT EXPENSES ARE UNPAID, WHO WILL FILE CLAIM FOR EXPENSES? (Name and Address)

21. TOTAL EXPENSE OF BURIAL, FUNERAL, TRANSPORTATION AND IF CLAIMED, BURIAL PLOT $	22. AMOUNT PAID $

23. WHOSE FUNDS WERE USED?

24A. HAS PERSON WHOSE FUNDS WERE USED BEEN REIMBURSED?
☐ YES ☐ NO (If "Yes," complete Items 24B and 24C)

24B. AMOUNT OF REIMBURSEMENT $

24C. SOURCE OF REIMBURSEMENT

25A. HAS OR WILL ANY AMOUNT BE ALLOWED ON EXPENSES BY LOCAL, STATE OR FEDERAL AGENCY?
☐ YES ☐ NO (If "Yes," complete Items 25B and 25C)

25B. AMOUNT $

25C. SOURCE

26. WAS THE VETERAN A MEMBER OF A BURIAL ASSOCIATION OR COVERED BY BURIAL INSURANCE?
☐ YES ☐ NO (Before answering read and comply with instruction 11)

VA FORM AUG 1982 **21-530**   EXISTING STOCK OF VA FORM 21-530, FEB 1982, WILL BE USED.

PART III - CLAIM FOR PLOT COSTS ALLOWANCE

IMPORTANT - Complete only if burial was NOT in a national cemetery or cemetery owned by the Federal Government.

27A. WAS BURIAL (WITHOUT CHARGE FOR PLOT OR INTERMENT) IN A STATE OWNED CEMETERY, OR SECTION THEREOF, USED SOLELY FOR PERSONS ELIGIBLE FOR BURIAL IN A NATIONAL CEMETERY? ☐ YES ☐ NO (If "Yes," complete Items 27A and 27B ONLY, then complete Part IV)	27B. PLACE OF BURIAL

28. COST OF BURIAL PLOT (Individual Grave Site) $	29A. DATE OF PURCHASE	29B. DATE OF PAYMENT	30A. HAVE BILLS BEEN PAID IN FULL? ☐ YES ☐ NO (If "No," complete Item 30B)	30B. AMOUNT UNPAID $

31. WHOSE FUNDS WERE USED?	32A. HAS PERSON WHOSE FUNDS WERE USED BEEN REIMBURSED? ☐ YES ☐ NO (If "Yes," complete Items 32B and 32C)	32B. AMOUNT OF REIMBURSEMENT $

32C. SOURCE OF REIMBURSEMENT	33A. HAS OR WILL ANY AMOUNT BE ALLOWED ON EXPENSES BY STATE OR FEDERAL AGENCY? ☐ YES ☐ NO (If "Yes," complete Items 33B and 33C)	33B. AMOUNT $	33C. SOURCE

PART IV - CERTIFICATION AND SIGNATURE

I CERTIFY THAT the foregoing statements made in connection with this application on account of the named veteran are true and correct to the best of my knowledge and belief.

34A. SIGNATURE OF CLAIMANT (If signed by mark, complete Items 40A thru 41B) (If signing for firm, corporation, or state agency, complete Items 34B and 35)	34B. OFFICIAL POSITION OF PERSON SIGNING ON BEHALF OF FIRM, CORPORATION, OR STATE AGENCY

35. FULL NAME AND ADDRESS OF THE FIRM, CORPORATION, OR STATE AGENCY FILING AS CLAIMANT

NOTE - Where the claimant is a firm or other unpaid creditor, Items 36A thru 39 MUST be completed by the individual who authorized services.

I CERTIFY THAT the foregoing statements made by the claimant are correct to the best of my knowledge and belief.

36A. SIGNATURE OF PERSON WHO AUTHORIZED SERVICES (If signed by mark, complete Items 40A thru 41B)	36B. NAME OF PERSON AUTHORIZING SERVICES (Type or Print)

37. ADDRESS (Number and street or rural route, city or P.O., State and ZIP Code)

38. DATE	39. RELATIONSHIP TO VETERAN

WITNESSES TO SIGNATURE IF MADE BY "X" MARK

NOTE: Signature made by mark must be witnessed by two persons to whom the person making the statement is personally known, and the signatures and addresses of such witnesses must be shown below.

40A. SIGNATURE OF WITNESS	40B. ADDRESS OF WITNESS
41A. SIGNATURE OF WITNESS	41B. ADDRESS OF WITNESS

PENALTY - The law provides severe penalties which include fine or imprisonment, or both, for the willful submission of any statement or evidence of a material fact, knowing it to be false.

VETERANS ADMINISTRATION HEADSTONES AND MARKERS

The Veterans Administration will furnish, upon request, a Government headstone or marker at the expense of the United States for the unmarked graves of certain individuals eligible for burial in a national cemetery, but not buried there. These individuals include any veteran with an other than dishonorable discharge who dies after service or any serviceman or servicewoman who dies on active duty. Certain other individuals may also be eligible for the headstone or marker. Headstones or markers for all individuals buried in a national or post cemetery are furnished automatically without request from the family.

In lieu of furnishing a headstone or marker for a veteran not buried in a national cemetery, the Veterans Administration may make a limited reimbursement for the cost of a privately purchased headstone or marker. The amount of reimbursement will not exceed the actual average cost of a Government headstone or marker.

For additional information and an application, contact the nearest Veterans Administration Office. Please state whether you wish to apply for a Government headstone or marker or whether you wish to apply for limited reimbursement for costs incurred in acquiring a non-Government headstone or marker.

S. GOVERNMENT PRINTING OFFICE 1983 381-488/3013

INSTRUCTIONS FOR COMPLETING APPLICATION FOR BURIAL BENEFITS
(UNDER 38, USC, Chapter 23)

IMPORTANT - READ THESE INSTRUCTIONS CAREFULLY

1. PROTECTION OF PRIVACY. No allowance of burial benefits may be granted unless this form is completed and returned as required by existing law (38 U.S.C., Chapter 23). The information requested by this form is considered relevant and necessary to determine maximum benefits provided under the law. Responses may be disclosed outside the VA only if the disclosure is authorized under the Privacy Act, including the routine uses identified in the VA system of records, 58 VA21/22/28, Compensation, Pension, Education and Rehabilitation Records - VA, published in the Federal Register.

2. BENEFITS PAYABLE

     a. <u>BASIC BURIAL ALLOWANCE</u> - An amount not exceeding $300 for expenses of burial and funeral of the deceased veteran. The term burial, as used in this form, includes all the recognized methods of interment including cremation, burial at sea, etc.

     b. <u>ELIGIBILITY FOR BASIC BURIAL ALLOWANCE</u> - The deceased veteran must have been discharged or released from service under conditions other than dishonorable and must have either:

         (1) Been in receipt of pension or compensation (or would have been in receipt of compensation, but for the receipt of military retirement pay; or

         (2) Had an original or reopened claim for pension or compensation pending and is found entitled from a date prior to date of death; or

         (3) Died while traveling under prior authorization or while properly institutionalized by the VA.

     c. <u>PLOT or INTERMENT ALLOWANCE</u> - The term interment, as used in this form, is synonymous with burial and is defined the same. The term plot means the final disposal site of the remains and includes a grave, mausoleum vault, columbarium niche, or similar place. The plot or interment benefit is payable as:

         (1) An additional allowance not exceeding $150 for incurred expenses of interment or plot <u>AND</u> the interment or burial was not made in a national cemetery or other cemetery under the jurisdiction of the United States.

         (2) An amount of $150, paid to a State or State agency or political subdivision, if a veteran died from nonservice-connected causes, and is buried (without charge for the cost of a plot or interment) in a State owned cemetery, or section thereof, used solely for persons eligible for burial in a national cemetery.

     d. <u>ELIGIBILITY FOR PLOT or INTERMENT ALLOWANCE</u> - In addition to persons for whom the basic burial allowance is payable, eligibility for only the plot or interment allowance exists when the veteran:

         (1) Was discharged or released from service under conditions other than dishonorable and must have either;

         (2) Served during a period of war; or

         (3) Been discharged from active duty for (or could have been discharged for) a disability incurred in or aggravated in the line of duty.

     e. BURIAL ALLOWANCE FOR SERVICE-CONNECTED DEATH - When the veteran's death occurs, as the result of a service-connected disability, an amount not exceeding $1,100 may be paid in lieu of the $300 basic burial allowance and the $150 interment and plot allowance.

     f. TRANSPORTATION COSTS - The cost of transporting the body to the place of burial may also be paid in addition to the above allowances when:

         (1) The veteran died of a service-connected disability or had a compensable service-connected disability and burial is in a national cemetery, or

         (2) The veteran died while in a hospital or domiciliary to which he/she had been properly admitted under authority of the VA, or while in a VA nursing home, or,

         (3) The veteran died enroute while traveling under prior authorization of the VA for the purpose of examination, treatment or care.

3. WHO SHOULD FILE CLAIM.

     a. CREDITOR - If expenses of the veteran's burial and funeral have not been paid, claim should be filed by the funeral director or crematory service by completion of Parts I, II, and IV. If the funeral director or crematory service has paid or advanced funds for or furnished the plot or interment expenses, the completion of Part II and inclusion of these items of expense on the statement of account will serve as claim for the $150 interment allowance. If the cemetery owner or other creditor has not been paid for the plot and the related interment expenses, he/she may file claim by completing Parts I, III, and IV. If both the funeral director and cemetery owner are unpaid, each must submit a separate VA Form 21-530 signed by the person who authorized services.

     b. PERSON WHOSE FUNDS WERE USED - If all creditors have been paid, claim should be filed by the person or persons whose personal funds were used to pay such expenses by completion of Parts, I, II, and IV.

     c. VETERAN'S ESTATE - If the expenses were paid from funds of the veteran's estate, claim should be filed by the executor or administrator thereof by completing Parts I, II, and IV, and submitting a copy of the letters of administration or letters testamentary certified over the signature and seal of the appointing court.

VA FORM **21-530**
AUG 1982

EXISTING STOCKS OF VA FORM 21-530,
FEB 1982, WILL BE USED.

d. STATE OR STATE AGENCY - If a veteran whose death occurred from nonservice - connected causes, was buried without charge for plot or interment in a State owned cemetery, or section thereof used for persons eligible in a national cemetery, claim may be filed by a State official by completion of Parts I, III (Items 27A and 27B), and IV.

4. HEARING - You have the right to a personal hearing at any stage of claims processing, either before or after a decision is made. This right may be exercised with regard to an original claim, supplemental claim or with regard to any subsequent action affecting your entitlement. All you need do is inform the nearest VA office as to your desires, and we will arrange a time and place for the hearing. You may bring witnesses if you desire and their testimony will be entered in the record. The VA will furnish the hearing room, provide hearing officials, and prepare the transcript of the proceedings. The VA cannot pay any of your expenses in connection with the hearing.

5. TIME LIMIT FOR FILING CLAIM. Claim must be filed with the Veterans Administration within 2 years from the date of the veteran's burial or cremation. In any case where a veteran's discharge was corrected, after death, to one under conditions other than dishonorable, claim must be filed within 2 years from date of correction.

6. SOCIAL SECURITY NUMBER. The number entered in Item 2A, Social Security Number, should be the deceased veteran's own social security number.

7. CAREFUL EXECUTION OF CLAIM NECESSARY. This application must be signed (Item 34A) by the claimant. All of the information required in this application should be answered fully and clearly. Answers must be written in a clear legible hand or typewritten. If you do not know the answer to any question, say so. If any of the questions are not clear and you desire further information before attempting to answer the question involved, you should write to the Veterans Administration for instructions.

8. COMPLETING OF CLAIM BY A FIRM, CORPORATION, OR STATE AGENCY. The claim must be executed in the full name of the firm, corporation, or State agency, and show the official position or connection with the firm, corporation, or State agency, of the individual who signs the claim in its behalf, e.g.:

STONE FUNERAL HOME
By: John Doe, President.

9. PROOF OF VETERAN'S DEATH TO ACCOMPANY CLAIM. The death of a veteran in a Government institution does not need to be proven by a claimant. Otherwise, the claimant must forward a copy of the public record of death or a copy of a coroner's report of death or of the verdict of a coroner's jury, certified by the custodian of such records. If proof of death has previously been furnished the Veterans Administration, it need not be submitted with this application.

10. STATEMENT OF ACCOUNT TO ACCOMPANY CLAIM.

a. FUNERAL DIRECTOR - This claim must be accompanied by a statement of account (preferably on the printed billhead of the funeral director) showing the name of the veteran for whom the services were performed; the nature and cost of services rendered, including any payments made to another funeral home (showing name and address) for initial services and merchandise; all credits; and the name of person or persons by whom payment in whole or in part was made.

b. TRANSPORTATION - If the body was transported by common carrier, a receipt from the railroad express company or airline should accompany the claim. All receipts covering transportation charges should show the name of the veteran whose body was transported, the name of the person who paid the charges, and the amount of the charges. The statement of account should be itemized to show the charge or charges made for all transportation expenses. Failure to itemize transportation charges may result in delay of payment or payment of a lesser amount than may otherwise be awarded.

c. ACCOUNT PAID IN FULL - WHERE TOTAL PAYMENT HAS BEEN MADE FOR THE SERVICES PERFORMED, THE STATEMENT OF ACCOUNT SHOULD BE RECEIPTED IN THE NAME OF THE FIRM OR INDIVIDUAL PERFORMING THE SERVICES. Bills or receipts filed in support of this claim become a part of the permanent record and may not be returned.

d. PLOT/INTERMENT ALLOWANCE ONLY - If claim is for the plot interment allowance only, the statement of account on the printed billhead of the cemetery or other creditor must show the cost of the veteran's individual gravesite or the total cost of the plot and the number of gravesites in the plot.

11. BURIAL ASSOCIATION OR BURIAL INSURANCE BENEFITS. If the deceased veteran was a member of a burial association or if any insurance company is obligated to pay all or part of the burial expenses, Item 26 should be answered "Yes". It will then be necessary to support the claim with a statement from the association or insurance company setting forth the terms of the contract and how and with whom settlement was made.

12. SERVICE RECORD. If the veteran never filed a claim with the Veterans Administration, a photocopy of his/her discharge certificate furnished with this claim will permit prompt processing.

13. IMPORTANT: Payment of burial benefits is prohibited if the funeral home or cemetery used is found to discriminate based upon race, color, or national origin (42 U.S.C. 2000(d)). The individual who authorizes services has the right to file a complaint with the nearest VA Regional Office if such discriminatory practices are encountered.

NOTE: The payment of any fee in the preparation of this claim is prohibited.

Form Approved
OMB No. 2900-0004

VA Veterans Administration	(DO NOT WRITE IN THIS SPACE) VA DATE STAMP

APPLICATION FOR DEPENDENCY AND INDEMNITY COMPENSATION OR DEATH PENSION BY SURVIVING SPOUSE OR CHILD
(INCLUDING ACCRUED BENEFITS AND DEATH COMPENSATION, WHERE APPLICABLE)

IMPORTANT - Read instructions carefully before completing this form. Answer all items fully. Detach and retain ONLY the instruction sheet. If more space is required, attach additional sheets and identify each answer by item number.

1. NAME OF DECEASED VETERAN *(First, middle, last) (Type or print)*

2. IF VETERAN PREVIOUSLY APPLIED TO THE VETERANS ADMINISTRATION FOR ANY BENEFIT, INSERT VA FILE NUMBER, IF KNOWN C–	3. SOCIAL SECURITY NUMBER OF VETERAN	4. RAILROAD RETIREMENT NO.	5. VETERANS ADMINISTRATION FILE NO. XC–

6A. NAME OF CLAIMANT *(First, middle, last) (Type or print)*	6B. TELEPHONE NO. *(Include Area Code)*

6C. MAILING ADDRESS OF CLAIMANT *(No. and street or rural route, city or P.O., State and ZIP Code)*	6D. RELATIONSHIP TO VETERAN *(Check one)* ☐ SURVIVING SPOUSE ☐ CHILD 6E. SOCIAL SECURITY NO. OF SURVIVING SPOUSE

PART I - IDENTIFICATION AND SERVICE INFORMATION OF VETERAN *(See Instructions, Paragraphs H & I)*

7. DATE OF BIRTH	8. PLACE OF BIRTH	9. DATE OF DEATH	10. PLACE OF DEATH

11A. CAUSE OF DEATH *(See Instructions, paragraph I)*	11B. ARE YOU CLAIMING THAT THE CAUSE OF DEATH WAS DUE TO SERVICE? ☐ YES ☐ NO

12A. ENTERED ACTIVE SERVICE		12B. SERVICE NO.	12C. SEPARATED FROM ACTIVE SERVICE		12D. GRADE, RANK OR RATING, ORGANIZATION AND BRANCH OF SERVICE
DATE	PLACE		DATE	PLACE	

13. IF VETERAN SERVED UNDER A NAME OTHER THAN THAT SHOWN IN ITEM 1, GIVE FULL NAME AND SERVICE RENDERED UNDER THAT NAME

PART II - INFORMATION RELATING TO MARRIAGE *(See instructions, Paragraph J)*
INFORMATION RELATING TO VETERAN

14. HOW MANY TIMES WAS VETERAN MARRIED?

15A. MARRIAGE		15B. TO WHOM MARRIED	15C. HOW MARRIAGE ENDED *(Death, divorce, etc.)*	15D. MARRIAGE ENDED	
DATE	PLACE			DATE	PLACE

INFORMATION RELATING TO SURVIVING SPOUSE

16. HOW MANY TIMES HAS SURVIVING SPOUSE BEEN MARRIED?	17. HAS SURVIVING SPOUSE REMARRIED SINCE DEATH OF VETERAN? ☐ YES ☐ NO

18A. MARRIAGE		18B. TO WHOM MARRIED	18C. HOW MARRIAGE ENDED *(Death, divorce, etc.)*	18D. MARRIAGE ENDED	
DATE	PLACE			DATE	PLACE

VA FORM 21-534
OCT 1982

SUPERSEDES VA FORM 21-534, MAR 1981, WHICH WILL NOT BE USED.

☆ U.S. GOVERNMENT PRINTING OFFICE: 1984-428-357

PART II — INFORMATION RELATING TO MARRIAGE *(Continued)*

NOTE: If claimant is not veteran's surviving spouse, omit Items 19 to 23 inclusive.

19. MAIDEN NAME OF VETERAN'S SURVIVING SPOUSE *(First - middle - last)* *(If applicable)*	20. DATE OF BIRTH

21. WAS A CHILD BORN OF SURVIVING SPOUSE'S MARRIAGE TO VETERAN? ☐ YES ☐ NO	22. DID SURVIVING SPOUSE LIVE CONTINUOUSLY WITH THE VETERAN FROM DATE OF MARRIAGE TO DATE OF DEATH? ☐ YES ☐ NO *(If "No," Complete Item 23)*

23. CAUSE OF SEPARATION *(Explain fully, giving reason, date of separation, duration, etc. If separation was by court order, attach a certified copy of such order.)*

PART III — INFORMATION CONCERNING CHILDREN *(See Instructions, paragraph K)*

IDENTIFICATION OF CHILDREN AND INFORMATION RELATIVE TO CUSTODY

NOTE — List below the name of each child of the veteran who is (1) under 18 years of age (or under 23 years of age if attending school) or (2) of any age if permanently incapable of self-support by reason of mental or physical defect. The term "child" includes an illegitimate, adopted, or stepchild of the veteran as well as any child whose marriage has been terminated by divorce, annulment, or death of a spouse. If the birth of a child of the veteran is expected, that fact should be stated.

24A. NAME OF CHILD *(First, middle initial, last)*	24B. DATE OF BIRTH *(Mo., day, yr.)*	24C. SOCIAL SECURITY NO. OF CHILD	24D. IDENTIFY *(Check each applicable category)*				
			MARRIED PREVIOUS-LY	STEPCHILD OR ADOPTED	ILLEGI-TIMATE	OVER 18 ATTENDING SCHOOL	SERIOUSLY DISABLED

25. NAME(S) OF ANY CHILD(REN) NOT IN YOUR CUSTODY	26. NAME AND ADDRESS OF PERSON(S) HAVING CUSTODY

NOTE: If the veteran died while in active service do not complete Parts IV, V or VI.

PART IV — NET WORTH OF SURVIVING SPOUSE AND/OR CHILDREN *(See Instructions, paragraph L, Items 27A to 27E, inclusive)*

ITEM NO.	SOURCE	AMOUNTS				
		SURVIVING SPOUSE OR CUSTODIAN OF CHILD/REN	NAME OF CHILD/REN			
27A.	STOCKS, BONDS, BANK DEPOSITS	$	$	$	$	$
27B.	REAL ESTATE *(Do not include residence)*					
27C.	OTHER PROPERTY					
27D.	TOTAL DEBTS					
27E.	NET WORTH	$	$	$	$	$

PART V - ANNUAL INCOME OF SURVIVING SPOUSE AND/OR CHILD/REN AND CUSTODIAN OF CHILD/REN						
IMPORTANT - Carefully read paragraph M of Instructions before completing this section.						

28A. HAVE YOU APPLIED FOR OR ARE YOU RECEIVING OR ENTITLED TO RECEIVE BENEFITS FROM THE SOCIAL SECURITY ADMINISTRATION ON YOUR OWN BEHALF OR ON BEHALF OF CHILD/REN IN YOUR CUSTODY? ☐ YES ☐ NO		28B. BEGINNING DATE *(Month,year)*	IF INCOME IS RECEIVED OR EXPECTED FROM ANY OTHER RETIREMENT PLAN, ANNUITY, OR ENDOWMENT INSURANCE, COMPLETE ITEMS 29-31.		
MONTHLY BENEFIT(S)	SURVIVING SPOUSE OR CUSTODIAN OF CHILDREN	EACH CHILD'S SHARE	29. BY WHOM PAID *(Name and Address)*	SURVIVING SPOUSE OR CUSTODIAN OF CHILD/REN	EACH CHILD *(If amounts or sources differ, explain in "Remarks.")*
28C. AMOUNT OF MONTHLY SOCIAL SECURITY CHECK	$	$			
28D. ADDITIONAL MEDICARE DEDUCTION					
28E. TOTAL MONTHLY BENEFIT(S) *(Sum of 28C and 28D)*			30. MONTHLY RATE		
28F. IS SOCIAL SECURITY BASED ON YOUR OWN EMPLOYMENT? ☐ YES ☐ NO			31. BEGINNING DATE		

ITEM NO.	SOURCE (A)	SURVIVING SPOUSE OR CUSTODIAN OF CHILD/REN (B)	AMOUNT OF INCOME			
			NAME OF CHILD/REN			
			(C)	(D)	(E)	(F)

INCOME RECEIVED FROM JANUARY 1 TO DATE OF DEATH OF VETERAN or, if claim is filed more than a year after the veteran died, income received from January 1 to date you sign this application.

32A	EARNINGS					
32B	SOCIAL SECURITY (GREEN CHECK)					
32C	OTHER ANNUITIES AND RETIREMENTS					
32D	DIVIDENDS, INTEREST, ETC.					
32E	SUPPLEMENTAL SECURITY INCOME (GOLD CHECK)					
32F	LIFE INSURANCE					
32G	ALL OTHER INCOME *(Specify source. For additional space, use Item 43, "Remarks")*					

INCOME EXPECTED FROM DATE OF DEATH OF VETERAN TO DECEMBER 31 OF THAT YEAR or, if claim is filed more than a year after the veteran died, income expected from the date you sign this application to December 31 of the same year.

33A	EARNINGS					
33B	SOCIAL SECURITY (GREEN CHECK)					
33C	OTHER ANNUITIES AND RETIREMENTS					
33D	DIVIDENDS, INTEREST, ETC.					
33E	SUPPLEMENTAL SECURITY INCOME (GOLD CHECK)					
33F	LIFE INSURANCE					
33G	ALL OTHER INCOME *(Specify source. For additional space, use Item 43, "Remarks")*					

INCOME EXPECTED FOR THE NEXT CALENDAR YEAR. If you are unable to state the exact amount, give approximate amounts expected.

34A	EARNINGS					
34B	SOCIAL SECURITY (GREEN CHECK)					
34C	OTHER ANNUITIES AND RETIREMENTS					
34D	DIVIDENDS, INTEREST, ETC.					
34E	SUPPLEMENTAL SECURITY INCOME (GOLD CHECK)					
34F	LIFE INSURANCE					
34G	ALL OTHER INCOME *(Specify source. For additional space, use Item 43, "Remarks")*					

PART VI — DEDUCTIBLE EXPENSES

NOTE: Your income may be reduced by the amount of unreimbursed expenses of the veteran's or his/her child's last illness and burial and the veteran's just debts which were paid by you . Be sure to include as income in Items 32G, 33G and 34G any reimbursement received on these expenses or debts. See paragraph O of Instructions for reporting payments and reimbursements made after filing of your claim.

35A. NAME AND ADDRESS OF PERSON TO WHOM PAID	35B. TOTAL AMT. OF EXPENSE OR DEBT	35C. NATURE OF EXPENSE OR DEBT	35D. DATE PAID	35E. AMOUNT PAID BY YOU
	$			$
	$			$
	$			$

PART VII — MISCELLANEOUS INFORMATION

36A. FULL NAME OF VETERAN'S MOTHER	37A. FULL NAME OF VETERAN'S FATHER
36B. ADDRESS, IF LIVING	37B. ADDRESS, IF LIVING

38. HAS THE SURVIVING SPOUSE OR CHILD FILED CLAIM FOR COMPENSATION FROM THE OFFICE OF WORKERS' COMPENSATION PROGRAMS BECAUSE OF DEATH OF VETERAN ON WHOSE SERVICE THIS CLAIM IS FILED?

☐ YES ☐ NO

39. IS A CLAIM OR COURT ACTION PENDING, OR HAS A COURT DECREE AWARDING DAMAGES ON A SETTLEMENT OR COMPROMISE OF A CLAIM BASED ON THE DEATH OF THE VETERAN BEEN MADE?

☐ YES ☐ NO *(If "Yes," explain in Item 43, "Remarks")*

40. IS A CLAIM FOR SURVIVOR BENEFIT PLAN (SBP) ANNUITY FROM A SERVICE DEPARTMENT PENDING OR AN AWARD OF THE SBP ANNUITY BEEN MADE BASED ON THE DEATH OF THE VETERAN.

☐ YES ☐ NO *("Yes," explain in Item 43, "Remarks")*

41A. HAS THE SURVIVING SPOUSE OR CHILD FILED CLAIM PREVIOUSLY WITH THE VETERANS ADMINISTRATION? ☐ YES ☐ NO *(If "Yes," complete Items 41B through 42B inclusive)*	41B. NAME OF PERSON ON WHOSE SERVICE CLAIM WAS MADE	41C. RELATIONSHIP TO CLAIMANT
42A. VA FILE NO.	42B. OFFICE WHERE CLAIM WAS FILED *(City and State)*	

PART VIII — CERTIFICATION AND ADDITIONAL COMMENTS

43. REMARKS *(If additional space is needed, attach separate sheet)*

CERTIFICATION: I CERTIFY THAT the foregoing statements are true and correct to the best of my knowledge and belief.

44. DATE SIGNED	45. SIGNATURE OF CLAIMANT, CUSTODIAN OR GUARDIAN

WITNESSES - If you sign by (X), it must be witnessed by two persons who know you personally and the signatures and addresses of such witnesses must be shown.

46A. SIGNATURE OF WITNESS	47A. ADDRESS OF WITNESS
46B. SIGNATURE OF WITNESS	47B. ADDRESS OF WITNESS

PENALTY - The law provides severe penalties which include fine or imprisonment, or both, for the willful submission of any statement or evidence of a material fact, knowing it to be false, or for fraudulent acceptance of any payment to which you are not entitled.

Form Approved
OMB No. 2900-0004

DEPARTMENT OF HEALTH AND HUMAN SERVICES	SOCIAL SECURITY ADMINISTRATION **APPLICATION FOR SURVIVORS BENEFITS** (PAYABLE UNDER TITLE II OF THE SOCIAL SECURITY ACT) *IMPORTANT - Read instructions before completing form. Detach and retain ONLY the instruction sheet.*	(DO NOT WRITE IN THIS SPACE) VA DATE STAMP

FIRST NAME - MIDDLE NAME - LAST NAME OF VETERAN *(Type or print)*	2. DATE OF DEATH

NOTE: If the veteran's Social Security No. is unknown, complete Items 4, 5, 6 and 7 about veteran.

SOCIAL SECURITY NO. OF VETERAN	4. DATE OF BIRTH	5. PLACE OF BIRTH

NAME OF FATHER	7. MAIDEN NAME OF MOTHER	8. DID THE VETERAN WORK IN THE RAILROAD INDUSTRY AT ANY TIME ON OR AFTER 1-1-37? ☐ YES ☐ NO

NOTE: The following information should be furnished for each period of the veteran's active service after September 7, 1939, in the Army, Navy, Air Force, Marine Corps or Coast Guard of the United States or service as a commissioned officer in the Public Health Service or the National Oceanic and Atmospheric Administration (formerly the Environmental Science Services Administration; Coast and Geodetic Service). If additional space is needed, attach separate sheet.

ENTERED ACTIVE SERVICE		9C. SERVICE NO.	SEPARATED FROM ACTIVE SERVICE		9F. GRADE, RANK, OR RATING, ORGANIZATION AND BRANCH OF SERVICE
9A. DATE	9B. PLACE		9D. DATE	9E. PLACE	

RELATIONSHIP OF APPLICANT TO VETERAN ☐ SURVIVING SPOUSE ☐ CHILD ☐ PARENT	11. DATE OF BIRTH OF APPLICANT	12. VETERANS ADMINISTRATION FILE NO.

CHILDREN: Show names of surviving children (including natural children, adopted children, and stepchildren) or dependent grandchildren (including stepgrandchildren) who at any time since the veteran died, were unmarried and (a) under age 18; (b) age 18 to 23 and attending school; (c) disabled or handicapped (18 or over and disability began before age 22).

13A.	13B.
13C.	13D.

I know that anyone who makes or causes to be made a false statement or representation of material fact in an application or for use in determining a right to payment under the Social Security Act commits a crime punishable under Federal law by fine, imprisonment, or both. I affirm that all information I have given in this document is true.

14. DATE *(Month, day, year)*	15. SIGNATURE OF APPLICANT *(First name, middle initial, last name) (Sign in ink)* SIGN HERE ▶

16. MAILING ADDRESS OF APPLICANT *(No. and street or rural route, city or P.O., State and ZIP Code)*	17. TELEPHONE NO.

WITNESSES REQUIRED ONLY IF SIGNATURE OF APPLICANT IS MADE BY "X" MARK ABOVE

18A. SIGNATURE OF WITNESS	18B. ADDRESS OF WITNESS *(No. and street, city, State and ZIP Code)*
19A. SIGNATURE OF WITNESS	19B. ADDRESS OF WITNESS *(No. and street, city, State and ZIP Code)*

ITEMS BELOW TO BE COMPLETED BY THE VETERANS ADMINISTRATION *(Use reverse for "Remarks")*

20. PROOFS RECEIVED *(Check)*	21. PROOFS REQUESTED FROM CLAIMANT OR OTHERS *(Specify)*
☐ DEATH ☐ MARRIAGE	☐ DEATH ☐ MARRIAGE
☐ AGE _____ (NAME)	☐ AGE _____ (NAME)
_____ (NAME)	_____ (NAME)
_____ (NAME)	_____ (NAME)
☐ OTHER *(Specify)*	☐ OTHER *(Specify)*

22. DATE	23. NAME AND ADDRESS OF TRANSMITTING VA OFFICE

FORM SSA-24
OCT 1982

SUPERSEDES SSA-24, MAR 1981,
WHICH WILL NOT BE USED.

634583

INSTRUCTIONS FOR COMPLETING FORM SSA-24, APPLICATION FOR SURVIVORS BENEFITS
(Payable Under Title II of the Social Security Act)

IMPORTANT: *PLEASE READ THE FOLLOWING BEFORE YOU COMPLETE THE SSA-24.*

This application form, SSA-24, is an Application for Survivors Benefits Payable Under Title II of the Social Security Act, as amended. Under authority of section 202(o) of the Social Security Act the application requests information in order to determine eligibility to social security benefits.

You do not have to complete this application; there are no penalties under the law if you do not complete part or all of the SSA-24. However, it is usually to your advantage to provide the information because not providing it could prevent an accurate and timely decision on your claim or could result in the loss of some benefits or insurance coverage.

If you do wish to supply the information requested on the SSA-24, this information will be forwarded to the Social Security Administration and used by them to determine whether social security benefits may be payable to a surviving dependent(s) of the veteran. Social Security will then contact you regarding any social security benefits payable based on the information given on this form.

Please understand that social security may, in certain instances, disclose the information on this form to another Federal, State or local agency or individual without your written consent. This would be done in order to:

- enable a third party or an agency to assist social security in establishing an individual's right to benefits or coverage;
- comply with Federal laws which require or authorize the release of information from social security records; and
- facilitate statistical research and audit activities necessary to assure the integrity and improvement of the social security programs.

If you should have any questions about entitlement to social security benefits, or the information you have provided on this form, please contact your local social security office.

Complete each item on the attached application, Form SSA-24, (except the Items 20 through 23). When signed and dated the form SHOULD BE LEFT ATTACHED to your completed application for dependency and indemnity compensation or death pension.

INSTRUCTIONS FOR VA FORM 21-534

READ VERY CAREFULLY, DETACH, AND RETAIN THIS SHEET FOR YOUR FUTURE REFERENCE.

PRIVACY ACT INFORMATION: Payment of death benefits cannot be made unless the information requested is furnished as required by existing law (38 U.S.C. Chapters 13 and 15. Subchapter III). The information requested is considered relevant and necessary to determine maximum benefits provided under the law. Responses may be disclosed outside the VA only if the disclosure is authorized under the Privacy Act, including the routine uses identified in VA system of records, 58 VA 21/22/28, Compensation, Pension, Education and Rehabilitation Records - VA, published in the Federal Register. Disclosure of claimant(s) Social Security number(s) is requested under the authority of Title 38 U.S.C. and is mandatory as a condition to receipt of Dependency and Indemnity Compensation (38 C.F.R. 1575). Social Security numbers will be used in the administration of veteran's benefits, in the identification of veterans or persons claiming or receiving Veterans Administration benefits and their records and may be used to verify Social Security benefit entitlement (including amounts payable) with the Social Security Administration and for other purposes where authorized by both Title 38 U.S.C. and the Privacy Act of 1974(5 U.S.C. 552a) or, where required by another statute.

A. PAYMENT OF BENEFITS - GENERAL

(1) Dependency and Indemnity Compensation may be payable when the veteran's death occurred in service, or when a veteran dies of a service-connected disability, or in certain circumstances if a veteran rated totally disabled from service-connected disability dies from non service-connected conditions.

(2) Pension may be payable when the death of a veteran with wartime service is not due to service, provided income is within applicable limits.

(a) The rate of pension paid depends upon the amount of family income and the number of dependent children, according to a formula provided by law.
(b) If there is no surviving spouse, pension may be payable on behalf of a child or children.
(c) Because benefit rates and income limits are frequently changed, it is not feasible to keep such information current in these instructions. Information regarding current income limitations and rates of benefits may be obtained by contacting your nearest VA office.

(3) A higher rate of Dependency and Indemnity Compensation is payable to a surviving spouse who is a patient in a nursing home or otherwise determined to be in need of regular aid and attendance or who is permanently housebound due to disability. Pension at a higher rate is also payable when the surviving spouse is in need of regular aid and attendance.

(4) Unless a claim is filed within one year from date of death, neither dependency and indemnity compensation nor pension is payable prior to the date the claim is received in the Veterans Administration.

B. ORGANIZATIONS AND ATTORNEYS - PAYMENT OF ANY FEE - You may be represented, without charge, by an accredited representative of any organization recognized by the Administrator of Veterans Affairs. While a claimant may also employ an attorney or claims agent recognized by the Veterans Administration to assist in prosecuting his/her claim, it is not necessary that he/she do so. Any attorney or agent so employed may not legally charge any fee other than that allowed under 38 U.S.C. 3404(c) and paid by the Veterans Administration (maximum $10), and which is deducted from benefits otherwise payable to the claimant.

C. HEARINGS - You have the right to a personal hearing at any stage of claims processing, either before or after a decision is made. This right may be exercised with regard to an original claim, supplemental claim or with regard to any subsequent action affecting your entitlement. All you need do is inform the nearest VA office as to your desires, and we will arrange a time and place for the hearing. You may bring witnesses if you desire and their testimony will be entered in the record. The VA will furnish the hearing room, provide hearing officals, and prepare the transcript of the proceedings. The VA cannot pay any of your expenses in connection with the hearing.

D. HOW TO COMPLETE THE APPLICATION - ALL THE INFORMATION REQUESTED MUST BE ANSWERED FULLY AND CLEARLY OR ACTION ON YOUR CLAIM MAY BE DELAYED. IF YOU DO NOT KNOW THE ANSWER, WRITE "UNKNOWN."

E. MINORS AND INCOMPETENTS - If the person for whom claim is being made is a minor or is incompetent, the application form should be completed and filed by the legal guardian or; if no legal guardian has been appointed, it may be completed and filed by some person acting on behalf of the minor or incompetent.

F. EVIDENCE - GENERAL - If you are unable to furnish with this application form any of the required evidence listed below, state why you are unable on a separate sheet. If public or church record evidence does not exist, do not establish such record for the purpose of this claim. Instead, the next lower class of evidence listed in paragraphs I, J and K, as required, should be furnished. Evidence filed previously in the Veterans Administration need not be filed in connection with this claim.

G. EVIDENCE-MEDICAL - A medical statement should accompany the application of a surviving spouse who is housebound or who requires the aid and attendance of another person if he or she is not a nursing home patient. A nursing home patient should furnish a statement signed by an official of the nursing home showing the date of admission and patient status. Also, indicate in Item 43, "Remarks" that you are a nursing home patient and give the name and address of the nursing home.

H. SERVICE INFORMATION (See application form, Items 12A, 12B, 12C and 12D) - Complete information should be furnished for each period of the veteran's active service including service as a commissioned officer, in the National Oceanic and Atmospheric Administration including officers of the Coast and Geodetic Survey and Environmental Science Services Administration or Public Health Service. If the veteran never filed a claim with the Veterans Administration, you should furnish the discharge or separation document issued by the service department for each period of service listed. If you do not have this document, we will obtain a copy.

I. PROOF OF DEATH (See application form, Item 11A) - Death of a veteran in active service or in a United States Government institution does not need to be proved by a claimant. Otherwise, the claimant should forward a certified copy of the public record of death, or a duly certified copy of a coroner's report of death, or a verdict of a coroner's jury.

J. INFORMATION RELATING TO MARRIAGE (See application form, Part II)
(1) PROOF OF WIDOWHOOD. The marriage of surviving spouse claimant to the veteran should be established by one of the following types of evidence in the order of preference indicated:

VA FORM 21-534
OCT 1982

SUPERSEDES VA FORM 21-534, MAR 1981,
WHICH WILL NOT BE USED.

(a) A certified copy of the public or church record of marriage to the veteran.
(b) Affidavit of the clergyman or magistrate who officiated.
(c) Original certificate of marriage.
(d) Affidavits of two or more eyewitnesses to the ceremony.

(2) HOW MARRIAGE ENDED. IMPORTANT—Complete information concerning all marriages entered into by either the surviving spouse or the veteran and the termination of such marriages must be furnished in Items 14 through 18D. Specific details as to date, place and manner of dissolution of each marriage must be included.

K. INFORMATION CONCERNING CHILDREN (See application form, Part III)

(1) PROOF OF AGE AND RELATIONSHIP OF CHILD. Evidence to establish the fact of birth of a child is required. It should consist of a certified copy of the public record of birth or a copy of the church record of birth or baptism showing date of birth of each child and the names of the parents.

(2) HELPLESS CHILD. If any child is claimed as being permanently incapable of self-support by reason of mental or physical defect, it must be shown that such incapacity existed prior to the date the child attained age 18. The nature and extent of the physical or mental impairment should be shown by a statement from the attending physician or other medical evidence, forwarded with the application.
NOTE: IF THE VETERAN DIED WHILE IN ACTIVE MILITARY, NAVAL OR AIR SERVICE, YOU NEED NOT COMPLETE PARTS IV, V AND VI OF THE FORM. DO NOT FURNISH THE INFORMATION REGARDING ANNUAL INCOME, DEDUCTIBLE EXPENSES OR NET WORTH DESCRIBED BELOW.

L. NET WORTH (See application form, Part IV)

(1) MINORS AND INCOMPETENTS.

(a) Custodian or Guardian of a Surviving Spouse - Report only the net worth of your ward.
(b) Custodian of Child(ren) - Report your net worth as well as the individual net worth of EACH CHILD for whom benefits are claimed.

(2) SURVIVING SPOUSE WITH CHILDREN. When a surviving spouse files application in his/her own right, the separate net worth of each child for whom benefits are claimed must also be reported.

(3) CHILDREN ALONE. When application is filed on behalf of a child in its own right, the child's net worth should be reported.
Item 27A - Include market value of stocks, checking accounts, bank deposits, savings and loan accounts, cash and currency.
Item 27B - Do not include the value of the single dwelling unit or that portion of real property used solely as your principal residence. On all other real estate reduce the market value by amount of the indebtedness thereon.
Item 27C - Report the total market value of all rights and interest in all other property not included in Items 27A and B. Do not include value of ordinary personal effects necessary for your daily living such as an automobile, clothing, furniture and the dwelling (single family unit) used as your principal residence.
Item 27D - Report all debts except mortgage(s) on real estate.
Item 27E - Report the total of Items 27A through 27C less 27D. This should be your net worth.

M. ANNUAL INCOME OF SURVIVING SPOUSE AND/OR CHILD(REN) (By Calendar Year) (See application form, Part V)

(1) MINORS AND INCOMPETENTS.
(a) Custodian or Guardian of a Surviving Spouse - Report only the income of your ward.
(b) Custodian of Child(ren) - Report your income as well as the individual income of each child for whom benefits are claimed.

(2) SURVIVING SPOUSE WITH CHILDREN. When a surviving spouse files application in his/her right, the separate income of each child for whom benefits are claimed must also be reported.

IMPORTANT

THERE ARE CERTAIN TYPES OF INCOME WHICH MAY BE EXCLUDED IN DETERMINING THE INCOME COUNTABLE FOR VA PURPOSES. HOWEVER, YOU MUST REPORT THE SOURCES AND AMOUNTS OF ALL INCOME BEFORE DEDUCTIONS. WE WILL DETERMINE ANY AMOUNT WHICH DOES NOT COUNT. INCLUDE ALL SEVERANCE PAY OR OTHER ACCRUED PAYMENTS OF ANY KIND OR FROM ANY SOURCE. WHEN NO INCOME IS RECEIVED OR EXPECTED FROM A SPECIFIED SOURCE, WRITE "NONE" IN THE APPROPRIATE BLOCK (ITEMS 32A THROUGH 34G). ATTACH SEPARATE SHEETS IF ADDITIONAL SPACE IS NEEDED.
Items 32G, 33G, 34G - When income is reported in these items, the source must be shown in "Remarks," Item 43. If that income is from two or more sources, list each amount separately and clearly indicate the source.

N. COURT OR CLAIM JUDGEMENT, SETTLEMENTS, OR COMPROMISES. Money or property received as a result of a claim or legal action for damages based upon the death of the veteran may affect payment of Dependency and Indemnity Compensation or Pension. You must report whether a claim or court action is pending or whether a court decree or settlement or compromise of a claim for damages has been made.

O. DEDUCTIBLE EXPENSES (See application form, Part VI)

(1) Any expenses of last illness and burial of the veteran or his/her child, or, just debts of the veteran paid by you, or reimbursement received after the filing of your claim, should be promptly reported to the office in which your claim is located.

(2) FAMILY UNUSUAL MEDICAL EXPENSES - These are amounts actually paid by you during the calendar year for unusual medical expenses for which you are not reimbursed by insurance or otherwise. In "Remarks" (Item 43), you should report the total unreimbursed amount you paid for medical expenses for yourself or for relatives you are under an obligation to support. You may include premiums paid for health, sickness or hospitalization insurance. In computing your income, the VA will deduct the amount you paid for medical expenses if they qualify for exclusion under the formula provided by law.

(3) EDUCATIONAL OR VOCATIONAL REHABILITATION EXPENSES. These are amounts paid for courses of education, including tuition, fees, and materials and may be deducted from the respective incomes of a surviving spouse and the earned income of a child if the child is pursuing a course of postsecondary education or vocational rehabilitation or training. If you or your school child(ren) paid these expenses, report the total amount(s) paid, dates of payment and state to whom the expenses apply.

(4) Unless a claim is filed within one year from date of death, neither dependency and indemnity compensation nor pension is payable prior to the date the claim is received in the Veterans Administration.

Form Approved
OMB No. 76-R0011

Veterans Administration	(DO NOT WRITE IN THIS SPACE) VA DATE STAMP

APPLICATION FOR DEPENDENCY AND INDEMNITY COMPENSATION BY PARENT(S)
(Including accrued benefits and death compensation, when applicable)

IMPORTANT - Read instructions before filling in form. Answer all items fully.

FIRST NAME - MIDDLE NAME - LAST NAME OF DECEASED VETERAN (Type or print)	2. VA FILE NUMBER XC -

ITEM NO.	RELATIONSHIP OF CLAIMANT (Check) (A)	FULL NAME OF CLAIMANT (B)	DATE OF BIRTH (C)	SOCIAL SECURITY NUMBER (D)
3	☐ MOTHER ☐ FOSTER MOTHER			
4	☐ FATHER ☐ FOSTER FATHER			

5. MAILING ADDRESS OF CLAIMANT(S) (Include No. and street or rural route, City or P.O., State and ZIP Code)	6A. WAS VETERAN SURVIVED BY (Complete Item 6B if applicable) ☐ WIDOW/WIDOWER ☐ CHILD UNDER 18 YEARS OF AGE ☐ NEITHER
	6B. NAME AND ADDRESS OF WIDOW/WIDOWER OR CHILD

PART I - INFORMATION RELATING TO VETERAN

7. RAILROAD RETIREMENT NUMBER OF VETERAN	8. SOCIAL SECURITY NUMBER OF VETERAN	9. IF VETERAN PREVIOUSLY APPLIED TO VETERANS ADMINISTRATION FOR ANY BENEFIT, INSERT VA FILE NUMBER, IF KNOWN

10. DATE OF BIRTH	11. PLACE OF BIRTH	12. DATE OF DEATH	13. PLACE OF DEATH

14. CAUSE OF DEATH (See Instructions, paragraph L)

NOTE - The following information should be furnished for each period of the veteran's active service in the Army, Navy, Air Force, Marine Corps, or Coast Guard of the United States or service as a commissioned officer in the National Oceanic and Atmospheric Administration, including officers of the Coast and Geodetic Survey and Environmental Science Services Administration or Public Health Service.

15A. ENTERED ACTIVE SERVICE		15B. SERVICE NO.	15C. SEPARATED FROM ACTIVE SERVICE		15D. GRADE, RANK OR RATING, ORGANIZATION AND BRANCH OF SERVICE
DATE	PLACE		DATE	PLACE	

16. IF VETERAN SERVED UNDER A NAME OTHER THAN THAT SHOWN IN ITEM I, GIVE FULL NAME AND SERVICE RENDERED UNDER THAT NAME

PART II - INFORMATION RELATING TO PARENTS OF VETERAN

17. MAIDEN NAME OF MOTHER	18. NAME OF FATHER

19. NAME OF FOSTER MOTHER (If none, write "NONE")	20. NAME OF FOSTER FATHER (If none, write "NONE")

21A. NAME(S) OF DECEASED PERSON(S) NAMED IN ITEMS 17, 18, 19, AND 20 (If any, fill in Item 21B)	21B. DATE(S) OF DEATH

22. WAS THE VETERAN A MEMBER OF YOUR HOUSEHOLD OR UNDER YOUR PARENTAL CONTROL AT ALL TIMES BEFORE HE/SHE REACHED 21 YEARS OF AGE?	23. DATES OF PARENTAL CONTROL:	
	A. BEGAN	B. ENDED
☐ YES ☐ NO (If "No," complete Items 23, 24 and 25)		

VA FORM
MAY 1980 **21-535**   EXISTING STOCKS OF VA FORM 21-535, NOV 1978, WILL BE USED.   605701

PART II - INFORMATION RELATING TO PARENTS OF VETERAN *(Continued)*

24. REASON VETERAN WAS NOT A MEMBER OF YOUR HOUSEHOLD OR UNDER YOUR PARENTAL CONTROL AT ALL TIMES BEFORE HE/SHE REACHED 21 YEARS OF AGE. *(Explain fully)*

25. NAME AND ADDRESS OF EACH PERSON WHO ASSUMED PARENTAL CONTROL OVER VETERAN AFTER DATE SHOWN IN ITEM 23B.

PART III - INFORMATION RELATING TO CLAIMANT(S)

26. IF REMARRIED, DATE OF MARRIAGE TO YOUR LAST SPOUSE	27. ARE YOU LIVING WITH YOUR SPOUSE? ☐ YES ☐ NO *(If "No," complete Item 28 or 29)*	28. DATE OF DEATH OF SPOUSE, IF DECEASED	29. DATE OF SEPARATION FROM SPOUSE

30. INDICATE WHICH OF THE FOLLOWING YOU OR YOUR SPOUSE MAY BE ENTITLED TO RECEIVE THIS YEAR OR NEXT YEAR BY PLACING "P" FOR YOURSELF OR "S" FOR YOUR SPOUSE IN THE APPROPRIATE BOX, OR "B" IF YOU BOTH ARE TO RECEIVE THAT ANNUITY INCOME

☐ SOCIAL SECURITY   ☐ CIVIL SERVICE   ☐ OTHER *(Specify)*

☐ RAILROAD RETIREMENT   ☐ U.S. ARMED FORCES   ☐ NONE

32. INCOME FROM SOCIAL SECURITY OR RAILROAD RETIREMENT	CLAIMANT	SPOUSE
MONTHLY ENTITLEMENT	$	$
MO. MEDICARE DEDUCTION *(If any)*	+	+
TOTAL MONTHLY ENTITLEMENT	$	$

31. If you or your spouse has applied or will soon apply for any benefit checked in Item 30, list the name(s) of the benefit(s) in Item A or B as appropriate and enter the date in Item C.

A. WILL SOON APPLY FOR

B. HAVE APPLIED FOR

C. DATE

ANNUAL INCOME *(By calendar year)*

NOTE: If income and medical expenses are not shown in dollars, enter name of money unit in Item 33. ➡

33. NAME OF MONEY UNIT *(Pesos, francs, pounds, liras, etc.)*

IMPORTANT

Read carefully paragraph C of instructions before answering questions. All items required to be filled in must be answered fully and completely.

34. INCOME RECEIVED-

Include income received from January 1 to date of veteran's death or if claim is filed more than a year after the veteran died, income received from January 1 to date you signed this application.

35. INCOME EXPECTED -

Include income expected from date of veteran's death to December 31 of that year, or, if claim is filed more than a year after the veteran died, income expected from the date you sign this application to December 31 of the same year.

36. INCOME EXPECTED FOR NEXT CALENDAR YEAR-

If unable to state exact amounts, give approximate amounts expected, or enter "Unknown."

LINE NO.	SOURCE (A)	PARENT (B)	SPOUSE *(If living together)* (C)	PARENT (D)	SPOUSE *(If living together)* (E)	PARENT (F)	SPOUSE *(If living together)* (G)
1	TOTAL WAGES *(Report total income and not take home pay)*	$	$	$	$	$	$
2	SOCIAL SECURITY *(Green check)*						
3	OTHER ANNUITIES OR RETIREMENT BENEFITS						
4	DIVIDENDS AND INTEREST						
5	SUPPLEMENTAL SECURITY INCOME *(Gold check)*						
6	UNEMPLOYMENT COMPENSATION						
7	NET INCOME FROM RENTALS						
8	NET PROFIT FROM SELF - EMPLOYMENT, BUSINESS OR FARM						
9	INSURANCE						
10	OTHER INCOME *(Explain in remarks)*						

ADDITIONAL INCOME INFORMATION *(Continued)*

TOTAL INCOME, WITHOUT DEDUCTING EXPENSES, RECEIVED FROM:						
11	RENTAL(S)					
12	SELF-EMPLOYMENT, FARM OR BUSINESS					

PART IV - MISCELLANEOUS INFORMATION

37. HAS CLAIMANT(S) FILED CLAIM FOR COMPENSATION FROM OFFICE OF FEDERAL EMPLOYEES COMPENSATION BECAUSE OF DEATH OF VETERAN ON WHOSE SERVICE THIS CLAIM IS FILED?

A. FATHER *(Claimant)*? ☐ YES ☐ NO

B. MOTHER *(Claimant)*? ☐ YES ☐ NO

38. HAVE YOU PREVIOUSLY FILED A CLAIM WITH THE VETERANS ADMINISTRATION BASED ON YOUR OWN SERVICE OR THE SERVICE OF ANY OTHER VETERAN?

☐ YES ☐ NO *(If "YES," complete Items 39, 40 and 41)*

39. NAME OF PERSON WHO SERVED

40. RELATIONSHIP TO CLAIMANT

41. VA FILE NO.

C-

42. HAS ANY FEE BEEN PAID OR WILL ANY FEE BE PAID TO ANY PERSON FOR ASSISTING IN THE PREPARATION OF THIS APPLICATION FORM?

☐ YES ☐ NO *(If "YES," complete Items 43 and 44)*

43. NAME AND ADDRESS OF PERSON ASSISTING

44. AMOUNT OF FEE

$

45. REMARKS *(Family unusual medical expenses, if any, may be shown here or on reverse of this page of form. See instructions, paragraph D.)*

CERTIFICATION AND SIGNATURE OF CLAIMANT

I CERTIFY that the foregoing statements are true and correct to the best of my knowledge and belief.

46. DATE

47. SIGNATURE OF MOTHER, FOSTER MOTHER, GUARDIAN, OR NEXT FRIEND

48. DATE

49. SIGNATURE OF FATHER, FOSTER FATHER, GUARDIAN OR NEXT FRIEND

WITNESS TO SIGNATURE OF CLAIMANT IF MADE BY "X" MARK

NOTE - Signature made by mark must be witnessed by two persons to whom the person making the statement is personally known, and the signature and addresses of such witnesses must be shown below.

50A. SIGNATURE OF WITNESS

51A SIGNATURE OF WITNESS

50B. ADDRESS OF WITNESS

51B. ADDRESS OF WITNESS

PENALTY - The law provides severe penalties which include fine or imprisonment, or both, for the willful submission of any statement or evidence of a material fact, knowing it to be false, or for the fraudulent acceptance of any payment to which you are not entitled.

Form Approved
OMB No. 76-R001

| DEPARTMENT OF HEALTH AND HUMAN SERVICES | SOCIAL SECURITY ADMINISTRATION **APPLICATION FOR SURVIVORS BENEFITS** (PAYABLE UNDER TITLE II OF THE SOCIAL SECURITY ACT) *IMPORTANT - Read instructions on reverse before filling in form.* | (DO NOT WRITE IN THIS SPACE) VA DATE STAMP |

1. FIRST NAME - MIDDLE NAME - LAST NAME OF VETERAN *(Type or print)* — 2. DATE OF BIRTH

NOTE: If the veteran's Social Security No. is unknown fill in Items 4, 5, 6, and 7 about veteran.

3. SOCIAL SECURITY NO. OF VETERAN — 4. DATE OF BIRTH — 5. PLACE OF BIRTH

6. NAME OF FATHER — 7. MAIDEN NAME OF MOTHER — 8. DID THE VETERAN WORK IN THE RAILROAD INDUSTRY AT ANY TIME ON OR AFTER 1-1-37?
☐ YES   ☐ NO

NOTE: The following information should be furnished for each period of the veteran's active service after September 7, 1939, in the Army, Navy, Air Force, Marine Corps or Coast Guard of the United States or service as a commissioned officer in the Public Health Service or the National Oceanic and Atmospheric Administration *(formerly the Environmental Sciences Services Administration; Coast and Geodetic Service)*. If additional space is needed, attach separate sheet.

ENTERED ACTIVE SERVICE		9C. SERVICE NO.	SEPARATED FROM ACTIVE SERVICE		9F. GRADE, RANK OR RATING, ORGANIZATION AND BRANCH OF SERVICE
9A. DATE	9B. PLACE		9D. DATE	9E. PLACE	

10. RELATIONSHIP OF APPLICANT TO VETERAN
☐ WIDOW   ☐ WIDOWER   ☐ CHILD   ☐ PARENT
11. DATE OF BIRTH OF APPLICANT
12. VETERANS ADMINISTRATION FILE NO.

CHILDREN: Show names of surviving children *(including natural children, adopted children, and stepchildren)* or dependent grandchildren *(including stepchildren)* who at any time since the veteran died, were unmarried and (a) under age 18; (b) age 18 to 23 and attending school; (c) disabled or handicapped *(18 or over and disability began before age 22).*

13A. — 13B.

13C. — 13D.

I know that anyone who makes or causes to be made a false statement or representation of material fact in an application or for use in determining a right to payment under the Social Security Act commits a crime punishable under Federal law by fine, imprisonment, or both. I affirm that all information I have given in this document is true.

14. DATE *(Month, day, year)* — 15. SIGNATURE OF APPLICANT *(First name, middle initial, last name) (Sign in ink)*
SIGN HERE ▶

16. MAILING ADDRESS OF APPLICANT *(No. and street or rural route, city or P.O., State and ZIP Code)* — 17. TELEPHONE NO.

WITNESSES REQUIRED ONLY IF SIGNATURE OF APPLICANT IS MADE BY "X" MARK ABOVE

18A. SIGNATURE OF WITNESS — 18B. ADDRESS OF WITNESS *(No. and street, city, State and ZIP Code.)*

19A. SIGNATURE OF WITNESS — 19B. ADDRESS OF WITNESS *(No. and street, city, State and ZIP Code.)*

ITEMS BELOW TO BE COMPLETED BY THE VETERANS ADMINISTRATION *(Use reverse for "Remarks")*

20. PROOFS RECEIVED *(Check)*
☐ DEATH   ☐ MARRIAGE
☐ AGE _____ (NAME)
_____ (NAME)
_____ (NAME)
☐ OTHER *(Specify)*

21. PROOFS REQUESTED FROM CLAIMANT OR OTHERS *(Specify)*
☐ DEATH   ☐ MARRIAGE
☐ AGE _____ (NAME)
_____ (NAME)
_____ (NAME)
☐ OTHER *(Specify)*

22. DATE — 23. NAME AND ADDRESS OF TRANSMITTING VA OFFICE

VA FORM
MAY 1980 **SSA-24**

EXISTING STOCKS OF SSA-24, NOV 1978, WILL BE USED.

605701

INSTRUCTIONS FOR COMPLETING FORM SSA-24, APPLICATION FOR SURVIVORS BENEFITS

(Payable Under Title II of the Social Security Act)

IMPORTANT: PLEASE READ THE FOLLOWING BEFORE YOU COMPLETE THE SSA-24.

This application form, SSA-24, is an Application for Survivors Benefits Payable under Title II of the Social Security Act, as amended. Under authority of section 202(o) of the Social Security Act the application requests information in order to determine eligibility to social security benefits.

You do not have to complete this application; there are no penalties under the law if you do not complete part or all of the SSA-24. However, it is usually to your advantage to provide the information because not providing it could prevent an accurate and timely decision on your claim or could result in the loss of some benefits or insurance coverage.

If you do wish to supply the information requested on the SSA-24, this information will be forwarded to the Social Security Administration and used by them to determine whether social security benefits may be payable to a surviving dependent(s) of the veteran. Social Security will then contact you regarding any social security benefits payable based on information given on this form.

Please understand that Social Security may, in certain instances, disclose the information on this form to another Federal, State or local agency or individual without your written consent. This would be done in order to:
- enable a third party or an agency to assist Social Security in establishing an individual's right to benefits or coverage;
- comply with Federal laws which require or authorize the release of information from social security records; and
- facilitate statistical research and audit activities necessary to assure the integrity and improvement of the social security programs.

If you should have any question about entitlement to social security benefits, or the information you have provided on this form, please contact your local social security office.

Complete each item of the attached application, Form SSA-24, (except the Items 20 through 23). When signed and dated the form SHOULD BE LEFT ATTACHED to your completed application for dependency and indemnity compensation or death pension.

INSTRUCTIONS FOR FILING CLAIM FOR DEPENDENCY AND
INDEMNITY COMPENSATION BY PARENT(S)

PRIVACY ACT INFORMATION - No benefits may be paid under this program unless this form is completed and returned as required by existing law (38 U.S.C. 415). The information requested by this form is considered relevant and necessary to determine maximum benefits to which you are entitled. The information submitted may be disclosed outside the Veterans Administration only as provided by law. Disclosure of Social Security number(s) of those for whom benefits are claimed is requested under the authority of Title 38, U.S.C. and is mandatory as a condition to receipt of Dependency and Indemnity Compensation (38 C.F.R. 1.575). Social Security numbers will be used in the administration of veterans' benefits, in the identification of veterans or persons claiming or receiving Veterans Administration benefits and their records and may be used to verify Social Security benefit entitlement (including amounts payable) with the Social Security Administration and for other purposes where authorized by both Title 38 U.S.C. and the Privacy Act of 1974 (5 U.S.C. 552a) or, where required by another statute.

The terms "father" and "mother" include a father, mother, father through adoption, mother through adoption, foster father or foster mother (including stepparents who stood in the relationship of parent to the veteran).

A. PAYMENT OF BENEFITS - GENERAL

1. Dependency and Indemnity Compensation. Dependency and Indemnity Compensation may be payable when the veteran dies:
(a) From *disease* or *injury* incurred or aggravated in line of duty while on active duty or active duty for training;
(b) From *injury* incurred or aggravated in line of duty while on *inactive* duty training; or
(c) From a disability compensable under laws administered by the Veterans Administration.

2. INCOME LIMITS AND RATES PAYABLE. The rate of Dependency and Indemnity Compensation paid depends upon the amount of income and number of dependent parents. Because benefit rates and income limits are frequently changed, it is not feasible to keep such information current in these instructions. Information regarding current income limitations and rates of benefits may be obtained by contacting your nearest VA office.

3. An additional amount is payable each month to a parent who is a patient in a nursing home or who is otherwise determined to be in need of regular aid and attendance.

Philippine Service Cases

In cases involving service in the Commonwealth Army of the Philippines or where a veteran enlisted as a guerrilla or in the Philippine Scouts under section 14, Public Law 190, 79th Congress, the amount of the parent's annual income and the rates of Dependency and Indemnity Compensation will be computed at a rate in Philippine pesos which is equivalent to $.50 for each dollar payable.

B. SOCIAL SECURITY NUMBERS

The father or mother completing this form should enter his or her social security number in Item 3D or Item 4D, as appropriate. The social security number of his or her spouse should be shown in the remaining box. The social security number of the deceased veteran should be entered in Item 8.

C. INCOME TO BE REPORTED

Report all income received including wages, interest and dividends. Also report the "source" of income: "Wages," "Old-age and survivors insurance," etc. In reporting wages or salary, report gross income and not "take home" pay. Do Not deduct amounts withheld under a retirement act or plan, or amounts withheld for income tax.

If room, board, or goods are received as part of your employment, you should report this fact and give the approximate value thereof.

(NOTE: If application is filed "As Guardian" or "As Custodian" of the parent, do not report your own income but only the income of the parent named on the application form.)

IMPORTANT

THERE ARE CERTAIN TYPES OF INCOME WHICH MAY BE EXCLUDED IN DETERMINING THE INCOME COUNTABLE FOR VA PURPOSES. HOWEVER, YOU MUST REPORT THE SOURCES AND AMOUNTS OF ALL INCOME BEFORE DEDUCTIONS. WE WILL DETERMINE ANY AMOUNT WHICH DOES NOT COUNT. INCLUDE ALL SEVERANCE PAY OR OTHER ACCRUED PAYMENTS OF ANY KIND OR FROM ANY SOURCE. WHEN NO INCOME IS RECEIVED OR EXPECTED FROM A SPECIFIED SOURCE, WRITE "NONE" IN THE APPROPRIATE BLOCK (ITEMS 34, 35, AND 36). ATTACH SEPARATE SHEETS IF ADDITIONAL SPACE IS NEEDED.

D. FAMILY UNUSUAL MEDICAL EXPENSES are amounts actually paid by you during the calendar year for unusual medical expenses for which you are not reimbursed by insurance or otherwise. You should report in Item 45, Remarks, the total unreimbursed amount you paid for medical expenses for yourself or for relatives you are under an obligation to support. You may include premiums paid for health, sickness or hospitalization insurance. In computing your income for Dependency and Indemnity Compensation, the VA will deduct the amount you paid for medical expenses if they qualify for exclusion under the formula provided by law.

E. REPRESENTATION - ORGANIZATIONS AND ATTORNEYS

You may be represented without charge, by an accredited representative of a service organization recognized by the Administrator of Veterans Affairs. While you may also employ an attorney authorized to practice in the United States or its territories or possessions to assist in prosecuting your claim, it is not necessary to do so. Any attorney so employed may not legally charge any fee other than that allowed and paid by the Veterans Administration, and which is deducted from benefits otherwise payable to the claimant.

F. HOW TO COMPLETE THE APPLICATION FORM

ALL THE INFORMATION REQUIRED IN THIS APPLICATION MUST BE FURNISHED AND THE QUESTIONS MUST BE ANSWERED FULLY AND CLEARLY. If you do not know the answer to any question say "Unknown." For additional space use Item 45, Remarks, or attach a separate sheet, indicating the item numbers to which the answers apply.

G. INCOMPETENTS

If the person for whom claim is being made is incompetent, the application form should be filled in and filed by the legal guardian or, if no legal guardian has been appointed, it may be filled in and filed by some person acting on behalf of the incompetent.

H. EVIDENCE - GENERAL

If you are unable to furnish with this application form any of the required evidence listed below, state why you are unable on a separate sheet. Evidence filed previously in the Veterans Administration need not be filed in connection with this claim.

I. EVIDENCE - NEED FOR AID AND ATTENDANCE

A statement from your doctor showing the extent of your disabilities should be furnished with your application if you require the aid and attendance of another person but are not a patient in a nursing home. If you are a nursing home patient, you should furnish a statement signed by an official of the nursing home showing the date of your admission and patient status. Also, indicate in Item 45, "Remarks" that you are a nursing home patient and give the name and address of the nursing home.

J. PROOF OF RELATIONSHIP OF NATURAL OR ADOPTIVE MOTHER OR FATHER

A copy of the public record of birth or church record of baptism showing the date of birth of the veteran and names of the parents and certified by the custodian of such records should be furnished. If neither of the records mentioned is obtainable, it is not necessary to establish one for the purpose of this claim. Instead, you should submit the affidavit of the attending physician or midwife or the affidavits of two persons who have personal knowledge of the facts to which he/she testifies. If the veteran was an adopted child, a copy of the court order of adoption, certified by the custodian of the court record, should be furnished.

K. FOSTER MOTHER OR FATHER (Persons, including stepparents, who stood in the relationship of parent to the veteran)

If the claimant is not the natural or adoptive parent of the veteran but was the last person who stood in the relationship of parent to the veteran during his/her minority for a period of not less than 1 year prior to his/her entrance into the active military or naval service, the claimant will be required to complete VA Form 21-524 which will be furnished upon receipt of the application.

L. PROOF OF DEATH AND SERVICE

Death of a veteran in active service of the Army, Navy, Air Force, Marine Corps, or Coast Guard, or in a United States Government institution does not need to be proved by a claimant. Otherwise, the claimant should forward a copy of the public record of death, certified by the custodian of such records, or a duly certified copy of a coroner's report of death, or a verdict of a coroner's jury.

If proof of death is required and the veteran never filed a claim with the Veterans Administration, you should also furnish a copy of the separation document for each period of service listed in Part I. If you do not have this document, we will obtain a copy.

Summaries of the Law of Wills for Each State*

The following section contains summaries of the law of wills for each state. These laws are always subject to change or to different legal interpretation. The executor should therefore consult a local attorney and not rely solely on the information presented in this section.

Alabama

MINIMUM AGE: Real Estate, 19; personalty, 18.

NUMBER OF WITNESSES: 2.

HOLOGRAPHIC WILLS: No provision.

NUNCUPATIVE WILLS: Restricted to property with a value not exceeding $500.[1]

REVOCATION BY OPERATION OF LAW:
 Marriage: A woman's will is revoked.
 Birth of Child: No provision.
 Divorce: Will provisions in favor of divorced spouse are revoked.

RIGHTS OF PRETERMITTED CHILDREN:
 Children Born After Execution of Will: Children[2] unprovided for in the will take intestate share.
 Children Born Before Execution of Will: No provision.

ELECTION AGAINST WILL: In lieu of provisions of will, widow may take dower in real estate and her intestate share of personalty.[3]

CHARITABLE GIFT LIMITATIONS: No provision.

RULE AGAINST PERPETUITIES: No provision; common law rule applied.

RULE AGAINST UNREASONABLE ACCUMULATION OF INCOME: 10 years, or for the minority of a minor beneficiary alive at the creation of the trust.

---

[1] Soldiers in actual service or mariners or seamen at sea may dispose of property without regard to the strict requirements generally governing the probate of nuncupative wills.

[2] Including posthumous and adopted children.

[3] If no children or their descendants survive, and the personal estate exceeds $50,000 in value, the widow takes the first $50,000, with the remainder distributed as provided in the will.

Alaska

MINIMUM AGE: 18.

NUMBER OF WITNESSES: 2.

HOLOGRAPHIC WILLS: Permitted.

NUNCUPATIVE WILLS: Restricted to soldiers in military service or mariners at sea without regard to the strict requirements generally governing the probate of nuncupative wills.

REVOCATION BY OPERATION OF LAW:
 Divorce: Will provisions in favor of divorced spouse are revoked. No other changes in a testator's circumstances affect his or her will.

RIGHTS OF PRETERMITTED CHILDREN: A child born or adopted after the execution of the will, and for whom the will makes no provision takes an intestate share, unless it appears from the will that the failure to provide for the omitted child was intentional, or the testator had a child when he or she executed the will and left substantially all his or her estate to the other parent of the omitted child, or the testator provided for the omitted child outside of the will.

ELECTION AGAINST WILL: The surviving spouse may elect to take against the will, and in such case is entitled to 1/3 of the augmented estate.

CHARITABLE GIFT LIMITATION: No provision.

RULE AGAINST PERPETUITIES: Common law rule established.

RULE AGAINST UNREASONABLE ACCUMULATION OF INCOME: No provision; permissible period of rule against perpetuities apparently applies.

Arizona

MINIMUM AGE: 18.

NUMBER OF WITNESSES: 2.

HOLOGRAPHIC WILLS: Permitted.

NUNCUPATIVE WILLS: Not permitted.

REVOCATION BY OPERATION OF LAW: Annulment, dissolution of a marriage, or divorce revokes provisions in favor of the ex-spouse. No other change in a testator's circumstances affects his or her will.

RIGHTS OF PRETERMITTED CHILDREN: A child born or adopted after the execution of the will, and for whom the will makes no provision, takes an intestate share, unless it appears from the will that the testator intended not to provide for such a child, or when the will was executed the testator had one or more children and left substantially all of his or her estate to the other parent of the omitted child, or the testator provided for the omitted child by transfer outside the will and the intent that the transfer be in lieu of a testamentary provision is shown by statements of the testator or from the amount of the transfer or other evidence.

ELECTION AGAINST WILL: No provision; community property state.

CHARITABLE GIFT LIMITATION: No provision.

RULE AGAINST PERPETUITIES: Common law rule established.

RULE AGAINST UNREASONABLE ACCUMULATION OF INCOME: No provision; permissible period of rule against perpetuities apparently applies.

Arkansas

MINIMUM AGE: 18.

NUMBER OF WITNESSES: 2.

HOLOGRAPHIC WILLS: Permitted.[1]

NUNCUPATIVE WILLS: No provision.

REVOCATION BY OPERATION OF LAW:
Marriage or Birth of Child: Will is not revoked; however, surviving widow may elect intestate share.
Divorce or Annulment: Will provisions in favor of divorced spouse or a spouse in an annulled marriage are revoked.

RIGHTS OF PRETERMITTED CHILDREN:
Children Born After Execution of Will: Children[2] unprovided for in the will, either specifically or as a member of a class, take intestate share.
Children Born Before Execution of Will: Children[3] unprovided for or mentioned in the will, either specifically or as member of a class take intestate share.

ELECTION AGAINST WILL: In lieu of provision of will, spouse may take intestate share.[4]

CHARITABLE GIFT LIMITATION: No provision.

RULE AGAINST PERPETUITIES: No provision; common law rule applies.

RULE AGAINST UNREASONABLE ACCUMULATION OF INCOME: No provision; permissible period of rule against perpetuities apparently applies.

---

[1] At least 3 witnesses must attest to the handwriting and signature of the testator.

[2] Including adopted children.

[3] Including issue of a deceased child.

[4] A devise of real property to a spouse is deemed to be in lieu of dower or curtesy.

California

MINIMUM AGE: 18.

NUMBER OF WITNESSES: 2.

HOLOGRAPHIC WILLS: Permitted.

NUNCUPATIVE WILLS: Restricted to soldiers in actual military service in the field or doing duty on shipboard at sea. Will apparently is valid to pass the proceeds of military life insurance up to the statutory limits or maximum of $1,000 whichever is smaller.

REVOCATION BY OPERATION OF LAW:
Marriage: Will is revoked unless provision is made for the spouse by marriage contract, or in the will or in such way mentioned therein as to show an intention not to make such provision.

Birth of Child: Marriage and the birth of a child revokes will provisions as to such issue unless provision has been made for issue by some settlement, or in the will or in such way mentioned therein as to show an intention not to make such provision.

Divorce: For purposes of a will, the former spouse of the testator, and that spouse's lineal descendants (but not the descendants of the testator), are deemed to have predeceased the testator, unless the will provides otherwise.

RIGHTS OF PRETERMITTED CHILDREN:
Children[1] Born After Execution of Will: Children unprovided for in the will or by any settlement and who have not had an equal proportion of the testator's property bestowed upon them by advancement, take intestate share unless it appears from the will that such omission was intentional.

ELECTION AGAINST WILL:
No statutory provision; community property state. It has been held, by case law, that as to community property, widow was required to make an election. Where widow elected to take under will, she was bound by such election although testator indicated an intention to dispose of the entire community property.

CHARITABLE GIFT LIMITATIONS:
Charitable bequests and devises to a nonprofit charitable corporation are invalid if contained in a will executed within six months prior to a filing of petition for a guardianship or conservatorship, when the corporation has been appointed the guardian or conservator.

RULE AGAINST PERPETUITIES:
Common law rule established, except that a period in gross of up to 60 years is allowed.

RULE AGAINST UNREASONABLE ACCUMULATION OF INCOME:
Permissible period of rule against perpetuities established.

---

[1] Including posthumous children and the issue of deceased children.

Colorado

MINIMUM AGE: 18.

NUMBER OF WITNESSES: 2.

HOLOGRAPHIC WILLS: Permitted.

NUNCUPATIVE WILLS: No provision.

REVOCATION BY OPERATION OF LAW:
Marriage: Will is not revoked.[1]
Birth of Child: Will is not revoked.
Divorce: Will provisions in favor of divorced spouse are revoked.[2]

RIGHTS OF PRETERMITTED CHILDREN:
Children Born After Execution of Will: Children unprovided for in the will take intestate share, unless it appears from the will that it was the intention of the testator to disinherit the child.

Children Born Before Execution of Will: No provision.

ELECTION AGAINST WILL:
The surviving spouse may elect to take against the will; and in such case is entitled to take a fraction of the augmented estate designated by the surviving spouse not greater than 1/2.

CHARITABLE GIFT LIMITATION:
No provision.

RULE AGAINST PERPETUITIES:
No provision; common law rule applies.

RULE AGAINST UNREASONABLE ACCUMULATION OF INCOME:
No provision; permissible period of rule against perpetuities applies.

---

[1] A common-law marriage will revoke a prior will.

[2] The effect of the revocation is the same as if the divorced spouse had died at the time of the divorce. A will, which by its terms is executed in contemplation of divorce, is not revoked by the divorce if the will expressly provides that it shall not be revoked by such divorce.

Connecticut

MINIMUM AGE: 18.

NUMBER OF WITNESSES: 2.

HOLOGRAPHIC WILLS: No provision.

NUNCUPATIVE WILLS: No provision.

REVOCATION BY OPERATION OF LAW:
Marriage, Birth[1] of Child, Annulment[2], or Divorce[2]: Will is revoked if no provision has been made for such contingency.

RIGHTS OF PRETERMITTED CHILDREN:
Children Born Before or After Execution of Will: No provision.

Election Against Will: Surviving spouse is entitled to a life estate in 1/3 the value of all of decedent's real and personal property. The surviving spouse's right to this portion of the estate cannot be defeated by will provisions devising it to others. However, by case law, if an election is made to take against the will, the surviving spouse's statutory share will be set off so as to do as little damage to the testator's intent as is possible.

CHARITABLE GIFT LIMITATION: No provision.

RULE AGAINST PERPETUITIES: Common law rule established except that permissible period is measured by actual rather than possible events.

RULE AGAINST UNREASONABLE ACCUMULATION OF INCOME: No provision; permissible period of rule against perpetuities applies.

---

[1] Or adoption of minor child, or child born as a result of artificial insemination.

[2] Divorce or annulment does not revoke testator's will where spouse was not a beneficiary thereunder.

Delaware

MINIMUM AGE: 18.

NUMBER OF WITNESSES: 2.

HOLOGRAPHIC WILLS: Not permitted.

NUNCUPATIVE WILLS: Not permitted.

REVOCATION BY OPERATION OF LAW: Annulment of marriage or divorce revokes all provisions in favor of the ex-spouse. No other change in a testator's circumstances affects his or her will.

RIGHTS OF PRETERMITTED CHILDREN: No provision. Moreover, a 1965 case denied an intestate share to a child of a testator born during a first marriage, when the child was not named clearly and unambiguously in the father's will disposing of his entire estate.

ELECTION AGAINST WILL: The surviving spouse may elect to take against the will, and in such case is entitled to $20,000 or 1/3 of the "elective estate", whichever is less, less the value of all property deemed transferred by the decedent to the surviving spouse *by virtue of death.* (e.g., jointly owned property that passes to the surviving spouse towards the purchase of which the surviving spouse contributed nothing, and any proceeds of insurance on the life of the decedent attributable to premiums paid by him or her.) The "elective estate" is the decedent's federal adjusted gross estate/less the value of all transfers made by the decedent during his or her lifetime that are included in the determination of the federal adjusted gross estate and

which were made with the written consent or joinder of the surviving spouse.

CHARITABLE GIFT LIMITATION: No provision.

RULE AGAINST PERPETUITIES: No provision; common law rule applies.[1]

RULE AGAINST UNREASONABLE ACCUMULATION OF INCOME: No provision; permissible period of rule against perpetuities applies.

---

[1] There is a specific statutory provision to the effect that powers of appointment are deemed to be created at the time of the exercise and not at the creation of the power of appointment.

District of Columbia

MINIMUM AGE: 18.

NUMBER OF WITNESSES: 2.

HOLOGRAPHIC WILLS: No provision.

NUNCUPATIVE WILLS: Restricted to persons in actual military or naval service, or a mariner at sea.

REVOCATION BY OPERATION OF LAW:
Marriage, and Birth of a Child: Revokes prior will.
Divorce: D.C. courts apply the common law doctrine of implied revocation, when a property settlement is coupled with a divorce, to revoke a prior will.

RIGHTS OF PRETERMITTED CHILDREN:
Children Born Before or After Execution of Will: No provision.

ELECTION AGAINST WILL: In lieu of bequest of personalty or devise of realty, spouse may elect dower.

CHARITABLE GIFT LIMITATION: Charitable bequests or devises invalid unless will executed at least 30 days before death.

RULE AGAINST PERPETUITIES: Common law rule established.

RULE AGAINST UNREASONABLE ACCUMULATION OF INCOME: No provision; permissible period of rule against perpetuities applies.

Florida

MINIMUM AGE: 18.

NUMBER OF WITNESSES: 2.

HOLOGRAPHIC WILLS: No provision.

NUNCUPATIVE WILLS: No provision.

REVOCATION BY OPERATION OF LAW:

Marriage: Will is not revoked.[1]

Birth of Child: Will is not revoked.

Divorce: Will provisions in favor of divorced spouse are revoked.

RIGHTS OF PRETERMITTED CHILDREN: A child born or adopted after the will was executed, and for whom no provision is made in the will, and who has not received a share of the decedent's estate by way of advancement, takes an intestate share unless it appears from the will that the failure to provide for the child was intentional, or the testator had one or more children when the will was executed and gave substantially all his or her estate to the parent of the omitted child.

ELECTION AGAINST WILL: The surviving spouse may elect to take against the will, and in such case is entitled to an amount equal to 30% of the fair market value of all property of the decedent, wherever located, that is subject to administration except real property located outside Florida.

CHARITABLE GIFT LIMITATION: Charitable bequests or devises may be challenged within eight months following testator's death by testator's spouse, natural or adopted children, or the descendants of either, unless will is executed more than six months before death, or unless a prior will, executed more than six months before his death, contained similar provisions.[2]

RULE AGAINST PERPETUITIES: No provision; common law rule applies.

RULE AGAINST UNREASONABLE ACCUMULATION OF INCOME: No provision; permissible period of rule against perpetuities applies.

---

[1] However, the surviving spouse does receive intestate share unless provision has been made for the spouse by marriage contract, or in the will, or the will discloses an intention not to make such provision.

[2] Charitable gift limitations do not apply to bequests or devises to institutions of higher learning.

Georgia

MINIMUM AGE: 14.

NUMBER OF WITNESSES: 2.

HOLOGRAPHIC WILLS: No provision.

NUNCUPATIVE WILLS: Permitted; applies to both real and personal property.

REVOCATION BY OPERATION OF LAW:

Marriage, Birth of Child, or Divorce: Will is re-

voked unless provision is made in the will in contemplation of such event.

RIGHTS OF PRETERMITTED CHILDREN:

Children Born Before or After Execution of Will: No provision.

ELECTION AGAINST WILL: In lieu of devise of realty in will, widow may take dower; however, the election does not bar her bequest of personal property unless expressed to be in lieu of dower.

CHARITABLE GIFT LIMITATIONS: No testator survived by a wife, child, or descendants of such child may make charitable bequests or devises totaling more than 1/3 of his estate, to the exclusion of such wife or child; and, in all cases, the devise must be executed at least 90 days before the testator's death.[1]

RULE AGAINST PERPETUITIES: Common law rule codified.

RULE AGAINST UNREASONABLE ACCUMULATION OF INCOME: No provision; permissible period of rule against perpetuities apparently applies.

---

[1] The status of this provision is uncertain. The 1977 Act, effective 7-1-77, was intended to repeal this provision, but the repealer appears to have been accidentally left out of the Act.

Charitable gift limitations do not apply to excess of estate over $200,000.

Hawaii

MINIMUM AGE: 18.

NUMBER OF WITNESSES: 2.

HOLOGRAPHIC WILLS: No provision.

NUNCUPATIVE WILLS: No provision.

REVOCATION BY OPERATION OF LAW:

Divorce: Will provisions in favor of divorced spouse are revoked. No other changes in a testator's circumstances affect his or her will.

RIGHTS OF PRETERMITTED CHILDREN: A child born or adopted after the execution of the will, and for whom the will makes no provision, takes an intestate share, unless it appears from the will that the testator intended not to provide for such a child, or when the will was executed the testator had one or more children and left substantially all of his or her estate to the other parent of the omitted child, or the testator provided for the omitted child by transfer outside the will/and the intent that the transfer be in lieu of a testamentary provision is shown by statements of the testator or from the amount of the transfer or other evidence.

ELECTION AGAINST WILL: Surviving spouse may elect against the will and take a 1/3 share of decedent's "net estate."[1]

CHARITABLE GIFT LIMITATION: No provision.

RULE AGAINST PERPETUITIES: No provision; common law rule applies.

RULE AGAINST UNREASONABLE ACCUMULATION OF INCOME: No provision; permissible period of rule against perpetuities applies.

---

[1] The net estate constitutes the estate disposed of by decedent's will or intestate succession minus all enforceable claims against the estate.

Idaho

MINIMUM AGE: 18. But an emancipated minor of any age may execute a will.

NUMBER OF WITNESSES: 2.

HOLOGRAPHIC WILLS: Permitted.

NUNCUPATIVE WILLS: Not permitted.

REVOCATION BY OPERATION OF LAW:
Divorce: Annulment of a marriage, or divorce revokes provisions in favor of the ex-spouse. No other change in a testator's circumstances affects his or her will.

RIGHTS OF PRETERMITTED CHILDREN: A child born or adopted after execution of the will, and for whom the will makes no provision, takes an intestate share, unless it appears from the will that the testator intended not to provide for such child, or the testator had a child living when the will was executed and left substantially all of his or her estate to the other parent of the omitted child, or the testator provided for the omitted child by transfer outside the will and/the intent that the transfer be in lieu of a testamentary provision is shown by statements of the testator or from the amount of the transfer or other evidence.

ELECTION AGAINST WILL: A surviving spouse who elects to take against the will is entitled to 1/3 of the augmented estate. In general, the Idaho augmented estate is the probate estate/plus 1/2 of the certain property transferred by the decedent during his or her life, plus 1/2 of property owned jointly by the decedent's death.

CHARITABLE GIFT LIMITATION: Charitable bequests or devises are invalid unless executed at least 30 days before death. Even if executed before such period, charitable gifts may not collectively exceed 1/3[1] of estate of a testator survived by lineal descendants.

RULE AGAINST PERPETUITIES: Lives in being plus 25 years. A statutory rule has replaced the common law rule against perpetuities.

RULE AGAINST UNREASONABLE ACCUMULATION OF INCOME: No provision; permissible period of rule against perpetuities apparently applies.

---

[1] This limitation does not apply where bequests or devises having an aggregate value of $100,000 or more made to testator's lineal descendants.

Illinois

MINIMUM AGE: 18.

NUMBER OF WITNESSES: 2.

HOLOGRAPHIC WILLS: No provision.

NUNCUPATIVE WILLS: No provision.

REVOCATION BY OPERATION OF LAW:
Marriage or Birth of Child: Will is not revoked.
Divorce: Will provisions in favor of divorced spouse are revoked, including appointment as executor or executrix, and will takes effect in the same manner as if the former spouse had predeceased the testator.

RIGHTS OF PRETERMITTED CHILDREN:
Children Born After Execution of Will: Children[1] unprovided for in the will take intestate share unless it appears by the will that it was the intention of the testator to disinherit the child.
Children Born Before Execution of Will: No provision.

ELECTION AGAINST WILL: In lieu of provisions of will, spouse may take 1/3[2] of the entire estate.

CHARITABLE GIFT LIMITATION: No provision.

RULE AGAINST PERPETUITIES: The common law rule applies, except as modified by the "State Concerning Perpetuities."

RULE AGAINST UNREASONABLE ACCUMULATION OF INCOME: Permissible period of rule against perpetuities established.

---

[1] Including adopted children.
[2] Or 1/2 if testator is survived by no descendants.

Indiana

MINIMUM AGE: 18, or member of armed forces, or merchant marine of U.S., or its allies.

NUMBER OF WITNESSES: 2.

HOLOGRAPHIC WILLS: No Provision.

NUNCUPATIVE WILLS: Restrictive to property with a value not exceeding $1,000.[1]

REVOCATION BY OPERATION BY LAW:
Marriage or Birth of Child: No provision.
Divorce: Will provisions in favor of divorced spouse are revoked. Annulment has the same effect.

RIGHTS OF PRETERMITTED CHILDREN:
Children Born After Execution of Will: Children[2] unprovided for in the will take intestate share unless it appears from the will that such omission was intentional, or unless when the will was executed, the testator had one or more children known to him to be living and devised substantially all his estate to his spouse.
Children Born Before Execution of Will: Children unprovided for in the will who, at the time of the will's execution, the testator believes to be dead, take intestate share unless it appears from the will or from other evidence that the testator would not have devised anything to such child had he known the child to be alive.

ELECTION AGAINST WILL: In lieu of provisions of the will, spouse may take ⅓ of the personal and real property.[3]

CHARITABLE GIFT LIMITATION: No provision.

RULE AGAINST PERPETUITIES: Common law rule against perpetuities codified.

RULE AGAINST UNREASONABLE ACCUMULATION OF INCOME: Permissible period of rule against perpetuities established.

---

[1] As to persons in active military, air, or naval service time of war, the limitation is $10,000.
[2] Including adopted and posthumous children.
[3] When the value of the property devised under the will is less than the amount the spouse would have received by exercising his or her election, the spouse may retain any of all specific devises and receive the balance in cash or property.
  If the surviving spouse is a second childless spouse, the election is for ⅓ the net personal estate plus a ⅓ life estate in real property.

Iowa

MINIMUM AGE: 18.

NUMBER OF WITNESSES: 2.

HOLOGRAPHIC WILLS: No provision.

NUNCUPATIVE WILLS: No provision.

REVOCATION BY OPERATION OF LAW:
Marriage or Birth of Child: No provision.
Divorce: Will provisions in favor of the divorced spouse are revoked.[1]

RIGHTS OF PRETERMITTED CHILDREN:
Children Born After Execution of Will: Children[2] unprovided for in the will take intestate share unless it appears from the will that such omission was intentional.
Children Born Before Execution of Will: No provision.

ELECTION AGAINST WILL: In lieu of provisions of will, spouse may elect ⅓ of real property;[3] all personal property in hands of family head exempt from execution, and ⅓ of all other personal property exempt.

CHARITABLE GIFT LIMITATIONS: Charitable bequests or devises in excess of ¼ of the estate invalid. Spouse, child, child of a deceased child, or parent may elect intestate share of excess.

RULE AGAINST PERPETUITIES: Common law rule against perpetuities codified.

RULE AGAINST UNREASONABLE ACCUMULATION OF INCOME: No provision; permissible period of rule against perpetuities applies.

---

[1] Adoption of a child may revoke a prior will.
[2] Including adopted and posthumous children.
[3] In lieu of interest in real property, spouse may elect to occupy the homestead.

Kansas

MINIMUM AGE: 18.

NUMBER OF WITNESSES: 2.

HOLOGRAPHIC WILLS: No provision.

NUNCUPATIVE WILLS: Permitted.

REVOCATION BY OPERATION OF LAW:
Marriage or Birth of Child: Either event, standing alone, will not revoke will. However, marriage, *and* birth[1] of a child revokes will.
Divorce: Will provisions in favor of divorced spouse are revoked.

RIGHTS OF PRETERMITTED CHILDREN:
Child Born Before or After Execution of Will: No provision.

ELECTION AGAINST WILL: In lieu of provisions of will, spouse may take intestate share.

CHARITABLE GIFT LIMITATION: No provision.

RULE AGAINST PERPETUITIES: No provision; common law rule applies.

RULE AGAINST UNREASONABLE ACCUMULATION OF INCOME: No provision; permissible period of rule against perpetuities apparently applies.

---

[1] Or adoption.

Kentucky

MINIMUM AGE: 18.[1]

NUMBER OF WITNESSES: 2.

HOLOGRAPHIC WILLS: Permitted.

NUNCUPATIVE WILLS: No provision.

REVOCATION BY OPERATION OF LAW:
Marriage: Will is revoked.[2]
Birth of Child: Will is revoked if testator had no child living when will was executed and an after-born child[3] is neither provided for nor mentioned in the will. The will is construed to take effect only if the child dies under age of 21 years, unmarried, and without issue.
Divorce: Revoked, apparently as to the entire will. There is an exception where the will was exercising testator's power of appointment and the property was to pass to his estate, heirs, or next of kin. Also, a will which made no bequest or devise to the former spouse is not revoked.

RIGHTS OF PRETERMITTED CHILDREN:
Children Born After Execution of Will: A child[3] born or adopted after execution of the will, for whom the will makes no provision, takes an intestate share unless it appears from the will that the testator intended not to provide for such child, or the testator had a child living when the will was executed and left substantially all of his or her estate to the other parent of the omitted child, or the testator provided for the omitted child by transfer outside the will, and the intent that the transfer be in lieu of a testamentary provision is shown by statements of the testator or from the amount of the transfer or other evidence.
Children Born Before Execution of Will: No provision.

ELECTION AGAINST WILL: In lieu of provisions of will, spouse may take intestate share.[4]

CHARITABLE GIFT LIMITATION: No provision.

RULE AGAINST PERPETUITIES: Common law rule established, except that permissible period is measured by actual rather than possible events.

RULE AGAINST UNREASONABLE ACCUMULATION OF INCOME: No provision; permissible period of rule against perpetuities applies.

---

[1] A father under 18 may, by will, appoint a guardian for his child.
[2] There are exceptions in limited cases where a will is made in exercise of a power of appointment.
[3] Including descendants and posthumous child.
[4] Except that as to real estate in which decedent held an interest, the spouse shall take a ⅓ share.
The spouse may receive an intestate share in addition to will provisions if such intention is expressed, directly or inferentially in the will.

Louisiana

MINIMUM AGE: 18 (or 16 and in prospect of death).

NUMBER OF WITNESSES [1]

HOLOGRAPHIC WILLS: Permitted.[2]

NUNCUPATIVE WILLS [1]

REVOCATION BY OPERATION OF LAW:
Marriage or Divorce: No provision.
Birth[3] *of Child:* Will is revoked unless the testator provides otherwise.

RIGHTS OF PRETERMITTED CHILDREN:
Children Born After Execution of Will: No provision.
Children Born Before Execution of Will: Children alive when will is executed may be disinherited only on certain specified grounds dealing, in the main, with disrespect or ill treatment of the parent by the child.

ELECTION AGAINST WILL: No provision; community property state.

CHARITABLE GIFT LIMITATION: No provision.

RULE AGAINST PERPETUITIES: 15 years from testator's death, or until beneficiary's death, whichever period is longer.

RULE AGAINST UNREASONABLE ACCUMULATION OF INCOME: No provision; permissible period of rule against perpetuities above applies.

---

[1] Louisiana provides for several kinds of wills. The *mystic* will is signed and declared by the testator before a notary and sealed in an envelope on which the notary, the testator, and three witnesses sign a superscription. In this state the *nuncupative* will is written. The private nuncupative will is written by the testator, or by someone at his dictation in the presence of five witnesses resid-

ing in the place where the will is received, or seven witnesses residing elsewhere, and is signed by two witnesses (the other witnesses may affix their marks). A public nuncupative will is dictated by the testator to a notary in the presence of three witnesses residing where the will is received, or five residing elsewhere, and is signed by the witnesses, or by one of them for himself and those who cannot write.

² Two competent witnesses must testify that the will was entirely written, dated, and signed in the testator's handwriting.

³ Or adoption.

Maine

MINIMUM AGE: 18, except that *any* married or widowed person may execute a will.

NUMBER OF WITNESSES: 2.

HOLOGRAPHIC WILLS: Permitted, whether or not witnessed, provided the signature and material provisions are in the testator's handwriting.

NUNCUPATIVE WILLS: Not permitted.

REVOCATION BY OPERATION OF LAW:
Marriage: Common law governs. Case law is that a will is not revoked by marriage.
Birth of Child: Common law governs. Case law is that a will is not revoked by the birth issue.
Divorce: Will is revoked as to provisions in favor of the former spouse, but are revived by testator's remarriage to the former spouse.

RIGHTS OF PRETERMITTED CHILDREN:
Children Born After Execution of Will: Children born or adopted after the execution of the testator's will and unprovided for in the will take intestate share unless it appears from the will that the omission to provide for such child was intended by the testator, or that when the will was executed the testator had at least one child and devised substantially all of his or her estate to the other parent of the omitted child, or the testator provided for the omitted child via transfer outside the will and evidence indicates the testator intended such a transfer to be in lieu of a testamentary provision.
Children Born Before Execution of Will: Children¹ not having any devise in the will take intestate share unless it appears that such omission was intentional, or was not occasioned by mistake, or that such child had "a due proportion" of the estate during the life of the testator. "The absence of a devise to a child . . . named in the will shall be regarded as conclusive that the absence of the devise was intentional." Children unprovided for in the will who, at the time of the will's execution the testator believes to be dead, take intestate share.

ELECTION AGAINST WILL: In lieu of provisions of will, spouse may take ⅓ of augmented estate.

CHARITABLE GIFT LIMITATION: No provision.

RULE AGAINST PERPETUITIES: Common law rule established, except that permissible period is measured by actual rather than possible events.

RULE AGAINST UNREASONABLE ACCUMULATION OF INCOME: No provision; permissible period of rule against perpetuities apparently applies.

---

¹ Including issue of deceased children.

Maryland

MINIMUM AGE: 18.

NUMBER OF WITNESSES: 2.

HOLOGRAPHIC WILLS: Valid only when made outside the United States by a member of the armed forces; becomes invalid after expiration of one year from the date of the testator's discharge, provided he is living at such time and possesses testamentary capacity.

NUNCUPATIVE WILLS: No provision.

REVOCATION BY OPERATION OF LAW:
Marriage and Birth¹ of Child: Will is revoked, if child or a descendant of the child survives the testator.
Divorce: Divorce on or after June 1, 1964, revokes will provisions in favor of former spouse unless will or divorce decree provide otherwise.

RIGHTS OF PRETERMITTED CHILDREN:
Children Born After Execution of Will: Children² unprovided for in testator's will take intestate share if the will provides for an existing child or children, or for the descendants of a deceased child.
Children Born Before Execution of Will: No provision.

ELECTION AGAINST WILL: In lieu of provisions of will, the surviving spouse may take an intestate share, limited in amount however to $4,000, plus ½ of residue. However, the election must be signed and filed with the court before the electing party's own death, or the election will be invalid.

CHARITABLE GIFT LIMITATION: No provision.

RULE AGAINST PERPETUITIES: Common law rule established, except that permissible period is measured by actual rather than possible events.

RULE AGAINST UNREASONABLE ACCUMULATION OF INCOME: No provision; permissible period of rule against perpetuities apparently applies.

---

[1] Or adoption.
[2] Including descendants of deceased children.

Massachusetts

MINIMUM AGE: 18.

NUMBER OF WITNESSES: 2.

HOLOGRAPHIC WILLS: No provision.

NUNCUPATIVE WILLS: Restricted to soldiers in actual military service or mariners at sea.

REVOCATION BY OPERATION OF LAW:
Marriage: Will is revoked unless it appears from the will that it was made in contemplation of the marriage.[1]
Birth of Child: Will is not revoked.
Divorce: Will is revoked as to provisions in favor of the former spouse, unless the will expressly provides otherwise.

RIGHTS OF PRETERMITTED CHILDREN:
Children Born Before or After Execution of Will: Children[2] unprovided for in the will take intestate share unless it appears that the omission was intentional and not occasioned by accident or mistake, or unless provided for by settlement in testator's lifetime.

ELECTION AGAINST WILL: In lieu of provisions of will, spouse may take elective share.[3]

CHARITABLE GIFT LIMITATION: No provision.

RULE AGAINST PERPETUITIES: Common law rule established, except that the period is measured by actual, rather than possible events.

RULE AGAINST UNREASONABLE ACCUMULATION OF INCOME: No provision; permissible period of rule against perpetuities apparently applies.

---

[1] There are limited exceptions applicable where the will is made in exercise of a power of appointment.
[2] Including posthumous children, or the issue of deceased children.
[3] If the surviving spouse makes the election, he or she is entitled to 1/3 of the decedent's real and personal property if the decedent left issue surviving; and if the decedent left no issue surviving, the spouse is entitled to $25,000, plus 1/2 of the remaining real and personal property, *provided that* if 1/2 of the remaining real and personal property exceeds $25,000 in value, the surviving spouse shall receive $25,000, plus real and personal property having value of $25,000 (or the case equivalent), plus a life estate in the then remaining personal property (which is to be held in trust) and real property.

Michigan

MINIMUM AGE: 18.

NUMBER OF WITNESSES: 2.

HOLOGRAPHIC WILLS: No provision.

NUNCUPATIVE WILLS: No provision.

REVOCATION BY OPERATION OF LAW:
Divorce: Divorce revokes will provisions in favor of former spouse unless will specifically provides otherwise.[1]

RIGHTS OF PRETERMITTED CHILDREN:
Children Born or Adopted After Execution of Will: Children unprovided for in the will take intestate share unless it is apparent from the will that it was the intention of the testator that no provision should be made for such child.[2]
Children Born Before Execution of Will: Children[2] unprovided for in the will take intestate share provided it appears that such omission was not intentional, but was occasioned by mistake or accident.

ELECTION AGAINST WILL: In lieu of the provisions of the will, the surviving spouse may elect to take 1/2 of his/her intestate share of the decedent's estate, reduced by 1/2 of the value of all property received from the decedent by any means other than testate or intestate succession at the decedent's death, or, if a widow, she may elect to take her dower right (life interest in 1/3 of decedent's realty).

CHARITABLE GIFT LIMITATION: No provision.

RULE AGAINST PERPETUITIES: Common law rule established.

RULE AGAINST UNREASONABLE ACCUMULATION OF INCOME: No provision; permissible period of rule against perpetuities apparently applies.

---

[1] No other charges will revoke the provisions of the will.
[2] Including adopted children, or the issue of deceased children.

Minnesota

MINIMUM AGE: 18.

NUMBER OF WITNESSES: 2.

HOLOGRAPHIC WILLS: Not permitted.

NUNCUPATIVE WILLS: Not permitted.

REVOCATION BY OPERATION OF LAW:
Marriage: Will is not revoked.

Birth of Child: Will is not revoked.

Divorce: Provisions of will in favor of divorced spouse are revoked.

RIGHTS OF PRETERMITTED CHILDREN:

Children Born After Execution of Will: Children[1] unprovided for in the will or otherwise take intestate share unless it appears that such omission was intentional and not occasioned by accident or mistake.

Children Born Before Execution of Will: Children[2] unprovided for in the will take intestate share unless it appears that such omission was intentional and not occasioned by accident or mistake.

ELECTION AGAINST WILL: In lieu of provisions of will, spouse may take intestate share.

CHARITABLE GIFT LIMITATION: No provision.

RULE AGAINST PERPETUITIES: Two lives in being codified as to real estate and leases; common law codified as to personalty.

RULE AGAINST UNREASONABLE ACCUMULATION OF INCOME: Accumulation of rents and profits of real estate valid to the same extent and for the same period permitted accumulation of income from personalty. No provision as to personalty; permissible period of rule against perpetuities apparently applies.

---

[1] Including posthumous children.

[2] Including adopted children, and the issue of deceased children.

Mississippi

MINIMUM AGE: 18.

NUMBER OF WITNESSES: 2.

HOLOGRAPHIC WILLS: Permitted.

NUNCUPATIVE WILLS: Permitted.

REVOCATION BY OPERATION OF LAW:

Marriage and Divorce: No provision.[1]

Birth of Child: Will is revoked if no child is living when will is executed and after-born child is neither provided for nor mentioned in will, unless the after-born child dies before 21 years of age, unmarried and without issue.[2]

RIGHTS OF PRETERMITTED CHILDREN:

Children Born After Execution of Will: Children[2] unprovided for by settlement, and neither provided for nor disinherited in the will, take intestate share, provided testator has a living child or children at the time of the execution of the will.

Children Born Before Execution of Will: No provision.

ELECTION AGAINST WILL: In lieu of provisions of will, spouse may take intestate share.[3]

CHARITABLE GIFT LIMITATIONS: Charitable bequests or devises of more than 1/3 of the estate are invalid where testator is survived by a spouse, child, or descendants. And all charitable gifts are void unless will is executed at least 90 days before death.

RULE AGAINST PERPETUITIES: No provision; common law rule applies.

RULE AGAINST UNREASONABLE ACCUMULATION OF INCOME: No provision; permissible period of rule against perpetuities applies.

---

[1] According to case law, a marriage will not revoke a prior will.

[2] Including posthumous children.

[3] However, even if the decedent spouse is not survived by issue, the surviving spouse may take at most only 1/2 of the decedent's real and personal estate.

Missouri

MINIMUM AGE: 18.

NUMBER OF WITNESSES: 2.

HOLOGRAPHIC WILLS: No provision.

NUNCUPATIVE WILLS: Restricted to property with a value not exceeding $500.

REVOCATION BY OPERATION OF LAW:

Marriage or Birth of Child: No provision.

Divorce: Will provisions in favor of divorced spouse are revoked.[1] However, will provisions for a spouse are not affected by divorce where the will is made prior to the testator's marriage.

RIGHTS OF PRETERMITTED CHILDREN:

Children Born After Execution of Will: Children[2] unprovided for or mentioned in the will, take intestate share, unless it appears from the will that such omission was intentional, or unless when the will was executed the testator had one or more children known to him to be living and devised substantially all his estate to the other parent of the omitted child, or the testator provided for the child by transfer outside the will and evidence indicates that such transfer was intended by the testator to be in lieu of a testamentary provision.

Children Born Before Execution of Will: Children unprovided for in the will take intestate share, provided, at the time the will was executed, the testator believed a child to be dead.

ELECTION AGAINST WILL: In lieu of provisions of will, spouse may take ½ of estate.[3]

CHARITABLE GIFT LIMITATIONS: No provision.

RULE AGAINST PERPETUITIES: No provision; common law rule applies.

RULE AGAINST UNREASONABLE ACCUMULATION OF INCOME: No provision; permissible period of rule against perpetuities apparently applies.

---

[1] Effect of revocation is the same as if divorced spouse had died at the time of the divorce.

[2] Including adopted and posthumous children.

[3] If the testator had lineal descendants, the spouse takes ⅓. Homestead allowance offset against survivor's share.

Montana

MINIMUM AGE: 18.

NUMBER OF WITNESSES: 2.

HOLOGRAPHIC WILLS: Permitted.

NUNCUPATIVE WILLS: Not permitted.

REVOCATION BY OPERATION OF LAW: Divorce revokes provisions in favor of the ex-spouse. No other change in a testator's circumstances affect his or her will.

RIGHTS OF PRETERMITTED CHILDREN: In general, if a testator fails to provide in his or her will for any of his or her children[1] or issue of a deceased child, the omitted child or issue receives an intestate share unless it appears from the will that the omission was intentional.

ELECTION AGAINST WILL: A surviving spouse may elect to take against the will, and in such a case is entitled to receive ⅓ of the augmented estate.

CHARITABLE GIFT LIMITATIONS: Charitable bequests or devises in excess of ⅓ of testator's estate invalid unless will executed within 30 days of death.

RULE AGAINST PERPETUITIES: Common law rule established.

RULE AGAINST UNREASONABLE ACCUMULATION OF INCOME: Permissible period of rule against perpetuities codified.

---

[1] Including adopted children.

Nebraska

MINIMUM AGE: 18[1].

NUMBER OF WITNESSES: 2.

HOLOGRAPHIC WILLS: Permitted.

NUNCUPATIVE WILLS: No provision.[2]

REVOCATION BY OPERATION OF LAW:
Marriage, Birth of Child: No provision.
Divorce: Will provisions in favor of former spouse are revoked.

RIGHTS OF PRETERMITTED CHILDREN:
Children Born After Execution of Will: Children[3] unprovided for in the will take intestate share, unless it is apparent from the will that it was the intention of the testator that no provision should be made for such child.
Children Born Before Execution of Will: Children[4] unprovided for in the will take intestate share where it appears that such omission was not intentional, but was occasioned by mistake or accident.[5]

ELECTION AGAINST WILL: In lieu of provisions of will, spouse may take ⅓ of the augmented estate.

CHARITABLE GIFT LIMITATIONS: No provision.

RULE AGAINST PERPETUITIES: No provision; common law rule applies.

RULE AGAINST UNREASONABLE ACCUMULATION OF INCOME: No provision; permissible period of rule against perpetuities applies.

---

[1] The minimum age limitation does not apply to married persons.

[2] Prior to 1974, nuncupative wills were permitted, and soldiers in actual service or mariners on shipboard were permitted to dispose of personal property without regard to the requirements that governed the probate of nuncupative wills.

[3] Including posthumous children.

[4] Including the issue of deceased children.

[5] Here, the burden is on the pretermitted child to prove that the omission was unintentional.

Nevada

MINIMUM AGE: 18.

NUMBER OF WITNESSES: 2.

HOLOGRAPHIC WILLS: Permitted.

NUNCUPATIVE WILLS: Restricted to property with a value not exceeding $1,000.

REVOCATION BY OPERATION OF LAW:

Marriage: Will is revoked unless provision is made for the spouse by marriage contract, in the will, or the spouse is mentioned in the will in such a way as to show an intention not to make such provision.

Birth of Child: No provision.

Divorce: Will provisions in favor of former spouse are revoked.

RIGHTS OF PRETERMITTED CHILDREN:

Children Born After Execution of Will: Children not provided for in the will, take intestate share.

Children Born Before Execution of Will: Children[1] unprovided for in the will take intestate share unless it can be shown that the omission was unintentional.[2]

ELECTION AGAINST WILL: No provision.

CHARITABLE GIFT LIMITATIONS: No provision.

RULE AGAINST PERPETUITIES: No provision; common law rule apparently applies.

RULE AGAINST UNREASONABLE ACCUMULATION OF INCOME: No provision; permissible period of rule against perpetuities apparently applies.[3]

---

[1] Including issue of deceased children.

[2] A presumption applies to the effect that the omission was intentional.

[3] The common law rule against perpetuities specifically applies to spendthrift trusts.

New Hampshire

MINIMUM AGE: 18.[1]

NUMBER OF WITNESSES: 3.

HOLOGRAPHIC WILLS: No provision.

NUNCUPATIVE WILLS: Permitted.

REVOCATION BY OPERATION OF LAW:

Marriage, Birth of Child, or Divorce: No provision.

RIGHTS OF PRETERMITTED CHILDREN:

Children Born Before or After Execution of Will: Children[2] not named or referred to in the will take intestate share.

ELECTION AGAINST WILL: In lieu of provisions of will and homestead rights, surviving spouse may elect to receive 1/3 of decedent's real and personal property, if there are surviving children of decedent or surviving issue of children.[3]

CHARITABLE GIFT LIMITATIONS: No provision.

RULE AGAINST PERPETUITIES: No provision; common law rule applies.

RULE AGAINST UNREASONABLE ACCUMULATION OF INCOME: No provision; permissible period of rule against perpetuities applies.

---

[1] The minimum age limitation does not apply to married persons.

[2] Including posthumous children, and the issue of deceased children.

[3] If no children or issue of children survive, but decedent's mother, father, sister or brother survive, the surviving spouse may elect to receive $10,000 in value of personalty and realty plus 1/2 the remaining value in excess of $10,000 of real and personal property. If no children, issue of children, mother, father, sister or brother of decedent survive, surviving spouse may elect to take $10,000 value of personalty and realty plus $2,000 per year for each full year of marriage plus 1/2 the remaining value in excess of the sum computed above of real and personal property.

New Jersey

MINIMUM AGE: 18.

NUMBER OF WITNESSES: 2.

HOLOGRAPHIC WILLS: No provision.

NUNCUPATIVE WILLS: No provision.

REVOCATION BY OPERATION OF LAW:

Marriage: Marriage does not, by implication, revoke a prior will.

Birth of Child: Will is revoked unless the will expresses a contrary intention.

Divorce: Provisions in the will in favor of the former spouse are revoked.

RIGHTS OF PRETERMITTED CHILDREN:

Children Born After Execution of Will: Children[1] neither provided for by settlement, nor disinherited by the testator, take intestate share, provided that testator has a living child when will is executed.

Children Born Before Execution of Will: No provision.

ELECTION AGAINST WILL: In lieu of provisions of will, surviving spouse may elect to take 1/3 of the augmented estate.

CHARITABLE GIFT LIMITATIONS: No provision.

RULE AGAINST PERPETUITIES: No provision; common law rule applies.

RULE AGAINST UNREASONABLE ACCUMULATION OF INCOME: No provision; permissible period of rule against perpetuities applies.

---

[1] Including child's issue.

New Mexico

MINIMUM AGE: 18.

NUMBER OF WITNESSES: 2.

HOLOGRAPHIC WILLS: Not permitted.

NUNCUPATIVE WILLS: Not permitted.

REVOCATION BY OPERATION OF LAW: Divorce revokes provisions in favor of the ex-spouse. No revocation if a testator fails to provide for a child. See below.

RIGHTS OF PRETERMITTED CHILDREN:

Children Born After Execution of Will: Children[1] not named or provided for in the will take intestate share unless intentionally omitted, or the testator had a child when he or she executed the will and left substantially all of his or her estate to the other parent of the omitted child, or the testator provided for the omitted child outside of the will.

Children Born Before Execution of Will: No provision; it has been held, by case law, that a child alive when will is executed, and unprovided for therein, takes intestate share.

ELECTION AGAINST WILL: No provision; community property state.[2]

CHARITABLE GIFT LIMITATIONS: No provision.

RULE AGAINST PERPETUITIES: No provision; common law rule apparently applies.

RULE AGAINST UNREASONABLE ACCUMULATION OF INCOME: No provision; permissible period of rule against perpetuities apparently applies.

---

[1] Including posthumous children, or the descendants of deceased children.

[2] Upon death, 1/2 of community property goes to the surviving spouse, 1/2 is subject to testamentary disposition.

New York

MINIMUM AGE: 18.

NUMBER OF WITNESSES: 2.

HOLOGRAPHIC WILLS: Restricted to members of the armed forces.

NUNCUPATIVE WILLS: Restricted to members of the armed forces.

REVOCATION BY OPERATION OF LAW:

Marriage: A surviving spouse is entitled to an intestate share regardless of the provisions in any will executed prior to September 1, 1930, unless the spouse is provided for in a written antenuptial agreement.

Birth of Child: See "Rights of Pretermitted Children" below.

Divorce: Divorce, annulment or other dissolution of the marriage revokes provisions of the will pertaining to the former spouse.[1]

RIGHTS OF PRETERMITTED CHILDREN:

Children Born After Execution of Will: Children[2] unprovided for in the will take intestate share unless no provision is made for children alive when the will is executed.[3]

Children Born Before Execution of Will: No provision.

ELECTION AGAINST WILL: In lieu of provisions of will, spouse may take 1/3 of net estate if decedent is survived by one or more issue, and 1/2 in all other cases.[4]

CHARITABLE GIFT LIMITATIONS: Charitable bequests or devises are limited to 1/2 of testator's estate if surviving issue or parents contest a disposition by the testator of the entire estate to charitable purposes.

RULE AGAINST PERPETUITIES: Common law rule established.

RULE AGAINST UNREASONABLE ACCUMULATION OF INCOME: Unless specifically authorized by statute, directions for the accumulation of income are void.[5]

---

[1] Revocation by this section is automatically revived by subsequent remarriage to same spouse.

[2] Including posthumous children.

[3] If there are other children alive when will is executed, the share of an after-born child is limited to the portion passing to living children under the will and, if possible, is to be of the same character. However, apparently where there is some concrete evidence that the after-born child was not inadvertently or unintentionally disinherited, he does not share in the estate.

[4] Where elective share does not exceed $10,000, spouse takes all; provisions apply to wills executed on or after September 1, 1966; different rules apply to wills executed before this date. Special rules apply regarding trusts.

[5] The statute permits directions for the accumulation of income if such accumulation will begin and end within the rule against perpetuities. A direction for accumulation of income in trust for religious, charitable, educational or benevolent purposes is generally valid without regard to the time at which it is to begin or end.

North Carolina

MINIMUM AGE: 18.

NUMBER OF WITNESSES: 2.

HOLOGRAPHIC WILLS: Permitted.[1]

NUNCUPATIVE WILLS: Permitted.[2]

REVOCATION BY OPERATION OF LAW:
Marriage: Will is not revoked.[3]
Birth of Child: Will is not revoked.
Divorce: Will provisions in favor of divorced spouse are revoked, including appointment as executor or executrix.

RIGHTS OF PRETERMITTED CHILDREN:
Children Born After Execution of Will: Children[4] unprovided for in the will, take intestate share unless it is apparent, from the will itself, that the omission was intentional.
Children Born Before Execution of Will: No provision; it has been held, by case law, that where a child is disinherited, it must be shown to be intentional.

ELECTION AGAINST WILL: In lieu of provisions of will, spouse may take intestate share but only if the will provisions and the value of the property interests passing outside the will to the spouse is less than ½ of the decedent's net estate where decedent is survived by a child, lineal descendants of a deceased child, or by a parent, or is less than ½ of the net estate where the surviving spouse is a second or successive childless spouse. In lieu of intestate share, spouse may take a life estate in ⅓ of real estate, including the homestead.

CHARITABLE GIFT LIMITATIONS: No provision.

RULE AGAINST PERPETUITIES: No provision; common law rule applies.

RULE AGAINST UNREASONABLE ACCUMULATION OF INCOME: No provision; permissible period of rule against perpetuities apparently applies.

---

[1] To be probated, the will must be found among the testator's valuable papers or effects, or in a safe deposit box for safekeeping. Three competent witnesses must testify that they believe the will was entirely written, dated, and signed in the testator's handwriting.

[2] Nuncupative wills of persons in military service are subject to the same general requirements as civilian nuncupative wills, including the requirement of contemplation of imminent death.

[3] However, the spouse may elect against the will in the same manner as if the will were executed after the marriage.

[4] Including adopted children.

North Dakota

MINIMUM AGE: 18.

NUMBER OF WITNESSES: 2.

HOLOGRAPHIC WILLS: Permitted.

NUNCUPATIVE WILLS: Not permitted.

REVOCATION BY OPERATION OF LAW: Divorce revokes provisions in favor of the ex-spouse. No other change in a testator's circumstances affect his or her will.

RIGHTS OF PRETERMITTED CHILDREN: In general, if a testator fails to provide in his or her will for any of his or her children or issue of a deceased child, the omitted child or issue receives an intestate share unless it appears from the will that the omission was intentional, or the testator had a child when he or she executed the will and left substantially all of his or her estate to the other parent of the omitted child, or the testator provided for the omitted child outside of the will.

ELECTION AGAINST WILL: A surviving spouse may elect to take against the will, and in such case is entitled to receive ⅓ of the augmented estate.

CHARITABLE GIFT LIMITATIONS: No provision.

RULE AGAINST PERPETUITIES: Common law rule codified.

RULE AGAINST UNREASONABLE ACCUMULATION OF INCOME: Permissible period of the rule against perpetuities is codified to be applicable.

Ohio

MINIMUM AGE: 18.

NUMBER OF WITNESSES: 2.

HOLOGRAPHIC WILLS: No provision.

NUNCUPATIVE WILLS: Permitted.

REVOCATION BY OPERATION OF LAW:
Marriage: A will executed by an unmarried person is not revoked by the person's subsequent marriage.
Birth of Child: No provision.
Divorce: No provision; it has been held, by case law, that a divorce and property settlement were not sufficient to revoke will.

RIGHTS OF PRETERMITTED CHILDREN:

Children Born After Execution of Will: Children[1] unprovided for in the will take intestate share unless it appears that such omission was intentional.

Children Born Before Execution of Will: No provision; case law appears to sanction the disinheritance of children alive when will is executed.

ELECTION AGAINST WILL: In lieu of provisions of will, surviving spouse may elect to take an intestate share not to exceed 1/3 of the net estate if two or more of decedent's children or issue of children survive, or not to exceed 1/2 of the net estate in all other cases.

CHARITABLE GIFT LIMITATIONS: Charitable bequests or devises in excess of 1/4 of the estate invalid if will executed within 6 months of the death of a testator survived by issue.

RULE AGAINST PERPETUITIES: Common law rule codified.

RULE AGAINST UNREASONABLE ACCUMULATION OF INCOME: No provision; permissible period of rule against perpetuities apparently applies.

---

[1] Including adopted children, or children's issue.

Oklahoma

MINIMUM AGE: 18.

NUMBER OF WITNESSES: 2.

HOLOGRAPHIC WILLS: Permitted.

NUNCUPATIVE WILLS: Restricted to property with a value not exceeding $1,000, and to persons "in actual military service in the field, or doing duty on shipboard at sea."

REVOCATION BY OPERATION OF LAW:

Marriage or Birth of Child: No provision; except some case law exists which suggests marriage may revoke a prior will.

Divorce: Will provisions in favor of divorced spouse are revoked.

RIGHTS OF PRETERMITTED CHILDREN:

Children Born After Execution of Will: Children[1] not provided for by advancement or settlement, and neither provided for nor in any way mentioned in the will, take intestate share.

Children Born Before Execution of Will: Children[2] unprovided for in the will take intestate share.

An intent to disinherit must appear on the face of the will in strong and convincing language before an omitted heir can be deprived of his (her) intestate share.

ELECTION AGAINST WILL: In lieu of provisions of will, spouse may take intestate share.

CHARITABLE GIFT LIMITATIONS: No provision.

RULE AGAINST PERPETUITIES: Common law rule established.[3]

RULE AGAINST UNREASONABLE ACCUMULATION OF INCOME: No provision; permissible period of rule against perpetuities apparently applies.

---

[1] Including posthumous children.

[2] Including issue of deceased children.

[3] As of the enactment of L. 1977, Ch. 5, effective 9-6-77, the statute was changed from *lives in being* to the common-law rule of *lives in being plus twenty-one years.*

Oregon

MINIMUM AGE: 18[1].

NUMBER OF WITNESSES: 2.

HOLOGRAPHIC WILLS: No provision.

NUNCUPATIVE WILLS: No provision.

REVOCATION BY OPERATION OF LAW:

Marriage or Divorce: Will is revoked by subsequent marriage and all provisions in favor of a former spouse are revoked by a divorce unless the will expressly declares a contrary intention.

Birth of Child: No provision.

RIGHTS OF PRETERMITTED CHILDREN:

Children Born After Execution of Will: Children born after the will is executed for whom the will makes no provision take an intestate share unless the testator had children alive when the will was executed and did not provide for those children in the will.

Children Born Before Execution of Will: No provision; case law suggests children unprovided for in the will take an intestate share.

ELECTION AGAINST WILL: In lieu of provision of will, spouse may elect to take the elective share, which consists of 1/4 of the testator's net estate, reduced by the value of property given to the spouse under the will.

CHARITABLE GIFT LIMITATIONS: No provision.

RULE AGAINST PERPETUITIES: No provision; common law rule applies.

RULE AGAINST UNREASONABLE ACCUMULATION OF INCOME: No provision; permissible period of rule against perpetuities apparently applies.

---

[1] The minimum age limitation does not apply to married persons.

Pennsylvania

MINIMUM AGE: 18.

NUMBER OF WITNESSES: 2.[1]

HOLOGRAPHIC WILLS: Permitted by case law.

NUNCUPATIVE WILLS: No provision.

REVOCATION BY OPERATION OF LAW:
Marriage: No provision. However, the spouse takes an intestate share unless the will provides a greater share.
Birth of Child: No provision.
Divorce: Will provisions in favor of divorced spouse are revoked.

RIGHTS OF PRETERMITTED CHILDREN:
Children Born After Execution of Will: Children[2] born after the will is executed for whom the will makes no provision take an intestate share unless it is apparent, from the will itself, that the omission was intentional.
Children Born Before Execution of Will: No provision; case law suggests a testator may disinherit his children.

ELECTION AGAINST WILL: In lieu of provisions of the will, spouse may take 1/3 of real and personal property.

CHARITABLE GIFT LIMITATION: No provision.

RULE AGAINST PERPETUITIES: Common law rule codified, except that permissible period is measured by actual rather than possible events.

RULE AGAINST UNREASONABLE ACCUMULATION OF INCOME: Permissible period of rule against perpetuities is codified to be applicable, except period is to be measured by actual rather than possible events.[3]

---

[1] The will is proved by the "oaths" or "affirmations" of the witnesses.

[2] Including adopted children.

[3] According to case law, the statute only permits accumulation of income for the benefit of a minor during an existing minority. The cases suggest that the accumulated funds must be the minor's and be paid to him at the termination of minority to be lawful *[Est. of Wright,* 227 Pa. 69, 75 Atl. 1026].

Rhode Island

MINIMUM AGE: 18.

NUMBER OF WITNESSES: 2.

HOLOGRAPHIC WILLS: No provision.

NUNCUPATIVE WILLS: Restricted to soldiers or airmen in actual military service or seamen at sea.

REVOCATION BY MARRIAGE, BIRTH OF CHILD, OR DIVORCE:
Marriage: Will is revoked unless made in contemplation of marriage.[1]
Birth of Child or Divorce: No provision.

RIGHTS OF PRETERMITTED CHILDREN:
Children Born After Execution of Will: Children[2] unprovided for in the will take intestate share unless the omission was intentional, and not occasioned by mistake or accident.
Children Born Before Execution of Will: No provision; case law suggests a testator may intentionally disinherit his children.

ELECTION AGAINST WILL: In lieu of provisions of the will, widow may take dower.

CHARITABLE GIFT LIMITATION: No provision.

RULE AGAINST PERPETUITIES: No provision; common law rule applies.

RULE AGAINST UNREASONABLE ACCUMULATION OF INCOME: No provision; permissible period of rule against perpetuities apparently applies.

---

[1] An exception applies where will is made in exercise of a power of appointment.

[2] Including posthumous children, or the issue of deceased children.

South Carolina

MINIMUM AGE: 18.

NUMBER OF WITNESSES: 3.

HOLOGRAPHIC WILLS: No provision.[1]

NUNCUPATIVE WILLS: Permitted.[1]

REVOCATION BY MARRIAGE, BIRTH OF CHILD, OR DIVORCE:
Marriage: Man's will is revoked unless the will is expressly made in contemplation of marriage and contains provisions for future wife and children, if any.[2]
Birth of Child: No provision.
Divorce: Provisions in favor of the former spouse

are revoked unless the will is expressly made in contemplation of divorce.

RIGHTS OF PRETERMITTED CHILDREN:
Children Born After Execution of Will: Children[2] unprovided for in the will take intestate share.
Children Born Before Execution of Will: No provision.

ELECTION AGAINST WILL: In lieu of provisions of the will, widow may elect dower.

CHARITABLE GIFT LIMITATION: No provision.

RULE AGAINST PERPETUITIES: No provision; common law rule applies.

RULE AGAINST UNREASONABLE ACCUMULATION OF INCOME: No provision; permissible period of rule against perpetuities apparently applies.

---

[1] Soldiers in actual military service or mariners or seamen at sea may dispose of property without regard to the strict requirements generally governing the probate of nuncupative wills.
[2] Either widow *or* issue must survive.

South Dakota

MINIMUM AGE: 18.

NUMBER OF WITNESSES: 2.

HOLOGRAPHIC WILLS: Permitted.

NUNCUPATIVE WILLS: Restricted to property with a value not exceeding $1,000.[1]

REVOCATION BY OPERATION OF LAW:
Marriage: Will is revoked unless provision has been made for the spouse by marriage contract, is provided for in the will, or is mentioned in such a way as to show an intention not to make such provision.
Birth of Child: Marriage *and* birth of a child[2] revokes will unless issue has been provided for by settlement, or in the will, or mentioned in the will in such a way as to show an intention not to make such provision.
Divorce: No provision; case law suggests that a divorce, coupled with a property settlement, will not revoke a prior will.

RIGHTS OF PRETERMITTED CHILDREN:
Children Born After Execution of Will: Children[3] unprovided for in the will, take an intestate share, unless it appears that such omission was intentional.
Children Born Before Execution of Will: No provision.

ELECTION AGAINST WILL: In lieu of provisions of will, spouse may elect to take the greater of ⅓ of the augmented estate or $100,000. Case law suggests except for support specifically provided by law, a widow has no rights in her husband's property. The same rule would probably apply to a surviving husband.

CHARITABLE GIFT LIMITATIONS: No provision.

RULE AGAINST PERPETUITIES: Lives in being.

RULE AGAINST UNREASONABLE ACCUMULATION OF INCOME: Void, except during minority of beneficiary.[4]

---

[1] Nuncupative wills of those in military service in the field or "doing duty on shipboard at sea" are subject to the same general requirements for probate, including contemplation or fear of immediate death.
[2] Including posthumous children.
[3] Including the issue of deceased children.
[4] Direction for accumulation must be made for benefit of minors in being, and terminate at age of majority.

Tennessee

MINIMUM AGE: 18.

NUMBER OF WITNESSES: 2.

HOLOGRAPHIC WILLS: Permitted. Witnesses must testify that will was written in testator's handwriting.

NUNCUPATIVE WILLS: Restricted to property with a value not exceeding $1,000.[1]

REVOCATION BY OPERATION OF LAW:
Marriage, Birth of Child, or Divorce: No provision. It has been held, by case law, that a divorce coupled with a property settlement agreement revokes a will.

RIGHTS OF PRETERMITTED CHILDREN:
Children Born After Execution of Will: Children[2] not provided for nor disinherited in the will, and not provided for by a settlement made in the testator's lifetime, takes an intestate share.
Children Born Before Execution of Will: No provision. Case law indicates that children may be disinherited, either expressly or by inference.

ELECTION AGAINST WILL: In lieu of provisions of the will, a surviving spouse may elect to receive ⅓ of decedent's net estate.

CHARITABLE GIFT LIMITATIONS: No provision.

RULE AGAINST PERPETUITIES: No provision; common law rule applies.

RULE AGAINST UNREASONABLE ACCUMULATION OF INCOME: No provision; permissible period of rule against perpetuities apparently applies.

---

[1] Persons in the military or naval service, in a will made outside the state or at sea while in such service, may dispose of personal property with a value not exceeding $10,000, without regard to the strict requirements generally governing the probate of nuncupative wills.

[2] Including posthumous children.

is his last will. If not "self-proved," two witnesses must testify that the instrument was written in the testator's handwriting.

[3] Including adopted or posthumous children.

[4] However, the will is not revoked unless such child dies within one year after the death of the testator.

[5] There are detailed provisions regarding homestead and exempt property.

Utah

MINIMUM AGE: 18.

NUMBER OF WITNESSES: 2.

HOLOGRAPHIC WILLS: Permitted.

NUNCUPATIVE WILLS: No provision.

REVOCATION BY OPERATION OF LAW:
Divorce: Will provisions in favor of divorced spouse are revoked. No other changes in a testator's circumstances affect his or her will.

RIGHTS OF PRETERMITTED CHILDREN:
Children Born After Execution of Will: Children,[1] not provided for by settlement, or in the will, or mentioned in the will, take intestate share.
Children Born Before Execution of Will: Children,[2] not provided for in the will, take intestate share unless such omission appears to be intentional.

ELECTION AGAINST WILL: In lieu of provisions of will, surviving spouse may elect to take 1/3 of the augmented estate.

CHARITABLE GIFT LIMITATIONS: No provision.

RULE AGAINST PERPETUITIES: No provision; common law rule applies.

RULE AGAINST UNREASONABLE ACCUMULATION OF INCOME: No provision; permissible period of rule against perpetuities apparently applies.

---

[1] Including posthumous children.

[2] Including adopted children, or the issue of deceased children.

Texas

MINIMUM AGE: 18.[1]

NUMBER OF WITNESSES: 2.[1]

HOLOGRAPHIC WILLS: Permitted.[2]

NUNCUPATIVE WILLS: Permitted.

REVOCATION BY OPERATION OF LAW:
Marriage: No provision; case law under an older statute suggests that marriage will not provoke a prior will, at least where there is a property settlement.
Birth of Child: Will is revoked where no child was living when will is executed, and an after-born child[3] is unprovided for or mentioned in the will.[4]
Divorce: Will provisions in favor of divorced spouse revoked, including appointment of spouse as executor or executrix.

RIGHTS OF PRETERMITTED CHILDREN:
Children Born After Execution of Will: Children,[3] unless provided for by settlement, take intestate share where testator has other children living at time of execution of will.
Children Born Before Execution of Will: No provision.

ELECTION AGAINST WILL: No specific provision; community property state.[5]

CHARITABLE GIFT LIMITATION: No provision.

RULE AGAINST PERPETUITIES: No provision; common law rule applies.

RULE AGAINST UNREASONABLE ACCUMULATION OF INCOME: No provision; permissible period of rule against perpetuities apparently applies.

---

[1] The minimum age limitation does not apply to persons presently or previously married, or to members of the U.S. armed forces or merchant marine.

[2] An holographic will may be "self-proved" at any time during testator's lifetime by an affidavit attached to the instrument that it

Vermont

MINIMUM AGE: 18.

NUMBER OF WITNESSES: 3.

HOLOGRAPHIC WILLS: No provision.

NUNCUPATIVE WILLS: Permitted.[1]

REVOCATION BY OPERATION OF LAW:
Marriage, Birth of Child, or Divorce: No provision.

RIGHTS OF PRETERMITTED CHILDREN:
Children Born After Execution of Will: Children[2] not provided for in the will take an intestate share unless it is apparent from the will that provisions should not be made for such child.
Children Born Before Execution of Will: Children[2] not provided for in the will take intestate share if it appears that such omission was made by mistake or accident.

ELECTION AGAINST WILL: In lieu of provisions of the will, spouse may elect dower or curtesy.

CHARITABLE GIFT LIMITATIONS: No provision.

RULE AGAINST PERPETUITIES: No provision; common law rule applies. A statute, apparently expanding upon the common-law rule, provides that the permissible period is to be measured by actual rather than possible events.

RULE AGAINST UNREASONABLE ACCUMULATION OF INCOME: No provision; permissible period of rule against perpetuities apparently applies.

---

[1] Soldiers in actual military service, or mariners or seamen at sea, may dispose of their property without complying with the strict requirements generally governing the probate of nuncupative wills.

[2] Including the issue of deceased children.

Virginia

MINIMUM AGE: 18.

NUMBER OF WITNESSES: 2.

HOLOGRAPHIC WILLS: Permitted.

NUNCUPATIVE WILLS: Restricted to soldiers in actual military service or mariners and seamen at sea without regard to the strict requirements generally governing the probate of nuncupative wills.

REVOCATION BY OPERATION OF LAW:
Marriage or Birth of Child: Will is not revoked.
Divorce: Will provisions in favor of former spouse are revoked.

RIGHTS OF PRETERMITTED CHILDREN:
Children Born After Execution of Will: If testator has no living children when will is executed, after-born children,[1] not provided for or mentioned in the will, take an intestate share.[2] If testator has a living child when will is executed, after-born children, or their descendants, not provided for in, nor

expressly excluded by, the will take an intestate share.
Children Born Before Execution of Will: No provision.

ELECTION AGAINST WILL: In lieu of provisions of the will, surviving spouse may elect dower.

CHARITABLE GIFT LIMITATION: No provision.

RULE AGAINST PERPETUITIES: No provision; common law rule applies.

RULE AGAINST UNREASONABLE ACCUMULATION OF INCOME: No provision; permissible period of rule against perpetuities apparently applies.

Washington

MINIMUM AGE: 18.

NUMBER OF WITNESSES: 2.

HOLOGRAPHIC WILLS: No provision.

NUNCUPATIVE WILLS: Restricted to members of the armed forces or persons employed on vessels of the U.S. Merchant Marine, and to property with a value not exceeding $1,000. The strict requirements governing probate of nuncupative wills generally are applicable.

REVOCATION BY OPERATION OF LAW:
Marriage: Will is revoked as to the spouse unless provision has been made for the spouse by marriage settlement, or in the will, or is mentioned in the will in such a way as to show an intention not to make such provision.
Birth of Child: No provision.
Divorce: Provisions of will regarding divorced spouse are revoked.

RIGHTS OF PRETERMITTED CHILDREN:
Children Born Before or After Execution of Will: Children,[1] not named or provided for in the will take intestate share.

ELECTION AGAINST WILL: No provision; community property state.

CHARITABLE GIFT LIMITATIONS: No provision.

RULE AGAINST PERPETUITIES: No provision; common law rule apparently applies.[2]

RULE AGAINST UNREASONABLE ACCUMULATION OF INCOME: No provision; permissible period of rule against perpetuities apparently applies.

___

[1] Including posthumous children or children's descendants.

[2] A statutory provision provides that if an instrument violates the rule against perpetuities, it will not be rendered invalid during any one of the following periods: (a) 21 years following the effective date of the instrument; (b) lives in being or portions thereof if measured by such a provision in the instrument, and (c) 21 years following the expiration of lives in being or portions thereof.

West Virginia

MINIMUM AGE: 18.

NUMBER OF WITNESSES: 2.

HOLOGRAPHIC WILLS: Permitted.

NUNCUPATIVE WILLS: Restricted to soldiers in actual military service or mariners or seamen at sea, without regard to the strict requirements generally governing the probate of nuncupative wills.

REVOCATION BY OPERATION OF LAW:
Marriage: Revokes prior will unless there is a provision for such contingency.
Birth of Child: No provision.
Divorce: Revokes prior will unless there is a provision for such contingency. Annulment has same result.

RIGHTS OF PRETERMITTED CHILDREN:
Children Born After Execution of Will: If testator has no child living when will is executed, after-born children,[1] not provided for or mentioned in the will, take an intestate share.[2] If testator has a child living when the will is executed, after-born children, or their descendants, not provided for nor expressly excluded by the will, take an intestate share.[2]
Children Born Before Execution of Will: No provision.

ELECTION AGAINST WILL: In lieu of provisions of the will, spouse may take dower and intestate share of personal property.

CHARITABLE GIFT LIMITATIONS: No provision.

RULE AGAINST PERPETUITIES: No provision; common law rule applies.

RULE AGAINST UNREASONABLE ACCUMULATION OF INCOME: No provision; permissible period of rule against perpetuities apparently applies.

___

[1] Including posthumous children or the children's issue.

[2] However, if an after-born child or descendant dies under the age of 18, unmarried and without issue, his portion of the estate,

or so much thereof as may remain unexpended in his support and education, shall revert to the beneficiaries under the will.

Wisconsin

MINIMUM AGE: 18.

NUMBER OF WITNESSES: 2.

HOLOGRAPHIC WILLS: No provision.

NUNCUPATIVE WILLS: Not permitted.

REVOCATION BY OPERATION OF LAW:
Marriage: A will is revoked by the subsequent marriage of the testator if the testator is survived by his or her spouse, unless the will indicates an intent that it not be revoked by subsequent marriage or was drafted under circumstances indicating that it was in contemplation of the marriage or makes provision for issue of the decedent; or testator and the spouse have entered into a contract before or after marriage that makes provision for the spouse or provides that the spouse is to have no rights in the estate of the testator.
Divorce: Annulment or divorce revokes any will provision in favor of the testator's former spouse.

RIGHTS OF PRETERMITTED CHILDREN:
Children Born After Execution of Will: Children[1] or their issue, unprovided for in the will, take an intestate share unless it is apparent from the will that it was testator's intention not to provide for such child.
Children Born Before Execution of Will: Children[2] unprovided for in the will take an intestate share if it appears that such omission was not intentional, but was made by mistake or accident.

ELECTION AGAINST WILL: Surviving spouse may elect to take 1/3 of the testator's net probate estate, reduced by the value of any property given outright to the surviving spouse under the testator's will. The net probate estate is the net estate, as defined in the Wisconsin Probate Code, including any property passing by intestate succession as well as under the will, but without deduction of the estate taxes.

CHARITABLE GIFT LIMITATION: No provision.

RULE AGAINST PERPETUITIES: Lives in being, plus 30 years.

RULE AGAINST UNREASONABLE ACCUMULATION OF INCOME: Statute permits any provision directing or authorizing trust income accumulation.

___

[1] Including, by case law, adopted children.

[2] Including the issue of deceased children.

Wyoming

MINIMUM AGE: 18.

NUMBER OF WITNESSES: 2.

HOLOGRAPHIC WILLS: Permitted.

NUNCUPATIVE WILLS: No provision.[1]

REVOCATION BY OPERATION OF LAW:

Marriage: No provision. It has been held, by case law, that marriage does not revoke will.

Birth of Child: No provision. It has been held, by case law, that a will is not revoked by birth of a child.

Divorce: No provision. It has been held, by case law, that an annulment coupled with a property settlement, revoked testator's will by implication.

RIGHTS OF PRETERMITTED CHILDREN:

Children Born Before or After Execution of Will: No provision.

ELECTION AGAINST WILL: In lieu of provisions of will, spouse may take ½ share of estate.[2]

CHARITABLE GIFT LIMITATIONS: No provision.

RULE AGAINST PERPETUITIES: Common law ruled codified.

RULE AGAINST UNREASONABLE ACCUMULATION OF INCOME: No provision; permissible period of rule against perpetuities apparently applies.

---

[1] Case law indicates nuncupative wills are invalid.

[2] Where testator is survived by a child or children of a previous marriage, or any descendants of such child or children, and no child or descendant of the marriage with the surviving spouse, the spouse may take no more than ⅓.

Summaries of the Intestacy Statutes for Each State*

This section of the appendix provides summaries of the intestacy statutes of each state. The most common survival situations are presented, such as where the decedent is survived by a spouse and children, a spouse with no children, or children with no spouse. These statutes are presented for your information only, and must be checked against current law by a local attorney, to make certain that these represent the law as it exists in your state at the death of the decedent.

Alabama

Spouse and Child(ren)[1]:

REAL ESTATE AND PERSONALTY: Surviving spouse takes the first $50,000 in value, plus 1/2 the balance of the intestate estate (if all issue are issue of the surviving spouse also). Otherwise, 1/2 to spouse; balance to the children[2] equally, or their issue *per stirpes*.

No Spouse, but with Child(ren):

REAL ESTATE AND PERSONALTY: All to the children[2] equally or their issue *per stirpes*.

Spouse and no Child(ren) but with Parents:

REAL ESTATE AND PERSONALTY: Surviving spouse takes first $100,000 in value plus 1/2 the balance of the intestate estate; balance to parents equally, or their issue *per stirpes*.

No Spouse or Child(ren), but with Parents:

REAL ESTATE AND PERSONALTY: All to the parents equally.

Spouse and no Child(ren) or Parents:

REAL ESTATE AND PERSONALTY: All to spouse.

No Spouse, Child(ren), or Parents:

REAL ESTATE AND PERSONALTY: All to brothers and sisters[3] equally, or their issue *per stirpes*. If none, 1/2 each to maternal and paternal kindred, or their issue *per stirpes*.

---

[1] Including adopted and posthumous children.

[2] Advancements to child or other descendants deducted from intestate share.

[3] Kindred of the half blood inherit equally with those of the whole blood in the same degree.

Alaska

Spouse and Child(ren)[1]:

REAL ESTATE AND PERSONALTY: If all of the children are children of the surviving spouse, the spouse takes the first $50,000, plus 1/2 of the balance of the estate. If some of the children are not children of the surviving spouse, the spouse takes 1/2 of the estate. In either case, the children share equally, the issue of any deceased child sharing *per stirpes*.

No Spouse, but with Child(ren):

REAL ESTATE AND PERSONALITY: All to the children[2] equally, or their issue *per stirpes.*

Spouse, and No Child(ren):

REAL ESTATE AND PERSONALITY: If no parent of the decedent is alive, the entire estate passes to the spouse. Otherwise, the spouse takes 1/2 of the estate, and the other 1/2 passes to the parent, or parents equally.

No Spouse, or Child(ren), but with Parents:

REAL ESTATE AND PERSONALITY: All to the parents equally, or the survivor.

No Spouse, Child(ren), or Parents:

REAL ESTATE AND PERSONALITY: All to brothers and sisters[3] equally, or their issue *per stirpes.* If none, all to the next of kin[3] in equal degree.

---

[1] Including adopted children.
[2] Advancements to child or issue deducted from intestate share.
[3] Kindred of the half blood inherit equally with those of the whole blood in the same degree.

Arizona

Spouse and Child(ren)[1]:

If the children are all children of the surviving spouse, the surviving spouse takes the decedent's separate property and his or her one-half of community property. If some of the children are not children of the surviving spouse, the surviving spouse takes 1/2 of the decedent's separate property but no part of the decedent's one-half of community property. In either case, the children take the balance of the estate equally, the issue of a deceased child sharing *per stirpes.*

No Spouse, but with Child(ren):

REAL ESTATE AND PERSONALITY: All to the children[2] equally, or their issue *per stirpes.*

Spouse and No Child(ren): All of the decedent's estate passes to the spouse.

No Spouse, or Child(ren), but with Parents: All of the decedent's estate passes to his or her parent, or parents equally.

No Spouse, Child(ren), or Parents:

REAL ESTATE AND PERSONALITY: All to brothers and sisters equally, or their issue *per stirpes.* If none, 1/2 each to maternal and paternal kindred and their descendants *per stirpes.*

---

[1] Including adopted children, and posthumous children and other posthumous descendants.
[2] Advancements to child deducted from intestate share.

Arkansas

Spouse and Child(ren)[1]:

REAL ESTATE: Life estate in 1/3 to spouse; balance to the children[3] equally, or their issue *per stirpes.*

PERSONALITY: 1/3 to the spouse, 2/3 to the children[3] equally, or their issue *per stirpes.*

No Spouse, but with Child(ren):

REAL ESTATE AND PERSONALITY: All to the children[3] equally, or their issue *per stirpes.*

Spouse and No Child(ren):

REAL ESTATE AND PERSONALITY: 1/2 to the spouse;[2] 1/2 to the parents equally, or the survivor. If neither parent survives, this 1/2 passes to brothers and sisters[4] equally, to grandparents, uncles and aunts and their descendants[4] in equal parts. If none, all to the spouse.

No Spouse, or Child(ren), but with Parents:

REAL ESTATE AND PERSONALITY: All to the parents equally, or the survivor.

No Spouse, Child(ren), or Parents:

REAL ESTATE AND PERSONALITY: All to brothers and sisters[4] equally, or their issue *per stirpes.* If none, to grandparents, uncles and aunts and their descendants[4] in equal parts.

---

[1] Including adopted and posthumous children.
[2] Regarding ancestral real estate, spouse takes a life estate of 1/2 against collateral heirs; 1/3 against creditors.
[3] Advancements to child deducted from intestate share.
[4] Kindred of the half blood inherit equally with those of the whole blood in the same degree; however, as to ancestral property, half bloods, unrelated by blood to the ancestor, do not inherit.

California

Spouse and One Child[1]:

SEPARATE REALTY AND PERSONALITY: 1/2 to the spouse, 1/2 to the child or its issue.[2]

COMMUNITY PROPERTY: All to the spouse.

Spouse and Children:

SEPARATE REALTY AND PERSONALITY: 1/3 to the spouse; 2/3 to the children equally, or their issue *per stirpes.*

COMMUNITY PROPERTY: All to the spouse.

No Spouse, but with Child(ren):

REAL ESTATE AND PERSONALITY: All to the children equally, or their issue *per stirpes.*

Spouse and No Child(ren):

SEPARATE REALTY AND PERSONALTY: 1/2 to the spouse; 1/2 to the parents equally or the survivor. If neither parent survives, to brothers and sisters[3] equally, or their issue *per stirpes*. If none, all to the spouse.

COMMUNITY PROPERTY: All to the spouse.

No Spouse, or Child(ren), but with Parents:[4]

REAL ESTATE AND PERSONALTY: All to the parents equally, or the survivor.

No Spouse, Child(ren), or Parents:[4]

REAL ESTATE AND PERSONALTY: All to brothers and sisters[3] equally, or their issue, *per stirpes*. If none to the next of kin[3] in equal degree, with exceptions.

---

[1] Including adopted children.

[2] Advancements to child *or other heirs* deducted from intestate share.

[3] Kindred of the half blood inherit equally with those of the whole blood in the same degree; however, as to ancestral property, half bloods, unrelated by blood to the ancestor, do not inherit.

[4] Where the decedent left no issue or spouse, but there are issue of the decedent's predeceased spouse, the portion of the decedent's estate attributable to the decedent's predeceased spouse (relating to separate property of the predeceased spouse which came to the decedent) shall go in equal shares to the issue of the predeceased spouse, *per stirpes*. If no issue, then such portion goes to the predeceased spouse's parents equally, or the survivor of them, or if both parents are dead, then in equal shares to the predeceased spouse's brothers and sisters (or their issue taking *per stirpes*). Notwithstanding the foregoing, that portion of the decedent's estate created from the separate property of a parent or grandparent shall pass to the same, or if dead, in equal shares to the heirs of such deceased parent or grandparent.

Where the decedent left no issue or spouse, but there are issue of the decedent's predeceased spouse, the portion of the decedent's estate attributable to the decedent's predeceased spouse (relating to community property) shall go in equal shares to the issue of the predeceased spouse, *per stirpes*. If no issue, then 1/2 of such portion goes to the decedent's parents equally, or the survivor of them, or if both parents are dead, then in equal shares to the decedent's brothers and sisters (or their issue taking *per stirpes*); the other 1/2 goes to the predeceased spouse's parents equally, or the survivor of them, or if both parents are dead, then in equal shares to the predeceased spouse's brothers and sisters (or their issue taking *per stirpes*).

Colorado

Spouse and Child(ren):[1]

If all of the children are children of the surviving spouse, the surviving spouse takes the first $25,000, plus 1/2 of the balance of the estate. If some of the children are not children of the surviving spouse, the surviving spouse takes 1/2 of the estate. In either case, the children take what remains equally, the issue of a deceased child sharing *per stirpes*.

No Spouse, but with Child(ren):

REAL ESTATE AND PERSONALTY: All to the children[2] equally, or their issue *per stirpes*.

Spouse and No Child(ren):

REAL ESTATE AND PERSONALTY: All to the spouse.

No Spouse, or Child(ren), but with Parents:

REAL ESTATE AND PERSONALTY: All to the parents equally, or the survivor.

No Spouse, Child(ren), or Parents:

REAL ESTATE AND PERSONALTY: All to brothers and sisters[3] equally, or their issue *per stirpes*. If none, 1/2 each to maternal and paternal kindred and their descendants,[3] *per stirpes*.

---

[1] Including adopted children, posthumous children and other posthumous descendants.

[2] Advancements to child deducted from intestate share.

[3] Collateral kindred of the half blood take a full share, except if there are also collaterals of the whole blood of the same class, in which case, half bloods take a one-half share.

Connecticut

Spouse and Child(ren):[1]

REAL ESTATE AND PERSONALTY: The first $50,000 to the surviving spouse, plus one-half of the balance; the children share the one-half of the balance equally, or their issue *per stirpes*. If one or more of the children are children only of decedent, the spouse takes one-half and the other half is shared by decedent's children equally.

No Spouse, but with Child(ren):

REAL ESTATE AND PERSONALTY: All to the children[2] equally, or their issue *per stirpes*.

Spouse and No Child(ren):

REAL ESTATE AND PERSONALTY: First $50,000 plus 3/4 of the balance to the spouse; the other 1/4 to the parents equally, or the survivor. If neither parent survives, all to the spouse.

No Spouse, or Child(ren), but with Parents:

REAL ESTATE AND PERSONALTY: All to the parents equally, or the survivor.

No Spouse, Child(ren), or Parents:

REAL ESTATE AND PERSONALTY: All to brothers and sisters[3] equally, or their issue *per stirpes*. If none, then to the next of kin[3] in equal degree.

[Statutory Reference Conn. Gen. Stat. §46-12]

---

[1] Including adopted children [Conn. Gen. Stat. §45-67] and, children born before marriage whose parents afterwards intermarry [Conn. Gen. Stat. §45-274(1)].

Children born out of wedlock can inherit from the mother also from the father, if: (1) father so adjudicated by court, and (2) he has acknowledged in writing under oath his parentage of the child [Conn. Gen. Stat. §45-274(b)(2)].

[2] Advancements to child or other descendants deducted from intestate share [Conn. Gen. Stat. §45-274(a)].

[3] Collateral kindred of the whole blood take in preference to those of the half blood [Conn. Gen. Stat. §45-276].

Delaware

Spouse and Child(ren)[1]:

If all of the children are children of the surviving spouse, the surviving spouse takes the first $50,000, plus 1/2 of the balance of the personal estate, plus a life estate in the real estate. If some of the children are not children of the surviving spouse, the surviving spouse takes 1/2 the personal estate, plus a life estate in the real estate. The children and the issue of a deceased child take *per stirpes.*

No Spouse, but with Child(ren):

REAL ESTATE AND PERSONALTY: All to the children[2] equally, or their issue *per stirpes.*

Spouse and No Child(ren): If the decedent is survived by parents, the surviving spouse takes the first $50,000 of the personal estate, plus 1/2 of the balance of the personal estate, plus a life estate in the real estate, and the parents take the balance equally. If the decedent is not survived by parents, the surviving spouse takes the entire estate.

No Spouse or Child(ren), but with Parents:

REAL ESTATE AND PERSONALTY: All to the parents equally, or the survivor.

No Spouse, Child(ren), or Parents:

REAL ESTATE AND PERSONALTY: All to brothers and sisters,[3] or their issue *per stirpes.* If none, to the next of kin[3] in equal degree *per stirpes.*

---

[1] Including adopted and posthumous children.

[2] Advancements to child or issue deducted from intestate share.

[3] Kindred of the half blood share equally with those of the whole blood in the same degree.

District of Columbia

Spouse and Child(ren)[1]:

REAL ESTATE: Life estate in 1/3 to spouse; the balance to the children[2] equally, or their issue *per stirpes.*

PERSONALTY: 1/3 to spouse; 2/3 to children[2] or their issue *per stirpes.*

No Spouse, but with Child(ren):

REAL ESTATE AND PERSONALTY: All to the children[2] equally, or their issue *per stirpes.*

Spouse and No Child(ren):

REAL ESTATE: Life estate in 1/3 to spouse; the balance to the parents equally, or the survivor. If neither parent survives, the balance passes to brothers and sisters[3] equally, or their issue *per stirpes.* If none, to collateral kindred[3] in equal degree. If none, to grandparents equally.

PERSONALTY: 1/2 to spouse; 1/2 in same manner as balance of real estate.

If the decedent is not survived by children, parents, grandchildren, brothers or sisters or their descendants, the surviving spouse takes the entire estate.

No Spouse, or Child(ren), but with Parents:

REAL ESTATE AND PERSONALTY: All to the parents equally, or the survivor.

No Spouse, Child(ren), or Parents:

REAL ESTATE AND PERSONALTY: All to brothers and sisters[3] equally, or their issue *per stirpes.* If none, to collateral kindred[3] in equal degree. If none, to grandparents equally.

---

[1] Including adopted children, posthumous children and other posthumous descendants.

[2] Advancements to child or other descendants deducted from intestate share.

[3] Kindred of the half blood share equally with those of the whole blood in the same degree.

Florida

Spouse and Child(ren)[1]:

REAL ESTATE AND PERSONALTY: If all the children are children of the surviving spouse, the first $20,000 worth of property, plus 1/2 the balance of the estate passes to the spouse. If some of the children are not children of the surviving spouse, the surviving spouse takes 1/2 of the estate. What remains passes to the children equally or to their issue *per stirpes.*

No Spouse, but with Child(ren):

REAL ESTATE AND PERSONALTY: All to the children equally, or their issue, *per stirpes.*

Spouse and No Child(ren):

REAL ESTATE AND PERSONALTY: All to the spouse.

No Spouse, or Child(ren), but with Parents:

REAL ESTATE AND PERSONALTY: All to the parents equally, or the survivor.

No Spouse, Child(ren), or Parents:

REAL ESTATE AND PERSONALTY: All to brothers and sisters[2] equally, or their issue *per stirpes.* If none, 1/2 each to paternal and maternal kindred[2] and their descendants, *per stirpes.*

---

[1] Including adopted children.
[2] Where collateral kindred of the whole and half blood survive, those of the half blood take only half shares.

Georgia

Spouse and Child(ren)[1]:

REAL ESTATE AND PERSONALITY: Spouse and each child[2] (or its issue *per stirpes),* take equal shares; the spouse takes a child's share, but widow[3] entitled to at least 1/5.

No Spouse, but with Child(ren):

REAL ESTATE AND PERSONALITY: All to the children[2] equally, or their issue, *per stirpes.*

Spouse and No Child(ren):

REAL ESTATE AND PERSONALITY: All to the spouse.[3]

No Spouse or Child(ren), but with Parents:

REAL ESTATE AND PERSONALITY: All to parents and brothers and sisters[4] equally, or their issue *per stirpes.*

No Spouse, Child(ren), or Parents:

REAL ESTATE AND PERSONALITY: All to brothers and sisters[4] equally, or their issue *per stirpes.* If none, all to nephews and nieces equally, or their issue, *per stirpes.* If none, to the paternal and maternal next of kin.

---

[1] Including adopted and posthumous children.
[2] Advancements to child deducted from intestate share.
[3] A widow, in lieu of her intestate share to real property, may elect to receive dower—a life estate in 1/3 of the realty.
[4] Brothers and sisters of the half blood, and their issue, inherit equally with those of the whole blood, and their issue.

Hawaii*

Spouse and Child(ren)[1]:

REAL ESTATE AND PERSONALITY: 1/2 to the surviving spouse; 1/2 to the children[2] equally.

No Spouse, but with Child(ren)[3]:

REAL ESTATE AND PERSONALITY: All to the children[2] equally, or their issue *per stirpes.*

Spouse and No Child(ren):

REAL ESTATE AND PERSONALITY: If there is also no surviving parent of the decedent, the surviving spouse takes the entire estate. If there are surviving parents, 1/2 to the surviving spouse; 1/2 to decedent's parents equally, or to the survivor.

No Spouse or Child(ren), but with Parents:

REAL ESTATE AND PERSONALITY: All to the parents equally, or the survivor.

No Spouse, Child(ren), or Parents:

REAL ESTATE AND PERSONALITY: All to brothers and sisters equally,[4] or their issue, *per stirpes.* If none, to grandparents in equal shares, or to the surviving grandparent. If no grandparents survive, to the uncles and aunts[4] equally.

---

* Governs descent and distribution of estates of decedents dying after 6-30-77.
[1] Including adopted and posthumous children.
[2] Advancements to child deducted from intestate share.
[3] If decedent is survived by several children, or one child and the issue of one or more other children, and a surviving child dies unmarried during minority, his intestate share is distributed, in equal shares, to other children of the same parent *per stirpes.*
[4] Kindred of the half blood inherit equally with those of the whole blood in the same degree; however, as to ancestral property, half bloods, unrelated by blood to the ancestor, do not inherit.

Idaho

Spouse and One Child:

SEPARATE REALTY AND PERSONALITY: If surviving issue is also issue of surviving spouse, first $50,000, plus 1/2 of balance to the spouse; remaining balance to the child; if surviving issue is not also issue of surviving spouse, 1/2 to spouse and 1/2 to child.

COMMUNITY PROPERTY: All to the spouse.[1]

QUASI-COMMUNITY PROPERTY: Surviving spouse receives 1/2, and also the remaining 1/2 if not otherwise disposed of by decedent's will.[2]

Spouse and Child(ren):

SEPARATE REALTY AND PERSONALITY: If surviving issue is also issue of surviving spouse, first $50,000, plus 1/2 of balance to spouse, remaining balance to children; if any of surviving issue is not also issue of surviving spouse, 1/2 to spouse and 1/2 to children equally.

COMMUNITY PROPERTY: All to the spouse.

QUASI-COMMUNITY PROPERTY: See "Quasi-Community Property" above.

No Spouse, but with Child(ren):

REAL ESTATE AND PERSONALITY: Everything to child or children.

Spouse and No Child(ren):

SEPARATE REALTY AND PERSONALITY: First $50,000, plus 1/2 of balance to the spouse; remaining balance to decedent's parents equally, or the survivor. If neither parent survives, all to the spouse.

COMMUNITY PROPERTY: All to the spouse.

QUASI-COMMUNITY PROPERTY: See "Quasi-Community Property" above.

No Spouse or Child(ren), but with Parents:

REAL ESTATE AND PERSONALTY: Everything to parents equally, or to surviving parent.

No Spouse, Child(ren), or Parents:

REAL ESTATE AND PERSONALTY: To brothers and sisters, or their issue. If none, 1/2 each to maternal and paternal kindred and their descendants *per stirpes*.

---

[1] Decedent's share of community property not otherwise disposed of by will passes in this order: (1) to surviving spouse; (2) if none, to decedent's children; (3) if none, to parents or parent; (4) if none, to brothers or sisters or their issue; (5) if none, to grandparents or their issue.

Any person who fails to survive the decedent by 120 hours is deemed to have predeceased the decedent for purposes of homestead allowance, exempt property and intestate succession, and the decedent's heirs are determined accordingly.

[2] Quasi-community property is property acquired by decedent while a nonresident of Idaho, which property would have been community property had decedent been a resident of Idaho, and the property acquired in exchange for such property.

Illinois

Spouse and Child(ren)[1]:

REAL ESTATE AND PERSONALTY: 1/2 to the surviving spouse, 1/2 to the children[3] equally, or their issue *per stirpes*.

No Spouse, but with Child(ren):

REAL ESTATE AND PERSONALTY: All to the children[2] equally, or their issue *per stirpes*.

Spouse and No Child(ren):

REAL ESTATE AND PERSONALTY: All to the surviving spouse.

No Spouse or Child(ren), but with Parents:

REAL ESTATE AND PERSONALTY: To the parents, brothers, and sisters equally. If only one parent survives, he receives a double share. The issue of deceased brothers and sisters[3] take *per stirpes*.

No Spouse, Child(ren), or Parents:

REAL ESTATE AND PERSONALTY: All to brothers and sisters[3] equally, or their issue *per stirpes*. If none, 1/2 each to maternal and paternal grandparents equally, or the survivor; if none surviving, to their issue *per stirpes*. If no surviving descendants

of grandparents, 1/2 each to maternal and paternal great-grandparents equally, or the survivor, and their descendants *per stirpes*. If no descendants of great-grandparents, then to the next of kin in equal degree.

[Statutory Reference: Ill. Rev. Stat. ch. 2, §1, Probate Act of 1975]

---

[1] Including adopted and posthumous children.

[2] Advancements to child or other descendants deducted from intestate share.

[3] Kindred of the half blood inherit equally with those of the whole blood.

Indiana

Spouse and One Child[1]:

REAL ESTATE AND PERSONALTY: 1/2 to the spouse;[2] 1/2 to the child[3] or its issue.

Spouse and Children:

REAL ESTATE AND PERSONALTY: 1/3 to the spouse;[2] 2/3 to the children[3] equally, or their issue *per stirpes*.

No Spouse, but with Child(ren):

REAL ESTATE AND PERSONALTY: All to the children equally, or their issue *per stirpes*.

Spouse and No Child(ren):

REAL ESTATE AND PERSONALTY: 3/4 to the spouse; 1/4 to the parents equally, or the survivor. If neither parent survives, all to the spouse.

No Spouse or Child(ren), but with Parents:

REAL ESTATE AND PERSONALTY: To the parents, brothers, and sisters equally, but each surviving parent takes at least 1/4. The issue of deceased brothers and sisters[4] take *per stirpes*.

No Spouse, Child(ren), or Parents:

REAL ESTATE AND PERSONALTY: All to brothers and sisters[4] equally, or their issue *per stirpes*. If none, then to the surviving grandparents equally. If none to uncles and aunts *per stirpes*.

---

[1] Includes adopted children, and posthumous children and other descendants.

[2] If decedent left a child or children of a former marriage, or descendants of such child or children, and no child by the marriage with the surviving spouse, the spouse takes a 1/3 life estate in realty; the spouse takes her statutory share of the personal property.

[3] Advancements to child *or other heirs* deducted from intestate share.

[4] Kindred of the half blood inherit equally with kindred of the whole blood.

Iowa

Spouse and Child(ren)[1]:

REAL ESTATE: 1/3 to spouse;[2] 2/3 to children[3] equally, or their issue *per stirpes.*

PERSONALTY: All property exempt from execution in hands of decedent as head of family at death, and 1/3 of remainder not necessary for payment of debts and charges to spouse;[2] balance to children[3] equally, or their issue *per stirpes.*

No Spouse, but with Child(ren):

REAL ESTATE AND PERSONALTY: All the children[3] equally, or their issue *per stirpes.*

Spouse and No Child(ren):

REAL ESTATE: 1/2 to spouse,[4] 1/2 to parents equally, or the survivor. If neither parent survives, this 1/2 goes to the parent's heirs,[5] *per stirpes.* If none, all to the spouse or spouse's heirs.

PERSONALTY: All property exempt from execution in hands of decedent as head of family at death, and 1/2 of remainder not necessary for payment of debts and charges to spouse;[4] balance to parents equally, or the survivor. If neither parent survives, this 1/2 goes to the parents' heirs,[5] *per stirpes,* or their issue *per stirpes.* If none, all to the spouse.

No Spouse or Child(ren), but with Parents:

REAL ESTATE AND PERSONALTY: All to the parents equally, or the survivor.

No Spouse, Child(ren), or Parents:

REAL ESTATE AND PERSONALTY: All to brothers and sisters equally, or their issue *per stirpes.* If none, to the ascending ancestors of the parents. If none, then to heirs of spouse of intestate.

---

[1] Including adopted children, posthumous children, and other posthumous heirs.

[2] Spouse entitled to $50,000 minimum of combined personal and real property.

[3] Advancements to child *or other heirs* deducted from intestate share.

[4] But spouse is entitled to a minimum of $50,000 in value from all non-exempt real and personal property and any remaining homestead interest plus 1/2 net value of estate over $50,000 and value of exempt personal property.

[5] e.g., decedent's brothers and sisters.

Kansas

Spouse and Child(ren)[1]:

REAL ESTATE AND PERSONALTY: 1/2 to the spouse; 1/2 to the children[2] equally, or their issue *per stirpes.*

No Spouse, but with Child(ren):

REAL ESTATE AND PERSONALTY: All to the children[2] equally, or their issue *per stirpes.*

Spouse and No Child(ren):

REAL ESTATE AND PERSONALTY: All to the spouse.

No Spouse or Child(ren), but with Parents:

REAL ESTATE AND PERSONALTY: All to the parents equally, or the survivor.

No Spouse, Child(ren), or Parents:

REAL ESTATE AND PERSONALTY: All to parents' heirs[3], *per stirpes.* If one parent died without heirs, all to heirs of the other parent.

---

[1] Including adopted and posthumous children.

[2] Advancements to children, *or other heirs,* deducted from intestate share. Children of the half blood inherit equally with children of the whole blood from the common parent.

[3] e.g., decedent's brothers and sisters.

Kentucky

Spouse and Child(ren)[1]:

REAL ESTATE AND PERSONALTY: 1/2 to the spouse;[2] 1/2 to the children[3] equally, or their issue *per stirpes.*

No Spouse, but with Child(ren):

REAL ESTATE AND PERSONALTY: All to the children[3] equally, or their issue *per stirpes.*

Spouse and No Child(ren):

REAL ESTATE AND PERSONALTY: 1/2 to the spouse; 1/2 to the parents equally, or the survivor. If neither parent survives, this 1/2 passes to decedent's brothers and sisters[4] or their issue *per stirpes.* If none, all to the spouse[5] equally.

No Spouse or Child(ren), but with Parents:

REAL ESTATE AND PERSONALTY: All to the parents equally, or the survivor.

No Spouse, Child(ren), or Parents:

REAL ESTATE AND PERSONALTY: 1/2 each to maternal and paternal kindred. First to grandmother and grandfather equally,[4] or the survivor. If none, then to uncles and aunts,[4] and their issue *per stirpes.* The order of succession is continued among lineal ancestors.

---

[1] Including adopted and posthumous children.
In addition to 1/2 fee interest in real property, spouse has a life estate in 1/3 of the realty. $7,500 of personalty first set aside for the minor children and spouse.

[3] Advancements to child or other descendants deducted from intestate share. $7,500 of personalty first set aside for spouse and minor children.

[4] Collateral kindred of the half blood inherit only half-shares.

[5] When the intestate dies without issue, owning real estate which is the gift of either parent, the parent making such gift inherits the whole of such estate.

Louisiana

Spouse and Child(ren)[1]:

SEPARATE PROPERTY: All to the children[2] equally, or their issue *per stirpes.*

COMMUNITY PROPERTY: One half passes outright to the spouse. In addition, the spouse has a usufruct interest during his or her life in the portion of community property that is inherited by issue of the decedent and surviving spouse. The usufruct ceases in the event the surviving spouse remarries, unless it has been confirmed for life or any other designated period by the decedent's will.

Spouse and no Child(ren):

SEPARATE PROPERTY: If no parents, brothers and sisters, or their descendants, all to the spouse.

COMMUNITY PROPERTY: If no descendants, all to the spouse. If descendants, spouse gets a usufruct in all community property.

No Spouse, but with Child(ren):

ALL PROPERTY: To the children[2] equally, or their issue *per stirpes.*

SEPARATE PROPERTY: 1/4 to each parent; 1/2 to the brothers and sisters, or their issue *per stirpes.* If only one parent survives, the brothers and sisters[3] equally, or their issue *per stirpes,* receive 3/4. Where neither parent survives, the brothers and sisters[3] equally, or their issue *per stirpes,* take all the separate property. If none, all to the surviving parent or parents. In the event decedent leaves no parent, brother, sister, nephew, or niece, the separate property passes to his more remote kindred; if no kindred, to the spouse.

COMMUNITY PROPERTY: 3/4 to the spouse; 1/4 to the parents equally, or the survivor. If neither parent survives, all to the spouse.

No Spouse or Child(ren), but with Parents:

ALL PROPERTY: All to parents equally or the survivor if no brothers or sisters. If surviving siblings, all to brothers and sisters equally, parents receiving a usufruct over the property.

No Spouse, Child(ren), or Parents:

ALL PROPERTY: All to brothers and sisters[3] equally, or their issue *per stirpes.* If none, to more remote kindred.

---

[1] Including adopted, posthumous, and duly acknowledged illegitimate children.

[2] Advancements to children or grandchildren deducted from intestate share.

If decedent dies "rich" leaving the surviving spouse in "necessitous" circumstances, the survivor may take a *marital portion* of the intestate's separate property. This equals 1/4 outright where decedent left no children, or a usufruct (similar to a *life estate* at common law) in a child's share (but not less than 1/4) if there are children.

[3] Brothers and sisters of the half blood take half shares. As to ancestral property, half-brothers or half-sisters, unrelated by blood to the ancestor, do not inherit.

Maine

Spouse and Child(ren)[1]:

REAL ESTATE AND PERSONALTY: Where all surviving issue of decedent are also issue of the surviving spouse, the first $50,000, plus 1/2 of the balance of the intestate estate goes to the surviving spouse; the other 1/2 of the balance goes to the surviving issue per capita at each generation.[2] Where there are surviving issue of the decedent at least one of whom is not an issue of the surviving spouse, 1/2 of the intestate estate goes to the surviving spouse, the other 1/2 goes to the surviving issue per capita at each generation.[2]

No Spouse, but with Child(ren):

REAL ESTATE AND PERSONALTY: All to the children[3] equally, or their issue per capita at each generation.[2]

Spouse and No Child(ren):

REAL ESTATE AND PERSONALTY: First $50,000, plus 1/2 of the balance to the spouse; the other 1/2 of the balance to the parents equally, or the survivor of them. Where neither parent survives, the entire intestate estate passes to the surviving spouse.

No Spouse or Child(ren), but with Parents:

REAL ESTATE AND PERSONALTY: All to the parents equally, or the survivor of them.

No Spouse, Child(ren), or Parents:

REAL ESTATE AND PERSONALTY: All to brothers and sisters[4] equally, or their issue per capita at each generation.[2] If none, to the surviving grandparents, 1/2 to the maternal grandparents and 1/2 to the paternal grandparents. If no surviving grandparents, then to the issue of the grandparents per capita at each generation.[2] If there is no surviving grandparent or the issue thereof on either the maternal or paternal side, the entire estate passes to the relatives on the other side in the same manner as the 1/2. If there is no surviving grandparent or the issue thereof, to the surviving great-grandparents, 1/2 to the maternal great-grandparents and 1/2 to the paternal great-grandparents. If no surviving great-grandparents, then to the issue of the great-grandparents per capita at each generation.[2] If there is no surviving great-grandparent or the issue thereof on either the maternal or paternal side, the entire estate passes to the relatives on the other side in the same manner as the 1/2.

---

[1] Including adopted and posthumous children.

[2] Issue of equal relationship to the decedent will take equal shares among themselves. Issue of a closer degree will never take a smaller share than more distant issue.

[3] Advancements to child and other descendants deducted from intestate share.

[4] Kindred of the half blood inherit equally with those of the whole blood in the same degree.

Maryland

Spouse and Child(ren)[1]:

REAL ESTATE AND PERSONALTY: 1/2 to the spouse, 1/2 to the children[2] equally. If no minor child, but surviving issue, the first $15,000 to the spouse plus 1/2 of the residue.

No Spouse, but with Child(ren):

REAL ESTATE AND PERSONALTY: All to the children[2] equally, or their issue *per stirpes.*

Spouse and No Child(ren):

REAL ESTATE AND PERSONALTY: The first $15,000 plus 1/2 of the residue to the spouse, 1/2 of the residue to the parents equally, or the survivor. If neither parent survives, all to the spouse.

No Spouse or Child(ren), but with Parents:

REAL ESTATE AND PERSONALTY: All to the parents equally, or the survivor.

No Spouse, Child(ren), or Parents:

REAL ESTATE AND PERSONALTY: All to brothers and sisters[3] equally, or to their issue *per stirpes.* If none, 1/2 each to the maternal and paternal grandparent or grandparents equally, or their issue *per stirpes.* If none, 1/4 to each pair of great-grandparents equally, or their issue *per stirpes.*

---

[1] Including adopted and posthumous children.

[2] Advancements to child or other descendants deducted from intestate share.

[3] Collateral kindred of the half blood share equally with those of the whole blood in the same degree.

Massachusetts

Spouse and Child(ren)[1]:

REAL ESTATE AND PERSONALTY: 1/2 to the spouse;[2] 1/2 to the children[3] equally, or their issue *per stirpes.*

Spouse and No Child(ren):

REAL ESTATE AND PERSONALTY: First $50,000, plus 1/2 the balance to the spouse;[2] the other 1/2 of balance passes to the parents equally, or the survivor. If neither parent survives, this 1/2 of balance passes to brothers and sisters[4] equally, or their issue *per stirpes.* If none, to the next of kin[4] in equal degree. If none, all to the spouse.[5]

No Spouse, but with Child(ren):

REAL ESTATE AND PERSONALTY: All to the children[3] equally, or their issue *per stirpes.*

No Spouse or Child(ren), but with Parents:

REAL ESTATE AND PERSONALTY: All to the parents equally, or the survivor.

No Spouse, Child(ren), or Parents:

REAL ESTATE AND PERSONALTY: All to brothers and sisters[4] equally, or their issue *per stirpes.* If none, to the next of kin in equal degree.

---

[1] Including adopted and posthumous children.

[2] The spouse, in lieu of his or her intestate share, may elect a 1/3 life estate in realty ("dower" and "curtesy").

[3] Advancements to child or other descendants deducted from intestate share.

[4] Kindred of the half blood inherit equally with those of the whole blood in the same degree.

[5] If the entire estate is less than $50,000, the spouse takes it all, even though there are kindred, but no issue.

Michigan

Spouse[1] and Child(ren)[2]:

REAL ESTATE AND PERSONALTY: Where all surviving issue of decedent are also issue of the surviving spouse, the first $60,000 plus 1/2 of the balance of the intestate estate goes to the surviving spouse; the other 1/2 of the balance goes to the surviving issue equally, if all are in the same degree of kinship, if not, those of more remote degrees take by representation. Where there are surviving issue of the decedent at least one of whom is not an issue of the surviving spouse, 1/2 of the intestate estate goes to the surviving spouse, the other 1/2 goes to the decedent's issue of the same degree equally. Again issue of more remote degrees takes by representation.

No Spouse, but with Child(ren):

REAL ESTATE AND PERSONALTY: All to the children[3] equally, or their issue *per stirpes.*

Spouse and No Child(ren):

REAL ESTATE AND PERSONALTY: The first $60,000[4] and 1/2 of the balance of the intestate estate to the surviving spouse, the other 1/2 of the balance to the parents equally, or the survivor.

Where neither parent survives, the entire intestate estate passes to the surviving spouse.

No Spouse or Child(ren), but with Parents:

REAL ESTATE AND PERSONALTY: All to the parents equally, or the survivor.

No Spouse, Child(ren), or Parents:

REAL ESTATE AND PERSONALTY: All to brothers and sisters equally, or their children, *per stirpes.* If none, to the surviving grandparents, 1/2 to the maternal grandparents and 1/2 to the paternal grandparents. If no surviving grandparents, then to the issue of the grandparents who are of the same degree of kinship.[5] Those of more remote degree take nothing.

---

[1] Should a Michigan-domiciled decedent die intestate leaving a surviving widow, she may elect to take either her intestate share or her dower right.

[2] Including adopted and posthumous children.

[3] Advancements to child or other descendants deducted from intestate share.

[4] In the case of partial intestacy the $60,000 is reduced by the amount received by the surviving spouse through the will.

[5] Kindred of the half blood inherit equally with those of the whole blood in the same degree.

Minnesota

Spouse and One Child[1]:

REAL ESTATE AND PERSONALTY: 1/2 to the spouse;[2] 1/2 to the child[3] or its issue.

Spouse and Children:

REAL ESTATE AND PERSONALTY: 1/3 to the spouse;[2] 2/3 to the children[3] equally, or their issue *per stirpes.*

No Spouse, but with Child(ren):

REAL ESTATE AND PERSONALTY: All to the children[3] equally, or their issue *per stirpes.*

Spouse and No Child(ren):

REAL ESTATE AND PERSONALTY: All to the spouse.[4]

No Spouse or Child(ren), but with Parents:

REAL ESTATE AND PERSONALTY: All to the parents equally, or the survivor.

No Spouse, Child(ren), or Parents:

REAL ESTATE AND PERSONALTY: All to brothers and sisters[5] equally, or their issue *per stirpes.* If none, to the next of kin[5] in equal degree.

---

[1] Including adopted and posthumous children.

[2] The spouse takes a life interest in the homestead, free of creditors, with the remainder interest to the children equally, or their issue *per stirpes.* A prenuptial agreement may modify the spouses intestate share.

[3] Advancements to child or other descendant deducted from intestate share.

[4] The spouse takes a fee interest in the homestead.

[5] Kindred of the half blood inherit equally with those of the whole blood in the same degree; however, as to ancestral property, half bloods, unrelated by blood to the ancestor, do not inherit.

Mississippi

Spouse and Child(ren)[1]:

REAL ESTATE AND PERSONALTY: Spouse and each child[2] (or its issue *per stirpes),* take equal shares; the spouse takes a child's share.

No Spouse, but with Child(ren):

REAL ESTATE AND PERSONALTY: All to children,[2] or their issue *per stirpes.*

Spouse and No Child(ren):

REAL ESTATE AND PERSONALTY: All to the spouse.

No Spouse or Child(ren), but with Parents:

REAL ESTATE AND PERSONALTY: All to parents and brothers and sisters equally, the issue of deceased brothers and sisters[3] taking *per stirpes.* If no brothers and sisters or issue, all to the parents equally or the survivor.

No Spouse, Child(ren), or Parents:

REAL ESTATE AND PERSONALTY: All to brothers and sisters[3] equally, or their issue *per stirpes.* If none, to grandparents and uncles and aunts equally. If none, to the next of kin[3] in equal degree.

---

[1] Including adopted children.

[2] Including children of a former marriage. Advancements to a child or other descendants deducted from intestate share.

[3] Kindred of the whole blood, in equal degree, are preferred to kindred of the half blood in the same degree.

Missouri

Spouse and Child(ren)[1]:

REAL ESTATE AND PERSONALTY: Where all surviving issue of decedent are also issue of the surviving spouse, the first $20,000, plus 1/2 of the balance of the intestate estate goes to the surviving spouse; the other 1/2 of the balance goes to the surviving issue equally, if all are in the same degree of kinship, if not, those of more remote degrees take by representation. Where there are surviving issue of the decedent at least one of whom is not an issue of the surviving spouse, 1/2 of the intestate estate goes to the surviving spouse, the other 1/2 goes to the decedent's issue of the same degree equally. Again, issue of more remote degrees take by representation.

No Spouse, but with Child(ren):

REAL ESTATE AND PERSONALTY: All to the children[2] equally, or their issue *per stirpes*.

Spouse and No Child(ren):

REAL ESTATE AND PERSONALTY: First $20,000, plus 1/2 of the balance of the intestate estate goes to the surviving spouse; the other 1/2 of the balance goes to the parents and brothers and sisters[3] equally, the issue of deceased brothers and sisters taking *per stirpes*. However, if neither parent survives, all to the surviving spouse.

No Spouse or Child(ren), but with Parents:

REAL ESTATE AND PERSONALTY: All to the parents and brothers and sisters[3] equally, the issue of deceased brothers and sisters taking *per stirpes*. If no brothers and sisters or their issue, all to parents, or the survivor.

No Spouse, Child(ren), or Parents:

REAL ESTATE AND PERSONALTY: All to brothers and sisters[3] equally, or their issue *per stirpes*. If none, to grandparents,[3] uncles,[3] and aunts[3] or their issue *per stirpes*.[4]

---

[1] Including adopted children, and posthumous children and descendants.

[2] Advancements to child or grandchild deducted from intestate share. However, property given by the decedent in the decedent's lifetime to an heir is an advancement only if the decedent declares it to be so in a contemporaneous writing, or the heir makes a written acknowledgment of the same.

[3] Regarding ascending and collateral kindred of decedent, those of the half blood inherit only half as much as those of the whole blood; however, if all collaterals are half bloods, they take whole portions, and ascendants double portions.

[4] Surviving spouse, or unmarried minor children of the decedent in the absence of a surviving spouse, can take a homestead allowance equal to the lesser of 1/2 the estate or $7,500. The intestate share of the recipient(s) of the homestead allowance will be offset by the allowance, but the allowance shall not be diminished if it is greater than the intestate share.

Montana

Spouse and One Child[1]:

REAL ESTATE AND PERSONALTY: If the child is not a child of the surviving spouse, the surviving spouse takes 1/2, the child[2] takes the other half, or its issue shares *per stirpes*. If a child of the surviving spouse, the surviving spouse takes all.

Spouse and Children:

REAL ESTATE AND PERSONALTY: If all the children are children of the surviving spouse, the surviving spouse takes all. If more than one of the children is not a child of the surviving spouse, the surviving spouse takes 1/3, and the children take

the balance, equally, the issue of deceased children sharing *per stirpes*.

No Spouse, but with Child(ren):

REAL ESTATE AND PERSONALTY: All to the children[2] equally, or their issue *per stirpes*.

Spouse and No Child(ren):

REAL ESTATE AND PERSONALTY: All to the spouse.

No Spouse or Child(ren), but with Parents:

REAL ESTATE AND PERSONALTY: All to the parents equally, or the survivor.[3]

No Spouse, Child(ren), or Parents:

REAL ESTATE AND PERSONALTY: All to the brothers and sisters[4] equally, or their issue *per stirpes*. If none, to the next of kin in equal degree.

---

[1] Including adopted and posthumous children.

[2] Advancements to child, or other descendants, deducted from intestate share.

[3] However, if an unmarried intestate dies while a minor, that portion of his estate derived by inheritance from a parent, descends to his brothers and sisters *per stirpes*.

[4] Kindred of the half blood inherit equally with those of the whole blood in the same degree; however, as to ancestral property, half bloods, unrelated by blood to the ancestor, do not inherit.

Nebraska

Spouse and Child(ren)[1]:

REAL ESTATE AND PERSONALTY: If all the children are children of the surviving spouse, the spouse takes the first $50,000, plus 1/2 of the balance of the estate. If some of the children are not children of the surviving spouse, the spouse takes 1/2 of the estate. In either case, the children share equally, the issue of any deceased child sharing *per stirpes*.

No Spouse, but with Child(ren):

REAL ESTATE AND PERSONALTY: All to the children equally, or their issue *per stirpes*.

Spouse and No Child(ren):

REAL ESTATE AND PERSONALTY: If no parent of the decedent is alive, the entire estate passes to the spouse. If either of the parents of the decedent survives, the spouse takes the first $50,000 plus 1/2 of the balance of the estate, and the parents or the survivor take the balance.

No Spouse or Child(ren), but with Parents:

REAL ESTATE AND PERSONALTY: All to parents equally, or the survivor.

No Spouse, Child(ren), or Parents:

REAL ESTATE AND PERSONALTY: All to brothers and sisters[3] equally, or their children *per stirpes.* If none, 1/2 each to paternal and maternal kindred or their descendants *per stirpes.*

---

[1] Including adopted and posthumous children.

[2] Advancements to children or other descendants deducted from intestate share.

[3] Kindred of the half blood inherit equally with those of the whole blood in the same degree.

Nevada

Spouse and One Child[1]:

SEPARATE REALTY AND PERSONALTY: 1/2 to the spouse; 1/2 to the child[2] or its issue.

COMMUNITY PROPERTY: All to the spouse.

Spouse and Children:

SEPARATE REALTY AND PERSONALTY: 1/3 to the spouse; 2/3 to the children[2] equally, or their issue *per stirpes.*

COMMUNITY PROPERTY: All to the spouse.

No Spouse, but with Child(ren):

REAL ESTATE AND PERSONALTY: All to the children[2] equally, or their issue *per stirpes.*

Spouse and No Child(ren):

SEPARATE REALTY AND PERSONALTY: 1/2 to the spouse; 1/2 to the parents equally, or the survivor. If neither parent survives, this 1/2 goes to brothers and sisters[3] equally, or their children *per stirpes.* If none, all to the spouse.

COMMUNITY PROPERTY: All to the spouse.

No Spouse, or Child(ren), but with Parents:

REAL ESTATE AND PERSONALTY: All to the parents equally, or the survivor.

No Spouse, Child(ren), or Parents:

REAL ESTATE AND PERSONALTY: All to brothers and sisters[3] equally, or their issue *per stirpes.* If none, to the next of kin[3] in equal degree.

---

[1] Including adopted, posthumous, and illegitimate children.

[2] Advancements to child *or any heir* deducted from intestate share.

[3] Kindred of the half blood inherit equally with kindred of the whole blood in the same degree; however, as to ancestral property, half bloods, unrelated by blood to the ancestor, do not inherit.

New Hampshire

Spouse and Child(ren)[1]:

REAL ESTATE AND PERSONALTY: If all of the children[2] are children of the surviving spouse, the spouse takes the first $50,000, plus 1/2 the balance of the estate. If some of the children are not chil-

dren of the surviving spouse, the spouse takes 1/2 of the estate. In either case, the children share equally, the issue of any deceased child sharing *per stirpes.*

No Spouse, but with Child(ren):

REAL ESTATE AND PERSONALTY: All to the children[3] equally, or their issue *per stirpes.*

Spouse and No Child(ren):

REAL ESTATE AND PERSONALTY: First $50,000, plus 1/2 of the balance to the spouse; the other 1/2 to the parents equally, or to the survivor.[3] If neither parent survives, all to the spouse.

No Spouse, or Child(ren), but with Parents:

REAL ESTATE AND PERSONALTY: All to the parents equally, or the survivor.

No Spouse, Child(ren), or Parents:

REAL ESTATE AND PERSONALTY: All to brothers and sisters equally, or their issue *per stirpes.* If none, 1/2 to paternal and maternal kindred or their descendants *per stirpes.*

---

[1] Including adopted, posthumous, and illegitimate children.

[2] Advancements to child *or any heir* deducted from intestate share.

[3] However, if an unmarried intestate dies while a minor, that portion of his estate derived by inheritance from a parent descends to his brothers and sisters equally, or their issue *per stirpes.*

New Jersey

Spouse and Child(ren)[1]:

REAL ESTATE AND PERSONALTY: Where all surviving issue of decedent are also issue of the surviving spouse, the first $50,000 plus 1/2 of the balance goes to the surviving spouse; the other 1/2 of the balance goes to the surviving issue equally, if all are in the same degree of kinship, if not, those of remote degrees take *per stirpes.* Where there are surviving issue of the decedent at least one of whom is not an issue of the surviving spouse, 1/2 of the estate goes to the surviving spouse; the other 1/2 goes to the decedent's issue of the same degree equally and those of more remote degrees would again take *per stirpes.*

No Spouse, but with Child(ren):

REAL ESTATE AND PERSONALTY: All to the children equally, or their issue *per stirpes.*

Spouse and No Child(ren):

REAL ESTATE AND PERSONALTY: The spouse takes the first $50,000 plus 1/2 of the balance. The other 1/2 of the balance to the parents equally, or the survivor. If neither parent survives, all to spouse.

No Spouse, or Child(ren), but with Parents:
REAL ESTATE AND PERSONALTY: All to the parents equally, or the survivor.

No Spouse, Child(ren), or Parents:
REAL ESTATE AND PERSONALTY: All to brothers and sisters[2] equally, or their issue *per stirpes*. If none, 1/2 each to maternal and paternal grandparents, or their issue.[2]

---

[1] Including adopted and posthumous children.
[2] Kindred of the half blood inherit equally with those of the whole blood.

NOTE: If a person who is entitled to a share of an intestate's estate received an advancement during the intestate's life, the value of the advancement at the time it was made is subtracted from the share to which the person would otherwise be entitled.

New Mexico

Spouse and Child(ren)[1]:
SEPARATE REALTY AND PERSONALTY: 1/4 to the spouse; 3/4 to the children[2] equally, or their issue *per stirpes*.

COMMUNITY PROPERTY: All to the spouse.

No Spouse, but with Child(ren):
REAL ESTATE AND PERSONALTY: All to the children equally, or their issue *per stirpes*.

Spouse and No Child(ren):
SEPARATE REALTY AND PERSONALTY: All to the spouse.

COMMUNITY PROPERTY: All to the spouse.

No Spouse, or Child(ren), but with Parents:
REAL ESTATE AND PERSONALTY: All to the parents equally, or the survivor.

No Spouse, Child(ren), or Parents:
REAL ESTATE AND PERSONALTY: All to brothers and sisters[3] equally, or their issue *per stirpes*. If none, 1/2 each to maternal and paternal grandparents, or their issue.[3]

---

[1] Including adopted and posthumous children.
[2] Advancements to child, *or any heir* deducted from intestate share.
[3] Kindred of the half blood inherit equally with those of the whole blood in the same degree.

New York

Spouse and One Child[1]:
REAL ESTATE AND PERSONALTY: First $4,000, plus 1/2 of the balance of the estate to the spouse;[2] other remaining balance to the child[3] or its issue.

Spouse and Children:
REAL ESTATE AND PERSONALTY: First $4,000, plus 1/3 of balance of the estate to the spouse; remaining balance to the children[3] equally, or their issue *per stirpes*.

No Spouse, but with Child(ren):
REAL ESTATE AND PERSONALTY: All to the children equally, or their issue *per stirpes*.

Spouse and No Child(ren):
REAL ESTATE AND PERSONALTY: The spouse takes the first $25,000, plus 1/2 the balance. The other 1/2 of the balance to the parents equally, or the survivor. If neither parent survives, all to the spouse.

No Spouse or Child(ren), but with Parents:
REAL ESTATE AND PERSONALTY: All to the parents equally, or the survivor.

No Spouse, Child(ren), or Parents:
REAL ESTATE AND PERSONALTY: All to brothers and sisters[4] or their issue *per stirpes*. If none, to grandparents equally, or their issue *per stirpes*. If none, to the next of kin[4] in equal degree.

---

[1] Including adopted children, and posthumous children or other posthumous heirs.
[2] The widow, in lieu of her intestate share may elect to receive dower—a life estate in 1/3 of the realty—provided the couple was married before September 1, 1930.
[3] Advancements to child *or other heirs* deducted from intestate share.
[4] Kindred of the half blood inherit equally with those of the whole blood in the same degree.

North Carolina

Spouse and One Child[1]:
REAL ESTATE: 1/2 to the spouse; 1/2 to the child,[2] or its issue *per stirpes*.

PERSONALTY: The spouse takes the first $15,000, plus 1/2 of the balance; remaining 1/2 of the balance to the child, or its issue *per stirpes*.

Spouse and Children:
REAL ESTATE: 1/3 to the spouse; 2/3 to the children,[2] or their issue *per stirpes*.

PERSONALTY: The spouse takes the first $15,000, plus 1/3 of the balance; remaining 2/3 of the balance to the children equally, or their issue *per stirpes*.

No Spouse, but with Child(ren):
REAL ESTATE AND PERSONALTY: All to the children[2] equally, or their issue *per stirpes*.

Spouse and No Child(ren):

REAL ESTATE: 1/2 to the spouse; 1/2 to the parents equally, or the survivor. If neither parent survives, all to spouse.

PERSONALTY: The spouse takes the first $25,000, plus 1/2 of the balance; remaining 1/2 of the balance to the parents equally, or the survivor. If neither parent survives, all to the spouse.

No Spouse, or Child(ren), but with Parents:

REAL ESTATE AND PERSONALTY: All to the parents equally, or the survivor.

No Spouse, Child(ren), or Parents:

REAL ESTATE AND PERSONALTY: All to brothers and sisters[3] equally, or their issue *per stirpes*. If none, 1/2 each to maternal and paternal grandparents, or their issue *per stirpes*.[3]

---

[1] Including adopted children, and posthumous children and other descendants.

[2] Advancements to child, *or any heir*, deducted from intestate share.

[3] Collateral relations of the half blood inherit equally with those of the whole blood.

North Dakota

Spouse and Child(ren)[1]:

REAL ESTATE AND PERSONALTY: If all the children are children of the surviving spouse, the spouse takes the first $50,000, plus 1/2 of the balance of the estate. If some of the children are not children of the surviving spouse, the spouse takes 1/2 of the estate. In either case, the children share equally, the issue of any deceased child sharing *per stirpes*.

No Spouse, but with Child(ren):

REAL ESTATE AND PERSONALTY: All to the children[2] equally, or their issue *per stirpes*.

Spouse and No Child(ren):

REAL ESTATE AND PERSONALTY: If there is no surviving parent, the spouse takes all. If there is a surviving parent or parents, the spouse takes the first $50,000, plus 1/2 of the balance of the estate; and the parents or the survivor take the balance.

No Spouse or Child(ren), but with Parents:

REAL ESTATE AND PERSONALTY: All to the parents equally, or the survivor.

No Spouse, Child(ren), or Parents:

REAL ESTATE AND PERSONALTY: All to the

brothers and sisters[3] equally, or their issue *per stirpes*. If none, 1/2 each to maternal and paternal grandparents or their issue *per stirpes*.

---

[1] Including adopted and posthumous children.

[2] Advancements to child or other descendants deducted from intestate share.

[3] Kindred of the half blood inherit equally with those of the whole blood in the same degree.

Ohio

Spouse[1] and One Child: The spouse receives the first $30,000 if he or she is the natural or adoptive parent of the child, the first $10,000 otherwise, plus in either case, 1/2 of the balance of the intestate estate. The balance passes to the child or the child's lineal descendants *per stirpes*.

Spouse[1] and Child(ren)[2]: The spouse receives the first $30,000 if he or she is the natural or adoptive parent of the child, the first $10,000 otherwise, plus in either case, 1/3 of the balance of the intestate estate. The balance passes to the children[3] equally, or to the lineal descendants of any deceased child *per stirpes*.

No Spouse, but with Child(ren):

REAL ESTATE AND PERSONALTY: All to the children equally, or their issue *per stirpes*.

Spouse and No Child(ren): If no issue of children, all to the spouse.

No Spouse, or Child(ren), but with Parents:

REAL ESTATE AND PERSONALTY: All to the parents equally, or the survivor.

No Spouse, Child(ren), or Parents:

REAL ESTATE AND PERSONALTY: All to brothers and sisters equally, or their issue *per stirpes*. If none, 1/2 to maternal grandparents equally or the survivor. If none, this 1/2 to their issue *per stirpes*. Other 1/2 to paternal grandparents equally, or the survivor. If none, to their issue *per stirpes*. If no surviving grandparents, or descendants, then to next of kin in equal degree.

---

[1] The surviving spouse may elect to receive, as part of the surviving spouse's share of the intestate estate, the entire interest of the decedent spouse in the mansion house. This election is personal to the surviving spouse and doesn't survive for the benefit of his or her estate.

[2] Including adopted and posthumous children.

[3] Advancements to children *or other heirs* deducted from intestate share.

Oklahoma

Spouse and One Child[1]:
REAL ESTATE AND PERSONALTY: 1/2 to the spouse;[2] 1/2 to the child[3] or its issue.

Spouse and Children:
REAL ESTATE AND PERSONALTY: 1/3 to the spouse;[2] 2/3 to the children[3] equally, or their issue *per stirpes.*

No Spouse, but with Child(ren):
REAL ESTATE AND PERSONALTY: All to the children[3] equally, or their issue *per stirpes.*

Spouse and No Child(ren):
REAL ESTATE AND PERSONALTY: 1/2 to the spouse;[4] 1/2 to the parents equally, or the survivor. If none, this 1/2 passes to brothers and sisters[5] equally, or their children *per stirpes.* If none, all to the spouse.

No Spouse or Child(ren), but with Parents:
REAL ESTATE AND PERSONALTY: All to the parents equally, or the survivor.[6]

No Spouse, Child(ren), or Parents:
REAL ESTATE AND PERSONALTY: All to brothers and sisters[5] equally, or the survivor *per stirpes.* If none, to the next of kin[5] in equal degree.

---

[1] Including adopted and posthumous children.
[2] However, if the decedent was married more than once, regarding property not acquired during the marriage with decedent, the surviving spouse takes only a child's share.
[3] Advancements to child or other descendants deducted from intestate share.
[4] Regarding real and personal property acquired by the joint industry of the decedent and his spouse during marriage, *all* such property goes to the survivor.
[5] Kindred of the half blood inherit equally with those of the whole blood in the same degree; however, as to ancestral property, half bloods, unrelated by blood to the ancestor, do not inherit.
[6] If the decedent is a minor, and his parents are not living together, the estate passes to the parent having had the care of the minor. If the decedent minor dies unmarried, that portion of his estate derived by inheritance from a parent, descends to his brothers and sisters equally, or their issue *per stirpes.*

Oregon

Spouse and Child(ren)[1]: The spouse takes a 1/2 interest in the net intestate estate, and the balance of the net intestate estate passes to the children equally, or to their issue *per stirpes.*

No Spouse, but with Child(ren):
REAL ESTATE AND PERSONALTY: All to the children[2] equally, or their issue *per stirpes.*

Spouse and No Child(ren):
REAL ESTATE AND PERSONALTY: All to the spouse.

No Spouse, or Child(ren), but with Parents:
REAL ESTATE AND PERSONALTY: All to the parents equally, or the survivor.[3]

No Spouse, Child(ren), or Parents:
REAL ESTATE AND PERSONALTY: All to brothers and sisters[4] equally, or their issue *per stirpes.* If none, to the next of kin in equal degree.

---

[1] Including adopted and posthumous children.
[2] Advancements to child or other descendants deducted from intestate share.
[3] If the decedent dies a minor without spouse or children, any real estate which descended to the intestate child from an ancestor passes to the heirs of his ancestor as if the child predeceased the ancestor.
[4] Kindred of the half blood inherit equally with those of the whole blood in the same degree.

Pennsylvania

Spouse and Child(ren)[1]:
REAL ESTATE AND PERSONALTY: If all the children are children of the surviving spouse, the spouse takes the first $30,000[2], plus 1/2 of the balance of the estate. If some of the children are not children of the surviving spouse, the spouse takes 1/2 of the estate. In either case, the children share equally, the issue of any deceased child sharing *per stirpes.*

No Spouse, but with Child(ren):
REAL ESTATE AND PERSONALTY: All to the children[3] equally, or their issue *per stirpes.*

Spouse and No Child(ren):
REAL ESTATE AND PERSONALTY: First $30,000, plus 1/2 of the balance to the spouse; other 1/2 of balance to the parents equally, or the survivor. If none, all to the spouse.

No Spouse, or Child(ren), but with Parents:
REAL ESTATE AND PERSONALTY: All to the parents equally, or the survivor.

No Spouse, Child(ren), or Parents:
REAL ESTATE AND PERSONALTY: All to brothers and sisters[4] equally, or their issue *per stirpes.* If none, 1/2 each to maternal and paternal grandparents equally, or the survivor. If none, to uncles or aunts[4] and their issue.

---

[1] Including adopted children, posthumous children and other posthumous heirs.
[2] Any property received by the surviving spouse under the will will satisfy pro tanto the $30,000 allowance in cases of partial intestacy.

[3] Advancements to any person are deducted from the person's share.

[4] Kindred of the half blood share equally with those of the whole blood in the same degree.

Rhode Island

Spouse and Children[1]:
REAL ESTATE: Life estate to widower; 1/3 life estate to widow; balance to children[2] equally, or their issue *per stirpes.*

PERSONALTY: 1/2 to spouse; 1/2 to children[2] equally, or their issue *per stirpes.*

No Spouse, but with Child(ren):
REAL ESTATE AND PERSONALTY: All to the children[2] equally, or their issue *per stirpes.*

Spouse and No Child(ren):
REAL ESTATE: Life estate to spouse. The court, in its discretion, may award $25,000 in fee to the spouse; balance to the parents equally, or the survivor. If none, the balance passes to brothers and sisters equally, or the survivor. If none, 1/2 each to maternal and paternal grandparents equally, or the survivor. If none, to aunts and uncles equally, or their issue *per stirpes.* If none, to more remote kindred. If none, all to the spouse.

PERSONALTY: First $50,000, plus 1/2 of the balance to the spouse; other 1/2 of balance to the parents equally, or the survivor. If none, his 1/2 of balance to brothers and sisters equally, or their issue *per stirpes.* If none, 1/2 each to maternal and paternal grandparents equally. If none, to more remote kindred. If none, all to the spouse.

No Spouse, or Child(ren), but with Parents:
REAL ESTATE AND PERSONALTY: All to the parents equally, or the survivor.

No Spouse, Child(ren), or Parents:
REAL ESTATE AND PERSONALTY: All to brothers and sisters equally, or their issue *per stirpes.* If none, 1/2 each to maternal and paternal grandparents equally. If none, to more remote kindred.

[1] Including adopted and posthumous children.

[2] Advancements to child or grandchild deducted from intestate share.

South Carolina

Spouse and One Child[1]:
REAL ESTATE AND PERSONALTY: 1/2 to the spouse;[2] 1/2 to the child[3] or its issue.

Spouse and Child(ren):
REAL ESTATE AND PERSONALTY: 1/3 to the spouse; 2/3 to the children[3] equally, or their issue *per stirpes.*

No Spouse, but with Child(ren):
REAL ESTATE AND PERSONALTY: All to the children[3] equally, or their issue *per stirpes.*

Spouse and No Child(ren):
REAL ESTATE AND PERSONALTY: 1/2 to the spouse; 1/2 to parents and brothers and sisters in equal shares, the issue of deceased brothers and sisters taking *per stirpes.* If no parents, 1/2 to brothers and sisters,[4] *per stirpes.* If no brothers and sisters, to the parents equally, or the survivor. If neither parents nor brothers or sisters survive, 1/2 to grandparents equally, or the survivor. If none, all to the spouse.

No Spouse, or Child(ren), but with Parents:
REAL ESTATE AND PERSONALTY: If no brothers and sisters, all to the parents equally or to the survivor.

No Spouse, Child(ren), or Parents:
REAL ESTATE AND PERSONALTY: All to brothers and sisters[4] *per stirpes.* If none, to grandparents equally, or the survivor. If none, to uncles and aunts equally, or their issue. If none, to the next of kin in equal degree.

[1] Including adopted children. Stepchildren take only in the absence of next of kin.

[2] A widow, in lieu of her intestate share, may elect dower—a 1/3 life estate in realty, or 1/6 absolute.

[3] Advancements to child or its issue deducted from intestate share.

[4] Brothers and sisters of the half blood take only in the absence of surviving parents and brothers and sisters of the half blood. In such event, the 1/2 passes to the half bloods and issue of brothers and sisters of the whole blood equally. In the absence of the latter, the half bloods take this 1/2.

South Dakota

Spouse and One Child[1]:
REAL ESTATE AND PERSONALTY: 1/2 to the spouse; 1/2 to the child[2] or its issue.

Spouse and Children:
REAL ESTATE AND PERSONALTY: 1/3 to the spouse; 2/3 to the children[2] equally, or their issue *per stirpes.*

No Spouse, but with Child(ren):
REAL ESTATE AND PERSONALTY: All to the children[2] equally, or their issue *per stirpes.*

Spouse and No Child(ren):
REAL ESTATE AND PERSONALTY: First $100,000, plus 1/2 of the balance to the spouse; other 1/2 of balance to the parents equally, or the

survivor. If none, this 1/2 of balance to brothers and sisters[3] equally, or their issue *per stirpes.* If none, all to the spouse.

No Spouse, or Child(ren), but with Parents:
REAL ESTATE AND PERSONALTY: All to the parents equally, or the survivor.

No Spouse, Child(ren), or Parents:
REAL ESTATE AND PERSONALTY: All to brothers and sisters[3] equally, or their issue *per stirpes.* If none, to the next of kin[3] in equal degree.

---

[1] Including adopted and posthumous children.
[2] Advancements to child or other descendant deducted from intestate share.
[3] Kindred of the half blood share equally with those of the whole blood in the same degree; however, as to ancestral property, half bloods, unrelated by blood to the ancestor do not inherit.

Tennessee

Spouse and Children[1]:
REAL ESTATE AND PERSONALTY: 1/3 or a child's share, whichever is greater, to the spouse; balance to the children equally, or their issue *per stirpes.*

No Spouse, but with Child(ren):
REAL ESTATE AND PERSONALTY: All to the children[2] equally, or their issue *per stirpes.*

Spouse and No Child(ren):
REAL ESTATE AND PERSONALTY: All to the spouse.

No Spouse, or Child(ren), but with Parents:
REAL ESTATE AND PERSONALTY: All to the parents equally, or the survivor.

No Spouse, Child(ren), or Parents:
REAL ESTATE AND PERSONALTY: All to brothers and sisters equally, or their issue *per stirpes.* If none, 1/2 each to maternal and paternal grandparents equally, or the survivor; if none surviving, to their issue *per stirpes.*

---

[1] Including adopted and posthumous children.
[2] Advancements to child deducted from intestate share.

Texas

Spouse and Child(ren)[1]:
SEPARATE REALTY: Life estate in 1/3 to the spouse; balance to the children[2] equally, or their issue *per stirpes.*

SEPARATE PERSONALTY: 1/3 to the spouse; 2/3 to the children[2] equally, or their issue *per stirpes.*

COMMUNITY PROPERTY: 1/2 to spouse; 1/2 to the children[2] equally, or their issue *per stirpes.*

No Spouse, but with Child(ren):
REAL ESTATE AND PERSONALTY: All to the children[2] equally, or their issue *per stirpes.*

Spouse and No Child(ren):
SEPARATE REALTY: 1/2 to the spouse; 1/2 to the parents equally. If only one surviving parent and brothers and sisters[3], the parent takes 1/4 with the other 1/4 divided equally among the brothers and sisters, or their issue *per stirpes.* If no brothers and sisters or issue, the surviving parent takes the entire 1/2. If no parents, the brothers and sisters, or their issue *per stirpes,* take this half. If no parents, brothers, sisters, or their issue survive, this 1/2 is divided equally among maternal and paternal kindred[3] (grandparents and their descendants). If none, all to the spouse.

SEPARATE PERSONALTY: All to the spouse.

COMMUNITY PROPERTY: All to the spouse.

No Spouse, or Child(ren), but with Parents:
REAL ESTATE AND PERSONALTY: All to the parents equally. If only one surviving parent, the survivor takes 1/2; the other 1/2 passes to brothers and sisters[3] equally, or their issue *per stirpes.* If no brothers or sisters or their issue, all to the surviving parent.

No Spouse, Child(ren), or Parents:
REAL ESTATE AND PERSONALTY: All to brothers and sisters[3] equally, or their issue *per stirpes.* If none, 1/2 each to maternal and paternal kindred[3] (grandparents and their descendants).

---

[1] Including adopted children, and posthumous children and other descendants.
[2] Advancements to child *or any heir* deducted from intestate share.
[3] Where collateral kindred of the whole and half blood survive, those of the half blood takes half shares. If only half bloods survive, they take whole portions.

Utah

Spouse and Child(ren)[1]:
REAL ESTATE AND PERSONALTY: If all the children[2] are children of the surviving spouse, the spouse takes the first $56,000 (includes $6,000 homestead allowance), plus 1/2 of the balance of the estate. If some of the children are not children of the surviving spouse, the spouse takes 1/2 of the

estate. In either case, the children share equally, the issue of any deceased child sharing *per stirpes*.

No Spouse, but with Child(ren):
REAL ESTATE AND PERSONALTY: All to the children[2] equally, or their issue *per stirpes*.

Spouse and No Child(ren):
REAL ESTATE AND PERSONALTY: First $106,000 (includes $6,000 homestead allowance), plus 1/2 the balance to the spouse; other 1/2 of balance to the parents equally, or the survivor. If neither parent survives, all to the spouse.

No Spouse or Child(ren), but with Parents:
REAL ESTATE AND PERSONALTY: All to the parents equally, or the survivor.

No Spouse, Child(ren), or Parents:
REAL ESTATE AND PERSONALTY: All to brothers and sisters[3] equally, or their issue *per stirpes*. If none, 1/2 each to maternal and paternal grandparents or their descendants, *per stirpes*. If none, to the next of kin[3] in equal degree.

---

[1] Including adopted and posthumous children.
[2] Advancements to child or other descendants deducted from intestate share.
[3] Kindred of the half blood inherit equally with those of the whole blood in the same degree.

Vermont

Spouse and One Child[1]:
REAL ESTATE: 1/2 to the spouse; 1/2 to the child[2] or its issue.

PERSONALTY: 1/3 to the spouse; 2/3 to the children[2] equally, or their issue *per stirpes*.

Spouse and Child(ren):
REAL ESTATE AND PERSONALTY: 1/3 to the spouse; 2/3 to the children[2] equally, or their issue *per stirpes*.

No Spouse, but with Child(ren):
REAL ESTATE AND PERSONALTY: All to the children equally, or their issue *per stirpes*.

Spouse and No Child(ren):
REAL ESTATE AND PERSONALTY: First $25,000, plus 1/2 of the balance to the spouse;[3] other 1/2 of the balance to the parents equally, or the survivor. If neither parent survives, this 1/2 of balance goes to brothers and sisters[4] equally, or their issue *per stirpes*. If none, this 1/2 of balance goes to the next of kin[4] in equal degree. If none, all to the spouse.

No Spouse or Child(ren), but with Parents:
REAL ESTATE AND PERSONALTY: All to the parents equally, or the survivor.

No Spouse, Child(ren), or Parents:
REAL ESTATE AND PERSONALTY: All to brothers and sisters[3] equally, or their issue *per stirpes*. If none, to the next of kin[3] in equal degree.

---

[1] Including adopted children.
[2] Advancements to child or other descendants deducted from intestate share.
[3] In the alternative, spouse may elect to take a 1/3 dower interest in decedent's real property.
[4] Kindred of the half blood inherit equally with those of the whole blood in the same degree.

Virginia

Spouse and Child(ren)[1]:
REAL ESTATE AND PERSONALTY: All to the spouse, unless one or more of the children or their descendants are not children or descendants of the surviving spouse, in which case 1/3 to the spouse; balance to the children[2] equally, or their issue *per stirpes*.

No Spouse, but with Child(ren):
REAL ESTATE AND PERSONALTY: All to the children[2] equally, or their issue *per stirpes*.

Spouse and No Child(ren):
REAL ESTATE AND PERSONALTY: All to the spouse.[3]

No Spouse, or Child(ren), but with Parents:
REAL ESTATE AND PERSONALTY: All to the parents equally, or the survivor.[3]

No Spouse, Child(ren), or Parents:
REAL ESTATE AND PERSONALTY: All to brothers and sisters[4] equally, or their issue *per stirpes*. If none, 1/2 each to paternal and maternal kindred. First to grandmothers and grandfathers equally, or the survivor. If none, to uncles and aunts[4] and their descendants. If no paternal (maternal) kindred, then all to maternal (paternal) kindred.[4]

---

[1] Including adopted children, posthumous children or other heirs, and children born as a result of artificial insemination.
[2] Advancements to child or other descendants deducted from intestate share.
[3] If an unmarried intestate dies without issue, owning real property derived by inheritance or gift from a parent, such property passes to kindred of that parent. If no such kindred, to kindred of other parent.
[4] Collateral kindred of the half blood inherit only half shares if kindred of the whole blood survive; if only collaterals of the half blood survive, lineal ancestors, if any, take double portions.

Washington

Spouse and Child(ren)[1]:

COMMUNITY PROPERTY: All to the spouse.

SEPARATE PROPERTY: 1/2 to the spouse; 1/2 to the children equally, or to their issue *per stirpes*.

No Spouse, but with Child(ren):

REAL ESTATE AND PERSONALTY: All to the children[2] equally, or their issue *per stirpes*.

Spouse and No Child(ren):

SEPARATE PROPERTY: 3/4 to spouse; 1/4 to parent or parents, or their issue.[3] If no parent or issue of parent, then all to the spouse.

COMMUNITY PROPERTY: All to the spouse.

No Spouse, or Child(ren), but with Parents:

REAL ESTATE AND PERSONALTY: All to the parents equally, or the survivor.

No Spouse, Child(ren), or Parents:

REAL ESTATE AND PERSONALTY: All to brothers and sisters[4] equally, or their children *per stirpes*. If none, then to grandparents[5] or their issue.

---

[1] Including adopted and posthumous children.
[2] Advancements to child or other descendants deducted from intestate share.
[3] Kindred of the half blood inherit equally with those of the whole blood in the same degree.
[4] However, if an unmarried intestate dies while a minor, that portion of his estate derived by inheritance from a parent descends to his brothers and sisters equally, or their issue *per stirpes*.
[5] If both maternal and paternal grandparents or a survivor are alive, 1/2 each to the maternal and paternal kindred.

West Virginia

Spouse and Child(ren)[1]:

REAL ESTATE: Life estate in 1/3 to spouse; balance to the children[2] equally, or their issue *per stirpes*.

PERSONALTY: 1/3 to the spouse; 2/3 to the children equally, or their issue *per stirpes*.

No Spouse, but with Child(ren):

REAL ESTATE AND PERSONALTY: All to the children equally, or their issue *per stirpes*.

Spouse and No Child(ren):

REAL ESTATE AND PERSONALTY: All to the spouse.

No Spouse, or Child(ren), but with Parents:

REAL ESTATE AND PERSONALTY: All to the parents equally, or the survivor.

No Spouse, Child(ren), or Parents:

REAL ESTATE AND PERSONALTY: All to brothers and sisters equally, or their issue *per stirpes*. If none, 1/2 each to paternal and maternal kindred. First to grandmothers and grandfathers equally, or the survivor. If none, to uncles and aunts and their descendants *per stirpes*. If no paternal (maternal) kindred, then to maternal (paternal) kindred.

---

[1] Including adopted and posthumous.
[2] Advancements to child or *any heir* deducted from intestate share.

Wisconsin

Spouse and One Child[1]:

REAL AND PERSONAL PROPERTY: If the child is the surviving spouse's child as well, the spouse takes the first $25,000, plus 1/2 of the balance of the estate. If the child is not the surviving spouse's child, the spouse takes 1/2 of the estate. In either case, the child takes the balance, or his issue shares *per stirpes*.

Spouse and Children:

REAL AND PERSONAL PROPERTY: If all of the children are children of the surviving spouse, the spouse takes the first $25,000, plus 1/3 of the balance of the estate. If some of the children are not children of the surviving spouse, the spouse takes 1/3 of the estate. In either case, the children share equally, the issue of any deceased child sharing *per stirpes*.

No Spouse, but with Child(ren):

REAL ESTATE AND PERSONALTY: All to the children[2] equally, or their issue *per stirpes*.

Spouse and No Child(ren):

REAL ESTATE AND PERSONALTY: All to the spouse.

No Spouse, or Child(ren), but with Parents:

REAL ESTATE AND PERSONALTY: All to the parents equally, or the survivor.[3]

No Spouse, Child(ren), or Parents:

REAL ESTATE AND PERSONALTY: All to brothers and sisters[4] equally, or their issue *per stirpes*. If none, all to the grandparents, or the survivor. If none, all to the next of kin in equal degree.

---

[1] Including adopted and posthumous children.
[2] Advancements to child or other heirs deducted from intestate share.
[3] However, if an unmarried intestate dies while a minor, that

portion of his estate derived by inheritance from a parent descends to his brothers and sisters equally, or their issue *per stirpes*.

⁴ Kindred of the half blood inherit equally with those of the whole blood in the same degree.

Wyoming

Spouse and Child(ren)[1]:

REAL ESTATE AND PERSONALTY: ½ to the spouse;[2] ½ to the children[3] equally, or their issue *per stirpes*.

No Spouse, but with Child(ren):

REAL ESTATE AND PERSONALTY: All to the children[3] equally, or their issue *per stirpes*.

Spouse and No Child(ren):

REAL ESTATE AND PERSONALTY: First $20,000, plus ¾ of the balance to the spouse;[2] the other ¼ of the balance to the parents equally, or

the survivor. If neither parent survives, this ¼ of balance to brothers and sisters[4] equally, or their issue *per stirpes*. If none, all to the spouse.

No Spouse or Child(ren), but with Parents:

REAL ESTATE AND PERSONALTY: All to the parents, brothers, and sisters[4] equally, the issue of any deceased brother or sister sharing *per stirpes*.

No Spouse, Child(ren), or Parents:

REAL ESTATE AND PERSONALTY: All to brothers and sisters[4] equally, or their issue *per stirpes*. If none, to the grandfather, grandmother, uncles and aunts[4] or their issue *per stirpes*.

---

[1] Including adopted and posthumous children.

[2] The homestead passes separately to the spouse.

[3] Advancements to child deducted from intestate share.

[4] Collateral kindred of the half blood take only a half-share if collaterals of the whole blood survive.

Summaries of the State Death Tax Laws for Each State*

This section contains summaries of the death tax laws of each state. Because tax laws are constantly changing, reference should be made to your state statutes by your local attorney.

ALABAMA
Type of Tax

Credit estate tax.

If all of a resident decedent's property is taxable in Alabama, the tax equals the maximum federal credit for state death taxes. There is no independent Alabama computation. Where a resident decedent leaves property not taxable in Alabama (such as realty or tangible personalty located outside the state), the Alabama tax generally bears the same ratio to the federal credit as decedent's Alabama property bears to the whole gross estate. Deductions are apportioned unless identified with specific property. A deduction traceable to specific Alabama property apparently may be taken in full, while the estate can take no part of a deduction identified with specific non-Alabama property. Any necessary computations by the Alabama department of revenue are based upon the figures shown in the decedent's federal estate tax return, a duplicate of which must be filed with the department by the executor. If the federal estate tax is increased, an amended federal estate tax return must be filed with the department, which will recompute the Alabama credit tax.

Payment

The tax is due and payable on or before 9 months after decedent's death. Time for payment may be extended (not exceeding 10 years) in hardship cases, in which event interest at the same rate set by the U.S. Secretary of the Treasury is assessed from the due date. There is no discount for early payment.

Ultimate Tax Burden

The tax is to be paid by the personal representative of the deceased, who is made liable for such payment. A statute provides for payment from residuary estate, even as to the tax assessed against property which does not pass to the personal representative, unless decedent's will provides otherwise.

Nonresident Decedents

Property of nonresident decedents dying subject to the tax includes "real estate or tangible personal property located within this state, or other item of personal property or interest therein lawfully subject to the imposition of an estate tax by the State of Alabama." However, the Act specifically exempts moneys, credits, securities and other intangibles not employed in carrying on a business

---

within the state, if the state of domicile extends a similar exemption to Alabama residents. Proportional exemptions are allowed nonresident decedents.

ALASKA
Type of Tax

Credit estate tax.

If all of a decedent's property is taxable in Alaska, the tax equals maximum federal credit for state death taxes. As to the estates of resident decedents who leave property located in another state, the tax is equal to the same proportion of the federal credit allowable as the Alaska property bears to the entire estate.

Payment

The tax is due and payable on or before 15 months after decedent's death. Time for payment may be extended (not exceeding five years) in hardship cases, in which event interest at 7% is assessed from the due date. There is no discount for early payment.

Ultimate Tax Burden

Each distributee or beneficiary bears his proportion of the tax unless decedent's will provides otherwise. The personal representative is made personally liable for payment if distribution of the estate is made before the tax is paid.

Nonresident Decedents

Property of nonresident decedents subject to the tax includes real and tangible personal property located in Alaska. Also, intangible personal property having a business situs as well as stocks, bonds, debentures, notes and other securities or obligations of Alaska corporations are subject to the tax. The Alaska law, however, provides an exemption for personal property, except tangible personal property having an actual situs in the state, of a nonresident decedent if his state of domicile extends a similar exemption to Alaska residents.

ARIZONA
Type of Tax

1. Credit estate tax. 2. Generation-skipping transfer tax.

If all of a decedent's property is taxable in Arizona, the tax equals maximum federal credit for state taxes. As to the estates of resident decedents who leave property located in another state, the tax is equal to the same proportion of the federal credit allowable as the Arizona property bears to the entire state.

Payment

The tax is due and payable 9 months after death. However, the Department of Revenue, with the Attorney General's approval, may abate small tax balances if the administration costs exceed the amount of the tax due. Whether or not an extension of payment is granted, interest, at the rate of 12% per annum, is assessed from expiration of 9 months after death. Payment can be extended either by obtaining an extension of payment on the federal tax due or upon a showing of good cause to the Commissioner. A penalty, not exceeding 25% of the tax, is assessed at the rate of 5% of the tax per month if the tax is not paid when the return, including any extension, is due.

Ultimate Tax Burden

Paid from residuary estate, unless decedent's will provides otherwise. The executor or administrator, together with sureties, is made personally liable for failure to pay the tax.

Nonresident Decedents

Real property and tangible personal property within the state is subject to the tax. Intangible personal property of nonresident decedents is not taxed.

Generation-Skipping Transfer Tax

Arizona has enacted a generation-skipping transfer tax. The Arizona tax is imposed upon all generation-skipping transfers, as defined in Ch. 13 of Subdivision B of the Internal Revenue Code, which occur on or after December 31, 1979. The tax affects real property situated in Arizona, tangible personal property actually located within Arizona, and intangible personal property owned by a trust having its principal place of administration in Arizona at the time of the generation-skipping transfer.

The tax is computed by multiplying the maximum credit allowable under IRC §2602, subsection (c), by a fraction, the numerator of which is the value of that portion of the property transferred in the generation-skipping transfer which is subject to Arizona credit estate tax and the denominator of which is the value of all the property (whether or not subject to Arizona credit estate tax) included in the generation-skipping transfer.

The taxpayer is required to file with the Arizona Department of Revenue a duplicate of his or her federal generation-skipping tax return on or before the last day prescribed for filing the federal return. Payment of the tax is also due on or before the last day prescribed for filing the federal return. However, the Department of Revenue, with the Attorney General's approval, may abate small tax balances if the administration costs exceed the amount of tax due.

ARKANSAS
Type of Tax

Credit estate tax.

If all of resident decedent's property is taxable in Arkansas, the tax equals maximum federal credit for state death taxes. As to estates of resident decedents who leave property located in another state, the tax is equal to the same proportion of the federal credit allowable as the Arkansas property bears to the entire estate. If the other state has a reciprocal provision which exempts property of nonresidents, the entire federal credit allowable is paid to Arkansas.

Payment

The tax is due and payable 9 months after the death of decedent unless an extension is granted, in which case interest at 10% per annum is assessed from due date. In case of deficiency, interest at 1/2 of 1% per month is charged, which figure is doubled if the deficiency resulted from negligence or fraud. No discount for early payment. The executor is required to file a return in all cases where the gross estate at the death of a citizen or resident of the U.S. exceeds $325,000 (1984), $400,000 (1985), $500,000 (1986), and $600,000 (1987 and thereafter) if a portion of the property is located in Arkansas. For a nonresident alien, the amount is $600,000.

Ultimate Tax Burden

Each distributee or beneficiary bears his proportion of the tax unless decedent's will provides otherwise. The personal representative is made personally liable for payment if distribution of the estate is made before the tax is paid.

Nonresident Decedents

All property, real and personal, tangible and intangible, located in Arkansas, is subject to the tax. The tax is an amount equal to the proportion of federal credit allowed for death taxes that the Arkansas property bears to the entire estate. An exemption is extended to all the property, real or personal, of a nonresident decedent who died resident of a state extending a similar exemption to Arkansas residents. The exemption is limited to such proportion of $100,000 as the Arkansas property bears to the entire estate.

CALIFORNIA
Type of Tax

1. Credit estate tax. 2. Generation-skipping transfer tax.

Whenever a federal estate tax is payable to the United States, there is imposed a California estate tax equal to the portion, if any, of the maximum allowable amount of the Credit for State Death Taxes, allowable under the applicable federal estate tax law, which is attributable to property located in the State of California. However, the estate tax imposed may not result in a total death tax liability to the State of California and the United States in excess of the death tax liability to the United States which would result if this section were not in effect.

In a case where a decedent leaves property having a situs in California and leaves other property having a situs in another state or states, the portion of the maximum state death tax credit allowable against the federal estate tax on the total estate by the federal estate tax law which is attributable to the property having a situs in California is determined in the following manner:

(a) For the purpose of apportioning the maximum state death tax credit, the gross value of the property is that value finally determined for federal estate tax purposes.

(b) The maximum state death tax credit allowable is multiplied by the percentage which the gross value of property having a situs in California bears to the gross value of the entire estate subject to federal estate tax.

(c) The product determined pursuant to subdivision (b) is the portion of the maximum state death tax credit allowable which is attributable to property having a situs in California.

"Estate" or "property" means the real or personal property or interest therein of a decedent or transferor, and includes all of the following:

(a) All intangible personal property of a resident decedent within or without the state or subject to the jurisdiction thereof.

(b) All intangible personal property in California belonging to a deceased nonresident of the United States, including all stock of a corporation organized under the laws of California or which has its principal place of business or does the major part of its business in California or of a federal corporation or national bank which has its principal place of business or does the major part of its business in California, excluding, however, savings accounts in savings and loan associations operating under the authority of the Division of Savings and Loan or the Federal Home Loan Bank board and bank deposits, unless those deposits are held and used in connection with a business conducted or operated, in whole or in part, in California.

Payment

The tax is due and payable at the date of the decedent's death. The tax is delinquent at the expiration of nine months from the date on which it becomes due and payable, if not paid within that time.

The tax does not bear interest if it is paid prior to the date on which it otherwise becomes delinquent. However, if that tax is paid after that date, that tax bears interest at the rate of 12% per annum from the date it became delinquent and until it is paid.

If the personal representative has obtained an extension of time for filing the federal estate tax return, the state filing is likewise extended.

If the return is not filed within the time period specified or the extension specified, then the personal representative must pay, in addition to the interest provided, a penalty equal to 5% of the tax due, for each month, or portion thereof, during which that failure to file continues, not exceeding 25%, unless it is shown that such failure is due to reasonable cause. If a similar penalty for failure to timely file the federal estate tax return is waived, that waiver constitutes reasonable cause.

Ultimate Tax Burden

The tax is payable by the personal representative to the extent of assets subject to his or her control. Liability for payment of the tax continues until the tax is paid.

Generation-Skipping Transfer Tax

California has enacted a generation-skipping transfer tax based on the federal generation-skipping transfer tax. The California tax is imposed on every generation-skipping transfer as defined by Ch. 13 of Subdivision B of the Internal Revenue Code, when the original deemed transferor is a California resident, or the real or personal property is located in California.

The tax equals the amount of the credit for state legacy taxes under Code §2602 of the federal generation-skipping provisions. A proportional reduction in the amount of the tax is permitted when any of the transferred property is real property in another state or personal property with a business situs in another state that imposes a tax payment for which credit is given against the federal generation-skipping transfer tax.

A return is required to be filed with the California Controller, when a return must be filed under the federal law. Payment is due on the date of a taxable distribution or termination as determined by the applicable federal generation-skipping tax provisions.

COLORADO
Type of Tax

1. Credit estate tax. 2. Generation-skipping transfer tax.

A tax in the amount of the federal credit is imposed on the gross estate of every domiciliary. If all of a domiciliary's property is taxable in Colorado, the tax equals the maximum federal credit for state death taxes. A domiciliary's real and tangible personal property located outside Colorado is not taxable. Intangible personal property is subject to tax regardless of where situated, except real property in a personal trust and such real property is located outside the state. Where Colorado domiciliaries have property taxable in other states, the Colorado tax is the amount of the federal credit minus the lesser of (1) the death tax paid to other states which is allowed as a credit against the federal estate tax, or (2) the federal credit multiplied by the proportion that the value of the domiciliary's gross estate less the value of the property of a domiciliary that is included in the domiciliary's gross estate bears to the value of the domiciliary's gross estate.

Payment

The person required to file a federal return shall file a return for the tax due and a copy of the federal return with the state department of revenue. The return is due within the time allowed for filing the federal tax return, including any extensions of filing time. Payment of the tax is due on or before the date the return is due. Election may be made to pay the tax in installments under the same guidelines as provided for a similar manner of payment of the federal tax.

If the tax is not paid within 9 months after the date of the decedent's death, the unpaid portion bears interest from such due date at the legal rate on late payments, regardless of any extension of time to pay the tax or election to pay the tax in installments. Additionally, absent reasonable cause, failure to file the return when due (including extensions) results in a penalty of 5% of the tax per month up to a 25% total.

Ultimate Tax Burden

The person required to file a return is directed to pay the tax. Both the person to whom the property is transferred and the person required to file are personally liable.

Nondomiciliary Decedents

Nondomiciliary decedents who are residents of the United States are taxed on the transfer of all real property located within the state and upon all tangible personal property located within the state. Intangibles having an actual or business situs within the state shall not be taxed. The tax is equal to the federal credit multiplied times a fraction, consisting of the value of the property located in the state which is included in the decedent's gross estate as the numerator and the decedent's entire gross estate as the denominator.

Generation-Skipping Transfer Tax

Colorado has enacted a generation-skipping transfer tax based on the federal generation-skipping transfer tax. The Colorado tax is imposed on every generation-skipping transfer as defined by Ch. 13 of Subdivision B of the Internal Revenue Code, when the real or tangible personal property is located in Colorado or intangible personal property is owned by a trust whose principal place of administration is within Colorado.

The tax is divided by multiplying the maximum amount of the credit for state legacy taxes under Code §2602 of the federal generation-skipping provisions by the proportion that the value of the aforementioned Colorado located property bears to the total value of property in the generation-skipping transfer.

A return is required to be filed when a return must be filed under the federal law. Payment is due on or before the date the return is due.

CONNECTICUT
Type of Tax

1. Inheritance tax. 2. A surtax of 30% of the inheritance tax. 3. A second additional surcharge of 10% of the inheritance tax. 4. Credit estate tax.

Exempted Property

Joint checking, savings, savings and loan, or credit union accounts, and United States war or saving bonds, are exempt if they aggregate less than $5,000; a fraction of the excess is taxable (see "Jointly Owned Property"). Property is exempt if transferred to the United States, or to any state, territory, or subdivision thereof; to any organization in trust to care for cemetery lots; or to any body formed for charitable, religious, educational, scientific, literary, or historical purposes, and organized in Connecticut or any state which grants reciprocity.

Taxable Property

IN GENERAL: The tax is imposed upon all real property and all tangible personal property within Connecticut, and all intangible personalty of Connecticut, residents wherever located.

DOWER OR STATUTORY SUBSTITUTE: Dower does not exist, but the surviving spouse's statutory share is taxable.

CONTEMPLATION OF DEATH: Such transfers are taxed. Transfers made within three years of decedent's death are presumed to have been made in contemplation of death.

TRANSFERS EFFECTIVE AT OR AFTER DEATH: If decedent gave property to another but reserved income or enjoyment, or a reversionary interest greater than 5%, or a power to revoke, alter, or amend, the property is taxed in his estate.

If decedent created a trust during his lifetime, and would have been an heir of the trust's terminal beneficiary, Connecticut holds that he retained a reversionary interest. The trust corpus, less any vested life interest, is taxable in his estate.

In the case of a joint bank account, Connecticut has held that such accounts are not taxable in their entirety as transfers intended to take effect in possession and enjoyment at or after death where the decedent did not intend the accounts to pass only at death, the decedent and the survivor both had access, and knew they had access to the funds in the account, and the account funds were occasionally used for common purposes.

JOINTLY OWNED PROPERTY: The statute exempts the first $5,000 in joint savings, including co-owned United States savings bonds and joint bank, savings-and-loan, and credit-union accounts. The balance of property held jointly with the right of survivorship is taxable to the extent of decedent's interest therein, to be determined by dividing the value of the property by the number of joint owners. Tenancies by the entirety are not specifically mentioned in the present statute, but they have been ruled taxable in the same manner as other joint property.

POWER OF APPOINTMENTS: Transfer of property after December 31, 1969 by the exercise or nonexercise of a power of appointment is taxable as if the property had belonged absolutely to the donee of the power and had passed by his will.

LIFE ESTATES AND ANNUITIES: Taxable at values based on the American Men's Ultimate Tables of Mortality, and 4% interest.

LIFE INSURANCE: Proceeds of policies payable to named beneficiaries, to a trustee under an inter vivos or testamentary trust, or to the estate are not taxable. Government life insurance is entirely exempt. Where life insurance polices payable to a named beneficiary are assigned as collateral security for a debt, the proceeds do not become a part of decedent's taxable estate, even though partly used to satisfy the debt. Also, the debt is a deductible estate item.

EMPLOYEE BENEFIT PLANS: Benefits payable to decedent's beneficiaries (other than his estate) from a qualified noncontributory employee plan are not taxable. Any portion of benefits attributable to the employee's contributions under a contributory plan, however, are taxable. Social Security, Railroad Retirement, Retired Serviceman's Family Protection Plan, and Survivor Benefit Plan benefits are exempt.

Deductions

Funeral expenses, costs of administration, executor's commissions, attorney's fees, debts which constitute lawful claims against the estate, unpaid mortgages, property taxes that were a lien at death, income taxes accrued prior to death.

Items specifically declared *nondeductible* include the federal estate tax and death taxes payable to other states, realty maintenance costs accrued subsequent to death, interest on obligations of decedent or the estate accrued subsequent to death, property taxes except as above, income taxes accrued subsequent to death, and taxes assessed and expenses incurred upon real estate located outside the state.

Valuation

IN GENERAL: Generally property is valued at its fair market value on the date of decedent's death. However, a chose in action reduced to possession within one year of decedent's death is its value as of the date of death plus any subsequent gain. The latter rule does not apply to corporate or government stocks or bonds or to accrued income after decedent's death.

SPECIAL USE VALUATION: Real property used as farmland may be valued as farmland if the farmland: (1) was transferred to class AA, A, or B beneficiaries, (2) belonged to the decedent or one of the designated beneficiaries for five of eight years immediately preceding decedent's death, and (3) was used by the decedent or the designated beneficiaries for active and substantial farming or agricultural operations for five of the eight years immediately prior to the decedent's death.

Exemptions

(Allowed for in following tax rate table. Note that the exemptions are allowed to the entire class, and not to the individuals within the class.)

	Amount of Exemption
Class AA:	
Husband or wife	$100,000 (For the class)
Class A:	
Parent, adoptive parent, grandparent, lineal or adopted descendant, legally adopted child and its lineal descendants	20,000 (For the class)
Class B:	
Husband or wife of natural or adopted child, widow or widower of deceased child, stepchild, brother or sister (natural or adoptive) of the full or half-blood or descendant thereof	6,000 (For the class)
Class C:	
All others	1,000 (For the class)

Tax Rates*

VALUE OF PROPERTY PASSING TO CLASS		CLASS AA		CLASS A	
From	*To*	*Tax on Col. 1*	*Rate on Excess*	*Tax on Col. 1*	*Rate on Excess*
$ 20,000	$ 25,000	$ 0	—%	$ 0	2.8%
25,000	100,000	0	—%	140	4.2%
100,000	150,000	0	4.2%	3,290	4.2%
150,000	250,000	2,100	5.6%	5,390	5.6%
250,000	400,000	7,700	7.0%	10,990	7.0%
400,000	600,000	18,200	8.4%	21,490	8.4%
600,000	1,000,000	35,000	9.8%	38,290	9.8%
1,000,000	Balance	74,200	11.2%	77,490	11.2%

VALUE OF PROPERTY PASSING TO CLASS		CLASS B		CLASS C	
From	*To*	*Tax on Col. 1*	*Rate on Excess*	*Tax on Col. 1*	*Rate on Excess*
$ 1,000	$ 6,000	$ 0	—%	$ 0	11.2%
6,000	25,000	0	5.6%	560	11.2%
25,000	50,000	1,064	7.0%	2,688	12.6%
50,000	150,000	2,814	7.0%	5,838	12.6%
150,000	250,000	9,814	8.4%	18,438	14.0%
250,000	400,000	18,214	9.8%	32,438	15.4%
400,000	600,000	32,914	11.2%	55,538	16.8%

| 600,000 | 1,000,000 | 55,314 | 12.6% | 89,138 | 18.2% |
| 1,000,000 | Balance | 105,714 | 14.0% | 161,938 | 19.6% |

* Includes 40% surtax on regular rates.

Payment

The tax is due at the death of the decedent, and payable within 9 months, at which time interest begins to run at the rate of 15% per annum, for any tax becoming due on or after July 1, 1980, but not later than June 30, 1981, and 12% per annum thereafter. Extensions will be automatically granted, unless the commissioner files a copy of an order denying or modifying the extension requested within sixty (60) days after his receipt of an application for extension. There is no discount for early payment. If an extension is granted, the tax shall bear interest at the rate of 11¼% per annum for any tax becoming due on or after July 1, 1980, but not later than June 30, 1981, and 9% per annum thereafter until the end of the extension; and after such extension expires at 15% for any tax becoming due on or after July 1, 1980, but not later than June 30, 1981, and 12% per annum thereafter until fully paid. The additional estate tax and the credit estate tax are subject to the same deadlines, rules and interest rates, except the commissioner may extend the time for payment of the credit estate tax, with or without interest, for such period as he may determine when good cause is shown.

Ultimate Tax Burden

The beneficiaries and the personal representative are personally liable for the tax, to the extent of the value of the property received by them. Federal and state estate taxes are apportioned among the beneficiaries, in the absence of a contrary stipulation in the will. Where a trust is created, or other temporary interest given, the estate tax is paid from the corpus.

Nonresident Decedents

Nonresidents are taxed on the transfer of real property and tangible personal property located within the state. There is no tax on the intangibles of nonresidents. Specific deductions are allowed to nonresident decedents. Exemptions allowed are the same as those allowed residents. Nonresidents are not subject to the additional estate tax.

DELAWARE
Type of Tax

1. Inheritance tax. 2. Credit estate tax.

Exempted Property

Transfers for charitable, religious, educational, hospital, historical or library purposes, or for the public benefit and improvement, are exempt from the tax.

Taxable Property

IN GENERAL: The gross estate of a resident decedent includes the value of all the decedent's real property located in Delaware and all of his or her personal property, wherever located, except tangible personalty having a situs outside Delaware. The gross estate of a nonresident decedent includes the value of all real and tangible personal property having a situs in Delaware.

DOWER OR STATUTORY SUBSTITUTE: Taxable.

CONTEMPLATION OF DEATH: The value of property given away by the decedent within 6 months of his or her death is includable in the decedent's gross estate unless the executor overcomes the presumption that such property was transferred in contemplation of death. There is no presumption that a transfer was made in contemplation of death if it was made more than 6 months before the transferor's death.

TRANSFERS EFFECTIVE AT OR AFTER DEATH: Property transferred by the decedent, reserving possession or enjoyment of the income therefrom, is taxable.

JOINTLY OWNED PROPERTY: The tax is imposed as if the property (including joint bank accounts and tenancies by the entirety) was owned absolutely by the decedent and devised by him to the survivors, except such portion as the survivors can show belonged originally to them. However, for up to $200,000 of the value of real property owned by the decedent and his or her surviving spouse as tenants by the entirety and personal property jointly owned by the decedent and his or her surviving spouse, one-half the value of such property shall be conclusively presumed to have been acquired from the decedent by the surviving spouse for an adequate and full consideration.

POWERS OF APPOINTMENT: Property passing under a general power of appointment is taxable in the appointor's estate.

LIFE ESTATES AND PRIVATE ANNUITIES: Taxable at values based upon United States Life and Actuarial Tables 1939–1941, with 3½% interest.

LIFE INSURANCE AND ANNUITY CONTRACTS: Life insurance (including Government life insurance) is taxable if payable to the estate, but exempt if payable to named beneficiaries. The value of a survivor's annuity generally is taxable to the extent the annuity is attributable to contributions made by the decedent or his or her employer. However, there is an exception to this rule for annuities, the value of which is excludable from the decedent's federal gross estate under Code §2039 is exempt. There is also an exception for annuities sponsored by any state or political subdivision.

REVOCABLE TRANSFERS: The gross estate includes the value of any property the decedent gave away during life if the decedent retained the power, exercisable at his or her death, to alter, amend or revoke the gift, or if the decedent relinquished such a power in contemplation of death and died within 6 months thereafter.

Deductions

Funeral and administration expenses, claims against the estate, unpaid mortgages on property included in the estate. Furthermore, there is a deduction, in general, for property included in the decedent's gross estate where such property was subject to the Delaware inheritance tax in a prior decedent's estate if the prior decedent died within two years of the decedent in question; the deduction is equal to the value of the property at the time of the prior decedent's death. Federal and state death taxes are not deductible.

Valuation

Property is valued at its market value on the date of decedent's death. A special use valuation is permitted for certain farm and ranch property.

Exemptions

(Allowed for in following Tax Rate Table.)

	Amount of Exemption
Class A:	
Husband or wife	$70,000
Class B:	
Grandparent, parent, child by birth, wife or widow of son, husband or widower of daughter, legally adopted child, lineal descendant of decedent	3,000
Class C:	
Brother or sister of the whole or half blood, or descendant of such brother or sister; aunt or uncle, or descendant of aunt or uncle	1,000
Class D:	
All others	None

Tax Rates

SHARE		CLASS A		CLASS B	
From	*To*	*Tax on Col. 1*	*Rate on Excess*	*Tax on Col. 1*	*Rate on Excess*
$ 0	$ 3,000	$ 0	—	$ 0	—
3,000	25,000	0	—	0	1%
25,000	50,000	0	—	220	2%
50,000	70,000	0	—	720	3%
70,000	75,000	0	2%	1,320	3%
75,000	100,000	100	2%	1,470	4%
100,000	200,000	600	3%	2,470	5%
200,000	Balance	3,600	4%	7,470	6%

SHARE		CLASS C		CLASS D	
From	*To*	*Tax on Col. 1*	*Rate on Excess*	*Tax on Col. 1*	*Rate on Excess*
$ 0	$ 1,000	$ 0	—	$ 0	10%
1,000	25,000	0	5%	100	10%
25,000	50,000	1,200	6%	2,500	12%
50,000	100,000	2,700	7%	5,500	14%
100,000	150,000	6,200	8%	12,500	16%
150,000	200,000	10,200	9%	20,500	16%
200,000	Balance	14,700	10%	28,500	16%

Credit for Gift Tax

There is a credit against the inheritance tax, equal in amount to the Delaware gift tax paid on any lifetime gift made by the decedent that is included in his or her estate. In general, the credit is applied against the tax imposed on the share of the beneficiary of the gift property, unless the decedent's will provides otherwise.

Payment

The inheritance tax is due and payable within 9 months of the date of the decedent's death. If not paid within 9 months, interest at the rate of 1% per month begins to run. The additional estate tax is due and payable within 15 months from date of death, after which interest of 1% per month is assessed; the tax and interest is prorated among the beneficiaries in the absence of a contrary stipulation in the will. There is no discount for early payment.

The Secretary of Finance, upon written request, may extend the time for payment of the inheritance or credit estate tax for a reasonable period.

Ultimate Tax Burden

The tax is paid by the executor or administrator, who deducts a share from each legacy or devise before distribution. By statute, the estate tax is apportioned among the beneficiaries with the tax assessed against a trust or other temporary interest paid from the corpus, unless the decedent's will otherwise directs.

Nonresident Decedents

The real and tangible personal property of non-resident decedent is taxed if located within the state. Full exemptions are allowed. Intangibles of nonresidents are not subject to the tax. The additional estate tax is not imposed upon the estates of nonresidents.

DISTRICT OF COLUMBIA
Type of Tax

1. Inheritance tax. 2. Credit estate tax.

Exempted Property

Property transferred exclusively for public or municipal purposes to the United States or the District of Columbia, or exclusively for charitable, religious or educational purposes, is exempt.

Taxable Property

IN GENERAL: The tax is imposed upon the transfer, in trust or otherwise, of all property, real or personal, tangible or intangible, having a taxable situs within the District of Columbia. A partnership interest in out-of-state property is taxable.

DOWER OR STATUTORY SUBSTITUTE: Taxable.

CONTEMPLATION OF DEATH: Such transfers are taxed. There is a presumption that transfers made within two years prior to death were made in contemplation of death, unless proven otherwise.

TRANSFERS EFFECTIVE AT OR AFTER DEATH: Transfers made by decedent, to take effect in possession or enjoyment at or after death, or reserving income or the right to designate those who shall enjoy the possession thereof or income therefrom, are taxable.

JOINTLY OWNED PROPERTY: Taxed on value ascertained by dividing the value of the property by the number of joint owners. One-half the property held in tenancy by the entirety is taxable.

POWERS OF APPOINTMENT: Transfers of property by exercise or nonexercise of a power of appointment are taxed as transfers from the donee of the power.

LIFE ESTATES AND PRIVATE ANNUITIES: Taxed at values based on the American Experience Table of Mortality, and 5% interest.

LIFE INSURANCE AND ANNUITY CONTRACTS: Proceeds of policies are taxable if (a) payable to the estate, or (b) taken out to provide for payment of inheritance or other taxes, or to benefit the estate, or (c) made payable to a named beneficiary who has predeceased the insured, or (d) the policies are annuities upon which the decedent received benefits during his lifetime, and upon which the full value did not terminate with his death, or (e) the policies were written by the United States Government, and any of the above provisions apply. Otherwise, death proceeds are exempt.

EMPLOYEE BENEFIT PLANS: Survivor benefits under employees' retirement plans or Civil Service Act are not taxable. However, a widow's annuity under the Retired Servicemen's Family Protection Act is taxable.

Deductions

Funeral expenses (to $1,000, unless will provides for more), cost of monument or memorial (if provided for by will), administration expenses, executor's commissions, attorney's fees, expenses incurred in distributing estate, taxes accrued before death, debts of decedent, federal estate tax.

Valuation

Property is valued at its market value on the date of decedent's death.

Exemptions

(Allowed for in following Tax Rate Table.)

	Amount of Exemption
Class A:	
Father, mother, husband, wife, children by blood, legally adopted children, lineal descendants or lineal ancestors	$5,000
All other	1,000

Tax Rates

SHARE		CLASS A		ALL OTHERS	
		Tax on	Rate on	Tax on	Rate on
From	To	Col. 1	Excess	Col. 1	Excess
$ 0	$ 1,000	$ 0	—	$ 0	—
1,000	5,000	0	—	0	5%
5,000	25,000	0	1%	200	5%
25,000	50,000	200	2%	1,200	10%
50,000	100,000	700	3%	3,700	14%
100,000	500,000	2,200	5%	10,700	18%
500,000	1,000,000	22,200	6%	82,700	22%
1,000,000	Balance	52,200	8%	192,700	23%

Payment

The tax is due and payable within 18 months of death of the decedent. If no personal representative is appointed, and the value of the share exceeds the personal exemption, the beneficiary is required to pay the tax on personal property within 9 months after death of the decedent, and the tax on real estate within 18 months. The tax on contingent remainders may be deferred until the estate vests in the remainderman. If not paid when due, the tax bears interest at ½ of 1% per month from such date. There is no discount for early payment. The additional estate tax is payable within 17 months of death of decedent, unless the time for payment of the federal tax is extended, in which case the estate tax is payable within 60 days from the expiration of the extended period.

Ultimate Tax Burden

The personal representative is directed to collect the tax from the beneficiary, or to withhold it from the share passing, before making distribution. If no personal representative is appointed, the beneficiary must pay the tax. Willful failure to pay may be punished by a fine of not more than $1,000 and imprisonment not exceeding one year.

Nonresident Decedents

The tax is imposed upon all property, real or personal, tangible or intangible, having a taxable situs within the District. However, intangibles of nonresidents (except nonresident aliens), not employed in carrying on a business within the District, are deemed to have their taxable situs in the state of domicile, and intangibles held by a trustee residing in the District are not deemed to have a taxable situs there by reason of such residence. The rates and exemptions are the same as those allowed to residents. The additional estate tax is not imposed upon nonresidents' estates.

FLORIDA
Type of Tax

1. Credit estate tax. 2. Generation-skipping transfer tax.

If all of a resident decedent's property is taxable in Florida, the tax equals the maximum federal credit for state death taxes. A resident's real and tangible personal property located outside Florida is not taxable. Intangible personal property is subject to tax regardless of where situated. Where Florida residents have property taxable in other states, the Florida tax is the amount of the federal credit minus the death taxes paid to other states. Any necessary computation by the Florida Comptroller, in his capacity as Commissioner of Revenue, is based upon the figures shown in the decedent's federal estate tax return, an executed copy of which must be filed with him by the executor. If the federal estate tax is increased, the executor must notify the Commissioner and pay any consequent increase in the Florida tax with ½% interest per month from the due date of the tax. Where the federal estate tax is overpaid and would result in an overpayment of the Florida tax, the Commissioner upon presentation of proof to his satisfaction will refund the overpayment without a formal claim for such.

Payment

The tax generally is due and payable 9 months after the decedent's death; however, payment of the tax may be deferred for up to 5 years (in 1-year periods) in cases of undue hardship.

If the tax is not paid when due, the unpaid portion bears interest at the rate of 1% per month. In the case of an extension of time to pay the tax, interest is charged at the rate of 1% per month.

Ultimate Tax Burden

The duty of payment is imposed upon the personal representative. State and federal taxes attributable to the probate estate are, in the absence of contrary stipulation in the will, charged against the residuary estate. If the assets of the residuary estate are insufficient to pay the taxes, the recipients of the balance of the estate must bear a share of the tax. In addition, recipients of nonprobate property must bear their share of the taxes.

Nonresident Decedents

Nonresident decedents who are residents of the United States are taxed on the transfer of all real property located within the state, upon tangible personal property located within the state, upon intangible personal property having a business situs within the state, and upon stocks, bonds, debentures, notes and other securities or obligations of corporations organized under the laws of the state.

Generation-Skipping Transfer Tax

Florida has enacted a generation-skipping transfer tax based on the federal generation-skipping transfer tax. The Florida tax is imposed on every generation-skipping transfer as defined by Ch. 13 of Subdivision B of the Internal Revenue Code, when the original transferor is a Florida resident, or the property transferred is real or personal property located in Florida.

Where the original transferor is a Florida resident upon the date of original transfer, the tax equals the amount of the credit for state legacy taxes under Code §2602 of the federal generation-skipping provisions, to the extent such credit exceeds the amount of taxes on the same transfer actually paid to other states. For nonresidents, where the property transferred includes real or personal property in Florida, a proportional reduction in the amount of the tax is permitted when any of the property transferred is real or personal property subject to the imposition of a tax payment from another state for which credit is allowed against the federal generation-skipping transfer tax.

The taxpayer is required to file with the Florida Department of Revenue a duplicate of his or her federal generation-skipping tax return on or before the last day prescribed for filing the federal return. Payment of the tax is also due on or before the last day prescribed for filing the federal return.

GEORGIA
Type of Tax

Credit estate tax.

If all of a resident decedent's property is taxable in Georgia, the tax equals the maximum federal credit for state death taxes. Where a resident decedent leaves property not taxable in Georgia (such as realty or tangible personalty located outside the state), the Georgia tax generally bears the same ratio to the federal credit as decedent's Georgia property bears to the whole gross estate. A resident decedent's intangible personal property is subject to tax regardless of where situated. Deductions allowable under the federal estate tax law and attributable to Georgia property will reduce the Georgia tax. Any necessary computations by the Georgia authorities are based upon the figures shown in the decedent's federal estate tax return, a duplicate of which must be filed with the state by the executor. If the federal estate tax is increased or decreased, an amended federal estate tax return must be filed with the state authorities, who will recompute the Georgia credit tax.

Payment

Payment is due on or before the date the return is due. The return is due within the time allowed for filing the federal estate tax return, including any extensions of filing time, but not to exceed 6 months after the federal filing date (not including extensions). In case of a late payment, interest is charged at a rate of 9% per annum.

Ultimate Tax Burden

Borne by the residuary estate, unless decedent's will provides otherwise.

Nonresident Decedents

All property located within the state is taxable. Included is intangible personal property, if it ac-crues out of or as an incident to property owned or a business conducted by a nonresident or his agent in Georgia. The Georgia tax generally bears the same ratio to the Federal credit as decedent's Georgia property bears to the entire gross estate. An example is a decedent's interest in a partnership located and doing business in Georgia. A flat 2% transfer tax on property of nonresident decedents has never been enforced, due to an Attorney-General's opinion that it is illegal. Provision is made for the reciprocal exemption of intangibles.

HAWAII
Type of Tax

Credit estate tax.

A tax in an amount equal to the federal death tax credit is imposed on the transfer of the taxable estate of every resident. If any property of a resident is subject to a death tax imposed by another state for which a federal credit is allowed, and if the tax imposed by the other state is not qualified by a reciprocal provision allowing the property to be taxed in the state of the decedent's domicile, the amount of the tax due under the law of Hawaii is credited with the lesser of: (1) the amount of the death tax paid the other state and credited against the federal estate tax; or (2) an amount computed by multiplying the federal credit by a fraction, the numerator of which is the value of the property subject to the death tax imposed by the other state, and the denominator of which is the value of the decedent's gross estate.

Payment

Payment is due on or before the date the return is due. The return is due within the time allowed for filing the federal estate tax return, including any extensions of filing time.

Ultimate Tax Burden

The duty of payment is based on the personal representative.

Nonresident Decedents

A tax is imposed on the transfer of the taxable estate located in Hawaii of every nonresident. The tax is computed by multiplying the federal death tax credit by a fraction, the numerator of which is the value of the property located in Hawaii, and the denominator of which is the value of the decedent's gross estate. The transfer of the property of a nonresident is exempt from tax to the extent that the property of residents is exempt from taxation under the laws of the state in which the nonresident is domiciled, except that real property located in Hawaii, a beneficial interest in a land trust which owns real property located in Hawaii, and tangible personal property located in Hawaii remain subject to tax.

IDAHO
Type of Tax

1. Inheritance tax. 2. Credit estate tax. 3. Generation-skipping transfer tax.

Exempted Property

One-half the community property belongs to the surviving spouse, and hence is exempt. In addition, such part of the remaining half as passes to the spouse is exempt. Decedent's separate property passing to the spouse is not exempt. Transfers to corporations, trusts, etc., exempted by law from taxation or to organizations or trusts engaged in benevolent, charitable, educational, public or like work not for profit, are exempt if for use within the state or if the organization or trust exists under the laws of the state. Transfers to similar out-of-state organizations or trusts are exempt if the state of domicile exempts transfers to Idaho organizations or trusts. Property passing to any person in Class A is exempt if the property was received, within 4 years prior to death, by decedent from another decedent of Class A, and provided a transfer tax was paid at that time.

Taxable Property

IN GENERAL: The tax is imposed upon all real property and all tangible personal property within Idaho, and all intangible personalty of Idaho residents wherever located.

DOWER OR STATUTORY SUBSTITUTE: Dower and curtesy have been abolished. Property passing under the homestead laws is taxable.

CONTEMPLATION OF DEATH: Transfers of property, or any interest therein, or income therefrom, in trust or otherwise, made by a resident in contemplation of death, are taxable. There is no presumption; the burden is on the state to prove contemplation of death.

TRANSFERS EFFECTIVE AT OR AFTER DEATH: Property transferred by decedent, reserving income or possession, is taxable. Revocable trusts (while not mentioned in the statute) are taxable, under the general rule.

JOINTLY OWNED PROPERTY: Community property is exempt, except such part of the decedent's half as does not pass to the surviving spouse. Property held in the joint names of two or more persons, with the right of survivorship, is taxable except to extent that the survivor can show original ownership. Bank accounts held jointly with the spouse are presumed to be community property, rather than held in joint tenancy. Tenancy by the entirety does not exist in Idaho since it is a community property state.

POWERS OF APPOINTMENT: Property passing by the exercise or nonexercise of a general power of appointment is taxed as if the property had belonged absolutely to the donee of the power, and had passed by his will. A power to consume, invade or appropriate property for the donee or other beneficiary, which is limited by an ascertainable standard relating to the health, education, support or maintenance of the donee or beneficiary is not a power of appointment, and therefore not a taxable transfer.

LIFE ESTATES AND PRIVATE ANNUITIES: Taxed at values ascertained by application of the tables and interest rate as set forth in I.R.C. §2031.

LIFE INSURANCE AND ANNUITY CONTRACTS: No statutory provision, but the general rule is that life insurance payable to the estate is taxable, while that payable to named beneficiaries is not. Government insurance is treated the same as other life insurance. Presumably, an annuity contract is valued in the same manner as a life estate.

EMPLOYEE BENEFIT PLANS: No statutory provision as to the taxation or exclusion therefrom of survivor benefits.

Deductions

Expenses of funeral and last illness (not to exceed $500 for memorial), debts and claims, state and municipal taxes which are liens at death, costs of administration, attorney's fees, executor's commissions, federal estate tax, state inheritance and estate taxes. Death taxes, funeral expenses and cost of administration (including attorney's and executor's fees) are deducted from decedent's one-half of the community property; community debts, expenses of last illness, and state and municipal taxes charged against community property, are deducted from the entire community estate.

Valuation

Property is valued at its market value on the date of decedent's death. Effective January 1, 1981, agricultural property which qualifies under Code §2032A can be valued according to use rather than market value.

Exemptions*

(Subtract from value of share before applying table.)

Class A:	Amount of Exemption
Surviving spouse	Unlimited
Minor child	$50,000
Lineal issue, lineal ancestors, adopted or mutually acknowledged children or their issue	30,000
Class B:	
Brothers, sisters, issue of brothers and sisters, wife or widow of son, husband of daughter	10,000
Class C:	
Uncles, aunts, their descendants	10,000
Class D:	
All others	10,000

* For transfers from decedents on or after January 1, 1981, should the total personal exemptions provided herein be less than the maximum amount of the federal estate tax exemption equivalent provided by the federal unified credit, property in the amount of the maximum exemption equivalent will be exempt from inheritance taxation. This additional exemption will be allocated among the distributees of the estate in the same proportion as the personal exemption provided each distributee bears to the total amount of such exemptions. Should a distributee's exemptions exceed the value of the property transferred thereto, the excess is allocated in the same manner as the additional exemption.

Tax Rates

SHARE IN EXCESS OF EXEMPTION		CLASS A		CLASS B	
From	To	Tax on Col. 1	Rate on Excess	Tax on Col. 1	Rate on Excess
$ 0	$ 25,000	$ 0	2%	$ 0	4%
25,000	50,000	500	4%	1,000	6%
50,000	100,000	1,500	6%	2,500	8%
100,000	200,000	4,500	8%	6,500	12%
200,000	500,000	12,500	10%	18,500	16%
500,000	Balance	42,500	15%	66,500	20%

SHARE IN EXCESS OF EXEMPTION		CLASS C		CLASS D	
From	To	Tax on Col. 1	Rate on Excess	Tax on Col. 1	Rate on Excess
$ 0	$ 25,000	$ 0	6%	$ 0	8%
25,000	50,000	1,500	9%	2,000	14%
50,000	100,000	3,750	12%	5,500	20%
100,000	200,000	9,750	15%	15,500	30%
200,000	500,000	24,750	20%	45,500	30%
500,000	Balance	84,750	25%	135,500	30%

Payment

The tax is due and payable within nine months from the death of the decedent. If not paid within 9 months, interest at 12% per annum is assessed from date of death. A discount of 5% is allowed if the tax is paid within 6 months of death. The tax on remainder interests may be deferred if bond is filed. Installment payments are permitted over a period of ten years or less at 8% interest upon a showing of reasonable cause.

Ultimate Tax Burden

The executor or administrator is made liable for payment, and is directed to collect the amount of the tax from the beneficiary, or deduct it from the share, before making distribution.

Nonresident Decedents

The tax is imposed on the transfer, by nonresident decedents, of all real property, and tangible personal property within the state, and all intangible personal property having a business situs in the state. A reciprocal exemption of intangibles is provided for decedents who died while residents of states not taxing intangibles of Idaho residents. Full exemptions are allowed to nonresidents.

Generation-Skipping Transfer Tax

Effective retroactively to January 1, 1977, where a federal generation-skipping transfer tax is payable to the U.S. and the inheritance tax payable to Idaho is less than the maximum state tax credit allowed by the federal generation-skipping transfer tax, a tax equal to the difference between this maximum credit and the inheritance tax payable is imposed. Where no inheritance tax is payable to Idaho, but a federal generation-skipping transfer tax is payable to the U.S., a tax in the amount of this maximum credit is imposed.

ILLINOIS
Type of Tax

Credit estate tax.

A tax is imposed upon the transfer of the estate of every decedent leaving an estate which is subject to the federal estate tax and which has, in whole or in part, a taxable situs in Illinois. The tax is equal to the maximum tax credit allowable for state death taxes against the federal estate tax imposed with respect to the portion of the decedent's estate having a taxable situs in Illinois, it being the purpose and intent of the tax to impose only such taxes as may be necessary to give Illinois the full benefit of the maximum tax credit allowable against the federal estate tax. If only a portion of a decedent's estate has a taxable situs in Illinois, the maximum tax credit is determined by multiplying the entire amount of the credit allowable against the federal estate tax for state death taxes by the percentage which the value of the portion of the decedent's estate which has a taxable situs in Illinois bears to the value of the entire estate.

The estate of a decedent consists of the property included in his gross estate (as defined by the Internal Revenue Code) for federal estate tax purposes, and the value of such property is that determined for federal estate tax purposes. With respect to estates of deceased residents, all property included in the gross estate of the decedent for federal estate tax purposes has a taxable situs in Illinois, excepting real estate and tangible personal property physically situated in another state.

Payment

The tax is due and payable at the time required for the filing of the federal estate tax return. Interest at the rate of 10% per annum is charged and collected for such time as the tax is not paid.

Ultimate Tax Burden

All executors, administrators and trustees are personally liable for the payment of the taxes and interest, and where there are proceedings for collection of taxes, the executors, administrators and trustees are personally liable for the expenses, costs, and fees of collection. They have full power to sell so much of the property of the decedent as will enable them to pay the tax, in the same manner as they may be enabled to do by law, for the payment of duties of their testators and intestates.

Nonresident Decedents

With respect to estates of decedents not residents of Illinois but residents of a state or territory of the United States, only real estate and tangible personal property physically situated in Illinois has a taxable situs in Illinois. With respect to estates of decedents who are not residents of a state or territory of the United States, real estate within Illinois, tangible personal property having an actual situs in Illinois, and intangible personal property evidenced by instruments physically present in Illinois have a taxable situs in the state for purposes of this tax.

INDIANA
Type of Tax

1. Inheritance tax. 2. Credit estate tax.

Exempted Property

All charitable transfers exempt under the federal estate tax [I.R.C., §2055(a)] are exempt under the Indiana inheritance tax. The widow's statutory allowance is not subject to inheritance tax. Property transferred to a cemetery association is exempt if used for cemetery purposes.

Taxable Property

IN GENERAL: The tax is imposed upon all real property and all tangible personal property within Indiana, and all intangible personalty of Indiana residents wherever located. A renounced legacy isn't subject to inheritance tax to the renouncer.

DOWER OR STATUTORY SUBSTITUTE: Dower has been abolished in Indiana. The statutory substitute, however, is taxable.

CONTEMPLATION OF DEATH: Transfers made within two years of death are presumed in contemplation of death unless the contrary is shown.

TRANSFERS EFFECTIVE AT OR AFTER DEATH: Property transferred by decedent reserving income or power to alter, amend, revoke or terminate, or where such power relinquished in contemplation of death, is taxed.

JOINTLY OWNED PROPERTY: Real estate held as tenants by the entireties is not taxed. Other property held jointly with right of survivorship is taxed in full, except that part proven as originally contributed by the survivor.

POWERS OF APPOINTMENT: Property passing under the exercise of a power of appointment is not taxed in the estate of the donee of the power.

LIFE ESTATES AND PRIVATE ANNUITIES: Taxed at values ascertained by reference to the federal estate tax tables set out in Subdivision E, Section 2 of this Service. If, at the time of death, a surviving spouse has been entitled for life to income from a property interest that was the subject of a previous transfer exempt from inheritance tax, then the value of the property interest at the surviving spouse's death is subject to state inheritance tax as if it were a transfer of property owned by the surviving spouse.

LIFE INSURANCE AND ANNUITY CONTRACTS: Proceeds of policies payable to the estate are taxable, but those payable to named beneficiaries or to a trust for the use of persons other than the estate are not. In practice, insurance proceeds used to meet inheritance taxes are not taxed. The proceeds of refund annuity contracts are taxable at commuted values as of date of death. Government life insurance is no doubt treated the same as other life insurance.

EMPLOYEE BENEFIT PLANS: Lump-sum death benefits payable under Social Security and Railroad Retirement Acts are exempt. Presumably, survivor benefits payable under these Acts are also exempt. The lump-sum death benefit which equals the employee's contribution under a publicly financed retirement plan is taxable. Also, that part of the value of a survivorship annuity attributable to the employee's contribution is taxable. Survivorship benefits under a plan in which the employee had nonforfeitable rights are taxable. Payments or annuities described in I.R.C., §2039(a) are exempt to the same extent as excluded under I.R.C., §2039.

Deductions

Funeral expenses (not exceeding $1,000 for a memorial); administration expenses, including reasonable attorney's fees; commissions of executors, administrators and trustees; debts of the decedent which are claims against the estate; the value of any property received by the surviving spouse in satisfaction of the $8,500 allowance; real and personal property taxes due at decedent's death; income taxes to the date of death; inheritance and transfer taxes paid or payable to other jurisdictions on tangible personal property (but not federal estate taxes); mortgages and special assessments (deducted from value of property). In the case of transfers other than by will, intestate laws, or trust (not to include taxable jointly owned property with right of survivorship), deductions are limited to liens, to which the transfer is subject and transfer taxes paid or payable to other jurisdictions on intangible personal property.

Valuation

Property is valued at its market value at the time of its appraisal date. The appraisal date is the date used to value the property for federal estate tax purposes.

Exemptions

(Deduct from value of property transferred before applying tax rates.)

Class A:	Amount of Exemption
Spouse	Value of all property transferred
Natural or legally adopted child under age 21	$10,000*
Natural or legally adopted child at least age 21 . . .	5,000
Parent	5,000
Other lineal ancestor or lineal descendant	2,000

Class B:	
Brother, sister, descendant thereof, wife or widow of son, husband or widower daughter	500

Class C:	
All others	100

In lieu of this exemption, an exemption is allowed for orphaned children under 20, equal to the product of $5,000 and the difference between the orphan's age and 21.

Tax Rates

VALUE OF PROPERTY INTERESTS TRANSFERRED		CLASS A	
From	To	Tax on Col. 1	Rate on Excess
$ 0	$ 25,000	$ 0	1%
25,000	50,000	250	2%
50,000	200,000	750	3%
200,000	300,000	5,250	4%
300,000	500,000	9,250	5%
500,000	700,000	19,250	6%
700,000	1,000,000	31,250	7%
1,000,000	1,500,000	52,250	8%
1,500,000	Balance	92,250	10%

SHARE IN EXCESS OF EXEMPTION		CLASS B	
From	To	Tax on Col. 1	Rate on Excess
$ 0	$ 100,000	$ 0	7%
100,000	500,000	7,000	10%
500,000	1,000,000	47,000	12%
1,000,000	Balance	107,000	15%

SHARE IN EXCESS OF EXEMPTION		CLASS C	
From	To	Tax on Col. 1	Rate on Excess
$ 0	$ 100,000	$ 0	10%
100,000	1,000,000	10,000	15%
1,000,000	Balance	145,000	20%

Payment

A discount of 5% is allowed if paid within one year of due date, which is usually date of death. Interest at 10% per annum is imposed from due date if tax is not paid within 18 months; subject to reduction to 6% where delay unavoidable or where bond given. The tax on remainder interests may be deferred.

The additional tax to absorb the federal credit, if levied, is payable within two years of death. Interest at 10% per annum is imposed for period overdue.

Ultimate Tax Burden

Borne by each beneficiary individually and deducted from his share by the executor or administrator, unless the beneficiary pays over his portion of the tax.

Nonresident Decedents

Taxed on real and personal property within the jurisdiction of Indiana. The same rates and exemptions apply as in the case of a resident estate. Deductions are limited to any taxes or liens against the property to which the transfer relates except, where property is transferred by will or intestate laws, if the total estate is insufficient to pay debts, all unpaid debts allowed by the state of the decedent's domicile are allowable deductions.

IOWA

Type of Tax

1. Inheritance tax. 2. Credit estate tax. 3. Generation-skipping transfer tax.

Exempted Property

Transfers to organizations existing under the laws of Iowa for charitable, religious or educational associations, or humane societies, or to veterans' organizations, are exempt. Provision is made for reciprocal exemption of property passing to charitable, etc., organizations organized under the laws of other states. No tax, if estate after deduction of liabilities, does not exceed $10,000.

Taxable Property

IN GENERAL: The tax is imposed upon all real property and all tangible personal property within Iowa, and all intangible personalty of Iowa residents wherever located.

DOWER OR STATUTORY SUBSTITUTE: Taxable.

CONTEMPLATION OF DEATH: Such transfers are taxed. Transfers made within three years of death are presumed in contemplation of death unless the contrary is shown.

TRANSFERS EFFECTIVE AT OR AFTER DEATH: Transfers intended to take effect in possession or enjoyment after death are taxable. Revocable trusts, though not mentioned in the statute, are held to be taxable.

JOINTLY OWNED PROPERTY: One-half of jointly held property of decedent and surviving spouse is not subject to tax. Also not subject to tax in any additional part which can be shown to have originally belonged to the survivor and never to have belonged to the decedent. United States savings bonds registered to decedent and his spouse as co-owners are taxed as jointly owned property.

POWERS OF APPOINTMENT: A gift of a general power of appointment is taxed at the donor's death as though the property passed to the donee. A gift of a special power is taxed as though the donee received a life estate; the remainder interests are taxed to those who take if the power is not exercised.

LIFE ESTATES AND PRIVATE ANNUITIES: Taxed at values by using current, commonly used tables of mortality and actuarial principles, pursuant to regulations prescribed by the director of revenue. Where a remainderman defers payment of his tax until the life tenant dies, he must pay tax upon the full value of the remainder then.

LIFE INSURANCE AND ANNUITY CONTRACTS: Proceeds of policies payable to the estate are taxable. Proceeds payable to named beneficiaries are exempt. Government life insurance has been held exempt since 1928. Proceeds of a refund annuity contract have been held taxable as a transfer taking effect in possession and enjoyment at death.

EMPLOYEE BENEFIT PLANS: Any portion of installment payments received by decedent's beneficiary under an employee's pension or retirement plan that is subject to Iowa income tax is exempt from inheritance tax.

Deductions

Funeral expenses, family allowance, costs of administration, debts and claims, local and state taxes accrued before the decedent's death, federal estate taxes, unpaid mortgages (deducted from value of property), and for resident decedents the costs of sale of real or personal property included in the estate. A credit against the inheritance tax is allowed to Class 1 and Class 2 beneficiaries for property received upon which an Iowa inheritance tax had been paid by decedent within two years of his death. The surviving spouse may deduct one-third of the tax for persons dying after 1985 and before 1987; two-thirds of the tax for persons dying after 1986 and before 1988; and the entire tax for persons dying after 1987.

Valuation

Property is valued at its market value on the date of decedent's death or on the alternate valuation date established under the federal estate tax law, unless a special valuation of qualified real property is elected under state law.

Exemptions

(Deduct from value of share before applying table.)

	Amount of Exemption
Class 1:	
Wife or husband	$180,000
Father or mother	15,000
Son or daughter, including adopted or illegitimate child entitled to inherit	50,000
Class 2:	
Brother, sister, son-in-law, daughter-in-law, stepchild	None
Class 3:	
Any person not in Class 1 or 2	None

Class 4:

Gifts to out-of-state institutions for charitable, etc.,
purposes . . . .   None*

Class 5:

Transfers to firms, societies or corporations organized
for profit . . . .   None

* But see reciprocal exemption provision under "Exempted Property."

Tax Rates

SHARE IN EXCESS OF EXEMPTION		CLASS 1		CLASS 2	
From	*To*	*Tax on Col. 1*	*Rate on Excess*	*Tax on Col. 1*	*Rate on Excess*
$ 0	$ 5,000	$ 0	1%	$ 0	5%
5,000	12,500	50	2%	250	5%
12,500	25,000	200	3%	625	6%
25,000	50,000	575	4%	1,375	7%
50,000	75,000	1,575	5%	3,125	7%
75,000	100,000	2,825	6%	4,875	8%
100,000	150,000	4,325	7%	6,875	9%
150,000	Balance	7,825	8%	11,375	10%

SHARE IN EXCESS OF EXEMPTION		CLASS 3		CLASS 4	
From	*To*	*Tax on Col. 1*	*Rate on Excess*	*Tax on Col. 1*	*Rate on Excess*
$ 0	$ 50,000	$ 0	10%	$ 0	10%
50,000	100,000	5,000	12%	5,000	10%
100,000	Balance	11,000	15%	10,000	10%

SHARE IN EXCESS OF EXEMPTION		CLASS 5	
From	*To*	*Tax on Col. 1*	*Rate on Excess*
$ 0	Balance	$ 0	15%

Payment

The tax must be paid, in general, within 12 months of death, at which time interest of 8% begins to run. If extension is granted for hardship, the interest is reduced to 6%. There is no discount for early payment. The additional estate tax is payable in the same manner, and bears the same interest.

Ultimate Tax Burden

The personal representative is directed to collect the amount of the tax from the beneficiary, or to deduct such amount from the bequest, before making distribution. Both the beneficiary and the representative are made personally liable for payment.

Nonresident Decedents

Transfers of real and personal property, tangible or intangible, are taxable if the property is within the state, or is subject to the jurisdiction of the state. Reciprocal exemption of intangibles is provided if the state of domicile levies an inheritance tax. Full exemptions are allowed to nonresident decedents. The additional estate tax applies to the Iowa property of nonresidents, as well as to resident estates.

Generation-Skipping Transfer Tax

Iowa has enacted a generation-skipping transfer tax based on the federal generation-skipping transfer tax. The Iowa tax is imposed on every generation-skipping transfer as defined by Ch. 13 of Subdivision B of the Internal Revenue Code, when the original transferor is an Iowa resident, or the real or personal property is located in Iowa.

The tax equals the amount of the credit for state legacy taxes under Code §2602 of the federal generation-skipping provisions. A proportional reduction in the amount of the tax is permitted when any of the transferred property is real property in another state or personal property with a business situs in another state that imposes a tax payment for which credit is allowed against the federal generation-skipping transfer tax.

A return is required to be filed when a return must be filed under the federal law. Payment is due within twelve months after the deemed transferor's death, if the transfer occurs at that time, or twelve months after the date on which the generation-skipping transfer occurred. If the tax is not paid when due, interest at the rate of 8% per annum is assessed until paid.

The tax is retroactive to any generation-skipping transfer made after 4-30-76, with certain exceptions patterned after the federal exceptions.

KANSAS
Type of Tax

1. Inheritance tax. 2. Credit estate tax.

Exempted Property

Transfers for public, religious, charitable, scientific, literary, educational, or other uses deductible for the federal estate tax under code §2055, are exempt. For the estates of decedents dying after December 31, 1980 and before January 1, 1986, the personal representative may elect to exclude from the decedent's gross estate a portion of the value of qualified real property (i.e. Kansas real property used either as a farm for farming purposes or used in a non-farm trade or business) (See "Qualified Real Property" below).

Taxable Property

IN GENERAL: The tax is imposed on all real property and all tangible personal property within Kansas, and all intangible property of Kansas residents, wherever located.

DOWER OR STATUTORY SUBSTITUTE: Taxable.

CONTEMPLATION OF DEATH: Transfers in contemplation of death are taxable. Transfers made within one year of decedent's death are presumed in contemplation of death. The first $10,000 of property transferred in contemplation of death is exempt, however, unless the property interest is included in the decedent's gross estate, or would have been included if such interest had been retained by the decedent as a retained right or reversionary interest.

TRANSFERS EFFECTIVE AT OR AFTER DEATH: Transfers by decedent intended to take effect in possession or enjoyment after death are taxable. Revocable trusts are also taxable, where enjoyment was subject to change, at the date of decedent's death, through exercise of a power by decedent (along with or in conjunction with another) to alter, amend, revoke or terminate, or where any such power was relinquished during the one-year period prior to the decedent's death.

JOINTLY OWNED PROPERTY: Property held in joint tenancy is taxable, except to the extent of the contribution which the survivor can prove he made. If the property is received by gift, bequest, devise, or inheritance, or in any other manner whereby the interests of the joint tenants is not fixed by law, decedent's interest is determined by dividing the value of the property by the number of joint tenants. Only one-half of a "qualified joint interest," as defined in Code §2040(b), is taxable. Notwithstanding the aforementioned, Code §2040(c) applies to the treatment of those joint interests which it covers for federal estate tax purposes. Where an election is made under Code §2040(d) to have Code §2040(b)(1) apply to a joint interest, the value included in the decedent's gross estate shall be one-half of the value of the joint interest. Tenancy by the entirety property is taxed in the same manner as joint tenancy property.

POWERS OF APPOINTMENT: The transfer of property subject to a power of appointment, or the exercise or relinquishment of a power of appointment is taxable, if the disposition is of such a nature that it would have been includable in decedent's estate, if it were a transfer of his property. The exercise of a power of appointment by creating another power is taxable if under local law an estate, interest, or absolute ownership or power of alienation is postponed or suspended by the exercise of such other power, for a period of ascertainable without regard to the date of the creation of the first power.

LIFE ESTATES AND PRIVATE ANNUITIES: Taxable at values based on American Experience Table of Mortality and 5% compound interest.

LIFE INSURANCE AND ANNUITY CONTRACTS: Insurance payable to the estate is taxable. Proceeds payable to named beneficiaries are taxed, if the decedent possessed any incidents of ownership in the policies at his death, exercisable either alone or in conjunction with another person. Government insurance would appear to be taxable to the same extent as other life insurance. Life insurance payable to named beneficiaries, including a trust for the benefit of beneficiaries other than decedent and his estate, are not taxed. The value of an annuity is includable in the decedent's gross estate to the extent that the decedent contributed to its cost.

EMPLOYEE BENEFIT PLANS: Exempt are employees' trusts, retirement annuity contracts purchased by employers, etc., which qualify under Code §§401(a), 403(a), or 501(a), or Chapter 73 of Title 10 of the U.S. Code, except that portion of such amounts attributable to decedent's contributions and payments is not excluded.

DEDUCTIONS: Funeral expenses, costs of administration, claims against the estate, federal state tax, unpaid mortgages (deducted from the value of property), property exempt from taxation by federal or state law, and uncompensated casualty losses on property, the value of which is included in decedent's gross estate.

Valuation

Property is generally valued at its market value on the date of decedent's death, although the executor or administrator has some flexibility to select alternative valuation dates. However, where a federal estate tax return is required to be filed, property is to be valued on the same date that was elected to value the property for federal estate tax purposes.

SPECIAL USE VALUATION: Real property used as farmland or in a closely-held business or trade may be valued as farmland or as property in a closely-held business use if the real property: (1) constitutes 50% or more of the adjusted gross estate, and (2) was being used for a qualified use, on the date of death, and (3) was acquired or passed from the decedent to a qualified heir; or (1) constitutes 25% of the adjusted gross estate, and (2) was owned by the decedent or a member of his family, used for a qualified use, and there was material participation of the decedent or a member of his family in the business during five of the eight years immediately preceding the decedent's death, and (3) was acquired or passed from the decedent to a qualified heir. The use of this special valuation provision may not reduce the decedent's gross estate by more than $750,000 [Added L. 1978, SB 549, §9]. For decedents dying after December 31, 1980, no special use valuation is permitted the decedent's estate if an election has been made to have the farm or business property excluded from the value of the estate. To qualify for this special use valuation, a similar federal election must be made.

Exemptions

(Deduct from value of Share before applying table.)

	Amount of Exemption
Class A1:	
Surviving Spouse	Unlimited
Class A2:	
Lineal ancestors, lineal descendants, step-children, adopted children, lineal descendants of adopted child, or stepchild, wife or widow of son, husband or widower of daughter, spouse or surviving spouse of adopted child or stepchild, stepparents	$30,000
Class B:	
Brother or Sister	$ 5,000
Class C:	
All other except those in classes A, B and D	None
Class D:	Totally
Charitable organizations	exempt

Tax Rates

SHARE IN EXCESS OF EXEMPTION*		CLASS A1		CLASS A2	
From	To	Tax on Col. 1	Rate on Excess	Tax on Col. 1	Rate on Excess
$ 0	$ 25,000	$ 0	.5%	$ 0	1%
25,000	50,000	125	1 %	250	2%
50,000	100,000	375	1.5%	750	3%
100,000	500,000	1,125	2 %	2,250	4%
500,000	Balance	9,125	2.5%	18,250	5%

SHARE IN EXCESS OF EXEMPTION*		CLASS B		CLASS C	
From	To	Tax on Col. 1	Rate on Excess	Tax on Col. 1	Rate on Excess
$ 0	$ 25,000	$ 0	3 %	$ 0	10%
25,000	50,000	750	5 %	2,500	10%
50,000	100,000	2,000	7.5%	5,000	10%
100,000	200,000	5,750	10 %	10,000	12%
200,000	500,000	15,750	10 %	22,000	15%
500,000	Balance	45,750	12.5%	67,000	15%

* No tax is imposed on a share with a value of $200 or less after all deductions.

In the event that the total of the inheritance taxes imposed upon the estate of the deceased does not equal the amount of the maximum credit allowed by §2011 of the 1954 Internal Revenue Code, as such Code existed on December 31, 1981, and as further amended by the Economic Recovery

Tax Act of 1981 (P. L. 97-34), against the tax imposed on the transfer of the taxable estate of the decedent by §2001 of the 1954 Internal Revenue Code, as such Code existed on December 31, 1981, and as further amended by the Economic Recovery Tax Act of 1981 (P. L. 97-34), whenever the federal estate tax is determined an additional tax is imposed upon the value of the taxable estate of the decedent as of the date of such determination equal to the difference between the total of the tax imposed under Kansas law and the amount of the maximum credit.

In the event that no tax is imposed upon the estate of the deceased, whenever the amount of the tax imposed upon the transfer of the taxable estate of the decedent by §2001 of the 1954 Internal Revenue Code, as such Code existed on December 31, 1981, and as further amended by the Economic Recovery Tax Act of 1981 (P. L. 97-34), is determined, a tax, equal to the amount of the maximum credit allowed against such tax on the transfer of the taxable estate of the decedent by §2011 of the 1954 Internal Revenue Code, as such Code existed on December 31, 1981, and as further amended by the Economic Recovery Tax Act of 1981 (P. L. 97-34), is imposed upon the taxable estate of the decedent as of the date of such determination.

Payment

The tax accrues and is payable within 9 months after decedent's death. If not paid at that time, interest at 18% per annum begins to run from the accrual date, except when the delay is not the fault of the legal representative. In that case, interest runs from the date of the filing of the return.

Ultimate Tax Liability

The personal representative and the beneficiary are made personally liable for payment. The representative is directed to collect the tax from the beneficiary or to deduct it from the share, before making distribution.

Nonresident Decedents

All real and tangible personal property within the state, and all intangibles within the jurisdiction of the state, are taxable. Reciprocal exemption of intangibles is provided if the state of domicile levies an inheritance tax and allows a similar exemption to residents of Kansas. Personal exemptions may be taken in the proportion that the Kansas property bears to the entire estate. The estate of a nonresident may qualify for the special use valuation.

Qualified Real Property

For the estate of decedents dying after December 31, 1980 and before January 1, 1986, the portion of the value of qualified real property which may be excluded from the decedent's gross estate is determined as follows:

VALUE OF QUALIFIED REAL PROPERTY		
From	To	EXCLUSION
$ 0	$250,000	Value of qualified property
250,000	300,000	$250,000 plus 85% of excess over $250,000
300,000	350,000	292,500 plus 60% of excess over $300,000
350,000	400,000	322,500 plus 30% of excess over $350,000
400,000	450,000	337,500
450,000	500,000	337,500 minus 35% of excess over $450,000
500,000	550,000	320,000 minus 70% of excess over $500,000
550,000	835,000	285,000 minus 100% of excess over $550,000
835,000	Balance	0

If the qualified heir, within five years subsequent to the decedent's death and before that heir's own death, disposes of any part of that heir's interest in the property to a nonfamily member or ceases to use that property for its qualified use, an additional tax is imposed on the same equal to what would have been the inheritance tax liability on that heir's interest or portion of interest absent this exclusion. This tax is due within six months after such a disposition or discontinuance of a qualified use.

KENTUCKY
Type of Tax

1. Inheritance tax. 2. Credit estate tax.

Exempted Property

Transfers to charitable, religious or educational institutions are exempt. Transfers to municipalities or public institutions within the state are also exempt. Payments by the federal government to the surviving spouse or heirs of any decedent due to the decedent's war service, and payments to beneficiaries of Retired Serviceman's Family Protection Plan or Survivor Benefit Plan, are exempt, as well.

Taxable Property

IN GENERAL: The tax is imposed upon all real property and all tangible personal property within Kentucky, and all intangible personalty of Kentucky residents wherever located. The interest of a Kentucky resident in a partnership located in another state is exempt from the Kentucky tax if the other state subjects the interest to its state death tax.

DOWER OR STATUTORY SUBSTITUTE: Taxable.

CONTEMPLATION OF DEATH: Transfers made within three years of death are presumed in contemplation of death unless the contrary is shown. A certificate of deposit, jointly owned and obtained within three years prior to death of the joint-owner, will not be presumed in contemplation of death, and tax will apply only to 50% of the transfer.

TRANSFERS EFFECTIVE AT OR AFTER DEATH: Transfers intended to take effect in possession or enjoyment after death, and transfers in trust, which the decedent had reserved power to revoke by will, are taxable.

JOINTLY OWNED PROPERTY: Property held jointly is taxed as if decedent and the survivor had held the property as tenants in common and the survivor had taken the decedent's interest by will. Tenancy by the entirety property is taxed in the same manner.

POWERS OF APPOINTMENT: The exercise or nonexercise of a power of appointment is taxed as though the property had belonged to the donee and passed by his will.

LIFE ESTATES AND PRIVATE ANNUITIES: Taxable at values ascertained by the United States Life Mortality Table, and 4% interest.

LIFE INSURANCE AND ANNUITY CONTRACTS: Proceeds of life insurance payable to the estate are taxable. Proceeds paid to named beneficiaries, including an inter vivos or testamentary trust, are exempt. Proceeds of a matured endowment contract held by the insurance company at time of decedent's death are not life insurance proceeds and thus are subject to inheritance tax. Government life insurance proceeds are exempt.

Annuities have been ruled not within the life insurance exemptions and, therefore, subject to the inheritance tax.

EMPLOYEE BENEFIT PLANS: Exempt are employees' trusts, retirement annuity contracts purchased by employers, etc., which qualify under §401(a), §403 or §501(a) of the Internal Revenue Code, or Chapter 73 of Title 10 of the U.S. Code. One statute exempts railroad retirement benefits.

Deductions

Funeral, monument and cemetery lot maintenance expenses (to $2,500), debts except those secured by property which Kentucky cannot tax, accrued taxes except those on property which Kentucky cannot tax, federal death taxes in the proportion which the net estate in Kentucky subject to federal estate tax bears to the entire net estate subject to federal estate tax, special assessments which constitute liens, cost of administration, attorney's fees, executor's commissions, property transferred to decedent within 5 years prior to death and on which an inheritance tax was paid.

Valuation

IN GENERAL: Property is valued at its market value on the date of decedent's death.

SPECIAL USE VALUATION: Real property used as horticultural or agricultural land may be valued as horticultural or agricultural land if the real property: (1) has been used as such land for five years prior to the decedent's death, (2) has a fair cash value which exceeds 50% of the gross taxable estate, and (3) passes to a qualified heir. This valuation may not reduce the gross estate by more than $500,000.

Exemptions

(Deduct from value of share before applying table.)

		Amount of Exemption
Class A:		
Surviving Spouse		$50,000
Natural or adopted minor or mentally disabled adult child		20,000
Parent, competent adult, natural or adopted child, stepchild, grandchild, stepchild's child, adopted child		5,000
Class B:		
Brother or sister of the whole or half blood, nephew or niece of whole or half blood, aunt, uncle, son-in-law, daughter-in-law		1,000
Class C:		
Educational, religious or other institutions, societies or associations, or to cities, towns, or public institutions (not exempt under K.R.S., §140.060) and all others		500

Tax Rates

SHARE IN EXCESS OF EXEMPTION*		CLASS A		CLASS B	
From	To	Tax on Col. 1	Rate on Excess	Tax on Col. 1	Rate on Excess
$ 0	$ 10,000	$ 0	2%	$ 0	4%
10,000	20,000	200	2%	400	5%
20,000	30,000	400	3%	900	6%
30,000	45,000	700	4%	1,500	8%
45,000	60,000	1,300	5%	2,700	10%
60,000	100,000	2,050	6%	4,200	12%
100,000	200,000	4,450	7%	9,000	14%
200,000	500,000	11,450	8%	23,000	16%
500,000	3,000,000*	35,450	10%	71,000	16%

SHARE IN EXCESS OF EXEMPTION*		CLASS C	
From	To	Tax on Col. 1	Rate on Excess
$ 0	$ 10,000	$ 0	6%
10,000	20,000	600	8%
20,000	30,000	1,400	10%
30,000	45,000	2,400	12%
45,000	60,000	4,200	14%
60,000	100,000	6,300	16%
100,000	200,000	12,700	16%
200,000	500,000	28,400	16%
500,000	3,000,000*	76,700	16%

* Estates of residents of Kentucky having a fair cash value of more than $3,000,000 are not subject to the inheritance tax. They are subject only to an estate tax equal to the federal credit.

Payment

The tax is due and payable at the decedent's death. If not paid within 18 months, interest at 10% is charged from date of accrual and executor must give bond. If delay unavoidable, interest at 6% is charged from the expiration of the 18-month period until cause of delay is removed, then 10% thereafter. A discount of 5% is allowed if the tax is paid within 9 months of death. The additional estate tax is payable in the same manner, and bears interest at the same rates.

Ultimate Tax Burden

The tax is paid by the beneficiary when he receives his share. Both the beneficiary and the personal representative are made personally liable for payment of the tax.

Nonresident Decedents

The tax is assessed against the transfer of all real property and tangible personal property within the state, and all intangibles that have acquired a taxable situs within the state. Provision is made for the reciprocal exemption of intangibles for decedents who died residents of states allowing a similar exemption to Kentucky. Personal exemptions are allowed only in the proportion that the Kentucky property bears to the entire estate. The additional estate tax applies to nonresidents as well as to residents. A statute taxing a nonresident decedent's stock in a Kentucky corporation at a flat 5% rate has been held unconstitutional.

LOUISIANA
Type of Tax

1. Inheritance tax. 2. Credit estate tax.

Exempted Property

Transfers to charitable, educational or religious organizations within the state are exempt. A reciprocal exemption of charitable, etc., transfers is made for states which allow an exemption to such organizations located in other states and territories of the U.S. Transfers to the state of Louisiana or subdivisions thereof for exclusively public purposes are exempt. One-half of the community property is not subject to the tax. The other half is valued after deducting the surviving spouse's usufruct (life estate) from it.

Taxable Property

IN GENERAL: The tax is imposed upon all real property and all tangible personal property within Louisiana, and all intangible personalty of Louisiana residents wherever located.

DOWER OR STATUTORY SUBSTITUTE: No dower, but if there are surviving issue of the marriage, and the decedent's community property is not completely distributed by will, the surviving spouse has a usufruct (life estate) in the part of the community property which the surviving issue inherit. This usufruct is tax-exempt. No homestead exemption.

CONTEMPLATION OF DEATH: Transfers made within one year of death are presumed in contemplation of death unless the contrary is shown.

TRANSFERS EFFECTIVE AT OR AFTER DEATH: The statute contains no provisions for taxing transfers intended to take effect in possession or enjoyment after death. In practice, such transfers are not taxed.

JOINTLY OWNED PROPERTY: Joint estates are not ordinarily recognized in Louisiana. U.S. bonds held in joint ownership are not taxed when purchased with community funds. Neither are they taxed when registered in beneficiary form.

POWERS OF APPOINTMENT: These are unknown to the civil law, and their taxability in Louisiana is an open question. The *common-law* rule is that powers of appointment are taxable in the estate of the donor, and not in that of the donee.

LIFE ESTATES AND PRIVATE ANNUITIES: Taxed at values based on the American Experience Table of Mortality and 6% interest.

LIFE INSURANCE AND ANNUITY CONTRACTS: Proceeds of policies payable to the estate are taxable, but those payable to named beneficiaries are not. If, in a policy payable to the estate, premiums were paid from community funds, only one-half the proceeds are taxable. Government life insurance paid to named beneficiaries is exempt. When paid to decedent's estate, however, it is taxable.

Proceeds of a refund annuity contract payable to a named beneficiary have been held taxable. The Attorney-General has ruled that an annuity is taxable if payment of the proceeds amounts to payment of a fund which the annuitant owned during his lifetime. An annuity purchased by a husband and wife out of community funds, payable to the husband during his life, and thereafter to his wife, is not subject to tax. Any annuity or guaranteed retirement income plan is exempt.

EMPLOYEE BENEFIT PLANS: Amounts received by any beneficiary (other than the estate) under any retirement, pension plan, trust, system or policy are exempt.

Deductions

Funeral expenses, costs of administration, executor's commissions, attorney's fees, debts and claims, unpaid mortgages (these deducted from value of property). If real estate is mortgaged in excess of one-half its value, a further deduction equally 20% of such mortgage is allowed.

If succession problems or substantial community debts render administration of all the community property essential, only half the costs of administering it are deductible. However, the Louisiana Supreme Court found all the administration expenses deductible where the whole community estate was administered, but where the sole purpose of administration was payment of federal and state death taxes.

Valuation

Property may be valued at its market value on the date of the decedent's death, or on an alternate date up to 6 months from the date of death.

Exemptions

(Deduct from value of share before applying table.)

	Amount of Exemption
Class A:	
Direct descendant by blood or affinity, ascendant or surviving spouse	$10,000 (1984)
	$15,000 (1985)
	$20,000 (1986)
	$25,000 (thereafter)
Class B:	
Collateral relation (including brothers, sisters, nephews and nieces by affinity)	1,000

Class C:

All others 500

Tax Rates

SHARE IN EXCESS OF EXEMPTION		CLASS A		CLASS B	
From	*To*	*Tax on Col. 1*	*Rate on Excess*	*Tax on Col. 1*	*Rate on Excess*
$ 0	$20,000	$. . . .	2%	$. . . .	5%
20,000	Balance	400	3%	1,000	7%

SHARE IN EXCESS OF EXEMPTION		CLASS C	
From	*To*	*Tax on Col. 1*	*Rate on Excess*
$ 0	$ 5,000	$. . . .	5%
5,000	Balance	250	10%

Payment

The tax is due and payable within six months after decedent's death unless application for formal administration is made within that period. Where formal administration is applied for within the six-month period, determination of the tax is held in abeyance until after payment of decedent's debts. Unless an extension of time for reasonable cause is granted, interest at .5% per month is charged for each month the tax remains unpaid, beginning with the 7th month after decedent's death and continuing until the 13th month, at which time the rate increases to 1% per month. Where a federal estate tax return must be filed, this is deemed reasonable cause for an extension of time until 15 months after decedent's death.

Ultimate Tax Burden

The personal representative collects the tax from the beneficiary, or deducts it from the amount of the share, before distribution. Both the beneficiary and the personal representative are personally liable for payment.

Nonresident Decedents

Transfers of real property and intangible personal property within the state are taxable. A nonresident's intangible property located outside the state is not taxed. Full exemptions are allowed in the case of nonresident decedents. The additional state tax applies to nonresidents, and is imposed upon all property of the decedent that is taxable for purposes of the inheritance tax.

MAINE

Type of Tax

1. Inheritance tax (phased out by 7-1-86). 2. Credit estate tax.

Inheritance Tax

(Phased Out by 7-1-86)

Exempted Property

Transfers to charitable, religious, benevolent or educational institutions within the state or for use within the state, or to those of other states that extend a similar exemption to Maine institutions, are exempt.

Taxable Property

IN GENERAL: The tax is imposed upon all real property and all tangible personal property within Maine, and all intangible personalty of Maine residents wherever located.

DOWER OR STATUTORY SUBSTITUTE: Dower no longer exists, but the statutory interest of the surviving spouse is taxable.

CONTEMPLATION OF DEATH: Transfers made in contemplation of death are taxable, the presumption being that transfers made within six months before death were so intended. Transfers made more than two years before death are not taxable unless intended to take effect in possession or enjoyment after death.

TRANSFERS EFFECTIVE AT OR AFTER DEATH: Transfers of property in which the decedent reserved income or enjoyment, or the power to revoke, alter, or amend, are taxable.

JOINTLY OWNED PROPERTY: Joint bank accounts, credit union accounts, and joint building and loan shares are taxed to the extent of decedent's contribution. To find the includable portion of any other property held in joint tenancy, divide the property's value by the number of joint tenants, without regard to contribution. Tenancy by the entirety does not exist in Maine. United States savings bonds purchased by the decedent in either co-owner or beneficiary form are subject to inheritance tax.

POWERS OF APPOINTMENT: Property passing by exercise or nonexercise of a limited power of appointment is not taxed in the estate of the donee. It is taxed in the donor's (creator's) estate. However, if property passes by exercise or nonexercise of a general power of appointment, it is taxed as though the donee had owned it absolutely.

LIFE ESTATES AND PRIVATE ANNUITIES: Taxed at values based on the United States life and actuarial tables, founded on the 1940 census, with 4% compound interest.

LIFE INSURANCE AND ANNUITY CONTRACTS: Proceeds payable to the estate are taxable, except where the surviving spouse or issue receive them by bequest or inheritance. Such proceeds passing ultimately to the spouse or issue, and proceeds payable to named beneficiaries, are exempt. Government insurance is treated the same as other insurance.

Since proceeds payable to a named beneficiary are exempt, the amount of premiums paid by decedent-insured within two years of death on a policy owned by another person is not a transfer in contemplation of death.

EMPLOYEE BENEFIT PLANS: Proceeds of qualified employee benefit plans received by decedent's spouse or children are exempt.

Deductions

Costs of administration, debts, funeral expenses, executor's commissions, attorney's fees, federal estate taxes; income, gift or property taxes accrued before death. Specific deductions are allowed to nonresident decedents.

Valuation

Property is valued at its market value on the date of decedent's death.

Exemptions

(Deduct from value of share before applying table)

Class A:	Amount of Exemption
Husband or wife	$50,000
Father, mother, child, adopted child, stepchild, adoptive parent, grandchild who is natural or adopted child of deceased natural or adopted child (if more than one such grandchild, only one exemption for group *per stirpes*)	25,000
Lineal ancestors, wife or widow of natural or adopted son or stepson, husband or widower of natural or adopted daughter or stepdaughter, grandchild who is child of a living son or daughter or stepchild, other lineal descendants	2,000
Class B:	
Brother, half-brother, sister, half-sister, uncle, aunt, nephew, niece, grandnephew, grandniece, cousin	1,000
Class C:	
All others	1,000

Tax Rates*

SHARE IN EXCESS OF EXEMPTION		CLASS A		CLASS B	
From	To	Tax on Col. 1	Rate on Excess	Tax on Col. 1	Rate on Excess
$ 0	$ 25,000	$ 0	5%	$ 0	8%
25,000	50,000	1,250	5%	2,000	8%
50,000	100,000	2,500	6%	4,500	10%
100,000	250,000	5,500	8%	9,500	12%
250,000	Balance	17,500	10%	27,500	14%

SHARE IN EXCESS OF EXEMPTION		CLASS C	
From	To	Tax on Col. 1	Rate on Excess
$ 0	$ 75,000	$ 0	14%
75,000	150,000	10,500	16%
150,000	Balance	22,500	18%

* Where death occurs after June 30, 1981, the total inheritance tax payable is the percentage of the tax otherwise due based on the following schedule:

85% where death occurs after June 30, 1981 and before July 1, 1982

75% where death occurs after June 30, 1982 and before July 1, 1983

65% where death occurs after June 30, 1983 and before July 1, 1984

55% where death occurs after June 30, 1984 and before July 1, 1985

45% where death occurs after June 30, 1985 and before July 1, 1986

No inheritance tax is payable where death occurs after June 30, 1986

Payment

The inheritance tax is due and payable at the end of 12 months from date of death where death occurs before July 1, 1981, and 9 months from date of death where death occurs after June 30, 1981. Extensions may be granted for cause. If not paid when due, interest at 3/4% per month is assessed from due date. A penalty of $5 or 5% of the tax, but not to exceed $25 or 25% of the tax (whichever is greater), is imposed for failure to make payment or file a return on the due date. The penalty is in addition to interest. No discount for early payment. The tax on remainder interests may be deferred, if bond is filed.

Ultimate Tax Burden

The personal representative is directed to collect the tax from the beneficiary before distribution. Both the representative and the beneficiary are made liable for the tax, with interest, until paid.

Nonresident Decedents

Real property and tangible personal property within the state are taxable. Intangibles of nonresidents are not taxed. Exemptions and deductions are allowed in the proportion which the Maine property bears to the entire estate.

Credit Estate Tax

A tax equal to the amount by which the federal credit for state death taxes under Code §2011 exceeds the lesser of (1) the death taxes actually paid to other states, or (2) the proportion of the federal credit as the value of the properties taxed by other states bears to the entire federal gross estate, is imposed on Maine residents.

Payment

The personal representative must pay the tax and file a return within 9 months after the date of the decedent's death. Extensions may be granted for cause. If not paid when due, interest at 3/4% per month is assessed from the due date. Additionally, a penalty of $5 or 5% of the tax, but not to exceed $25 or 35% of the tax (whichever is greater), is imposed for failure to make payment or file a return on the due date. There is no discount for early payment. The tax on remainder interests may be deferred, if bond is filed.

Ultimate Tax Burden

The personal representative is directed to collect the tax from the beneficiary before distribution. Both the representative and the beneficiary are made liable for the tax, with interest, until paid.

Nonresident Decedents

Property of nonresident decedents subject to the tax includes real and tangible personal property located in Maine. For nonresident estates, the Maine tax bears the same proportion to the federal credit as decedent's Maine property bears to the total federal gross estate.

MARYLAND
Type of Tax

1. Inheritance tax. 2. Credit estate tax.

Exempted Property

Transfers to the state or subdivision thereof, or to any corporation, etc., organized in any part of the United States and operated for religious, charitable, etc., purposes, if a substantial part of the activities of such organization are carried on in Maryland, or in any state which likewise exempts transfers to Maryland organizations, are exempt. The family allowance is also exempt.

Taxable Property

IN GENERAL: The tax is imposed upon all real property and all tangible personal property within Maryland, and all intangible personalty of Maryland residents wherever located.

DOWER OR STATUTORY SUBSTITUTE: Dower has been abolished in Maryland. The statutory substitute, however, is taxable.

CONTEMPLATION OF DEATH: Such transfers are taxed. Transfers within two years prior to death are presumed in contemplation of death unless proven otherwise. If decedent and his spouse transferred tenancy-by-the-entirety property in contemplation of his death, one-half the property is taxable.

TRANSFERS EFFECTIVE AT OR AFTER DEATH: Property transferred by decedent, reserving income or enjoyment, or the power to revoke, is taxable. Where decedent reserved a life estate in the transferred property, a tax is payable.

JOINTLY OWNED PROPERTY: Property held jointly with right of survivorship by decedent and any person other than his spouse (including joint bank accounts and United States savings bonds in co-ownership form) is taxable to the extent of decedent's fractional interest. However, property held jointly with right of survivorship (including United States bonds regardless of registration form) by decedent and spouse is exempt.

POWERS OF APPOINTMENT: Property subject to a power of appointment is taxed in the estate of the donor of the power, and not in the donee's estate. Property passing under a power of appointment is considered received from the donor of the power, not the donee.

LIFE ESTATES AND PRIVATE ANNUITIES: Taxed at values ascertained by reference to the federal estate tax tables set out in Subdivision E, Section 2 of this Service. According to the Attorney-General, where a transfer gives a life tenant full power to sell, mortgage, etc., with remainder to another, the remainderman takes a vested interest subject to divestment. If his interest is not divested, he is liable for inheritance tax at the life tenant's death.

LIFE INSURANCE AND ANNUITY CONTRACTS: Insurance payable to the estate is taxable. If payable to named beneficiaries, it is exempt. Government insurance is treated the same as other life insurance.

EMPLOYEE BENEFIT PLANS: Payments and annuities under public and private employee's pension and benefit plans are not subject to tax, if not taxed for purposes of the federal estate tax. However, in the case of public or private employee's pension or benefit plans, the authority to designate the beneficiary or annuities or other payments does not constitute dominion so as to make such interests taxable.

Deductions

Funeral expenses, costs of administration, executor's commissions, attorney's fees, debts, federal estate tax, death taxes paid to other states, unpaid mortgages, property and income taxes accrued before death.

Valuation

Property is valued at its market value on the date of distribution to recipient. Special use valuation is permitted on certain farmland and certain historic properties.

Exemptions

Class 1:
Parent, stepparent, husband, wife, legitimate or adopted child, stepchild, or other lineal descendant, is not taxed if the transfer does not exceed $150. If the share exceeds that amount, there is no exemption.

Class 2:
All others are not taxed if their share does not exceed $150. If their share exceeds that amount there is no exemption.

Tax Rates*

Class 1: 1%

Class 2: 10%

* Where a savings account jointly owned by the decedent and a spouse of a lineal descendant passes to such spouse upon the decedent's death, the tax rates are: 1% of the amount up to $2,000, and 10% on the amount in excess of $2,000. The rate of 1% also applies to the value of a bequest to a corporation of which all the shareholders are lineal descendants of the decedent.

Payment

The tax is due and payable before the personal representative makes distribution of the property, or within 15 months from the date letters of administration are granted. The additional estate tax is due 15 months after decedent's death. Interest at a rate of one-twelfth of the adjusted annual rate of interest established under I.R.C., §6621 (not to exceed 1.25% per month nor be less than 1%) on both taxes begins to run from the due date. No discount for early payment. The tax on remainder interests may be deferred.

Ultimate Tax Burden

The personal representative is required to pay the tax when due. He forfeits his commission if the tax is unpaid 15 months after his appointment. If the beneficiary does not remit his share, the representative is authorized to sell the property.

Nonresident Decedents

All real property and tangible personal property within the state, and all intangible personal property having acquired a business situs in the state, are subject to the tax. The additional estate tax does not apply to nonresidents. Provision is made for reciprocal exemption of intangibles. The only deductions allowed to nonresidents are administration expenses, but full exemptions may be claimed.

MASSACHUSETTS
Type of Tax

1. Estate tax. 2. Credit estate tax. 3. Generation-skipping transfer tax.

Exempted Property

Property received from the federal government by beneficiaries of missing servicemen is exempt from taxation; this law applies to tax years ending on or after February 28, 1961. See also "Taxable Property" and "Deductions" below.

Taxable Property

Taxable property includes all property that would be includable in the federal gross estate, except real and personal property having a situs outside Massachusetts.

Deductions

The same deductions allowable in computing the federal taxable estate generally are allowable in computing the Massachusetts taxable estate. However, the Massachusetts marital deduction is limited to one-half of the Massachusetts adjusted gross estate. (To compute the Massachusetts adjusted gross estate, one first computes the Massachusetts gross estate, which is the federal gross estate less the value of real and personal property having a situs outside Massachusetts. To arrive at Massachusetts adjusted gross estate, one then subtracts the expenses, indebtedness, taxes and losses allowed as deductions by I.R.C., §§2053 and 2054.)

Valuation

Property in the Massachusetts gross estate is valued as of the date of death, or the alternate valuation date provided by federal law, whichever date has been selected for valuing the federal gross estate.

Exemptions

An exemption of $30,000 is allowed to all estates, but if the Massachusetts net taxable estate (which equals the Massachusetts gross estate less: (1) funeral expenses; (2) claims against the estate; and (3) unpaid mortgages) is *less* than $60,000, the exemption is equal to the Massachusetts net estate.

Tax Rates*

| Taxable Estate | | Tax on | Rate on |
From	To	Col. 1	Excess
$ 0	$ 50,000	$ 0	5%
50,000	100,000	2,500	7%
100,000	200,000	6,000	9%
200,000	400,000	15,000	10%
400,000	600,000	35,000	11%
600,000	800,000	57,000	12%
800,000	1,000,000	81,700	13%
1,000,000	2,000,000	107,000	14%
2,000,000	4,000,000	247,000	15%
4,000,000	Balance	547,000	16%

* The tax under this table may not exceed 20% of the amount by which the Massachusetts net estate exceeds $60,000.

Payment

Payment is due within 9 months after death. Certain extensions may be granted. However, if not paid when due, interest of 18% per annum, or such other adjusted rate under Code §6621 that is in effect for the taxable year, is assessed from the due date.

Ultimate Tax Burden

The tax is to be paid by the executor. Transferees of estate assets are liable for the tax to the extent of the value of property they receive if the tax is not paid when due.

Nonresident Decedents

Real property and tangible personal property of a nonresident decedent, if situated in Massachusetts, are subject to the tax. Intangibles of nonresidents are not taxed. The exemption and deductions may be taken only in the proportion that the Massachusetts gross estate bears to the federal gross estate.

MICHIGAN
Type of Tax

1. Inheritance tax. 2. Credit estate tax. 3. A surtax of 1/2 of 1% on the total inheritance and credit estate tax.

Exempted Property

Transfers to charitable, religious, educational or public institutions within the state, or within a state extending a reciprocal exemption to transfers to Michigan institutions, are entirely exempt, as are transfers to persons or corporations exempted from real or personal property taxes. Shares of less than $100 are exempt. Transfers to surviving spouses which qualify for the federal estate tax marital deduction are also exempt.

Taxable Property

IN GENERAL: The tax is imposed upon all real property and all tangible personal property within Michigan, and all intangible personalty of Michigan residents wherever located.

DOWER OR STATUTORY SUBSTITUTE: The Revenue Department taxes a widow's dower interest, although the statute is silent on the point and the Michigan Supreme Court has not decided the question.

CONTEMPLATION OF DEATH: Such transfers are taxed. Transfers made within two years of death are presumed to have been made in contemplation of death, unless the contrary is shown.

TRANSFERS EFFECTIVE AT OR AFTER DEATH: The tax extends to transfers intended to take effect in possession or enjoyment after death. A revocable trust is not taxable if, during decedent's lifetime, one or more beneficiaries became eligible to receive the trust income.

JOINTLY OWNED PROPERTY: Joint bank accounts, United States savings bonds in co-ownership form, and all property held in joint tenancy or in tenancy by the entirety, are *not* taxable.

POWERS OF APPOINTMENT: Property passing by the exercise or nonexercise of a power of appointment is taxable.

LIFE ESTATES AND PRIVATE ANNUITIES: Taxed at values based on special table prepared by the Commissioner of Insurance, and 5% interest. Latest revision of the special table is applicable to decedents dying on and after July 1, 1965.

LIFE INSURANCE AND ANNUITY CONTRACTS: Life insurance payable to the estate is taxable. The Attorney-General has ruled that proceeds payable to a named beneficiary at the death of the insured are not taxable. By statute, proceeds payable to a trustee for the benefit of beneficiaries named in the trust instrument are exempt. Government insurance is probably treated the same as other life insurance.

EMPLOYEE BENEFIT PLANS: Amounts received by a surviving spouse from a survivor benefit plan, an annuity, retirement plan or pension by reason of decedent's death are not taxed. Amounts to others from such plans may be taxable based upon a case under prior law wherein a decedent's share in a profit-sharing trust passing to his designated beneficiary was held taxable.

Deductions

Funeral expenses, costs of administration, executor's fees, attorney's fees, debts, taxes accrued before death. Inheritance taxes paid to other states are not deductible unless paid to secure the transfer of corporate stock, in which event such taxes are deductible from the value of such stock. Federal estate tax is not deductible.

Valuation

Property is valued at its market value on the date of decedent's death.

Exemptions*

Class 1:	Amount of Exemption
Husband or wife (widow allowed additional $5,000 for each minor child to whom no property is transferred)	$65,000, plus additional $10,000 exemption
Grandparent, parent, child, brother, sister, wife or widow of son, husband of daughter, adopted child, mutually acknowledged child, lineal descendant (but not lineal issue of adopted child)	10,000
Class 2:	
All others	None

---

* The share of any beneficiary is exempt if less than $100.

The transfer of qualified farm real property is exempt from inheritance taxes at 50% of the clear market value of such farmland, if the qualified heir executes a farmland development rights agreement. The taxes which are due on the remaining 50% can be deferred for 10 years without penalty or interest. No tax lien will attach until the end of the deferral period.

Tax Rates*

SHARES		CLASS 1		CLASS 2	
From	To	Tax on† Col. 1	Rate on Excess	Tax on† Col. 1	Rate on Excess
$ 0	$ 50,000	$	2%	$	12%
50,000	250,000	1,000	4%	6,000	14%
250,000	500,000	9,000	7%	34,000	14%
500,000	750,000	26,500	8%	69,000	17%
750,000	Balance	46,500	10%	111,500	17%

* Add .5% of total tax.

† From total tax, for a surviving spouse, subtract the $65,000 exemption from the top applicable bracket rate in the Class 1 table for the property share. Also, subtract the additional $10,000 exemption that is given to surviving spouses from the lowest bracket rate on the Class 1 table. For all other Class 1 beneficiaries, subtract the $10,000 exemption from the lowest bracket rate on the Class 1 table.

Payment

The tax accrues at death, and is due and payable within 9 months. Failure to pay the tax within 9 months results in both penalty and interest being added to the amount due. The penalty is $5 or 5% of the tax due, whichever is greater, for the first month or fraction of month that the overdue tax remains unpaid, with an additional 5% for each month or fraction during which the failure to pay continues, to a maximum of 25%. The interest added is 3/4 of 1% per month on the amount of tax, and generally the interest runs from the time the tax was accrued until the date of payment. The personal representative may defer payment of inheritance tax for up to 10 years without penalty or interest if the decedent was a professional artist and reasonable cause is demonstrated to the probate court.

Ultimate Tax Burden

The person receiving the property, and the personal representative, are personally liable for payment. The executor is directed to deduct the tax before distribution of the property.

Nonresident Decedents

All real property and tangible personal property within the state are subject to the tax. Reciprocal exemption of intangibles is provided for decedents who die residents of states which do not tax intangibles of Michigan residents or which provide a similar exemption. Deductions are allowed only in the proportion that the Michigan property bears to the entire estate, but the full personal exemption is allowed. Nonresidents are not subject to the additional estate tax.

MINNESOTA
Type of Tax

Estate tax *or* Credit estate tax, whichever is greater.

Exempted Property

Transfers for public or government purposes within the United States, or for charitable, religious, educational, literary, scientific or public cemetery purposes (including the encouragement of art and prevention of cruelty to children or animals), are fully exempt if the transferee operates within the state, or if the state of domicile extends a similar exemption to Minnesota organizations. Property, valued at $1,000 or less, which is transferred to a clergyman for performance of religious ceremonies and pay accrued by a decedent serviceman while missing in action are exempt. Survivor benefits under the Social Security, Veterans Burial Benefit and Railroad Retirement Acts are exempt. Property devised to an ESOT is exempt. To the extent included in the federal gross estate, payments are exempt which are received from (1) pension or retirement plans which were qualified under the code when the decedent separated from employment (or plan termination, if earlier); (2) benefit plans for employees of the U.S. and its agencies and instrumentalities, Federal Reserve Bank, and the state of Minnesota (or any of its subdivisions); or (3) a benefit plan for Minnesota volunteer firefighters' relief association members.

Taxable Property

IN GENERAL: The Minnesota taxable estate equals the federal gross estate, as defined in IRC §2031, including the value of property located in Minnesota, yet not disclosed on the federal return, and minus the value of property located outside Minnesota upon decedent's death, the exemptions and deductions allowed herein, and the sum $275,000 (for deaths in 1983), $325,000 (1984), $400,000 (1985), $500,000 (1986), and $600,000 (thereafter); provided that, where property passes from a nonresident decedent, this amount is multiplied by a fraction which has as its numerator the value of the Minnesota gross estate and as its denominator the value of the federal gross estate.

DOWER OR STATUTORY SUBSTITUTE: Dower does not exist, but the statutory interest of the surviving spouse is taxable.

CONTEMPLATION OF DEATH: Transfers of property made within three years of death are presumed in contemplation of death.

TRANSFERS EFFECTIVE AT OR AFTER DEATH: Transfers intended to take effect in possession or enjoyment at or after death are taxable. Revocable trusts are taxable if made in contemplation of death or to take effect in possession, etc., after death.

JOINTLY OWNED PROPERTY: The taxation of jointly owned property follows the federal rule as found in Code §2040.

POWERS OF APPOINTMENT: Property subject to a power of appointment held by the decedent is taxed under the federal law.

LIFE ESTATES AND PRIVATE ANNUITIES: Taxed at values ascertained by reference to the federal estate tax tables.

LIFE INSURANCE AND ANNUITY CONTRACTS: The taxation of life or accident insurance proceeds other than government life insurance, follows the federal rule. Where the beneficiary is the owner of life insurance upon the life of her husband, the death proceeds will not be included in his estate merely because he signed the application consenting to his life being insured. Government life insurance and Servicemen's group life insurance are exempt. Proceeds of a refund annuity contract are taxable as a transfer taking effect in possession and enjoyment at death.

EMPLOYEE BENEFIT PLANS: Payments made to a deceased employee's spouse, minor or dependent child are exempt if received from a qualified trust or annuity plan or from a retirement annuity contract which had been purchased for an employee by a charitable, religious or educational organization. Only the portion of payments attributable to employer contributions is exempt.

Deductions

The Minnesota taxable estate is determined by deducting from the Minnesota gross estate (i.e., the federal gross estate plus property located in Minnesota and not disclosed on the federal return and minus property located outside Minnesota) the value of any property interest (except a Code §2056(b) terminable interest) passing from the decedent to surviving spouse to the extent included in determining the Minnesota gross estate and not exempt from taxation. This marital deduction is unlimited. Additional deductions are allowed for funeral expenses, administration expenses, expenses of the last illness, valid claims and debts, the portion of the federal estate tax allocable to Minnesota (which is equal to an amount obtained by multiplying the federal estate tax due by a fraction, the numerator of which equals the Minnesota gross estate reduced by applicable deductions and exemptions, and the denominator of which equals the federal taxable estate), taxes, and liens and mortgages.

Credits

A credit is allowed for inheritance or estate taxes paid on property which was transferred within 5 years prior to decedent's death, but may not exceed the present estate tax of the decedent attributable to such property. A credit is also allowed for gift taxes paid on transfers within 3 years of decedent's death, but may not exceed the present estate tax of the decedent attributable to such property. If both of these credits apply to the same property, when added together, they may not exceed the present estate tax of the decedent attributable to that property.

Valuation

Generally, property is valued as of the date of decedent's death. However, the personal representative may elect an alternate valuation date of 6 months later. Certain farm and business property, which qualifies under I.R.C. §2032(A), can be valued according to use rather than market value.

Exemptions

There are no personal exemptions.

Tax Rates* (death in 1984)

Taxable Estate		Tax on Col. 1	Rate on Excess
From	To		
$ 0	$ 75,000	$ 0	8%
75,000	175,000	6,000	9%
175,000	375,000	15,750	10%
375,000	875,000	37,500	11%
875,000	Balance	96,250	12%

* The tax imposed is the greater of the tax computed by applying the tax rate schedule to the taxable estate, or a tax equal to the maximum credit allowable under Code §2011 for state death taxes as the Minnesota gross estate bears to the value of the federal gross estate.

Payment

The tax generally is due and payable 9 months after death. Failure to pay the tax on or before the due date results in the addition of a penalty in the amount of 10% of the unpaid tax (unless an extension of time to pay is granted), and interest at 8% from the time when payment was due. The penalty itself also accrues interest at 8% from the due date.

Where the tax is at least $5,000, it may be paid in five annual installments at the election of the taxpayer. Interest is paid at the specified rate from the date when payment of the tax should have been made if no election to pay the tax in installments had been made.

In cases of hardship, the payment of the tax (or the first installment payment) may be deferred for two years.

Ultimate Tax Burden

The duty of collection and payment is on the personal representative, who may sell the property to pay the tax. In the event the personal representative cannot or does not pay the tax due, the transferee must pay.

Nonresident Decedents

Real property and tangible personal property, within the state or its jurisdiction, are taxable. Intangibles of nonresidents are not taxed. Only those deductions and exemptions specifically incurred within the state are allowed.

MISSISSIPPI
Type of Tax

1. Estate tax. 2. Credit estate tax.

Exempted Property

Annuity proceeds or other payments received by a beneficiary under a military family protection plan, survivor benefit plan, or other similar plan are exempt. Similarly, pay and allowances due MIA's of the armed forces for service in Vietnam from the date of their missing in action to their determined date of death are also exempt. Where any tax has been paid on such MIA pay or allowances, a claim for refund for the same must be filed by January 1, 1982.

Taxable Property

IN GENERAL: The tax is imposed upon all real property and all tangible personal property within Mississippi, and all intangible personalty of Mississippi residents wherever located.

DOWER OR STATUTORY SUBSTITUTE: Taxable.

CONTEMPLATION OF DEATH: Transfers made within three years of death are presumed in contemplation of death unless the contrary is shown.

TRANSFERS EFFECTIVE AT OR AFTER DEATH: Transfers intended to take effect in possession or enjoyment after death are taxable. Revocable trusts are taxable if intended to take effect in possession, etc., after death.

JOINTLY OWNED PROPERTY: Property held jointly (including tenancies by the entirety and joint bank accounts) with the right of survivorship is taxable except to the extent the survivor can show original ownership. If the decedent and his spouse are the only joint-owners, it is presumed that each contributed equally, and only 50% is taxable, unless the surviving spouse can show a greater contribution than one-half.

POWERS OF APPOINTMENT: Property passing under the exercise of a general power of appointment, by will or deed, is taxable in the estate of the donee of the power.

LIFE ESTATES AND PRIVATE ANNUITIES: Taxable at values ascertained by reference to the American Experience Table of Mortality and 5% interest.

LIFE INSURANCE AND ANNUITY CONTRACTS: Insurance payable to the estate is taxable. Proceeds payable to named beneficiaries are exempt up to $20,000, but any excess is taxed if the decedent possessed at his death any incidents of ownership exercisable either alone or in conjunction with any other person. Government insurance is taxable to the same extent as other life insurance.

EMPLOYEE BENEFIT PLANS: No statutory provision as to the taxation or exclusion therefrom of survivor benefits.

Deductions

Funeral expenses, debts and claims, unpaid mortgages, administration expenses, executor's commissions, attorney's fees, family allowance; taxes accrued and payable at death (except state and federal death taxes); property subject to estate tax within two years prior to decedent's death or property received in exchange for such property; losses incurred during settlement of estate arising from casualty or theft, to extent uncompensated by insurance.

The estate may also deduct transfers to the state of Mississippi, or subdivisions thereof, for exclusively public purposes, or to any religious, charitable, scientific, educational or literary organization, or to trustees for such organization. For Mississippi residents, this deduction applies whether the transfer is to a Mississippi or out-of-state organization, but an alien legatee does not qualify.

Valuation

Generally, property is valued at its market value on the date of decedent's death. However, if the personal representative elects the alternative valuation date, the federal rule will generally apply. For Mississippi residents only, certain farm and business property, which qualifies under I.R.C.,

§2032A, can be valued according to use rather than market value.

Exemptions

There are no personal exemptions. A decedent's property is exempt as follows:

Year of Death	Amount of Exemption
1978	$ 120,666
1979	134,000
1980	147,333
1981	161,563
1982 and thereafter	175,625

Tax Rates

(On net estate after deducting exemption.)

Taxable Estate		Tax on*	Rate on*
From	To	Col. 1	Excess
$ 0	$ 60,000	$ 0	1 %
60,000	100,000	600	1.6%
100,000	200,000	1,240	2.4%
200,000	400,000	3,640	3.2%
400,000	600,000	10,040	4 %
600,000	800,000	18,040	4.8%
800,000	1,000,000	27,640	5.6%
1,000,000	1,500,000	38,840	6.4%
1,500,000	2,000,000	70,840	7.2%
2,000,000	2,500,000	106,840	8 %
2,500,000	3,000,000	146,840	8.8%
3,000,000	3,500,000	190,840	9.6%
3,500,000	4,000,000	238,840	10.4%
4,000,000	5,000,000	290,840	11.2%
5,000,000	6,000,000	402,840	12 %
6,000,000	7,000,000	522,840	12.8%
7,000,000	8,000,000	650,840	13.6%
8,000,000	9,000,000	786,840	14.4%
9,000,000	10,000,000	930,840	15.2%
10,000,000	Balance	1,082,840	16 %

* The tax shall not be less than the federal state death tax credit allowed for the federal estate tax.

Payment

The tax is due and payable nine months after decedent's death, subject to extension of not more than six months in hardship cases. Interest at .5% per month begins to run from due date. No discount for early payment. In the case of qualified farms and closely held businesses, the tax thereon is due and payable when the federal tax is due and payable.

Ultimate Tax Burden

Borne by residuary estate, unless decedent's will provides otherwise. The personal representative of the deceased is made personally liable for payment of the tax.

Nonresident Decedents

All real property and tangible personal property within the state are subject to the tax. The personal representative generally must compute the gross estate, most deductions, and the specific exemption in the proportion which the Mississippi property bears to the entire estate. In this event, however, he takes the full deduction for Mississippi property previously taxed, and deducts charitable, etc., bequests to the extent they are given to Mississippi organizations. Alternatively, he may compute the tax upon the Mississippi property alone, with no deductions or exemptions.

MISSOURI
Type of Tax

1. Credit estate tax (applicable to estates of decedents dying on or after 1-1-81). 2. Generation-skipping transfer tax (applicable to estates of decedents dying on or after 1-1-81).

Credit Estate Tax

If all of a resident decedent's property is taxable in Missouri, the tax equals the maximum federal credit for state death taxes. A resident's real property and tangible personal property located outside Missouri is not taxable. Intangible personal property is subject to tax regardless of where situated. Where a resident decedent leaves property not taxable in Missouri, the Missouri tax bears the same ratio to the federal credit as decedent's Missouri tax situs property bears to the whole gross estate.

Payment

For residents, a tax return must be filed by every personal representative required to file a federal estate tax return. For nonresidents, a tax return must be filed by every personal representative who is required to file a federal estate tax return if the decedent's gross estate having a tax situs in Missouri exceeds $10,000. The tax generally is due and payable 9 months after the decedent's death; however, payment of the tax and filing the return may be extended by the director of revenue for a reasonable period of time, not to exceed four years for paying the tax, and six months for filing the tax return. Where the taxpayer has been granted an extension of time for filing the federal estate tax return, filing a copy of such extension with the director of revenue automatically extends the due date for filing the state return. Where the taxpayer has been granted an extension of time for paying the federal estate tax, filing a copy of such extension with the director of revenue automatically extends the time for paying the state tax up to four years.

Ultimate Tax Burden

The personal representative of the decedent is personally liable for the tax until it is paid. However, the personal representative collects the tax from the beneficiaries or deducts it from their shares.

Nonresident Decedents

Nonresident decedents are taxed on the transfer of all real property and tangible personal property located in Missouri. The intangible personal property of a nonresident decedent is not taxable regardless of where situated.

Generation-Skipping Transfer Tax

Missouri has enacted a generation-skipping transfer tax for generation-skipping transfers which occur on or after January 1, 1981. The tax is imposed on the generation-skipping transfer of every deemed transferor whose property included in such a transfer consists entirely, or in part, of real property or tangible personal property located in Missouri; and intangible personal property, wherever located, in the case of resident transferors. The tax shall be the maximum credit for state death taxes allowed under Code §2602(c)(5)(C). A proportional reduction in the amount of the tax is permitted when any of the transferred property has a tax situs outside Missouri, by multiplying the tax by a fraction having as its numerator all property having a tax situs in Missouri and as its denominator, the decedent's gross estate.

For residents, a return must be filed by every personal representative who is required to file a federal generation-skipping tax return. For nonresidents, a return must be filed by every personal representative who is required to file a federal generation-skipping tax return if that part of the gross estate having a tax situs in Missouri exceeds $10,000. Filing of the return and payment of the tax is due within 9 months after the decedent's death. Extensions of time in filing the return or paying the tax are permitted if granted by the director of revenue or if an extension has been granted pursuant to the federal generation-skipping tax return.

MONTANA
Type of Tax

1. Inheritance tax. 2. Credit estate tax.

Exempted Property

Transfers to the state of Montana or a political subdivision thereof are exempt. Also exempt are transfers to charitable, religious or educational organizations organized in Montana. A reciprocal exemption of charitable, etc., transfers is made for states which allow an exemption to Montana organizations.

Also, the clear market value of all the property distributed or passing to a decedent's surviving spouse is exempt.

Transfers of property owned by a member of the armed forces who was killed in action, or who died as a result of wounds, disease or injury incurred in a combat zone are exempt.

Taxable Property

IN GENERAL: Real property within the state is taxable. Tangible personal property is, under the statute, taxable wherever located. However, an exemption is provided if the state of location actually levies a death tax on the property. Intangible personalty of Montana residents is taxable wherever located.

DOWER OR STATUTORY SUBSTITUTE: Taxable.

CONTEMPLATION OF DEATH: There is a presumption that property transferred within three years prior to death was transferred in contemplation of death. Transfers made more than three years before death may not be held in contemplation of death.

TRANSFERS EFFECTIVE AT OR AFTER DEATH: Property transferred by decedent, reserving income or enjoyment, or power to revoke, either alone or in conjunction with another, is subject to the tax.

JOINTLY OWNED PROPERTY: Property held jointly with the right of survivorship (including tenancies by the entireties, joint bank accounts and Government bonds held jointly) is taxable to the extent of one-half or other proper fraction, as if held as tenants in common, except such part as can be shown to have originally belonged to the survivor. In one case, prior to a 1951 amendment, it was held that the exception did not apply because it was the source of the title and not the source of the funds which was important. Cases after the 1951 amendment, however, have held that where the survivor can show that decedent made no contribution to the joint property, the exception will apply.

POWERS OF APPOINTMENT: Transfer of property by the exercise or nonexercise of a power of appointment is taxable as if the property had belonged absolutely to the donee of the power and had passed by his will.

LIFE ESTATES AND PRIVATE ANNUITIES: Taxed at values based on the American Experience Table with interest at 5%.

LIFE INSURANCE AND ANNUITY CONTRACTS: Proceeds of insurance policies in excess of $50,000 are taxable, whether payable to the estate or to named beneficiaries. The $50,000 exemption is prorated among named beneficiaries, including trustees. A death benefit under an annuity contract is considered insurance and entitled to the exemption. However, where decedent left matured endowment proceeds with the company at interest, and with the principal payable at her direction, the principal did not qualify for the $50,000 insurance exemption, since she could have withdrawn it at maturity. Government insurance is treated the same as other life insurance.

EMPLOYEE BENEFIT PLANS: No statutory provision as to the taxation or exclusion therefrom of survivor benefits.

Deductions

Expenses of funeral and last illness, costs of administration, attorney's fees, executor's commissions, debts, unpaid mortgages (deducted from estate and not from value of property); federal, Montana, and local taxes due at death; federal estate tax; other states' death taxes (not to exceed amount Montana would have charged). The child of a male decedent, receiving from such decedent's widow property which she inherited from him, takes credit for a proportional share of the tax she paid at his death, provided she died within ten years after his death.

Valuation

Property is valued at its market value on the date of decedent's death. If an election is made within 18 months of decedent's death, certain qualified farmland or closely held business can be valued by alternate methods.

Exemptions

(Deduct from bottom bracket)

	Amount of Exemption
Class 1:	
Spouse, child, or lineal descendant of the decedent	All property
Adult lineal ancestor of the decedent	$7,000

Class 2:
Brother, sister, descendant of brother or sister, wife of son,
  husband of daughter   1,000

Class 3:
Uncle, aunt, first cousin . . . .   None

Class 4:
All others . . . .   None

Tax Rates

| SHARE | | CLASS 1† | | CLASS 2 | |
| | | *Tax on | Rate on | *Tax on | Rate on |
From	*To*	*Col. 1*	*Excess*	*Col. 1*	*Excess*
Exemption	$ 25,000	$	2%	$	4%
25,000	50,000	500	4%	1,000	8%
50,000	100,000	1,500	6%	3,000	12%
100,000	Balance	4,500	8%	9,000	16%

| SHARE | | CLASS 3 | | CLASS 4 | |
| | | *Tax on | Rate on | *Tax on | Rate on |
From	*To*	*Col. 1*	*Excess*	*Col. 1*	*Excess*
Exemption	$ 25,000	$	6%	$	8%
25,000	50,000	1,500	12%	2,000	16%
50,000	100,000	4,500	18%	6,000	24%
100,000	Balance	13,500	24%	18,000	32%

---

* Subtract from total tax, the exemption at appropriate first bracket rate.
† Does not include spouse.

Payment

The tax is due and payable at the death of decedent. If not paid within 18 months, interest at 10% is assessed from date of death, subject to reduction to 6% if delay unavoidable until cause of delay is removed, when the 10% rate attaches. If paid within 18 months of death, a discount of 5% is allowed. The additional estate tax is payable at the same time as the federal tax, and bears the same rate of interest. The tax on remainder interests may be deferred if bond is filed.

The tax is apportioned among the shares of beneficiaries in proportion to the amounts beneficiaries receive unless the will provides otherwise.

For certain qualified farmland and closely held businesses, an installment plan can be elected.

Ultimate Tax Burden

The beneficiary and the personal representative are made personally liable for payment. The representative either collects the tax from the beneficiary, or withholds it from the legacy, before distribution.

Nonresident Decedents

The real property and tangible personal property within the state, and intangible personal property that has gained a business situs within the state, is subject to the tax. Reciprocal exemption of intangibles is provided for decedents who die residents of states which do not tax intangibles of Montana residents or which provide a similar exemption. Exemptions and deductions can be taken only in the proportion that the Montana property bears to the entire estate. Nonresidents are not subject to the additional estate tax.

NEBRASKA
Type of Tax

1. Inheritance tax. 2. Credit estate tax.

Exempted Property

Transfers to political subdivisions or governmental agencies are exempt. Nebraska also exempts transfers to religious, charitable, scientific, or educational organizations, *provided* the gift is limited for use within the state, or the organization was formed in Nebraska or in a state which grants reciprocity.

Taxable Property

IN GENERAL: The tax is imposed upon all real property and all tangible personal property within Nebraska, and all intangible personalty of Nebraska residents wherever located.

DOWER OR STATUTORY SUBSTITUTE: The surviving spouse's marital exemption equals her family allowance and homestead interest, plus the share she would receive if she renounced decedent's will or he died intestate. This share varies from 1/4 to 1/2 the net estate.

CONTEMPLATION OF DEATH: Transfers made within three years of death are presumed to be made in contemplation of death. Transfers made more than three years before death may not be held in contemplation of death. These provisions do not apply to joint tenancies.

TRANSFERS EFFECTIVE AT OR AFTER DEATH: Transfers intended to take effect in possession or enjoyment at or after death are taxable. Transfers in trust, reserving income for life, are taxable.

JOINTLY OWNED PROPERTY: Property held jointly with the right of survivorship generally is taxable to the extent the survivor cannot show original ownership. If the decedent and his or her surviving spouse were the only owners of joint tenancy property, it is presumed that each spouse furnished one-half the consideration for the property, unless the surviving spouse proves that his or her contribution was greater than one-half. Property held as tenants in common is taxable to extent of decedent's interest. Property acquired under the (repealed) community property laws is taxable to extent of one-half its value upon the death of the spouse.

POWERS OF APPOINTMENT: Property subject to a power of appointment is taxed in the donor's (creator's) estate at his death. The donee or appointor is considered beneficiary, unless the donor has limited the possible appointees to specific persons or classes of persons. In that event, such persons or classes are deemed the beneficiaries. Nebraska does not tax such property in the donee's (appointor's) estate.

LIFE ESTATES AND PRIVATE ANNUITIES: Valued in accordance with the federal estate tax tables.

LIFE INSURANCE AND ANNUITY CONTRACTS: Insurance payable to the estate is taxable. If payable to named beneficiaries, it is exempt. Government insurance no doubt would be treated just as other life insurance.

EMPLOYEE BENEFIT PLANS: An employee death benefit is exempt from the Nebraska inheritance tax to the extent it consists of (a) life insurance proceeds that are otherwise exempt, or (b) a benefit that is not subject to the federal estate tax pursuant to Code §2039.

Deductions

Expenses of funeral and last illness, costs of administration, executor's commissions, attorney's fees, debts, unpaid mortgages, federal estate taxes, income and property taxes accrued before death; the amount of inheritance taxes paid on the previous transfer of property received by decedent in any manner from a person who died within five years prior to decedent's death.

Valuation

Property is valued at its market value on the date of decedent's death.

Exemptions

(Allowed for in following Tax Rate table.)

	Amount of Exemption
Class 1:	
Husband or wife	Unlimited
Father, mother, child, brother, sister, wife or widow of son, husband of daughter, legally or informally adopted child, lineal descent born in lawful wedlock or legally adopted	$10,000

Class 2:

Aunt, uncle, nephew, or niece, related to the deceased by blood or legal adoption, or lineal descendant of same 2,000

Class 3:

All others, except charitable institutions 500

Tax Rates

SHARE		CLASS 1		CLASS 2	
From	*To*	*Tax on Col. 1*	*Rate on Excess*	*Tax on Col. 1*	*Rate on Excess*
$ 0	$ 2,000	$ 0	. . . .	$ 0	. . . .
2,000	5,000	0	. . . .	0	6%
5,000	10,000	0	. . . .	180	6%
10,000	20,000	0	1%	480	6%
20,000	50,000	100	1%	1,080	6%
50,000	60,000	400	1%	2,880	6%
60,000	Balance	500	1%	3,480	9%

SHARE		CLASS 3	
From	*To*	*Tax on Col. 1*	*Rate on Excess*
$ 0	$ 500	$ 0	. . . .
500	2,000	0	6%
2,000	5,000	90	6%
5,000	10,000	270	9%
10,000	20,000	720	12%
20,000	50,000	1,920	15%
50,000	60,000	6,420	18%
60,000	Balance	8,220	18%

Payment

The tax is due and payable at death. If not paid within 12 months, interest at the rate of 14% is charged from date of death. The tax on remainder interests is due immediately, but the beneficiary can give bond to pay when he comes into possession. There is no discount for prompt payment. The additional estate tax is due and payable within 12 months of death, with interest at 14% from death, if not paid when due.

Ultimate Tax Burden

The beneficiaries and the personal representative are liable for payment of the tax. The representative is directed to collect the tax from the beneficiary or deduct it from his share before distribution. Federal and state estate taxes are apportioned among the beneficiaries, in absence of a contrary stipulation in the will.

Nonresident Decedents

The statute purports to tax real and personal property within the state. However, the statute limits the jurisdiction over the estate of a nonresident decedent to the County Court of the county in which the real estate of the nonresident decedent is situated. It would appear that if the decedent owned no real estate within the state, there would be no procedure for taxing the personal property.

Reciprocal exemption of intangibles is provided by the present law. Full personal exemptions are allowed, but only the local (Nebraska) deductions may be taken. Effective 1-1-77, the credit estate tax applies to the transfer of Nebraska real estate owned by a nonresident.

NEVADA
Type of Tax

None

NEW HAMPSHIRE
Type of Tax

1. Inheritance tax. 2. Credit estate tax.

Exempted Property

Transfers to a city or town in New Hampshire for public municipal purposes, and transfers for the care of cemetery lots, are exempt. Reciprocal exemption is made for transfers to or for the use of educational, religious, cemetery or other out-of-state public charitable institutions.

Taxable Property

IN GENERAL: The tax is imposed upon all real property and all tangible personal property within New Hampshire, and all intangible personalty of New Hampshire residents wherever located.

DOWER OR STATUTORY SUBSTITUTE: Not taxable.

CONTEMPLATION OF DEATH: Transfers within two years of death are presumed in contemplation of death unless the contrary is shown.

TRANSFERS EFFECTIVE AT OR AFTER DEATH: Transfers intended to take effect in possession or enjoyment after death, and transfers reserving income, etc., to decedent, are taxable.

JOINTLY OWNED PROPERTY: Property passing by the right of survivorship is taxable to the survivor in the proportion which the contribution of decedent bears to the entire purchase price. Note that if the survivor is the spouse of decedent, such property is not taxable. Tenancy by the entirety does not exist in New Hampshire.

Decedent's share of a homestead, jointly owned, and occupied as a residence by decedent and a brother or a sister, will be exempt if the homestead was so owned and occupied for at least a year prior to decedent's death, and it passes to or for the use of the brother or sister.

POWERS OF APPOINTMENT: Statute silent, but the common-law rule is that such transfers are taxable in the estate of the donor, and not in that of the donee. However, the Attorney General has power to compromise and settle these claims.

LIFE ESTATES, ANNUITIES AND REMAINDERS: The value of a life estate, any intermediate estate, an annuity and any remainder interest is determined in accordance with IRS regulations and tables in effect at the decedent's death.

LIFE INSURANCE AND ANNUITY CONTRACTS: No definite statutory provision. Insurance payable to the estate has, in practice, been taxed. If payable to named beneficiaries, the proceeds are exempt. Death benefits under annuity contracts are subject to tax. Government insurance receives the same treatment as other life insurance.

EMPLOYEE BENEFIT PLANS: No statutory provision as to the taxation or exclusion therefrom of survivor benefits.

Deductions

Expenses of funeral and last illness, cost of administration, executor's commissions (up to 2½% of value of real and personal property sold to pay debts), income and property taxes accruing prior to death, federal estate taxes, state death taxes (except when paid on specific bequest of property located in such states), mortgages. A beneficiary who has a claim against decedent, evidenced by a contract in writing, for board, maintenance, care, etc., covering a period of more than six months, may deduct the amount of claim from his share, provided the contract specified a time for payment within decedent's lifetime.

Valuation

Property is valued at its market value on the date of decedent's death, or at the alternate valuation date allowed by federal law.

Exemptions

Property received by a spouse, or lineal ancestor or descendant, or by a spouse of a lineal ancestor or descendant, and all property passing by will from a stepparent to a stepchild or a stepchild's spouse or vice versa, is entirely exempt.

Tax Rates

Property received by nonexempt individuals is taxed at a rate of 15%.

Payment

The tax is due and payable at the expiration of 12 months after decedent's death, with interest of 1.25% per month. No discount is allowed for prompt payment. The additional estate tax is payable at the same time as the federal tax, and bears the same interest for the same period. As to non-resident decedents—the tax on transfer of real property is due at the time of the transfer with 1.25% per month interest until paid. If such transfer is not made within 15 months of decedent's death, the 1.25% per month interest is charged from that time.

Ultimate Tax Burden

The personal representative and the beneficiaries are personally liable for the tax, with interest, until paid. The representative is directed to collect the tax from the beneficiary or to deduct it from the share before distribution. He has power to sell the property to pay the tax.

Nonresident Decedents

The tax is imposed upon the real property and tangible personal property within the state and intangible personal property that has acquired a taxable situs in the state. Under the statute, the following intangibles are not taxable: the stocks and bonds of domestic corporations whose business is carried on outside the state, and deposits in banks and trust companies within the state. Provision is made for the reciprocal exemption of intangibles. Full exemptions are allowed on transfers of real property within the state, but no exemption exists as to personal property. Deductions on the real property may be taken in the proportion that the real property in the state bears to the entire estate.

NEW JERSEY
Type of Tax

1. Inheritance tax. 2. Credit estate tax.

Exempted Property

Property transferred to the state or a subdivision thereof for exclusively public purposes is exempt. Also exempt are transfers to nonprofit educational institutions, churches, hospitals, orphan asylums, public libraries, Bible and tract societies, religious, benevolent and charitable organizations located in New Jersey, or any state which grants reciprocity to New Jersey residents.

Taxable Property

IN GENERAL: The tax is imposed upon all real property and all tangible personal property within New Jersey, and all intangible personalty of New Jersey residents wherever located.

DOWER OR STATUTORY SUBSTITUTE: Dower has been abolished in New Jersey. The statutory substitute, however, is taxable.

CONTEMPLATION OF DEATH: Transfers made within three years of death are presumed in contemplation of death unless the contrary is shown. Transfers made more than three years before death are *not* made in contemplation of death, for purposes of the New Jersey tax.

TRANSFERS EFFECTIVE AT OR AFTER DEATH: Tranfers by grant or gift, intended to take effect in possession or enjoyment at or after death, are taxable. This includes revocable trusts, and transfers in which the decedent reserved the income for his life.

JOINTLY OWNED PROPERTY: Property held jointly with the right of survivorship, including joint bank accounts (but not including tenancies by the entirety), is taxable in full, except to the extent the survivor can show original ownership. Real property held in tenancy by the entirety is exempt. Also excluded from taxation is the right of a spouse, as a surviving joint tenant with the deceased spouse, to the immediate ownership or possession and enjoyment of a membership or stock in a cooperative housing corporation which ownership enabled the surviving spouse and decedent to occupy real estate as their principal residence.

POWERS OF APPOINTMENT: Transfers by power of appointment are not taxable in the donee's (appointor's) estate, but are taxed as if the property had passed under the will of the donor of the power.

LIFE ESTATES AND PRIVATE ANNUITIES: Taxed at values ascertained by reference to the U.S. Life Tables after December 10, 1970, Single Life Male 6% and Single Life Female 6%, with interest at 6% per annum.

LIFE INSURANCE AND ANNUITY CONTRACTS: Insurance payable to the estate is taxable. If payable to named beneficiaries, either directly or in trust for such beneficiaries, it is exempt. The transfer, exercise, relinquishment or surrender of the right to nominate or change the beneficiary of an insurance policy is exempt. Government life insurance is also exempt. Dividends and refunds on life insurance policies are not part of the proceeds and are taxable as transfers taking effect at or after death.

Amounts paid to a beneficiary under refund and retirement annuity contracts are not life insurance and are taxable.

EMPLOYEE BENEFIT PLANS: Exempt from taxation is the value of any pension, annuity, retirement allowance, or return of contributions paid to decedent's surviving spouse due to decedent's employment under a plan qualified under Code §§401(a),(b), or (c) or 2039(c), and not otherwise exempt. Civil Service, Retired Serviceman's Family Protection Plan, or Survivor Benefit Plan benefits are exempt [N.J. Rev. Stat. §54:34-3(h),(i)]. Also, payments from any of the state retirement plans are exempt according to a pamphlet released by the New Jersey Tax Bureau. However, the benefit payable under the Supplemental Annuity Plan of the state's Public Employees' Retirement system is taxable.

Deductions

Expenses of funeral and last illness, costs of administration, attorney's fees, executor's commissions, state (but not federal) death taxes, mortgages (deducted from value of property), debts (but only to excess of value of property by which it is secured, if outside New Jersey).

Valuation

Property is valued at its market value on the date of decedent's death.

Exemptions

	Amount of Exemption
Class A:	
Parent, grandparent, spouse, child or adopted child or his issue, stepchild, child mutually acknowledged for 10 years commencing at or before his 15th birthday	$15,000
*Class C:**	
Brother, sister, wife or widow of son, husband or widower of daughter	None (But no tax if the share is less than $500)
Class D:	
All others	None (But no tax if the share is less than $500)

Tax Rates

SHARE		CLASS A	
From	*To*	*Tax on Col. 1*	*Rate on Excess*
$ 15,000	$ 50,000	$ 0	2%
50,000	100,000	700	3%
100,000	150,000	2,200	4%
150,000	200,000	4,200	5%
200,000	300,000	6,700	6%
300,000	500,000	12,700	7%
500,000	700,000	26,700	8%
700,000	900,000	42,700	9%
900,000	1,100,000	60,700	10%
1,100,000	1,400,000	80,700	11%
1,400,000	1,700,000	113,700	12%
1,700,000	2,200,000	149,700	13%
2,200,000	2,700,000	214,700	14%
2,700,000	3,200,000	284,700	15%
3,200,000	Balance	359,700	16%

SHARE		CLASS C*		CLASS D	
		Tax on Col. 1	*Rate on Excess*	*Tax on Col. 1*	*Rate on Excess*
From	*To*				
0**	$ 700,000	$ 0	11%	$ 0	15%
$ 700,000	1,100,000	77,000	11%	105,000	16%
1,100,000	1,400,000	121,000	13%	169,000	16%
1,400,000	1,700,000	160,000	14%	217,000	16%
1,700,000	Balance	202,000	16%	265,000	16%

* There is no Class B. Class B was repealed on July 1, 1963.

** Even though there is no exemption, no tax is due if the beneficiary's share is less than $500.

Payment

The tax is due and payable at the death of decedent. However, where the decedent's death was caused by a wrongful act, neglect, or default, the tax which is due with respect to any sum recovered as compensation therefor is due on the date that a settlement is reached or an award of damages is received. If the tax is not paid within 8 months of death or within 30 days of award or settlement, the beneficiaries and personal representative are required to give bond, and interest at 10% is charged thereafter. If the delay is unavoidable, the interest rate will be 6% until the cause of delay is removed, at which time the 10% rate attaches. If decedent died a member of the armed forces, interest does not begin to run until eight months after receipt by next of kin of notification of death. There is no provision for discount for early payment. The additional estate tax is due at death, and payable within 18 months thereafter, at which time interest at 6% is charged until paid. The tax on contingent remainder interests may be deferred if bond is filed.

Ultimate Tax Burden

The personal representative, and "grantees, donees and vendees," are personally liable to pay the tax. Thus, it appears that the beneficiary would not be personally liable unless he is a donee, but the enforcement provisions leave no doubt that the beneficiary's share is liable for the tax. The representative is directed to deduct the amount of the tax from the share, or to collect it from the beneficiaries, before distribution.

Nonresident Decedents

All real property and tangible personal property within the state is subject to the tax. Intangibles of nonresidents are not taxed. The additional estate tax is not imposed on nonresident decedents. The same exemptions and deductions as are allowed to resident decedents are allowed to nonresidents if the property is specifically devised. If not specifically devised, the same rates and exemptions apply, but the tax is computed on the entire estate of the nonresident and that proportion taken which represents the proportion of the taxable property located in New Jersey to the total estate.

NEW MEXICO
Type of Tax

Credit estate tax.

If all of a decedent's property is taxable in New Mexico, the tax equals maximum federal credit for state taxes. As to the estates of resident decedents who leave property located in another state, the tax is equal to the same proportion of the federal credit allowable as the New Mexico property bears to the entire estate.

Payment

The tax is due and payable on or before 9 months after decedent's death. If not paid within this time limit, interest at 6% per year is assessed from the due date. There is no discount for early payment. Payment may be made in the form of works of art if directed by the decedent's will or elected by the personal representative.

Ultimate Tax Burden

Each distributee or beneficiary bears his proportion of the tax unless decedent's will provides otherwise. The personal representative is made personally liable for payment if distribution of the estate is made before the tax is paid.

Nonresident Decedents

Property of nonresident decedents subject to the tax includes real and tangible personal property located in New Mexico. Also, intangible personal property having a business situs as well as securities of New Mexico corporations are subject to tax. The New Mexico law, however, provides a reciprocal exemption for the property of a nonresident decedent if the decedent's state of residence likewise provides such an exemption to nonresidents.

NEW YORK
Type of Tax

1. Estate tax. 2. Credit estate tax.

Exempted Property

Since New York has an estate tax similar to the federal estate tax, there is no exempted property as such.

Taxable Property

IN GENERAL: The tax is imposed upon all real property and all tangible personal property within New York, and all intangible personalty of New York residents wherever located.

The New York taxable estate equals the New York gross estate, less the New York deductions. The New York gross estate equals the federal gross estate, less real and personal property outside New York and amounts included in the federal gross estate under Code §2044, plus amounts in connection with limited powers of appointment created prior to September 1, 1930 and amounts transferred within three years of death under Code §2035(d).

DOWER OR STATUTORY SUBSTITUTE: Taxable.

CONTEMPLATION OF DEATH: The concept has been abandoned in favor of a provision similar to the federal rule. Certain transfers made within three years of death are now includable in the decedent's estate, except those made as a bona fide sale for full and adequate consideration, or those made (other than the transfer of an interest in a life insurance policy) which the decedent was not required to file a gift tax return for under Code §6019. The decedent's gross estate is increased by the gift taxes paid on such transfers which are includable in the decedent's gross estate.

TRANSFERS EFFECTIVE AT OR AFTER DEATH: Property transferred by decedent, reserving income or power to alter, amend, revoke or terminate, or where such power was relinquished during the three-year period ending on the date of the decedent's death, is taxable. However, property transferred prior to March 10, 1931, will not be taxed merely because possession or enjoyment was reserved.

JOINTLY OWNED PROPERTY: Tenancies by the entirety and joint tenancies with right of survivorship (including such joint bank accounts) are taxed to the extent the survivor cannot show original ownership. If tenants by the entirety took their property by gift, devise, bequest, or inheritance, one-half is taxable. If joint tenants acquired their property thus, the taxable portion equals the whole property divided by the number of joint tenants. In the case of a "qualified joint interest" (any interest in property held by the decedent and his spouse as joint tenants or tenants by the entirety subject to certain limitations), only one-half is taxable.

POWERS OF APPOINTMENT: Property subject to a power of appointment held by the decedent is taxed as under the federal law. Property passing under a general power of appointment created after October 21, 1942, is taxable in the estate of the donee of the power.

LIFE ESTATES AND PRIVATE ANNUITIES: Same as federal law.

LIFE INSURANCE: Proceeds of policies upon decedent's life, if the executor receives them, are includable in the gross estate. It has been held that proceeds payable to a creditor beneficiary are as if payable to the executor, and not entitled to exemption. Proceeds received by named beneficiaries are includable to the extent decedent possessed incidents of ownership when he died.

ANNUITY CONTRACTS: On inclusion of annuity payments. New York law is the same as federal law.

EMPLOYEE BENEFIT PLANS: Generally the same as federal law.

Deductions

The deductions are those allowed under Code §§2046, 2053, 2054, 2055, and 2056, and adjusted as provided in N.Y. Estates, Powers & Trusts §§956(b) and (c) and 957(c), reduced by the portion thereof attributable to real and tangible personal property with a situs outside New York.

Valuation

Property is valued at its market value on the date of decedent's death, except the federal alternative valuation date may be used if a federal estate tax return is filed. The Federal alternative valuation date may also be used if it would have been available, but no federal return was filed because of the size of the estate. Certain farm and business property, which qualifies under I.R.C., §2032A, can be valued according to use rather than market value.

Tax Rates

NET ESTATE				Of Amount
From	To	Tax is	Plus	Over
Exemptions	$ 50,000	$ 0	2%	Exemptions
$ 50,000	150,000	1,000	3%	$ 50,000
150,000	300,000	4,000	4%	150,000
300,000	500,000	10,000	5%	300,000
500,000	700,000	20,000	6%	500,000
700,000	900,000	32,000	7%	700,000
900,000	1,100,000	46,000	8%	900,000
1,100,000	1,600,000	62,000	9%	1,100,000
1,600,000	2,100,000	107,000	10%	1,600,000
2,100,000	2,600,000	157,000	11%	2,100,000
2,600,000	3,100,000	212,000	12%	2,600,000
3,100,000	3,600,000	272,000	13%	3,100,000
3,600,000	4,100,000	337,000	14%	3,600,000
4,100,000	5,100,000	407,000	15%	4,100,000
5,100,000	6,100,000	557,000	16%	5,100,000
6,100,000	7,100,000	717,000	17%	6,100,000
7,100,000	8,100,000	887,000	18%	7,100,000
8,100,000	9,100,000	1,067,000	19%	8,100,000
9,100,000	10,100,000	1,257,000	20%	9,100,000
10,100,000	Balance	1,457,000	21%	10,100,000

Credits

A general credit is allowed the estate of every decedent as follows:

Amount of Tentative Tax	Credit
$ 0 to $2,750	Amount of the tax
2,750 to 5,000	Amount by which $5,500 exceeds tax
5,000 to Balance	$500

A credit is also allowed for the exemption value of qualified property in a qualified use. That exemption value equals the first $200,000 and ½ the excess over $400,000 in value of qualified property, which was owned by the decedent and has vested in a qualified heir, and which is employed in a qualified use. When the exemption value is used to compute the marital deduction, this exemption value is limited to the excess of this exemption amount over total New York deductions, as adjusted by N.Y. Estates, Powers & Trusts Law, §956(c), concerning the partial or complete disallowance of the New York marital deduction. In either case, once this exemption amount is determined, the credit for it is the *excess* of (1) an amount equal to 2% of the first $50,000 ($1,000), 3% of the next $100,000 ($3,000), 4% of the next $100,000 ($4,000), and 5% of the next $100,000 ($5,000), *over* (2) the amount of the general credit.

Credit is also given for previously taxed New York property, reduced by the general credit, and the qualified property credit. This credit is generally determined in the same manner as the federal credit for prior transfers under Code §2013.

Credit is also allowed in the amount of gift tax paid on any amount thereafter required to be included in a decedent's New York gross estate. The credit is generally determined in the same manner as the federal credit for gift tax under Code §2012. Code §2012 applies to gifts made prior to December 31, 1982, for purposes of the New York law.

Payment

The tax is due and payable at the time of decedent's death. If at least 80% of the tax is not paid within six months, interest on the unpaid tax is charged at 1/2% for the seventh month, 1% for the eighth month, and 11/2% for the ninth month. If not paid within nine months, interest on the unpaid tax is payable from date of death at the rate established by the tax commission (but not less than 6% per annum). Where the tax exceeds 5% of the net estate, an extension may be granted. Interest is charged if the tax is not paid within the extension period. If the tax is not paid within nine months, a penalty of 1/2% is added to the amount of tax due for the tenth month, with an additional 1/2% for each additional month or portion thereof, up to a total of 25%.

Ultimate Tax Burden

Both the New York and federal estate taxes are apportioned by the New York Decedent Estate Law to those receiving taxable property, in the same proportion as their individual shares bear to the total taxable estate, with allowable exemptions and deductions, unless the decedent's will provides otherwise.

Nonresident Decedents

The tax laws contain no provisions for taxing intangible property to nonresidents. A New York constitutional provision limits the power of the state to tax intangible property of nonresident decedents to those cases where the property is used in a business in the state, or where no other state has jurisdiction to tax such property. Where real or tangible personal property is situated in the state, the tax is determined as follows: Ascertain what the tax would have been if the decedent had been a resident with all his property situated within the state, except real and personal property with actual situs outside the state. The tax payable is the product obtained by multiplying this ascertained figure by a fraction, the denominator of which is the gross estate as ascertained above, and the numerator of which is the value of the real and personal property situated within the state. No credits are allowed against the tax. The tax on the transfer of a nonresident's artworks located in New York for exhibition purposes and either includable in the nonresident's federal gross estate, or would be in-

cludable in the nonresident's New York gross estate (under limited powers of appointment provisions) if a resident, is equal to the death taxes imposed on the transfer if the artworks were located in the nonresident's state. If the nonresident's state imposes a death tax on artworks located in New York for exhibition purposes, then the artworks are not subject to the New York tax.

NORTH CAROLINA

1. Inheritance tax. 2. Credit estate tax. 3. Generation-skipping transfer tax.

Exempted Property

Property passing to the United States, any state, or territory, or political subdivision thereof, or to the District of Columbia exclusively for public purposes, or to charitable, religious, benevolent or educational institutions within the state, or to such organizations located in other states, if such other states do not tax transfers to North Carolina organizations.

Taxable Property

IN GENERAL: The tax is imposed upon all real property and all tangible personal property within North Carolina, and all intangible personalty of North Carolina residents wherever located. An interest in partnership realty is considered intangible personalty.

DOWER OR STATUTORY SUBSTITUTE: Taxable.

CONTEMPLATION OF DEATH: Transfers exceeding 3% of decedent's estate, made within three years of death, are presumed in contemplation of death unless the contrary is shown. The Attorney-General has ruled that the presumption applies only to single gifts. Thus, a number of gifts may be made within this period, the aggregate of which exceeds 3% without subjecting them to the inheritance tax, so long as no single gift is above this limit. The statute was amended in 1977 to conform with this opinion. The law now exempts the first $3,000 of transfers to any one donee when made by deed, grant, sale, or gift within three years of donor's death. If a gift tax has been paid on the prior transfer, the amount of gift tax will be allowed in reduction of the inheritance tax, and any additional tax found due on this transfer shall be paid by the estate, and not by the beneficiary.

TRANSFERS EFFECTIVE AT OR AFTER DEATH: Transfers of property by the decedent, intended to take effect in possession or enjoyment after death, or in which he reserved the income, or the power to revoke or to change the beneficiaries, are taxable.

JOINTLY OWNED PROPERTY: One-half the value of property, including real property, held by the entirety is taxable. North Carolina does not recognize common-law joint tenancies. Where, however, property passes by a contractual right of survivorship, it is taxable to the extent of decedent's contribution. This rule applies to joint bank accounts, to joint savings and loan accounts, and to face-amount certificates. It also applies to statutory joint tenancies without right of survivorship. United States savings bonds registered in co-ownership form are taxable to the extent of decedent's contribution. Bonds registered in beneficiary form are taxed in the purchaser-owner's estate.

POWERS OF APPOINTMENT: Property subject to a power of appointment held by the decedent is taxed as under the federal law. Property passing under a general power of appointment created after October 12, 1942, is taxable in the estate of the donee of the power. Property subject to a special power of appointment is not taxed to the donee.

LIFE ESTATES AND PRIVATE ANNUITIES: Taxed at values based on statutory tables with 6% interest.

LIFE INSURANCE AND ANNUITY CONTRACTS: Federal rule generally applies. Insurance payable to the estate is taxable. Insurance on the life of a decedent payable to named beneficiaries (subject to certain exemptions) is taxable if the insured possessed at his death any of the incidents of ownership, exercisable alone or in conjunction with any other person. A reversionary interest as defined in the federal law is included within the term "incident of ownership."

The entire amount of insurance payable to the state, or charitable, etc., organizations, is exempt. Up to $20,000 of commercial life insurance payable to decedent's estate or any named beneficiary is also exempt if the insured's death is caused by enemy action in a military engagement. If a beneficiary who owns the policy predeceases the insured, the cash surrender value is includable in the beneficiary's gross estate, since her death effected a transfer to the contingent beneficiary. Accidental death insurance proceeds are taxed as life insurance proceeds. When life insurance proceeds are used to satisfy a mortgage or improvement loan on entirety real property, one-half of such proceeds are includable.

Government life insurance is not taxable if the insured served in World War I or II or any subsequent military engagement. This includes NSLI payable to the insured's estate. However, federal employees' group life insurance is taxed the same as other life insurance.

Annuity proceeds are taxable, and do not qualify for the life insurance exemption.

The total value or proceeds of an annuity payable to any beneficiary (but the executor) under a military family protection or survivor benefit plan is exempt. Also exempt is the total value of proceeds of an annuity or other payment receivable by any beneficiary, other than the estate, under a federal employee retirement program to which the employee made contributions during his working years.

EMPLOYEE BENEFIT PLANS: Benefits received from an employee plan are exempt from inheritance tax if such plan is qualified under federal law and the benefits are taxable under state income tax law. However, the value of benefits attributable to the deceased employee's contributions are taxable. (Deductible employee contributions under I.R.C. §72(0)(5) are not considered to have been contributed by the decedent, and thus are exempt.) IRAs are exempt in the same manner as other exempt benefits. Certain lump-sum distributions of retirement benefits described in Code §402(e)(4) are exempt.

Benefits received from a nonqualified plan and not subject to state income taxation are generally taxable. Where, however, decedent does not have the right to designate or change beneficiary and has no vested interest in the death payments, they are exempt.

Deductions

Funeral expenses (not to exceed $2,500 for monument and including bequests to a trust, the entire income of which is used to care for burial grounds, not to exceed the smaller of $1,250 or 2% of the gross estate), debts and claims, administration expenses, executor's commissions, attorney's fees, mortgages, taxes accrued at time of death, state inheritance and estate taxes, gift taxes paid upon a prior transfer which is subject to inheritance tax. *A tax credit* is allowed transferees if the property received from decedent had been taxed to him within five years prior to his death.

Valuation

Generally, property is valued at its market value on the date of decedent's death. However, if the personal representative elects the alternate valuation date, the federal rule will apply.

Exemptions

(Effective 7-1-79, all personal exemptions are replaced by a tax credit.)

Class A: Surviving spouse, lineal issue, adopted child, stepchild, lineal ancestor or son-in-law or daughter-in-law whose spouse is not entitled to any beneficial interest in the property of the deceased.

	Amount of Credit
(1) Surviving spouse	Tax credit of $3,150
(2) Children under 18 years of age, and mentally or physically incapacitated children who are unmarried and living with the decedent at the time of his death or institutionalized on account of the disability	Amount of credit unused by (1), above, on a pro rata basis
(3) Other Class A beneficiaries	Amount of credit unused by (1) and (2), above, on a pro rata basis

Class B:
Brother or sister or descendant of same, aunt or uncle by blood . . . . None

Class C:
All others . . . . None

Tax Rates

SHARE		CLASS A		CLASS B	
		Tax on	Rate on	Tax on	Rate on
From	*To*	*Col. 1*	*Excess*	*Col. 1*	*Excess*
$ 0	$ 5,000	$ 0	1%	$ 0	4%
5,000	10,000	50	1%	200	5%
10,000	25,000	100	2%	450	6%
25,000	50,000	400	3%	1,350	7%
50,000	100,000	1,150	4%	3,100	8%
100,000	200,000	3,150	5%	7,100	10%
200,000	250,000	8,150	6%	17,100	10%
250,000	500,000	11,150	6%	22,100	11%
500,000	1,000,000	26,150	7%	49,600	12%
1,000,000	1,500,000	61,150	8%	109,600	13%
1,500,000	2,000,000	101,150	9%	174,600	14%
2,000,000	2,500,000	146,150	10%	244,600	15%
2,500,000	3,000,000	196,150	11%	319,600	15%
3,000,000	Balance	251,150	12%	394,600	16%

SHARE		CLASS C	
		Tax on	Rate on
From	*To*	*Col. 1*	*Excess*
$ 0	$ 5,000	$ 0	8%
5,000	10,000	400	8%
10,000	25,000	800	9%
25,000	50,000	2,150	10%
50,000	100,000	4,650	11%
100,000	200,000	10,150	12%

200,000	250,000	22,150	12%
250,000	500,000	28,150	13%
500,000	1,000,000	60,650	14%
1,000,000	1,500,000	130,650	15%
1,500,000	2,000,000	205,650	16%
2,000,000	2,500,000	285,650	16%
2,500,000	3,000,000	365,650	17%
3,000,000	Balance	450,650	17%

Payment

The tax is due and payable at death. If not paid within 9 months, interest at 6% is charged from the expiration of the 9 month period. There is no provision for discount for prompt payment. The additional estate tax is payable in the same manner, and the same penalties attach.

Ultimate Tax Burden

No personal representative is required to file a return when the gross estate is less than $75,000 and all the beneficiaries are Class A beneficiaries. The personal representative is directed to collect the tax from the beneficiary, or to deduct it from the share, before distribution. Both the representative and the beneficiary are made liable for the tax. If a foreign corporation transfers on its books securities owned by a resident decedent, exceeding $200 par value, before the tax has been paid, it becomes liable for such tax. Domestic corporations transferring securities of either resident or nonresident decedents, without the consent of the Commissioner, become liable for the tax and a penalty not to exceed $1,000.

Nonresident Decedents

All real property and tangible personal property within the state, and all intangible personal property having a business situs within the state, are taxable, except that intangibles held in trust by a resident are not deemed to have acquired a taxable situs merely because the trustee is a resident. Shares of stock in domestic corporations, held by a nonresident decedent, are not taxable unless they have acquired a business situs within the state. There is no reciprocal exemption of intangibles. To find the tax, compute the gross tax upon the whole estate, using North Carolina rates, deductions, and exemption. Then determine the proportion which the North Carolina property bears to the entire estate. This is the net tax payable.

Generation-Skipping Transfer Tax

North Carolina has enacted a generation-skipping transfer tax. The North Carolina tax is imposed upon all generation-skipping transfers, as defined in Ch. 13 of Subdivision B of the Internal Revenue Code, which occur after July 1, 1979, when at the time of the transfer, the original transferor is a North Carolina resident, or the real or personal property is located in North Carolina.

The tax equals the amount of the credit for state legacy taxes under the federal generation-skipping provisions of Code §2602 to the extent such credit exceeds the aggregate amount of all taxes actually paid on the same transfer to any state other than North Carolina.

The taxpayer is required to file with the North Carolina Secretary of Revenue a duplicate of his or her federal generation-skipping tax return on or before the last day prescribed for filing the federal return. Payment of the tax is also due on or before the last day prescribed for filing the federal return.

NORTH DAKOTA
Type of Tax

Credit estate tax.

Credit Estate Tax

If all of a resident decedent's property is taxable in North Dakota, a tax is imposed on the transfer of a North Dakota taxable estate (i.e., all property in a decedent's federal gross estate that has a situs in North Dakota) at a rate equal to the maximum federal credit for state death taxes. If only part of the decedent's property has a taxable situs in North Dakota, the maximum federal credit equals the allowable credit against the federal estate tax for state death taxes multiplied by a fraction that has as its numerator the value of the portion of the decedent's estate having a taxable situs in North Dakota, and that has as its denominator the value of the decedent's entire estate.

Payment

The tax is due and payable at the death of the decedent. If not paid within 15 months, interest of 1% per month begins to run. There is no discount for prompt payment.

Ultimate Tax Burden

The personal representative and the beneficiaries are personally liable for the tax. If the personal representative pays the tax, he has a right to recover from the beneficiaries their proportionate part. Decedent may provide directions for payment of the tax.

Nonresident Decedents

Nonresidents are treated the same as residents.

OHIO
Type of Tax

1. Estate tax. 2. Credit estate tax. 3. Generation-skipping transfer tax.

Exempted Property

Since Ohio has an estate tax somewhat similar to the federal estate tax, there generally is no exempted property. However, certain police, firemen's, and State Highway Patrol pension fund payments are exempt. Property transferred to charitable, etc. institutions are deductible from decedent's gross estate. Pay and allowances due a member of the armed services, while missing in action in Vietnam prior to his (her) death between Feb. 28, 1961 and July 1, 1973, are exempt.

Taxable Property

IN GENERAL: The tax is imposed upon all real property and all tangible personal property within Ohio, and all intangible personalty of Ohio residents wherever located.

DOWER OR STATUTORY SUBSTITUTE: Taxable.

CONTEMPLATION OF DEATH: Transfers made within three years of death are presumed in contemplation of death unless the contrary is shown. Sales, transfers of property that would not be included in the decedent's gross estate if retained until death, transfers of property that are not required to be reported for federal gift tax purposes, federal or state gift taxes, and proceeds of insurance payable under an employer death benefit plan (unless paid to the estate) are excluded from application of the contemplation of death provision.

TRANSFERS EFFECTIVE AT OR AFTER DEATH: Transfers of property, in trust or otherwise, reserving income to the grantor, or intended to take effect in possession or enjoyment after death, or where the grantor reserves the right to amend or revoke, are taxable.

JOINTLY OWNED PROPERTY: Property passing by right of survivorship is taxable in full, unless it can be shown that the property, originally belonged to the survivor. Where the joint tenants are husband and wife, one-half the property is taxable.

POWERS OF APPOINTMENT: The value of all property, to the extent the decedent held a general power of appointment on the date of his death, is taxable.

LIFE ESTATES AND PRIVATE ANNUITIES: Such interests are valued by the usual methods of valuation, including the use of tables of mortality and actuarial principles, under rules and regulations prescribed by the tax commissioner.

LIFE INSURANCE AND ANNUITY CONTRACTS: Insurance payable to the estate is taxable. Insurance, including government life insurance, payable directly to named beneficiaries or in trust is exempt. Insurance paid to a guardian or custodian for the benefit of an incompetent or minor is also exempt. Matured endowments are not exempt insurance. Annuity death benefits generally are taxable, excluding certain government annuities. Employer death benefit insurance otherwise includable in decedent's gross estate is reduced by $2,000 if payment is made by reason of the death of a plan participant.

EMPLOYEE BENEFIT PLANS: So much of the value of an annuity or other payment as is proportionate to employer contributions is includible in the Ohio gross estate if it is excludable from the federal gross estate under Code §2039 and if the annuity or other payment was payable to the decedent or the decedent possessed the right to receive such an annuity or payment for his/her life or for any period not ascertainable without reference to his/her death or for any period which does not in fact end before his/her death.

Deductions

Funeral expenses, costs of administration, claims against the estate which are outstanding and unpaid as of the date of decedent's death, and bequests to the United States, any state or political subdivision thereof, or to a charitable institution are deductible. Unpaid mortgages, when the subject property value is included in the gross estate undiminished by the mortgage debt, are also deductible. Property passing to a surviving spouse qualifies for a marital deduction equal to the lesser of (1) the amount allowed by the federal estate tax marital deduction or (2) the greater of 1/2 of the difference between the value of the gross estate and the deductions allowed by §5731.160F of the Ohio Revised Code, or $500,000.

Valuation

Property is valued at its market value on the date of decedent's death, or an alternate valuation date of six months after death, unless special valuation of qualified real farm property is elected.

Tax Rates

| NET ESTATE | | | | Of Amount |
From	To	Tax Is	Plus	Over
$ 0	$ 40,000	$ 0	2%	$ 0
40,000	100,000	800	3%	40,000
100,000	200,000	2,600	4%	100,000
200,000	300,000	6,600	5%	200,000
300,000	500,000	11,600	6%	300,000
500,000	Balance	23,600	7%	500,000

Credit

A credit is allowed against the tax equal to the lesser of $500 or the amount of the tax.

Payment

The taxes are due and payable 9 months after the death of the decedent. After the expiration of 9 months, interest is charged at the rate of 6% until payment is made. There is no discount for early payment. The credit estate tax is collected in the same manner. The tax on remainder and reversionary interests may be deferred, if the executor so elects. Penalties are provided for late filing.

Ultimate Tax Burden

The personal representative is personally liable for payment of the tax. The representative is directed to deduct the tax from the share of the beneficiary before distribution.

Nonresident Decedents

Real property and tangible personal property within the state, and intangible personal property used in carrying on a business within the state, are taxable. Reciprocal exemption is provided for intangibles.

OKLAHOMA
Type of Tax

1. Estate tax. 2. Credit estate tax.

Exempted Property

The statute exempts transfers to the state or any of its subdivisions, to religious, charitable, or educational bodies organized in Oklahoma, and to nonprofit Oklahoma youth groups or medical research foundations. Transfers to similar institutions in other states are exempt if such states grant Oklahoma reciprocity. Also exempt are transfers for the education, support, and relief of poor, blind, or crippled residents of Oklahoma.

Also exempted is the net value of any interest in the decedent's estate, beneficial or otherwise, that vests in his or her surviving spouse. This exemption applies with respect to both resident and non-resident decedents.

Taxable Property

IN GENERAL: The tax is imposed upon all real property and all tangible personal property within Oklahoma, and all intangible personalty of Oklahoma residents wherever located.

DOWER OR STATUTORY SUBSTITUTE: Statutory estates in lieu of dower or curtesy are taxable.

CONTEMPLATION OF DEATH: Transfers made within three years of death are presumed in contemplation of death unless the contrary is shown, but if a gift tax has been paid on the transfer, it is allowed as a credit. If decedent exercised or released a general power of appointment in contemplation of death, the affected property is taxed in his estate.

TRANSFERS EFFECTIVE AT OR AFTER DEATH: Property transferred by decedent, reserving income, or intended to take effect in possession or enjoyment after death, is taxable. Revocable trusts fall within this definition. Proceeds of a matured endowment left at interest are also includable.

JOINTLY OWNED PROPERTY: Property held jointly with the right of survivorship (including tenancies by the entirety and joint bank accounts) is taxable to the extent of decedent's interest therein.

POWERS OF APPOINTMENT: If decedent possessed a general power of appointment when he died, the property subject thereto is taxed in his estate.

LIFE ESTATES AND PRIVATE ANNUITIES: The American Experience Table of Mortality, with interest at 5%, is used to compute taxable value.

LIFE INSURANCE AND ANNUITY CONTRACTS: Insurance payable to the estate is taxable. There is a special $20,000 exemption for insurance paid to named beneficiaries of decedents dying before July 1, 1974. After that date, no exemption is available. The proceeds are taxable, provided decedent had power either to change the benficiary or to convert the policies to his own use. A remote reversionary interest alone, without present incidents of ownership, will not bring a policy into the insured's gross estate. Where decedent had gained an interest in another's policy through premium payments, such interest is excluded. Government life insurance is entirely exempt.

EMPLOYEE BENEFIT PLANS: Death benefits from annuities and retirement plans are included in decedent's estate to the extent of contributions made by the employee-decedent. The value of *all* such benefits, however, are excluded where the beneficiary is decedent's surviving spouse.

Deductions

Expenses of funeral and last illness (not to exceed $1,000 for a burial lot, crypt, or mausoleum and $500 for a gravestone), debts, administration costs, executor's commissions, attorney's fees, property subject to Oklahoma gift or estate tax within five years before decedent died, and certain unpaid taxes. Deductible taxes include property taxes, federal and state income taxes to the date of decedent's death, federal gift tax, and other states' death taxes on intangibles. If decedent left out-of-state property, these deductions may be taken only in the proportion which the Oklahoma property bears to the whole estate. The federal estate tax is not deductible.

There is a *tax credit* for all or part of the Oklahoma estate tax paid with respect to property includable in the decedent's estate that was transferred to the decedent by a person who died within 10 years before or 2 years after the decedent.

Valuation

Property is valued at its market value on the date of decedent's death or, at the election of the executor, an alternative valuation date six months after death.

Exemptions

PERSONAL EXEMPTIONS—Class one: Father, mother, child, child of husband or wife, adopted child or lineal descendant of decedent or of such adopted child, not in excess of a total aggregate of $175,000. Exemptions are deducted from the net estate before the tax is applied.

Class two: All others. There are no exemptions for this class.

There is a complete exemption of any interest passing to a spouse who is an Oklahoma resident, except for the purposes of calculating the credit estate tax.

Tax Rates

(On net estate after deductions and exemptions.)

Estate Tax*

NET ESTATE (after deductions and exemptions) Col. 1		CLASS ONE Tax on Col. 1	Rate on Excess	CLASS TWO Tax on Col. 1	Rate on Excess
$ 0 $	10,000	$ 0	1%	$ 0	2%
10,000	20,000	100	2%	200	4%
20,000	40,000	300	3%	600	6%
40,000	60,000	900	4%	1,800	8%
60,000	100,000	1,700	5%	3,400	10%
100,000	250,000	3,700	6%	7,400	12%
250,000	500,000	12,700	6.5%	25,400	13%
500,000	750,000	28,950	7%	57,900	14%
750,000	1,000,000	46,450	7.5%	92,900	14%
1,000,000	3,000,000	65,200	8%	127,900	15%
3,000,000	5,000,000	225,200	8.5%	427,900	15%
5,000,000	10,000,000	395,200	9%	727,900	15%
10,000,000	. . . . . .	845,200	10%	1,477,900	15%

* If the total net value of the estate within Oklahoma is less than $100, the estate is exempt from tax.

Payment

The tax is due and payable within nine months after death of decedent. If not paid within such time, interest at 1% per month is assessed from the expiration of nine months, unless the delay is caused by litigation or dispute as to the value of the estate, in which case the tax upon the disputed portion shall be ½ of 1% per month. There is no discount for early payment. No estate tax return need be filed where decedent's surviving spouse receives all of decedent's property, or where an Oklahoma district court issues an order releasing estate tax liability. The additional estate tax is payable in the same manner, and with the same penalties, as the estate tax.

Ultimate Tax Burden

The personal representative is personally liable for the tax on any part of the estate which he transfers without collecting the tax thereon. The beneficiaries are personally liable for the tax on property received by them.

Nonresident Decedents

The property of nonresident decedents which is subject to the tax includes all real property and tangible personal property within the state, and all intangible personal property having a business situs in the state, or which is held in trust by a resident, when the nonresident died resident of a state which does not tax similar transfers by citizens of Oklahoma. Exemptions and deductions may be taken in the proportion which the Oklahoma property bears to the total estate.

A nonresident decedent's partnership interest in Oklahoma-based property is intangible personal property having a business situs therein. However, it is not taxed if decedent's state of residence contains a reciprocal exemption for such property.

OREGON

Type of Tax

1. Inheritance tax. 2. Credit estate tax. (The inheritance tax is to be phased out by 1987; its elimination will not affect the credit estate tax.)

Exempted Property

Transfers to the state of Oregon or any of its political subdivisions are exempt. Transfers to the United States, any state, or territory and any political subdivision of them for an exclusively public purpose are exempt. Transfers to charitable, benevolent, religious, scientific, or educational institutions wherever located are also exempt. Social Security benefits are not subject to the state inheritance tax.

Taxable Property

IN GENERAL: The tax is imposed upon all real property and all tangible personal property within Oregon, and all intangible personalty of Oregon residents wherever located.

DOWER OR STATUTORY SUBSTITUTE: Taxable.

CONTEMPLATION OF DEATH: Transfers made within three years before death are subject to taxation, whether made in contemplation of death or not. Transfers made more than three years before decedent's death are not taxable if: (1) no gift taxes were due on such transfers, or (2) assessed gift taxes were paid when due.

TRANSFERS EFFECTIVE AT OR AFTER DEATH: Transfers of property by decedent, reserving income, or intended to take effect in possession or enjoyment after death, are taxable.

JOINTLY OWNED PROPERTY: One half of jointly owned property that passes by right of survivorship to the surviving spouse is included in the decedent's taxable estate. Also, ½ of real property held in tenancy by the entirety is included in the taxable estate. Where decedent and his spouse sold property under an executory or installment contract, their right to the unpaid balance of the purchase price is taxed as entirety property.

POWERS OF APPOINTMENT: A transfer by exercise of a general power of appointment is taxed in the donee's (appointor's) estate.

LIFE ESTATES AND PRIVATE ANNUITIES: Taxable at values ascertained by reference to the 6% Federal Mortality Tables.

LIFE INSURANCE AND ANNUITY CONTRACTS: All insurance proceeds from policies in which the decedent has retained any incidents of ownership are taxable. Incidents of ownership include a reversionary interest, but only if the value of the reversionary interest exceeds 5% of the value of the policy immediately before decedent's death.

EMPLOYEE BENEFIT PLANS: The benefits payable to each beneficiary, other than decedent's estate, under the Social Security Act, National Railroad Retirement Act; any pension or retirement plan established by the federal or state government or any of its political subdivisions, or any qualified employee plan, are exempt, but only to the extent that the benefit value is attributable to employer or owner-employee contributions. IRAs under I.R.C., §408(a), individual retirement annuities under I.R.C., §408(b), and retirement bonds under I.R.C., §409(a) are also exempt.

Deductions

Expenses of funeral (not to exceed $1,000 for memorial), administration expenses (if not taken as deductions under state income tax law), executor's commissions, reasonable attorney's, appraiser's, trustee's and accountant's fees, debts, mortgages, state, county and municipal taxes which are a lien at death; accrued state or federal income and gift taxes (but not federal estate tax); decedent's debts owing at death paid or payable from property included in the estate are deductible. No deduction is allowed for interest expenses accruing after the time of death.

There is a credit for inheritance taxes previously paid on property in the decedent's estate which he received from related individuals within 5 years of his death.

Valuation

Property is valued at its market value on the date of decedent's death. Property tax provisions govern the valuation of forest land.

Exemptions

An exemption from the inheritance tax is allowed in an amount determined by the year decedent dies as follows:

Year of Decedent's Death	Amount of Exemption
1978	$ 50,000
1979 and 1980	70,000
1981 and 1982	100,000
1983 and 1984	200,000
1985 and 1986	500,000

Tax Rates

A uniform inheritance tax rate of 12% is imposed on amounts exceeding the exemption. The rate on all estates of decedents dying after January 1, 1987 is zero. (The inheritance tax will thereby be eliminated as of January 1, 1987.)

Credits

A credit is allowed against the inheritance tax for each beneficiary who is a surviving spouse, a child or stepchild under age 18 at his parent's death, or a child or stepchild judicially deemed to be physically or mentally incapacitated. The amount of the credit is the lesser of the amount of the tax or the amount determined by reference to the following table:

Year of Decedent's Death	Amount of Credit
1978	$54,000
1979 and 1980	51,600
1981 and 1982	48,000
1983 and 1984	36,000
1985 and 1986	—0—

Payment

The return and payment are due within 9 months after the date of death. There is a penalty equal to 5% of the amount of tax for failure to file a return within the 9-month period. An additional penalty of 20% of the tax is imposed if the failure to file extends beyond 3 months after the due date. The 5% and 20% penalties do not apply to the amount of tax paid within the 9-month period. *Interest* at the rate of 1% per month or fraction of month accrues on any tax not paid within 9 months of the date of death. *Interest* at the rate of 3/4% per month or fraction of a month accrues on any tax due, but postponed by an approved extension of payment.

Ultimate Tax Burden

The personal representative of the decedent, and the beneficiary, are personally liable for the tax. The representative is directed to deduct the amount of the tax from the share, or to collect the amount from the beneficiary, before distributing the property.

Nonresident Decedents

Real property and tangible personal property located within the state, and intangible personal property that has gained a business situs within the state, are taxable. A reciprocal exemption is provided for intangibles of nonresidents. Full exemptions are allowed to nonresidents, but deductions may be taken only in the proportion that the value of the Oregon property bears to the entire estate.

PENNSYLVANIA
Type of Tax

1. Inheritance tax. 2. Credit estate tax.

Exempted Property

The statute exempts: (1) transfers to the United States, the Commonwealth of Pennsylvania, or any of its subdivisions; (2) transfers to bodies organized exclusively for religious, charitable, scientific, literary, or educational purposes (including encouragement of art and prevention of cruelty to children or animals); (3) transfers to lodges for religious, charitable, scientific, literary or educational purposes; (4) transfers to certain veterans' organizations; and (5) payments due as a result of decedent's service in the Vietnam conflict after August 5, 1964 while missing in action prior to death.

Benefits payable to a self-employed decedent's beneficiary from a Keogh plan are not subject to the inheritance tax.

Taxable Property

IN GENERAL: The tax is imposed upon all real property and all tangible personal property within Pennsylvania, and all intangible personalty of Pennsylvania residents wherever located.

DOWER OR STATUTORY SUBSTITUTE: Taxable.

CONTEMPLATION OF DEATH: A transfer in excess of $3,000 made within one year of death is taxed.

TRANSFERS EFFECTIVE AT OR AFTER DEATH: Transfers of property, reserving income to decedent, are taxable. So are transfers intended to take effect in possession or enjoyment after death, provided the decedent retained at least a 5% reversionary interest. If decedent transferred property during his lifetime but reserved a life estate, the property is taxed at the rate prevailing when he signed the deed or trust instrument. A revocable transfer with a reserved life estate is taxed at the rate prevailing when the transfer became irrevocable.

If decedent created a revocable trust, its corpus is not taxed at his death unless he retained a vested or contingent life estate.

JOINTLY OWNED PROPERTY: Property held jointly with the right of survivorship (except property held jointly with the spouse) is taxable to the extent of decedent's interest therein, to be determined by dividing the value of the property by the number of joint owners. Estates by the entirety in real and personal property (including joint bank accounts) are not taxable, unless they fall within the contemplation-of-death provisions. United States savings bonds registered in co-ownership form are considered joint property and taxed accordingly. However, if decedent furnished the entire purchase price and his co-owner never had access to the bonds, they are fully taxable.

POWERS OF APPOINTMENT: The transfer of property subject to a power of appointment is not taxable to the estate of the donee. The property is taxed in the estate of the donor of the power, notwithstanding any blending of such property with the donee's estate. In computing the tax, use the relationship between the donor and appointee, and the value at the donee's death.

Where the income beneficiary of a life insurance trust possessed a general power of appointment over the corpus and exercised it in her will, the corpus was not taxed at her death. Since she was donee of the power, the tax did not reach these funds in her estate, and they were exempt life insurance proceeds in the insured's (donor's) estate.

LIFE ESTATES AND PRIVATE ANNUITIES: Valued in accordance with the federal estate tax tables.

LIFE INSURANCE AND ANNUITY CONTRACTS: All life insurance proceeds are exempt. The proceeds of a previously matured endowment are not exempt as life insurance.

All government life insurance proceeds are exempt.

An annuity cannot qualify as life insurance; hence, the sum payable to a refund-annuity beneficiary at the annuitant's death is taxable.

EMPLOYEE BENEFIT PLANS: A statute provides that payments made to decedent's designated beneficiaries under a pension, stock-bonus or profit-sharing plan, or a Keogh plan or IRA, are exempt from inheritance tax to the extent that decedent before his death did not otherwise have the right to possess (including proprietary rights at termination of employment), enjoy, assign or anticipate the payments so made, or to the extent the benefits are exempt from federal estate tax. A payment which would otherwise be exempt for federal estate tax purposes if it had not been made in a lump sum is exempt even if paid in a lump sum. Where decedent had retired but died before all retirement payments had been received, the remainder paid to a named beneficiary under the statute was exempt. The statute further provides that life insurance proceeds, otherwise exempt, shall not be subject to inheritance tax because they are paid under a plan. Likewise, lump-sum death benefits under the Social Security or Railroad Retirement Acts are exempt even if paid to decedent's estate. It has been held that accumulated pension benefits paid to an incompetent veteran's estate and then distributed to his heirs are exempt. Also, the proceeds of the Public School Employee's Retirement Fund are exempt even when paid to decedent's estate.

Case decisions on the pre-1961 law generally followed the rules established by the 1961 statute. Where, however, the court found that the decedent possessed a power of appointment in the employer's contributions at death, or possessed a substantial ownership of his allocated share of a profit-sharing trust prior to his death, or could have assigned his interest in a deferred compensation contract prior to his death, the amount received by the beneficiary was subject to inheritance tax.

Retirement benefit payments paid to a surviving spouse pursuant to a Keogh plan, where death occurs prior to the retirement of the plan participant, are an exempt retirement annuity under §2485-316 and are not taxable.

Deductions

Funeral expenses (including reasonable cemetery and gravestone costs, and bequests for masses), the $2,000 family exemption, administration costs, debts, taxes which were debts of decedent, death taxes of other states and foreign countries to the extent attributable to property which is subject to this tax, and nonreimbursed medical expenses. Pennsylvania does *not* permit deduction of the federal estate tax, litigation expenses of beneficiaries, contractual claims of a spouse or former spouse, or debts to the extent they are secured by realty or tangible personalty located outside the state.

Valuation

Property is valued at its market value on the date of decedent's death. A reduction in value is allowed for federal income taxes paid on income in respect of the decedent.

Effective December 10, 1980, the value of land owned by the decedent and devoted to agricultural use, agricultural reserve, or forest reserve shall be its value for its particular use, rather than its fair market value. To achieve this valuation for land devoted to agricultural use requires that the land have been so used during the three years preceding the decedent's death and be at least ten contiguous acres in area or have an anticipated yearly gross income from such use of $2,000. Where the land is presently devoted to agricultural reserve or forest reserve, it must be at least ten contiguous acres in area for the particular use valuation to apply. Finally, the contiguous tract of land sought to be valued in this manner must not be less than the entire contiguous area of the owner used for agricultural use, agricultural reserve, or farm reserve purposes.

Exemptions

Class A: None. A $2,000 family exemption is allowed as a deduction, however.

Class B: None.

Tax Rates

CLASS A: Grandparents, parents, spouse, lineal descendants (including descendants by adoption and of stepchildren), stepchildren, wife or widow of son, husband or widower of daughter.

The rate of tax imposed on Class A beneficiaries is a flat 6%.

CLASS B: All persons not in Class A.

The rate of tax imposed on Class B beneficiaries is a flat 15%. A bequest to a corporation is taxed at the 15% rate regardless of the relationship of stockholders to decedent.

If a will directs that inheritance tax on a specific or general legacy be paid from the residuary estate, the amount of residue so used is not an additional legacy to the specific or general legatee.

Payment

The tax is due and payable at the death of decedent. A discount of 5% is allowed if the tax is paid within three months after becoming due. If the estate tax is not paid within 9 months, or the inheritance tax is not paid within 9 months after death, interest at the federal rate is charged from such time. Payment of tax due on the transfer of a small business interest may be paid in quarterly installments beginning 9 months after the decedent's death.

Ultimate Tax Burden

The personal representative of the estate is personally liable for the tax. He is directed to collect the tax from the beneficiaries before distribution unless there is a contrary direction in the will or other instrument of transfer, and except for those beneficiaries who receive specific or general devises and bequests. The inheritance tax on specific or general devises, and bequests, unless directed otherwise by the testator, is paid from the residuary estate and charged in the same manner as a general administration expense.

Nonresident Decedents

The transfer of real property and tangible personal property having its situs in Pennsylvania is taxed. Intangibles of nonresidents are not taxable if the state or country of residence does not tax intangibles of nonresidents or if the state or country of residence provide for a reciprocal exemption of intangibles. The tax on nonresidents' property may be computed by one of two methods: (1) take the value of the Pennsylvania property in excess of any unpaid property taxes, liens and mortgages, without any deductions, and apply the applicable rate; or (2) take the value of the entire estate and compute the tax just as though the decedent was a resident and then pay tax in an amount which bears the same ratio to the total tax as the Pennsylvania property bears to the entire estate. The additional estate tax does not apply to a nonresident decedent's estate unless he is a resident of a foreign country.

PUERTO RICO
Type of Tax

Estate Tax. Puerto Rico has a community property law. However, at the death of either spouse the entire community property is included in the decedent's gross estate for the purpose of attributing to the survivor the proportional amount of debts, liens, and obligations.

Exempted Property

Because Puerto Rico has an estate tax, there is no exempted property as such. Property transferred to charitable, etc. institutions is deductible from decedent's gross estate.

Taxable Property

IN GENERAL: The tax is imposed upon all of decedent's property, real or personal, tangible or intangible, wherever located. A credit is allowed for property not located in Puerto Rico and taxed in such jurisdiction.

DOWER OR STATUTORY SUBSTITUTE: Dower does not exist. Puerto Rico has a community prop-

erty law. The surviving spouse's one-half of a community property is deductible.

TRANSFERS EFFECTIVE AT OR AFTER DEATH: Transfers of property by decedent, reserving income, or intended to take effect in possession or enjoyment after death, are taxable.

JOINTLY OWNED PROPERTY: Property held jointly with right of survivorship is taxable in full except to the extent the survivor can show original ownership.

POWERS OF APPOINTMENT: No statutory provision.

LIFE ESTATE AND PRIVATE ANNUITIES: No statutory provision.

LIFE INSURANCE AND ANNUITY CONTRACTS: Life insurance on which the decedent had paid the premiums directly or indirectly, or in which he owned any incident of ownership, is included in the gross estate. If, however, the proceeds are payable to decedent's administrator, surviving spouse, or heirs, a deduction not to exceed $10,000 is allowed. The value of any annuity contract to the extent received by a survivor is included in decedent's gross estate. Also, any life insurance amounts payable to the surviving spouse are deductible to the extent of 50% of the total amounts payable as life insurance on the decedent.

EMPLOYEE BENEFIT PLANS: Any amount paid to decedent's survivors under a private retirement system is includable in the gross estate. Amounts paid under a retirement fund subsidized by Puerto Rico or from the United States are exempt up to the first $2,500 per annum.

Deductions

Transfers to Puerto Rico, the United States or any of its states including political subdivisions thereof for public purposes; transfers to religious, charitable, scientific, literary, educational, and cultural organizations; transfers to lodges for religious, charitable, scientific, literary, or educational purposes; transfers to veterans' organizations are all deductible. Property received by a surviving spouse from the decedent if the value of such property was included in the decedent's gross estate, and undistributed amounts accumulated in the decedent's IRA up to a maximum of $100,000, are also deductible. Decedent's debts, taxes that were due at his death, mortgages, funeral expenses, losses, and the first $60,000 of property are also deductible. 50% of the value of property included in the gross estate which has been invested for a period of three years or more in a qualified enterprise for a greater development of the Puerto Rico economy is deductible. Otherwise, up to $200,000 may be deducted for eligible investments improving the Puerto Rican economy.

An agricultural deduction is permitted. This deduction from the decedent's gross estate is equivalent to 100% of the value of agricultural, poultry, or farm-livestock production property. However, the decedent must have derived more than 50% of net income from such farm business during the three years prior to death, and these farm production units must remain active as such for at least ten years after the decedent's death.

One-half of all the community property is deductible.

Administration expenses such as fees for attorneys, accountants, appraisers, surveyors, partitioners, and the executor are deductible subject to a maximum as follows:

Value of Gross Estate:

Not over $100,000 . . . . . .   3 %
$100,000 to $ 500,000 . . . .   2½ % or $ 3,000, whichever is higher
$500,000 to $1,000,000 . . . .   2 % or $15,000, whichever is higher
Over $1,000,000 . . . .   1½ % or $20,000, whichever is higher

Valuation

Property is valued at its market value on the date of decedent's death. However, the executor, administrator or trustee may elect an alternate valuation date six months after the decedent's death.

Exemptions

No personal exemptions allowed. The first $60,000 is deductible from the gross estate.

Tax Rates

(On taxable estate plus adjusted gifts.)

From	To	Tax on Col. 1	Rate on Excess
$ 0	$ 10,000	$ 0	18%
10,000	20,000	1,800	20%
20,000	40,000	3,800	22%
40,000	60,000	8,200	24%
60,000	80,000	13,000	26%
80,000	100,000	18,200	28%
100,000	150,000	23,800	30%
150,000	250,000	38,800	32%
250,000	500,000	70,800	34%
500,000	750,000	155,800	37%
750,000	1,000,000	248,300	39%
1,000,000	1,250,000	345,800	41%
1,250,000	1,500,000	448,300	43%
1,500,000	2,000,000	555,800	45%
2,000,000	2,500,000	780,800	49%
2,500,000	Balance	1,025,800	50%

Credits

A unified credit of up to $121,800 is allowed. A credit is allowed for any property included in decedent's gross estate which he received as an inheritance or gift within 10 years of his death. This credit is an amount that bears the same ratio to the estate tax previously paid with respect to the value of the transferred property, less an amount which bears the same ratio of such transfer with the taxable estate or taxable gift, as the case may be, decreased by any other estate or gift taxes paid in connection with said estate. However, the credit is reduced by 20% for each full two years by which the death of the prior decedent preceded the decedent's death.

Another credit is allowed for the tax paid to the United States or any jurisdiction for property which is also included in the Puerto Rico estate. There is also a credit for taxes paid on gifts made in 1967 and 1968 where such property is included in decedent's gross estate. This latter credit is limited, however, by an amount which is the difference between the estate tax, computed by including the value of the gifts, and the estate tax computed without the value of the gifts.

Payment

The tax is due and payable without notice or assessment within 270 days after decedent's death. Payment may be delayed as much as six years if an extension is granted. There is no discount for prompt payment. Interest at the rate of 6% per year is charged on the first three years of extension and 9% thereafter. If a tax deficiency is assessed, interest at the rate of 9% runs from the date of assessment. Where an extension is granted because decedent's assets are in a family business, 6% interest is charged. The interest rate is changed to one equivalent to 2% (for individuals) or 5% (for partnerships or corporations) over the maximum interest rate established by Board of Interest and Finance charges for personal loans. Certain real and personal property may be used, in addition to or in lieu of money, for the partial or full payment of estate taxes. Such property must be certified as having great, historical, cultural importance to Puerto Rico, or be property which the government has declared an interest in expropriating for public purposes, or is already in the government's possession and engaged in public use. Furthermore, such property must be based within a period of one year following the filing of the estate tax return. At the expiration of this one year period, this property will no longer be accepted as payment for the estate tax instead of cash.

Ultimate Tax Burden

Decedent's personal representative is liable for the tax unless relieved of such liability by the Secretary. If no personal representative is appointed, or he is relieved of responsibility of tax payment, the heirs, donees, or beneficiaries are responsible for the full amount of the tax until it is paid. The personal representative, when responsible, has a right to recover the proportionate amount of tax from any heir, etc. and he may sell any of the estate's property to obtain funds to pay the taxes.

Nonresident Decedents

The tax reaches all real and personal property, including intangibles, located in Puerto Rico. Certain securities of Puerto Rico are exempt if the transferee is also a nonresident. Deductions are allowed in the proportion that Puerto Rico property bears to the total gross estate. Where the estate of the nonresident decedent, not located in Puerto Rico, is subject to taxation in his or her country of origin, the tax equals the maximum tax credit that the country of origin grants to the estate of the nonresident decedent (not located in Puerto Rico) on the property located in Puerto Rico.

RHODE ISLAND
Type of Tax

1. Estate tax. 2. Additional estate tax. 3. Credit estate tax. 4. Special tax on contingencies. 5. Generation-skipping transfer tax.

Exempted Property

Transfers exempted under the basic estate tax include property transferred to corporations, associations or institutions in the state which are exempted, by charter or law, from taxation, or to any corporation, institution or association located outside the state, if the state of domicile allows an exemption to similar Rhode Island organizations, or to any person in trust for the same, or for use by the same for charitable purposes, or to any Rhode Island city or town for public purposes, or estates of servicemen missing in action. Similarly, U.S. civil and federal military service annuity payments are exempt. Also, there shall be exempted from the estate tax a marital deduction in the amount of $175,000 for interests passing to decedent's surviving spouse, providing such interests are included in decedent's gross estate. Furthermore, there shall be

exempted from the estate tax an orphan's deduction similar to the one allowed under federal law. Limited powers of appointment are not subject to tax.

Taxable Property

IN GENERAL: The tax is imposed upon all real property and all tangible personal property within Rhode Island, and all intangible personalty of Rhode Island residents wherever located.

DOWER OR STATUTORY SUBSTITUTE: Formerly, the statute expressly stated that dower and curtesy in property located in Rhode Island were taxable. For estates of decedents dying on or after October 1, 1980, however, this language has been deleted from the statute.

CONTEMPLATION OF DEATH: Gifts made in contemplation of death are taxable. Property transferred within two years of death is presumed to have been transferred in contemplation of death, unless the contrary is proven.

TRANSFERS EFFECTIVE AT OR AFTER DEATH: Transfers of property by decedent, reserving income or power to revoke, or intended to take effect in possession or enjoyment after death, are taxable.

JOINTLY OWNED PROPERTY: Property held jointly with right of survivorship, including tenancy by the entirety, is taxable to the survivor, except to the extent that the spouse can show original ownership.

POWERS OF APPOINTMENT: Transfers by the exercise, nonexercise, disclaimer, or renunciation of a general power of appointment are taxed as if the property belonged absolutely to the donee and passed by his will. Limited powers of appointment are not subject to tax.

LIFE ESTATES AND PRIVATE ANNUITIES: Taxed at values based on the mortality tables used in Reg. §20.2031-10, with interest at 6%.

LIFE INSURANCE AND ANNUITY CONTRACTS: Insurance, whether payable to a trustee, executor, administrator, or any other named beneficiary, is fully taxable, provided the insured possessed incidents of ownership in the policies when he died. Prior to 6-1-78, the first $50,000 of life insurance was exempted.

EMPLOYEE BENEFIT PLANS: No statutory provision as to the taxation or exclusion therefrom of survivor benefits.

Deductions

Funeral expenses, debts and claims, costs of administration, attorney's fees, executor's and trustee's commissions, family allowance, unpaid mortgages, death taxes of other states, other state and local taxes owing at time of death, losses incurred during administration in reducing intangibles (except stocks and bonds) to possession.

Valuation

Property is valued at its market value on the date of decedent's death.

Exemptions

(Allowed for in the Tax Rate Tables)

Decedent's estate is allowed an exemption of $25,000 in computing the net estate.

Tax Rates

ESTATE TAX

NET ESTATE		Tax on	Rate on
From	To	Col. 1	Excess
$ 0	$ 25,000	$ 0	2%
25,000	50,000	500	3%
50,000	100,000	1,250	4%
100,000	250,000	3,250	5%
250,000	500,000	10,750	6%
500,000	750,000	25,750	7%
750,000	1,000,000	43,250	8%
1,000,000	Balance	63,250	9%

ADDITIONAL ESTATE TAX[1]

NET ESTATE		Tax on	Rate on
From	To	Col. 1	Excess
$ 0	$ 250,000	$ 0	0%
250,000	300,000	0	1.4 %
300,000	500,000	700	2.2 %
500,000	700,000	5,100	3.0 %
700,000	900,000	11,100	3.8 %
900,000	1,000,000	18,700	4.6 %
1,000,000	1,500,000	23,300	5.24%
1,500,000	2,000,000	49,500	6.04%
2,000,000	2,500,000	79,700	6.84%
2,500,000	3,000,000	113,900	7.64%
3,000,000	3,500,000	152,100	8.44%
3,500,000	4,000,000	194,300	9.24%
4,000,000	5,000,000	240,500	10.12%
5,000,000	6,000,000	341,700	10.92%
6,000,000	7,000,000	450,900	11.72%
7,000,000	8,000,000	568,100	12.52%
8,000,000	9,000,000	693,300	13.32%
9,000,000	10,000,000	826,500	14.12%
10,000,000	Balance	967,700	14.92%

[1] Where the tax imposed under this table is less than the credit allowed under I.R.C., §2011, then a tax is imposed such that the total of all taxes paid is equal to the credit allowed by Code §2011.

Special Tax

A special tax of 2% is imposed in the case of contingencies which make it impossible to determine the tax immediately. This tax is paid by the estate, and is for the privilege of awaiting the contingency before having the final tax on the remainder interest determined. This 2% tax is in addition to any legacy tax that may be due when the contingency happens.

Payment

The two estate taxes and the inheritance tax are due and payable ten months after the date of death. Extensions of time to pay the tax, not to exceed four years from the due date, may be allowed in cases of undue hardship. There is no discount for early payment. If the taxes are not paid within ten months from the date of death, 8% interest is charged, without regard to any extensions granted. A penalty shall be added to the tax if not paid when due (determined without regard to extensions) of .5% of the tax due per month up to a maximum of 25%, unless reasonable cause for the failure to pay, and not willful neglect, can be shown.

Ultimate Tax Burden

The personal representative is made personally liable for the tax, and is directed to collect the amount of the tax from the beneficiaries, or deduct it from their shares, before distribution. Beneficiaries are not personally liable. The tax, however, is a lien upon the property transferred.

Nonresident Decedents

Real property and tangible personal property having an actual situs within the state are taxable, but intangibles of nonresidents are not taxed. The $25,000 exemption, orphan's deduction, $175,000 marital deduction, and other deductions are granted to nonresidents in the proportion which the Rhode Island property bears to the entire estate.

Generation-Skipping Transfer Tax

Rhode Island has enacted a generation-skipping transfer tax based on the federal generation-skipping transfer tax. The Rhode Island tax is imposed on every generation-skipping transfer as defined by Ch. 13 of Subdivision B of the Internal Revenue Code, where the original and deemed transferors are Rhode Island residents, or the real or personal property transferred is located in Rhode Island.

The tax equals the amount of the credit for state

legacy taxes under Code §2602 of the federal generation-skipping provisions. Where the property transferred is real property located in another state or personal property having a taxable situs there, which is subject to the imposition of a tax payment from another state for which credit is allowed against the federal generation-skipping transfer tax, a proportional reduction in the Rhode Island tax due is permitted based on the value that the property taxable in the other state bears to the value of the gross generation-skipping transfer for federal purposes.

A return is required to be filed with the Director of the Division of Taxation on or before the last day prescribed for filing the federal return. Payment is due on the date of a taxable distribution or termination as determined by the applicable federal generation-skipping tax provisions.

SOUTH CAROLINA
Type of Tax

1. Estate tax. 2. Credit estate tax. 3. Generation-skipping transfer tax.

Gross Estate

The South Carolina gross estate is determined and valued in the same way as the federal gross estate, except that real or personal property that has an actual situs outside the State at the time of the decedent's death is excludable.

Taxable Estate

The South Carolina taxable estate is determined by deducting from the value of the gross estate the deductions allowed for federal estate tax purposes pursuant to §2051 and §§2053 through 2055, inclusive, of the Internal Revenue Code of 1954, as amended through December 31, 1975, and §2056 of the Code, as amended through December 31, 1982. The South Carolina marital deduction is unlimited. However, if property includable in the federal gross estate is excluded from the South Carolina gross estate because it is located outside the State, each deduction allowable under the I.R.C. shall be reduced, for purposes of computing the South Carolina taxable estate, in the proportion that the value of real and tangible personal property having an actual situs outside the State bears to the total value of the gross estate including such property.

Exemptions

Decedent's estate is allowed an exemption of $120,000 in addition to the deductions and exemp-

tions provided for in S.C. Code §12-15-60, in computing the taxable estate.

Tax Rates

(On the taxable estate)

From	To	Tax on Col. 1	Rate on Excess
$ 0	$ 40,000	$ 0	6%
40,000	100,000	2,400	7%
100,000	Balance	6,600	8%

[S.C. Code §12-15-10]

Credits

If decedent's estate includes property on which a prior tax was paid his estate may take a credit.

(1) If the decedent died less than ten years before the present decedent, and South Carolina estate tax was paid on the property, the present decedent's estate may take a credit on the tax attributable to the property according to the following table:

100% if within the first or second year preceding the present decedent's death;
80% if within the third or fourth year;
60% if within the fifth or sixth year;
40% if within the seventh or eighth year;
20% if within the ninth or tenth year.

The full credit is computed as follows: it is an amount which bears the same ratio to the prior decedent's South Carolina tax plus credit for previously taxed property as the value of the property transferred bears to the South Carolina estate reduced by all death taxes and increased by the exemption.

(2) If the prior decedent died less than ten years before the present decedent, and tax was paid on the property under the death tax law in effect prior to January 1, 1962, the credit is the amount of such tax with regard to the percentages in (1) above.

Payment

The tax is due and payable nine months after decedent's death, subject to extension of not more than five years in hardship cases.

Ultimate Tax Burden

Absent a contrary direction in decedent's will, the representative may recover from each beneficiary the pro-rata share of the total tax paid, as the value of each respective share bears to the sum of the taxable estate and the $120,000 exemption. When the beneficiary is the surviving spouse, whose share was computed using the marital deduction, the recovery is limited to the amount of tax attributable to the property received in excess of the amount of the marital deduction.

Nonresident Decedents

All real property and personal property having a situs within the state are taxable. This includes intangibles which have a business situs within the state. Provision is made for the reciprocal exemption of intangibles. A nonresident's South Carolina taxable estate is computed by subtracting from the value of the decedent's federal gross estate the value of real and personal property with a situs outside the state, with additional adjustments by proportional allowance of exemptions and deductions. Deductions and the exemption are allowed in the proportion that South Carolina property bears to the total gross estate. An exemption of $120,000 is allowed, in addition to the other proportional deductions and exemptions, in computing the nonresident's taxable South Carolina estate.

Generation-Skipping Transfer Tax

South Carolina has enacted a generation-skipping transfer tax based on the federal generation-skipping transfer tax. The South Carolina tax is imposed on every generation-skipping transfer as defined by Ch. 13 of Subdivision B of the Internal Revenue Code, which occurs on or after March 21, 1980, when the original transferor is a South Carolina resident, or the real or personal property is located in South Carolina.

The tax equals the amount of the credit for state legacy taxes under Code §2602 of the federal generation-skipping provisions. A proportional reduction in the amount of the tax is permitted when any of the transferred property is real property in another state or personal property with a business situs in another state that imposes a tax payment for which credit is allowed against the federal generation-skipping transfer tax.

The taxpayer is required to file with the South Carolina tax authorities a duplicate of his or her federal generation-skipping tax return on or before the last day prescribed for filing the federal returns. Payment of the tax is also due on or before the last day prescribed for filing the federal return.

SOUTH DAKOTA
Type of Tax

1. Inheritance tax. 2. Credit estate tax.

Exempted Property

Transfers to public charitable, religious or educational institutions are exempt. Also exempt are transfers for county, township or municipal purposes. Transfers to similar institutions in other states are exempt if these states exempt such transfers to South Dakota institutions. Also transfers of property of less than $10,000 to charitable and religious societies not already eligible for exemption as a public charitable, religious, or educational institution are exempt. Property transferred to the spouse which qualifies for the federal estate tax marital deduction is also exempt from tax.

Taxable Property

IN GENERAL: The tax is imposed upon all real property and all tangible personal property within South Dakota, and all intangible personalty of South Dakota residents wherever located.

DOWER OR STATUTORY SUBSTITUTE: Taxable.

CONTEMPLATION OF DEATH: Transfers made in contemplation of death are taxable. The statute provides that property will be presumed to have been transferred in contemplation of death if the deed was delivered, or delivered out of escrow, or recorded, at or after death of the decedent, and the burden will fall on the person claiming under the transfer to prove otherwise.

TRANSFERS EFFECTIVE AT OR AFTER DEATH: Property transferred by decedent, reserving income, or intended to take effect in possession or enjoyment after death, is taxable.

JOINTLY OWNED PROPERTY: Property held jointly with the right of survivorship (except between husband and wife) is taxable in full to the survivor except such part as he can prove originally belonged to him. Where the property is held jointly between spouses, with right of survivorship, one-half thereof is taxable. United States saving bonds issued to co-owners but purchased and retained by decedent-purchaser are taxable as transfers taking effect at death.

POWERS OF APPOINTMENT: Property transferred by the exercise or nonexercise of a power of appointment is taxed in the donee's estate.

LIFE ESTATES AND PRIVATE ANNUITIES: Taxable at values ascertained by a table to be selected by the Commissioner. In practice, the American Experience Table with interest at 5% is used.

LIFE INSURANCE AND ANNUITY CONTRACTS: Insurance payable to the estate is taxable, but that payable to named beneficiaries is exempt. Government insurance is probably treated the same as other life insurance. The Attorney-General has ruled that no tax is due upon the annuity received by a joint and survivor annuitant.

EMPLOYEE BENEFIT PLANS: No statutory provision as to the taxation or exclusion therefrom of survivor benefits.

Deductions

Expenses of funeral, last illness and administration, debts, property and income taxes accrued before death, unpaid mortgages (if property is devised free of liens, but if devised subject to liens, the mortgage is deducted from value of property). Neither the federal estate tax, nor inheritance taxes paid to other states, are deductible.

Valuation

Property is valued at its market value on the date of decedent's death.

Exemptions

(Allowed for in the following Tax Rate tables.)

	Amount of Exemption
Class 1:	
Surviving Spouse . . . . Value of all property transferred	
Lineal issue of decedent, legally adopted child, child mutually acknowledged for 10 years provided relationship began prior to child's 15th birthday	30,000
Class 2:	
Lineal ancestor	3,000
Class 3:	
Brother, sister, descendant of either, wife or widow of son, husband of daughter	500
Class 4:	
Brother or sister of father or mother, or descendant of same	200
Class 5:	
All others	100

Tax Rates

SHARE		CLASS 1	
		Tax on	Rate on
From	To	Col. 1	Excess
$ 0	$ 30,000	$ 0	—
30,000	50,000	0	3¾%
50,000	80,000	750	6 %
80,000	100,000	2,550	6 %
100,000	Balance	3,750	7½%

SHARE		CLASS 2		CLASS 3*	
		Tax on	Rate on	Tax on	Rate on
From	To	Col. 1	Excess	Col. 1	Excess
$ 0	$ 500	$ 0	—	$ 0	—
500	3,000	0	—	0	4%
3,000	10,000	0	3%	100	4%
10,000	15,000	210	3%	380	4%
15,000	50,000	360	7%	580	10%
50,000	100,000	2,810	12%	4,080	16%
100,000	Balance	8,810	15%	12,080	20%

SHARE		CLASS 4		CLASS 5	
		Tax on	Rate on	Tax on	Rate on
From	To	Col. 1	Excess	Col. 1	Excess
$ 0	$ 100	$ 0	—	$ 0	—
100	200	0	—	0	6%
200	500	0	5%	6	6%
500	3,000	15	5%	24	6%
3,000	10,000	140	5%	174	6%
10,000	15,000	490	5%	594	6%
15,000	50,000	740	12½%	894	15%
50,000	100,000	5,115	20%	6,144	24%
100,000	Balance	15,115	25%	18,144	30%

* Where a surviving brother or sister of the decedent was continuously engaged in business or farming with the decedent at least 10 years and such brother or sister receives from the decedent an additional interest in real or personal property related to that farm or business, then such additional interest is taxed as follows:

SHARE		Tax on	Rate on
From	To	Col. 1	Excess
$ 0	$ 500	$ 0	—
500	15,000	0	3%
15,000	50,000	435	7%
50,000	100,000	2,885	12%
100,000	Balance	8,885	15%

Payment

The tax is due and payable when the amount is determined, except that the tax on contingent remainders is due when the remainderman comes into possession. If not paid within one year from date of death, interest at 1.5% per month is charged from date of death unless waived or compromised because of unavoidable delay. No discount is allowed for prompt payment.

Ultimate Tax Burden

The beneficiary and personal representative are made personally liable for the tax, and the representative is forbidden to deliver any property without first collecting the tax thereon. If a bank or person holding assets of decedent delivers them to the personal representative of decedent without first obtaining the consent of the Department of Revenue, such company or person is liable for the payment of the inheritance tax. A domestic corporation transferring on its books shares of stock belonging to a nonresident decedent without the consent of the Division of Taxation becomes liable for the tax due, plus a 10% penalty.

Nonresident Decedents

Real, tangible and intangible personal property within the state or its jurisdiction is taxable. A reciprocal exemption of intangibles is provided. Exemptions are allowed to nonresidents in the proportion which the South Dakota property bears to the total estate, but are reduced by the value of property located outside the state passing to same beneficiary.

TENNESSEE
Type of Tax

1. Inheritance tax. 2. Credit estate tax. 3. Generation-skipping transfer tax.

Exempted Property

Transfers to the United States, to the State of Tennessee, or any subdivision thereof for public purposes, and transfers to charitable, educational, or religious organizations therein, are exempt. A reciprocal exemption of charitable, educational, and religious transfers is made for states which allow an exemption to such Tennessee organizations.

Taxable Property

IN GENERAL: The tax is imposed upon all real property and all tangible personal property within Tennessee, and all intangible personalty of Tennessee residents wherever located.

DOWER OR STATUTORY SUBSTITUTE: Taxable.

CONTEMPLATION OF DEATH: Transfers made within three years of decedent's death are taxable, regardless of whether made in contemplation of death, except those falling within the annual gift tax exclusion, or those made as a bona fide sale for a full and adequate consideration, which are wholly excluded. The decedent's gross estate is increased by the amount of the gift taxes paid on such transfers includable in the gross estate. In addition, these gift taxes paid are allowed as a credit against the tax.

TRANSFERS EFFECTIVE AT OR AFTER DEATH: Transfers of property by the decedent, reserving income or power to alter, amend or revoke, or intended to take effect in possession or enjoyment after death, are taxable. Where a settlor reserved part of the trust income for life, the entire trust corpus was taxed at his death.

JOINTLY OWNED PROPERTY: For property held jointly with right of survivorship (including tenancies by the entirety), the entire value of the property will be considered to be transferred from the decedent to the survivor(s) and such transfer is subject to inheritance tax. Where the decedent and the survivor are husband and wife, one-half of the value of the property is deductible. However, where the property was originally acquired for an adequate and full consideration, that part of the value of the taxable transfer proportionate to the survivor's contribution to such consideration is deductible. And where the property was not originally acquired for an adequate and full consideration, a deduction is allowed for the fractional part of the value of the taxable transfer which the survivor(s) had originally acquired.

POWERS OF APPOINTMENT: Property subject to a power of appointment is taxable to the same extent as taxed under Code §2041. However, an unexercised general power of appointment that was granted by will (which was probated before November 1, 1978) and held by the decedent who died on or after May 1, 1980, but before May 28, 1981, is not a taxable transfer. Furthermore, a credit is allowed against the tax liability resulting from the transfer of property by an unexercised general power of appointment which was irrevocable before November 1, 1978, providing the property so transferred had been previously included in the taxable estate of decedent spouse.

LIFE ESTATES AND PRIVATE ANNUITIES: Taxable at values based on the Actuaries' Combined Experience Table of Mortality, with interest at 6% in use by the IRS at time of decedent's death.

QUALIFYING INCOME INTEREST FOR LIFE PROPERTY: Property in which the decedent held a "qualifying income interest for life," as defined in I.R.C., §2056(b)(7)(B)(ii), if a federal deduction was allowed for the original transfer to the decedent, is treated as a taxable transfer of that property by the decedent.

LIFE INSURANCE AND ANNUITY CONTRACTS: Insurance payable to the estate is taxable. Proceeds payable to named beneficiaries are taxable if the insured possessed any incident of ownership at his death. Annuity benefits are also taxable. Government insurance is taxable to the same extent as other life insurance.

EMPLOYEE BENEFIT PLANS: Benefits are taxable to the same extent as taxed under Code §2039(a),(b). Benefits excluded under Code §2039(c),(e) are exempt, as are benefits under Chapter 73 of Title 10 of the U.S. Code. Survivor benefits paid under social security, civil service and railroad retirement are exempt.

Deductions

IN GENERAL: Funeral expenses, debts (not secured by out-of-state property), costs of administration, executor's commissions, attorney's fees, trustee's commissions, mortgages, taxes and assessments which were a lien at death, federal income taxes accrued before death, death taxes paid to other states on intangible property, widow's support. Property decedent received, within five years before death, from a prior decedent's estate, or property received in exchange for such property, is deductible as a credit against the tax, if a tax was paid on the prior transfer.

MARITAL DEDUCTION: The surviving spouse is allowed an unlimited marital deduction, but in no event to exceed the spouse's actual interest included in computing the gross estate. Code §2056(b) and (c) is generally applicable.

Valuation

Property is valued at its market value on the date of decedent's death or 6 months after death if so elected by the personal representative. Property that has been distributed, sold, exchanged, or otherwise disposed of before 6 months, will be valued as of the date of distribution or sale. Certain farm and business property, which qualifies under I.R.C. §2032A, can be valued according to use rather than market value.

Exemptions

(Allowed for in following Tax Rate table.)

	Amount of Exemption
Class A: Husband, wife, child or legally adopted child, lineal ancestor or lineal descendant (including those related as a result of adoption), brother, sister, stepchild, son-in-law, or daughter-in-law	$325,000 (1984)
	$400,000 (1985)
	$500,000 (1986)
	$600,000 (1987 and thereafter)
Class B: All others	$ 10,000

Only one exemption is allowed to each class. The exemption is prorated among the beneficiaries of each class, who also share the tax. A common-law spouse of decedent is a Class B beneficiary.

Tax Rates*

NET ESTATE PASSING TO CLASS		CLASS A		CLASS B	
From	To	Tax on Col. 1	Rate on Excess	Tax on Col. 1	Rate on Excess
$ 0	$ 40,000	$ 0	5.5%	$ 0	6.5%
40,000	50,000	2,200	6.5%	2,600	6.5%
50,000	100,000	2,850	6.5%	3,250	9.5%
100,000	150,000	6,100	6.5%	8,000	12 %
150,000	200,000	9,350	6.5%	14,000	13.5%
200,000	240,000	12,600	6.5%	20,750	16 %
240,000	440,000	15,200	7.5%	27,150	16 %
440,000	Balance	30,200	9.5%	59,150	16 %

* The tax is computed on the share which passes to the class.

Payment

The tax is due and payable 9 months after date of death. If not paid within such time, interest is charged at the rate determined by the Commissioner of Revenue. In addition, a penalty of 1/2 of 1% per month is charged if still unpaid after 9 months, but the Commissioner can waive the penalty for good cause shown by written application for waiver before penalty attaches. The additional estate tax is payable in the same manner, and at the same time, as the federal estate tax, and bears interest at the same rate. If not paid when due, a penalty of 25% of the tax, exclusive of interest, is charged. The additional estate tax is charged proportionately to the beneficiaries, in the absence of a contrary stipulation in the will. The tax on contingent remainder interests may be deferred, if bond is given.

Ultimate Tax Burden

The personal representative of the estate is personally liable for payment of the tax. He is directed to deduct the pro rata share of taxes from the distributive shares. The tax is a lien on the property transferred. Unless otherwise provided by will, if any part of the gross estate consists of property the value of which is includable in the gross estate as property for which a marital deduction was previously allowed, the decedent's estate may recover from the person receiving the property the amount by which: (1) the total state tax which has been paid exceeds (2) the total state tax which would have been payable if the value of such property had not been included in the gross estate.

Nonresident Decedents

The tax is imposed on real property and tangible personal property situated within the state. Intangibles of nonresidents are not taxed. Exemptions may be claimed only in the proportion that the Tennessee property bears to the total estate. The marital deduction for a nonresident's estate is similarly apportioned. Nonresident decedents are not subject to the additional estate tax.

Generation-Skipping Transfer Tax

Tennessee has enacted a generation-skipping transfer tax based on the federal generation-skipping transfer tax. The Tennessee tax is imposed on every generation-skipping transfer as defined by Ch. 13 of Subdivision B of the Internal Revenue Code, when the original transferor is a Tennessee resident, or the real or personal property is located in Tennessee.

The tax equals the amount of the credit for state legacy taxes under Code §2602 of the federal generation-skipping provisions. A proportional reduction in the amount of the tax is permitted when any of the transferred property is real property in another state or personal property with a business situs in another state that imposes a tax payment for which credit is allowed against the federal generation-skipping transfer tax.

A return is required to be filed when a return must be filed under the federal law. Payment is due on the date of a taxable distribution or termination as determined by the applicable federal generation-skipping tax provisions.

TEXAS
Type of Tax

1. Credit estate tax. 2. Generation-skipping transfer tax.

A tax equal to the amount of the federal credit for state death taxes is imposed on the transfer at death of the property of every resident. Property of a resident includes real property having an actual situs in Texas whether or not held in trust; tangible personal property having an actual situs in Texas; and all intangible personal property, wherever the notes, bonds, stock certificates, or other evidence may be physically located, except that realty in a personal trust is not taxed if the realty has an actual situs outside Texas.

Credit Estate Tax Credit

A credit against the tax is permitted when the estate of a resident is subject to a death tax imposed by another state or states for which the credit is allowable. The amount of the credit is the lesser of the amount of the death tax paid the other state or states and that is allowable as the federal credit, or an amount determined by multiplying the federal credit by a fraction, the numerator of which is the value of the resident's gross estate less the value of the property of a resident that is included in the gross estate and the denominator of which is the value of the resident's gross estate.

Payment

Payment is due nine months after the date of the decedent's death, unless extended under federal law. A penalty of 5% is assessed against delinquent taxes, and if not paid within 30 days after the due date, an additional 5% penalty is charged. The personal representative of the decedent is liable for payment of the tax.

Nonresident Decedents

A tax is imposed on the transfer at death of the property located in Texas of every nonresident or alien. The tax is an amount determined by multiplying the federal credit by a fraction, the numerator of which is the value of the property located in Texas that is included in the gross estate and the denominator of which is the value of the nonresident's or alien's gross estate. Property located in Texas of a nonresident or alien includes realty having an actual situs in Texas, whether or not held in trust and tangible personal property having an actual situs in Texas. For nonresidents, intangibles that have an actual situs in Texas are not taxable, but this rule does not apply to aliens (to the extent that the property is included in the alien's gross estate).

Generation-Skipping Transfer Tax

A tax is imposed on every generation-skipping transfer for which a credit for state taxes is allowed under I.R.C., 2602(c)(5)(C). The tax is an amount determined by multiplying the generation-skipping transfer tax credit by a fraction, the numerator of which is the value of the property located in Texas included in the generation-skipping transfer and the denominator of which is the value of all property included in the generation-skipping transfer. The taxes on generation-skipping transfers are due at the same time as the federal tax on such transfers. Penalties for delinquent taxes are the same as under the Texas Credit Estate Tax.

UTAH
Type of Tax

Credit estate tax.

Utah Taxable Estate

A tax in the amount of the federal credit is imposed on the taxable estate of every resident decedent reduced by certain credits.

Utah Estate Tax Credit

A credit against the tax is permitted when any of the resident decedent's real property or tangible personal property located in Utah, or intangible personalty wherever located, is subjected to another state's death tax which is allowed as a federal credit, and the other state's tax is not qualified by a reciprocal provision permitting taxation by Utah. The amount of the credit is the lesser of the amount of the death tax paid the other state, or an amount computed by multiplying the federal credit by a fraction with the value of property taxed by the other state as numerator and the value of decedent's gross estate as the denominator.

Payment

The tax is due and payable on the date the federal estate tax is required to be filed (9 months from decedent's death), with interest thereafter at 12%. Extensions, not to exceed five years, may be granted for good cause. A penalty of 5% per month, not to exceed a maximum of 25% of the tax, is imposed in addition to the 12% interest when the return is not timely filed.

Ultimate Tax Burden

The personal representative of the decedent's estate has the duty to pay the tax, and is personally liable for the tax, including penalties and interest if it is not paid.

Nonresident Decedents

Real property and tangible personal property having an actual situs within the state, intangible personal property having a business situs within the state, and securities of any corporation or entity organized under Utah law are taxable. Provision is made for the reciprocal exemption of intangibles. The amount of the tax is determined by multiplying the federal credit by a fraction with the nonresident's Utah property value as numerator and the nonresident's gross estate as denominator.

VERMONT
Type of Tax

Credit estate tax.

If all of a resident decedent's property is taxable in Vermont, the tax equals the maximum federal credit for state death taxes. Where the decedent leaves property not taxable in Vermont (such as realty or tangible personal property located outside the state), the Vermont tax is the amount by which the maximum federal credit exceeds the lesser of: (1) the total amount of state death taxes actually paid to other states, which qualifies for the credit, or (2) the same ratio to the federal credit as the value of the property taxed by other states, which qualifies for the credit, bears to the value of the decedent's federal gross estate. A resident decedent's intangible personal property is subject to tax regardless where situated. Deductions allowable under the federal estate law and attributable to Vermont property will reduce the Vermont tax.

Payment

The tax is due and payable 15 months after decedent's death, subject to extension of not more than five years where it is shown that payment would result in undue hardship to the estate. If the tax is not paid when due, interest at 1% per month on the unpaid amount of tax is charged (except where the undue hardship extension has been granted). A penalty equal to the lesser of $5,000 or 25% of the tax due may be imposed in addition to the 1% interest if the tax is not timely paid.

Ultimate Tax Burden

Absent a contrary direction in decedent's will, the federal rule as to the liability of the personal representative, together with the lien provision, and liability of beneficiaries applies.

Nonresident Decedents

Nonresidents are taxed on all real and tangible personal property located within the state. The value of intangible personal property owned by the decedent is excluded from taxation. In the case of a nonresident, the Vermont tax is equal to such proportion of the maximum federal credit as the value of Vermont real and tangible personal property taxed in Vermont, which qualifies for the credit, bears to the value of the decedent's federal gross estate.

VIRGINIA
Type of Tax

1. Credit estate tax. 2. Generation-skipping transfer tax.

A tax in the maximum amount of the federal credit for state death taxes allowable by Code §2011 is imposed on the estate of every resident decedent, dying on or after 1-1-80, reduced by certain credits.

Credit Estate Tax Credit

A credit is permitted against the tax when any of the resident decedent's real or tangible personal property located in Virginia, or intangible personal property wherever located, is subject to another state's death tax allowed as a credit against the federal estate tax. The amount of the credit is the lesser of the amount of death tax paid the other states, or an amount computed by multiplying the federal credit by a fraction with the value of property taxed by the other state as the numerator, and the value of decedent's entire gross estate as the denominator.

Payment

The tax is due and payable on the date the federal estate tax is required to be filed (9 months from decedent's death), with interest thereafter at the rate of 1% per month. Extensions are granted if federal extensions are granted; a copy of the federal extension must be provided the state.

Ultimate Tax Burden

The personal representative of the decedent's estate has the duty to pay the tax, and is personally liable for the tax, including interest for late payment, if it is not paid.

Nonresident Decedents

Property of nonresident decedents subject to the tax includes real property, real property interests, and tangible personal property located in Virginia. For nonresident estates, the Virginia tax bears the same ratio to the federal credit as decedent's Virginia property bears to the whole gross estate.

Generation-Skipping Transfer Tax

Virginia has enacted a generation-skipping transfer tax based on the federal generation-skipping transfer tax. The Virginia tax is imposed on every generation-skipping transfer as defined by Ch. 13 of Subdivision B of the Internal Revenue Code, when the original transferor is a Virginia resident, or the real or personal property is located in Virginia.

The tax equals the amount of the credit for state legacy taxes under Code §2602 of the federal generation-skipping provisions. A proportional reduction in the amount of the tax is permitted when any of the transferred property is real property in another state or personal property with a business situs in another state that imposes a tax payment for which credit is allowed against the federal generation-skipping transfer tax.

A return is required to be filed when a return must be filed under the federal law. Payment is due on the date of a taxable distribution or termination as determined by the applicable federal generation-skipping tax provisions.

WASHINGTON
Type of Tax

Credit estate tax.

A tax in an amount equal to the federal credit is imposed on the transfer of the net estate of every resident. For nonresidents, the tax is computed by multiplying the federal credit by a fraction, the numerator of which is the value of the property located in Washington, and the denominator of which is the value of the decedent's gross estate.

Payment

The Washington tax return must be filed on or before the due date for the federal return, including any extension of time for filing the federal estate tax return. The taxes are due when the return is to be filed. Delinquent taxes are charged an interest of 12% and the personal representative is to pay a penalty of 5% of the tax due for each month the report has not been filed. No penalty may exceed 25% of the tax.

Ultimate Tax Burden

The personal representative of every estate subject to the Washington estate tax who is required to file a federal estate tax return must file a Washington return.

WEST VIRGINIA
Type of Tax

1. Inheritance tax. 2. Credit estate tax.

The credit estate tax is equal to the difference between the maximum credit for state death taxes allowed by federal law and the total amount of state death taxes paid to all states.

Exempted Property

Transfers to the state or any of its political subdivisions for public purposes are exempt. Also exempt are transfers for educational, charitable, religious, scientific or literary purposes. Provision is made for reciprocal exemption of property passing to charitable, etc., organizations organized under the law of other states. Up to $2,500 in joint bank accounts or in joint shares or savings in state or federal savings and loan associations which pass to Class A beneficiaries and transfers of $100 or less are exempt.

Taxable Property

In General: The tax is imposed upon all real property and all tangible personal property within West Virginia, and all intangible personalty of West Virginia residents wherever located.

Dower or Statutory Substitute: Statute is silent, but the Tax Commission considers such property taxable.

CONTEMPLATION OF DEATH: Transfers made with three years of death are presumed in contemplation of death unless proven otherwise.

TRANSFERS EFFECTIVE AT OR AFTER DEATH: Transfers of property by the decedent, reserving income or the power to revoke, alter or amend, and transfers not intended to take effect in possession or enjoyment until after death, are taxable.

JOINTLY OWNED PROPERTY: Property held jointly with the right of survivorship is taxed to the extent of decedent's contribution. However, if he held such property jointly with his surviving spouse, no more than one-half is taxable. The law specifically exempts $2,500 from joint bank accounts or in joint shares or savings in state or federal savings and loan associations with Class A beneficiaries.

POWERS OF APPOINTMENT: Transfers by the exercise or nonexercise of a power of appointment are taxable as if the property had belonged absolutely to the donee of the power, and has passed by his will.

LIFE ESTATES AND PRIVATE ANNUITIES: Taxed at values based upon special tables found in Art. 2, Chap. 43, Code of 1955.

LIFE INSURANCE, ANNUITY AND INVESTMENT CONTRACTS: Life insurance and accident insurance payable to named beneficiaries, directly or in trust, are exempt from tax. Pro rata exemption is afforded the proceeds of annuity and investment contracts payable to named beneficiaries where premiums have been contributed by the beneficiary or where the contract has been assigned for a valuable consideration or as security. Life insurance payable to the estate is taxable. Government life insurance is entirely exempt.

Also exempt are payments received by any beneficiary under an employee's trust qualified under I.R.C., §401(a), or under a retirement annuity qualified under I.R.C., §403(a), or under retirement annuities purchased by certain employers and are exempt from tax under I.R.C., §501(a) for their employees, or under an annuity from the Retired Serviceman's Family Protection Plan or Survivor Benefit Plan, or under a savings plan for which a deduction is allowed under I.R.C., §219, or under a pension or relief fund for policemen and firemen.

EMPLOYEE BENEFIT PLANS: No statutory provisions as to the taxation or exclusion therefrom of survivor benefits. Lump-sum social security death benefits are exempt.

Deductions

Funeral expenses, debts incurred in good faith, costs of administration, executor's commissions, attorney's fees, federal estate tax, property and income taxes due at death, mortgages, property subjected to inheritance taxation within three years prior to decedent's death (deductible only as to Classes A and B).

Valuation

Property is valued at its market value on the date of decedent's death. However, the value of the decedent's residential property is based on its potential rental value under normal conditions given its locality. Farm property is valued according to its actual use and potential rental value.

Exemptions*

(Deduct from appropriate bottom bracket)

	Amount of Exemption
Class A:	
Wife, husband	$30,000
Child, stepchild, father, mother	10,000
Grandchildren	5,000
Class B:	
Brother or sister of the whole or half blood	10,000
Class C:	
Persons further removed in relationship to decedent than brother or sister	None
Class D:	
Strangers and institutions	None

Tax Rates

		CLASS A		CLASS B	
SHARE		*Tax on	Rate on	Tax on	Rate on
From	*To*	*Col. 1*	*Excess*	*Col. 1*	*Excess*
Exemption $	50,000	$	3%	$	4%
$ 50,000	150,000	1,500	5%	2,000	6%
150,000	300,000	6,500	7%	8,000	8%
300,000	500,000	17,000	9%	20,000	10%
500,000	1,000,000	35,000	11%	40,000	14%
1,000,000	Balance	90,000	13%	110,000	18%

		CLASS C		CLASS D	
SHARE		Tax on	Rate on	Tax on	Rate on
From	*To*	*Col. 1*	*Excess*	*Col. 1*	*Excess*
Exemption $	50,000	$	7%	$	10%
$ 50,000	150,000	3,500	9%	5,000	12%
150,000	300,000	12,500	11%	17,000	14%
300,000	500,000	29,000	15%	38,000	18%
500,000	1,000,000	59,000	20%	74,000	24%
1,000,000	Balance	159,000	25%	194,000	30%

* Subtract from total tax 3% of the exemption. The difference between the amount of exemption and the first $50,000 is taxed at 3%. That portion of the estate in excess of $50,000 is taxed at the indicated higher rates. In one case a taxpayer unsuccessfully contended that the first $50,000 after deduction of the exemption was taxable at the first bracket rates.

Payment

The tax is due and payable at the death of the decedent. If paid within 10 months, a discount of 3% is allowed. If not paid within 11 months, interest at the rate of 8% per annum, computed from the expiration of 11 months from the date of death is added, and if late payment is due to willful neglect, an additional 1/2% per month is added (but not to exceed 25% in the aggregate), but payment may be suspended by the Commissioner on such terms and conditions as he may require. If the return is not filed due to willful neglect, a penalty of 5% of the tax due is added for each month the filing is late (but not to exceed 25% in the aggregate). The tax on remainder interests may be deferred.

Ultimate Tax Burden

Both the personal representative and the person to whom the property is transferred are liable for the tax. The representative is directed to pay the tax upon the transfer of property. The tax is a lien on the property for ten years after decedent's death.

Nonresident Decedents

Real property and tangible personal property within the states are taxable. Intangibles, including bonds, securities, shares of stock and choses in action kept within the state for investment, safekeeping or otherwise, are taxable. Stock of domestic corporations is taxable, whether the certificates be within or without the state. However, provision is made for the reciprocal exemption of nonresidents' intangibles. Exemptions and deductions may be taken in the proportion which the West Virginia property bears to the entire estate.

WISCONSIN
Type of Tax

1. Inheritance tax. 2. Credit estate tax.

Exempted Property

Transfers to the State of Wisconsin or one of its municipalities, or to any other state, the United States, or any political subdivision of a state or the United States are exempt. Also exempt are transfers to corporations, trusts, voluntary associations or foundations organized and operated exclusively for religious, humane, charitable, scientific or educational purposes; or to any such organization existing for the direct financial benefit of any Wisconsin municipality.

Taxable Property

IN GENERAL: The tax is imposed upon all real property and all tangible personal property within Wisconsin, and all intangible personalty of Wisconsin residents wherever located.

DOWER OR STATUTORY SUBSTITUTE: Taxable.

CONTEMPLATION OF DEATH: Transfers made within *two years* of death are presumed in contemplation of death unless the contrary is shown.

TRANSFERS EFFECTIVE AT OR AFTER DEATH: Property transferred by decedent, reserving the right to alter, amend, revoke or terminate, or to designate the beneficiary, or reserving the income, or which transfer was intended to take effect in possession or enjoyment after death, is taxable.

JOINTLY OWNED PROPERTY: In general, the right of surviving joint tenants to the immediate ownership of jointly owned property upon the death of a fellow joint tenant is deemed to be a taxable transfer. The amount subject to tax is the property's clear market value.

However, there are two exemptions pertaining to jointly owned property. First, the fractional interest of the survivor or survivors (determined by dividing the property's clear market value by the number of joint tenants, including the decedent) is an exemption that is subtracted from the property's clear market value before the inheritance tax rates are applied. Second, with respect to joint bank accounts, where the creation of the survivorship interest or interests was not subject to the Wisconsin gift tax because there was an incomplete transfer, the proportionate part of the account contributed by the surviving tenant or tenants is an exemption that is added to the appropriate exemption shown on AUS page 3-94 and is applied to the lowest inheritance tax brackets. The first of these exemptions does not apply to joint bank accounts.

POWERS OF APPOINTMENT: Property passing by exercise or nonexercise of a power of appointment is taxed in the donee's (appointor's) estate, as though it had belonged to him and passed by his will. Also, if the decedent releases a power of appointment over property or creates another one, the property is taxed.

LIFE ESTATES AND PRIVATE ANNUITIES: Taxed at values ascertained by reference to the federal estate tax tables.

LIFE INSURANCE AND ANNUITY CONTRACTS: Proceeds are taxable if the decedent possessed any incident of ownership. Government life insurance receives the same treatment as other life insurance. The statute includes accidental death insurance proceeds.

EMPLOYEE BENEFIT PLANS: The value of any benefit received by decedent's beneficiary, other than his estate, that would be excluded from decedent's gross estate under the federal estate tax is exempt from inheritance tax.

Deductions

Debts allowed by the court, medical expenses of last illness not claimed as an income tax deduction, reasonable funeral expenses, administration expenses not claimed as an income tax deduction, real estate taxes accrued during the year of death, the federal estate tax as it is finally determined, and first $10,000 of household property transferred are deductible.

Valuation

Property is valued at its market value on the date of decedent's death.

Exemptions†

(Deduct from appropriate bottom bracket)

	Exemption	Tax Saved
Spouse	$ unlimited	
Class A:		
Lineal issue, lineal ancestor, adopted child, mutually acknowledged child, lineal issue of adopted or mutually acknowledged child, wife or widow of son, husband or widower of daughter	10,000	250 (each)
Class B:		
Brother, sister, descendant of brother or sister	1,000	50 (each)
Class C:		
Brother or sister of father or mother, descendant of same	1,000	75 (each)
Class D:		
All others	500	50 (each)

† Effective for transfer or deaths occuring after July 1, 1979.

Tax Rates

		CLASS A		CLASS B	
SHARE		Tax on	Rate on	Tax on	Rate on
From	To	Col. 1*	Excess	Col. 1*	Excess
$ 0	$ 25,000	$	2.5%	$	5%
25,000	50,000	625	5 %	1,250	10%
50,000	100,000	1,875	7.5%	3,750	15%
100,000	500,000	5,625	10 %	11,250	20%
500,000	Balance	46,625	12.5%	91,250	25%

		CLASS C		CLASS D	
SHARE		Tax on	Rate on	Tax on	Rate on
From	To	Col. 1*	Excess	Col. 1*	Excess
$ 0	$ 25,000	$	7.5%	$	10%
25,000	50,000	1,875	15 %	2,500	20%
50,000	100,000	5,625	22.5%	7,500	30%
100,000	500,000	16,875	30 %	22,500	30%
500,000	Balance	136,875	30 %	142,500	30%

* Subtract from total tax the tax on the exemption at appropriate first bracket rate.

In no case shall this tax exceed 20% of the value of the property which the beneficiary receives.

Payment

The tax is due and payable at time of death. If not paid within one year, interest at the rate of 9% is charged from date of death. There is no discount for early payment. Installment payments, not to exceed 15 years from decedent's death, are permitted where the distributee is authorized to pay federal estate taxes in periodic payments under Code §6166.

Ultimate Tax Burden

The personal representative has the power to withhold and pay the tax on any property to be distributed to a beneficiary. He also has the power to sell the property to obtain the tax. The trustee of an existing trust which contains taxable property at the time of decedent's death is liable for the tax. A beneficiary having taxable property not under the control of the personal representative or a trustee must pay the tax to the personal representative. The latter has the power to enforce payment. The tax on property transferred which contains a life estate and remainder is taken from the corpus of the property.

Nonresident Decedents

The tax is imposed upon all real property and tangible personal property within the state, and all intangibles having a taxable situs within the state. Intangible property has a taxable situs in the state when held there in trust, or when it consists of stock in Wisconsin corporations. Reciprocal exemption, however, is made for intangibles of nonresidents. Nonresidents are not subject to the additional estate tax. Exemptions may be taken in the proportion that the Wisconsin property bears to the entire estate.

WYOMING

Credit estate tax.

A tax is imposed on the transfer of property constituting the Wyoming gross estate of every decedent. The amount of tax is the maximum state death tax credit allowed to a Wyoming estate as a credit against federal estate taxes under the laws of the United States for estate, inheritance, legacy and succession taxes actually paid to the several states, times the ratio which the Wyoming gross estate bears to the value of the federal gross estate, or the maximum state death tax credit allowable to a Wyoming gross estate, whichever is greater. "Wyoming gross estate" means the value of the federal gross estate of a decedent excluding the value of real or tangible personal property which has an actual situs outside Wyoming at the time of death of the decedent, and excluding the value of intangible personal property owned by a decedent not domiciled in Wyoming.

Payment

Returns must be filed and Wyoming estate tax paid at the time federal tax returns are required to be filed and federal estate taxes paid under the laws of the United States, including any extensions of time for filing or payment granted by the federal authorities.

Ultimate Tax Burden

The personal representative of an estate, a portion of which constitutes Wyoming gross estate, must file with the commissioner a duplicate of all federal estate tax returns and notices required to be made to the federal authorities, and pay the Wyoming estate tax to the commissioner.

Worksheets

Property in Gross Estate

Key: S = Separate
    CP = Community Property
    J = Joint Survivorship Rights (including tenancy by the entireties)

L = Liquid
SL = Semiliquid
NL = Nonliquid
MD = Marital Deduction

P = Probate
NP = Nonprobate

PROPERTY IN GROSS ESTATE	S, CP OR J	ESTATE TAX VALUE	AMOUNT PASSING TO SPOUSE IN MANNER QUALIFYING FOR M.D.	Value			Value	
				L	SL	NL	P	NP
Item ( )								
( )								
( )								
( )								
( )								
( )								
( )								
( )								
( )								
( )								
( )								
( )								
( )								
( )								
( )								
( )								
( )								
TOTALS								

Property Not in Gross Estate	Values
( )	
( )	
( )	
( )	

Calculations & Comments

This form is reproduced through the courtesy of The American College and is used as part of its **Advanced Estate Planning I and II courses.**

Determination of Cash Requirements

   (1) Gross estate . . . . $ _____

Minus

   (2) Funeral and administration expenses
     (estimated as _____ % of
     _____) . . . . ._____✓

   (3) Debts and taxes . . . . ._____✓

   (4) Losses ._____

      Total deductions . . . . $ _____ _____

Equals

   (5) Adjusted gross estate . . . . _____

Minus

   (6) Marital deduction (form 103,
     line 3) . . . . ._____

   (7) Charitable deduction . . . . ._____

      Total deductions . . . . $ _____ _____

Equals

   (8) Taxable estate . . . . _____

Plus

   (9) Adjusted taxable gifts (post-1976
     lifetime taxable transfers not
     included in gross estate) . . . . _____

Equals

   (10) Tentative tax base (total of taxable
     estate and adjusted taxable
     gifts) . . . . _____

Compute

   (11) Tentative tax (apply form 111 rates
     to line 10) ._____

Minus

   (12) Gift taxes payable on post-1976
     gifts* . . . . ._____

Equals

   (13) Federal estate tax payable before
     credits . . . . _____

Minus

   (14) Tax credits
     (a) Unified credit   _____
     (b) State death tax   (b-1)_____ ✓
       credit†   _____   (State death
                 tax **payable**)

(c) Credit for foreign
   death taxes   _____

(d) Credit for tax on
   prior transfers   _____

                Total reduction _____   _____

Equals

(15) Net federal estate tax payable . . . .   _____ ✓

Plus

(16) Total cash bequests . . . .   _____ ✓

Equals

(17) Total cash requirements (sum of 2,
    3, 14(b-1), 15, and 16) . . . . $ _____

* The computation of this amount is to be made as if the rate schedule applicable on the date of the decedent's death was also applicable when the gifts were made.

† Apply line 8 figure (taxable estate) directly to form 112 rates to determine 14 state death tax credit.

This form is reproduced through the courtesy of The American College and is used as part of its **Advanced Estate Planning I and II courses.**

Determination of Cash Requirements (Community Property)

      (1) Gross estate . . . . $ _____

Minus

      (2) Funeral and administration expenses
          (estimated as _____ % of
          _____) . . . . ._____ ✓

      (3) Debts and taxes . . . . ._____ ✓

      (4) Losses . . . . ._____

                 Total deductions . . . . $ _____   _____

Equals

      (5) Adjusted gross estate . . . .   _____

Minus

      (6) Marital deduction (form 103,
          line 3). . . . . ._____

      (7) Charitable deduction . . . . ._____

                 Total deductions . . . . $ _____   _____

Equals

      (8) Taxable estate . . . .   _____

Plus

      (9) Adjusted taxable gifts (post-1976
          lifetime taxable transfers not
          included in gross estate) . . . .   _____

Equals

      (10) Tentative tax base (total of taxable
           estate and adjusted taxable
           gifts) . . . .   =======

Compute

      (11) Tentative tax (apply form 111 rates
           to line 10) . . . . ._____

Minus

      (12) Gift taxes payable on post-1976
           gifts* . . . . ._____

Equals

      (13) Federal estate tax payable before
           credits . . . .   _____

Minus

      (14) Tax credits
          (a) Unified credit   _____
          (b) State death tax   (b-1)_____ ✓
              credit†   _____   (State death tax **payable)**

(c) Credit for foreign
   death taxes   _____
(d) Credit for tax on
   prior transfers   _____
                Total reduction _____   _____

Equals

(15) Net federal estate tax payable . . . .   ════════ √

Plus   (16) Total cash bequests . . . .   _____ √

(In states
where
appropriate)   (17) Spouse's share of community expenses
       (a) Administration expenses
          (estimated as _____ % of
          _____) . . . . _____
       (b) Debts and taxes . . . . _____
                Total costs . . . .   _____ √

Equals   (18) Total cash requirements (sum of 2,
          3, 14(b-1), 15, 16, and 17) . . . . $ ════════

* The computation of this amount is to be made as if the rate schedule applicable on the date of the decedent's death was also applicable when the gifts were made.

† Apply line 8 figure (taxable estate) directly to form 112 state death tax credit rates.

This form is reproduced through the courtesy of The American College and is used as part of its **Advanced Estate Planning I and II courses.**

Determination of Whether Estate Qualifies for Current Use

Valuation of Farm Real Estate or Business Real Estate

               (1) Gross estate (Form 102, line 1)* . . . . $ _____

Less

               (2) Unpaid mortgages or indebtedness on property included in estate at gross value (Fact Finder, pp. 4, 5, 6, 20) . . . . . $ _____

Equals

               (3) Adjusted value of gross estate . . . . $ _____

               (4) 50% of adjusted value of gross estate . . . . $ _____

               (5) 25% of adjusted value of gross estate . . . . $ _____

               (6) Value of real and personal property of farm or closely held business (Fact Finder, pp. 4 & 5) . . . . $ _____

Less

               (7) Unpaid mortgages or indebtedness on farm or closely held business real or personal property included in estate at gross value (Fact Finder, pp. 4, 5, 6, 20) . . . . $ _____

Equals

               (8) Adjusted value of real and personal property of farm or closely held business . . . . $ _____

               (9) Qualified real property (Form 101) . . . . . . $ _____

Less

              (10) Unpaid mortgages or indebtedness on qualified real property included in estate at gross value (Fact Finder, pp. 4, 5, 20) . . . . $ _____

Equals

              (11) Adjusted value of qualified real property . . . . $ _____

REAL PROPERTY OF FARM OR CLOSELY HELD BUSINESS QUALIFIES FOR CURRENT-USE VALUATION IF LINE 8 EQUALS OR EXCEEDS LINE 4 **AND** LINE 11 EQUALS OR EXCEEDS LINE 5.

This also assumes that (a) the decedent was a U.S. citizen or resident, (b) the real property passes to a qualified heir, and (c) for 5 out of the last 8 years before the decedent's death, the real property was used in the farm or closely held business, and the decedent or a family member materially participated in the farm or business operation.

* The full highest and best-use value and not the current-use value is used in determining the value of the gross estate for the 50% and 25% tests.

This form is reproduced through the courtesy of The American College and is used as part of its **Advanced Estate Planning I and II courses.**

Valuation of Business Interest

CLOSE CORPORATION ☐   PARTNERSHIP ☐   SOLE PROPRIETORSHIP ☐

Book Value

ASSETS			LIABILITIES		
Real Property			Mortgages (Real)		
Equipment and Fixtures			Mortgages (Chattel)		
Inventory			Loans (Current)		
			Loans (Seasonal)		
Accounts Receivable			Accounts Payable		
Notes Receivable			Notes Payable		
Cash Value Life Insurance			Deferred Compensation		
Cash			Accrued Taxes		
Other			Other		
Total			**Total**		

Total assets . . . . $_____
Less total liabilities . . . . _____
Book value . . . . _____

Forced Sale Value*

ASSETS			LIABILITIES		
Real Property[1]			Mortgages (Real)		
Equipment and Fixtures[2]			Mortgages (Chattel)		
Inventory[3]			Loans (Current)		
			Loans (Seasonal)		
Accounts Receivable[4]			Accounts Payable		
Notes Receivable			Notes Payable		
Cash Value Life Insurance			Deferred Compensation		
Cash			Accrued Taxes		
Other			Other		
Total			**Total**		

Total assets . . . . $_____
Less total liabilities . . . . _____
Forced sale value . . . . . _____

*Forced Sale Values Recoverable

1. **Real Property**
   Forced sale values depend on location of property, type of buildings, purposes to which buildings can be put, and other circumstances. Forced sale values may *vary from 50% to 90% of the fair market value* of the property, taking into account real estate commissions, legal fees, and other transfer costs.

2. **Equipment and Fixtures**
   The forced sale value of fixtures and equipment generally *varies from 10% to 25% of the fair market value* of these items. The Central West Distributors' Adjustment Bureau states: "These items, which usually must be disposed of

through secondhand dealers, are sold for only a fraction of their original value."

3. **Inventory**
Forced sale value *approximately 50%.* The National Association of Retail Credit Men states: "There is a shrinkage of about 50% between the value at the death of the owner and the time of actual sale."

4. **Accounts Receivable**
The forced sale value of accounts receivable generally *varies from 25% to 75%.* The Retailers' Credit Association states: "It is almost impossible to collect a dead man's bills. People simply will not pay after a store has changed hands. A 50% collection is unusual; 25% would be nearer the actual figure."

This form is reproduced through the courtesy of The American College and is used as part of its **Advanced Estate Planning I and II courses.**

Estimated Going-Concern Value

(1) Average annual net earnings of the business (total salaries
     paid to all owners + amount added to surplus + amount
     of dividends paid) .... $ _____

Less

(2) Sum of (a) estimated replacement salaries
             (for all owners) .... $ _____

            (b) earnings on book value
               _____% × $ _____ = $ _____

                             Total _____ $ _____

(3) Annual average net earnings due to goodwill, past activity,
     and risk of capital .... $ _____
     (1) − (2)

(4) Capitalized value of (3) $ _____ × _____ yrs. .... $ _____

Plus

(5) Book value .... $ _____

Equals

(6) TOTAL GOING-CONCERN VALUE .... $ ═══════
     (4) + (5)

---

1. Return on Book Value
    The return on book value (the use of capital) should vary directly with
the risk. The higher the risk, the greater the return. Although these
amounts can vary considerably, for a stable well-established business
a return of 12–18% might be used; for an average business, 15–25%;
and for a new or speculative business, 20–40%.

2. Capitalized Value

The capitalized value of goodwill should vary inversely with the risk. Thus it is suggested that for a stable well-established business with consistently high profits an 8–12 year factor might be used; for an average business, 5–8 years; and for a new or speculative business, 1–5 years.

Tax Schedules

UNIFIED RATE SCHEDULE FOR ESTATE AND GIFT TAXES
(for decedents dying and gifts made in years 1977–1981
and for 1985–1988 if estate does not exceed $2,500,000)

If the amount with respect to which the
tentative tax to be computed is: *The tentative tax is:*

Not over $10,000 . . . . 18% of such amount.

Over $10,000 but not over $20,000 . . . . $1,800 plus 20% of the excess
of such amount over $10,000.

Over $20,000 but not over $40,000 . . . . $3,800 plus 22% of the excess
of such amount over $20,000.

Over $40,000 but not over $60,000 . . . . $8,200 plus 24% of the excess
of such amount over $40,000.

Over $60,000 but not over $80,000 . . . . $13,000 plus 26% of the excess
of such amount over $60,000.

Over $80,000 but not over $100,000 . . . . $18,200 plus 28% of the excess
of such amount over $80,000.

Over $100,000 but not over $150,000 . . . . $23,800 plus 30% of the excess
of such amount over $100,000.

Over $150,000 but not over $250,000 . . . . $38,800 plus 32% of the excess
of such amount over $150,000.

Over $250,000 but not over $500,000 . . . . $70,800 plus 34% of the excess
of such amount over $250,000.

Over $500,000 but not over $750,000 . . . . $155,800 plus 37% of the excess
of such amount over $500,000.

Over $750,000 but not over $1,000,000 . . . . $248,300 plus 39% of the excess
of such amount over $750,000.

Over $1,000,000 but not over $1,250,000 . . . . . . $345,800 plus 41% of the excess
of such amount over $1,000,000.

Over $1,250,000 but not over $1,500,000 . . . . . . $448,300 plus 43% of the excess
of such amount over $1,250,000.

Over $1,500,000 but not over $2,000,000 . . . . . . $555,800 plus 45% of the excess
of such amount over $1,500,000.

Over $2,000,000 but not over $2,500,000 . . . . . . $780,800 plus 49% of the excess
of such amount over $2,000,000.

Over $2,500,000 but not over $3,000,000 . . . . . . $1,025,800 plus 53% of the excess
of such amount over $2,500,000.

Over $3,000,000 but not over $3,500,000 . . . . . . $1,290,800 plus 57% of the excess
of such amount over $3,000,000.

Over $3,500,000 but not over $4,000,000 . . . . . . $1,575,800 plus 61% of the excess of such amount over $3,500,000.

Over $4,000,000 but not over $4,500,000 . . . . . . $1,880,800 plus 65% of the excess of such amount over $4,000,000.

Over $4,500,000 but not over $5,000,000 . . . . . . $2,205,800 plus 69% of the excess of such amount over $4,500,000.

Over $5,000,000 . . . . $2,550,800 plus 70% of the excess over $5,000,000.

(See following page for rates in succeeding years on estates in excess of $2,500,000.)

UNIFIED RATE SCHEDULE FOR ESTATE AND GIFT TAXES
(for decedents dying and gifts made in years following 1981)

For 1982
In the case of decedents dying and gifts made in 1982, the following substitution should be made in the rate schedule:

Over $2,500,000 but not over $3,000,000 . . . . $1,025,800, plus 53% of the excess over $2,500,000.

Over $3,000,000 but not over $3,500,000 . . . . $1,290,800, plus 57% of the excess over $3,000,000.

Over $3,500,000 but not over $4,000,000 . . . . $1,575,800, plus 61% of the excess over $3,500,000.

Over $4,000,000 . . . . $1,880,800, plus 65% of the excess over $4,000,000.

For 1983
In the case of decedents dying and gifts made in 1983, the following substitution should be made in the rate schedule:

Over $2,500,000 but not over $3,000,000 . . . . $1,025,800, plus 53% of the excess over $2,500,000.

Over $3,000,000 but not over $3,500,000 . . . . $1,290,800, plus 57% of the excess over $3,000,000.

Over $3,500,000 . . . . $1,575,800, plus 60% of the excess over $3,500,000.

For 1984, 1985, 1986, or 1987
In the case of decedents dying and gifts made in 1984, 1985, 1986, or 1987, the following substitution should be made in the rate schedule:

Over $2,500,000 but not over $3,000,000 . . . . $1,025,800, plus 53% of the excess over $2,500,000.

Over $3,000,000 . . . . $1,290,800, plus 55% of the excess over $3,000,000.

For 1988 and later years
In the case of decedents dying and gifts made in 1988 and later years, the following substitution should be made in the rate schedule:

Over $2,500,000 . . . . $1,025,800, plus 50% of the excess over $2,500,000.

MAXIMUM CREDIT TABLE FOR STATE DEATH TAXES

The amount of any state death taxes paid may be subtracted from the federal estate tax as determined under the preceding table, provided, however, that the maximum to be subtracted may not exceed the maximum determined under the following table:*

If the taxable estate is:	The maximum tax credit shall be:
Not over $150,000	8/10ths of 1% of the amount by which the taxable estate exceeds $100,000.
Over $150,000 but not over $200,000	$400 plus 1.6% of the excess over $150,000.
Over $200,000 but not over $300,000	$1,200 plus 2.4% of the excess over $200,000.
Over $300,000 but not over $500,000	$3,600 plus 3.2% of the excess over $300,000.
Over $500,000 but not over $700,000	$10,000 plus 4% of the excess over $500,000.
Over $700,000 but not over $900,000	$18,000 plus 4.8% of the excess over $700,000.
Over $900,000 but not over $1,100,000	$27,600 plus 5.6% of the excess over $900,000.
Over $1,100,000 but not over $1,600,000	$38,800 plus 6.4% of the excess over $1,100,000.
Over $1,600,000 but not over $2,100,000	$70,800 plus 7.2% of the excess over $1,600,000.
Over $2,100,000 but not over $2,600,000	$106,800 plus 8% of the excess over $2,100,000.
Over $2,600,000 but not over $3,100,000	$146,800 plus 8.8% of the excess over $2,600,000.
Over $3,100,000 but not over $3,600,000	$190,800 plus 9.6% of the excess over $3,100,000.
Over $3,600,000 but not over $4,100,000	$238,800 plus 10.4% of the excess over $3,600,000.
Over $4,100,000 but not over $5,100,000	$290,800 plus 11.2% of the excess over $4,100,000.
Over $5,100,000 but not over $6,100,000	$402,800 plus 12% of the excess over $5,100,000.
Over $6,100,000 but not over $7,100,000	$522,800 plus 12.8% of the excess over $6,100,000.
Over $7,100,000 but not over $8,100,000	$650,800 plus 13.6% of the excess over $7,100,000.
Over $8,100,000 but not over $9,100,000	$786,800 plus 14.4% of the excess over $8,100,000.
Over $9,100,000 but not over $10,100,000	$930,800 plus 15.2% of the excess over $9,100,000.

Over $10,100,000 . . . . $1,082,800 plus 16% of the excess over $10,100,000.

* This table resembles the table contained in IRC Section 2011(b), but it is not the same. The table in the Code is based on the *adjusted taxable estate,* defined as the taxable estate reduced by $60,000. This table is a modification of that table and can be used directly from the *taxable estate.*

INCOME TAX RATE SCHEDULES AND OTHER ITEMS INDEXED FOR 1985

ZERO BRACKET AMOUNT:	Married, filing jointly	$3,540
	Married, filing separately	1,770
	Other filing status	2,390

| PERSONAL EXEMPTION: | $1,040 |

SCHEDULE X—SINGLE INDIVIDUALS AND CERTAIN MARRIED INDIVIDUALS LIVING APART

Taxable Income		Tax on Lower Amount	Tax Rate on Excess
$ -0- to $ 2,390		$ -0-	0%
2,390 to 3,540		-0-	11
3,540 to 4,580		126.50	12
4,580 to 6,760		251.30	14
6,760 to 8,850		556.50	15
8,850 to 11,240		870.00	16
11,240 to 13,430		1,252.40	18
13,430 to 15,610		1,646.60	20
15,610 to 18,940		2,082.60	23
18,940 to 24,460		2,848.50	26
24,460 to 29,970		4,283.70	30
29,970 to 35,490		5,936.70	34
35,490 to 43,190		7,813.50	38
43,190 to 57,550		10,739.50	42
57,550 to 85,130		16,770.70	48
85,130 to		30,009.10	50

SCHEDULE Y(J)—JOINT RETURNS AND SURVIVING SPOUSES

Taxable Income		Tax on Lower Amount	Tax Rate on Excess
$ -0- to $ 3,540		$ -0-	0%
3,540 to 5,720		-0-	11
5,720 to 7,910		239.80	12
7,910 to 12,390		502.60	14
12,390 to 16,650		1,129.80	16
16,650 to 21,020		1,811.40	18

Taxable Income		Tax on Lower Amount	Tax Rate on Excess
21,020 to	25,600	2,598.00	22
25,600 to	31,120	3,605.60	25
31,120 to	36,630	4,985.60	28
36,630 to	47,670	6,528.40	33
47,670 to	62,450	10,171.60	38
62,450 to	89,090	15,788.00	42
89,090 to	113,860	26,976.80	45
113,860 to	169,020	38,123.30	49
169,020 to	....	65,151.70	50

SCHEDULE Y(S)—MARRIED FILING SEPARATELY

Taxable Income		Tax on Lower Amount	Tax Rate on Excess
$ -0- to $	1,770	$ -0-	0%
1,770 to	2,860	-0-	11
2,860 to	3,955	119.90	12
3,955 to	6,195	251.30	14
6,195 to	8,325	564.90	16
8,325 to	10,510	905.70	18
10,510 to	12,800	1,299.00	22
12,800 to	15,560	1,802.80	25
15,560 to	18,315	2,492.80	28
18,315 to	23,835	3,264.20	33
23,835 to	31,225	5,085.80	38
31,225 to	44,545	7,894.00	42
44,545 to	56,930	13,488.40	45
56,930 to	84,510	19,061.65	49
84,510 to	....	32,575.85	50

SCHEDULE Z—HEAD OF HOUSEHOLD

Taxable Income		Tax on Lower Amount	Tax Rate on Excess
$ -0- to $	2,390	$ -0-	0%
2,390 to	4,580	-0-	11
4,580 to	6,760	240.90	12
6,760 to	9,050	502.50	14
9,050 to	12,280	823.10	17
12,280 to	15,610	1,372.20	18

Taxable Income	Tax on Lower Amount	Tax Rate on Excess
15,610 to 18,940	1,971.60	20
18,940 to 24,460	2,637.60	24
24,460 to 29,970	3,962.40	28
29,970 to 35,490	5,505.20	32
35,490 to 46,520	7,271.60	35
46,520 to 63,070	11,132.10	42
63,070 to 85,130	18,083.10	45
85,130 to 112,720	28,010.10	48
112,720 to	41,253.30	50

TAX RATE SCHEDULE FOR ESTATES AND TRUSTS

Taxable Income	Tax on Lower Amount	Tax Rate on Excess
$ -0- to $ 1,050	$ -0-	11%
1,050 to 2,100	115	12
2,100 to 4,250	241	14
4,250 to 6,300	542	16
6,300 to 8,400	870	18
8,400 to 10,600	1,248	22
10,600 to 13,250	1,732	25
13,250 to 15,900	2,395	28
15,900 to 21,200	3,137	33
21,200 to 28,300	4,886	38
28,300 to 41,100	7,584	42
41,100 to 53,000	12,960	45
53,000 to 79,500	18,315	49
79,500 to 106,000	31,300	50
106,000 to	44,550	50

TAX RATE SCHEDULE FOR CORPORATIONS

Taxable Income	Tax on Lower Amount	Tax Rate on Excess
$ -0- to $ 25,000	$ -0-	15%
25,000 to 50,000	3,750	18
50,000 to 75,000	8,250	30
75,000 to 100,000	15,750	40
100,000 to	25,750	46
1,000,000 to 1,405,000	-0-	5

Tax Planning Checklist

	Person responsible	Date accomplished

Estate Tax Elections

1. Payment of tax through "flower" bonds (bonds redeemed by the federal government at par value to satisfy part or all of tax due). _____ _____

2. Exercise of spouse's election against will. Surviving spouse can take specified share of estate to secure marital deduction if not otherwise available. _____ _____

3. Disclaimer to reduce surviving spouse's estate (by renouncing all or a portion of her legacy, the surviving spouse can decrease the size of her potential estate and shift assets, gift tax free, to those beneficiaries who would take under the will had surviving spouse died before the decedent spouse). Likewise, if certain powers or rights will attract taxation in the surviving spouse's estate, consider having spouse disclaim such powers in order to avoid taxation. Likewise, other beneficiaries can disclaim. This may result in larger gifts

Estate Tax Elections	*Person responsible*	*Date accomplished*

passing to charity or to a surviving spouse. _____ _____

4. Alternate valuation date, the date 6 months after an individual dies, may be elected for federal estate tax purposes in order to increase the tax "basis" (the starting point for determining gain or loss on a future sale). _____ _____

5. Special use valuation allows reduction of value for federal tax purposes not only of family farmland but also of real estate held in a closely held business. _____ _____

6. Debts and expenses incurred with respect to nonprobate assets should be paid prior to the date for filing the federal estate tax return. _____ _____

7. Consider payment of federal estate taxes in installments. _____ _____

8. If sole beneficiary is also executor, compute relative advantage of "waiving commissions" and do so in writing in order to save personal income tax or accept commissions (which are deductible for federal estate tax purposes) and save death taxes at the cost of additional income taxes. Note also that executor's fees may be taken on the estate's income tax return. _____ _____

9. Administration expenses may be taken totally or partially as an estate income tax deduction or partially or totally as an estate tax deduction. If income tax deductions make sense, "time" payment to derive maximum income tax

	Person	*Date*
Estate Tax Elections	*responsible*	*accomplished*

advantage. Alternatively, if commissions, counsel fee and other administration expenses are taken in the last tax year the estate is open, "excess deductions" will be created. These excess deductions may be distributed to the beneficiary and taken on his or her personal income tax return.

10. Medical expenses may be deducted on the surviving spouse's income tax return if they are paid by her. Alternatively, the estate can pay the medical expenses of the decedent and these can be deducted on the federal estate tax return. A third possibility is for the estate to pay medical expenses within a year of the individual's death and take a deduction on the final income tax return of the decedent.

11. If the value of closely held stock in the estate exceeds 35 percent of the decedent's adjusted gross estate, a Section 303 stock redemption can be made within 3 years and 90 days of filing the return.

12. Consult with the beneficiary of any qualified pension or profit-sharing plan, HR-10 or IRA as to whether to receive payments in a lump sum (thereby qualifying for a special 10-year income averaging but losing the federal estate tax exclusion for such death benefits) or taking the payments over more than 1 tax year (in which case death benefits would qualify for the exclusion

	Person responsible	Date accomplished

Estate Tax Elections

which is limited to $100,000). An alternative is for the beneficiary to take the money in a lump sum but elect to forgo special income tax treatment and thereby qualify the first $100,000 of proceeds for the federal estate tax exclusion).

13. Interest earned on life insurance can be excluded (up to $1,000 a year) if the surviving spouse elects to take insurance proceeds in installments.

14. Executor should consider whether or not to file a joint return with the survivor spouse for the year of the decedent's death.

15. Consider whether or not a fiscal year other than a calendar year should be selected for federal income tax purposes. This may make it possible to delay the payment of tax and time income and deductions advantageously.

16. An income tax exemption of $600 is allowed to an estate in its first and last tax years even if those years are "short." This planning, of course, may make income tax savings possible.

17. Time distribution of income so that the various parties (including trusts and the estate itself) receive income/deductions in a way that maximizes the exemption allowed to each and increases the number of taxable entities, while also taking maximum advantage of the relative rates of each taxpayer.

Estate Tax Elections	*Person responsible*	*Date accomplished*
18. Discuss with estate's accountant whether United States savings bond interest should be accrued on the final income tax return of the decedent.	_____	_____

GENERAL ERRORS

_____Was the gross estate $500,000 or less at the date of death? If so, only 2 of the 17 schedules in IRS Form 706 need to be filed. Did you file the proper schedules?

_____Are all required signatures on the 706?

_____Are all questions answered?

_____Has a *certified* copy of the will (and other required documents) been attached?

_____Does the return take into account prior taxable gifts? (Check gift tax returns back to 1976.)

_____Did you compute the credit for state death taxes properly? (Be sure to subtract $60,000 from the taxable estate before applying the rates.)

_____Should you request an extension of time to file the return or pay the tax? (This must be done before the return is due.)

Schedule A—Real Estate

_____Was the appraiser qualified and did he or she list the factors considered in determining value? (List the appraiser's credentials.) The appraiser should discuss:

(a) size of plot	(e) comparable sales, if any
(b) improvements	(f) assessed value
(c) replacement value	(g) actual or potential value
(d) zoning requirements	

_____Was mortgage erroneously deducted from fair market value of real estate? (See Instructions to 706.)

Schedule B—Stocks and Bonds

_____Is stock accurately described (e.g., was common stock described as preferred)? (Copy description directly from stock certificate.)

_____Were there dividends payable on stock owned by the decedent that are not listed? (Have the decedent's stockbroker confirm this information.)

_____Did you include data to support the valuation you placed on closely held or unlisted stock? (Balance sheets and profit and loss statements for the 5 years preceding death must be attached to the 706.)

_____Have you attached any buy-sell agreement affecting closely held stock to the Form 706?

Schedule C—Mortgages, Notes, and Cash

_____Did you fail to list interest on a bank account because it was not credited in the decedent's bankbook? (Obtain and attach written confirmation from bank officer as to the date-of-death balance and earned interest.)

_____Did you submit data to support the true value of the decedent's interest in a promissory note or mortgage?

Schedule D—Life Insurance on Decedent's Life

_____Did you file a Form 712 (Life Insurance Statement) for each policy listed on the return? (This form will be provided free by the insurer upon request of the personal representative. It must be filed even for small estates where Schedule D itself doesn't have to be filed.)

_____Was there a policy on the decedent's life that was not listed? (Include proof that the insured had no incidents of ownership. For example, include copy of the absolute assignment [gift or sale] form or a letter from the insurer.)

Schedule E—Jointly Owned Property

_____Have you reported the form of ownership correctly? (Was the property owned only by husband and wife? Did you submit documents proving the amount or percentage of the surviving tenant's contribution to the purchase price of the asset?)

Schedule F—Other Miscellaneous Property

_____Did you include any state or federal income tax refunds in the list of assets?
_____Did you submit documents to substantiate a contention that a particular asset should not be included in the gross estate? (For example, certain employer-generated post-death payments to survivors are not includable in the decedent-employee's gross estate).

Schedule G—Transfers During the Decedent's Lifetime

_____Did you include gift taxes paid on gifts made within 3 years of death? (Examine the last 3 years' gift tax returns and separate gift taxes paid on gifts more than 3 years prior to death from taxes on gifts made within 3 years of death.)

Schedule H—Powers of Appointment

_____Did you submit a certified copy of any trusts, etc., if you included (or excluded) property subject to a general (or special) power of appointment? You must submit the certified copy even if you feel the property subject to the power is not includable.

Schedule I—Annuities

_____Did you include copies of any annuity contract or a letter from the trustee or insurance company supporting the exclusion of all or a portion of the annuity from the estate tax?

Schedule J—Funeral Expenses
Incurred in Administering Property Subject to Claims

_____Did you claim an amount of executor's commissions for federal purposes which exceeds the amount that is allowable under state law?

Schedule K—Debts of Decedent and Mortgages and Liens

_____Did you enclose photostats of canceled checks to show payment of debt or documents to show existence and amount of loan(s)?

Schedule L—Net Losses During Administration and Expenses Incurred in Administering Property Not Subject to Claims

_____Have you listed expenses incurred with respect to the transfer of title to life insurance or jointly held real estate?

Schedule M—Bequests, etc., to Surviving Spouse

_____Can ostensibly nonqualified terminable interests be made into Q.T.I.P. (qualified terminable interest property)? An executor can now elect to make property that might otherwise not qualify for the federal marital deduction qualify.

Schedule N—Section 2032A Valuation

_____Have you filed the appropriate statements? An executor must submit (a) a notice that special use valuation of farm or business real estate is desired and (b) an agreement to the terms of this election signed by all parties who have any interest in the property.

Schedule O—Charitable, Public, and Similar Gifts and Bequests

_____Have you filed a statement—with respect to any charitable gifts for which deductions are claimed—that no suits have been filed or action contemplated that could affect the charitable deduction?

Schedule P—Credit for Foreign Death Taxes

_____Have you attached Form 706CE to support a claim for a credit for death taxes paid to that foreign country? Form 706CE must be attached even for estates of $500,000 and under, where Schedule P is not required.

Schedule Q—Credit for Tax on Prior Transfers

_____Have you checked your computations?

_____Have you overlooked a tax paid by someone who died within the last 10 years and left property to the present decedent? (Even certain life estates may qualify for the credit, although it technically isn't in the present decedent's estate. Have estate's attorney check Rev. Rul. 59-9, 1959-1C.B.232.)

_____If you are filing under the "small estate" rules, have you filed a Schedule Q?

WHERE TO LIST AN ASSET

Schedule A

Crops
House(s) in sole name of decedent
Mineral rights
Oil royalties
Real property in decedent's name
Accrued rents

Schedule B

Bonds
Uncashed bond coupons
Debentures
Stock dividends
Mutual funds
Stocks
Warrants

Schedule C

Bank accounts in sole name of decedent
Cash
Checking accounts in sole name of decedent
Uncashed checks
Accrued interest
Mortgages (owed to decedent)
Promissory notes owed to decedent
Savings accounts in decedent's name

Schedule D

Life insurance on decedent's life

Schedule E

Checking accounts owned jointly
House(s) owned jointly

Schedule F

Accounts receivable
Art
Automobiles
Coin collections
Copyrights
Death benefits other than life insurance
Equipment
Guns
Household goods
Inventions
Inventories
Leasehold interests
Livestock
Notes receivable
Options
Partnership interests
Patents
Personal property
Refunds
Royalties
Stamp collections
Trademarks

Schedule G

Gifts
Property in trust
Property transferred

Schedule H

Power of appointment
Property interests

Schedule I

Annuities
Pensions

ITEM	SCHEDULE				
	J	K	L	M	O
Abstract fee	X				
Accountant's fee	X				
Ambulance cost		X			
Appraiser's fee	X				
Attorney's fee	X				
Burial expenses	X				
Casualty losses			X		
Charge accounts		X			
Charitable deductions					X
Court costs	X				
Debts of decedent		X			
Doctors' bills		X			
Executor's fee	X				
Filing costs	X				
Flowers for funeral	X				
Funeral expenses	X				
Gifts					X
Hospital bills		X			
Illness, expenses of		X			
Insurance	X				
Leases, unexpired		X			
Loans		X			
Marital deduction				X	
Medical expenses		X		'	
Mortgages		X			
Notes payable		X			
Personal property taxes		X			
Publication costs	X				
Real estate taxes		X			
Repairs	X				
Taxes (unpaid income)		X			

ITEM	SCHEDULE				
	J	**K**	**L**	**M**	**O**
Telephone bills	X	X			
Thefts			X		
Transfer fees	X				
Travel, executor's	X				
Utility bills	X	X			

United States Estate Tax Return

Form **706** (Rev. March 1985) Department of the Treasury Internal Revenue Service	**United States Estate Tax Return** Estate of a citizen or resident of the United States (see separate instructions) To be filed for decedents dying after December 31, 1981, and before January 1, 1988. Section references are to the Internal Revenue Code.	OMB No. 1545-0015 Expires 12-31-87

Decedent's first name and middle initial (and maiden name, if any) JAMES W.	Decedent's last name ATKINS	Date of death 11/28/84
Domicile at time of death Pennsylvania	Year domicile established 1977	Date of birth	Decedent's social security no. 280 22 4263

Name of executor (see instructions) Charles Stephans	Executor's address (number and street including apartment number or rural route, city, town or post office, state and ZIP code) 722 Moore Avenue Bryn Mawr, PA 19010
Executor's social security number (see instructions) 158 32 0846	

Name and location of court where will was probated or estate administered Register of Wills of Delaware County, Pennsylvania	Case number 43-84-2538

If decedent died testate, check here ▶ ☒ and attach a certified copy of the will.   If Form 4768 is attached, check here ▶ ☐

Authorization to receive confidential tax information under regulations section 601.502(c)(3)(ii), to act as the estate's representative before the Internal Revenue Service, and to make written or oral presentations on behalf of the estate if return prepared by an attorney, accountant, or enrolled agent for the executor:

Name of representative (print or type) Charles K. Parker	State PA	Address (number and street, city, state and ZIP code) Suite 100 Office Center Bldg. Philadelphia, PA 19103

I declare that I am the attorney/accountant/enrolled agent (strike out the words that do not apply) for the executor and prepared this return for the executor. I am not under suspension or disbarment from practice before the Internal Revenue Service and am qualified to practice in the State shown above—

Signature	Date 6/20/85	Telephone number (215) 265-7370

Tax Computation

1	Total gross estate (from Recapitulation, page 3, item 10).	**1**	439,336	82
2	Total allowable deductions (from Recapitulation, page 3, item 20)	**2**	34,663	48
3	Taxable estate (subtract line 2 from line 1).	**3**	404,673	34
4	Adjusted taxable gifts (total taxable gifts (within the meaning of section 2503) made by the decedent after December 31, 1976, other than gifts that are includible in decedent's gross estate (section 2001(b))).	**4**	−0−	
5	Add line 3 and line 4	**5**	404,673	34
6	Tentative tax on the amount on line 5 from Table A in the instructions	**6**	123,388	94
7	Total gift taxes payable with respect to gifts made by the decedent after December 31, 1976. Include gift taxes paid by the decedent's spouse for split gifts (section 2513) only if the decedent was the donor of these gifts and they are includible in the decedent's gross estate	**7**	−0−	
8	Gross estate tax (subtract line 7 from line 6)	**8**	123,388	94
9	Unified credit against estate tax from Table B in the instructions **9** 96,300 00			
10	Adjustment to unified credit. See instructions **10**			
11	Allowable unified credit (subtract line 10 from line 9).	**11**	96,300	00
12	Subtract line 11 from line 8 (but do not enter less than zero).	**12**	27,088	94
13	Credit for State death taxes. Do not enter more than line 12. Compute credit by using amount on line 3 less $60,000. See Table C in the instructions and **attach credit evidence** (see instructions).	**13**	6,949	55
14	Subtract line 13 from line 12.	**14**	20,139	39
15	Credit for Federal gift taxes on pre-1977 gifts (section 2012) (attach computation) . **15**			
16	Credit for foreign death taxes (from Schedule(s) P). (Attach Form(s) 706CE) . . **16**			
17	Credit for tax on prior transfers (from Schedule Q) **17**			
18	Total (add lines 15, 16, and 17).	**18**	−0−	
19	Net estate tax (subtract line 18 from line 14)	**19**	20,139	39
20	Prior payments. Explain in an attached statement. **20**			
21	United States Treasury bonds redeemed in payment of estate tax **21**			
22	Total (add lines 20 and 21)	**22**	−0−	
23	Balance due (subtract line 22 from line 19)	**23**	20,139	39

Note: *Please attach the necessary supplemental documents. **You must attach the Death Certificate.***

Under penalties of perjury, I declare that I have examined this return, including accompanying schedules and statements, and to the best of my knowledge and belief, it is true, correct, and complete. Declaration of preparer other than the executor is based on all information of which preparer has any knowledge.

Signature(s) of executor(s)	Date

Signature of preparer other than executor	Address (and ZIP code)	Date

For Paperwork Reduction Act Notice, see page 1 of the instructions.   Form **706** (Rev. 3-85)

Form 706 (Rev. 3-85)

Estate of: James W. Atkins

Elections by the Executor

Please check the "Yes" or "No" box for each question.	Yes	No
1 Do you elect alternate valuation?	X	
2 Do you elect special use valuation?		X
If "Yes," complete and attach Schedule N and the agreements required by the instructions to Schedule N.		
3 Are you excluding from the decedent's gross estate the value of a lump-sum distribution described in section 2039(f)(2)?		X
If "Yes," you must attach the information required by the instructions.		
4 Do you elect to claim a marital deduction for qualified terminable interest property (QTIP) under section 2056(b)(7)?.		X
If "Yes," please attach the additional information required by the instructions.		
5 Do you elect to pay the tax in installments as described in section 6166?		X
If "Yes," you must attach the additional information described in the instructions.		
6 Do you elect to postpone the part of the tax attributable to a reversionary or remainder interest as described in section 6163?		X
7 Do you elect to have part or all of the estate tax liability assumed by an ESOP as described in section 2210?		X
If "Yes," enter the amount of tax assumed by the ESOP here $ -------------------- and attach the supplemental statements described in the instructions.		

General Information

1   Death certificate number and issuing authority (attach a copy of the death certificate to this return).

    085901C

2   Decedent's business or occupation. If retired check here ▶   [X]   and state decedent's former business or occupation.

    Banker

3   Marital status of the decedent at time of death:

    ☐   Married

    [X]   Widow or widower—Name and date of death of deceased spouse ▶   Elise Atkins, died 9/2/80

    ☐   Single

    ☐   Legally separated

    ☐   Divorced—Date divorce decree became final

4a Surviving spouse's name	4b Social security number	4c Amount received (see instructions)

5   Individuals (other than the surviving spouse), trusts, or other estates who receive benefits from the estate (do not include charitable beneficiaries shown in Schedule O) (see instructions). For Privacy Act Notice (applicable to individual beneficiaries only), see the Instructions for Form 1040.

Name of individual, trust or estate receiving $5,000 or more	Identifying number	Relationship to decedent	Amount (see instructions)
Jonathan Dougherty	158-56-2632	Nephew	

All unascertainable beneficiaries and those who receive less than $5,000 . . . . ▶	
Total	

(Continued on next page)

Form 706 (Rev. 3-85)

Estate of: James W. Atkins

Please check the "Yes" or "No" box for each question.	Yes	No
6 Does the gross estate contain any section 2044 property (see instructions)?		X
7a Have Federal gift tax returns ever been filed?		X
If "Yes," please attach copies of the returns, if available, and furnish the following information:		
7b Period(s) covered 7c Internal Revenue office(s) where filed		

If you answer "Yes" to any of questions 8-16, you must attach additional information as described in the instructions.

	Yes	No
8a Was there any insurance on the decedent's life that is not included on the return as part of the gross estate?		X
8b Did the decedent own any insurance on the life of another that is not included in the gross estate?		X
9 Did the decedent at the time of death own any property as a joint tenant with right of survivorship in which (1) one or more of the other joint tenants was someone other than the decedent's spouse and (2) less than the full value of the property is included on the return as part of the gross estate?		X
10 Did the decedent, at the time of death, own any interest in a partnership or unincorporated business or any stock in an inactive or closely held corporation?		X
11 Are any of the contents of any safe deposit box which the decedent either owned or had access to not included on the return as part of the gross estate?		X
12 Did the decedent make any transfer described in section 2035, 2036, 2037 or 2038 (see the instructions for Schedule G)?		X
13 Were there in existence at the time of the decedent's death:		
a Any trusts created by the decedent during his or her lifetime?		X
b Any trusts not created by the decedent under which the decedent possessed any power, beneficial interest or trusteeship?		X
14 Did the decedent ever possess, exercise or release any general power of appointment?		X
15 Was the marital deduction computed under the transitional rule of Public Law 97-34, section 403(e)(3) (Economic Recovery Tax Act of 1981)? . . . . If "Yes," attach a separate computation of the marital deduction, enter the amount on item 18 of the Recapitulation, and note on item 18 "computation attached."		N/A
16 Was the decedent, immediately before death, receiving an annuity described in the "General" paragraph of the instructions for Schedule I?		X

Recapitulation

Item number	Gross estate	Alternate value		Value at date of death	
1	Schedule A—Real Estate	23,500	00	23,500	00
2	Schedule B—Stocks and Bonds	93	04	93	04
3	Schedule C—Mortgages, Notes, and Cash	-0-		-0-	
4	Schedule D—Insurance on the Decedent's Life (attach Form(s) 712)	8,744	93	8,744	93
5	Schedule E—Jointly Owned Property (attach Form(s) 712 for life insurance)	-0-		-0-	
6	Schedule F—Other Miscellaneous Property (attach Form(s) 712 for life insurance) . .	5,981	84	5,981	84
7	Schedule G—Transfers During Decedent's Life (attach Form(s) 712 for life insurance) .	401,017	01	419,455	87
8	Schedule H—Powers of Appointment	-0-		-0-	
9	Schedule I—Annuities	-0-		-0-	
10	Total gross estate (add items 1 through 9). Enter here and on page 1, line 1	439,336	82	457,775	68

Item number	Deductions	Amount	
11	Schedule J—Funeral Expenses and Expenses Incurred in Administering Property Subject to Claims	31,678	40
12	Schedule K—Debts of the Decedent	2,985	08
13	Schedule K—Mortgages and Liens.	-0-	
14	Total of items 11 through 13	34,663	48
15	Allowable amount of deductions from item 14 (see the instructions for item 15 of the Recapitulation)	34,663	48
16	Schedule L—Net Losses During Administration	-0-	
17	Schedule L—Expenses Incurred in Administering Property Not Subject to Claims	-0-	
18	Schedule M—Bequests, etc., to Surviving Spouse	-0-	
19	Schedule O—Charitable, Public, and Similar Gifts and Bequests	-0-	
20	Total allowable deductions (add items 15 through 19). Enter here and on page 1, line 2	34,663	48

Form 706 (Rev. 3-85)

Estate of: James W. Atkins

SCHEDULE A—Real Estate

(For jointly owned property that must be disclosed on Schedule E, see the Instructions for Schedule E.)
(Real estate that is part of a sole proprietorship should be shown on Schedule F.)

Item number	Description	Alternate valuation date	Alternate value	Value at date of death
1	Premises: 272 Overhill Road, Upper Dublin Township, Delaware County, Pennsylvania (appraisal attached)	5/28/85	23,000.00	23,000.00
2	Decedent's 50% interest in Block 31, Lot 2, on 4th Street, Woodbridge Commons, Gloucester County, New Jersey (appraisal attached)	5/28/85	500.00	500.00
	Total from continuation schedule(s) (or additional sheet(s)) attached to this schedule			
	TOTAL. (Also enter on the Recapitulation, page 3, at item 1.)		23,500.00	23,500.00

(If more space is needed, attach the continuation schedule from the end of this package or additional sheets of the same size.)

United States Estate Tax Return

Form 706 (Rev. 3-85)

Estate of: James W. Atkins

SCHEDULE B—Stocks and Bonds

(For jointly owned property that must be disclosed on Schedule E, see the Instructions for Schedule E.)

Item number	Description including face amount of bonds or number of shares and par value where needed for identification. Give CUSIP number if available.	Unit value	Alternate valuation date	Alternate value	Value at date of death
1	U. S. Series E Bond $25.00 face value, dated 8/1/63, due 5/71		5/28/85	46.41	46.41
2	U. S. Series E Bond $25.00 face value, dated 9/1/63, due 6/71		5/28/85	46.63	46.63
	Total from continuation schedules(s) (or additional sheet(s)) attached to this schedule . . .				
	TOTAL. (Also enter on the Recapitulation, page 3, at item 2.)			93.04	93.04

(If more space is needed, attach the continuation schedule from the end of this package or additional sheets of the same size.)

Schedule B—Page 5

Form 706 (Rev. 3-85)

Estate of: James W. Atkins

SCHEDULE C—Mortgages, Notes, and Cash

(For jointly owned property that must be disclosed on Schedule E, see the Instructions for Schedule E.)

Item number	Description	Alternate valuation date	Alternate value	Value at date of death
1	N O N E.			
	Total from continuation schedule(s) (or additional sheet(s)) attached to this schedule . . .			
	TOTAL. (Also enter on the Recapitulation, page 3, at item 3.)		−0−	−0−

(If more space is needed, attach the continuation schedule from the end of this package or additional sheets of the same size.)

Schedule C—Page 6

Form 706 (Rev. 3-85)

Estate of: James W. Stkins

SCHEDULE D—Insurance on the Decedent's Life

Item number	Description	Alternate valuation date	Alternate value	Value at date of death
1	Prudential Life Insurance Co. Group No. 34-200, payable to Decedent's Revocable Trust	5/28/85	3,514.93	3,514.93
2	Metropolitan Life Insurance Policy No. 9230257, cash value payable to Decedent's Estate	5/28/85	230.00	230.00
3	John Hancock Life Insurance Policy No. 4418017, proceeds payable to Decedent's Estate	5/28/85	5,000.00	5,000.00
	Total from continuation schedule(s) (or additional sheet(s)) attached to this schedule . . .			
	TOTAL. (Also enter on the Recapitulation, page 3, at item 4.)		8,744.93	8,744.93

(If more space is needed, attach the continuation schedule from the end of this package or additional sheets of the same size.)

Form 706 (Rev. 3-85)

Estate of: James W. Atkins

SCHEDULE E—Jointly Owned Property

PART I.— Qualified Joint Interests—Interests Held by the Decedent and His or Her Spouse as the Only Joint Tenants (Section 2040(b)(2))

Item number	Description For securities, give CUSIP number, if available.	Alternate valuation date	Alternate value	Value at date of death
	N O N E			
	Total from continuation schedule(s) (or additional sheet(s)) attached to this schedule.			
1(a)	Totals.			
1(b)	Amounts included in gross estate (½ of line 1(a))			

PART II.— All Other Joint Interests

2(a)   State the name and address of each surviving co-tenant. If there are more than 3 surviving co-tenants list the additional co-tenants on an attached sheet.

	Name	Address (Number and street, city, State, and ZIP code)
A.		
B.		
C.		

Item number	Enter letter for co-tenant	Description (including alternate valuation date if any) For securities, give CUSIP number, if available.	Percentage includible	Includible alternate value	Includible value at date of death
		N O N E			
		Total from continuation schedule(s) (or additional sheet(s)) attached to this schedule			
2(b)		Total other joint interests			
Total includible joint interests (add lines 1(b) and 2(b)). Also enter on the Recapitulation, page 3, at item 5 .				−0−	−0−

(If more space is needed, attach the continuation schedule from the end of this package or additional sheets of the same size.)

Schedule E—Page 8

United States Estate Tax Return

Form 706 (Rev. 3-85)

Estate of: James W. Atkins

SCHEDULE F—Other Miscellaneous Property Not Reportable Under Any Other Schedule

(For jointly owned property that must be disclosed on Schedule E, see the Instructions for Schedule E.)

		Yes	No
1	Did the decedent, at the time of death, own any articles of artistic or collectible value in excess of $3,000 or any collections whose artistic or collectible value combined at date of death exceeded $10,000? . . . . If "Yes," full details must be submitted on this schedule.		X
2	Has the decedent's estate, spouse, or any other person, received (or will receive) any bonus or award as a result of the decedent's employment or death?. . . . . If "Yes," full details must be submitted on this schedule.		X
3	Did the decedent at the time of death have, or have access to, a safe deposit box?. . . . . If "Yes," state location, and if held in joint names of decedent and another, state name and relationship of joint depositor.		X

If any of the contents of the safe deposit box are omitted from the schedules in this return, explain fully why omitted.

Item number	Description For securities, give CUSIP number, if available.	Alternate valuation date	Alternate value	Value at date of death
1	Guns per appraisal by Samuel T. Freeman & Co.	5/28/85	1,030.00	1,030.00
2	Household furnishings – sales price	5/28/85	2,750.00	2,750.00
3	Medicare and other medical reimbursements	5/28/85	746.64	746.64
4	Uncashed Social Security checks for Aug. 1979; Sept. 1979; Oct. 1979, and May 1980.	5/28/85	1,455.20	1,455.20
	Total from continuation schedule(s) (or additional sheet(s)) attached to this schedule . . .			
	TOTAL. (Also enter on the Recapitulation, page 3, at item 6.)		5,981.84	5,981.84

(If more space is needed, attach the continuation schedule from the end of this package or additional sheets of the same size.)

Schedule F—Page 9

Form 706 (Rev. 3-85)

Estate of: James W. Atkins

SCHEDULE G—Transfers During Decedent's Life

Item number	Description For securities, give CUSIP number, if available.	Alternate valuation date	Alternate value	Value at date of death
	A. Gift tax paid by the decedent or the estate for all gifts made by the decedent or his or her spouse within 3 years before the decedent's death (section 2035(c))	X X X X X		
	B. Transfers includible under sections 2035(a), 2036, 2037 or 2038:			
1	Under date of August 5, 1977, decedent created a Revocable Deed of Trust with The Bryn Athen National Bank and Daniel P. Tias as Trustees. The composition and value of the Trust corpus is shown on attached Exhibit "A"	5/28/85	402,990.52	421,429.38
2	Income on hand and accrued to date of death	5/28/85	(1,973.51)	(1,973.51)
	Total from continuation schedule(s) (or additional sheet(s)) attached to this schedule			
	TOTAL. (Also enter on the Recapitulation, page 3, at item 7.)		401,017.01	419,455.87

SCHEDULE H—Powers of Appointment

Item number	Description	Alternate valuation date	Alternate value	Value at date of death
1	Decedent possessed an income interest in a Trust under Will of Paul T. Furlong which terminated at death with no further value.			
	Total from continuation schedule(s) (or additional sheet(s)) attached to this schedule			
	TOTAL. (Also enter on the Recapitulation, page 3, at item 8.)		−0−	−0−

(If more space is needed, attach the continuation schedule from the end of this package or additional sheets of the same size.)

Form 706 (Rev. 3-85)

Estate of: James W. Atkins

SCHEDULE I—Annuities

Note: *The total combined exclusion for lump sum distributions and "Annuities Under Approved Plans" is $100,000 for the estates of certain decedents dying after December 31, 1982. No exclusion is generally allowed for the estates of decedents dying after December 31, 1984 (see instructions).*

Item number	Description Show the entire value of the annuity before any exclusions.	Alternate valuation date	Includible alternate value	Includible value at date of death
1	Decedent was receiving a pension from The Bryn Athyn National Bank which terminated at death with no further value.			
	Total from continuation schedule(s) (or additional sheet(s)) attached to this schedule . . .			
	TOTAL. (Also enter on the Recapitulation, page 3, at item 9.)		−0−	−0−

(If more space is needed, attach the continuation schedule from the end of this package or additional sheets of the same size.)

Schedule I—Page 11

Form 706 (Rev. 3-85)

Estate of: James W. Atkins

SCHEDULE J—Funeral Expenses and Expenses Incurred in Administering Property Subject to Claims

Note: *Do not list on this schedule expenses of administering property not subject to claims. For those expenses, see the Instructions for Schedule L.*

If executors' commissions, attorney fees, etc., are claimed and allowed as a deduction for estate tax purposes, they are not allowable as a deduction in computing the taxable income of the estate for Federal income tax purposes. They are allowable as an income tax deduction on Form 1041 if a waiver is filed to waive the deduction on Form 706 (see Form 1041 instructions).

Item number	Description	Expense amount	Total Amount
1	**A. Funeral expenses:** Nason's Funeral Home - Funeral services Less: Social Security Death Benefit	3,985.00 (255.00)	
	Total funeral expenses		3,730.00
	B. Administration expenses:		
1	Executors' commissions—amount estimated/agreed upon/paid (Strike out the words that do not apply.) . .		13,450.00
2	Attorney fees—amount estimated/agreed upon/paid. (Strike out the words that do not apply.)		10,000.00
3	Accountant fees—amount estimated/agreed upon/paid. (Strike out the words that do not apply.)		
4	Miscellaneous expenses:	Expense amount	
	Register of Wills of Delaware County - Letters Testamentary, Short Certificates, etc.	82.00	
	Real Estate Liability Insurance	14.24	
	Acme Newspapers, Inc. - Legal Advertising	30.00	
	Delaware County Legal Journal - Legal Advertising	35.00	
	Samuel T. Freeman & Co. - Appraisal fee	109.00	
	Quality Appraisal Assoc. - Appraisal fee	110.00	
	W. E. Savers - Appraisal fee	350.00	
	Expenses re: Sale of Securities	1,859.95	
	Expenses re: Preservation & Protection of Real Estate : John G. Ronson - Maintenance expense PECO - Services PSW Co. - Services	143.60 176.00 38.61	
	Additional Administration expenses	1,000.00	
	Garison Auction - Commission	550.00	
	Total miscellaneous expenses from continuation schedule(s) (or additional sheet(s)) attached to this schedule		
	Total miscellaneous expenses		4,498.40
	TOTAL. (Also enter on the Recapitulation, page 3, at item 11.)		31,678.40

(If more space is needed, attach the continuation schedule from the end of this package or additional sheets of the same size.) **Schedule J—Page 12**

Form 706 (Rev. 3-85)

Estate of: James W. Atkins

SCHEDULE K—Debts of the Decedent, and Mortgages and Liens

Item number	Debts of the Decedent—Creditor and nature of claim, and allowable death taxes	Amount
1	PECO - Service	176.00
2	PSW Co. - Service	71.49
3	Margaret Williams, LPN - Nursing services	816.00
4	EMT Ambulance Service, Inc. - Services	10.00
5	Ema Herron - Nursing services	672.00
6	Constance D. Thompkins, LPN - Nursing services	60.00
7	Kastome Convalescent Center - Final bill	495.98
8	Delaware County Tax Claim Bureau - 1983 Real Estate Tax	251.01
9	Insurance Co. - Homeowners Ins., 272 Overhill	432.60

Total from continuation schedule(s) (or additional sheet(s)) attached to this schedule . . . .

TOTAL. (Also enter on the Recapitulation, page 3, at item 12.) **2,985.08**

Item number	Mortgages and Liens—Description	Amount
1	N O N E	

Total from continuation schedule(s) (or additional sheet(s)) attached to this schedule . . . .

TOTAL. (Also enter on the Recapitulation, page 3, at item 13.) . . . .

SCHEDULE L—Net Losses During Administration and Expenses Incurred in Administering Property Not Subject to Claims

Item number	Net losses during administration (Note: Do not deduct losses claimed on a Federal income tax return.)	Amount
1	N O N E	

Total from continuation schedule(s) (or additional sheet(s)) attached to this schedule . . . .

TOTAL. (Also enter on the Recapitulation, page 3, at item 16.) . . . .

Item number	Expenses incurred in administering property not subject to claims (Indicate whether estimated, agreed upon, or paid.)	Amount
1	N O N E	

Total from continuation schedule(s) (or additional sheet(s)) attached to this schedule . . . .

TOTAL. (Also enter on the Recapitulation, page 3, at item 17.) . . . .

(If more space is needed, attach the continuation schedule from the end of this package or additional sheets of the same size.)

Schedules K and L—Page 13

Form 706 (Rev. 3-85)

Estate of: James W. Atkins

SCHEDULE M—Bequests, etc., to Surviving Spouse

		Yes	No
1	Did any property pass to the surviving spouse as a result of a qualified disclaimer?.		
	If "Yes," attach a copy of the written disclaimer required by section 2518(b).		

Item number	Description of property interests passing to surviving spouse	Value
1		

| Total from continuation schedule(s) (or additional sheet(s)) attached to this schedule . . . . | |

2	Total	
3	(a) Federal estate tax payable out of property interests listed above	
	(b) Other death taxes payable out of property interests listed above	
	(c) Add items (a) and (b).	
4	Net value of property interests listed above (subtract 3(c) from 2). Also enter on the Recapitulation, page 3, at item 18.	−0−

(If more space is needed, attach the continuation schedule from the end of this package or additional sheets of the same size.)

Schedule M—Page 14

United States Estate Tax Return

Form 706 (Rev. 3-85)

Estate of: James W. Atkins

SCHEDULE N—Section 2032A Valuation

Enter the requested information for each party who received any interest in the specially valued property. **Also complete and attach the required agreements described in the instructions.**

	Name	Address
A		
B		
C		
D		
E		
F		
G		
H		

	Identifying number	Relationship to decedent	Fair market value	Special use value
A				
B				
C				
D				
E				
F				
G				
H				

SCHEDULE O—Charitable, Public, and Similar Gifts and Bequests

		Yes	No
1(a)	If the transfer was made by will, has any action been instituted to have interpreted or to contest the will or any provision thereof affecting the charitable deductions claimed in this schedule?		
	If "Yes," full details must be submitted with this schedule.		
1(b)	According to the information and belief of the person or persons filing the return, is any such action designed or contemplated?		
	If "Yes," full details must be submitted with this schedule.		
2	Did any property pass to charity as the result of a qualified disclaimer?		
	If "Yes," attach a copy of the written disclaimer required by section 2518(b).		

Item number	Name and address of beneficiary	Character of institution	Amount
1			

Total from continuation schedule(s) (or additional sheet(s)) attached to this schedule . . . .

3 Total . . . .

4 (a) Federal estate tax payable out of property interests listed above . . . .

   (b) Other death taxes payable out of property interests listed above . . . .

   (c) Add items (a) and (b) . . . .

5 Net value of property interests listed above (subtract 4(c) from 3). Also enter on the Recapitulation, page 3, at item 19 . . .

(If more space is needed, attach the continuation schedule from the end of this package or additional sheets of the same size.)

Schedules N and O—Page 15

Form 706 (Rev. 3-85)

Estate of: James W. Atkins

SCHEDULE P—Credit for Foreign Death Taxes

List all foreign countries to which death taxes have been paid and for which a credit is claimed on this return.

If a credit is claimed for death taxes paid to more than one foreign country, compute the credit for taxes paid to one country on this sheet and attach a separate copy of Schedule P for each of the other countries.

The credit computed on this sheet is for _____
(Name of death tax or taxes)

_____ imposed in _____
(Name of country)

Credit is computed under the _____
(Insert title of treaty or "statute")

Citizenship (Nationality) of decedent at time of death _____

(All amounts and values must be entered in United States money)

1	Total of estate, inheritance, legacy and succession taxes imposed in the country named above attributable to property situated in that country, subjected to these taxes, and included in the gross estate (as defined by statute)	
2	Value of the gross estate (adjusted, if necessary, according to the instructions for item 2)	
3	Value of property situated in that country, subjected to death taxes imposed in that country, and included in the gross estate (adjusted, if necessary, according to the instructions for item 3)	
4	Tax imposed by section 2001 reduced by the total credits claimed under sections 2010, 2011, and 2012 (see instructions)	
5	Amount of Federal estate tax attributable to property specified at item 3. (Divide item 3 by item 2 and multiply the result by item 4.)	
6	Credit for death taxes imposed in the country named above (the smaller of item 1 or item 5). Also enter on page 1, line 16	

SCHEDULE Q—Credit for Tax on Prior Transfers

	Name of transferor	Social security number	IRS office where estate tax return was filed	Date of death
A				
B				
C				

Check here ▶ ☐ if section 2013(f) (special valuation of farm, etc., real property) adjustments to the computation of the credit were made (see instructions).

Check here ▶ ☐ if section 2013(g) (generation-skipping transfers) adjustments to the computation of the credit were made (see instructions).

Item	Transferor			Total A, B, & C
	A	B	C	
1 Transferee's tax as apportioned (from worksheet, (line 7 ÷ line 8) x line 35 for each column) . . .				
2 Transferor's tax (from each column of worksheet, line 20)				
3 Maximum amount before percentage requirement (for each column, enter amount from line 1 or 2, whichever is smaller)				
4 Percentage allowed (each column) (see instructions).	%	%	%	
5 Credit allowable (line 3 x line 4 for each column)				
6 TOTAL credit allowable (add columns A, B, and C of line 5). Enter here and on line 17 of the Tax Computation.				

Sample Account

The following form of account is the model form approved by the Pennsylvania Supreme Court and is acceptable in all counties throughout Pennsylvania. It is reprinted for general reference only. You must check with local court rules to ascertain the form of account that is acceptable in your jurisdiction.

Start page 1

COURT OF COMMON PLEAS OF NORTHWEST COUNTY,
PENNSYLVANIA ORPHANS' COURT DIVISION

NO.

_____

Estate of JOSEPH B. DUNN, Deceased
Late of Southeastern Township

_____

FIRST AND FINAL ACCOUNT OF
JANE R. DUNN, EXECUTOR

Date of Death: July 7, 1971   Will No. 85-71
Letters Granted: July 15, 1971
First Complete Advertisement of Grant of Letters: July 19, 1971
Account Stated to September 30, 1972

SUMMARY & INDEX

Pages

	Pages	
PRINCIPAL		
Receipts	3	$188,663.80
Net Gain or (Loss) on Conversions	3–4	1,115.00
Adjusted Balance		$189,778.80

Less Disbursements	4	− 33,630.65	
Balance before Distributions		$156,148.15	
Distributions to Beneficiaries	5	− 28,120.00	
Investments	5		
Capital Changes	5–6	_____	
Principal Balance Remaining	2		$128,028.15
INCOME			
Receipts	7	$ 7,946.12	
Less Disbursements	7	− 868.16	
Balance before Distributions		$ 7,077.96	
Distributions to Beneficiaries	8	− 5,000.00	
Income Balance Remaining	2		$ 2,077.96
COMBINED BALANCE REMAINING			$130,106.11

[GENERAL NOTES: *Itemization.* A number of payments that have been received from the same source or disbursed to the same recipient for the same purpose over a period of time need not be itemized but may be stated in total amounts with dates of beginning and ending of the period covered.

Real Estate. Reference should be made to last deed or other instrument of title and place of recording.

Additional schedules, such as a separate account of transactions relating to real estate or specifically devised property or an invested income account may be included when the accountant believes it is desirable for reasons of clarity or to facilitate presentation of a question that will arise or an award that the Court will be requested to make.]

Start page 2

COMPOSITION OF NET BALANCES

PRINCIPAL

	Value 9-30-72	Account Value
Real Estate		
47 Main Street, Hometown, Pa.—conveyed to decedent by deed dated Jan. 14, 1968, recorded in Northwest Co. Deed Book 312, p. 73 et seq. (9-30-72 value estimated)	37,500.00	35,000.00
Bonds		
$20,000 Zepher Co. 6%, due 1-15-95	20,000.00	20,000.00
Stocks		
500 shs Alpha Tel. & Tel. Co., com.	26,000.00	25,000.00
1000 shs Beta Million Uranium Mines, com.	2,200.00	2,000.00
1000 shs Pure Gold Medical Center Inc., com.	40,000.00	38,000.00

Cash

Safety First Savings Bank, savings	6,500.00	6,500.00
Old Faithful Bank, checking	1,528.15	1,528.15
TOTAL PRINCIPAL	133,728.15	128,028.15

INCOME

Stocks

35 shs Alpha Tel. & Tel. Co., com.	1,820.00	1,767.50

Cash

Old Faithful Bank, checking	310.46	310.46
TOTAL INCOME	2,130.46	2,077.96
TOTAL PRINCIPAL AND INCOME	135,858.61	130,106.11

[NOTE: In accounts of personal representatives, the column of current values is optional with the accountant and may be omitted.]

Start page 3

PRINCIPAL RECEIPTS

Inventory Filed

9- 4-71	Per Copy of Inventory Attached		188,382.30

Adjustments to Account Values

10- 8-71	Mathematical error in Inventory —decrease	(100.00)	
12- 2-71	100 shs Pyramid Clubs of America —declared worthless	(100.00)	(200.00)

Subsequent Receipts

10-12-71	Internal Revenue Service—1970 Income Tax Refund	385.50	
12-30-71	Medicare Payment	96.00	481.50
	TOTAL PRINCIPAL RECEIPTS		188,663.80

[NOTES: *Inventory, Previous Award or Original Transfer*—The first account of a personal representative or guardian will normally begin with the assets included in the inventory. These may be itemized separately or a copy of the inventory may be attached as an exhibit to the account. Subsequent accountings by personal representatives or guardians and all trustees' accounts will normally begin with the assets awarded on the prior account or received from the settlor in the case of an inter-vivos trust, itemized separately.

Adjustments to Account Values—Any corrections in the inventory or previous accounting values and any eliminations of worthless or abandoned assets should be shown here.

Subsequent Receipts—This should itemize assets not inventoried or included in the previous award or original transfer, additions to principal made by the settlor or others, transfers from income and any other miscellaneous receipts.]

PRINCIPAL CONVERSIONS INTO CASH

			Gain	*Loss*
2-12-72	200 shs Alpha Tel. & Tel. Co., com.			
	Proceeds	10,315.00		
	Inventoried at	10,000.00	315.00	—
2-15-72	$10,000 U.S. Treasury Bills			
	Matured	9,800.00		
	Carried at	9,800.00	—	—
3-15-72	$10,000 U.S. Treasury Bills			
	Matured	9,900.00		
	Carried at	9,900.00	—	—
3-21-72	800 shs Beta Million Uranium Mines, com.			
	Inventoried at	1,600.00		
	Proceeds	1,400.00	—	200.00
4- 1-72	1000 rts Pure Gold Medical Center, Inc., com.			
	Proceeds	1,000.00		
	Carried at	1,000.00	—	—

Start page 4

			Gain	*Loss*
5-15-72	$10,000 Ajax Minerals 8% Bond, due 11-15-90			
	Called at	10,000.00		
	Inventoried at	9,000.00	1,000.00	—
	TOTAL		1,315.00	200.00
	Net Gain Transferred to Summary			1,115.00

PRINCIPAL DISBURSEMENTS

7-15-71	Register of Wills, Probate and Short Certificates		50.00
7-16-71	Bar Association Journal, Advertising		8.50
7-16-71	Daily Newspaper, Advertising		10.50
7-19-71	Patrick Green, Tax Collector, Real Estate Taxes		620.00
8- 9-71	Postage and Insurance		4.60
8-10-71	Register of Wills, Certified Copy of Will		3.00
8-10-71	Honest John Realty—Appraisal, Real Estate		75.00
8-10-71	Local Hospital—Balance Due		297.85
8-10-71	Friendly Undertaker—Funeral Bill		1,678.00
8-10-71	Gone Auctioneers—Appraisal, Personalty		75.00
8-10-71	John Goodheart, M.D.—Services		30.00
8-11-71	Jane R. Dunn, Family Exemption		1,500.00
9- 4-71	Register of Wills, fee for filing Inventory		6.00
10- 4-71	Register of Wills, Agent		
	Pa. Inheritance Tax—gross	9,473.68	
	Less Discount	(473.68)	9,000.00
10-12-71	Jane R. Dunn, reimbursement for:		
	Bea Helpful, R.N.	44.00	
	Penna. Electric Co.—Service	45.00	
	Warm Home Oil Co.—Service	89.00	
			178.00
12-14-71	Department of Vital Statistics, Death Certificate		2.00
12-15-71	Carver Stone—Gravemarker		105.00
3-28-72	Register of Wills, Agent		
	Balance of Pa. Inheritance Tax		624.04
3-28-72	Register of Wills, fee for filing Statement of Debts and Deductions		3.00
3-28-72	Internal Revenue Service—Federal Estate Tax		3,629.16
3-28-72	Jones & Jones, Notary Fees		8.00
5-24-72	Jane R. Dunn, Executor's Commission		7,500.00
5-24-72	Jones & Jones, Attorney Fee		7,500.00
7-20-72	Patrick Green, Tax Collector, Real Estate Taxes		622.00
9-30-72	Jones & Jones, Advance for:		
	Notary fees	5.00	
	Reg. Wills, Filing Account	96.00	101.00
	TOTAL PRINCIPAL DISBURSEMENTS		33,630.65

[NOTE: No separation into categories is required unless the estate is insolvent in which event disbursements shall be separated into administration expenses, family exemption, preferred debts, taxes, and other debts.]

Start page 5

PRINCIPAL DISTRIBUTIONS TO BENEFICIARIES

7-15-71	Jane R. Dunn	
	Personal Possessions	1,120.00
12-13-71	Joseph B. Dunn, Jr.	
	Cash Bequest	1,000.00
12-13-71	Elaine S. Dunn	
	Cash Bequest	1,000.00
7-14-72	Jane R. Dunn and Old Faithful Bank, Trustees	
	U/W Joseph B. Dunn	
	Partial Funding of Marital Trust	25,000.00
	TOTAL PRINCIPAL DISTRIBUTIONS	28,120.00

[NOTE: Distributions may be listed chronologically or grouped by recipient.]

PRINCIPAL INVESTMENTS

12-15-71	$10,000 U.S.A. Treasury Bills,	
	due 2-15-72 at 98	9,800.00
2-16-72	$10,000 U.S.A. Treasury Bills,	
	due 3-15-72 at 99	9,900.00
3-20-72	Deposited in Savings Account	
	Safety First Savings Bank	10,000.00

PRINCIPAL CAPITAL CHANGES

Alpha Telephone & Telegraph Co., com.

			Account Value
	350 shs	Inventoried at	35,000.00
8-15-71	350 shs	Received on 2-1 split, record 8-8-71	
	700 shs		35,000.00
11-15-71		Received 35 shs 5% stock dividend, transferred to income	
2-12-72	200 shs	Sold	10,000.00
	500 shs		25,000.00

Beta Million Uranium Mines, com.

	1500 shs	Inventoried at	3,600.00
9- 4-71	300 shs	Received 20% stock dividend, record 8-2-71	
	1800 shs		3,600.00
3-21-72	800 shs	Sold	1,600.00
	1000 shs		2,000.00

Start page 6

Pure Gold Medical Center, Inc., com.

	1000 shs	Inventoried at	39,000.00
3-26-72		Received 1000 rights carried at	1,000.00
	1000 shs		38,000.00
	1000 rts		1,000.00
			39,000.00
4- 1-72	1000 rts	Sold	1,000.00
	1000 shs		38,000.00

Safety First Savings Bank

	Inventoried at	28,880.00
3-20-72	Deposit	10,000.00
		38,880.00
3-22-72	Withdrawal	4,500.00
		34,380.00
5-23-72	Withdrawal	2,380.00
		32,000.00
7-14-72	Withdrawal	25,500.00
		6,500.00

Start page 7

INCOME RECEIPTS

[NOTE: If an income account is omitted or is stated for only part of the period covered by the principal account, an appropriate notation should be made. A waiver of income accounting signed by the parties entitled to income or their representatives may be filed with the Court.]

Alpha Telephone & Telegraph Co., com.

| 8-15-71 | Dividend on 350 shs | 525.00 |
| 11-15-71 | Dividend on 700 shs | 525.00 |

11-15-71	5% stock dividend received		
	35 shs carried at	1,767.50	
2-14-72	Dividend on 735 shs	551.25	
5-14-72	Dividend on 535 shs	401.25	
8-14-72	Dividend on 535 shs	535.00	4,305.00

$10,000 Ajax Minerals 8% bond, due 11-15-90

11-15-71	Interest	284.45	
5-15-72	Interest	400.00	684.45

U.S. Treasury Bills—matured

2-15-72	$10,000 at 98	200.00	
3-15-72	$10,000 at 99	100.00	300.00

Safety First Savings Bank

9-30-71	Interest	250.00	
3-31-72	Interest	680.00	
9-30-72	Interest	500.00	1,430.00

$20,000 Zepher Co. 6% bond, due 1-15-95

7-15-71	Interest	26.67	
1-15-72	Interest	600.00	
7-15-72	Interest	600.00	1,226.67
	TOTAL INCOME RECEIPTS		7,946.12

[NOTE: Income receipts should normally be grouped under the particular investment to which they relate. If the account contains very few investments or covers a short period of time, a chronological listing may be used.]

INCOME DISBURSEMENTS

4-12-72	Internal Revenue Service	
	Fiduciary Income Tax	177.00
4-12-72	Department of Revenue	
	Pennsylvania Fiduciary Income Tax	37.06
4-30-72	Patrick Green, Tax Collector	
	1972 Personal Property Tax	256.79
9-30-72	Jane R. Dunn, Income Commissions	397.31
	TOTAL INCOME DISBURSEMENTS	868.16

Start page 8

INCOME DISTRIBUTIONS TO BENEFICIARIES

TO: Jane R. Dunn

7-15-72	3,000.00	
9-15-72	2,000.00	5,000.00
TOTAL INCOME DISTRIBUTIONS		5,000.00

Jane R. Dunn

Start page 9

COMMONWEALTH OF PENNSYLVANIA :

SS

COUNTY OF NORTHWEST :

JANE R. DUNN , being duly sworn according to law, deposes and says that the Account as stated is true and correct and that the Grant of Letters and the first complete advertisement thereof occurred more than six (6) months before the filing of the Account.

Sworn to and Subscribed
before me this   day
of   A.D. 1972.

Notary Public

[NOTE: Accounts should be signed by all accountants and verified by at least one of them.]

Start page 10

REGISTER OF WILLS
NORTHWEST COUNTY

COMMONWEALTH OF PENNSYLVANIA   :

SS

COUNTY OF NORTHWEST   :

    JANE R. DUNN, being duly sworn according to law, deposes and says that the items appearing in the following Inventory include all of the decedent's real estate in the Commonwealth of Pennsylvania and all of the decedent's personal assets wherever situate; that the valuation placed opposite each item in said Inventory represents its fair value as of the date of decedent's death; and, that decedent owned no real estate outside the Commonwealth of Pennsylvania except that which appears in a memorandum at the end of this Inventory.

S/ _____

Jane R. Dunn

Sworn to and subscribed
before me this 4th day of
September, A.D. 1971

  S/Jane Secretary

Notary Public

My commission expires 3-13-73

    INVENTORY of the assets of the Estate of JOSEPH B. DUNN, Deceased, late of Southeastern Township, Northwest County.

Real Estate

1. 47 Main Street, Hometown, Northwest County—
    Conveyed to decedent by deed dated Jan. 14, 1968,
    recorded in Northwest Co. Deed Book 312, p. 73 et seq.
	$35,000.00

Bonds

2. $10,000 Ajax Minerals 8%, due 11-15-90	9,000.00
3. Accrued Interest	115.55
4. $20,000 Zepher Co. 6%, due 1-15-95	20,000.00
5. Accrued Interest	573.33

Stocks

  6. 350 shs. Alpha Telephone & Telegraph Co.   35,000.00
  7. 1500 shs. Beta Million Uranium Mines   3,600.00
  8. 1000 shs. Pure Gold Medical Center, Inc.   39,000.00
  9. 100 shs. Pyramid Clubs of America   100.00

Cash

10. Safety First Savings Bank, savings   28,880.00
11. Old Faithful Bank, checking   15,893.42

Miscellaneous

12. Personal effects   1,120.00

                         TOTAL   **$188,382.30***

* The total is mathematically incorrect in order to permit the Sample Account to show an adjusting entry. Correct total is $188,282.30.

End of Form of Account

Index